THE ROWLAND BURDONS

To Ann
from Maureen TG

Published under licence 2017 by Searching Finance Ltd.

ISBN: 978-1-907720-22-2

Typeset and designed in the UK by Deirdré Gyenes

Printed in UK by Searching Finance

THE ROWLAND BURDONS

North Country Gentlefolk

Maureen Taylor-Gooby

CONTENTS

CONTENTS

INTRODUCTION
by David Taylor-Gooby

I have helped with the editing and arrangement of the text and
Maureen has asked me to write an introduction.

The book gives a very comprehensive account of the lives of the
Burdon Family who lived in Castle Eden from 1758 until 1944. The
family originates from Stockton, so there is a chapter about that but
the main focus of their activities were Newcastle and Castle Eden
itself.

The book paints a wide canvass of what life was like during
that period, and more importantly, how it changed. Castle Eden
was originally a small agricultural society, but this changed both
with the development of agriculture, and then the arrival of coal
mining. The book shows too how society changed, and it is fitting
to see towards the end of the book how the position of the Burdons
in society was eclipsed by the leader of local government and the
miners, Peter Lee. The new town named after Peter Lee now occupies much of what was originally the Burdon estate. It is interesting
to speculate how things might have turned out differently if the
Burdon family had not been wiped out by the First World War and
had been able to maintain its influence in the area.

The Burdon family did not just look after their estate. They and
their relations were involved in many contemporary events, from
the Civil War, to the wars in India, the abolition of the Slave Trade,
mining disputes and of course the First World War. The Burdons
were also responsible for building the Turnpike (now the A19) and
the first Wearmouth Bridge in Sunderland (although there was an

ongoing dispute as to actually designed it.) The book gives fascinating insights to all these events. The family too took part in social and political life in both Newcastle and London.

A picture emerges too of a family which was concerned about, and cared for their local community, albeit in a paternalistic way. The Burdons were involved in the construction of railways, Hartlepool docks, and perhaps most importantly Hartlepool hospital. They also helped many local charities and community organisations on a smaller scale.

The book gives an insight into a way of life which has passed away, and provides much information for those interested in the political and social history of the period and this area. Like so many landowning families the advent of the First World War wiped out many of their sons who would have continued the line. Rowland Burdon VII who would have inherited the estate was one of the many who were slaughtered, although ironically in an aeroplane accident rather than in combat.

Now the family home has become flats and the church where the family was buried has been closed. It is therefore important that we remember the contribution the Burdons made to East Durham.

A note about the text. All the landowners at Castle Eden except one (John Burdon) were called "Rowland Burdon", so in order to avoid confusion they are referred to as Rowland Burdon I, II and so on. It is not likely they were referred to in this way by their contemporaries, although local accounts refer to "Rowland Burdon, the seventh of that name". The numbering is to help the reader.

The chapters correspond to the lives of the various Burdons, although some, where they lived a long time and were very active, have been split into several. Again to help the reader the chapters have been split up into different topics.

Three generations, Spring 1893

Rowland Burdon

CHAPTER ONE

The First and Second Burdons

A Gimer Hogg

In 1604, the first Rowland Burdon inherited a 'gimer hogg' from his maternal great uncle Gyles Weatherel. Rowland's sisters Alice and Elizabeth both inherited a 'lambe'. Gyles Weatherel of Stockton-on-Tees, made his will on 12th July 1604 when he was "sick in body but good and perfect in memory blessed be God therefore". Gyles Wetherel was a farmer and kept sheep and cows. Leaving animals as an inheritance would not be unusual in 1604, so Grandfather Gyles was in his right mind when he made his will. A gimer hogg is a young female sheep that had never lambed. This would be a good inheritance for a young man as he could breed from that young ewe. Alice and Elizabeth would both be pleased with their lambs.

The Burdon family was 'perhaps the oldest in the connection with the county of Durham, (Tristram page 3) the earliest references to the Burdon family being in Stockton-on-Tees. On November 15th 1337, the Bishop of Durham, Richard de Bury, gave a 'grant of a messuage and two oxgangs of land to Thomas Bordon."[1] An oxgang of land was the land an ox could plough in one day, so the amount varied according to the cultivation of the land. Twenty acres of the land would be the average, a figure to be used. The messuage, a dwelling with gardens, usually an orchard and outbuildings plus the 30 acres of land, was situated just south of the church in Sedgefield was "was still in the possession" of the "Rowland Burdon in 1796".[2]

In 1486 there are references to a Thomas Bordon and also in 1485 to John Bordon. This Thomas Bordon was Mayor of Stockton in 1485. After these dates the surname changes to Burdon. About

1564, in the time of Queen Elizabeth, William and Henry Burdon live in adjoining houses, numbers 8 and 9, in the main street of Stockton.

In 1574, a William Burdon is born who becomes Mayor of Stockton in 1621. William's son Henry married Elizabeth, daughter of Rowland Wetheral. Rowland's brother Gyles was an ancestor of the Smith's of Burn Hall.

Rowland Burdon inherited his forename from his maternal grandfather Rowland Wetherel, Gyles Wetheral's brother.

Rowland Wetheral inherited animals including cows as well as his brother's good agricultural land in Newbye in the County of York. Various others like young Rowland Burdon inherited sheep. This would indicate Gyles Wetheral, their great uncle, owned quite a lot of animals and may have been considered to be a man of substance.

If Rowland Burdon had a young ewe and his sisters had lambs, their father Henry Burdon would also have land where they could keep their animals

Rowland Burdon's father, Henry died in 1632. Two years later in 1634 Rowland married Elizabeth Swainston, probably enabling him the use of her dowry to buy an oxgang, 20 acres, of land. Rowland Burdon and Elizabeth had several daughters and two sons, George and Henry.

More land was acquired. From 11th December, 1645, brothers Rowland and Robert Burdon jointly rented 4 ½ oxgangs, about 90 acres of land in Stockton as well as several fields at a cost of 125/- a year. The brothers must have had some wealth to rent so much land.

Rowland Burdon progressed from inheriting a gimer hogg, his young female sheep. Between 1641 and 1655 he was Mayor of Stockton nine times.

The mayor was elected by a majority of burgesses; the owners of land and tenancies, each year on the first Tuesday after 29th September. Rowland Burdon must have been a competent mayor to have been elected nine times. Other members of his family had been mayor before him; William Burdon in 1621, Rowland

Wetherell and Giles Wetherell. The Burdon and Wetherell families must have been of some note in 17th Century Stockton.

Troubled Times

There was trouble during the time when Rowland Burdon was Mayor of Stockton. Civil War broke out in 1642 and Stockton was a Royalist stronghold. Although Rowland Burdon was a 'staunch Royalist' he received a letter in September 1644 stating he "was well affected by Parliament."[3] Despite this, his name was one of the signatories on a petition to Parliament on January 14th 1651 'for the establishment of a college at Durham', yet he did not sign "the address to the "Lord General Cromwell" on April 28th 1653, nor to that to the Lord Protector, April 21st 1658."[4]

This Rowland Burdon, Mayor of Stockton when Oliver Cromwell was marching north is reputed to have vowed that, 'If Cromwell comes to the town he will never pass through the city gates.' Cromwell did not pass through the city gates.

But the Scots did. The Scots had invaded England in 1640 and defeated the King's Troops at Newburn and occupied Newcastle. The Scots used the Tees as a frontier. When Rowland Burdon was bailiff of Stockton, the Bishop's Palace, a fortified Manor House known as the Castle, was captured by the Scots in 1644, surrendering to Lord Calendar without any resistance on 24th July 1644. The Scots garrisoned there until 1646. After Parliament's treaty with Scotland in 1646 and a payment of £200,000 the Scots withdrew back to Scotland.

Rowland Burdon was Mayor during these times of unrest. The Scots had not only passed through the city gates but also occupied the city. At the end of the Civil War Oliver Cromwell ordered the destruction of the Bishop's Castle. Despite these setbacks, Rowland Burdon continued as Mayor until 1655. Cromwell had not passed through Stockton's gates but part of the gates did not remain at the entrance to the city. These gates originally had two tall pillars made from Frosterley marble. This marble was highly prized when cut and polished and frequently used in churches and sometimes cathedrals. The marble at the city gates must have had a bluish tinge, as Mayor Rowland Burdon had the pillars removed from the gates and used in his house to support a balcony and from henceforth this house became known as 'Blue Posts.' The house was demolished in 1870 and when the pillars were bought by Rev John Webster, vicar of Kelloe, he had them fashioned into lampstands for his drawing room. As the Websters and Burdons were related by marriage, when Rev Webster died, the pillars were bequeathed to the Rev John Burdon who erected them on each side of the front door of the Castle in Castle Eden. They were still there in the Castle porch in 1920.

Rowland Burdon II

Mayor Rowland Burdon had two sons, George and Henry. George, baptised on the 3rd December 1648, married Elizabeth Hutchinson. When George Burdon died he was succeeded by his only surviving son Rowland who was baptised in January 1679. Aged 18, Rowland Burdon 11, of Sedgefield, matriculated at Lincoln College, Oxford on 27th March 1699, obtaining his BA in 1702. This Rowland married Sarah the daughter of John Reeve of Great Milton, about six miles from Oxford so it is possible Rowland met Sarah while he was studying at University. John Reeve was a man of great wealth and this Rowland Burdon inherited a "priceless drinking relic, the drinking cup of the last Abbot of Bury, a large goblet of Dutch glass mounted in silver, to which a (silver) lid had been added probably by the Reeves." It was still in the possession of the Burdon family in 1901.[5]

John Reeve was Abbott of Bury-St-Edmunds from 1513 to 1539, the time of the Dissolution of the monasteries during the reign of Henry VIII. In 1538, the Royal Commissioners stripped the Abbey of most of the gold, silver and valuable items. In 1539, the remaining valuable items were sold by the Commissioners for almost £413.

Abbott Reeve, or Abbott Melford as he was sometimes called, was forced to surrender the Abbey on November 4th 1539. He had lived in a magnificent palace and was removed to a small house at the top of Crown Street. The Abbott was given a pension of £333, but he died shortly after the event. It would appear the Abbott had managed to retain the priceless drinking cup as it had not been confiscated by the Commissioners. This relic appeared to have been passed down the family until it reached Sarah Reeve, daughter of wealthy John Reeve of Milton. The pension of £333 may have been passed down the family also and contributed to this great wealth.

The second Rowland Burdon who inherited the priceless relic through his marriage to Sarah Reeve, had taken holy orders and lived for some time at Sedgefield. The town was known as Ceddesfield in Medieval times, probably because of large amounts of sedge that grew in the area. The parish church of St. Edmund's dates back to the 13th Century.

There is a legend attached to Sedgefield church regarding the death of Rev. J. Carnage, Rector of St. Edmund's who died in 1747.[6] The tithes were due about one week after he had died and his 'cunning' wife devised a plan for obtaining the money. She told no-one of his death and 'salted' his body where no-one could see her in the act. She dressed his body in clothes and propped him up in a chair in the window where all could see him. As nobody suspected the Rector had died, so the tithes were paid. After she had received the entitlements of the living, the Rector's wife announced her poor husband had died.

Legend has it that the 'apparition' of the 'pickled parson ....was presumed to infect the neighbourhood of the rector's hall, "making night hideous." At about 2 am on the morning of December 31st 1792, a fire broke out in the Rectory and most of the building was destroyed before the blaze could be extinguished. From the day the 'apparition' was seen no more.

A new Rectory, Ceddesfield Hall, was built by the Barrington brothers; their nephew Rev. George Barrington becoming Rector and living in the fine mansion which is now a Community Centre.

The second Rowland Burdon died in 1750 and was buried in Sedgefield Church.

Rowland and Sarah had three children; another Rowland baptised on January 7th 1724, John who took holy orders and became curate of Sedgefield who died unmarried and a daughter, Elizabeth who also died unmarried.

CHAPTER TWO
The third Rowland Burdon

Rowland Burdon 3rd was born in 1724 in Stockton. Stockton had been a market town since Bishop Bek opened a market in 1310. It was also a port. A large wooden ship was constructed for a Bishop of Durham in 1470. These Bishops were powerful: they were Prince Bishops.

Rowland Burdon had a large house in Stockton referred to as the Blue Posts. The house, situated on the west side of the main street was dated 1475, indicating the Burdons' would have lived in Stockton during the time of the Prince Bishops. Another large Stockton house, west of the church was inhabited by the Websters,the family related to the Burdons by marriage.

Stockton

Stockton was a port. The main ports of call were London, Hull, Leith and Sunderland. Coal was picked up from nearby Sunderland and transported to other places like London. As well as coal, the main exports were farm produce like wheat flour, corn, rye, butter, cheese and bacon but there were also exports of ale, oak-timber, flax, linen, linen and worsted yarns and lead. Some ships exported abroad mainly to Rotterdam and the Baltic. There were imports of timber from Norway and the Baltic and wines from places like Oporto, Lisbon and Malaga.

There were problems at the docks in 1740. In June a detachments of soldiers were sent to several seaports to stop grain the export of grain to France as the Government considered the grain was needed for the home market. The Howard's regiment was sent to Stockton because great numbers of people had gathered at the port opposing the export of corn. In August, two women and a man were transported for seven years for attempting to steal large quantities of wheat from a ship docked in Stockton.

Bread had become very expensive because grain harvests were down because of extremely bad weather. The spring and winters of 1739 and 1740 were severely cold. The River Thames was frozen over for eight weeks. In February 1739 the ice on the River Wear was so thick that it could take the weight of oxen and horses. A fox ran down the ice during a hunt and was pursued by hounds and riders.

There was a famine in Ireland when frost destroyed potato crops. Europe too saw problems like the insurrection that occurred in Liege because bread had become so expensive.

In June 1740, troops sent to places like Stockton appear to have little effect in preventing violence and tumult. The populace were more afraid of the consequences of the lack of bread than they were of the troops. To alleviate this fear, during the disorder the merchants of Stockton offered corn for sale at reduced prices. This offer had no effect and the militia proceeded from Sedgefield to legally attempt to appease and disperse the crowd. It is probable that during this time the militia arrested the three people attempting to steal grain from a ship. These people were desperate but they quickly received the harsh sentence of seven years transportation as a possible deterrent to dispel the unrest.

Rowland Burdon goes to Newcastle

Rowland Burdon 3rd probably witnessed some of this unrest before he left Stockton in 1742 to go to Newcastle as an apprentice merchant indentured to Ambrose Surtees of Newcastle. His father, George would have paid a substantial sum of money to have him apprenticed with Ambrose Surtees, a merchant in Newcastle. There was a Robert Surtees who owned and rented out land in Stockton at this time. It is possible this Robert Surtees introduced Rowland to Ambrose Surtees as it was customary at this time for such an apprentice to obtain his position by such a method.

John Wesley in Newcastle

Rowland Burdon would have just arrived in Newcastle in 1742 the year that John Wesley visited Newcastle. John's brother Charles joined him between 1743 and 1751. People of the wealthy class like Rowland Burdon may not have heard John Wesley or his brother Charles preach when they were in Newcastle. He was more likely to have purchased in 173 from a bookseller for threepence a published copy which set down the notions of the Methodists. As a wealthy merchant Rowland Burdon probably attended the Church of England regularly. Merchants made their wealth through shipping. Newcastle shipping was mainly based around coal. Poor workers like those living in coal mining villages would be more likely to be affected by the words of John Wesley.

Rowland Burdon became a corn, food and drink merchant. He had seen the importance of the corn market in the unrest in Stockton but an added incentive to become a corn merchant may have resulted from the cattle epidemic of 1749. After the severe epidemic, many farmers around the Stockton area ploughed up their meadow land and grew corn. There was a ready new harvest for a corn merchant to access. Rowland Burdon probably took advantage of this especially as his experience in Stockton had shown the importance of corn.

Rowland Burdon married Elizabeth Smith in August 1755 in Elvet Church, Durham. Elizabeth's sister married Anthony Salvin of Sunderland Bridge, near Croxdale, leading to a family connection between the Burdons and the Salvins.

Elizabeth had lived with her father George Smith in Burn Hall near Croxdale and she brought with her a fortune of £1,000 when she married Rowland. There was a distant family connection between the Burdons and the Smiths going back to the 1600's, when Elizabeth Wetheral's brother Giles Wetheral married into the Smith family.

Rowland Burdon 3rd and his wife, Elizabeth had a house in Pilgrim Street, Newcastle. Their son, another Rowland was born in1756 and baptised in Newcastle on 30th December.

Early on the morning of Saturday 3rd December 1757, an express coach arrived in Newcastle to inform Rowland Burdon that his wealthy uncle John Reeve had died in London. John Reeve had been Sheriff of Newcastle, so he was considered an important man as well as wealthy, leaving a fortune of about £100,000, a massive amount made from being a considerable wholesale linen draper in Newgate Street, Newcastle. Rowland Burdon had been sent for because his uncle had died in London, so he would probably have to arrange procedures after his uncle's death.

This fortune of £100,000 was left by Rowland's maternal uncle John. There were a considerable number of benefactors including Rowland's mother Sarah, a widow since 1750, who received an annuity of 300 pounds during her lifetime, which would be another 30 years as she died in March 1780. Elizabeth Burdon, Rowland's sister received an annuity of £200. The rest and residue of the estate went to Rowland Burdon, so he would receive a large inheritance.

Shortly after this large inheritance, Rowland's marriage had a sad ending when in April 1758 his wife Elizabeth died giving birth to a daughter, Elizabeth Christian, who sadly died at the same time as her mother. The newspaper described Elizabeth as having, "every virtue, and through an amiable disposition gave constant assistance to the poor, who never applied without immediate relief, by whom her loss will be severely felt, as it is justly regretted by her Friends and Acquaintances. Yesterday her corpse, after lying in state, was carried to Sedgefield in a grand manner for interment."[1]

This announcement is so different from one might expect today. The loss for the family does not appear to be stressed in such announcements. Probably at that time the family loss would be unspoken and taken for granted and such announcements would attempt to portray the person in a good light. Her forename, Elizabeth, is not mentioned. She was the Lady of Rowland Burdon. She helped and poor. They would miss her, as would her friends and acquaintances but she would be solely missed by her husband and family especially as she had died at such a young age and in what should have been a joyous event but turned out to be tragedy.

In the October of 1758, not long after the death of his wife, Rowland Burdon's sister went to Great Milton in Oxfordshire, birthplace of her mother Sarah Reeve, to visit relatives. During her stay, Rowland's sister died. Now Rowland Burdon had lost his wife, his new born baby daughter and his sister. Two year old Rowland jnr had lost his mother, so he would probably never remember her. He had lost his sister and his aunt. His grandmother Sarah, another lady of great benevolence and charity died aged 85 in March 1780. Young Rowland may have had the comfort of a kind grandmother when he was growing up.

Giving to the Poor

The obituaries of Rowland's wife and sister emphasised how generous they were to the poor. When wealthy people gave money to the poor it was reported in the newspapers. It was almost as if giving was a duty but it had to be noted so that it could be recognised who had fulfilled their duty.

This was particularly true at Christmas when for example, a relative, John Burdon of Hardwicke Esq, a man, "whose exemplary benevolence is always extended... (in) his usual goodness and humanity, (has) given a handsome sum of money to be distributed among the poor of the parish of Kelloe to enable them to cheerfully celebrate he joyful nativity of our common Redeemer."[2]

On the 23rd December 1758, Rowland Burdon gave a large piece of beef and a 12 penny loaf to a great number of poor families. Another contributor has given meat and a 6d loaf to the poor. These would be Christmas contributions but their report in the newspapers suggests giving to the poor especially at Christmas had become almost a competition. The more one gave, the worthier one was. They would be most welcome by the poor, especially for a Christmas dinner, but there appears to be the need to be seen doing good as well as doing good for its own sake. One could also suppose that the poor should be grateful to those who donated to their wellbeing and did not question why some were so rich and they were so poor.

Giving to the poor can be viewed in two different ways. William Blake did this with his poems, 'Holy Thursday'. Workhouse children "their innocent faces clean' and 'radiance all their own' attend the Maundy Thursday service in St. Paul's Cathedral whilst, "Beneath them sit the aged men wise guardians of the poor.' This sentiment is turned on its head by Blake in the 'Songs of Experience' when he questions;

"Is this a holy thing to see,
In a rich and fruitful land,
Babes reduced to misery,
Fed with the cold and usurious hand."

The plight of the poor was accepted as being the norm. Those who gave to the poor did so willingly but probably through a sense of duty. They did not consider the need to change the system so that 'babes' were not 'reduced to misery'.

It should not be dismissed that the wealthy did give to the poor. The price of wheat was still very high in January 1758, it was reported that the 'prices of grain are still out of compass of the poor man's pockets'. The poor would welcome the large quantities of grain they received from John Burdon of Hardwicke in Durham. The newspaper felt by giving relief to the poor this act would "give pleasure to the benevolent of mind."[3]

Wealth in Newcastle

Rowland Burdon was wealthy. He had gone to Newcastle apprenticed to a merchant where he learned his trade. He became a member of the Company of Merchant's Adventurers of Newcastle and greatly increased his fortune. In partnership with Ambrose Surtees, he established a bank. On October 13th 1757, both Rowland Burdon and Ambrose Surtees were admitted to the company of Hostmen. As a wealthy man, Rowland Burdon could afford to give to the poor.

Shipping coal may have been one source of the wealth in Newcastle. Coal production had been in the area for a long time.

By the 13th Century, coal mining had become established along the Tyne, especially at Whickham, then in County Durham and nearby Winlaton. From as early as 1305, coal was shipped from the Tyne quickly to London.

By 1334, Newcastle was the fourth wealthiest town in England after London, Bristol and York. By 1378 Newcastle shipped 15,000 tons of coal each year to many parts of Europe. Iron ore was imported from Sweden.

By 1547, Newcastle's population was around 10,000. A group of powerful merchants called the Hostmen had control of the export of coal. By 1615, 200 ships carried coal to London and another 200 ships carried coal to other parts of the country.

Alkali development started in the 1700's. In 1807 alkali works were established by Losh, Wilson and Bell at Walker-on-Tyne. The manufacture of bleaching powder began in 1830 and the Losh Company soon manufactured half the soda in England. Alkali works opened up at the Tyne Docks in 1822, Felling Shore in 1826 and 1834 and Friars' Goose at Gateshead in 1828. Pollution from the emission of hydrochloric acid was a great problem with alkali works, so tall chimneys were built. In 1833 the tallest chimney in England was built at Friar's Goose.

In 1787, the Northumberland Glass Company opened Lemington's Glass Works. Other glass works followed and by the middle of the 19th Century the glass industry on Tyneside and Wearside produced a considerable part of the national output of glass.

Potteries were located along the riverside of the Tyne. Proximity to the river enabled raw materials and the finished products had easy access off and onto ships.

There was shipbuilding on the Tyne from as early as 1294, when a galleon for the fleet of King Edward was built in Newcastle. The firm that became Swan and Hunter began building ships at Walker on the Tyne in 1852. Their works extended to Wallsend in 1873.

The Directory of 1801 informs that "considerable colour manufactories have been established and various other works such as earthen–ware, sugar, cordage, lamp black, coal-tar, white red and shot lead, oil and several smelting works."

There is one surprising inclusion in the above list. Works had been established that produced sugar. John Graham Clarke of Newcastle owned plantations in Jamaica. At his death he owned 13 plantations. Slaves worked on these plantations. This was the reason that sugar and rum were imported and exported from ships on the Tyne.

John Graham Clarke had multiple business interests as an industrialist. One interest involved the refinement of sugar. He also owned several ships. Two of his ships the "Arabella" and the "Mayflower" bound for Jamaica in February 1794 advertised 'excellent accommodation' (1st) in the Newcastle Courant for passengers. The advert also wanted a millwright, a 'complete master of the business'4 who was needed to work on a plantation in Jamaica.

By the 18th Century, ships sailed mainly to London, Riga, Hamburg, Rotterdam and Le Havre heavy laden with coal and some coal from local pits was shipped out to Caribbean islands, like Jamaica, probably due to the connection with James Graham Clarke.

Coal was the main export but other exports included worked iron, copperas and grindstones. Butter, bacon and salmon were shipped to London to supply the London markets.

The main imports in 1801 were timber, iron, flax, hemp, tar, tallow, wines, spirits and sugars. In 1800, about 900 ships were employed throughout the year in the coal trade and 7,969 ships were cleared from the Custom House.

Sailing was dangerous. In 1756, it was reported; "Newcastle, Oct. 9. On Tuesday morning about one o'clock we had a violent hurricane, whereby several houses were blown down, others unroofed, many stripped of their chimney pots etc. The damage done on the river is very deplorable, viz. about forty keels were either sunk or driven to sea, and several men on board lost. The 'Welcome Messenger' of London was driven to sea with her ports open, with three men and two boys on board. The 'Sarah' and 'Margaret' of London were also driven to sea with her ports open, and no accounts are heard of either since. A Danish vessel laden with iron for the factory at Swalwell (a village in Gateshead), was sunk at Burdon's Key. The 'Blessing of Whitby' was overset at Jarrow Key, and four boys drowned. By travellers from Aldstone Moor we are told, the people there would have it that the earth shook, so that they ran under the hedges for safety; but were soon dislodged from thence by the breaking of trees, the tumbling of stones etc."[5]

The above sounded like a devastating storm. Ships that were moored in the harbour and river were affected so the consequences of a storm like this would have been catastrophic at sea.

'Burdon's Key' is mentioned in the article. This may be an indication that merchandise from ships they were involved with docked at this quay.

Rowland Burdon, a wealthy gentleman lived in Newcastle but he may have wanted to escape the grime, noise and clamour of Newcastle for the life of a country gentleman as well as continuing his business interests in Newcastle. It was decided a country estate was necessary, so one was purchased.

CHAPTER THREE
The Castle Eden Estate

Rowland Burdon bought the Castle Eden Estate in 1758 from representatives of the Rt. Hon William Bromley who had been secretary of state under Queen Anne. The Manor had been unoccupied for 150 years. About half of the land, amounting to about 1,700 acres was unenclosed and laying in waste, so work was needed to enclose and improve the land. The Church had been without a roof and in ruins for a long time. The old castle of Robert de Brus had long gone and the subsequent manor house was in ruins.

Rowland Burdon had inherited money from his Uncle John so decided to invest in land and an estate. There was much work to be done. He enclosed and improved the land and built a church before building a residence for himself. The church, St. James' was completed only six years after Rowland Burdon bought the manor. This Rowland Burdon's son later added two aisles and gallery to the church.

The Rowland Burdon residence, referred to as the Castle, was considered to be a mansion house. Mock battlements round the roof of the house styled the building like a castle, probably harking back as a reminder that a castle was once on the estate.

Rowland Burdon must have seen the need for a country estate as many wealthy men did at that time. He maintained his house in Newcastle but may have seen the countryside as being a healthier place to spend some time. His wife and sister had died in 1758. He may have considered the increasing industry dirt and pollution along the Tyne made the city a less healthy place than the countryside.

As well as buying the Castle Eden Estate, Rowland Burdon bought land from the four surviving daughters and co-heirs of Sir Baldwin Conyers, who had owned the manor of Horden, lands in Preston in Skerne and Little Thorpe. Preston Le Skerne is hamlet within agricultural land near Aycliffe. These lands were conveyed to Rowland Burdon on 23rd November 1767 for £20,000, a considerable sum of money in 1767. Rowland Burdon also spent money to conduct extensive renovation and restoration of the land on the Castle Eden Estate. He must have been very wealthy at this time.

Castle Eden

The Castle Eden estate had been occupied by Robert de Brus who owned a substantial amount of land in the land in the area, including land in Hartlepool. He was reputed to have a castle near Castle Eden. When Robert de Brus returned to Scotland he returned with plunder including prisoners of both sexes taken from Hartlepool. When he returned to attack a year later, many castles, probably including the fortress at Castle Eden, were raised to the ground.

During 1143–1152 when William St. Barbara was Bishop of Durham, Robert de Brus granted the chapel of Eden to the monks of St. Cuthbert. In 1764, a small chancel was built in St. James' Church. Whilst enlarging this chancel in 1896, two local limestone grave covers of a peculiar design, dating from between 1150 and 1180, were unearthed. Both these stones, possibly from the time of the earlier chapel, were placed inside the church against the East wall of the organ-chamber. A coin was also found during these alterations. It was dated between 1162 and 1176 and was proved to be a denier from the time of Henry 1 and during the time of the Archbishop of Rheims. This coin was sent to the British Museum.

In 1318, Eustace de Eden gave half of his land to St. Cuthbert (the Monastery of Durham) and 10/- out rent from the moiety he received. This donation he made in discharge of 17 marks, which the Monks of Durham had paid to release him from Leo, the Jew of York.[1]

In Catholic Doctrine of the time, lending money for interest was considered the sin of usury so Jews became moneylenders. The interest would increase over time, so those who borrowed would have an incentive to repay as quickly as possible. Eustace de Eden had 17 marks, probably meaning 17 loan transactions, which he had made and was made to repay the money. The sum he owed must have been vast if he had to forfeit so much to enable him to repay these loans. Eustace could not forfeit the land to Leo the Jew, as Jews were not permitted to own land. Instead, Eustace de Eden gave the land and income from some rents so they could forward the money he owed to Leo in York. Leo was probably rich but possibly not as rich as Aaron of Lincoln had been in the 12th Century when he was considered the wealthiest man in Britain. In this way, the Church obtained half of the estate previously owned by Eustace de Eden.

There were much earlier occupations in the area by Vikings when the lands between Jodene (Yoden) and Billingham were given to Scula, a Viking Captain by King Reinewald. This was a time of excessive tribute demanded by Scula ,making some Vikings wealthy. It may have been at this time that a wealthy Viking lost a gold armband in the vicinity of what is now Shotton Hall. The gold armband was made originally by the Romans but additions had been made by Viking craftsmen. The wealthy Viking and his servants, or slaves, may have looked to no avail for the valuable armband because it was not uncovered until 1881 when it was found in the garden of Shotton Hall.

There was another valuable find but this time it had not been lost, it had been buried. In 1765, labourers laying a hedge on the estate unearthed human remains and a glass vase or beaker. A letter written by Rowland Burdon dated November 6th, 1775 describes the event; "This glass vase was found about the year 1775 at Castle Eden, in the County of Durham, in throwing down a hedge back about 100 yards north of the bridge leading to the Castle, and near where two ash trees now stand upon an eminence near the roadside. The mouth of the vase was applied to the skull of a human figure so near the surface as to leave the bottom of the vase exposed in the gutter of the hedge, which was mistaken by the labourer who found it for the bottom of a broken bottle. The body had lain horizontally east to west, the head towards the east, and had been covered with a heap of ordinary field stones. The labourer said that the skull and bones appeared entire, but he was ordered by the clergyman of the place to make no further search. I had the curiosity however, on my return to Castle Eden soon after, to open the ground, where I found the heap of stones remaining with such a cavity as might be supposed to contain an ordinary body, and a quantity of deep-coloured soil, which I presumed to have been the ashes of the bones."[2]

The labourers would have received quite a shock when they unearthed a skeleton. One of their first thoughts must have been to ask the local clergyman what to do. Instructions to leave the remains alone did not appear to influence the inquisitive Rowland Burdon. He 'found a heap of stones' and a mound of earth covering a cavity large enough to contain a body. The remains were Anglo-Saxon and his discovery appears to indicate the cairn of stones covered by a mound of earth was a small tumulus. The body had been buried with grave goods; a vase which first mistaken for the remains of a bottle. This artefact was given to the British Museum in October 1947 by a descendent, Mrs. Sclater-Booth. It identified as a late 5th AD Frankish claw beaker, so called because of 'claws' that have been attached to the thin glass. The beaker is made from 'pale greenish-blue glass with 'trails of royal blue in the neck and base.' The Museum considers the claw beaker being in 'pristine condition' and must have been the treasured possession of the Anglo-Saxon with whom it was buried. The beaker is rare; 'the only one of its kind ever found in England.'

The Anglo Saxon who was buried with this claw beaker must have been wealthy or important to own such a treasure. Rowland Burdon describes the position of the body as lying 'horizontally east to west.' This is the position usually used for a Christian burial. The head is usually positioned towards the west. Those holding church positions like clergymen have their head positioned towards the east so on the day of the Resurrection, they are facing the souls rising from the dead. This body had the head facing towards the east, so it is possible the person buried was not only very wealthy but also had a connection with the Christian Church. The estate bought by Rowland Burdon had considerable history.

Rowland Burdon the third, spent time both in Newcastle and Castle Eden. He was wealthy and had wealthy relatives other than his deceased Uncle John Reeve whose wealth he had inherited. Because of his wealth, he would mix with wealthy people. He was wealthy enough to go into partnership with Aubone Surtees.

The Exchange Bank

This had been founded by Ralph Carr in 1755. Thirteen years later, in 1768 Rowland Burdon and Aubone Surtees founded the Exchange Bank in Newcastle. Rowland Burdon had probably known Aubone Surtees from when he became apprentice to Aubone's father Ambrose Surtees in 1742 with Rowland probably working alongside Aubone in his Ambrose Surtees' business. Rowland and Aubone decided to open a bank together.

Both men had earlier been in business together earlier in what was described as a shop.[3] In 1776, Surtees and Burdon were robbed by thieves who had broken into their shop. This 'shop' was broken into during the hours of darkness in late November 1757, when thieves entered the shop by the roof, probably through a skylight window. There was broken glass in the counting house and several traces of blood, so at least one of them must have been injured whilst breaking in. The thieves stole silver and money. This 'shop' appears to have been dealing in coins and silver. Merchants like Surtees and Burdon were respected. They kept money and goods like silver and gold. This was the beginning of banking. They would be known to clients when they issued shares to open the Exchange Bank in 1768 in Moseley Street Newcastle. Crimes were still committed. On 8th July 1777 a box was stolen or lost from a stage wagon between Edinburgh and Newcastle. The box, containing Newcastle bank notes and on its way to Messrs Bell Cookson and Messrs Surtees and Burdon was put into stage at Edinburgh on 15th January but not missed in Newcastle until Monday the 20th. There must have been a considerable amount of money in the box as there was reward of £50 for information. Some of the contents of the box were recovered but it is uncertain whether Henry Howey's money was returned. If Surtees and Burdon, as merchants and bankers, were transporting the money in a named box so they were may have had some responsibility for not ensuring its security during transit. They would have wanted to secure the return of the box belonging to Henry Howey to safeguard their reputations, especially with their shareholders like John Graham Clarke, the ship and plantation owner who was one of the principal shareholders in the Exchange Bank and would have been well known to Rowland Burdon and Aubone Surtees and other wealthy people.

Entertainments in Newcastle

Newcastle catered for wealthy people. Some if not all of the following entertainments and events may have been enjoyed or witnessed by both father and son Rowland Burdon during their lives in Newcastle.

A theatre opened at the Turk's Head in 1747. Celebratory banquets were held at the Turk's Head. Cock-fighting was widespread at this time and the Turks Head was one of the venues.

There was a theatre in Castle Garth from 1781. A Theatre Royal (not the present Theatre Royal in Grey Street) was built in Moseley Street by subscription. Advertisements for the purchase of shares appeared in local newspapers. The shares were £30 each and eighty subscribers bought 130 shares. More adverts appeared but there was still insufficient finance to build the theatre. A committee was formed to negotiate loans of £2,500 from Newcastle banks, with committee members acting as security for the loan. The total cost of the building, including land purchase and conveyances amounted to £6,281 17s 6d. The money was raised and the theatre opened. Stephen Kemble managed the Theatre Royal from 1792-1806. His sister, Sarah Siddon and other members of the Kemble family like Charles and John Kemble were also actors. A Sunderland born comic actor John Emery who worked in Covent Garden also performed in the theatre as did Master Betty, a child actor, who was so popular he drew in the sum of £213.

In 1760 the New Ranelagh Pleasure Gardens opened in Newcastle. The first Ranelagh Pleasure Garden rivalling the Vauxhall Gardens, opened in 1742 adjacent to the Royal Hospital in

London. Pleasure Gardens became very popular. They had a social season that included, balls, public breakfasts, concerts, masquerades and firework displays.

Brodies' Long Room, in the Big Market held various functions, meetings and celebratory dinners. There was a meeting about American Affairs in March 1778 where a petition to the government was signed by 60 people. There was a court martial there in 1779.

Well attended balls were held. There were entertainments with cold collations and several concerts. There were fund raising activities that frequently included dinners after the event. In July 1788, a confirmation service at St. Nicholas held by the Bishop of Durham was followed by a dinner at Brodies Long Room. There were other fund raising church services. Stewards of the Infirmary had Church services with collections afterwards to raise money. A good sermon was necessary to encourage donations. £26 1s 2d was raised in 1776 but only £14 19s 3d ½ was contributed one year later apparently because of a pathetic sermon entitled 'Let us not weary in well doing' preached by the Rev. Robert Thorp, M.A., Vicar of Chillingham. The congregation must have been so wearied by his sermon that they did not feel inclined to 'do well' by giving to charity but many of them joined the stewards in a celebratory dinner, again at Brodies Long Room, an expensive place to eat. The celebratory dinner would have cost much more than what was contributed in the collection. Someone was so bored they gave a halfpenny, but many were enlivened enough to have a sumptuous repast at Brodies.

The practice of a Church service in order to raise money for the Infirmary continued with the service still followed by a dinner. Rowland Burdon jnr became a steward, so he would have attended these services and enjoyed the celebratory dinners.

On the afternoon of 5th August 1798, Rowland Burdon, as a steward of the Infirmary, attended the service in St. Nicholas' Church. The Infirmary served the sick, lame and poor of Durham, Newcastle-upon-Tyne and Gateshead. He was joined by his fellow stewards, some of whom were, Sir Thomas J Clavering Bart, Rev

John Fawcett, Mr. Anthony Surtees, Chas John Brandling, and Job Bulman. Rowland Burdon was in distinguished company. After service the stewards and those who had bought tickets costing 10/6d enjoyed a celebratory dinner at Brodies. It is to be wondered whether they entered into the annual celebration to listen to the sermon of Rev. Prosser and contribute to the collection or enjoy the company and good food afterwards at Brodies.

Lectures were also held in the Long-room. In March 1783 Mr. Clark gave a Philosophical lecture to a large audience who had paid to attend this lecture, the first in a series of eight, costing 10s 6d for all eight lectures or 2s for a single lecture. The first lecture, including an experiment was about an engine for drawing coals. The new coal engine was exhibited for the whole course of the eight lectures. The lectures appear to have been well received and well attended.

The topic of James Graham's lecture in 1783 was pills, potions and electrical baths. It included a demonstration of a 'celestial' electromagnetic bed stuffed with stallion hair. The celestial bed which included music that came from organ pipes, oriental fragrances and a release of 'ethereal' gases from a dome at the top was supposedly an aid to conception. The Mayor, Mr. Atkinson must have considered his lectures and demonstrations improper because he banned any future lectures by James Graham but he did return for a demonstration of a mud bath exhibition in 1791.

As an Honorary Member of the Literary and Philosophical Society, Rowland Burdon jnr may have attended these lectures in their venue in Groat Market. As well as a venue for lectures, there was an extensive library and collections of curiosities. Many years later there were lectures and demonstrations by people such as Stephenson, Swan and Brunel.

In 1778 in Newcastle, there were five coffee and punch houses in Sandhill. Henry Bourne described Sandhill in 1736 as a, 'spacious place and adorned with buildings very high and stately, whose rooms speak the ancient grandeur being very large and magnificent.' Aubone Surtees, partner of Rowland Burdon lived in 41-44 Sandhill, one of the high stately buildings, indicative of his wealth and status.

If theatre, inns, coffee houses and pleasure gardens did not suffice, there were many booksellers in Newcastle. After the lapse of the Licensing Act in 1695, Newcastle became the most important printing centre after London. In the 1770's more children's books were published in Newcastle than anywhere outside London. By 1790 there were; 20 printers, 12 booksellers and stationers, 13 bookbinders, and 3 engravers including Thomas Bewick in Newcastle. There were also 7 subscription libraries, St. Nicholas' parish library with its 5,000 books, 3 circulating libraries and Joseph Barber's library at Amen Corner with its stock of 5,000 books. There was plenty to read.

If the gentleman preferred horse racing to reading, there plenty of accessible race courses like those at Morpeth, Scarborough, Durham, Newcastle, Kelso and Hexham. Rowland Burdon owned race horses. Some of these were a brown mare called Duchess, Smart a bay colt, Frolic, Dorcas and Orpheus. Being an owner, he probably went to the courses, particularly when his horses were running.

Rowland Burdon jnr was a member of the Masons, so he attended Masonic events and was poll bearer at the funerals of other masons, like that of William Reed an eminent wine and corn merchant. At his funeral in St Nicholas Church, the other pall bearers were Sir Walter Blackett Matthew Ridley, Edward Collingwood, John Erasmus Blackett, and Christopher Fawcett Francis Forster, all eminent gentlemen.

Lunardi's Balloon

Newcastle appeared to be a lively, entertaining place, a place where someone like Lunardi, the aeronaut may come to exhibit his balloon. Many, probably including Rowland Burdon, would have read of Lunardi's exploits and eagerly anticipated the forthcoming event advertised in the Newcastle Courant of September 1786 [4] when Lunardi would "ascend to the aetherial regions in a balloon."

The balloon would ascend from the Spittal in Westgate Street. Tickets costing 3/- would be available for those wanted to enter the area where the balloon was to be filled with gas and made ready to take off. The tickets could be bought from the Subscription Coffee Rooms, Bella's Coffee House, Mr. Fishers, Mr. Hodgson's and J. Whitfield Booksellers. For an extra one shilling entrance fee; "A substantial scaffold for ladies with convenient seats, will be erected near the place where the balloon will be filled; and to prevent its being crowded with improper persons, every one having an equal right, Mr. Lunardi had been advised to let the builder charge 1/- admittance upon the scaffold, to defray the expense of erection."

There are two reasons for the extra shilling. The first is to deter 'improper persons 'from crowding the area where 'ladies' were to sit. The advert hastens to add that everyone has an equal right to sit with the ladies but it implies that extra cost will deter 'improper persons' from doing so. Improper persons probably included pickpockets, who would be certain to show their presence at a large gathering.

For another shilling one could visit Brodies' Long Room where the balloon and car were to be exhibited prior to its flight. A further 5/- would purchase a copy of the 'Scotch Sky'; a series of letters to Lunardi's Guardian Chevalier Compagni and a portrait of Mr. Lunardi etched by the 'celebrated Mr. Burke.'

The total outlay for all the events, including a seat in the scaffold would cost ten shillings, way beyond the remit of many of the inhabitants of Newcastle but for those with wealth, this occasion would be eagerly anticipated.

This flight was to be an occasion for the whole city of Newcastle. A flag was to be hoisted 'On the old castle at the very moment the Apparatus for filling his Aerostatic Machine' was to be 'set to work'. Those who could not afford to enter the enclosure would be able to view the balloon as it rose above the city.

Lunardi's exploits had appeared in many newspaper and many would know that Vincent (Vincenzo) Lunardi was the first man to navigate the skies of England. He was an Italian but he lived in Britain working as the secretary to Prince Caramanico, the Neapolitan Ambassador.

This proposed ascent in Newcastle was not Vincenzo Lunardi's first ascent in a balloon. In September 1784 this ascent took place from Moorfield in London. Such huge crowds gathered to witness the event that; [5] "not a plain, or an eminence, a window or a roof, a chimney or a steeple, within the sight of Bedlam, but what were populously thronged."

It would appear dangerous for people to climb on roofs, steeples and chimneys but this would be the first time a man would take to the air. Some thought Lunardi must be mad to attempt such a dangerous feat. The newspapers used Lunardi's name as a pun for Lunatic; there was a reference to Bedlam in the account quoted, Bedlam being a noted Lunatic Asylum in London.

One hundred and fifty thousand spectators witnessed the flight. Among them was the Prince of Wales. He arrived in the Artillery Ground at half past one in the afternoon. The Prince viewed the apparatus and the balloon before retiring to the Artillery Suite with his followers and others who had paid the high cost of admission. Those who could not afford the admission rented out windows in nearby houses to view the spectacle.

The Duke and Duchess of Richmond, in company with Mr. Pitt, paid fifty guineas to occupy an apartment in a floor-cloth manufactory, in the City Road.

His Majesty the King did not have to pay as he viewed the balloon through a telescope from the Queen's Presence Chamber.

Filling the balloon had commenced the previous evening under the direction of Dr. George Fordyce. The 'rarified air' as they called hydrogen was produced using zinc, oil of vitriol (Sulphuric acid check), and steel shavings.

An accountant of this first flight, written by Lunardi, appeared in the 'Scot's Magazine' of 1st October 1784. Lunardi said that both himself and his assistant Mr. Biggins intended to make the first flight; Biggins to undertake 'the philosophical experiments and observations' and Lunardi to ensure 'the conduct of the machine and the use of the vertical oars in depressing the balloon at pleasure."

That was the intention. However, Lunardi considered the 'multitude' was 'impatient' so it was decided to set off before the balloon was filled to capacity. This meant one person could be lifted by the balloon, resulting in Biggins being unable to go. Lunardi did take a cat, a dog and a pigeon in a cage.

As Lunardi was ready to go, everyone watching from the Gallery of the Artillery Suite, including the Prince of Wales, raised their hats in salute. A gun fired at five past two. Lunardi [5] "embraced his friends. All matters (were) adjusted. A second gun was fired as the signal of ascension. Insensible must the heart be which did not feel itself anxious and interested at that moment for his fate.

The machine was launched into the air; and after having mounted about twelve yards, reclined to its native earth. Mr. Lunardi took his seat in the gallery with great composure and confidence on the balloon's being launched; but finding himself too equally poised, he discharged a part of the ballast, which consisted of small bags of white sand, and by that means relieved his weight and caused a regular and most beautiful ascension. There was cheers and applause."

When it reached a height of 20 yards it was 'depressed by the wind', making it appear to 'pause majestically before the departure." Lunardi discharged some of the ballast and the balloon rose up to 200 yards.

As he did so, Lunardi "saluted the populace with a great elegance and gallantry, by waving a blue flag, which he had taken for that purpose, and seemingly bidding them a friendly adieu."[5]

Reaching this height meant that the huge crowd of 150,000 people outside the confines of the Artillery Ground could begin to see the balloon. The mass of people, 'rent the air with their acclamation and applause'.

Lunardi 'worked the oars' however one of the oars broke and fell to the ground. He had a thermometer on board and the temperature became colder as the balloon rose into the air. As it grew colder, he decided to have a few glasses of wine. He ate a leg of chicken with his wine but the bread he had brought with him had been mixed with sand from the ballast, so the bread was inedible.

Lunardi recorded what he saw and how he felt. He had 'not the slightest sense of motion from the machine. There was a 'stillness' and an 'extent and magnificence to the scene.' The 'horizon seemed a perfect circle' and the 'terminating line' appeared' several hundred miles in circumference.'

He had 'soared from the apprehensions and anxieties of the Artillery Ground, and felt as if (he) had left behind all the cares and passions that molest mankind.' This description has echoes of how it must have felt as man made the first flight in to space.

Lunardi said that 'the face of the countryside had a mild and permanent verdure to which Italy is a stranger.' He considered the view was,' such as the ancients supposed Jupiter to have of the earth.' He looked down on this earth, the rivers meandering, the sea glistening with the rays of the sun, the immediate district beneath (him), spotted with cities, towns, villages and houses, pouring out their inhabitants to hail my appearance.'[6]

Lunardi used his remaining oar for about half an hour before becoming 'fatigued'. After these exertions he 'again had access to (his) bottle; this (he) emptied to the health of my friends and bene-factors from the lower world.' He then sat down and wrote 'four pages of desultory observation to (his) friend and patron Prince Caramanio.'

His cat was badly affected by the cold so he decided to descend using his oar. When he was about 300 yards from the ground he 'spoke through his trumpet to some country people.' These people probably got quite a shock and surprise at seeing the balloon descending and hearing a voice from the sky.

About half past three, Lunardi descended into a cornfield in South Mimms. His cat, 'the poor animal' was 'badly affected', so he 'landed it'. Whether it survived or was taken care of is uncertain.

The pigeon had already escaped and flown away, so he just had the dog for company as he once again ascended into the air by throwing out ballast from the balloon. As he rose, 'the clouds to the eastward rolled beneath (him) in masses immensely larger that the waves of the sea.' He journeyed on before making his final descent and landing in a 'spacious meadow' in Stondon near Ware in Hertfordshire.

When Lunardi landed there were labourers working in the meadow. He called for their assistance; they exclaimed they would have "nothing to do with one who came in the devil's house, or on the devil's horse'. He 'could not distinguish which of these phrases they used.' The labourers must have been terrified as they saw him not as a god like Jupiter but rather as someone associated with the devil.

He did receive help. He owed his 'deliverance to the spirit and generosity' of a 'young woman who was with an old wife in the field.' She 'took hold of a cord' he had 'thrown out'. The young woman called to the men and they 'yielded that assistance to her.' They helped her secure the balloon by holding cords and ropes. A 'crowd of people from the neighbourhood soon assembled' and they were 'very obliging' as they helped him to 'disembark.'

Five 'gentlemen' on horseback had followed him from London. They helped Lunardi secure the balloon to the ground. The 'inflammable air was let out by an incision and produced a most offensive stench which is said to have affected the atmosphere of the countryside.' This 'stench' may have convinced the labourers who at first would not help him that he had indeed come from the devil. They may have said that only someone from the devil could have had such a stench so bad that it 'affected the atmosphere' where they lived and worked.

Mr. Biggins did get to ascend in the balloon from the George's Fields on 3rd July 1785. The gondola of the balloon was differently designed to accommodate four people; Lunardi, Biggins, Colonel Hastings and Mrs. Letitia Ann Sage.

Mrs. Letitia Ann Sage was an actress who performed in Drury Lane Theatre. She was reportedly a beauty and much admired. Unfortunately the balloon could only carry a certain weight, and Mrs Letitia Ann Sage, described as Junoesque, weighed in excess of 200 pounds. It was evident on the day that the balloon would not ascend carrying these four people. Colonel Hastings stepped down. There was still a problem. George Biggins had been disappointed twice already, so Lunardi decided his friend and assistant George could accompany Mrs. Letitia Ann Sage on the flight.

Mrs Letitia Ann Sage, wife of Cheapside haberdasher, was dressed for the occasion wearing a very low cut silk dress supposedly to be more wind resistant and a large feathered hat. She stepped through the door of the gondola, closely followed by George Biggins.

The door of the gondola needed to be laced with threads to close it securely but once George entered, the balloon commenced its ascent with the door not completely fastened. The balloon sailed over Piccadilly. Those watching got a full view of Letitia Ann on all fours frantically lacing the door with George Biggins close behind her. Some viewers probably did not realise they were making the door secure and possibly reached a different conclusion. It may said that Mrs. Letitia Ann Sage was England's the first female aeronaut. The Northampton Mercury 4 July 1785 reported the balloon, 'took its course westward, and made a very beautiful appearance over Westminster Bridge; and after it had been launched about a quarter of an hour, it altered its course, and was seen very plain in Fleet Street, Newgate Street, Holborn etc, and almost all over London; the direction then was North West.'

George Biggins, a young wealthy Old Etonian was probably used to comfort. There were pillows to sit on and a picnic lunch of cold chicken and Italian wine. They sailed over the countryside and landed ninety minutes later in a field near Harrow.

Unfortunately the gondola of the balloon scraped along the ground as it landed. The couple were fine but the farmer's crops were damaged causing him great annoyance.

The day was saved when a group of boys from Harrow School, who had been watching the flight of the balloon, raced into the field. They all chipped in money to compensate the farmer for his loss and he left the scene reasonably happy.

Once the balloon was secured, Mrs Letitia Ann Sage alighted from the gondola. She, despite her weight, was reportedly hoisted aloft on the young gentlemen's shoulders and they carried her off to the nearest inn. George Biggins had intended to resume the flight but by this time there were so many spectators around the spectacle of the balloon, that he abandoned this idea.

The aerial travellers alighted in perfect safety a few minutes after three o'clock in Harrow Field, after a very agreeable journey, they were received by the young gentlemen and neighbours with the utmost politeness friendly attention. It was the intention of Mr. Biggins to have proceeded further, after having parted with his companion, but he was prevented by the people about him.

The balloon was exhibited in the Pantheon in Oxford Street. There was, of course, an entrance fee. Mrs. Letitia Ann Sage was in attendance to talk about her adventurous aerial flight. She had received publicity as the first female to make an aerial voyage in England, so she capitalised on the event. For one shilling one could purchase a copy of a letter she wrote to a female friend. In this letter she described 'the general appearance and effects of her expedition.'[7] An engraving of Mrs. Sage taken from a portrait painted by Shelley could be purchased for half a crown to accompany Lunardi's etching. Both could be purchased together.

Vincenzo Lunardi made five flights in Scotland in his Grand Air Balloon. The balloon was made from green, pink and yellow silk and was exhibited fully expanded and floating state in the nave of St. Mungo's Cathedral in Glasgow.

The first of these flights occurred in October 1785, witnessed by huge crowds thronging the grounds of the George Heriot School in Edinburgh to witness the take-off of the hydrogen balloon. The flight lasted 46 miles, across the Firth of Forth and landing in Coaltown. The Scots Magazine reported this event and commented that "The beauty and grandeur of the spectacle could only be exceeded by the cool, intrepid manner in which the adventurer conducted himself; and indeed he seemed infinitely more at ease than the greater part of his spectators."

It is to be doubted that Lunardi retained this composure when he made a return visit to Edinburgh in December 1785. Again the balloon ascended from Herriot's Garden with Lunardi as the occupant. This time the balloon did not sail over land. It sailed towards the German Ocean (North Sea). An observer watched the flight across the sea through his telescope as the balloon drifted further and further away before finally dropping into sea. Lunardi was afloat in the water for about one and a half hours before being picked up by a fishing boat about five miles off Gullness. Lunardi could not have held out much longer and he was lucky to be rescued.

During the rescue, the balloon had to be cut away from the car. It rose rapidly in the air and rapidly disappeared from view. It was later found by Captain Air's cutter about 12 miles from the island of May and the remains of the balloon were carried to Anstruther.

This misadventure did not deter Lunardi. In January 1786, he returned to London to construct a new machine. He was going to visit Newcastle and ascend from the new balloon above Newcastle and the surrounding countryside.

Lunardi's visit to Newcastle would have been eagerly awaited. Each of the twelve flights he had made previously had been witnessed by many crowds of people. When the balloon took off from the Spittal in Sept 1786 , "every eminence in this town" was present , "and every place adjoining the Spittal crowded with people."[8]

The Burdon family were amongst the 'eminence' of Newcastle. Female members of the family who attended would have paid the extra shilling to excitedly sit in their seats in anticipation of a flight into the air they had read about in newspapers but would now witness themselves.

The procedure to fill the balloon commenced. It was half filled by about 1 pm and when just over half filled, a number of 'gentlemen were employed in holding down the balloon by the netting in which it was enclosed.' Spectators watched as the balloon gradually expanded.

The feelings of anticipation and excitement changed suddenly into apprehension as Mr. Lunardi, "Introduced the remaining part of the acid and the effervescence being at that time remarkably strong, forced a great quantity of inflammable air in through the hole, which was only 4" in diameter, before the plug could be replaced. This gave out such an alarm to some the gentlemen on that side of the balloon, who thought it was on fire, that they immediately quitted their hold of the net, and flew from it to the other side, alarming those stationed there also…. The balloon being liberated on one side made a rapid stretch upwards, whereby a considerable opening was torn in its neck; this occasioned a loud noise and a considerable discharge of inflammable air; Mr. Lunardi ran to the opposite side, and desired the gentlemen there to keep their hold, assuring them there was not the least danger; the consternation however soon became general and the balloon being set at liberty, ascended with great rapidity."[9]

Unfortunately, Mr. Ralph Heron jnr had twisted a rope and fastened the top round his arm. The balloon dragged him up 500 feet. The netting dislodged itself from the balloon at this height. The netting and rope attached to Ralph Heron plummeted to the ground and fell into a nearby garden. Ralph Heron was fatally injured and he died a few hours later.

The day had commenced with an expectation of a magnificent flight into the air. To the horror of the spectators it became a "scene of grief and commiseration." Lunardi was inconsolable and in a state of "deep mourning."

Lunardi had been publicly acclaimed as the 'daredevil aeronaut.' He was now so heavily criticised that he left Britain. He continued as an aeronaut in Italy, Spain and Portugal. He died in poverty in a Lisbon Monastery in 1806. The people of Newcastle never witnessed the wonder of flight. All they would remember was a tragic accident. Other gathered to witness this events may have also remembered being victims of crime.

Crime in Newcastle

There was crime in Newcastle like the pickpockets who had flocked to Spittal on the day of the supposed flight. Pickpockets gathered whenever crowds assembled. In September 1786 Henry Jennings was executed by hanging on the Town Moor for horse stealing. The Newcastle Courant recorded when he died he was, very penitent and admonished the wicked and unwary to take warning by his sad and untimely death.

Henry Jennings was executed for stealing a horse. Horse stealing had affected Rowland Burdon. In February 1755 Rowland Burdon of Stockton advertised the loss of a horse. The horse is described as being, a strong chestnut gelding with a white face, 15 hands high, hog-mained, a scab on his back hurt by a cart-saddle, lame before, and 21 years old." [9] It would appear the elderly horse may not have been kindly treated if it had been injured by a cart saddle as well as being lamed previously. Yet he offered a 'handsome reward' for intelligence that would 'secure the person who stole him.' Horse thieves like Harry Jennings were frequently hung for their crime.

Crowds witnessed his hanging of Henry Jennings in Newcastle. Thomas Brown, a millwright and Thomas Hamilton, a cordwainer, were both standing almost directly under the gallows watching the hanging. During the event, Thomas Hamilton had 6s 6d stolen out of his left pocket. About three minutes later the pocket of Thomas Hamilton was also picked. A constable was summoned and a man arrested.

There were pickpockets at the execution of Jane Jameson, this time for murder rather than theft. The account of the procession that left the prison bound for the execution is gruesomely reported. The procession was led by the Town Sergeants dressed in black with black cocked hats and wearing swords. The Town Marshall followed wearing his official dress. The cart containing the prisoner followed next. She sat in the cart on top of her coffin. To make sure she did not escape, in the cart on either side there were 8 javelin men and 10 constables with staves guarding her. After the cart came the mourning coach with its occupants; Rev R. Green the Chaplain, Mr. Adamson the Under Sheriff, Mr. Sopwith the Gaoler and the Clerk of St. Andrew's Mr Scott. The newspaper reported that; "The unhappy woman kept her eyes shut all the way, as she had been directed, that her thoughts might not be distracted by sight of the crowd. The procession arrived at the gallows, which was erected at the usual place, on a part of the Town Moor near the Barracks, at a few minutes before 10 o'clock. The Rev. R. Green, on reaching the fatal spot, prayed with her, and a psalm was sung. The worthy chaplain then asked her if she died in charity with all mankind, and she said she did. To his question whether she had the same faith in Jesus Christ for the salvation of her soul which she had before expressed, she also answered in the affirmative. The reverend gentleman recommended her to continue to pray until the last moment, which she appeared to do, then shook hands with her, and bidding her fare well, said, 'May Almighty God have mercy on your soul.' She appeared until the last remarkably firm, and when the cap was placed over her face, she got on a stool upon the platform in the cart, and when the cord was adjusted about her neck, she said in a steady tone, 'I am ready', then stooping as if to meet her fate, she was launched into eternity, expiring in almost an instant without a struggle. After she had hung nearly an hour, the body was taken down and conveyed to the Surgeon's Hall for dissection, where lectures have since been given upon it. This unfortunate woman was very ignorant, and her course had been extremely vicious. It was given in evidence in the trial that her mother had charged her with destroying her two illegitimate children; and it is currently reported that in one of her mad drunken fits she had attempted to kill her father. The crowd that attended to witness the execution was immense, 20,000 more than half of them women." [10]

Death of Rowland Burdon III

Rowland Burdon the third died in 1786, long before the gruesome execution of Jane Jameson. His will stipulated that he wanted to be buried "without pomp in the East End of the choir in Sedgefield Church in which vault (lie) the remains of my late dear wife, father, brothers, daughter," wishes that were carried out. His body was given a respectful funeral, not given to the surgeon's for dissection. Rowland Burdon had led a privileged life both in Newcastle and in Castle Eden but he had faced misery in his life with the early loss of both his wife and baby daughter as well as the early death of his sister but he was laid to rest in the family vault at Sedgefield. Although his son Rowland Burdon IV was his father's sole heir, there were other bequests. A yearly annuity of £200, out of the manor of Horden, was to be paid to Ann Griffith the housekeeper who may have been his housekeeper for many years. The other bequests were quite small, so Rowland Burdon IV became a wealthy man.

Rowland Burdon third's death in October 1786 was announced in several national newspapers so he appears to have been of some note; "On Wednesday last died Rowland Burdon one of the Proprietors of the Exchange Bank, a considerable benefactor to the Infirmary and the poor in general. His large property, together with his interest in the bank, devolve on his only son Rowland Burdon Esq." [11]

While his father was alive Rowland Burdon IV was referred in the newspapers as Rowland Burdon jnr. He had now inherited property, wealth and his father's interest in the bank. He was junior no longer and as a proprietor of the Exchange Bank had a great deal of responsibility.

CHAPTER FOUR

Rowland Burdon IV

Rowland Burdon was baptised on the 30th December 1756 in Newcastle. His mother died when he was very young. Rowland attended the Royal Grammar School in Newcastle. This school was founded in 1525 by Thomas Horsley, the Mayor of Newcastle, and awarded a royal foundation by Queen Elizabeth I. When Rowland Burdon was in attendance, the eminent scholar Rev Hugh Moises, was Headmaster. John Scott and his elder brother William attended this school at the same time as Rowland Burdon. All three went to Oxford University. Rowland Burdon and John Scott, supposedly remained life-long friends with, John Scott aged 15 and Rowland Burdon at 16, going to University College Oxford at the same time. John Scott was bright, winning the annual prize for prose competition in 1771. John Scott would rise to become Earl Eldon and his brother William, Lord Stowell.

John Scott and Bessie Surtees

Rowland 's father and Aubone Surtees had known each other very well for a long time. They were probably friends as well as working partners. In 1772 Aubone Surtees probably confided in Rowland Burdon senior, over his concern on a serious family matter. Aubone's daughter Elizabeth, Bessie as she was known, had fallen in love with John Scott. He was bright but he was the young son of a coal trader. John's father was reasonably wealthy but he was a coal trader, so his son John was just not a suitable match for Aubone's daughter. Aubone forbad Bessie from seeing John, but one night

53

when everyone was asleep, Bessie climbed down from her bedroom and eloped to Scotland with her beloved John. Once in Scotland, they married.

One may wonder how John Scott met Bessie Surtees. Rowland Burdon IV knew both, probably very well, so he may have been not only instrumental in their meeting but also in helping them to elope.

When John and Bessie returned to Newcastle they were reconciled with Bessie's father. John trained in law. John Scott became a Member of Parliament. In 1793 he was Attorney General. By 1799 he was appointed Lord Chief Justice. Aubone Surtees was probably proud of John Scott's political rise but died one year before John Scott was made Lord Eldon in 1801 and became Lord Chancellor of England. Bessie had made a good choice when she fell in love with John Scott and eloped with him to Scotland. Brother-in law William also did well. He too went into law and became Lord Stowell; Judge of the High Court of the Admiralty.

The Grand Tour

After University, in 1779, Rowland Burdon began a Grand Tour with several friends, one of whom was Thomas Bowdler. They met up with architect John Soane and paid for him to accompany them as a draughtsman. The travellers left Naples on 11th April 1779. On 21st they boarded a Swedish ship and sailed to Palermo to begin their tour of Sicily where they visited many ancient sites. John Soane was apparently greatly influenced by the ancient Greek ruins like those in Agrigento. After visiting Agrigento they headed to Licate and sailed to Valletta in Malta. On 2nd June they left Malta and returned to Sicily reaching the port of Syracuse and journeyed to Etna, Taormina, Messina and the Lipari Islands before returning to Naples.

In August 1779 Soane and Rowland Burdon on his two year Grand Tour forged what would supposedly become a lifelong friendship. Whilst in Rome he had his portrait painted by Pompeo Battoni, a highly fashionable portrait painter, especially favoured by the British tourists on the Grand Tour.[1]

Reputedly the artist coveted Burdon's new and probably very fashionable green coat which he left behind after the sittings. As Battoni had not returned the coat after frequent requests, Burdon sent a 'rather peremptory message' so Battoni returned the coat with a message suggesting the coat was a 'dirty old thing... not fit for a gentleman to wear.' This message about a new, fashionable bright green coat convinced the family that Battoni had intended 'to keep it.[2] The portrait shows Rowland Burdon as a young man, wearing his green coat and a golden coloured waistcoat. He does look a very fashionable young man.

On Burdon's return to England, he had developed a taste for high fashion. Such young men were called macaronis because time spent in Italy had given them a taste for pasta, something unusual in Britain at that time. Macaroni was considered fashionable, so these young men considered themselves highly fashionable, wearing brightly coloured clothes and high powdered wigs. They were the precursors of the dandy. Rowland Burdon was not as extreme as a macaroni; he was what was considered a macaroni manque, a fashionable young man without the extreme affectations of a full blown macaroni.

Rowland in Newcastle

The Grand Tour cost a great deal of money, so when John Soane returned to England, he was £120 in debt. He tried in vain to obtain architectural commissions, so he turned to his friends for help. Rowland Burdon IV tried to help him. On his return from the Grand Tour, Rowland had been made a partner in the Exchange Bank but his resources were limited so Soane's plans for new stables and a new house at Castle Eden were never executed.

Rowland then sought help from his grandfather George Smith of Burn Hall near Croxdale. Rowland Burdon introduced him to his grandfather on a visit to Burn Hall on 22nd July 1783. George Smith needed a new cow barn so Soane also measured the existing house at Burn Hall and produced plans for a new building. This plan was not executed.

George Smith, Rowland's grandfather, was a banker in Durham. In 1788 together with John Curre he founded the Monmouthshire Bank in Gwent. He needed somewhere in the area to live, so John Soane was commissioned to design Piercefield House. The country house was designed in a neo-classical style, probably influenced by buildings he had seen on his grand tour. The declaration of war with France on February 11th 1793 led to a financial panic. The Monmouthshire bank failed and George Smith became bankrupt. John Soane had to stop work on the house and he never finished building Piercefield House. These setbacks aside, he obtained commissions through other friends until he established himself as a noted architect.

Rowland Burdon IV married shortly after his return from his Grand Tour. In July 1780 he married Margaret Brandling, daughter of Charles John Brandling of Gosforth.

The Brandling family fortune came mainly from coal mining on their land in Felling and Gosforth. The family seat of Gosforth House was built around 1760. There had been coal workings in Felling since about 1670. In 1763 Charles Brandling advertised the letting of land for coal mining at Gosforth and Felling. The Brandlings sunk a deep mine in Felling in 1779. In 1825 sinking of the Brandling Pit began at Gosforth. The owner of this pit was a family member, Rev. R.H. Brandling.

Charles John Brandling was born in 1733. He married Elizabeth Thompson of Shotton in 1756. Elizabeth was the daughter of John Thompson, a gentleman farmer. The Thompson family had owned land in Shotton since the reign of Elizabeth I.

About 1760 a mansion house called Shotton Hall, now in Old Shotton village Peterlee, was built for Charles Brandling and Elizabeth. Shotton Hall is very near Castle Eden so the Burdons and Brandlings would be neighbours.

Charles Brandling of Gosforth House was High Sheriff of Northumberland during 1781-2. He also kept race horses and had a horse named Gosforth that ran in a race at Hambleton in 1774. He would have moved in the same circles as the Burdon's.

Shortly after his marriage in July, 1780, September saw Rowland appointed as a steward for Morpeth Races. He later became steward at Newcastle races. His fellow racing enthusiast at Morpeth was Lord Algenon Percy. Lord Algenon was the second son of Hugh Percy, the 1st Duke of Northumberland.

As well as being steward of Morpeth races in 1780, Lord Algenon Percy was also elected as Tory M. P. for Northumberland. He left Parliament in 1786 when he inherited the Barony of Lovaine and in 1790 he became the Earl of Beverley.

Rowland Burdon jnr continued as partner in the Exchange Bank. In 1783 he and his father-in-law Charles Blanding were amongst the list of proprietors of the Newcastle upon Tyne Fire Office. He was also a Justice of the Peace for County Durham at Castle Eden.

When his father died in 1786 Rowland Burdon did take on more responsibility at the Exchange Bank but he had not trained as a merchant or banker as his father had and he appeared interested in wider issues. In 1788 Rowland Burdon produced a plan for a turnpike road that led from Sunderland, through Easington and ending at Stockton where he still owned land. The meeting he held was well attended and well received.

Subscribers bought shares in the road and Rowland Burdon guaranteed any shortfall in funds. The 26 miles of road between Sunderland and Stockton was sponsored. The road passed Rowland Burdon's estate. He also led later campaigns for a seven mile road from Sunderland to South Shields and the eleven mile road from Sunderland to Newcastle.

The roads were run by boards of trustees and tolls were auctioned annually. The meetings of the Trustees and annual auctions for the Sunderland to Stockton road took place in the Castle Inn in Castle Eden.

Rowland Burdon IV and politics

Rowland Burdon was becoming increasingly interested in projects outside of banking. It is possible that Rowland Burdon's association with Lord Percy sparked an interest into becoming a Tory MP himself.

Rowland Burdon raised his political profile. In January 1789 a meeting was held in Morpeth Town Hall to consider sending a letter of congratulations to Prime Minister William Pitt concerning his handling of the Regency Crisis. The Newcastle Courant reported Rowland Burdon as the main speaker. There was opposition to sending a letter. Sir Charles Grey asked what had Mr. Pitt done that warranted thanks and as such he saw no reason for sending a letter. Sir George Liddell did not see what Mr. Pitt had done for the county in particular. Sir Charles Grey was a Whig. He would become Prime Minister in November 1830. Liddell and Grey probably saw that writing a letter to Pitt was a political move by the Tory instigators.

Rowland Burdon persisted. He assured the meeting that there was nothing of faction or party in writing a congratulatory letter. He also assured the meeting that no influence had been brought to bear to bring freeholders to the meeting. Sir Charles Grey still saw no reason to write a letter.

Rowland Burdon again replied that the two houses of Parliament had adopted Pitt's resolutions and these resolutions were founded on the true principles of the constitution. Sir Charles Grey viewed writing a congratulatory letter to Pitt as being a political move. This meeting was held during the first Regency Crisis. King George III was physically and mentally incapacitated. The Whigs were in favour of a speedy passing of the Regency Bill. Once passed ,the Whigs, who supported the Prince, thought Pitt would be dismissed as Prime Minister leading the way open for a Whig. Pitt was anxious the King recovered rapidly so the progress of the bill had been delayed.

Sir Charles Grey and his Whig contemporaries wanted a swift resolution that would result in the Prince of Wales becoming Regent thus enabling them to depose the Tory Government. Rowland Burdon argued that the throne was not vacant, so there was no need to give the Prince more Regal Power. He emphasised that Pitt had seen this and had carried that grand point and because of that and other striking merits of his administration Mr. Pitt should be thanked. He moved the reading of the letter. This was seconded.

Sir Frances Blake was averse to Pitt making the Prince of Wales Regent with contracted powers as this would make the Regent subservient to a Party and the Party could dismiss the Regent and appoint another in his place if they disapproved of him. This would give the power of the Throne to the Party, meaning Pitt and the Tory Party, and that if that happened he would not give a week's purchase for the liberties of the country. Sir Francis opposed the motion and hoped the address to Pitt would not be sent.

Rowland Burdon replied that this could not happen as the present Parliament was constitutionally elected and it acted within the limits of the known laws of the country.

Sir Frances Blake suggested opening the discussion to the meeting and after much loud debate it was resolved that Mr. Burdon should sign the address. The address was then read to the meeting.

Sir W. Middleton and Mr. Grey were spending late hours in the house to serve the country. They felt that the address would put an adverse censure on their conduct in Parliament. Mr. Jonathan Thompson suggested that Mr. Pitt's name should be removed from the address. After fierce arguments this amendment was withdrawn with a show of hands following resulting in the meeting voting against sending the address. Sir Henry George Liddell, then in the chair, thanked the county members. As a supporter of Pitt, Rowland Burdon had lost this argument in Morpeth.

The argument was won elsewhere. In December 1788 a meeting of the boroughmen, freemen, freeholders and inhabitants in the borough of Gateshead, and others in the County of Durham had been held at Methuen's Long Room in Gateshead. The meeting was chaired by Rowland Burdon. It was resolved, "That the thanks of this meeting be given to the Right Honourable William Pitt, and the 267 worthy Members of the honourable House of Commons, who have so nobly stood forth in the support of the true principles of the Revolution, in constitutionally providing for the exercise of the Royal authority, unhappily interrupted by the much lamented disposition of our beloved Sovereign, and for the zealous and ardent attention which Mr. Pitt has ever manifested for the inesti-mable rights and privileges of British subjects."[3]

In the same publication as the account of the meeting Morpeth, the following replies from William Pitt to the above resolution were reported; "The above resolution sent by Rowland Burdon received a reply from William Pitt. It was addressed to Rowland Burdon and included the words;

> 'May I beg the favour of you to assure them (the above mentioned group), how much I feel myself flattered by their approbation of the principles on which I have thought it my duty to act on the present important occasion, and by favourable sentiments they have been pleased to express regarding my public conduct; allow me, at the same time, to return to you, personally, my thanks for the very obliging manner in which you made this communication.
>
> I am, Sir
>
> Your most obedient and most humble servant'
>
> William Pitt
>
> To Rowland Burdon Esq [4].

This was a reply direct from William Pitt to Rowland Burdon. There were two more resolutions. Although the first was addressed to Matthew Hedley, Master of Trinity House in Newcastle, it had been sent by Mr. Brandling, possibly at Rowland Burdon's suggestion.

This address had been forwarded on behalf of the master pilots and seaman of Newcastle. Another similar reply from Pitt was to the Lordship of a meeting of magistrates, clergy, gentlemen, freeholders and merchant adventurers of the town and vicinity of Sunderland, again County Durham.

Only the reply to Rowland Burdon had the added personal thanks.

The King recovered before the Regency Bill entered the House of Lords, so the bill was withdrawn on this occasion. The public-ity given to the sending of this address and the subsequent replies would have positively boosted Rowland Burdon's suitability as a politician. He was elected as Sheriff of Northumberland in 1789. He also began his election campaign to be elected as a Member of Parliament.

Rowland Burdon IV stands for Parliament

There appeared to more support for him in County Durham so Rowland Burdon decided to attempt to be elected to represent the county at Parliament. The following letter, dated April 1789 and addressed to the gentlemen, clergy and freeholders of County Durham, included the following;

"*GENTLEMEN,*

Permit me to declare to you my intention of offering my services to the county of Durham whenever a dissolution of Parliament shall take place; my motive is to submit to your choice, a person whose principles would urge him, to support with industry and independence, the continuation of the system of administration, which has so happily conducted this nation, through a most alarming crisis and merited the praises and countenance both of the sovereign and the kingdom at large."[5]

This is quite a clever letter as it reminds the readers of the complimentary letter he had received from William Pitt and also emphasises the relief people were feeling at the apparent recovery of the King.

There were two vacancies. One of the sitting MPs, Sir Thomas Clavering stood down because of ill-health. The other sitting member was Sir John Eden who had represented County Durham for 15 years. There were three candidates for two seats; Rowland Burdon, Ralph Milbanke and Sir John Eden.

Letters from the three men appeared regularly in newspapers. There were two vacancies as members for Durham County so much canvassing was done. Rowland Burdon visited every freeholder in the County as part of his canvass.

He was getting a lot of support from those whose support had perhaps been overlooked by Milbanke and Eden. Eden expected support from the freeholders as they frequently supported him in the past. Milbanke wrote that his campaign was successful but publicly apologised to the freeholders he had been unable to visit personally. He blamed the vast distances that had to be covered, something which the freeholders would probably not accept. Burdon gratefully acknowledged in newspapers the amount of enthusiastic support for his nomination he had received from every part of the county. He had visited every part of the county probably giving the impression that if he was elected he would work hard to include and represent all areas electors in the county.

By the end of 1789 Sir John Eden was becoming anxious. He recognised how well Rowland Burdon was progressing in gaining support, so he sought the help of Lord Lisburne. He had estates in the North and connections with Berwick but his Parliamentary seat was in Cardiganshire. Sir Ralph Milbanke canvassed hard and he had much support from leading Whig families.

But Rowland Burdon had support from his father-in-law, Charles Brandling MP for Newcastle, the Bishop of Durham who would bring in the votes of the Clergy, and the 2nd Earl of Darlington who had been a Whig MP for County Durham between 1753 and 1758. He was now Lord Lieutenant of the County and also a supporter of William Pitt.

Parliament was dissolved in June 1790. The election campaign began in earnest. Throughout the campaign Sir John Eden complained that rumours he was about to withdraw were untrue. These rumours must have had a source and had been widely circulated. Sir John Eden answered these rumours in the press saying; "As my conduct has been uniformly independent, I trust such conduct will secure me the favour of the independent electors of the county of Durham. From them I am promised and expect support, as I am well satisfied they are neither to be awed by lordly menaces, nor induced by courtly bribes to desert an old friend who has spent the greatest and best part of his life in your services." [7]

This appeal seems desperate. He appears to be accusing his opponents of menace and bribery. He may have been partly referring to press statements from Milbanke and Burdon. They both advertised that carriages would be available to transport their voters to the poll. Rowland Burdon's advertisement was even cleverer. The advert was headed by the High Sheriff on behalf of Rowland Burdon, probably implying that the High Sheriff would pay for the carriage transport thus emphasising his support for Rowland Burdon. There were also allegations from the supporters of Sir John Eden that every 'bottle' drunk by electors was at the 'candidates, expense'. The word, 'bottle' suggests bottles of wine.

The poll commenced in June 1790. It was the longest and most expensive poll in the country. Sir Ralph Milbanke supposedly spent £15,000 and to meet the debt had to mortgage his property.

The poll finally closed and the result was declared on the 8th July. Rowland Burdon topped the poll with 2,073 votes. Sir Ralph Milbanke received 1799 but Sir John Eden was not elected as he received 1,696 votes. Instead of two Whigs being returned to Parliament the members were now one Tory representative in Rowland Burdon and the Whig Sir Ralph Milbanke.

Anonymous letters appeared in the newspaper; some critical, some defending the result of the election. There were accusations from those supporting Sir John Eden that there was a 'secret junction' between Milbanke and Burdon. Each elector had two votes but it was not customary to vote along party lines. The ballot was not secret and records were kept in Poll Books. A 'secret junction' between two candidates to keep out a third, although frowned upon, could occur. Both Rowland Burdon and Ralph Milbanke were supported by the greatly influential Earl of Darlington. Many freeholders were also tenants who rented from a large landowner like the Earl of Darlington. Tenants were usually expected to follow the voting preference of the landowner so Burdon and Milbanke probably received votes from the Freeholders in the estate of the Earl of Darlington.

The Bishop of Durham and most of the Clergy had votes. The Bishop supported Burdon but also supported Sir John Eden.

This appears to rule out a 'secret junction' between Burdon and Milbanke. One letter writer suggested that if Burdon and Milbanke had entered a 'secret junction', Sir John Eden would have lost by a much larger number of votes.

Polls could be very expensive so it was in candidates interests to avoid a poll. If a candidate withdrew before the poll money would be saved. Sir John Eden was always bottom of the poll. The poll lasted for ten days. Ralph Milbanke led for the first three days with Rowland Burdon second. Rowland Burdon overtook Ralph Milbanke who then remained in second place. It was customary for a candidate in the situation of Sir John Eden to stand down and thus avoid an expensive poll. He did not because it is alleged many freeholders had promised to vote for him. These promised votes would have secured him a lead of hundreds over his opponents. The promised votes did not materialise. He had been misled.

One writer suggests a fair advocate influenced voters. He likened this lady to the 'Duchess of Devonshire' who 'has been much celebrated for her electioneering abilities'. The letter writer believed even the Duchess, never went further putting her questions home than a certain fair advocate. The fair advocate's name was not mentioned but she was probably Ralph Milbanke's daughter the Viscountess Melbourne, a close friend of the Duchess of Devonshire, who herself had considerable political influence.

Sir John Eden's supporters considered he should have won the election, however one letter writer suggested that, Sir John was to blame for his inattentiveness in his constituency and his lack of canvassing. It was claimed he had not even ventured to Weardale to seek the support of many new voters. Consequently not one of the Weardale Freeholders had given him their vote.

The Sheriff considered the election was conducted with decorum, regularity and uprightness. The bells of St. Nicholas' Church Newcastle and those of churches in Gateshead ran out on Thursday 8th July until after midnight when the result was announced. On 10th July a ball, attended by a large number of ladies and gentlemen was held at the Assembly Rooms in Sunderland to celebrate Rowland Burdon's victory. The celebrations lasted until after four o'clock the next morning. Rowland Burdon was now a Member of Parliament.

Rowland Burdon had married Margaret Blandling in July 1780. In January 1783 at his father's Rowland's house in Pilgrim Street, Rowland's wife Margaret gave birth to a daughter. Margaret was now a mother but she was also the wife of the Member of Parliament for Durham and the daughter of the Member for Newcastle. Life may have looked good.

Tragedy Strikes

There were sorrowful times to come. Rowland and Margaret's daughter Elizabeth was now eight years old. In early 1791, she was staying in Fenham at the house of her mother's sister Eleanor Ord, when she took ill. Elizabeth's mother and father were probably there as well as they could have been visiting over the festive period.

This must have been a sudden illness as Rowland and Margaret's daughter died on January 30th and was buried in the chancel of Gosforth Church. Her parents would have been distraught. In February, it would have been time for Rowland to return to London and Parliament. Margaret decided to accompany him and they set off in a coach to make their journey to London. They probably had their own coach but there were coaches which travelled to London from Newcastle.

The Royal Charlotte Coach was supposedly elegant and could speedily travel from Newcastle to London in 44 hours. Travelling by coach was uncomfortable. Roads were often bumpy and uneven so The Royal Charlotte claimed to be a soft coach', probably because of the upholstery of the seats. Highwaymen waylaid coaches, so there were guards on the coach. The coach would be travelling through the night, so lamps on the coach lit the way. The coachman and horses could not drive the coach all the way to London so although coachmen and horse would be changed there would be only six changes of coachmen all the way from Newcastle to London. Passengers need not travel the whole of the distance if they were fatigued. They could alight from the coach along the way and rest for the day until the next available coach with vacant accommodation came along. For three months in the winter during December, January and February, the coach would stop overnight at Doncaster and resume the journey at 5 am in the morning.

In 1798 the cost of this journey was £4. 4s for a seat inside and £2.10 to sit outside. Sitting inside for forty four hours on a bumpy road with little sleep would be difficult but sitting outside in the cold and wet especially when dark would be extremely unpleasant and difficult.

The mail coach would be faster as it only stopped for the delivery of mail.

The mail coaches also had a guard armed with a blunderbuss and two pistols. They would accompany the coach for the whole journey sitting outside and there are instances of guards freezing to death from hypothermia in extremely cold weather. The Burdons travelled in the Royal Charlotte coach, a private coach with guards as this would be more comfortable but as safe as the mail coach with its armed guard.

It was February when Rowland and Margaret Burdon set off by London, so as it was winter they would probably have stayed overnight. The coach would be travelling along the Great Road, the coaching route used for mail coaches that ran from Edinburgh, Newcastle and York to London. There would be inns on the road used as staging posts. These inns offered accommodation, stabling for the horses, and replacement horses for coaches continuing the journey. Because it was winter the Burdon's coach probably had an overnight stay at Doncaster. The next morning about five am they continued their journey to London.

Margaret was not feeling well. They stopped the coach at Newark, not too far from Doncaster so Rowland and Margaret could alight from the coach. Margaret became worse. She had a fever. Over a week the fever was much worse. Margaret died on February 17th 1791. She was buried in the chancel of the church in Nottingham. When Rowland Burdon returned to Castle Eden on March 1st he requested the details of the deaths of his daughter and wife be placed in the Church Register at Castle Eden.

It must have been very difficult for him to visit the incumbent of Castle Eden to request the inclusion of the deaths of his 8 year old daughter and 31 year old wife who had died within such a short time. Margaret had a fever which suggests an infectious disease. It is possible both Elizabeth and Margaret died from the same cause. Rowland's father-in-law Charles Brandling would also have felt the loss of his daughter and granddaughter.

The events did not stop Rowland Burdon being involved in events and charities locally. In 1793 and 1794 he had kept the connection with Stockton when he became Mayor of the town. He was still on the committee of the Infirmary in Newcastle. In March, both he and Ralph Milbanke donated £50 each towards the establishment of a ward for patients at the Durham Dispensary. Racing was included in these events as in July he subscribed 10 guineas for winnings for hunters at Durham races. He may not have attended the races but he still showed an interest.

Burdon's involvement in Parliament and the Slave Trade issue

Rowland Burdon continued attending Parliament. He supported the gradual abolition of slaves in the slave trade debate on 18th April but by 25th April 1792 he supported immediate abolition.

There were moves in the area for the abolition of the slave trade. A meeting was held on Tuesday 28th February in the Guildhall Durham, chaired by William Shields the Mayor. This meeting was addressed to the Gentlemen, Clergy and Freeholders of County Durham demonstrates the strength of feeling at this time. The meeting resolved unanimously to forward a petition with the following resolution to the House of Commons for the Abolition of the Trade, "That the trade to Africa for slaves is destructive of lives of thousands of unhappy natives, and of great numbers of British seamen; is in principle, subversive of the dearest rights of humanity, and is expressly repugnant to the law of God."

The petition was left in the Town Hall to be signed before it and the resolution was transmitted by the Chairman to the City Members John Tempest and William Henry Lambton for them to present it to the House of Commons. Copies of the petition and resolution would also have been sent by the Chairman to the County Members, Rowland Burdon and Ralph Milbanke. It was hoped the four Members would exert their best endeavours to obtain the object of the petition.

Rowland Burdon and the Sunderland Bridge

In 1790 there was also a Campaign in Sunderland to build a bridge across the River Wear. A committee was appointed to investigate the "inconvenient and dangerous state of the ancient ferry in the middle of the harbour at Wearmouth" and it being decided that a bridge should be substituted, arrangements were made for erecting one of stone, although this intention was subsequently abandoned. The cost may have proved too expensive and beyond the committees finances.

Although the committee abandoned the idea, Rowland Burdon, now an MP, became massively involved in the construction of a bridge over the River Wear. At that time the only way of crossing the river was by the use of ferry boats. There were two boats; the Pann-boat that was situated just below where the present bridge stands and the Low-boat which crossed the river nearer the harbour. In 1790 Rowland Burdon instigated the building of an arched bridge over the river. His plan would need an Act of Parliament before it could be built.

As the bridge, according to the principal ship owners would need an arch with a span of no less than 120 feet with a minimum height of 80 feet if ships were safely to passage under the bridge, so Ralph Milbanke MP and Rowland Burdon MP contacted several architects for their opinions on building a suitable bridge.

Meetings were called to gain support for a petition to go to Parliament in support of an Act to enable the building of a suitable bridge across the river. By January 1792, they had gained much support for the project. A meeting was held to give notice that Rowland Burdon in conjunction with Ralph Milbanke intended on 26th January to bring forward a petition to erect a bridge to Parliament.

There were numerous people at this meeting when Rowland Burdon set out the main reasons for the building of a bridge across the river. There had been a rapid increase in the population and trade at Sunderland. A bridge would enable the improvement of the market of Sunderland. This argument would appeal to men of trade if they could the see the advantage of an easy increase in trade.

It has been suggested Rowland Burdon had an additional reason to build a bridge across the River Wear. There was a story that appeared in the press about a 100 years after the supposed event; "An interesting account of a story which used to be current as to how it was that Rowland Burdon built the bridge over the Wear at Sunderland has recently been given. He was courting Miss Brandling, of Gosforth, who afterwards became his wife. The father and mother said, "How can we expect our daughter to go to such an out-of-the-way place as Castle Eden? There is no road to it. Miss Brandling said until there was a road by which her parents could drive their carriage to come and see her, or she could go and visit them, she would not marry Rowland Burdon. He supposedly replied, "But I will make a road," and she replied, "But how are you going to get across the Wear?" He said, "I will build a bridge," and he at once set to work and made a road from Castle Eden. There was a road as far as Easington but it was not a highway. He had to get an Act of Parliament to build the bridge."[8]

This seems a romantic tale reported so long after the event but still it would be considered interesting in 1893. Both the road and the bridge were built and the couple married. If there is a grain of truth in this romantic tale, then Rowland Burdon must have wanted to marry Elizabeth very much, so much that was prepared to spend a fortune building a bridge so her relatives could visit her in Castle Eden.

A bridge was needed to cross the river.[9] The two ports of Sunderland and Wearmouth were different in their trade and connexions with other parts of the country and abroad. A bridge over the river would enable the flourishing of 'reciprocal accommodation' between the ports. Transportation over a bridge would be much quicker and easier than using ferries from one side of the river to the other.

The area. Coal mines abounded but these only gave employment to men. There the 'reciprocal accommodation' would tempt those with capital to invest in was little employment for women and children and this lack of employment affected the poor rates. More employment for women and children would 'ease the poor rates'. The audience he addressed would be affected by having to pay the 'poor rates'. If there were fewer women and children to support their rates would be reduced. A reduction in poor rates would appeal to such an audience.

To satisfy the sceptics that such a bridge could not be built, Rowland Burdon informed the meeting that Mr. Milbanke had recommended Mr. Nash who Burdon described as an 'architect of eminence in South Wales'. Mr. Nash was ready to produce his plan on the 26th January to demonstrate that it was practicable to build the bridge that would suit navigation on the river. At this time John Nash was working on the building of Carmarthen Prison, St David's Cathedral and country houses in Wales. He had not worked on bridges and his more important building projects would occur at a later date but Burdon would have impressed the audience by describing Nash as an 'architect of eminence in South Wales'.

There was opposition in the meeting to Burdon's proposal and arguments. Sir Hedworth Williamson considered a bridge would of great risk and impediment to navigation not only during construction but when it was completed. Burdon pointed out that bridges had been successfully built on rivers with equal or even greater risks to navigation; rivers like the River Thames. He cuttingly suggested that if everyone had these apprehensions, bridges would never be built.

The coal owners saw no advantage in a bridge. They had coal supplies from both sides of the river and used keel boats and lighters to load their ships.

Some were even apprehensive that the bridge may even fall down once built.

Support came from the gentlemen, fitters, ship owners and principal inhabitants of Sunderland and Wearmouth. An address, dated 21st November 1791, headed Rowland Burdon and Ralph

Millbanke, had been forwarded to Parliament.[10] It was published in the press together with the notice of another meeting to be held in the Assembly Rooms in Sunderland, hopefully encouraging more to attend the Assembly Rooms and add their names to the petition.

The shipowners and others mentioned above were primarily concerned about improving safety on the river. A suitable bridge would do this. They stressed the great dangers and bad consequences on the river that especially occurred near the landing stages of the ferries because of the great number of ships moored in the harbour. In the rapid tides the ropes of these ships rendered it very difficult and dangerous. It was felt that if the specified bridge was built lives and properties would be saved. They believed a bridge would extend communication on the river as the larger ships could pass through the arch with no natural delay. Smaller craft like the keel boats loaded with coal would be prevented by the abutments from being injured by rugged faces of rocks at the side of the river where the currents were very strong.

The loss of properties and injuries to boats is mentioned but the ship owners and others emphasise the danger to the lives of workers. This address may have had quite an effect on the outcome of subsequent meetings.

Other meeting were occurring at the same time when Mr Burdon would acquaint those who were interested in the townships mentioned in the proposed roads and those interested in navigation of the River Wear that meeting would occur. A Bill in Parliament would be necessary to bring in the building of Turnpike Roads to link Sunderland, Newcastle and South Shields. Such roads and a bridge would extend the turnpike road from Sunderland and Stockton built by Burdon. It would extend to Newcastle and South Shields, making transport by road much easier and speedier. Rowland Burdon may have had this in mind when he advocated a bridge across the River Wear.

Despite some opposition the Act to build a bridge over the River Wear was passed in 1792. Building could begin.

As well as being the instigator and principal investor in the Wearmouth Bridge, Rowland Burdon also wanted to design the bridge himself. He approached Walkers of Rotherham, the firm that held Thomas Paine's designs for an iron bridge. At the time he supposedly considered that Walkers would have more expertise than the iron forges around Newcastle and Sunderland.

Rowland Burdon wanted to design an iron bridge. He had spent a year of his Grand Tour with John Soane the architect, who would become his lifelong friend. They had visited many sites of ancient architecture in Italy and Sicily. John Soane was the draughtsman but he also instructed Burdon in design and architecture during the year they were together. Burdon did have an understanding of design. Joseph Walker who worked the iron, urged Burdon to submit a patent for the final design of Wearmouth Bridge. Ralph Milbanke had suggested Nash as architect to build a stone bridge that had been designed by Robert Shout, an engineer. The Bridge Committee dismissed the idea of building a stone bridge as the cost was prohibitive and the plans did not seem feasible. Rowland Burdon was not deterred. The Bridge Committee agreed with Rowland Burdon that a bridge could be made from cast iron so Burdon approached Messrs Walkers of Rotherham. Messrs Walkers of Rotherham was the same foundry used by Thomas Paine to build an iron bridge in a field in Marylebone Road London. Paine had hoped this demonstration bridge would enable him obtain funding to build a bridge across the River Thames. There was no little interest in his bridge so the bridge was dismantled and the iron returned to Walker's in Rotherham. Rowland Burdon's patent for the bridge was submitted in 1795.

The foundation stone of the bridge was laid in September 1793. Burdon would fund £30,000 to the building of the bridge. The laying of the foundation stone was a Masonic occasion when Grand Master William Henry Lambton led a 200 strong procession of masons from the Worshipful Masters of Phoenix and Sea Captains Lodges, commencing from the Phoenix Lodge. As a leading mason Rowland Burdon would have been there.

The masonry abutments were commenced in October 1793. This was a huge task as some of the blocks of stone weighed as much as seven or eight tons. The bridge abutments were finished in 1795.

Once the abutments were in place the cast iron work forged at Rotherham took only a short while to span across the river. It was now ready for placing the woodwork, and throughout March 1795, advertisements for carpenters appeared in the press requesting house carpenters to apply immediately for work on the bridge at a wage of twelve shillings a week.

The platform across the bridge was made from a strong frame of timber. Once erected, this timber was covered with a composition made from tar, chalk and sand before marl and gravel then made it suitable for carriages. The footpaths were made from freestone.

The bridge's arch had a span of 236 feet and a breadth 32 feet, measurements greatly exceeding the requirements specified by the ship owners. The spring of the arch was only 33 feet, forming a very small segment of a circle. It contained about 250 tons of iron, 210 cast with the remainder wrought. The two piers which supported the ironwork were so high that ships might pass under on a level with the ground on each side. The south pier was founded on a high projecting rock, the north on a foundation level with the bed of the river.

The Opening of the Bridge

Wearmouth Bridge opened for the use of the public on Tuesday 9th August 1796. Huge crowds gathered to witness the opening of what was then the largest single span iron bridge in the world. At least 50,000 people from near and far, some coming from 'all parts of the kingdom', came to Wearmouth on that day.[11]

The ceremony began at 9am when a salute was fired from the battery by the Sunderland Volunteers. The Committee of the Provincial Grand Lodge of Masons for the County of Durham had organised a procession. The participants set off from 'Mr. Irvine's Inn' towards the south entrance of the bridge. The procession was headed by some of the artisans and labourers who had worked on the bridge. They were followed by; constables with staves, a martial band, two union flags, the colours of the Sea Captains Lodge at Sunderland, uniformed Sunderland Volunteers who were not Free Masons, two Tylers with swords, a steward with his wand, two banners, a Company of Free Masons wearing aprons and gloves marching two by two and carrying two banners, the lodge secretaries marching two by two, treasurers, past Masters of the Lodges, and Loyal Sunderland Volunteers who were Free Masons wearing uniforms and aprons. Another martial band was followed by two banners, a Grand Steward and wardens with their columns, Masters with their truncheons, Past Grand Stewards and Past Warders, the Architect carrying his tools on a cushion, followed by the Grand Architect, the Grand Treasurer with his staff and the Grand Secretary with his bag. Then came another Tyler with a sword followed by two Masters of Lodges carrying the Corinthian, Ionic candlesticks and lights. The Lodge followed, led by the Master of the Lodge with a doric candlestick and light, the Master of the Lodge carrying a Bible and accompanied by two Grand Stewards chaplains, the Book of Constitutions carried by two Grand Stewards, Grand Wardens, two banners and the Grand Sword Bearer. This huge Masonic Procession reached its climax with His Royal Highness Prince William of Gloucester walking between Rowland Burdon and the Grand Master of Durham Mr. Alderman Pinch. There were two Tylers with swords that ended the Masonic Grand Procession. After them came Clergymen in their gowns walking in twos, Magistrates, Officers of the Navy and Army, Commissioners and finally Constables.

A huge number of people took part in this procession. It must have been very grand with the parade of Masons and their regalia, men in uniforms, banners, lighted candles, two bands playing loud music as they marched along, and a Royal presence, Prince William of Gloucester. Such a procession would never have been witnessed in Sunderland before.

The procession finally reached the south end of the bridge when they walked through an arch, decorated with flowers erected for the occasion. Scaffolding with seating for the ladies had been erected so they could have a good view of the opening ceremony.

Once through the arch, the procession was reversed so the Grand Masters led the procession over the bridge to the north side of the river, marched up to the Limekilns, down to the Low Road and back to the bridge. Once the Lodge was formed in the centre of the bridge the Rev Nesfield, Grand Master and Chaplain made a speech. Trumpeters sounded from the centre of the bridge. At this signal the Lincoln Militia fired three vollies into the air.

The procession left the bridge and proceeded to a service in the Church led by Rev Mr. Brewster. After this service, the procession proceeded to the Assembly Rooms. Luckily the weather had been fine so those who participated in the long procession would welcome the 'elegant cold collation' when they reached the Assembly Rooms.

The bridge became a tourist attraction. Iron Bridge in Coalbrookdale was the first iron bridge in the world but the bridge crossing the River Wear was, at that time, the longest iron bridge in the world. It was described by the Gentleman's Magazine as being, "uncommonly light and beautiful. It has been visited since its erection by visitors from distant countries, and will remain a monument of the great improvements which have been made in the most useful arts."

"The bridge soon became famous, and its image upon the pottery made on Wearside rendered its appearance familiar far beyond the immediate neighbourhood. The praises of its inventor were sung in verse and rhyme, and no book which professed to describe the notable sights of the county of Durham omitted to mention the bridge as one amongst the principal. When the Grand Duke Nicholas, who afterwards became Emperor of Russia, visited England in the year 1816, he came to Sunderland along with the Grand Duke Michael and a retinue. "As the Emperor took hold of the rails and read the inscription, *Nil Desperandum Auspice Deo*, he seemed to be struck with wonder at the magnificence of the lofty structure from which he gazed upon the tapering masts lying beneath him. Indeed, words fail to describe the beauty and elegance of the original fabric, which seemed to be fanciful ornament in design rather than a passage way to sustain enormous burdens which pass to and fro in a seaport town."[12]

The Grand Duke Nicholas was not the only important visitors amongst the many tourists who came to marvel at the iron bridge. Over 1,500 people stood on the bridge when the Duke of Wellington visited to pass over the bridge. The bridge was strong. It was calculated that if each of those people weighed 10 stone the bridge held a weight of 112 tons on that day.

The article that described the bridge in 1885 says that, "the praises of its inventors were sung in verse and rhyme," like the following;

> "Ye sons of Sunderland, with shouts that rival ocean's roar,
> Hail Burdon in his iron boots, who strides from shore to shore!
> O may ye firm support each leg, or much, O much I fear, Poor
> Rowland may o'erstretch himself in striding 'cross the Wear!
> A patent quickly issue out, lest some more bold than he,
> Should put on larger iron boots, and stride across the sea!
> Then let us pray for speedy peace, less Frenchmen should come over,
> And, fol'wing Burdon's iron plan, from Calais stride to Dover."[13]

Controversy over the design of the bridge

This poem gives Rowland Burdon the credit for the bridge. His 'iron boots' have built a bridge that can stretch from 'shore to shore'. He had largely financed the scheme himself but controversy over the design of the bridge lasted for many years. Long before the patent was taken out by Burdon in 1795, rumours and rumblings abounded about the originator of the design of the bridge. Many believed the designer to be Thomas Paine who had submitted his designs to Walkers of Rotherham. The poem written around this time suggests Paine may have designed the bridge;

> "A patent quickly issue out, lest some more bold than he,
> Should put on larger iron boots, and stride across the sea!

*Then let us pray, for speedy peace, lest Frenchmen should come
over,
And fol'wing Burdon's iron plan, from Calais stride to Dover."*

The poem had references about Rowland Burdon not taking
out a patent for the design of the bridge. It also referred to someone
from across the sea taking the credit. This referred to Thomas Paine
who had submitted designs to Walkers of Rotherham and also had
a model for an iron bridge made to cross the river at Philadelphia.
This model bridge was cast under direction from him by Messrs
Walkers at Rotherham. When finished it was brought to London
and exhibited for some time at a bowling green at Pancras, near the
old church. The American speculator faulted in his payment so it
was alleged these materials were afterwards used in constructing
the Wearmouth Bridge.

At this time Thomas Paine was not known for his work on
bridge building. He was unpopular amongst many in Britain at this
time for his writings and political activity. Paine was born in 1737 in
Thetford Norfolk. He emigrated to America in 1774, and became
a journalist writing a pamphlet advocating America's independence from Great Britain. In some eyes this pamphlet was integral in
America's fight for Independence from Britain.

Whilst in America, Paine designed an iron bridge to cross the
river in Philadelphia. He returned to London in 1787 to unsuccessfully raise funds to build the bridge. He did commence building an
iron bridge over the River Don in South Yorkshire but this was not
completed. Payne also built an iron bridge in the field in Marylebone
Road. A model of the proposed bridge for Philadelphia was on
display in London for about one year.

When the French Revolution began he moved to France. In
1792 he was elected to the French National Convention and granted
honorary French citizenship. Paine wrote 'The Age of Reason',
a book advocating reason and freethinking but arguing against
organised religion. This was followed by his book, "The Rights of
Man." He was considered seditious in England.

According to Lady Hester Stanhope, William Pitt "used to say that Tom Paine was quite in the right: but he would add, 'What am I to do? If the country is overrun with all these men, full of vice and folly, I cannot exterminate them. It would be very well, to be sure, if everybody had sense enough to act as they ought; but, as things are, if I were to encourage Tom Paine's opinions, we should have a bloody revolution; and after all, matters would return pretty much as they are." [13]

Thomas Paine's opinions were regarded in Britain as a force that would lead to 'bloody revolution.' Thomas Paine started his career as an excise officer, spending a short time as a school teacher before leaving for America in 1774. The American Revolution commenced on April 19th 1775. Paine's writing was seen as anti-monarchy and his pamphlet "Common Sense" which presented a powerful argument for independence was so influential that George Washington used it to inspire the American soldiers during the war.

In 1787, Thomas Paine left for Paris to seek sponsorship for his design of a single- span iron bridge. This is the design supposedly used for the construction of Sunderland Bridge. Whilst in Paris, Paine became involved in the French Revolution and was given honorary French citizenship because of work, "The Rights of Man." But Paine was against the death penalty that led to mass killing and was very outspoken at the execution of the King. He was arrested, sentenced to death and imprisoned in the Luxembourg Prison, once a palace, and for a prison a luxurious place, where he was housed in a large room with two windows. By an oversight, when the cross on the door for his execution went unnoticed, Paine escaped the guillotine. When he was released mainly by the intervention of President James Munroe, he returned to America. When Paine wrote "The Age of Reason" it was seen as being an attack on organised religion and his popularity rapidly waned. He died a poor man in New York in 1809.

The Bridge controversy continues

During his absence from Britain, Paine communicated with a friend of his, Sir R. Smith saying he thought that Millbanke and Burdon

4 | ROWLAND BURDON IV

had been making free with his bridge when they constructed the Wearmouth Bridge. Paine wrote to Millbanke because he thought he had been involved with the construction. The letter he wrote appeared to wish for a gratuity for his input into building the bridge and he thought Paine was just seeking money from him.

Paine wrote a letter to Sir S. Stainton explaining that in a stone bridge, they begin at the bottom on the extremity of the arch, and work forwards meeting at the crown. In an iron one begins at the crown by a line perpendicular and then work downwards. Although this letter implies he had worked on the building of an iron bridge, he was not in England when the Wearmouth Bridge was constructed. Yet Paine supposed that the persons who constructed the Iron Bridge at Sunderland had made free with his model which was at the Iron Works where the Sunderland Bridge was cast.

The above information led to confusion about who designed the Wearmouth Bridge. In May 1796, the Gentlemen's Magazine wrote that; the "public should be informed that Rowland Burdon is not only the inventor of the principle on which the bridge was erected but the patron by whose munificence it was chiefly carried into execution." Rowland Burdon has the credit at that time.

In September 1796, a letter addressed to Rowland Burdon and signed by John Rastrick, a civil engineer who lived in Morpeth was published; "You must recollect that, in the year 1791, after you had heard that I had invented a plan of a cast-iron bridge on a new construction (the principle of which has been followed in the erection of that at Wearmouth), you wrote to me respecting an interview, and that I met you by your own desire at several places to explain to you my plan. After some lapse of time when I knew my plan had been pursued, I made a demand of my charge, which you refused to pay. I twice made an offer to you of leaving the settlement of the amount to two experienced engineers in London but to the proposal you never deigned to return an answer. I now again thus publicly request your definitive decision respecting that proposal and hope you will not by your silence compel me to bring this case forward in a more offensive manner." [14]

John Rastrick appears to suggest Burdon had heard of him and his plans for such As bridge as early as 1791, the time Burdon had started to consider the possibility of constructing an iron bridge. At Burdon's request Rastrick had several meetings between them when plans were discussed in detail with explanations. Burdon, according to Rastrick said he would pay with thanks. Rastrick considered this meant a financial reward. The money was not forthcoming and Rastrick raised the matter once more in another letter, on 10th September, addressed to the printer of the Newcastle Chronicle saying that Rowland Burdon had 'not condescended to reply' to his previous letter. He also responded to a previous letter in the newspaper regarding the patent on the bridge suggesting this report was erroneous.

On 27th August Walkers of Rotherham had published details about the patent for the building of Wearmouth Bridge. Walkers had forged the iron work but Joshua Walker said the patent was granted solely to Rowland Burdon Esq. "The iron work was done by (Rowland Burdon's) order and under his direction, whose invention we believe the principle on which Wearmouth's Bridge confirmed to be, and different from either that of CoalBrookdale or Thomas Paine's. We suggested to Mr. Burdon the propriety of taking out a patent, which is granted only on the oath of the party; and believe that he is the first and true inventor." Joshua Walker, the iron worker, was publicly endorsing Rowland Burdon as the 'true inventor' of the Wearmouth Bridge. [14]

John Rastrick said in his publication that the letter from Joshua Walker 'renders it necessary…to enlarge upon and explain the circumstances." He was 'far from willing to attribute to Messrs Walker any base intention, in declaring their belief that Mr. Burdon was the first and true inventor of the Iron Bridge."

Rastrick alludes to the inference that Wearmouth Bridge was built on the principle of a model of Paine's. He asserted this model came to Burdon's house from London one evening when he, Rastrick, was visiting Castle Eden along with several, intimate and particular friends of Mr. Burdon's who all approved of Rastrick's plan.

Rastrick tried to discredit Rowland Burdon when he passed his opinion that, "All acknowledge Mr. Burdon's talents (though great) are not suited to Mechanics. Many people have told me I must have taken infinite pains to make Mr. Burdon understand my invention. I certainly carefully explained to him everything relative to bridge building."[15] Rastrick continued with the statement, 'far from willing to attribute to Messrs Walker any base intention, in declaring their belief that Mr. Burdon was the first and true inventor of the Iron Bridge." After a polite beginning he suggests that the 'human memory is so very defective and he then implies that Joseph Walker appears to have forgotten that in the early summer of 1791, Joseph Walker had requested to meet John Rastrick in Covent Garden to view Rastrick's plan for an iron bridge. Rastrick said that Walker had highly admired his plan and had said, 'it was a most wonderful invention' and 'he would do all in his power to serve' him. Several months later Mr. Burdon had seen Rastrick's 'drawing'. Because both Walker and Burdon had seen his 'drawing' Rastrick says he told Mr. Burdon that Walker was aware of the plan and it was because of this that Burdon had gone to the Rotherham firm of Messrs Walkers for the casting. Rostrick asserts Walkers gave oath to the patent not because they had any 'real design' to serve Mr. Burdon but they had the "intention of monopolising all future favours." The statements implies Walkers would gain extra business because Mr. Burdon understands my invention. I certainly carefully explained to him everything relative to bridge building." Rastrick continued with the statement, "I hope to prove...that the inventor of the Wearmouth Bridge belongs to me and no one else, and that I was applied to build a bridge on this plan before Mr. Walker knew it."

Rastrick then complicates matters yet again. According to him Mr. Scarth, Burdon's Steward, read Joseph Walker's letter in which he affirmed Burdon was the 'first and true inventor' of Wearmouth Bridge. Rastrick said when Mr. Wilson the Superintendent of Works heard this he jumped up and shouted that Mr Burdon was not the sole inventor and he wanted to 'claim to his share of the merit of invention'. Scarth's supposedly replied to Wilson that 'they would settle that privately betwixt themselves."

A letter from Wilson and Scarth dated 12th December 1800 reads that they; "inform Mr. Burdon they claim no right to the Patent right of 'arches' as inventors but are entitled as one third each under Mr. Burdon's assignments as a consideration for their exertions."[16]

This idea could have originated from the settling between Wilson and Scarth after Scarth publicly read Joseph Walker's letter. The outcome of the allegations by Rastrick and the letter from Scarth and Wilson are uncertain but both situations open up a lot of unanswered questions.

Rastrick complicates things even further when he adds a post-script to the end of his letter which reads; "Any gentleman wishing to encourage the engraving of a plan, elevation and section on a large scale for an iron bridge, much superior to that at Wearmouth in strength and appearances, at one guinea each, may signify their patronage to J. Rastrick, Engineer, Morpeth."

This postscript hints at Rastrick having the ulterior motive of trying to obtain work especially as he asserts his bridge would be 'much superior' to the bridge at Wearmouth. He had hinted there would be a settlement between Scarth and Wilson. He probably wanted such a settlement for himself.

The Commissioners of the bridge acknowledged Rowland Burdon as the inventor of the bridge when it opened in 1796. The *Encyclopædia Britannica* in 1803 concluded that he was the 'inventor' and architect 'of that magnificent and elegant arch which has been erected.

The controversy continued. The bridge had undergone several repairs but after a severe flood major work was needed. Between 1857 and 1859, workmen under the direction of Robert Stephenson stripped back the bridge to its six iron ribs and raised the abutments in order to level the hump. The six original iron ribs were retained, so they must have been of a good design.

In 1859 the then Rowland Burdon v wrote to Robert Stephenson in an attempt to settle the controversy. The letter refers to; "information on my respected father as inventor of the bridge. Many parties claim the honour for Tom Paine and it is high time this question should be settled and I will forward anything in my possession to clear up this matter.

PS You will be aware this bridge was illuminated at your birth."[17]

This is an interesting post script that when Robert Stephenson was born, to acknowledge Robert's father George's great achievements, the bridge was lit up as a sign of celebration.

Rowland Burdon's letter to Robert Stephenson requests an answer to the controversy but underlines that the then Rowland Burdon considered his father was the 'inventor of the bridge.'

Robert Stephenson apparently had insufficient time to research the matter, so he handed it on to one of his assistants, George H. Phipps who replied; "Being now in possession of copies of Paine's patent for the construction of Bridges as well as those of Burdon and Burdon and Wilson the chief link required to establish the identity of Paine's invention with that of Burdon and Burdon and Wilson is wanting."[18]

Phipps expanded on technical details before reaching this conclusion; "We should probably make a fair division of the honour connected with the unique Bridge at Sunderland by conceding to Burdon all that belongs to a care for elaboration and improvement upon the designs of another, to the boldness of taking upon himself the great responsibility of applying his idea at once, on so magnificent a scale, and to his liberality and public spirit in furnishing the requisite funds, but we must not deny to Paine the credit of conceiving the construction of iron bridges of far longer span than had been made before his time or of the important examples both as models and large construction he caused to be publicly exhibited."

A further letter came from Robert Stephenson apologising for being unable to investigate the matter personally but he was satisfied with the "accuracy of all the important points" and he quite agreed with the conclusion. Stephenson further added; "Whilst upon the subject of inventions generally, I should wish to add that so far as my own observations have led me, there is scarcely ever an instance perhaps where any important (so called) is strictly the production of a single individual arising from the necessity of this application of invention keeping pace with the progress of Science and of Manufactory, Art, and none of us probably, are so far in advance of others, in our Inventions as the World is apt to suppose. But I have always considered those amongst us capable of collecting together the scattered and desultory results of the reasoning and experiments of others, when combined with a fair amount of original invention as constituting by far the most useful class in the mechanical world and would instance such men as Smith in the well-known Screw Propeller, your father and the erection of the Sunderland Bridge as leading examples." [19]

Whilst these letters from Robert Stephenson and his assistant George Phipps they both acknowledge the important part Burdon played in the building of the bridge. Stephenson likens Rowland Burdon's role as similar to that of Smith and the invention of the screw propeller.

Francis Petit Smith was a farmer who had constructed model boats from childhood but he was not a trained engineer. He submitted a patent for a screw propeller in 1836 which became the driving force behind the construction of the world's first screw-propelled steamship SS Archimedes, ordered by the Admiralty in "fear of France, America or some other nation"[20] taking the "lead of us in the adoption of the screw apparatus to ships of war. Ericsson, a Swedish engineer, submitted a patent six weeks later. Ericsson was the first to couple the engine to the propeller shaft. Ericsson was commissioned by Captain Robert Stockton of the United States Navy to build two iron ships fitted with his design of screw propeller in Birkenhead. Ericsson emigrated to New York where he designed the first iron turret ship "Monitor."

There were propellers long before 1836. The Chinese had used them on their sailing crafts, one being brought to England in the 17th Century. Several other inventors had ideas on the screw propeller, some even submitting patents including; James Watt in 1770, the Austrian Joseph Ressel, the Frenchman Frederic Sauvage, Richard Trevethick in 1815, Joseph Swan and a Mr. Woodcroft whose experiments were patented in 1826.

The controversy continued over many years. Possibly Stephenson included this example to demonstrate that over many years many great brains had been involved in perfecting the screw propeller, Smith being one of those foremost in its invention and eventual usage. This argument continued; "The day is not distant when it will hardly be credited, that side wheels have been used propulsion, and nature's beautiful provision neglected. The propeller is the tail of the fish – which gives to the salmon to make its wonderful leaps, and the dolphin its beautiful flights, to the swordfish to exhibit its tremendous force, and the leviathan of the deep to move its immense bulk with a velocity beyond race-horse speed.... That some modification of the screw, whether Archimedean or Ericssonian is not for us to say."[21]

The writer almost waxes lyrical on the importance and power of the invention but he cannot determine who was the inventor of the screw propeller but suggests it was between the 'Archimedean', probably referring to Smith's ship SS Archimedes and the reference to Ericsson.

Perhaps Robert Stephenson was trying to soften the blow by linking Rowland Burdon to Smith. Smith's input was highly important, so was Burdon's. Rowland Burdon would have known that Smith was a farmer and Ericsson an engineer, so this knowledge may not have been helpful. Rowland Burdon had spent a year with John Soane, the architect in his Grand Tour. There was an inlaid architect's table in the Castle. The Burdon family still insisted for many years after this decision by Robert Stephenson that their Rowland Burdon had been the person who not only secured the Act for building the bridge against much opposition, financed it at great cost to himself, but was responsible for the design.

Credit or not the bridge was still being admired as late as 1885 when this article on the history of the bridge appeared in the *Sunderland Daily Echo and Shipping Gazette*.

"What a bridge is that iron bridge over the Wear!" exclaimed a tourist. "Now, stand down here and tell me, fellow traveller, did you ever see anything so like a spider's web, flowing airily in mid-air across a stream, as that bridge; it is all iron, but it seems all filigree work; and how nobly and proudly the ships seem to sail under its stretching arch, without doing nuisance to it by lowering masts!

The little streamer on the top mast of that brig, now sailing under the bridge seems to be sporting with the iron circles that fill up the spandrills of the arch. In like manner to this bridge, poetry can throw a charm over the darkest waters and the dullest commerce."

The Burdons had the last word: "Yet we presume Mr. Stephenson will not feel uneasiness lest in succeeding generations the bridge over the Menai or the St. Lawrence be attributed to the genius of Tom Paine while his name is struck out of the roll of inventors and consigned to oblivion."[22]

At the time of the Paine controversy, Thomas Paine was considered a radical and revolutionary, connected with the American and French Revolutions.

The Effect of the French Revolution in the North East

Tom Paine had been at the forefront during the French Revolution. This revolution had stirred up anxiety, apprehension and fear of radicalism amongst many in Britain with fear that riots and disorder could occur in England.

Riots that had occurred in Birmingham in July 1791 would still be fresh in people's minds. This riot, apparently against dissenters resulted in numerous buildings being burned to the ground and properties looted.

A few days after these riots, handbills, considered highly treasonable, had been distributed. These handbills stressed the extravagance of the Royal Family, Ministers of State, Bishops and the Clergy. The riots recommenced. More houses were destroyed and looted. The mob approached the residence of Dr. Joseph Priestley, a Unitarian theologian and scientist. Luckily he had been forewarned by the son of John Ryland and they escaped before the rioters arrived. The house was burned to the ground and completely destroyed. One rioter was killed by falling rubble and two others were injured.

At the same time as this was happening a group of rioters went to Squire Taylor's house where the servants gave them all the food in the house as well as 15 guineas. The rioters departed shouting and yelling as they went back to town where they assembled in a public house and spent the seven guineas on ale. They were now completely drunk and returned to Squire Taylor's house and burned it to the ground.

Constables appeared and a battle ensued with rioters wielding broken chair and table legs as weapons. The park was covered with broken bottles and drunken or wounded men. The constables left.

The mob assembled at John Ryland's house, aware that his son had informed Dr Priestley and enabled his escape. The rioters were offered money to leave but they refused and forced their way into the cellars to imbibe everything stored there. They proceeded to set fire to his newly refurbished mansion and all the furniture. Constables arrived. There was another battle where many were injured and one man killed. After the fire had burned down, several bodies of rioters were discovered in the ruins of the cellars. They had burned to death, probably too drunk to notice the fire and escape. One victim could only be recognised by the buckle on his shoe.

The riots did subside but the damage was enormous. Mansions and houses were completely destroyed. Up to 100 dwellings had been at least attacked and ransacked.

There was trouble again in Birmingham in May 1792 in the aftermath of the murder of a dragoon. After the man was charged, boys assembled outside the house of the accused murderer, a butcher, and it was damaged. The crowd grew into a mob that terrorised the area creating mayhem and destruction as it progressed and grew larger. The riot act was read in four parts of town but more houses were demolished.

This time dragoons were drafted in to deal with the rioting. With swords drawn they drove the rioters off. The rioters headed for a graveyard at St. Bartholomew's. A trooper was thrown from his horse and badly injured on a gravestone.

The trouble and damage to property continued throughout the next day. The Riot Act was read again in several places. Three more troops of Dragoons were drafted in. They rode furiously towards the rioters through the ripped off gates of the Churchyard. The railings and the gravestones offered no protection for the rioters and many of them were severely injured. One man had his hand nearly severed as he had raised it to his head to protect himself. Peace was now restored but at a cost. Many of the wounded had to apply to the Hospital or Workhouse for assistance and help with their injuries.

Cheap copies of Paine's 'Rights of Man' had been published in Manchester. Paine's ideas were leading to a mass support for democratic reform. On 25th January, Lord Lauderdale and Charles Grey formed a society, the 'London Corresponding Society' to advocate democratic reform, stressing this should be achieved without public disturbance. By November that year there were 87 branches of the society with their members mainly drawn from artisans and shopkeepers.

In June 1792 it was announced in the 'Newcastle Courant' that several gentlemen had signed a requisition to the High Sheriff of Northumberland requesting a meeting to discuss the Proclamation of King George III when he had warned against "divers wicked and seditious writing, referring to those in Paine's Rights of Man." A notice, printed in newspapers and signed by Charles Grey, Member of Parliament for Northumberland notified all the Gentlemen, Freeholders, and Clergy of Northumberland that such a meeting would be held on the 29th June in Morpeth Town Hall. Charles Grey urged members of his constituency to attend this meeting.

The members did. When the High Sheriff arrived a huge crowd had gathered in the streets outside the Town Hall. He and a constable found it impossible to gain access into the building. Others who had assembled were frequently prevented from approaching the entrance.

Mr. Trevelyan said a way had been made clear for the High Sheriff to enter but this was not taken up. It was suggested the Town Hall was too small a venue and a larger venue be found elsewhere. This idea was supported by Charles Brandling and Rowland Burdon. The High Sheriff cancelled the meeting. Charles Grey published a statement that appeared in the Newcastle Journal on the 14th of July. He made four points. The first was that the, "concourse of people round the doors of the Town Hall consisted almost entirely of Freeholders – of men who all had an equal right to admittance, and whose behaviour showed nothing more than earnestness and

4 | ROWLAND BURDON IV

anxiety to obtain an entrance immediately after the High Sheriff.
It is conceivable that Charles Grey may have known some of the
freeholders but others there would have probably informed him
that there were only a few people there who were not freeholders. His second point was that there was no riot or disorder during
the whole day. This appears to be true but the High Sheriff may
have been alarmed at the large number of men crowding round
the Town Hall. Thirdly, Mr Grey emphasised by writing in italics
that a passage had been made for the High Sheriff and that the
entrance had been free. There may have been room enough for the
High Sheriff to enter but he was reluctant to do so because he was
reporting as saying, "that his getting in could be of no use, unless
the Gentlemen who had come to attend the Meeting could accompany him." This reply to Charles Grey outside the Town Hall seems
to indicate that the High Sheriff was afraid the Gentlemen would
not be able to enter the meeting. The Town Hall was small and if
all the Freeholders squashed in after him there would be insufficient room to accommodate his supporters. Fourthly, he refused
to hold the meeting in a larger venue even when this proposal was
supported by Mr. Brandling and Mr. Burdon. The crowd may have
panicked him and he did not really want to hold the meeting when
so many freeholders were present. Grey's fifth point is that because
no meeting had been held, any address to Parliament could not be
said to have come from the County. Finally Grey had held a meeting
outside with the Freeholders because he wanted to keep his promise to them. Presumably none of the High Sheriff's Gentlemen were
at this meeting outside, as he says he addressed 'the Freeholders in
the open street.' Grey concluded by saying he wanted an 'opportunity of arguing the propriety of the measure proposed' but 'he
saw such disposition' on the part of certain gentlemen. There is the
suggestion that he felt they did not wish the meeting to take place
as if it had he may have received a considerable amount of support
from the Freeholders.

A large number of freeholders had gathered outside the Town
Hall to attend the meeting. They were not rioters or disorderly but
such was the fear of riots and disorder at the time that the High

Sheriff had abandoned the meeting. Charles Grey was not deterred. He addressed the Freeholders outside the Town Hall. He may have received support from them for his ideas on Parliamentary Reform.

The Banking Crisis of 1793

There was a widespread problem with money in 1793. On 19th February the Bank of England refused a paper of Lane, Son and Frazer. The next day this bank failed. Panic resulted. Other London bankers failed. The London panic spread outside the capital. Holders of notes flocked to London desperate to seek gold.

In Newcastle the Commercial Bank suspended payment on April 8th. The same day there was a public meeting of Gentlemen, Merchants and Freeholders of Newcastle and Neighbourhood held in the Merchant's Hall. Representatives from Banks attended this meeting including those from the Exchange Bank of Burdon and Surtees. A committee of sixteen was appointed. Sufficient pledges to meet the notes of £230,000 were raised to be used if needed. The banks were sound and despite the offer of support, gold was demanded. There was alarm and distress.

Highwaymen

Rowland Burdon was in London because of parliamentary duties. News reached him that there were difficulties with the bank in Newcastle and needed gold supplies, so he set off from London with £10,000 worth of gold stored beneath a carriage rug.

There had been horse racing at Newmarket and George Baker of Elemore Hall had won a considerable amount of money. He accompanied Rowland Burdon so far but because of the threat from footpads he decided to stop overnight in an inn on the north road. Rowland Burdon was alone in the carriage except for £10,000 worth of hidden gold.

Rowland slept whilst the carriage hastened through the darkened roads. About one or two o'clock in the morning, he awakened with a start. The coach had stopped and someone was clambering in beside him. He quickly leant forward and grasped a couteau de chasse (a French dagger) he had hidden in the front carriage pocket. The intruder, a highwayman, tackled Rowland Burdon, pinning down his arms. Burdon struggled and his strength enabled him to free his arm and strike his assailant in the shoulder. The highwayman placed the muzzle of his pistol against the back of Burdon's head. Burdon did not panic. He remained cool and struck a bargain with the highwayman, offering to give him the 25 guineas he was carrying for travelling expenses as well as a gold watch if the highwayman and his two companions would go away quietly and leave.

The highwayman agreed. He got out of the carriage and summoned his two accomplices. The two men had thrown Burdon's valet who was travelling on the box into a ditch where he had laid terrified until the ordeal was over. They threatened the coachman who also stayed where he was. On hearing the ringleader's orders, the three highwaymen rode off into the night, probably pleased with their haul of 25 guineas and a gold watch. Little did they know that a huge amount of gold had been hidden in the carriage very close to where the highwayman had tackled Rowland Burdon.

The highwayman was wounded. Rowland Burdon's nightcap was covered on blood. The highwayman's wound must have been superficial as the three highwaymen crossed to another road and committed another robbery.

This robbery took place in the Epping Forest just past the Baldfaced Stag Inn. The highwaymen stopped the horses and threatened to shoot the two occupants of the carriage before robbing them of £1,500 worth of notes and cash. The highwaymen were apprehended and although there was sufficient evidence to proceed with the robbery of Rowland Burdon they were convicted for the second time so his case did not proceed. The three men were hung.

The highwaymen, unaware of the contents of Rowland Burdon's stage, had only taken 25 guineas and a gold watch, so the crime was reported in the newspapers as being the theft of 25 guineas and a gold watch with no mention of the hidden money. Rowland Burdon knew of the money bags hidden away in rugs very close to where the highwayman had been inside the coach. He kept his head and his secret. He had saved the bank's gold.

Rowland Burdon marries Cotsford Mathews

Rowland Burdon had saved the bank's money and the bank from ruin. He would be pleased about that but he would also be pleased because, despite the early death of his first wife and child, he had met someone he wanted to marry. A letter dated 14th December, 1793, from a Miss Wilson of Ayton suggests; "It is not impossible that Miss Mathews may settle in the Co. of Durham. Mr. Burdon, of Castle Eden, a man of very respectable character, is at present wishing to obtain her as a partner for life. I hope his endeavours to gain her favour will prove successful. The chances of her marrying well are so very great."[23]

It would appear if Cotsford's chances of 'marrying well' were 'so great', there may have been other suitors. She chose Rowland Burdon. They were married on February 20th 1794 in St Mary Le Bone London. Cotsford was nineteen years old and a minor, so her two testamentary guardians, William Cooke and Jeffery Jackson had to assent to her marriage.

CHAPTER FIVE

Cotsford Mathews and Rowland Burdon

Cotsford Mathews was orphaned as a child. In 1782 when she was about seven years old her father Richard Mathews wrote his will naming testamentary guardians that included those mentioned above who had signed the register for her marriage to Rowland Burdon.

Cotsford's father General Richard Mathews married Cotford's mother Elizabeth Cotgrave on 3rd December 1773 in Fort St George India. Cotsford would have been born in India between 1774 and 1775. Her unusual forename, Cotsford was her wealthy godfather's surname. A letter written to a friend by Richard Mathews, Cotsford's father, on December 23rd 1781 says; "It is long since we heard of the departure of Mr. Cotsford from Madras – some accident may have happened to him, and as I have some reason to think that he has not forgotten his god daughter… But I hope that he will return and enjoy his wealth in peace."

Edward Cotsford, Cotsford Mathews' godfather, "distinguished himself at the sieges of Pondicherry and Manilla; and likewise during many subsequent campaigns in India.[1] He transferred to the Company's Civil Service, and seeking promotion wrote from Madras to Robert Palk. Patronage must have been the way to secure promotion in the East India Company.

In December 1781, Edward Cotsford had left Madras and returned to England taking his considerable fortune with him. This fortune was increased when his mother died in November. At this time he was unmarried, possibly the reason Richard Mathews had called his daughter Cotsford, in hope she as Edward Cotsford's goddaughter would inherit a considerable amount of his fortune. Edward Cotsford did marry in 1787, at the age of about 47, he was married for the first time by special licence to Miss Lydia Manning, daughter of Rev Mr. Manning. By this time after two unsuccessful attempts he had been elected MP for Midhurst in Essex.

Edward Cotsford died in 1810. As he had no children most of his fortune went to his wife Lydia.[2] She inherited at least £20,000, various properties and land, as well as "all her watches, jewels, ornaments and… paraphernalia." Lydia inherited all the household goods, furniture, gold and silver plate, pictures, musical instruments, books and ornaments. There were some other bequests. Lydia' relatives received legacies. The two daughters of Colonel James Carter, late of Madras in the East India Company recieved £2000 each. The servants received small amounts. Cotsford Mathews had received Edward Cotsford's name but his god daughter, Cotsford received nothing else. She may not even had known her father had hoped she would inherit from her god father.

When Cotsford was still very young she was sent to England to be educated in England. It would appear from this letter that Cotsford was in the 'charge' of the recipient of the letter, George Jackson. One of her guardians was Jeffry Jackson of Woodford Bridge Essex. He had captained an East Indian ship and this is probably how he knew Richard Mathews. Jeffery Jackson had made a fortune in the East India Company and had retired to Wood Ford Bridge.

When Cotsford sailed to England, she was accompanied by her cousin, Elizabeth Cotgrave whose father John was a Major in the East India Army. Cotsford and Elizabeth may have both been educated in the same establishment.

Cotsford's cousin, Elizabeth returned to India and married a Mr. Ashburner. Only shortly afterwards she was left a widow with a small daughter Eliza. Elizabeth remarried Sir Charles Forbes of Newe, head of the merchantile house Forbes and Company based in Bombay. The family returned to England and Charles Forbes became a Member of Parliament for 20 years. During that time he took a keen interest in India, at one stage procuring a huge sum of money to supply pure water for the people of Bengal. After his death in 1849 a statue in his honour was erected in Bombay. Cotsford Mathews probably kept in contact with her cousin Elizabeth. They may have talked of times together when they were both very young and lived in India.

General Richard Mathews, Cotsford's father

Cotsford Mathews father, Brigadier General Richard Mathews was Commander-in- Chief of the East India Military Company in Bombay. Although he lived in India for more than twenty years, he did visit England when he purchased, or rented a house in Christleton near Chester. Richard's first wife Elizabeth Cotgrave had relatives in and around Chester, so they may have moved there for her to be near family.

Richard Mathews' father had died when he was young and his mother, Phillis had since remarried twice, each time being widowed. When he returned to India his mother, Phillis Stiles was living in his house at Christleton.

Elizabeth, Richard Mathew's wife and Cotsford's mother, died. By the time Richard wrote his will in 1782, he had recently remarried. He was then a Brigadier General in the service of the Honourable East India Company and now a resident of Bombay.

The East India Company had a fleet of ships, the Bombay Marine. Bombay was a deep-water port so large vessels could dock there. Trade from Bombay would include things like; raw cotton, silk, indigo dye, salt, saltpetre, tea, pepper and opium. Contracts for luxury goods were made with Indian merchants and craftsmen. Some local rulers benefitted from this trade. By 1782 the East India Company had taken over the administration of large parts of India. A large military presence was necessary to protect the trade of the East India Company.

Richard Mathews had amassed a fortune during his time in the East Indian Army. He made a will when he returned to India in 1782. This will states that he confirmed the settlement made on his marriage to his present wife. This statement suggests his previous wife, Elizabeth, the mother of Cotsford had died and he had recently remarried. As well as the settlement, his present wife, whose forename is not mentioned will inherit all her jewels and ornaments. Richard Mathews made an annuity for his mother of £100 a year in two half yearly payments. He made provision for an indenture of £2000 to be paid to the estate of Augustus de Morgan.

Augustus de Morgan was born in 1741. He was a Captain in the Madras Army of the East India Company. In 1769 he married Christiana Huttenan, the daughter of a Danish missionary. They had three children, although one died as a baby in 1774, about the same time as his mother. Sons, George Augustus and John, were only three and two years old. Four years later on 11th October 1778, Captain Augustus de Morgan was blown up and killed at the siege of Pondercherry.

When their father was killed the boys were already in school in England, supposedly in the care of guardians. These guardians appeared unaware that the school went bankrupt and it was some time before it was realised that the two boys were no longer in the school.

There was a search in London involving Bow Street Officers. The two boys now aged seven and six, were eventually found living in Monmouth Street in the household of an elderly couple who sold old clothes. The couple had found the boys living on the street and taken them in and looked after them for so long that the boys considered them as their parents, knowing no other.

Monmouth Street was noted for the selling of old clothes and boots. It was in a poor part of London and houses consisted mainly of overcrowded slums. Despite this the boys had been lucky to have been taken in and looked after.

Once found they would have been sent to a better school but would have been old enough to remember some of their life in Monmouth Street. It is uncertain whether Richard Mathews had been one of the boys' guardians at that time but when he allocated £2000 in his will to their dead father's estate in 1782, this indicates he may have been paying towards the boys' education, perhaps out of guilt at what had happened to them. George Augustus de Morgan and his brother John both joined the East Indian Army.

George was killed aged 19 and in 1789 John was serving as a cadet in Ceylon (now Sri Lanka). Their commissions would have been paid for from their father's estate, possibly with the help of the £2000 given by Richard Mathews.

These two boys had gone to school in England at a very early age. The same probably happened to Cotsford Mathews. In her father's will of 1782, he said the rest of his estate was to be for the "maintenance and education or otherwise for the benefit and advantage of my daughter Cotsford Mathews until she shall attain the twenty one years or be married."[3] Until this time, the estate was to be administered by the "survivor or survivors of those joint executors Guardians of the personal fortune and estate of the said Cotsford Mathews in Great Britain." There were five potential testamentary guardians and three of these were eligible at the time of her father's death because they were living in Great Britain. He did not want an absent testamentary Guardian responsible for his daughter's well-being. Richard Mathew's death came sooner than he probably anticipated.

Conflict in India

Richard Mathews had returned to India with his new wife in 1782. Shortly after landing in Madras, he was ordered to the Malabar Coast to command the Army to penetrate into the dominions of Hyder Ali. Under the command of General Mathews, 1,500 Sepoys and 400 Europeans sailed from Bombay aboard HMS Africa. They arrived there at their destination on the 12th December 1782.

Sultan Hyder Ali ruled the Kingdon of Mysore. Tippoo was his eldest son. Both he and his father were allied to the French and their army had been trained by the French. They were a formidable fighting force and Tippoo was especially well trained by the French in military combat.

In 1780, a vicious battle at Pollilur between the army of the East India Company led by William Baillie and the much larger Mysore Army of Hyder Ali and Tippoo resulted in a catastrophic British defeat. Many prisoners were taken. Baillie and other officers, often held in chains, were incarcerated in Seringapatum; Hyder and

Tippoo's capital of Mysore. Baillie had been wounded in the battle and died in captivity in 1782. The Sepoys were imprisoned in Hyder Hagur.

Richard Mathews appeared concerned over the poor wages and lack of money by his troops. He wrote a list of foods and their costs to illustrate the high cost of living in India for those of limited income.

Those with money led an extravagant life style. Mathews was in Bombay in August 1782. He wrote a letter illustrating this concerning "a jollyboat boy who belonged to the Nassau Indiaman. Upon his arrival here he had the good fortune to find his brother who is a young subaltern of the Bengal detachment. His discharge was immediately procured from the Ship, his greasy jacket, tarry trousers, check shirt and every honest mark of servitude were thrown into the sea and the new made gentleman equipped in scarlet. The next day he made his appearance mounted upon a charger attended by two Peons, a horse-keeper and a man with a Punkah to prevent the rays of the sun from doing any further injury to his weather-beaten countenance – you may from this circumstance form an opinion of the extravagance of officers of the higher rank." [4]

On October 1782 Mathews wrote a letter to George Jackson saying that the state of things in India were "rather unpleasant." Newspaper accounts illustrate the situation was more serious than just 'unpleasant.'

"This day the guns fired, for the capture of Hyder Hagur and the Bedanore country by Gen. Mathews. By this success three battalions of Sepoys, taken with Colonel Baillie, have been liberated, and added to the British Army."

The French fleet are gone from Cuddalore, except a line of battle ships and a frigate. ...There is still a talk of peace with Tippoo." [5]

With the success of General Mathews in 1783, the Sepoys who were imprisoned in Hyder Hagur were liberated. Cannon was captured from different forts. In Hyder Nagur 8,000 new weapons were discovered along with great quantities of powder, shot and other stores.

Before capturing Bedenore, Mathews had secured four ships almost ready for launching. Three of these ships had 50 guns and a larger one was equipped with 64. The ships had been built under the direction of a French ship-builder and would have presented a huge naval threat.

The Governor of the Bedanore country had surrendered under terms very advantageous to the East India Company on condition the he remained as Governor. He relinquished his loyalty to Tippoo Sultan, gave up Bedanore and other strongholds, giving large sums of money to the troops in lieu of plunder and agreeing to pay an annual tribute to the East India Company.

Tippoo

The guns rang out on March 3rd 1783 to celebrate what appeared to be a great victory. The Tippoo, now Sultan after his father's sudden death in 1782 was not jubilant. When Mathews took possession of Bedenore he ordered the destruction of all public books, papers and archives. He removed valuables and treasure from the fort and allegedly sent it to his wife in her residence of safety. Tippoo Sultan was reputedly incensed to a violent degree and bent on revenge.

Tippoo Sultan approached the fortress with a huge force of French, cavalry infantry and cannons. Tipoo's forces of between 100,000 and 150,000 covered the hills as far as the eyes could see. Mathews' forces were 1,200 Sepoys, less than 400 Europeans and five cannons. Mathews requested reinforcements, dated 20th March 1783, stating that 50,000 men with 25 cannons were east of them.

It must have terrifying for the force defending the fort to be surrounded by so many fighting men bent on revenge. The numbers of the 'force' appeared so huge that an accurate estimate could not be made.

An account of the battle underlines the terrifying events when Tipoo's forces began throwing rockets. These rockets were about one foot long, with an iron tube fixed to a bamboo, filled with combustibles and able to fly through the air a t great speed. These were deadly weapons and with only a touch could kill or wound three or four at a time, frequently taking off an arm or a leg. It was not uncommon for the surgeon to have to amputate seven legs and arms in a morning. There was no cover for the men so the fort was difficult to defend.

The battle tactics of rocket throwing has a connotation of an unfair. The troops did not meet each other on the battlefield but there is the suggestion that Tippoo and his forces did not play by the conventional rules of battle.

These rockets had devastating effects with the surgeon kept busy amputating limbs. There would be no anaesthetic so the pain would have been unbearable, accompanied by noise, not only of men screaming in agony but also of a saw cutting through bone. The importance of cleanliness and hygiene was not understood at that time. There were no antibiotics to fight possible infection. Many of these men would die through trauma of the operation or infection.

The battle and noise of the conflict would continue during the work of the surgeon and his assistants. They themselves may have felt they were fighting a losing battle in their attempts to save lives.

Against the odds of such a huge approaching force, General Mathews and his troops were forced to retreat inside the fortress. The attack on the fort was relentless. They were under siege. After seventeen days there were no provisions and all ammunition was expended. Many had been killed or wounded. They were surrounded by a vast army of at least 100,000 horse and foot soldiers as well as a large number of batteries. There was no possibility of retreat. Help and reinforcements were not expected.

Ambassadors left the fort to negotiate a truce and propose terms of capitulation with Tippoo. Fighting had ceased for four days before the Ambassadors returned with positive news that Tippoo had agreed terms of surrender.

The following is reported to be 'an authentic account' of an 'extract of a letter from John Hubbard Lieutenant of the 12th Battalion of Sepoys late secretary to General Mathews and Chaplain to the army of Mr. Shirley Woolmer of Exeter dated 31st May 1784.[6]

"(Tippoo) found a pretence to violate the treaty; he suffered us to march out of the fort with drums beating and colours flying in front of which we were to lay down our arms and halt a small distance from it, till the General pleased to return to our settlements. We had not arrived at our ground one hour, before we perceived three or four battalions of Sepoys moving towards us, who soon drew up with fixed bayonets and completely hemmed us in. The General (who had his fears before) and the army now saw through Tippoo's treachery and that our prospect of going to Bombay was frustrated. The next morning the General was sent for by the Nabob, with the officers engaged in making the treaty, when after a conference they were (instead of returning to us) confined in separate apartments and their papers, money etc taken from them; soon after an order came from the Town Mayor, our Paymaster, and two Commissionaires; who were likewise detained; it was expected the Secretary (the writer of the letter) would be next but whether I was overlooked in the hurry, or whether my good fortune in escaping may be computed to the ignorance of the importance of so ostensible a post, I will not pretend to say.

The day following, we were all taken before some of the head Brahmins, and stripped of all our money, apparel, baggage etc. My own loss was very heavy, being above 1,000 pagodas (or £500 sterling), besides, two fine horses etc. After they had plundered us of everything but a slender covering, we were conducted under a strong guard to some old barracks, where they kept us a day without victuals; at last the Nabob ordered us a seer (an Indian weight) of rice a man, and two pice (a monetary unit), about 1d, sterling."

This probably means they ordered a seer of rice to feed everyone and the soldiers were allotted a quantity of rice each to the value of 1d. This would be a small amount of rice for a daily ration.

"This was our daily allowance. The sudden change of diet, quitting the profusion of the General's table, to descend to rice and water, had a sensible effect on me, for in a day or two I had a violent flux come on me, attended with a fever, in which weak state I was obliged to march with the rest, an order having come for us to be in readiness. Before we set out, they sent all the captains away. As we thought, to have better treatment, amongst whom a few subalterns squeezed themselves, in hopes of becoming better off.

We were taken prisoners on the 1st May, 1783, and marched off from Nagur or Bidanore, the 9th with our bundles on our backs. The villains hurried us on in the heat of the sun, at the rate of 20 or 25 miles a day, and those that fell sick on the road, and were not able to keep up, were beat about, and dragged up by the hair by the savage Sepoys, till they got the men, dead or alive, it was all the same to them. We lost three of our officers, who actually dropped down dead on the road through over fatigue, with their burdens on their backs. The brutes would hardly let us stop for a drink of water, when almost famished without a stroke on the back to make us haste. When we halted to eat, it was without shade in the day, and slept on cold ground, exposed to the open air, without any cove. One night a terrible storm came on of thunder, lightning, hail and rain, just as we were in our first sleep; it continued with great violence for some hours, so that we were soon up to our knees in water. The next morning they forced us to march to Chittledroog; we arrived there on the 21st May, after eleven days, hard march; when we came to prison, we were put in separate apartments, near each other, but totally unconnected; our number was about seventy officers so the fixed us by halves in two houses. Only conceive to yourself what must have been the feelings on entering this dreary cell, and beholding the prospect I had before me, of dragging on a miserable existence, and pining away in wretchedness what short period I thought I could breathe out. On our leaving Nagur, we were immediately hand-cuffed with heavy rusty irons, two and two; and in that most painful, disagreeable manner were marched all the way to prison, like felons going to the gallows, sleeping linked to another man, and being obliged to perform all offices together. We were taken into prison on the evening of the 21st and one by one had our irons knocked off our hands, and others ten times as heavy put on our legs; mine indeed weighed me down so much, that I was obliged to lie on my back almost all day; as to bed we had none. Only picture yourself one moment, the only truly deplorable and unpitied situation we were in, bearing the oppressive weight of rude heavy irons, with all the horrors of a dungeon to dread. No relief if attacked by sickness; our bed the cold ground, with rats and other vermin in abundance; our fare course rice and water, and subject to the insults of black rascally sepoys, who were always tantalizing us with false reports, and were adding to our distress by ill usage at the time.

On the 6th August we were paid a visit by some of Tippoo's head people, when they invited us to go into the Nabob's service, and promised us very handsome wages; we did not hesitate a moment to treat his offer with scorn; we were offered service again, and were threatened on refusal, to be put to death; some of our officers were taken out three times, and were mounted on gallows, with the ropes about their necks, but they were firm in their behaviour, and with manly fortitude refused to the last. News of peace was brought us when we were just on the verge of despair; we were fearful it was only a blind to move us peaceably to another fort; however, Lady day (the 25th March, which I shall always remember) confirmed the truth of their story in that point' the 23rd they knocked our irons off and the 25th we were marched out of prison, with hearts longing for liberty; the conduct of the Nabob's people was altered to us, and they behaved as courteous as before austere. The Nabob has detained several of our officers and men, notwithstanding his engagement to deliver us all and has been privately murdered others, whom he reports to be dead in the list. Amongst the number, my good friend and patron, the General was, who was confined at Siringgapatan, Hyder's capital; he was secretly poisoned, and so were all those captains, Town Major, two Commissionaries, and all that went from us, to have, (not as supposed) better treatment; the Paymaster likewise shared the same fate. The General's brother also, a brave Lieutenant with him, were taken out of their beds carried to the woods, and there had their throats cut; such is the cruelty, and arbitrary proceedings of a despotic Prince.

When the people came to administer the poisons to the officer, (which was composed of the milk of the coconut balm), they peremptorily refused taking it, when the ruffians held their hands and shoulders, and forced it down; it is most inveterate poison. When they had all drank the fatal draught but three, one of them Captain Richardson, begged on his knees they would wait, and send to the Nabob for a confirmation of the order, or a pardon, but they said it was positive, and must be put to execution; so they were compelled to follow the rest, and all expired, in the greatest agonies.

Poor Mrs Mathews is insane for the loss of her husband. Had not the peace been concluded at the time it was, we should have all been put to death; the order was issued for that purpose, but was recalled. I was extremely ill after all the march from Tippoo's country to our own, with a flux and fever; and had I not had interest enough to procure a conveyance, I certainly must have dropped, and died on the road. You can only imagine how rejoiced we were in joining our own officers, and finding ourselves safe of the enemy's country. Finding myself very ill, I obtained leave of the General to proceed to Madras immediately, to have advice, and medicines; I was expeditiously sent in a proper conveyance and arrived the second instant, in the morning, heartily glad that my sufferings and difficulties were over.

The East India Army's officers and men were captured and imprisoned. General Richard Mathews was imprisoned in Seringapatam, Tippoo's capital city.

Tippoo Sultan wanted the plundered treasure returned. It is alleged Tippoo Sultan had Richard Mathews forced by a gun at his head and a dagger at his breast, to sign letters to Mrs Mathews. These letters, contrary to the truth, insisted the General and his fellow officers were being well treated. The letters also contained an earnest invitation from the General to come and see him, bring all his property and valuables with her. Mrs Mathews believed the contents of the letters to be true. She was about to follow her husband's supposed instructions but her friends thought otherwise. They knew about the treachery that had been practised by Tippoo Sultan in the past and persuaded her not to go.

Tippoo's plan had not succeeded. Richard Mathews was allegedly tortured. Still the treasure was not returned. Mathews was confined in a prison in Bednore and poisoned on 16th August 1784. Some officers, like Richard's brother Captain Mathews were taken out into the woods and had their throats cut or were hacked to pieces."

The above account appears to show brutality inflicted on the military force of the East India Company Army. The brutality was not one-sided. The campaign led by General Mathews began on 5th January 1783 with the capture of the city of Onore. The city was taken by storm and every man was put to the sword. The writer continues; "The carnage was great: we trampled thick on the dead bodies that were strewed in the way; it was rather shocking to humanity; yet such are but secondary considerations – and to a soldier, whose body glows with heroic glory, they are thought accidents of war."

The carnage continued with the defeat of Annapur, where the population, including women, were slaughtered. All the men, except one wounded horseman who managed to escape, were put to the sword. Four hundred women jumped from the fort into the moat. Some were killed in the fall. Others were violated before being bayoneted to death.

This was blood lust and cruelty. The Chaplain explained his feelings under fire; "The first time I saw an angry shot fired, and was standing in the ranks where they flew hot about, I did not know how my feelings would operate; but after a few shot were fired, I thought nothing of it; and in the intentness of your mind, in the heat of action, the sight of an officer dropping by your side is not regarded; in eager are we to decide the gain or loss of the day."

After a 'few shots' were fired, he 'thought nothing of it.'

The Chaplain had soon become accustomed to the horrors of war. The conflict did end culminating in a Treaty. The Chaplain escaped with his life, unlike many others.

General Mathews did not escape criticism. Some though he ought to have saved his army by retreating in time to Magalore, where he might have saved all his fame and credit; but his principle failing was being obstinate. He was a man of sound sense, and some excellent qualities, and was very discerning: but his first error was, when he set out with too great a contempt of his enemy, his want of intelligence, by not paying enough for it, and in spreading his army in detachments, by which means he had them cut up in detail. His time and attention were too much taken up about the money he had command of. In the rooms of the Durbar (or

Prince's palace), there were chests of treasure, silver and gold, rough diamonds and other valuables. There were about 48 sacks of gold pagodas. A great part of this money belonged to the officers, and there was a great stir about it, but the General kept it secure for a long time, and no one knew what became of it. This was a great deal of plunder amassed by Colonel Mathews. The subaltern's expected their usual share of the plunder, amounting to around £3,000 each, equivalent to £168,090 in 2005.[7] The subaltern's were disgruntled because their share did not materialise. Newspapers commented on this and another aspects concerning Colonel Mathews; "In the fate of General Mathews we have the affliction of knowing that it was the lust of plunder that accelerated, if not produced his fate. That curse which has occasioned all our calamities in India, attended his fatal expedition. He amassed an enormous treasure, and concealed it. He fell a victim to his own avarice." Comments were also made on his supposed cruelty; "If what has been published in some of the newspapers be true, that a unfortunate General in the East Indies, during the success of his arms, ordered all the men in a fortified town to be put to the sword, and the public records to be burnt, while the Army following the dispositions of their General used the women with greatest barbarity, and murdered two peaceable Brahmins, one of whom esteemed sacred by the inhabitants, can it be called cruelty; when this Army were taken prisoners by the natives, to put the General to the sword, as he had others; or was it barbarity to despatch the authors of the greatest calamities to poison? Surely, let it rather be called Justice." [8]

It is to be hoped Cotsford Mathews did not read comments like this about her father. He had amassed a great fortune in India and had made his will before he died. His wife would receive the money agreed in the marriage settlement and also any jewels and ornaments she possessed. Whether these jewels and ornaments included any acquisitions from recent plunder is uncertain. She may never have received any. It was suggested in newspapers that Mrs Mathews was 'quite insane at the death of her husband'. It is uncertain whether this means she was extremely upset or whether the events surrounding his death had affected her mentally and she was clinically insane.

General Mathews wrote his own account in a letter to Sir David Blair, sent via an Indian, washerwoman;[9] "I am sorry for the misfortune of my friends. Rumley is dead. Featherstone was killed. I was a Brigadier-General and Commander-in-Chief on the Makabar Coast. Mangalore has a very good garrison, and I think will hold out until relieved from Madras. Our Fleet is superior to the French in India. Our Army victorious in the Carmatic, likewise in the Cuddapah country. Lang, a Brigadier-General, has taken Karur, and has 10,000 good men under him. Our affairs were a tolerable aspect. The Mahrattas have made peace and alliance with us. I had 300 Europeans and 800 Sepoys, effective at Nagram, and made a treaty with Tippoo, which he broke, plundered us, and made us close prisoners. I think that Tippoo wishes for peace, and that something towards it may take place in November. I am used ill, but not in irons. I have neither pen, ink, nor paper and it is dangerous to correspond...We know not our situation. If we had, I should not have been a prisoner... For myself, two European servants and one black, I am allowed one panam and a half per day, with one seer of meat, three of bad rice, and three of ghee. I am compelled to receive what they give and not allowed to buy any other from the Bazaar. I cannot procure anything but through the Harrikar. Should anything happen to my life, I beseech you to remember the Company owe me for money advance by me during my command 33,000 rupees, besides all my pay and allowances from time of my arrival in India. The troops that were with me are, some in the Nabob's services, the rest sent in irons to different parts of the country."

Colonel Mathews wrote of friends who were dead. He continued with victories by others and the superiority of the Fleet. Mathews believes because of the treachery of Tipoo, he is not a part of this. He has not died in battle, neither has he been victorious. Instead he has been taken prisoner, as have some of his men, whilst others have joined the enemy. He has servants in prison but their existence is pitiful, living on meagre rations and being treated 'ill'. Mathews considers his fate, and what may happen to him. He appears to think he may be killed. If this does happen he begs Sir David Baird to ensure any money owed to him by the Company is recognised, presumably to be forwarded to those in his will.

The Death of Colonel Richard Mathews

Colonel Mathews did die. "There is no case more pathetic than that of General Mathews, who was compelled to partake of food and drink that he knew had been poisoned. The words he uttered at the time of his death are most heart-rending. One mournful memorial was brought to light at the time of his death in the compartment of an old spice-box found in the Palace of Tippoo Sultan. It was in the well-known writing of the unfortunate General, and simply contained the date of his murder."[9]

The washerman had brought the account of the death. He was put in irons. When he became aware he was to be poisoned, he refused food. Some guards and servants gave him some of their food, so he remained alive. This was discovered and stopped. Poisoned food was brought daily. Mathews did not eat the food until he realised the choice was die quickly by poison or starve slowly to death. There was no choice. He ate the poisoned food and drank the poisoned liquid he had been given. Despite this it took six hours for him to die. Three days after his death, the British discovered the officers who had been sent to Mysore had been poisoned with 20 others meeting a similar death two days after that at Kavel Drug. Soldiers would not expect to die like this.

Cotsford Mathews

Cotsford Mathews would probably have been at school in England when her father was murdered. It is uncertain who would act as her day to day guardian. Cotsford, now an orphan did have a step mother who lived in India. Richard Mathews's new wife was not named as Cotsford's guardian in her father's will. It is even possible the new Mrs Mathews was 'insane at the death of her husband' so could not have looked after her at all. Cotsford did have an elderly grandmother living in England who was not named as a guardian but may have had contact with Cotsford. In 1782 grandmother, Phillis Stiles; Stiles being the surname of her late third husband, lived in Christleton just outside Chester in the house of her son Richard Mathews. She later moved to Petersham in Surrey where she died 1787.

Cotsford did have other relatives. Her uncle William Mathews had been killed in India in 1784. His wife Sarah was Cotsford 's aunt. She died in 1790 but there were cousins, including her cousin William who became a Major in the Indian Army and Phillis Augusta who married Hugh Griffiths in India.

Cotsford's mother was the sister of General Cotgrave. When Cotsford was sent to England to be educated she was accompanied by her cousin Elizabeth. Cotsford and Elizabeth probably attended the same school and became very close friends as well as cousins. They probably kept in contact.

In 1861, Cotsford cousin, now Elizabeth Ashburner aged 88 and a baronet's widow, lives in Chester House. Three of her children are in the household together with several servants, including a butler. The house has two separate buildings, one to house the gardener and his family and the other for the coach-house with living accommodation for the coachman's household. This family was rich and they too had treasures brought back from India by Elizabeth's father, including an uncut ruby ring encircled with diamonds, a celebrated pearl necklace worth a king's ransom and pearl earrings.

Cotsford's granddaughter, Elizabeth Burdon stayed with Elizabeth's children in her youth, particularly remembering Miss Eliza Ashburner as being very kind to her as a "small child. The families evidently kept in touch. Elizabeth had been promised the pearl earrings in an inheritance but unfortunately for her this was not to be.

Cotsford Mathews did have testamentary guardians who lived in England. Jeffery Jackson lived in Woodford Bridge, Essex. He had been a Captain in the East India Company the same time as Cotsford's father. Jeffery Jackson became a ship owner. He left silver, plate, furniture, books as well as money and other interests in his will. He probably made his money from his expeditions in India.

William Cooke, another of Cotsford's testamentary guardians was a surgeon. He may have been the surgeon who amputated many limbs in a morning during the heat of battle. William Cooke married when he returned to England and had three children with his wife Jane. His will includes jewels, ornaments, books, a piano, a silver gilt snuff box, a cornelian ring and a seal received as a gift from the Nawab of Oudh. It is probable some of this wealth came from India.

William Cooke also provided in his will for four natural children who were all born in India. This was not uncommon. In Thackeray's "Vanity Fair" there is a discussion as to whether Jos Sedley should marry Becky Sharp ;

"Let Jos marry whom he likes" Mr. Sedley said; "it's no affair of mine. This girl has no fortune, no more had Mrs. Sedley. She seems good-humoured and clever, and will keep him in order, perhaps. Better she, my dear, than a black Mrs. Sedley, and a dozen of mahogany grandchildren."[10]

This arrangement did not seem to be uncommon. Sometimes the mother of children was provided for, even though, like William Cooke, the couple were not legally married. In his will, William Cooke made provision for Bebee Nancy of Monghier. A Bibi refers to an Indian wife or mistress. If Cooke provided for them in his will, he probably also provided for them during his lifetime. The children were all given his surname of Cooke. Their mother was probably Indian.

It was not unusual for those connected with the East Indian Company at that time to have Indians wives or mistresses. Information of the wills of officials of the East India Company from the 1780's show that more than one third of British men were leaving money to Indian wives or mistresses.

They had money to leave, probably from privateering which appeared to amass fortunes, probably that of Cotsford's, the jewellery and treasures of her cousin Elizabeth's family, and that of William Cooke illustrate the fortunes that could be made or 'acquired' by connections with the East India Company.

At the age of 19, Cotsford Mathews was of marriageable age and probably much sought after. She did have a considerable fortune left to her by her father. She had had a good education, so probably had all the refinements expected of a young lady.

Cotsford's Schooldays

Cotsford left India at an early age to attend boarding school in England. Accounts of expenses incurred at a Boarding School in Queen's Square were sent to one of her guardians, Jeffrey Jackson. One bill for £259 12s includes; [11]

"Board and Lodging for Miss Mathews and two servants with the use of the carriage £150

Wages of two servants....£20

Masters half the year for dancing French Music and drawing....£75 [12]

Keeping a horse for Miss Mathews....£14"

There was also £50 a year to be paid towards the town lodging of the Master.

This appears to have been an expensive, exclusive school where Miss Cotsford was treated as a young lady of substance. She had servants, the use of a carriage and a horse. This appears to have been a privileged education. She was taught dancing, music and drawing all considered essential attributes for a young lady.

In September 1783, £18 18s 5d was paid by Mr Jackson for various items including; an English prayer book, a spelling catechism and collect book and payment to the Minister were all linked to the Church. It would appear sewing was involved as there were purchases of materials, satin, silks, lace, muslin, gauze as well as pins and needles. Cotsford learnt French, so money was needed for a French spelling book and payment to the French Master. Writing books were also purchased. She was given allowance money but gloves, a collar and a purse had been purchased on her behalf. There was a payment of 2s 6d for 'Breaking up at Xmas.' It is possible this amount may have contributed to some kind of celebration, like a party.

A further bill of £32 16s 3d, also paid by Mr. Jackson, includes some of the above items as well as; 'The History of England' probably a book, a collection of 'songs set to music, materials for 'drawing on silk the deserted village' with a 'small frame for work', an extra' drawing and stencil set, geography, use of the globes, and music double time.' Cotsford could probably now make her own tea as there was a charge of 17s 6d for 'tea and sugar.' This bill was for a term that led up to Whitsuntide as there was an item categorised as 'breaking up at Whitsuntide.'

Cotsford's musical abilities are being extended to singing. The syllabus also included an interest in geography and history. A further undated bill of £142 16s 2d includes; £3 14s 6d for a picture probably painted by her drawing master, money for the Dancing Master's Ball, additional music teaching, a coat-maker's bill for £7 12s 9s, hosiers 1s 4s, shoemaker and mending £10s, stay-maker £1 11s 6d, gloves £2 11s 3d, milliner's £20 7s 2d, linen drapers £7 9s 9d, collar maker 11s, books £5, earrings 11s 6d, plain work and haberdashers £1 14s, sundries £1 13d, wine £1 4s, contributions to the sick in church 10s 6d, staying over during the Whitsunday holidays £3 3s, £5 5s for cash in hand, the cost of garters, pins and laces amounted to 4s 6d, and the hire of a coach cost £2.

Some of these purchases like stays, earrings and a large bill for millinery suggest an older Cotsford, possibly ready to leave school. There is payment for a ball organised by the dancing teacher. She has purchased a picture. She has had additional music lessons possibly to advance her musical skills before she leaves education. She has progressed from tea and sugar and is now drinking wine as well. She goes out in a coach. As a Church goer Cotsford is donating to the sick of the parish maybe on her own volition or because this is what society expects from a wealthy young lady. She has stayed over the Whitsuntide holidays, possible to be with her friends before she leaves school as an accomplished young lady able to draw, sing, play the piano and sew fine needlework. She could probably have developed an interest in History and Geography and be able to speak and read French.

Cotsford would not have been left school for very long before she met Rowland Burdon. The letter about Rowland wanting to make Cotsford his 'partner for life' was written to Commodore William Wilson from his sister who lived in Ayton Hall, Yorkshire. Commodore Wilson had married George Jackson's youngest sister Rachel Jackson. They bought Ayton Hall in North Yorkshire. The young James Cook worked as a stable boy at Ayton Hall for the Wilson family.

Rachel's brother George Jackson had encouraged the young James Cook to serve in the Navy. He continued to encourage his protégé. In return Cook, when a Lieutenant in 1770, named the first European settlement in Australia Port Jackson which is now the natural harbour of Sydney.

George Jackson became Secretary to the Commissioners of the Royal Navy. He was a friend of Cotsford's father General Richard Mathews. George's younger sister Dorothy had married Jeffrey Jackson Cotsford's testamentary guardian. Dorothy Jackson was born just before the youngest sister Rachel Wilson so she probably visited her in Great Ayton, especially as their brother Ralph lived five miles away in Guisborough. Cotsford may have accompanied her guardian's family on such visits. A reminder of the letter which read; "December 14th 1793. It is not impossible that Miss Mathews may settle in the Co. of Durham. Mr. Burdon of Castle Eden, a man of very respectable character, is at present wishing to obtain her as partner for life. I hope his endeavours to gain her favour will prove successful. The chances of her marrying so well are very great. Should you write to Woodford Bridge, do not notice this affair till you hear of it from that quarter."

Woodford Bridge Essex was the residence of Cotsford's guardian Jeffrey Jackson. The mention of Woodbridge Bridge suggests she lived there with the Jackson family at some time.

Miss Wilson appears to have been acquainted with Rowland Burdon and hopes that he will marry Cotsford Mathews. Miss Wilson requests that her brother should not mention what she has told him to the occupants of Woodford Bridge. Jeffery Jackson, one of Cotsford Mathews testamentary guardians, lived in Woodford

Bridge. Commodore William Wilson communicated with Jeffery Jackson by letter so they must have been well acquainted. If he was a friend of Jeffrey Janckson and visited Woodbridge, he probably also knew Cotsford as it would appear she may have spent some time in that household.

Cotsford was described as; "a very remarkable woman, of great intellectual powers and decided individuality of character.... She was in the best sense of the word a strong-minded woman. She had thrown herself with an intensity of her own, into the political life of the twenty years of her husband's political career. She was, in the best sense of the word, a strong-minded woman."

Rowland Burdon as a "consistent Tory and steady supporter of William Pitt, of whom he was a close personal friend, and who had great confidence in his judgement, and often consulted him as to the probable reception of any proposal by the country.... His personal friendship for Pitt was also cemented by the close intimacy of Mrs. Burdon with Lady Hester Stanhope." [13]

It is uncertain how close the friend ship was between William Pitt and Rowland Burdon. In his book, "William Pitt the Younger" William Hague does not record Rowland Burdon as a member of Pitt's inner circle of friends. There does appear to be some credence in the 'close intimacy' between Cotsford Burdon and Lady Hester Stanhope, so both statements probably have an element of truth. This may have been connected to how Cotsford and Rowland met through Cotsford's supposed intimate friendship with Lady Hester Stanhope.

Lady Hester Stanhope was William Pitt's niece. She was born in March 1776, so was of an age with Cotsford Burdon, born in 1775.

Lady Hester Stanhope

Lady Hester Stanhope was the eldest of three children from the first marriage of the third Earl of Stanhope. Her mother, Hester Pitt, was supposedly the favourite sister of William Pitt the elder. Their father was the Earl of Chatham. Lady Hester's mother died when she was only four years old. Cotsford's Burdon's mother had died when she was very young so they both had the experience of a motherless childhood.

Earl Stanhope was remarried just over six months later to his late wife's cousin Louisa Grenville; who according to Cleveland 'did not commend herself to her little step-daughters'. Cleveland describes Louisa as being, "stiff and frigid, with a chilling conventional manner." She suggests the children, 'Never became fond of her, and she never gained any influence over them – least of all Hester. As for their father, he apparently did not even attempt to do so; he merely gave his orders, and took care they were obeyed." He was a busy man so they saw little of him anyway. Cleveland suggests the children were brought up in an 'unhappy home'.[14]

Cleveland says Hester was; 'highly gifted' with an 'intellect of rare scope and power'. This intelligence and enquiring mind was shared by Cotsford who was described as also being 'highly intelligent'.

Lady Hester had faults one of which was, 'her father's imperious and impetuous temper, with his indomitable and inflexible will." Cotsford was strong minded and stories appear to suggest she too may have had a similar impetuous temper. It would appear both Cotsford and Lady Hester were similarities in temperament and in an early unhappy home life.

After the death of her grandmother, and a tour of Europe, Hester went to live with her uncle William Pitt. Prior to his mother's death, William Pitt had insisted he could, 'under no circumstances' 'offer her a home' in his 'own house'. Faced with the emergency of a homeless niece, he relented and took in Hester; 'his favourite sister's child'. "Henceforth she sat at the head of his table, and assisted him in doing the honours to his guests…. He came to regard her with almost a father's affection, and she, on her part, quickly formed for him a strong and devoted attachment."[15]

Hague describes Lady Hester as; "Tall and 'handsome' rather than beautiful" and she "abounded in wit and mimicry."[16] Lady Hester's exploits after 1810 when she left England for good demonstrate a life of travel and many adventures. One such was when she dressed as Bedouin and travelled through a potentially hostile desert accompanied by a caravan of 22 camels. The journey was not hostile. She was welcomed by Emir Mahannah el Fadel and became known as Queen Hester. In 1815, she obtained permission from the Ottoman authorities to conduct an archaeological excavation looking for a great treasure supposedly hidden under the ruins of a mosque in Ashkelon. This was the first archaeological excavation in Palestine.

Lady Hester finally settled near Sidon a coastal town in what is now Lebanon. She lived in a succession of three monasteries. She remained there until her death.

Hester Stanhope was supposedly a very close friend of Cotsford Mathews. It is possible she met Rowland Burdon, a supporter of William Pitt through these associations.

In 1794, Cotsford, aged about 19, married Rowland Burdon nearly twenty years her senior, in St. Martin in Fields Westminster Middlesex. When in London, they lived in 35, Grosvenor Square, the corner house.

Rowland was twice her age but both had experienced grief in their past lives.

Cotsford had suffered a traumatic childhood with the loss of both her parents. She never really knew her mother and her father had died in horrific circumstances. Rowland's mother and baby sister had died when he was two. His wife and daughter had both died three years ago. Their past grief may have drawn them together.

Cotsford was young but she was very intelligent and well educated. She was interested in art and painted herself. Rowland Burdon was also well educated. He had travelled on the Continent and was an accomplished linguist.

Rowland Burdon was considered a fashionable young man; even a 'macaroni manque'. Fashions had changed and he probably dressed fashionably but in a more sober manner. Cotsford too appeared fashionable and well-dressed. When she married she had a fine trousseau, including "a worked muslin gown and piece the same...cloaks...a Brussels lace veil...Beaver Hatts...a Canterbury Gown...morning caps trimmed with lace..(and) a satin dress."[17]

As a friend of Lady Hester Stanhope, Cotsford and possibly other women amongst their circle of friends, may have discussed current affairs and even politics. Rowland Burdon was a Member of Parliament and Cotsford "threw herself, with an intensity all her own, into the political life of her husband's parliamentary career." [18]

Rowland Burdon in Parliament: William Pitt

Rowland Burdon was reportedly a close friend of William Pitt. This friendship supposedly deepened by Cotsford's close friendship with Lady Hester Stanhope, the niece of William Pitt.

The closeness of the friendship between William Pitt and Rowland Burdon is uncertain. Hague does not mention Rowland Burdon as being one of the close friends of William Pitt, but there are pointers that there was a strong link between Pitt and Rowland Burdon.

Burdon had begun his canvass in Durham emphasising his strong support for Pitt. In return Pitt influenced government support for Burdon. Throughout his time as a Member of Parliament Burdon generally supported Pitt. There are numerous instances reported in the Press that demonstrate this support.

Burdon was frequently named in the reports of debates that had occurred in the House. As well as being well known in his constituency of Durham, he must have been known in the country and amongst the Press. Accounts of voting demonstrate this. Mr. Burdon appears as named amongst other notable members. The majority of members are unnamed, just being recorded as members whose names are not known. Mr. Burdon was named. He was known and probably considered an important Member of the House.

Burdon was a 'very steady and good friend' (parliamentary of Burdon) of Henry Dundas. Dundas was a very close friend of Pitt who considered him 'indispensable'. Newspaper reports often link Dundas and Burdon together in their support of Pitt.

Some Northern Industry

In 1792, Burdon secured an Act of Parliament to build the bridge across the River Wear to would connect the turnpike roads between Stockton and Sunderland, another of his projects. Burdon played an integral part in the funding and probably design of the Wearmouth Bridge. In the 18th Century, the riverside between Sunderland and Bishopwearmouth was the main focus of commerce and industry, including shipbuilding, potteries, glass and bottle manufacturing, rope making, lime kilns and the manufacture of copperas. The port was busy with exports including coal from nearby coal mines.

This already busy area expanded rapidly when the both banks of the river were linked by the Wearmouth Bridge erected in 1796. By 1814, Sunderland overtook Newcastle to become the nation's largest shipbuilder. The potteries expanded. By the year 1818 Wearside was exporting 300,000 pottery objects each year. By 1868 there were six major potteries in Wearside. The building of the bridge brought increased prosperity and expansion to the town.

Ropemaking: The Websters

One of the manufacturers of ropes was Webster and Co. whose plant located at Deptford. Rowland Webster was related to Rowland Burdon through a previous marriage of the Burdon female line. Webster was originally in partnership with Michael Scarth, Ralph Hill and John Grimshaw. Michael Scarth was Rowland Burdon's Land Agent. John Grimshaw was a great innovator. Between 1796 and 1802 he was granted three patents that improved ropemaking. The manufactory was financed by Rowland Burdon, so took the Webster and Co. name. By 1817, the Deptford factory was solely owned by the Websters because Grimshaw, a Quaker had left the company as he did not wish to supply ropes to the Navy.

In 1805, the cast iron bridge in Sunderland needed repairs. The bridge had been designed without bracing causing the ribs to move out of alignment and making the bridge unstable. John Grimshaw undertook repairs to the cast iron bridge by inserting iron diagonal braces between the ribs. Grimshaw considered that the bridge would have collapsed if this work had not been done. The original design of the bridge appears to have been not as effective as it should have been. The lack of engineering knowledge adds weight to the claim that Rowland Burdon not only funded the bridge but designed it as well.

Webster and Co.'s rope factory was the first in the world to produce machine made ropes. It was also the first factory in Sunderland to use steam to power the machines. Rowland Webster (1751-1809) financed and named the company that include Michael Scarth, John Grimshaw and Ralph Hill. Rope had previously been hand made using rope walks. Machines enabled the considerably faster manufacture of ropes producing about 500 tons of rope a year. Five of Sunderland's other nine rope manufactures converted to machine produced rope but using horse rather than steam power. Previously Sunderland had imported rope but now became almost self-sufficient for the large quantities needed for ship building, sails and in coal-mining. Webster's experimented with the production of iron wire ropes from 1830. These were produced about 1842. An iron rope, 'made of steel wire' they produced in 1892 was a 'sensation' according to the 'Sunderland Echo' because it was 'six miles long and weighing over 25 tons, destined for Whitehaven Colliery, required 35 horses to draw it to the goods station at Monkwearmouth.'

The Webster family married into the Maling family. The Maling pottery business was founded in North Hylton near Sunderland in 1762, producing mainly functional ware. The business was moved to Newcastle in 1817 and the ware became more decorative.

Rowland Webster, the rope manufacturer had married Mary Maling in Bishopwearmouth on 26th October 1802. Rowland Burdon was probably at the wedding. He now had connections with the rope manufacturing of his relative Rowland Webster and the Maling family. Burdon's securing and Act to build the bridge at Sunderland could have benefitted both businesses.·

The Abolition of Slaves and the Slavery Link

Throughout Rowland Burdon's time as a Member of Parliament, there were many debates about the abolition of slavery. On April

1791 he voted for the gradual abolition of the slave trade but his views against slavery were strengthened by April 1792 when his support for immediate abolition or limitation began, with four more votes in the House recorded for support of abolition.

Newcastle does not at first appear to have links with the Slave Trade. It is a port but it mainly traded with London, Rotterdam, Riga, Hamburg and Le Havre. The Trevelyans of Wallington Hall had connections through a marriage in 1757 with major sugar producers in Granada. There were many other notable North East families that had interests and connections in plantations in the Caribbean. The Graham Clarke family was one with major interests in sugar plantations in Jamaica.

John Graham Clarke was a major shareholder in the Exchange Bank run by Burdon and Surtees. The Graham Clarke's owned sugar plantation estates in Jamaica. As the world's leading sugar producer, sugar was Jamaica's most important crop. In 1805, 101,600 tonnes of sugar were produced. The production of sugar was labour intensive. Slaves, including children often from the early ages of three or four were forced to labour incessantly to produce these huge amounts of sugar.

John Graham Clarke had interests in thirteen plantations and owned several ships. Ships sailed across the Atlantic loaded with cargo like coal, glass, pottery and linen. They returned mainly with sugar and rum but also with products like hard wood, pimento and indigo. Graham Clarke advertised the scale of some of his goods in newspapers like the Newcastle Courant. Such an advertisement appeared in November 1806 where Graham Clarke, 'importer' offered for sale, 'three casks of fine Jamaican sugar, fit for the scale, to be put up into small lots for the convenience of the purchaser.' The sugar could be sampled the day before the sale at Mr. Loftus' Rooms in the Haymarket.

There were other items for sale. Jamaican rum, sugar, coffee, logwood and fustic a dye producing plant were all offered for sale by 'private contract.'

There were many other notable families who were owned plantations and slaves in the West Indies. There were other aspects of the trade where many were involved. Graham Clarke owned two of the three sugar refineries in Newcastle and Gateshead and the Crowleys who operated iron-foundries at Winlaton and Swalwell made slave restraints and tools for the plantations.

Graham Clarke owned ships. Two of these, the 'Ariel' and the 'Ambuscade' were to sail from Newcastle to Jamaica in February 1792. These were only two of his several ships. Both vessels had 'excellent accommodation for passengers' as well as facilities for cargo. It is probable that one of these ships returned to Newcastle with passengers that included the six children of a slave woman called Elissa Peters and George Goodwin Barrett. The six children were sent to Newcastle to be looked after by John Graham-Clarke because there was a family connection between the Barretts, through a marriage of John Graham Clarke's daughter Mary. It is uncertain what they feel about leaving their mother and Jamaica to start a new life in a completely different environment. They may have been shipped off to England in 1792 because a year later George Barrett, aged thirty three, married while still living in Jamaica. He died two years later at the age of thirty five.

One of the six children was called Samuel. He would have been a baby when he left Jamaica. He was committed to an asylum in 1806. In the 1851 Census, Samuel Peters now aged 59 is recorded as living in a Belle Grove Retreat, a small private Lunatic Asylum next to Spital Tongues in Newcastle. Samuel Peters was recorded as being born in Jamaica and a 'gentleman'. There were few inmates; one other 'gentleman', three men recorded as once being articled attorneys, a curate and several men who had served in the army, probably because the Retreat was in close proximity to Fenham Barracks the base for the Northumberland Fusiliers. Those who were looked after in the Retreat had money, so their lives in this lunatic asylum may have been more comfortable than those who were destitute. They would have been housed in the Newcastle Lunatic Hospital.

In 1824 the Newcastle Lunatic Hospital was described by the Newcastle upon Tyne Common Council as grossly overcrowded and ill-ventilated. Chains were in use, there were iron bars on the windows and the cells resembled dungeons. There was no differentiation between the sexes and restraint and coercion were to be seen everywhere.

This Samuel Peters, born in Jamaica lived his last days in a private lunatic asylum. He died just over one year after the Census in October 1852.

The above may have been the fate of one of the children of George Burdett but this was not shared by the six illegitimate children of Jacob Graham. Jacob Graham was Joseph Graham's uncle. Jacob owned the Lapland estate in St. James, Jamaica. When Jacob died, aged ninety in 1816 he had lived seventy years in Jamaica. Although he left his estate to his nephew Joseph, he also left small plots of land and houses to his six mixed-race children. Jacob lived and died in Jamaica and his children were able to stay in Jamaica.

Passengers travelled to and from Jamaica but workers were needed on the plantations. Employment opportunities were advertised. There was need for a millwright, a house carpenter, a stone mason who was a 'good waller' preferably with bricks, a good blacksmith with experience of copper and plumbing, a cooper, a gardener, a husbandman and a watchmaker. Most of the employment offered would suggest building work. The husbandman would look after animals and horses in particular. Employment for a watchmaker appears more uncertain.

Shipping had more sinister tasks than transportation of cargo and passengers to the West Indies. The National Archives records that a ship called "The Fly" set sail from Newcastle in 1776 bound for Africa. It was a ten gunned ship with a crew of twelve. One hundred and nineteen slaves were purchased. By its arrival in Pensacola in Florida, 26 of the slaves had died on the voyage. 'The Fly' returned to England in July 1777.

The twenty six slaves would have died on board ship probably from disease or lack of adequate food. Their bodies would have been thrown overboard. Not such a death for the Graham Clarkes. They lived a good life surrounded by wealth and privilege.

John Graham Clarke died in 1818. The contents of his will illustrate his wealth. His wife was left with a good income, being able to remain in the house with sole use of the household furniture during her lifetime. She was bequeathed all the 'wines, spirits and malt liqueur' in her husband's private cellar. She also inherited the carriage and carriage horse, the cows, the hay in the hay lofts and the granaries. This was wealth. There was more than one carriage with a number of horses. There was land to graze cattle and granaries in which to store wheat. Graham Clarke left his cousin and his two sons a substantial amount of money and the ownership of the furniture, plate, linen, china, printed books, pictures and prints. They also inherited the plantations on estates in St. James in Jamaica. This included the "slaves, goods, cattle, chattels and effects." John Graham Clarke had left his wife the horses and cows in England. The "slaves" and "cattle" on his plantations were inherited by his cousin and two sons. The "slaves" and "cattle" are linked together as if they were of equal value to each other. The "slaves" do not have a value as people. They are classed as being of same value as the cattle.

His five daughters, three of whom were unmarried, also inherited considerable sums of money.

The exploitation of these slaves, considered by him in the same category as his cattle, had brought prosperity to John Graham Clarke. He had land and property in England and Jamaica. He also had land and property in Yorkshire plus shares and interests in glassworks in Newcastle and Northumberland.

His two sons and his cousin inherited but so did his five daughters. The three unmarried daughters inherited eight thousand pounds each. The two married daughters had received marriage settlements. Their inheritance was the same amount minus the marriage settlement.

Mary, one of John Graham Clarke's daughters had married Edward Moulton Barrett. Edward Barrett was related to George Goodwin Barrett who had sent his mixed race children to England. In 1805 Mary Graham Clarke was married to Edward Moulton Barrett in Gosforth Church. They both came from families who owned sugar plantations and slaves.

Edward and Mary Barrett rented Coxhoe Hall which the previous owner, John Burdon, had previously renovated. An advertisement containing a description of Coxhoe Hall appeared in NC 7th June 1800. It read; "The Mansion House called Coxhoe Hall, situated one mile from the Turnpike Road heading with the Out-Offices, Coach-Houses, Stabling for 13 horses, Dove-Cote, Dog Kennel, Cold-Bath, Pleasure-Ground, and about 70 acres of meadow and pasture adjoining.

The Manor of Coxhoe, which abounds with Game, and the fishery of Kelloe Burn (the stream running through the Manor, and producing excellent re Trout) will be reserved to the Occupier of the House.

The Mansion and Offices contain every requisite Convenience for the Residence of a respectable Family, in a cheap and pleasant County, good Neighbourhood, and a short distance from the Sea, and within five miles of good Coals.

The situation is peculiarly desirable for a Sportsman, being in the hunting Country, near several covers, hunted by the Earl of Darlington's hounds and within easy distances of others hunted by Mr. Lambton's; and the Manor and Neighbourhood afford remarkably good Hare Hunting. More or less land, if desired be had with the Estate.

The advertisement does not describe the interior of the house. Instead it underlines the desirability of the estate for a 'Sportsman' defined as being a man who enjoys hunting to foxes to hounds, hunting hares presumably with the dogs kept in his kennels and fishing. There is name dropping in the advertisement; the Earl of Darlington and the Lambton's, implying that the man who rented this estate would be mixing in such circles.

The Earl of Darlington supported Rowland Burdon's election campaign. He would know both him and the Lambton family. It is probable Rowland Burdon associated with Edward Moulton Barrett when he lived in Coxhoe Hall. The Hall was very near Castle Eden, so they could be considered almost neighbours.

It was here their first child Elizabeth Barrett was born in 1806. Elizabeth was baptised privately one year later but in 1808 she was baptised publicly along with her brother in Kelloe Church. Elizabeth Barrett married Robert Browning in 1846. There is a plaque in St. Helen's Church that commemorates that she was baptised in the church.

The Barrett family moved to Hertfordshire in 1809 but Elizabeth Barrett who was to become Elizabeth Barrett Browning spent her very early years in Coxhoe Hall.

Rowland Burdon probably knew or had connections with people who owned plantations and therefore slaves. He may even have known the owner of the 'Fly', the ship that transported slaves from Africa to Florida. He did support at first the gradual abolition of the slave trade and had moved towards complete abolition by 1793.

Moves towards Abolition

There were abolitionists in the North East. Thomas Clarkson headed an Abolition Committee in London. In 1788 information on the brutality of the Slave Trade was sent to Mayors throughout the country urging them to petition Parliament.

On Feb 12th Newcastle Common Council carried forward a resolution to draw such a resolution from the corporation to Parliament, "to take into serious consideration the hardships which many of the natives of Africa suffer by means of the trade carried on for purchasing slaves to cultivate the lands in the West Indies." [19]

In 1791 Thomas Clarkson came to Newcastle and William Turner became responsible for organising and co-operating with the London Abolition Committee. In late 1791 a society was formed in Newcastle for the "purpose of co-operating with the London and other Societies to obtain the Abolition of the Slave Trade upon the coast of Africa, particularly by purchasing and distributing such books as are best calculated to inform the public at large in this town and the adjacent counties, respecting the real nature of this horrid traffic." [20]

A considerable number of people in Newcastle were Methodists. John Wesley had preached four times in Newcastle. Many would have read his "Thoughts on Slavery" that he wrote as early as 1774. This may have been one of the information pamphlets distributed.

They published 2,000 copies of Clarkson's 'Abstract of Evidence against the Slave Trade'. Thomas Bewick, himself an abolitionist, engraved the frontispiece of the tract. Clarkson also had commissioned the iconic illustration that showed the gross overcrowding on board the ship 'Brooks.'

The Unitarian William Batson, a wealthy corn merchant, is mentioned many times in the Newcastle Courant as receiving subscriptions for the cause. Many of the subscribers were named in the newspaper with the subscription amount, next to their names. This was customary at that time but a considerable number of subscribers were recorded as being anonymous. They did not want recognition for their generosity as the giving was of the greatest importance. Most of the leaders of the Anti-Slave Trade movement like William Batson had strong religious connections. They were mainly Unitarians, Quakers, Methodists and Presbyterians.

There were also addresses in meetings and sermons delivered in chapels and churches that would inform the public and raise awareness of the horrors of the Slave Trade. The numbers of petitions to Parliament began to accumulate.

One such petition recorded in 25th Feb 1792 reports a petition containing upwards of 3,160 signatures for the Abolition of the Slave Trade from Newcastle and its neighbourhood had been sent to Parliament. Newcastle was not the only place involved in raising petitions. Great numbers were signing petitions including, Alnwick, Belford, Wooler, Warkworth, Rothbury and Hexham. It was suggested that every market town in the North of England expressed that abhorrence towards a trade that so directly violated every religious and humane principle.

The raising of petitions was not limited to market towns. They came from many towns and their surroundings areas in the North East. Subscriptions were raised to pay for the printing of pamphlets, tracts, advertising and books.

Letters were written to newspapers. Many would read such letters and be persuaded to join the cause for abolition. A published letter [21] written by James Field Stanfield was probably one of the works many people would have read.

Although born in Dublin in 1749, James Field Stanfield eventually came to live in Sunderland. He was a seaman and at one time had been involved in the Slave Trade, working on the slave ship "Brooks".

He left the sea in 1782 and became an actor, living in Sunderland until his death in 1824. A plaque was erected on the building erected on the site of his former house. It reads; "JAMES FIELD STANFIELD (1749 -1824) Actor, author and campaigner against the Slave Trade lived in a house on this, site which was also the birth of his son Clarkson Stanfield R.A, a marine and landscape painter. James Field called his son Clarkson, probably after Thomas Clarkson, a prominent abolitionist.

In 1788 J.F. Stanfield recorded his experiences in the form of letters addressed to the Rev Thomas Clarkson. These letters were published in 1789 entitled, *"The Guinea voyage. A poem in three books."*

James Stansfield had gone to sea on a vessel engaged in the slave trade. He describe the ship as a 'floating dungeon' and recorded the horrors he had witnessed on board ship. He wrote of the "sadism of the captain who, ill in bed from Africa to the West Indies, had a female servant flogged before him in his cabin for a minor offence. As the unwilling sailor administering the punishment was judged to be too lenient, the sailor himself was flayed and the woman was flogged 'until her back was full of holes'... He had spent time in Benin" and argued against the lies perpetuated by some that a life of slavery in the West indies was better than life in Africa arguing that "he had never seen a happier race of people than those in the Kingdom of Benin with its well-stocked markets of food and other commodities."

Stanfield's writings "were serialised in newspapers in Britain and America and shocked their readers." The writer of this letter to the newspaper had read Stanfield's account and recorded his thoughts; "His writings on the subject of slavery, will afford greater information than I am able to give. I have not seen the pale quivering lip of fatal disease hang on the dejected African, torn from all that is dear to him, whilst grim death stalks over the deck, and seizes alike on the African Slave and the British Seaman, who also fall prey to this infernal trade. The relentless Master of the Slave Ship, deaf to the cries of nature, becomes so hardened to cruelty, that he even has no feeling for his own countrymen, purloined from their wives by his deceitful hypocrisy. Need we wonder then that he feels not for the unhappy African, whom he impiously deems of an inferior order of creation…no loss suffered by our revenue ought to be put in competition with the misery of a whole species of the human race; for what is a small loss to the revenue in particular, considering the many resources of a commercial country, without having no recourse to that dire one of trading in our fellow creatures: perhaps that revenue raised on the exportation of the unhappy negro, from his native home, from all the endearing comforts of a social life, torn from his friends, his family, his country; exposed to all the dire effects and disease in the midst of the ocean, where, devoid of human aid, he drags on a wretched existence, amidst the dying shrieks of his expiring neighbours, who, if he chances to survive all these hardships, is doomed to linger in wretched captivity in a foreign land, and to feel all the rigours of slavery in the extreme perhaps the revenue raised from this unhappy wretch, or rather from numbers of these unhappy creatures, is given to feed the pride, or pamper the arrogance of some courtly minion, who will pretend to deny the existence of these facts, because he lives upon the produce of the misfortunes they cause."

This letter illustrates the profound effect that anti-Slave Trade publications had on the literate public. An iconic illustration commissioned by Thomas Clarkson showed the terrible overcrowding in the slave ship 'Brooks' would have a profound effect.[22]

By 1792 over 500 petitions with over 400,000 signatures were forwarded to Parliament. A letter writer in the Newcastle Chronicle on 25th February 1792 summed up the argument for and against the Abolition of the Slave Trade in the following words; "Humanity against, and interest for the trade are the two principal leading features in the contest.

The promotion of the abolition of Slavery have depicted in strong colours the miserable condition of the Slaves, and have given us an animated description of the beauty of the universal philanthropy, they have exhibited to the nation upon the oaths of many respectable persons the most astonishing unheard of system of cruelty daily and hourly exercised by the Hunters, Kidnappers, Dealers, Merchants, Captains of Ships, Purchasers, Owners, Overseers, and Drivers of Slaves too painful to recite, too distressing to be read, what must it be to endure? They argue that the trade should be abolished, and humane efficacious Laws enacted for the government and happiness of those now in slavery.

The defenders of the trade allege that the slaves are happier in their present state, than in their own country; that the plantations cannot be beneficially cultivated without their labour, that the revenue may be injured; that other nations will take up the traffic to our loss, and that the impulse of benevolence should give way to public utility."

There were many who were on the side of 'public utility'. Debates held in the House of Lords as early as 1788, demonstrated these views.

Lord Rodney, "condemned the bill as not only unnecessary, but impolitic. The French were at this moment giving bounty to ships employed in the African Slave Trade...by abolishing or restraining it would as much benefit our enemies as we injured ourselves."[23]

The Earl of Sandwich in the same year extended this argument when he was reported as saying, "A very valuable branch of commence which had for many years not only benefited our West India Islands, but had found employ for almost every branch of our home manufactures, and throw those advantages into the hands of the ranch or the Dutch."

An example of one type of commerce comes from a petition presented to Parliament on behalf of Messrs. Dawsons of Liverpool. The firm had entered into a contract with the King of Spain to supply the Spanish colonies with 5,000 slaves annually. If the Bill was passed this commerce would be lost.

The Earl of Sandwich underlined his opinion that, "the cry for abolition of the Slave Trade was made by persons wholly ignorant of the consequences that would result from the attainment of their wishes."

These arguments and feelings were still present when an Abolition Bill was presented to Parliament again after receipt of all the petitions and campaigning throughout the country. "Humanity" lost. "Public utility" won. The Bill was defeated.

Efforts were praised in 1793 when part of a report of a meeting was recorded;[24]

"That Rowland Burdon and Ralph Millbanke Esquires Representatives in Parliament for this county, be desired to continue their exertions to obtain this important and much desired object; and that copies of these Resolutions be transmitted to them by the Chairman, with the thanks of this meeting for their having supported the immediate Abolition.

That the thanks of this Meeting are due to William Wilberforce, Esquire, for his great exertions in bringing forward this subject, and to every Member of the House of Commons, who supported him herein."

People like Rowland Burdon and Ralph Millbanke continued their 'exertions' and William Wilberforce continued his 'great exertions' abolition of the British Slave Trade was not achieved until 1808. Stanfield then published a combined edition of his two works to mark the passing of the Abolition of the Slave Trade. It was dedicated to Sir Ralph Millbanke MP for County Durham, whom Stanfield records as seconding Wilberforce's Abolition Bill. Both Millbanke and Burdon had supported William Wilberforce.

Campaigning continued until nearly thirty years later it resulted in the abolition of slavery in the British Empire. Those who owned slaves did not lose out. Twenty million pounds was granted as compensation for the loss of property to owners of all West Indian slaves. In 1788 there were 410,000 slaves in the British West Indies; 174,000 of these were in Jamaica; many owned by the Graham Clarke family at their plantations. John Graham Clarke received £1,187 8s 11d compensation from the National Debt Office for the 62 slaves he owned on the Westmorland; one of his plantations in Jamaica; an average of about £19 for the cost of a single member of 'humanity'.

Some owned less like many middles class families including people like country vicars and iron manufacturers. Others, like John Gladstone father of William Gladstone would receive huge amounts of money. He owned 2,508 slaves so he received £106,769 compensation, equivalent today to the huge amount of £83 million pounds.

The compensation of 1834 amounted to 40% of the Treasury's actual spending budget, amounting to a staggering modern equivalent of about £16.5 billion.

The Duke of York

Money was needed at an earlier time to finance the expenditure of the Duke of York and the Royal Family. This matter was discussed in the House of Commons in the 1790's. In March 1792 Pitt suggested to the House that His Highness the Duke of York should be allocated a budget of £18,000 per annum and his wife the Duchess should receive £8,000. Rowland Burdon and others objected to this large amount. Burdon considered an annual income of £10,000 was more than adequate for His Highness to spend.

In February 1795, there was a criticism of Pitt for his handling of the financial claims of the Prince of Wales. In 1795 what was to be a disastrous marriage between the Prince and Princess Caroline took place. It was an extremely lavish affair; Princess Caroline's dress was made from silver tissue and lace and her velvet robe was trimmed with ermine. The dress was so heavy she could barely stand during the ceremony. The dress did not improve the Prince of Wales feelings towards Caroline as he was in a state of drunken collapse on his wedding night. The Prince's extravagant spending was increased when by 1795 repairs and renovations to the newly acquired Carlton House in Pall Mall had run up bills of £17,000. The Prince of Wales debts were soaring but he continued buying paintings and expensive furniture.

In May 1795 the House argued for a reduction of the proposed grant to the Prince of Wales. They voted for Sumner's amendment to payment of Prince's debts. The Prince was allocated an increase of income on his marriage. He would now receive £125,000 annually. However, to pay off his debts, £65,000 of this amount was to be deducted as well as the £13,000 income he received from the Duchy of Cornwall. As a bachelor, the Prince's yearly income received £18,000 a year more than it would be now as a married man. This reduction in income would not sweeten his feeling towards Princess Caroline.

During the debate in the House in May, Rowland Burdon proposed a retrenchment in the salaries to noblemen and gentlemen in the Prince's establishment, which now stood at £25,000 a year. Mr. Fox spoke for two hours against the plan. He proposed a new plan for the sale of the Duchy of Cornwall which he estimated as being worth £600,000. Fox proposed £300,000 should be used to purchase a life annuity for the Prince of Wales, and the other £300,000 should be reverted to the public.

Fox's proposal was not adopted but probably led to the House deciding income from the Duchy should be used to pay off the Prince's debts. If Fox had carried the day, the Duchy of Cornwall would not have been the property of any Prince of Wales.

Debts and Taxation

Parliament reduced the income of the Prince of Wales in order to reduce his debts. Britain had debts. After suffering defeat to America in their War of Independence Britain's national debt was extreme; £234 million pounds. The annual tax revenues totalled £13 million pounds so £8 million of this paid interest on the vast national debt.

William Pitt introduced eleven new taxes between 1784 and 1786. A stamp duty was placed on hair powder for wigs. A licence costing £1 1s to use hair powder was introduced in 1795. This raised £177,000 in the first year but the tax led to the gradual ending of the fashion of wearing wigs and by 1869 the tax had finished. Perfumes and cosmetics were taxed for 14 years. A tax on hats introduced in 1784 lasted 27 years.

Clocks and watches were taxed for only one year as the tax was ruining the trade but the tax on horses lasted for 91 years. The Game licence continued for 223 years. Pawnbrokers needed a licence until 1949.

More money was needed to finance the army and navy when France declared war in 1793. Between 1795 and 1798 four new assessed taxes were introduced.

This included a dog tax that lasted 192 years. Duties on houses, horses, male servants, carriages and windows were increased. Income tax was introduced in 1799. In March 1798, Parliament debated an increase in window tax. Rowland Burdon argued that as watch and clock tax was to be given up the money saved could be used to offset the tax on windows. The new plan charged on a sliding scale dependent on the number of windows ranging from 10shillings for seven windows increasing through stages reaching £20 10s for fifty windows, £37 for 100 windows and £61 for 180 and above windows.

Rowland Burdon insisted he visited every freeholder in his election campaign. There would be few, if any, who had 180 windows and could afford to pay extra tax. He knew this tax would be unpopular amongst the less wealthy freeholders in his constituency when he addressed the House by reportedly saying,[25] "The Chancellor of the Exchequer should have the opportunity of giving some relief to country gentlemen who were subjected to great hardships in consequence of the number of windows in their houses." The window tax was increased. It is uncertain how many windows were in Burdon's house in Castle Eden but it would have been a substantial number. Perhaps he included himself as one of the 'country gentlemen' who would have been affected by paying for the number of windows in his residence. His income would be reduced as well as that of the Prince of Wales.

Hardships for Many: the Deserving Poor

The Prince of Wales' income would be reduced. The 'country gentlemen with small fortunes' would have more to pay in tax. Some of these 'country gentlemen with small fortunes' may have been amongst Rowland Burdon's circle of friends. In 1801 it was reported that Rowland Burdon Esq MP was entertaining his friends but he was also contributing in the support of the poor in the neighbourhood of Castle Eden, near Durham. The poor throughout the country would need support. Times were very hard. Bad harvests had continued for a number of years.[26] "We can assure the public that, on account of the very great loss the farmers must have sustained by the badness of the harvest, and the late very heavy falls of rain, Rowland Burdon of Castle Eden Esq.; has generously stepped forward, and amply relieved all the sufferers on his estate at Westharle."

Shortages had led to a high demand and food prices were soaring so rapidly they were beyond the reach of many of the poor. The price of potatoes was high in 1800 mainly because of the poor harvest due to unfavourable weather. The weather in April was extremely unfavourable when there was a bitter easterly wind with snowstorms and heavy rain. The bad weather continued throughout the year. Scarcity of animal feed killed many ewes, lambs and young sheep. Pasture was bare causing suffering to cattle.

Sowing seed had been delayed because of poor weather. The summer was remarkably cold and wet. Some grain, especially rye, had not ripened by the severe frosts that appeared in a very cold October.

It was not only grain that was affected; butter, cheese, bacon, pickled pork, rice and potatoes were also limited in quantity and quality.

There had been a bad harvest that led to food riots in 1795. What was called a riot in happened in Birmingham in February, 1800. [27]

"On Thursday, in our market, an attempt was made by some women and boys (for we must do men the justice to say they took no part in these disgraceful proceedings) to create a riot in consequence of the price of potatoes. The disturbance was, however, soon put an end to."

The writer appears to praise men for not taking any part in this attempted 'riot'. Potatoes were part of the staple diet of the poor.

Women may have been desperate to feed their families. Their sons, probably younger sons were possible involved in this attempt to obtain food for the family. This was an attempted riot and 'soon put an end to.' But it demonstrates how the desperation felt by the poor at this time.

These food shortages had continued for many years. Meat was expensive in 1795. Shortly after shearing sheep at the usual time there had been a succession of extremely cold nights which had killed many animals.

Cattle for sale at the early markets and fairs were thin and lean before of lack of winter feeding.

Crops were scanty but many considered this was only part of the problem for the high price of provisions. Many thought like Pitt in his June speech in Parliament in 1796 that the enormous price of grain was out of all proportion with the scarcity. Some considered that farmers were holding wheat from the market in order to drive up the price. There was also the view that merchants were illegally entering into a monopoly to increase the price of corn.

Rowland Burdon was aiding the poor in Castle Eden whilst others were also helping those where they lived. Eighteen measures were being taken throughout many towns and cities in the country; "In consequence of the high price of potatoes which have risen in proportion with other provisions, a dealer in that article has engaged with the corporation of the city of London to sell to the public at large the best potatoes at three farthings per pound, and an inferior sort at one halfpenny, provided the corporation furnishes him with a warehouse for the purpose of retailing them, together with weights and scales, which they will be at liberty at all times to prove are just. The sale commenced on Tuesday morning, in Honey-Lane market, where large quantities were disposed of. The good effect may be judged from what took place yesterday. As soon as the other dealers found that all their customers applied to this new warehouse, they reduced their potatoes to the same price, boasting at the same time that they could afford and would supply the public at a cheap a rate as their new opponent."

It was not only the potato crop that had suffered. Grain was expensive and the price of bread rose dramatically. Charities that provided for the 'industrious poor' were advised to attempt to diminish the consumption of bread by substituting 'soup and other food, cheaper and equally wholesome with that of bread.'

Wrexham had a different solution as they had, 'entered into a very liberal subscription for the relief of the poor, and are now supplying them with soup, coal and potatoes at reduced prices."[29]

Rowland Burdon and his wife also subscribed into such a scheme set up in their locality, when they subscribed ten guineas for potato, soup and rice and rice for the benefit of the industrious poor of Durham and its neighbourhood. The industrious poor were considered the deserving poor and they needed help. The situation appeared to improve a little by 1803 when Mary Hale, whom we shall meet later wrote; [30] "Poor old England has fought a tough fight, and 'tis high time she should take breath a little. To complete our happiness, the last Season has been highly productive of all the necessities of life, more Corn having been reaped than was ever remembered. Of course the price of provisions is lowering very fast, and 'tis expected Wheat will be as low as five shillings the Bushel, a good hearing for this extensive family, for whom I was obliged to purchase it as high as a Guinea per Bushel before the new; Corn was got in; while the poorer class were unable to procure any food but potatoes, they were even scarce and dear, and the meagre countenances of the people sufficiently indicated their want and misery."

There were many instances reported of help for the 'industrious poor'. Soup was made in soup kitchens and sold to the poor at a reduced price;[31] "Yesterday the sale soup shop in this town opened. All the soup made in the two kitchens was sold in the course of an hour."

Individuals contributed money. Thomas Wilkinson, Esq, a recent Captain in the Durham militia, had just received his final six months' pay, so he contributed one hundred pounds worth of stock with an annual yield of three per cent. Half of the donation went to the Durham Infirmary and the remainder to the poor of his own parish of Brancepeth. Charitable Institutions like hospitals, schools, dispensaries and infirmaries were supported by donation. At this time Thomas Wilkinson saw the need to give half of his charitable donation to the poor in the parish of Brancepeth.

There are many examples recorded in newspapers including the New Year's Day's distribution of a large quantity of beef and bread to the poor at Whickham by the Earl of Strathmore. Lady Iddrell, of Urpeth House, had excellent soup made in her own kitchens and this was distributed twice a week to the poor in her neighbourhood. At the beginning of winter Lady Iddrell had also had members of her household make a large quantity of woollen clothing which she had distributed to pensioners in her district.

These events were recorded in the newspaper, possibly to demonstrate those with wealth who looked after the deserving poor. It could serve another purpose. In December 1799[32] the Duke of Northumberland donated one hundred pounds for the relief of the poor at Alnwick. The article gave him praise for this action. He was described as having "munificence which has peculiarly distinguished his Grace on every occasion when administering of comfort and happiness to the lower orders of the people." The article reports the 'principal inhabitants of the town, cordially uniting with the Duke made very liberal subscriptions for the same cause." The Duke had donated a large amount of money. It then followed that those 'principal inhabitants of the town' were expected to do the same. The publicity of the Duke and those others who gave led to the expectations that those of superior status should help the 'lowers orders of the people'.

Others had different ideas about helping the poor. Ratepayers were contributing towards poor relief to aid paupers, the deserving poor of the parish. The article suggested that the poor should not be allowed to keep dogs. The writer cited one hamlet in Suffolk where there were 53 dogs kept in the 20 houses. He considered this practice was a scandal because the paupers' dogs would be devouring the food should not keeping dogs that ought to have been fed to their half-starved children. He further argued that these dogs would be supported by people who were paying the poor relief for the paupers. Farmers were amongst these ratepayers. The paupers' dogs worried the farmers' sheep so farmers were doubly hit by the effect of the dogs. They paid into poor relief to feed the dogs and lost sheep because of worrying so the writer argued the farmers were paying to get their own sheep worried. The conclusion was that no pauper should be allowed to keep a dog.

It was said of Rowland Burdon that [33] "His charities were munificent and widely extended but in one respect he was far in advance of his age – in endeavouring to help those who helped themselves…together with his intimate friends Bishop Barrington of Durham and Sir Thomas Bernard Bart the last Governor of Massachusetts, he founded a 'Society for Battering the Condition of the Poor'…a society that was the pioneer of all the modern schemes for the reform of the abuses of the old Poor Law, and for the Factory Acts. His leading idea was to teach the poor to help themselves… (by joining) Friendly Societies' for securing help in sickness and old age. Castle Eden Friendly Society was founded in 1793, and the Mongewell Friendly Society in Oxfordshire founded by Bishop Barrington on his private estates at the same time were the first organisations of the kind in Britain." The Friendly Society in Castle Eden kept going until 1860. It would be easy for those in extreme poverty in the early 1800's to even find sufficient funds to join a friendly society. Fuel as well as food was increasingly expensive.

Coal

Coal, a vital commodity for warmth and cooking had also become increasingly costly. In March 1800, concerns were voiced over the cost of coal. Coal had been sold in London the previous winter at what was considered the exorbitant sum of £8 a chaldron, a measure of coal. This high price would affect poorest most.

Parliament a considered the high price of coal was of national importance so a committee was appointed to enquire into the state of coal trade. This committee included; Mr. Manning, Sir Matthew Ridley, William Wilberforce and Mr. Burdon.

Rowland Burdon knew many of the coal mine owners in Northumberland and Durham. Burdon was a merchant and Sir

Ridley the 1st Baronet was Governor of Newcastle-Upon-Tyne Company of Merchants. Both men had set up banks in Newcastle. Rowland Burdon was reported attending meetings and functions with knew him. Rowland Burdon's father would have known Sir Ridley's father. Matthew Montagu. Matthew Robinson was orphaned. When he was taken in by his aunt Mrs. Montagu, he took her surname. Elizabeth Montagu lived in Mayfair but her husband Edward Montagu had mining interests in Northumberland including the Montagu or Caroline Pit. When her husband died about 1775, Mrs. Montagu took over the running of the mines. When in Northumberland East Denton Hall was the family residence. Although a great socialite, Mrs. Montagu preferred her society friends in London to the society in the North who she is alleged to have patronised for their practical conversation. To alleviate the tedium of northern visits she invited several notable guests to her Newcastle residence, including Dr Samuel Johnson, Joshua Reynolds, Goldsmith and David Garrick. Elizabeth Montagu stopped visiting East Denton Hall in 1789, so her heir Matthew Montagu would become more involved in the mining interests. At her death in 1800, Mrs. Montagu's coal yearly income exceeded £10,000. There was money to be made from coal. At the time of the debates about coal, Matthew Montagu, known to Rowland Burdon, would be owner of the coal interests in Northumberland. Matthew Montagu had been a Member of Parliament and would be again. Although he was out of office for ten years from 1796, he still moved amongst the Pitt circle. Burdon was reportedly also in this circle, so probably knew him socially.

Burdon had associates and relatives like the Brandlings and Ords in the North who were coal owners. Charles Brandling, Burdon's father-in-law, from his first marriage, was Member of Parliament for Newcastle. Charles Brandling had coal resources on his estates at Felling. Rowland Burdon had married Charles' daughter, Margaret Brandling. Two of his Charles' other daughters had married into the Ord family. Eleanor married William Ord and Barbara married Rev. James Ord. The Ord family had interests in Benwell Colliery. Rowland Burdon would have many other connections with other mine owners. This would give him experience to serve on this committee to ascertain the reasons for the high price of coal. There were other matters to be investigated.

In the House Manning sought an enquiry into the exorbitant price of coal. Burdon sat on the Committee of the two enquiries in May and November of 1800. Manning's Regulation Bill of 11th March 1801 failed when Burdon amongst others, mainly defended the interests of the Northern coal owners by arguing against the Bill.

Cold Bath Field Prison

There were other enquiries that involved Rowland Burdon. He was one of the investigators who personally delved into allegations of the mistreatment of Col. Despard whilst he was in custody in Cold Bath Field Prison. Despard was arrested on suspicion of involvement if Irish rebellion. He was imprisoned whilst he was held for trial for nearly three years under the suspension of habeus corpus, a measure supported by Burdon. During his imprisonment Despard raised instances of cruelties and brutality he considered had occurred in Cold Bath Fields prison.

Cold Bath Field prison was rebuilt in 1794. The prison was meant to house men, women and children who had been given short sentences of up to two years. There were separate blocks for felons, those who had committed misdemeanours and vagrants. It was also used as a debtors' prison. The prison became notorious for its strict regime of silence and use of the treadmill.

It was alleged that prisoners were; beaten by turnkeys, chained in irons for several months, starved to near the point of death, placed in solitary confinement for minor misdemeanours and faced exorbitant charges for the basic necessities,

Despard himself complained of maltreatment. He was allowed no fire, candle, chair, table, knife, fork or book to read. His window was unglazed. It was so cold that his wife Catherine said his feet were frostbitten.

A case was brought before the court that highlighted what were considered atrocities. Mary Rich, a 14 year old girl had been held in prison, as a witness. She had accused a lawyer of rape. Until the trial, it was customary to allow the accused perpetrator to remain free but the witness was placed in prison to await trial, so the accused lawyer was allowed his freedom but Mary Rich was placed in Cold Bath Fields prison for one month to await the trial.

The court was shocked at her appearance at the trial. She was so frail and pale that she was unable to stand. She had been fed only bread and water for one month. Her cell had no fire and the window was unglazed so her cell was freezing. The bed coverings provided were scant so no warmth could be had in the bed.

In March 1799 it was reported that,[34] "Mr Burdon said, that as the prison in Cold Bath Fields had been the subject of much public discussion, and as examination had lately taken place into the situation of that prison, and the treatment of prisoners confined there... he wished that the subject matter of this examination be laid before the house'. A select committee was formed to inquire into the prison but Rowland Burdon was unable to serve on this committee as he was a member of the Secret Committee on Conspiracies. William Dundas took up Burdon's call for an enquiry into the prison.

Although Colonel Despard was moved from Cold Bath Field Prison, the enquiry did not help him. He was tried and convicted of treason. He was executed, along with others in February 1803, when;[35] "About half past eight the prisoners were brought upon the scaffold, Colonel Despard closing the melancholy procession. On coming forward he turned to the right and left, and repeatedly bowed to the multitude, some few of who, that had placed themselves in a phalanx directly opposite the door of the prison, returned the salute with a kind of shout, which was, however, overpowered by the solemn murmur of disapprobation.

The ropes being put round the necks of the unfortunate men, the Colonel advanced about two steps, and in a firm tone of voice declared his innocence of the crimes of which he had been accused - that he was brought there to receive the reward of thirty years faithful service of his country – that the cause for which he died was that of liberty, justice and humanity; for which more he apprehended might suffer, ... A profound stillness prevailed while the

Colonel was speaking, and when he had done faint applause was heard from about twenty or thirty persons; the rest observed a melancholy silence ... In about a quarter of an hour the platform fell, and left the bodies suspended; in which state they remained about half an hour, when they were cut down and decapitated with an axe, the operation beginning with that of the Colonel, after which the heads were successively exhibited by the executioner, making the usual proclamation – 'This is the head of a traitor' and designating each by his name. A little after ten the whole of the fatal ceremony was over... The bodies were placed in coffins arranged in a row to receive them. It was altogether an awful spectacle, and it is hoped the dreadful necessity will never recur of exhibiting to the eyes of Englishmen such another."

This reported account of the hanging is shocking but the writer appears to have had some sympathy for the fate of Colonel Despard in particular. He writes that 'the rest' of the gathering 'observed a melancholy' silence while the Colonel was speaking. There were reportedly 20,000 spectators who had gathered on that day to witness the event. That is a large number of people to have 'observed a melancholy silence'. It is probably there was some public sympathy amongst the crowd.

Colonel Despard was an Irish soldier who served gallantly in the British Army. He was imprisoned in 1798 under suspicion of involvement in the Irish Rebellion but released without charge in 1801. In late 1802, he along with six others, were named by Government informers and disaffected soldiers as being members of a conspiracy to seize the Tower of London, the Bank of England an assassinate King George III. There was scant evidence to substantiate these accusations. Lord Nelson knew Colonel Despard and he gave a character witness in favour of the Colonel at the trial. Colonel Despard and the six others were found guilty and subsequently executed.

Rowland Burdon had spearheaded the examination of conditions in Cold Bath Field Prison. In March 1799, Mr Burdon reportedly said; [36]

"That as the prison in old Bath Fields had been the subject of much public discussion, and as examinations had lately taken place into the situation of the prison, and the treatment of prisoners conditions there, by the Magistrates of the county of Middlesex, in consequence of the Lord Lieutenant's direction, he therefore wished that the subject matter of those examinations be brought before the House. He accordingly moved, that an humble address be presented to his Majesty, that he maybe graciously pleased to give directions for laying before the House, copies of the examinations respecting the prison in Cold Bath Fields, taken by the magistrates of the county of Middlesex at their last quarter sessions, and returned to the office of the Secretary of State."

Rowland Burdon had an interest in prisons. He was a magistrate in County Durham so had a considerable amount of experience. He became one of the many who gave donations of money and food to prisoners. This information appeared in newspapers always accompanied by words that indicated the usual and expected gratitude of the prisoners for these donations; [37] "The prisoners in Durham Goal return sincere thanks to Rowland Burdon Esq MP for a good dinner, a 3d loaf, 3 gills of ale, and one shilling each."

Although he had an interest in prison welfare and had brought the complaints to Parliament, Rowland Burdon was a Member of the Secret Committee so he could not serve on a Select Committee to further investigate conditions in Cold Bath Field Prison.

He served on other committees. In March 1797 Mr. Pitt had moved for a Secret Committee on the country's finances. There was a lengthy ballot to select members that lasted until almost six o'clock. There were 15 members chosen and eleven of these members were recorded in the newspaper including William Pitt, William Wilberforce with Rowland Burdon appearing third in a list of distinguished company.

A ballot for a Secret Committee to consider the papers presented by the Chancellor of the Exchequer took place in April 1801 (Bury and Norwich Post). Twenty one members were selected, including Rt. Hon William Pitt, Rt Hon H Addington, Lord Viscount Castlereagh, Rt. Hon. H. Dundas, William Wilberforce

Esq and Rowland Burdon Esq. The reporting newspaper added that all those appointed on the secret committee are in the ministerial interest.

Seaman's Strike at Shields

In 1799 Rowland Burdon was appointed to serve on the Select Committee on Wet Docks. He had been involved in maritime matters. In November 1792, he was credited with resolving the riots of seamen that had occurred in Shields. A letter written by Burdon gives some information about the gravity of the situation;[38] "Castle Eden Nov 3rd 1792. The sailors from the Ports of the Tyne had been on strike for nearly three weeks because they considered their pay insufficient. They would not suffer any ships to put to Sea, unless their owners would sign a promise of payment of four guineas per voyage during the winter months."

Burdon had witnessed events in Shields harbour when sailors in a 'determined systematic manner' proceeded to 'take the officer's out of their ships.'

Together with the Mayor of Newcastle and his father-in-law Charles Brandling MP for Newcastle Rowland Burdon attended a meeting of the Ship Owners in Trinity House Newcastle on Oct. 24th. The outcome was 'to allow £3 per Voyage for four winter months which offer being made to the Sailors was treated with contempt'.

Burdon then described what he considered to be conditions in South Shields at the time; [39] "Every day as the light ships return from London, these men board them, & oblige the officers & sailors to join in their revolt. South Shields has risen so rapidly, from the spirit of Commerce, as to contain at least 14,000 inhabitants without a single magistrate to control it. None of its inhabitants are of a description to qualify for that office, and few would be active or hardy enough.... Not a single soldier is there to protect a great, & increasing property; novel establishments have flourished to such a degree, that the property in Shipping of the Shields (there was a North and South Shields separated by the River Tyne) has multiplied itself within 30 years from 30 Sail of Colliers to not less than 120. The Magistrates of Newcastle are either diffident of their power, or unwilling to exert it. North Shields had the protection of Barracks, & Magistrates of activity in its Neighbourhood – South Shields as I have already stated is totally unprotected. I am conscious that this representation won't come with more propriety from the Magistrates of Newcastle, but as a Magistrate of the County of Durham (South Shields was in County Durham) & employed in its Representation (as a Member of Parliament) having been at South Shields on Oct. 26, & seeing distinctly the unprotected Situation of its Trade."

To add to what Burdon sees as a possible inflammatory situation he points out that alcohol consumption could aggravate the situation as, "In South Shields we have about 160 Public Houses" with only a force of "3 soldiers on an average" to keep order. He suggested "Government ought to be at the expense of Barracks here." He had been in communication with the Bishop of Durham and this letter had led Burdon to believe that '4 or 5 Companies of Soldiers' are "necessary in addition to those already in the Neighbourhood, and I can advise you in the most earnest wish of all people here to have the Mob quelled".

As to the Corporation of Newcastle, I concur they feel little anxiety about this Riot – but we will now determine to make them feel our resent for there I am much obliged will be guided.

We also have in contemplation, a letter from the Bishop in regard to the force requested to quell this riot. I should really think 4 or 5 Companies of Soldiers necessary in addition to those already in the Neighbourhood, and I can advise you in the most earnest wish of all people here to have the Mob quelled." [40]

The unrest continued with sailors in South Shields objecting to sail for wages less than four guineas. Meetings continued but the sailor extended their demands and their language was extremely insolent. The feeling was that the Government should give 'a police' to these commercial towns facing the maritime unrest.

Rowland Burdon was a magistrate well as being a Member of Parliament and it was in both capacities that he enabled a satisfactory outcome to the dispute. His "indefatigable exertions" demonstrated what "one firm and industrious Magistrate" is capable of doing. [40]

The dispute was about the amount of money paid to the seamen for each voyage. The Ship Owners held a public meeting in Newcastle and agreed to the seamen's first demands of £3 a voyage for six months. The sailors then rejected this. They wanted payment of three guineas a voyage for one year. The Ship-Owners convened another meeting. The dispute had lasted five weeks. They wanted it settled.

Rowland Burdon, as Magistrate was called in to intervene in order to bring the seamen to a sense of their duty and to lay their case before Parliament. It was hoped Rowland Burdon might be able to obtain a Bill for relief by the end of May. With an added small concession, Burdon persuaded the seamen to agree with the Ship Owner's. The Ship-Owners consented to the concession.

Mr. Burdon left the meeting room in the Town Hall, South Shields, and spoke to the sailors waiting outside informing them an agreement to their last request had been made by the Ship Owners. However Burdon added a warning to the sailors that they should be satisfied with what had been agreed and he would undertake no further negotiations on their behalf. He also reminded them that as a magistrate, he had treated them with mildness, and if any further action like violently boarding ships or maltreating their fellow seaman was to occur, he would resort to justice so law and order could prevail.

Rowland Burdon meant what he said. He pressed to make the agreements between the Masters and Seamen more strict and regular because in doing this he considered such an agreement would benefit both parties. Some seamen had neglected to sign to sign the agreement of the act. This had led to them boarding ship but refusing to sail until they were given higher wages. He, a magistrate, wanted greater powers to deal with similar situations. Although he appeared fair to the cause of the seamen and negotiated their cause with the Masters, he was definitely on the side of the Masters and wanted more powers to enforce their cause.

The Militia

There was violence at home. There had been food riots. Seamen had rioted over their rates of pay. There was an even greater threat of violence from abroad with a great fear of invasion by the French. Rowland Burdon was involved in the Militia augmentation Bill of 6th March 1794. He put forward a proposition to raise a Volunteer Corps. Burdon welcomed the Militia Enlistment Bill of 30th December, 1797 moving quickly to form a Volunteer Group. By September 1798 they were presented with a standard when on;[41] "Sunday morning last, the Easington Ward Yeomanry Cavalry were presented with the elegant standard by Mrs Burdon, who on that occasion, complimented the Corps on the spirited and ready manner in which they originally volunteered their service, as well as their subsequent conduct extending its limits and increasing the number to a squadron of two troops. The Major-Commandant, after a compliment to the Ladies of this country expressed his confidence that the Easington Ward Cavalry would on all dealings do their duty, should their actual services be called forth; in defence of their King, their Country, all that was dear to them; pointed out to the Corps the service rendered by the Yeomanry in Ireland, as a noble example; and concluded by exhorting them to do their duty both in their military and civil capacities, with a proper confidence in the protection of Divine Providence, which he inculcated by giving to their standard the motto of the Bridge, at Wearmouth, Nil desperandum Auspice Deo –After the ceremony was over, the Corps attended Divine Service and heard an occasional Sermon; after which, on their return, they fired three volleys and lowered the standard with military etiquette, "The following evening being the Anniversary of the laying of the foundation of Wearmouth Bridge. Mrs. Burdon gave a Ball and Cold Collation at Castle Eden Inn, to upwards of 200 persons, consisting of volunteers, tenants, and respectable young people of the neighbourhood; and the evening was concluded with the utmost harmony and decorum."

Mrs. Burdon is involved even to the extent of giving a Ball including a cold collation at the Castle Eden Inn.

Others, including William Pitt, raised Battalions. He took an active part in parades and drill. So much so that General Dundas was extremely impressed by Mr. Pitt's newly raised 1st Battalion. Lady Hester Stanhope probably knew General Dundas as military and naval personnel were frequent guests at the home of William Pitt. Pitt himself took an active part in his Battalion

Others were involved in raising militia. In Northumberland, by August 1799 the Rt Hon Earl Percy had raised 600 men. On 5th January 1799, the Newcastle Courant published an account of the presentation of colours and standard by Lady Ridley to the Newcastle Armed Association in their exercising ground at the Nuns fields. As the field was situated behind Mr. Brodies' Long Room, a wooden platform under the windows along the whole length of the building was erected by the corps so invited ladies could view the ceremony.

The event was quite a spectacle, probably much to the delight of the ladies.

The ladies would probably have been friends or acquaintances of Lady Ridley and Mrs. Cotsford Burdon would most likely have been present as Rowland Burdon, a Captain took part in the proceedings.

The ceremony began at 11am. A parade of eight companies of infantry and a troop of cavalry proceeded to Nun's field. The three hundred strong rank and file of the militia formed a line at 12 o'clock, with the troop of horses at the rear. General Cowell and his retinue attended the parade. John Clayton Cowell served in the 1st Royals. He became Lieutenant Colonel of the foot soldier regiment; A.D.C. to the Duke of Kent and Governor of St Thomas Island. John Clayton Cowell was related through his mother to the Clayton family of Newcastle, so because of his connections and military status he was appointed General of the newly formed Newcastle Armed Association.

The march past, with a salute to Lady Ridley was viewed by the ladies from their prime position outside Brodie's Long room. The troops then formed three sides of a square with the troop of horses to the rear.

Lady Ridley presented the colours to the newly formed Newcastle Armed Association, considering this an honour and praising those who had volunteered to offer their services in defence of their Country in this time when there was the threat and danger of invasion, by an imperious and desperate foe.

The fear of the danger of invasion by the French was very real. The Militia was being raised throughout the country. Lady Ridley continued her speech including her thoughts that when these men eventually returned to their peaceful pursuits and respective dwellings and various occupations they would have performed the most sacred duty and would deserve to feel gratitude from their countrymen.

Colonel Ridley replied to his wife's speech, addressing her as Madam and saying he felt infinite pleasure to receive the Colours for such an honourable detachment of men, emphasising once more the worthiness of the men in fulfilling their patriotic duty. He continued in similar vein concluding with in the event of invasion he knew they would do their duty and face any conflict with honour.

The threat of invasion by France appeared real. Lady Ridley and her companions on the platform would be relieved that such a show of force could be relied upon for their defence and protection. The troops on hearing this would be spurred on by the thought that they were not only being patriotic but they were also in the Militia to protect, not only these ladies but their own wives and children from what they considered to be the impending danger.

The Colonel, Sir Ridley then delivered a considerable address to the troops, underlining how their volunteering demonstrated their patriotism in a time when there was a strong impression of danger that was felt by all men of whatever rank or condition of life. The important necessity of being united in what was considered the same glorious cause was strongly emphasised.

The Colonel is implying the volunteers are all equal in this glorious cause and equal in their patriotism. They were volunteers yet the Colonel spoke at some length linking their volunteering with the actions of our brave countrymen of the army and navy engaged in the war with France. He is raising the troops' status from volunteer to regular soldier. He reminds them of victories by men such as Jervis, Duncan, Nelson and Warren. There was a need for vigilance and prepare for internal defence. He asked the troops to look around at all those who had come to the ceremony; to consider all those most dear to us; wives, children, parents, relatives or friends. He urged them to feel that that it is for their protection and security they would fight even at the risk of danger to their own lives. Lord Ridley reminded them that in these ranks he saw so many men of every description in society who were united in arms in the same cause. This gave him a sense of pride that he too could rank himself amongst them as a fellow citizen. After this stirring speech Colonel Ridley delivered the Colours to the officers and the Battalion presented arms.

Colonel Ridley's speech linked himself and other officers with the ranks of many men of every description in society as fellow citizen fighting together in defence of those most dear to them whose lives they would defend to the death. The Colonel suggested this was a just war as in his opinion God was on their side. These words would raise the morale of the ranks.

They would also raise the morale of those in the concourse as well as those on the platform. Relatives of the ranks saw the parade, although from not as good a vantage point as the ladies on their specially built platform. Relatives and friends listening to the speeches would take a sense of well-being that officers and men were fellow citizens there to protect their safety if an invasion occurred.

After the presentation of the Colours, the escort of the horse advanced to the platform. Lady Ridley addressed Captain Burdon before presenting him with the Standard. He replied with sincere gratitude and concluded his address underling they had taken arms in defence of their country, its religion, liberty and laws and with a determination to follow the banners with ardour. Captain Burdon took the Standard and addressed the Troop with a statement that he in his honour and integrity had pledged himself to her Ladyship, on behalf of the assembled volunteers.

The determined spirits of those witnessing the events would be heightened by the words. The cavalry would be there to support the Troop. The Captain of the *Newcastle Association Light Horse* had given his assurance.

The infantry resumed their ground on the opposite side of the field and fired three volleys into the air. The parade assembled. With bands playing the whole Corps escorted their colours to the Colonel's House in Westgate Street before proceeding with the Standard to Captain Burdon's house in Northumberland Street.

At four o'clock the General and the Staff of the district, the Officers of the Association of the Gentlemen Volunteers, and of all the Military Bodies in the neighbourhood, with many Members of the Association, to the number of about 200, sat down to an elegant dinner at Brodie's, Colonel Ridley in the chair, and the afternoon was spent in the utmost, conviviality and harmony. The following, amongst other toasts were given:-

The King; the Queen and Royal Family; Lady Ridley; Colonel Blakeney and the Newcastle Volunteers; Colonel Ridley and the Armed Association; the Navy; Duke of York and Army; Lord Nelson; Prosperity to the County of Northumberland; the Members for Newcastle; May the English Standard never suffered from the French fire; the 2nd Northumberland Militia; Marquis Cornwallis; Mr. Buddle and the Wall's End Band (one of the bands in the parade); Lord Stanley and the 2nd Lancashire Militia, Colonel Murray and the Perthshire; Captain Monkhouse and the Newcastle Volunteer Cavalry; Captain Bell and the Morpeth Volunteers; Mayor and Corporation of Newcastle; Both Sides of the Tweed; a Speedy and Honourable Peace; Sir John Borlace Warren; General Cowell and the Staff, North East District.

A song composed and sung by Mr. Thompson, on the occasion, met with much applause.

In the evening there was an elegant assembly at the Rooms, in honour of Lady Ridley.

After all that toasting one may question how many of the illustrious gentlemen who enjoyed their 'elegant dinner' attended Lady Ridley's 'elegant assembly'.

The "elegant dinner" with its toasting, songs, "conviviality and harmony" was strictly for the gentlemen. The ladies had an elegant assembly in the evening.

Despite the insistence on all being fellow citizens who were all prepared to fight for their country, liberties and laws, an elegant dinner was enjoyed by the gentlemen and in evening there was an elegant assembly for the ladies. There was no mention of celebrations organised for those who were not ladies and gentlemen. Members of the ranks along with their families and friends of lower status did not warrant such elegant celebrations. Their fellow citizenship did not extend as far as dinner at Brodies.

There may have been some celebration like that in May 1799 at Seaton Delaval. The Volunteers were householders who resided in houses belonging to Lord Delavel. After the parade the Volunteers were in the marble hall of Seaton Delavel by his Lordship, accompanied by Lord and Lady Tyrconnel and Lady Susan Carpenter. The wives and daughters of the volunteers were invited to enjoy the festivities of the day" and given a welcoming reception by the ladies.

Earlier in the year on January 5th, 1799, the Gibside Volunteer Corps of Cavalry, commanded by the Right Hon. Earl Strathmore, had a general muster, and went to Whickham Church, where a sermon was preached on the occasion. And on New Year's day the Corps were hospitably entertained with a dinner at Gibside House, his Lordships' seat when many loyal toasts were given and songs sung, in particular a song made on the occasion by the Earl of Tyrconnel, was sung by him with great applause At the same time Lord Strathmore's showed his benevolence by distributing a great quantity of beef, bread and ale to the poor of the parish..

Those mentioned above may have been the subject of much gossip at Lady Ridley's elegant assembly" Sarah Delavel, the daughter of Lord John Deleval had married George Carpenter who became the 2nd. Earl of Tyrconnel. Lady Susan Carpenter was their daughter. There would have been much gossip about Lady Tyrconnel. After her affair with Frederick Duke of York she had a relationship with Earl Strathmore of Gibside, openly living with him at Gibside.

This relationship does not seem to have affected her husband the Earl of Tyrconnell, as he not only attended Strathmore's celebration but composed a song for the occasion and appeared to have sung it with gusto.

Lady Tyrconnel died one year later in October 1800. Her obituary written by her father, insisted she died at Delavel Hall even though she died at the Gibside, the home of her lover Lord Strathmore. Earl Tyrconnel appears to have had a friendship with Lord Strathmore but this did not extend to his consenting to Strathmore's request to marry his daughter, nineteen year old Lady Susan after her mother's death. The affairs of this family would fuel a considerable amount of gossip for the ladies of Newcastle their elegant assemblies.

The Arrival of Napoleon

The militia had strong presence in the Easington Ward; of which Castle Eden was a part. Local people would be well aware of their presence. The fear of invasion by the French would probably have been felt by local people. An account illustrates the feelings of agricultural workers in Castle Eden;[42] "One day before the battle of Trafalgar, Mr. Burdon being from home, his butler dressed himself up in his master's court dress and cocked hat, and went out into a hayfield at the edge of the Dene, where he electrified the assembled haymakers by announcing himself as Napoleon Buonaparte, and that he had just landed. The alarm may be imagined. Scarth, the agent, in hot haste called out the troop of yeomanry which Mr. Burdon commanded, and led them down to the foot of the Dene to see if the French really had landed. The further history of that butler has not been preserved."

This appears to be quite a comical story. Maybe the butler considered it would be quite a lark to pretend to be Napoleon. The lark backfired because at the time the fear of invasion was very real. Haymakers must have raced to inform Mr. Scarth the agent of what they were convinced was a sighting of Napoleon and the landing of the French. Mr. Scarth was Captain of the Militia and responsible in the absence of Burdon. In 'hot haste' and probably quite a panic, Scarth called out the 'troop of yeomanry'. It is about a four mile walk from Castle Eden to the 'foot of the Dene.' They would have travelled through the Dene, a densely wooded area to reach the coast that lies at the 'foot of the dene.' The troop may not have walked. They may have hurried at a quick march, with great apprehension. There would have been relief when they reached the coast and discovered there was not a trace of a French landing. Mr. Scarth and no doubt Mr. Burdon would not have found the incident amusing. The story ends wryly with; "The further history of that butler has not been preserved". The 'Napoleon' butler's employment may have been short lived after that incident.

Road Building

Rowland Burdon frequently travelled by coach between Castle Eden and London and he was probably in London at the time of the 'Napoleon' butler. Burdon had an interest in roads. He had constructed the turnpike road from Sunderland to Stockton, having an interest in Stockton as his family had connections from early days, and also being Mayor of Stockton in 1793 and 1794. Burdon probably anticipated that the development at Sunderland would greatly benefit from greatly improved infrastructure. There were no roads, just country lanes, leading to the ferries across the River Wear. Wheeled vehicles had great difficulty on these country lanes. A year after he became MP, Rowland Burdon procured an Act of Parliament to construct a road. Shortly after the road was completed, he extended the road northwards from Sunderland to Newcastle and southwards from Stockton to Thirsk.

As there was only a ferry across the River Wear to connect the comparatively small town of Sunderland to the even smaller Bishopwearmouth and Monkwearmouth on the north side of the river the Wearmouth Bridge was commissioned by Burdon and it stretched across the River Wear. The roads and bridge opened up communications and was a prime mover not only in facilitating the rapid growth of industry that grew up along the banks of the river but also led to the huge expansion of Sunderland as a town.

Burden saw the need for improved infrastructure. In April 1800 he addressed Parliament on the state of the roads in England. He had experience of travelling a great distance from Castle Eden to London. He also had an interest in roads, but he considered that although improvement was needed for all the highways in Britain the roads towards London were in such a shameful state that some efficacious steps should speedily be taken for their improvement. If this was not done it would soon be altogether impracticable to travel.

Burdon was appointed on a select committee to consider means of improving the roads and examining the existing turnpike laws. There seemed to be little interest by other members to consider recommendations as there was a lack of quorum on the three occasions the report was to be considered.

Turnpike Acts were needed to create Turnpike Trusts. The public invested in the Trusts and the tolls collected were used for profits for the shareholders and maintenance of the roads, so passing of a Turnpike Act supposedly led to improvements in road condition. By 1800 there were over 700 Turnpike Trusts increasing to over 1,000 by 1830 covering about 30,000miles in England and Wales with 800 toll collection points. They were unpopular with many, especially the poorer members of the community who found it expensive to move themselves and livestock up and down roads.

Burdon travelled a considerable distance to London to Parliament. He wanted the roads improvement, especially around London. Others do not seem to have shared his enthusiasm. They may have been more concerned with the effects of the wars with France.

Pitt's Resignation

This preoccupation with France probably included William Pitt. In February 1801, Pitt resigned as Prime Minister, ostensibly because of his inability to secure the emancipation of Catholics in Ireland that had been pledged to them by Marquis Cornwallis and Lord

Castlereagh. This could not be followed through as the King had refused his consent. The opening of Parliament was delayed to give ministers time to come to some understanding on the matter. Pitt felt in the circumstances he could not continue as Prime Minister.

This may not have been the whole reason. Pitt's health was bad. There had been riots and unrest because of the dearth of basic food-stuffs and the rapid rise in the cost of living. It was suggested in the Morning Post) in February 1801 that;[43] "Some persons, we know, ...entertain that opinion, can hardly be persuaded that the Catholic question is the real cause of Mr. Pitt's resignation...They think it is the bloody business of 8 years of fatal war that alarms him into retreat....it is the millions which these conquests have cost us.... In his hands peace is impossible."

Both the King and Pitt agreed Addington should succeed as Prime Minister. Rowland Burdon transferred his support to Addington but by September 1801, he announced he would not stand as Member for County Durham at the next election.

Rowland Burdon tries to stand down from Parliament

Lord Eldon, Burdon's friend from school, told his brother;[44] "I have had a letter from Burdon. He assigns no reason but a love of retire-ment. He adds only...that his support for the treason and sedition bills, and the stronger measures of government, have created him bitter, fierce and unrelenting enemies, in a country in which he seems to say ... all good men are inconceivably timid."

Burdon was probably referring to Addington as the 'good' but 'timid' man. He did not have the forcefulness or power of oratory ascribed to William Pitt. Burdon suggests he had enemies. He had lost many of his friends who had resigned with Pitt. Henry Dundas was one of these. Dundas had tried to persuade the King that his Coronation Oath in no way conflicted with Catholic Emancipation. This argument was futile so Dundas resigned. Lord Liverpool suggested that Dundas had wanted to retire from the war depart-ment so some time but Pitt and the King did not accept this, so he resigned. However Addington thought Dundas resigned because he not only found himself in disfavour but was having health problems and found a public pretext for resigning. On his resignation Dundas received a pension of £2000 from the East India Company and he was made Viscount Melville on 24th December 1802.

Whatever the reasons for the resignations of Pitt, Dundas and other Cabinet Members, Rowland Burdon may have felt at a loss without his friends and allies in Parliament, especially when he considered he had made "fierce and unrelenting enemies." Burdon was determined to resign but others had different ideas.

Judith Millbanke, wife of Ralph Millbanke the Whig MP for Durham may have heard conversations of her husband when she claimed Burdon's real reason for retiring was that he had got a contract under government to supply the navy with rope. She argued that if the war continued, he would have found this contract very profitable, but now peace was being made, the contract was little more than worthless. Rowland Burdon was still involved with rope making, so this story may have been common gossip.

Addington did not secure the shaky peace agreement in the Treaty of Amiens until 1802 but he possibly knew of negotiations in September 1801 when he decided not to seek re-election.

Newspapers in various parts of the country reported his decision not to stand. The announcement of Rowland Burdon's retirement published in the "*Morning Post*" was placed in the 'gossip column' beside an announcement that the Marchioness of Headfort, and part of her family, had arrived in London, to direct the furnishing of her Ladyship's new house. This juxtaposition confines Burdon's proposed retirement to an item of gossip.

The Voters, especially the Freeholders, in Durham had different ideas. Burdon was very popular. He had come top of the Poll. As they wanted him to remain as one of their representatives in Parliament, they began an intensive campaign throughout County Durham.

The campaign was extended to the area in and around London, where some of the wealthier land and householders of Durham resided most of the time. Meetings were called like to consider the best way of effectively securing the nomination and election for Rowland Burdon. However Rowland Burdon was apparently still not persuaded to stand for election despite his electorate thinking otherwise. The Morning Chronicle found the situation odd;[45] "Many very extraordinary contests have appeared during the present General Election, but that for the County of Durham is certainly most singular. Mr. Burdon some time ago publicly declared his intention of retiring from Parliament at the general election. Several of the principal towns in the county have since applied to him to offer himself as a candidate again for the county, which he declines to do: the Freeholders, however are canvassing with great activity to elect him."

Despite saying he would not stand, the Freeholders were canvassing for him. Many eligible to vote would return from London to the County to do so. Finally Burdon was persuaded to stand and the day before the election, Sir Henry Vane Tempest considered that Rowland Burdon had been persuaded to stand because the sentiments of the County of Durham so strongly in favour of him remaining as their Member of Parliament. Rowland Burdon and the now Sir Ralph Millbanke were returned as Members unopposed.

There had been great pressure from many of his supporters to make Rowland Burdon change his mind. *The Morning Post* considered he was being coquettish in the first place;[46] "Mr. Burdon, it now appears, was only coquetting with the Durhamites, when he declined their representation. He had better take care that invitation is not meant as an Oliver for his Rowland." In the Charlemagne cycle of legends, Oliver is one of his paladins. His close friendship with Rowland began after the end of a prolonged and undecided battle. Perhaps the writer is warning Rowland Burdon that if he says he will stand down, someone may decide to challenge him for his seat if Burdon decides to continue.

The above 'announcement' was placed in the 'gossip section', this time between Mr. And "Mrs. Milner left Manchester Square last week for Dover. The family is going on a tour through France and Italy," and "Lord Limerick has fitted up his house in Mansfield Street in a style of uncommon elegance."

The information about the Milner family and Lord Limerick are simple enough to understand but the apparently sarcastic comment

5 | COTSFORD MATHEWS AND ROWLAND BURDON

on Burdon appears even more obscure now but would have been relevant and poignant at that time. The newspaper gave his motive as coquettishness and such behaviour could backfire against him.

Burdon may have changed his mind when he realised the amount of support he had. He may have reconsidered because he realised he would miss political life. It is probable both Rowland and his wife Cotsford would also miss their life in London where they appeared to move amongst society.

Social life: fashionable gatherings

In 1803, Rowland Burdon and his wife were amongst four hundred others from the fashionable world who attended an assembly organised by Duchess of Marlborough. Lady Hester Stanhope was there together with at least three of the attendees, Lady Salisbury, the duchess of Rutland and Lady Stafford whom she referred to as being the forerunners of fashion.

Entering the magnificent Marlborough family mansion in Pall Mall, guests walked through the brilliantly illuminated hall, festooned with a vast number of variegated lamps and ornamented with a great number of orange trees and sweet smelling shrubs. The Duke of York's band played martial music in the centre of the gallery for several hours. The assembly started about half past nine and continue until two o'clock in the morning.

Only those considered the most notable of the 400 guests were named. These included Ambassadors from Spain and Portugal, Dukes, Duchesses, Countesses, Lords, Ladies including Lord Stanhope and his wife. Mr. Pitt was amongst the untitled dignitaries. Mr. Burdon was listed next to Mr. Pitt. Only those considered most notable amongst the 400 guests. Cotsford Burdon attended and this was noted in the newspaper, so she too must have been recognised by the press.

The reporter was impressed by the event; [47] "Every preparation had been made to give eclat to the scene. On entering from the porch the eye was struck with the appearance of 12 servants, all dressed in new and superb state liveries, embroidered and trimmed with gold lace. They formed a lane for the company to pass through.

The running footman likewise in full dress, with the gold stick, stood at the top of the second flight of steps, in the hall, to announce the visitors. The hall was brilliantly illumined by a vast number of very large crystal lamps; but the principle novelty which charmed the eye, ravished the senses, was a great variety of orange trees, bearing the finest fruit, many of them above seven feet in height (all brought from the Duke's hot houses, at Blenheim.) These trees were placed in a conspicuous situation to the left of the entrance. There were likewise several myrtle trees, of an astonishing size, and nearly five feet high; and rose trees, and mignionette in abundance. The apartments of state were in usual style and splendour. This was one of the most brilliant assemblies ever witnessed at Marlborough House. The company exceeded six hundred personages, of the very first rank and distinction; and the ladies, who always form the major part on these occasions, were dressed in a style of more than ordinary taste and magnificence, so splendidly indeed were they dressed, that it reminded one of the Installation Ball. Among the number conspicuous were, the Dowager of Rutland, in white and silver head dress, a bandeau of laurel leaves, composed of a diamonds, and a diamond plume. Countess of Kenmare, in purple robe and silver; her fine hair confined in front by brilliants, and drop a bandeau of diamond chains," with a "profusion of very small diamond stars, interspersed over the head; a necklace of tree rows of very large brilliants, and drop diamond earrings; her ladyship looked beautiful. Countess of Grosvenor, plain white dress; head dress, a bandeau of laurel leaves; her ladyship's beautiful dark brown hair appeared too much advantage with no other orna- ment... Lady Hobart, in a plain white dress; a bandeau of diamond laurel leaves. Mrs. Methuen, blue crape robe' head dress, a bandeau of black velvet, with diamond stars, and white ostrich feathers. A great number of beautiful women were present; among whom we noticed the Countess of Barrymore and Miss Coghlan."

This was an occasion to be talked about like the assembly in Pall Mall on 28th June 1804. There was a similar description of servants and the impressive surroundings the article included that her Grace and her beautiful daughter Lady E Spencer received the company in the principal drawing room. This probably also happened on the occasion when the Burdon's were known to attend. In June there were 394 carriages for those attending so the grand court yard was only accessible for chairs. The Prince of Wales and Prince William of Gloucester, the Spanish Ambassador and titles personages were listed as attending on this occasion but it is possible the Burdons were also here in the presence of Royalty. If so, they would have had much to gossip about, especially as Prince Esterhazy was present. He was a wealthy Hungarian Prince rumoured to had more than 200 mistresses and to have fathered about 100 children.

The Burdons were noted as being present at many other functions so they were not only considered amongst the "very first rank and distinction, but they were also well known and were amongst the few individually named in the press from the large numbers present.

Fashion at the time

The apparel of the ladies present at this assembly has been carefully recorded in newspapers. People, especially the ladies would have been interested by descriptions of what those of rank were wearing. This would set the fashion.

Adverts in the press took advantage of this;[48] "T. Hannan is making a new and large assortment of Italian corsets, which for their ease and elegance, exceed any that have been offered to the nobility, and answer every purpose to improve the shape."

To wear fashionable clothes some may have considered they first needed an improvement in their shape. T. Hannan's corset was advertised as the answer to this problem. Once the lady had improved her shape, she would then have to decide what to wear and would need to know the latest fashions.

"The contest between muffs and muslins is at present very severe among the Ladies, most of whom condescend to keep the hands warm, though the cold, and thin clothing, shall die parts of their body in Imperial purple popularity of Indian muslin."[49]

Ladies are being ridiculed for following fashion by wearing thin clothes made from Indian muslin, even in weather cold enough to warrant the wearing of muffs. Fashion was important but not only for women as men also followed the latest fashions which according to the Morning Post seemed to be dictated by Paris. [50]

"All our young men of fashion now wear a frock coat of dark blue cloth, dark green or dark brown, with metal buttons, a little convex, a round hat with a broad brim short breeches and white stockings or large pantaloons with Russian boots high upon the leg."

The fashion for brightly coloured waistcoats and jackets as worn by the macaronis has changed for frock coats of darker much more subdued colours. (He probably dressed in fashion as described. There were fashions for certain occasions; "Riding coats are very large and full. At the balls they wear a black coat, and white waistcoat, black breeches, white stockings, and a cocked hat."[51]

Descriptions of fashions for ladies, like the following, appear many times in *The Morning Post*; "The ladies still wear the silver broaches in the headdresses of black or sky blue crepe, the shape of which is not entirely so long as usual – Some of the dress their heads d l'Egyptian with a small band enriched with pearls, which passes round the neck, and envelopes the chin. Others have adopted the Paysannes of lace, a rustic peasant look; but the most general headdress is the veil, upon the front of which we observe a large flower, with a headdress in hair, or a tuft of crepe, with a capote or black feather. The fashion of long waist maintains its ground. The trains are still extremely long, and it is bon top not to tuck them up, but to have them full length."[51]

There is a foreign influence in these fashions; Russian and Egyptian. The British had military coalition with Russia against the French. The British Museum, opened in 1759, had some Egyptian objects on display. After Nelson's victory against the French at the Battle of the Nile in 1798 and the surrender of the French, other Egyptian antiquities found by the French, including sculptures, became the property of Britain and, like the Rosetta Stone, were donated to the British Museum. Some ladies took to the fashion of dressing their heads "d l'Egyptian'; a French take on ancient Egyptian fashion. Egyptian style chairs and furniture also became the height of fashion.

"The newest fashion is after the Egyptian style, the backs resembling a scroll, which extends over after the manner of the Grecian couches; they are stuffed in the centre, and are surmounted by a rich tablet. The elbows are made very full with an easy sweep from the top, and are supported by whole length antique chimeras, or female figures. The seats of these singularly elegant and antique chairs are thinly stuffed, to contain a very thick cushion, the frame of the chairs are a mixture of bronze or or-moulu, the coverings are of crimson or black velvet, after the style of Mt. Thomas Hope's splendid mansion, in Duchess-street, but then they are enriched by very beautiful specimen of needle-work or embroidery."[52]

Furniture inspired by other ancient sources also became fashionable.

"Pier tables – are of statuary marble, inlaid with gold ornaments, richly chased and supported by a single console or leg; the latter idea is taken from the model of those found in the ruins of Herculaneum.

Ladies work tables – are made upon the same principle as the latter article, but under a smaller scale, with tops to imitate marble ornamented with bronze, or or-moulu feet. The fashionable shape is oblong, after the antique."[52]

London would be the city for those in the height of fashion. As a young man Rowland Burdon had been called 'a macaroni manqué', a follower of fashion and influenced by fashionable tastes. A macaroni was a man who followed fashion in clothes, eating and gambling. A manqué was a person with aspirations for that status but someone who did not exactly achieve this aspiration. Rowland Burdon was influenced by fashionable tastes but did not quite succeed in becoming a fully-fledged 'macaroni'. He had been on the Grand Tour, mainly in Italy, for two years so may have developed a taste for Italian food as well as a taste for high fashion. A macaroni was the precursor of the dandy, a later term for a man who set or followed high fashion. Although probably not a dandy, it is probable that the more mature Rowland Burdon still took a keen interest in fashion at that time.

There were shops in the North of England but London would be regarded as the place to buy the most fashionable goods. Lord Limerick's house in Mansfield Square had been furnished in an elegant style. It was also newsworthy that Marchioness Headfort and part of her family had travelled from Ireland to London to furnish her new house.

People did have clothes made for them at home. Records show that Charles Brandling of Shotton Hall, brother-in-law of Rowland Burdon by his first marriage was billed the sum of £6 18s 6s from a local trader. The itemised bill was the cost of materials including a rich dove satin, white satin, lace and lace trimmings. There was an added cost of 15s for the making of a dress and a cape. Some satin was not used so it was 'sent home' and the cost reduced by 2 shillings, making the amount payable £6 16s 6d.

In 1823, later than when the Burdons were in London, Mrs. Brandling had a shopping trip to London. She visited a straw hat manufacturer at 336, Oxford Street who supplied bonnets to Her Majesty and the Princesses. Mrs Brandling spent £4 on two bonnets and three shillings on a box for the bonnets. She spent £19 10s 6d at Howell and James in Pall Mall, made eight purchases from Charles Turner that amounted to almost £64 and purchased £4 17s worth of lace from I.W. Hayward who sold lace to the Royal Family.

Howell and James moved from Pall Mall to Regent Street and were considered to be the first department store. There were four departments. The first sold furs and fans; the second haberdashery including silks, muslins, lace and gloves; the third jewellery, ornaments and French clocks whilst the fourth was the millinery and dress department. The staff on the shop floor would be men as there were no female shop assistants at this time. That did not seem to have hindered Mrs. Blanding spending money on her purchases.

London was a fine place for shopping. There were functions, balls and assemblies thrown by the elite of society. Cotsford may have attended parties thrown by Lady Hester Stanhope. Supposedly her bosom friend, Cotsford may have been included in the guest list. Thackeray mentions these parties in 'Vanity Fair.'[52]

"Ladies, are you aware that The Great Pitt lived in Baker Street? What would your grandmothers have given to be asked to Lady Hester's parties in that now decayed mansion?.....I have dined in it... I peopled the chamber with ghosts of the mighty dead... the shade of Dundas...Addington sate bowing and smirking in a ghastly manner...Wilberforce's eyes went up to the ceiling... Yes, Lady Hester once lived in Baker Street, and lies asleep in the wilderness."

The Burdons were never recorded as dining in this household amongst this company but if Cotsford was a close as friend and, as suggested, Rowland Burdon possibly did.

Other entertainments

There was other various forms of entertainment at that time. The Vauxhall Gardens were a great attraction. [54]

"The gardens great attraction arises from their being splendidly illuminated at night with about 15,000 glass lamps. These being tastefully hung among the trees, which line the walks, produce an impression similar to that which   is called upon reading of the stories in the Arabian Nights Entertainments. On some occasions there have been upwards of 19,000 persons in them, and this immense concourse most of whom are well dressed seen in connection with the illuminated walks, and not a little to the brilliant and astonishing effect of the whole scene."

Thackeray added more to this description in "Vanity Fair"; "... all the delights of the Gardens; of the hundred thousand extra lamps, which were always lighted; the fiddlers in cocked hats, who played ravishing melodies under the gilded cockle-shell in the middle of the Gardens; the singers, both of comic and sentimental ballads, who charmed the ears there; the country dances, formed by bouncing cockneys and cockneyesses, and executed amidst jumping, thumping, and laughter; the signal which announced Saqui was about to mount skyward on a slack-rope ascending to the stars the hermit that always sat in the illuminated hermitage; the dark walks, so favourable to the interviews of young lovers;" Madame Saqui, the tightrope walker did not appear at Vauxhall until 1816, but the account indicates the types of entertainment, ranging from sailing matches to concerts, to be had at the Gardens. Crowds flocked to these events. They were sometimes so well attended that some hopeful spectators could not obtain tickets.

There were performances at the theatre by the best artists of the day.

In 1801, Harry Siddons made his first appearance in a new comedy. He was the son of the acting family William and Sarah Siddons. His mother, Sarah, mainly a Shakespearean actress was famous for her role as Lady Macbeth. Sarah, formerly Sarah Kemble was sister of Stephen Kemble who managed the Theatre Royal in Newcastle from 1791-1806. Well-known actors were attracted to appear at Newcastle but most prestigious performances occurred in London.

There were also entertainments involving what was advertised as a horse circus or equestrian events. If one's taste involved opera rather than horses and acrobats many operas were performed at Covent Garden.

Mrs. Billington and Nancy Storace were two highly paid operatic sopranos. Mrs. Billington sang wholly at Drury Lane. During 1801 she made £10,000 to £15,000 said her fortune amounted to £65,000.

Nancy Storace was also highly paid. She received a payment of £1,500 for the season. It was suggested that Storace was as fond of her gold as she was of her notes. Anna Selina (known as Nancy) Storace was born in London and she performed from an early age becoming a child prodigy at the age of 12. Her first leading role was in Florence at the age of 15. She was so well known that Mozart created the role of Susanna for her in his opera 'Le nozze di Figaro'. The first performance featured her in the role. Her brother Stephen Storace wrote comic opera that was very popular at the time.

If lectures were an interest you could attend the South East Side Royal Exchange. At twelve noon the lectures would be in Latin and if you waited until 1 pm you could hear lectures in topics including; English, Divinity, Civil Law, Astronomy, Music, Geometry, Rhetoric or Physics.

Entertainment in the North

There was entertainment in the north, particularly in Newcastle. There were assembly rooms in Westgate Street, Theatres, a circus and riding school and musical concerts and entertainments. In October 1792, Durham Music Festival was held under the patronage of the Honourable Right Reverend the Lord Bishop of Durham. Four Members of Parliament; Rowland Burdon, Ralph Milbanke , Rowland Burdon, John Tempest and W.H. Lambton were all stewards of this Music Festival so they would have been in attendance. The Festival took place in St. Mary-Le–Bow Church in Durham to mark the opening of the Organ at Bow. There was a great selection of sacred music directed by the Rev. Edward Parker.

Horse Racing

Rowland Burdon was involved in Northern horse racing events for many years. As a young man he had been described as a 'macaroni manque'. One of the attributes of a 'macaroni' was a tendency to gamble. He owned and raced a succession of horses like his chestnut horse, Centaur entered in June 1791 to run at the Spring Meeting at Manchester. There were a number of Northern race courses such as York, Hexham, Newcastle, Durham, Alnwick and Morpeth where his horses ran. He was a steward at Newcastle racecourse, Morpeth race course with Lord Algernon Percy and also served as steward with Ralph Milbanke at Durham. As well as being steward he also subscribed towards the prize money at the races, especially at those held in Durham.

On 15th May 1784, Rowland Burdon jnr entered a horse to run in the Noblemen and Gentlemen's Sweepstakes. Charles Brandling and Mr. Ord also had horses running. Burdon appeared to enjoy horse racing and the company of those who attended horse racing meetings.

At the races, there were rules laid out for the 'selling of alcohol. Scaffolds, tents and huts could be set up on the Town Moor for a subscription of 5s for a freeman and 10s for a non-freeman. To discourage those from outside the town setting up facilities to retail liquors, a charge of £50 was made. This charge was eventually dropped and only those publicans and innkeepers who resided in Newcastle could sell refreshments.

There were two other rules. Everyone who set up a scaffold, tent or hut for the races had to remove it and level the ground within three days after the event or they would be totally excluded from selling liquors on the ground. The race course was in good order so to maintain the good condition of the ground no carriage or horse-back riding was allowed, other than those participating in the races.

As well as the races entered by many horses there appeared to be private races between two horses. The prize money was usually fifty guineas. There was a match between the Duke of Hamilton's bay horse 'Disguise' and Mr. Bowes's grey horse 'Icelander' at this event. The race was over four miles, 'for 500 guineas each, half forfeit.' There was money to be made and lost at the racecourse.

In November 1783, Rowland Burdon jnr, as a magistrate attended a meeting of magistrates at the General Quarter Sessions in the city of Durham when The Grand Jury of the county made a representation about, the pernicious consequences that resulted from petty horse racing and cock-fighting in the county. These activities were seen to corrupt the morals of what was considered the already depraved inferior classes. Such activities by these lower orders deprived the community of the benefit of their labour as they wasted their time pursuing idle amusements instead of working hard to support themselves and their families.

The Court of magistrates deliberated upon the subject and came to the following resolutions that horse racing they considered petty as well as all cock-fighting ought to be totally suppressed and abolished throughout the county." The Magistrates would also prosecute all a keepers of alcoholic establishments in County Durham who permitted cock-fighting or any other unlawful gaming on their premises.

Similar proceedings had occurred in Newcastle July 1781. Petty Horse-Racing was defined as racing where the prize money was less than £50. Offenders would be proceeded against and could be fined £200.

There appears to be a different attitude towards horse racing and petty horse racing. Horse racing is only for the wealthy. The legislation that came about through an Act of George II was designed to restrain and prevent the excessive increase of horse races. Horse racing by law specified that the plate, prize or sum of money should have a minimum value of £50. Petty horse-racing did not fall into this category so penalties to deter this could be recovered by action at law. A fine of £100 was recommended by the Act for advertising or holding a petty horse-race and that half of the fine should go to the informer, and the other half to the poor of the parish. The offence of cockfighting became punishable by a fine or imprisonment.

Newcastle brought in similar regulations but their fine for petty horse racing was increased to £100. These measures would be a deterrent against petty horse-racing.

It was considered that petty horse racing would corrupt the morals of the already depraved inferior classes and make them pursue idle amusement instead of employment.

Those, like Rowland Burdon junior, who had issued these condemnations enjoyed and participated in horse racing. This was not petty. Prizes of £500 were on offer in a two horse race. Those with wealth did not see themselves as pursuing idle amusement instead of being gainfully employed. They considered, like the magistrates at Newcastle in 1781, that drunkenness, gambling, profane cursing and swearing, quarrelling, and fighting, only occurred when a great number of idle lower class people gathered together. A 'macaroni mangue' would not do that.

Agricultural society

From an early time, Rowland Burdon had an interest in agriculture. There was an Agricultural Society in County Durham. Sir John Eden was President, Rowland Burdon jnr and Christopher Hill were both Vice-Presidents, Burdon becoming President in 1791. Rewards are given to winners of various categories like prize of ten guineas or a silver cup of the same value going to the farmer who demonstrated the most skilful mode of cultivation and the best condition. There were prizes for the best meadows, best crops of turnips, cabbages, winter tares and rye grass. Specifications were given for the growing of the turnips. The turnips were not allowed to have more than a specified amount of dung used as manure. The quality and quantity of compost used on the turnips had to be specified by the Society.

At this time, a prize of three guineas would be awarded to the person who could discover the cheapest and most effectual method of destroying wild oats. Wild oats must have been a problem and difficult to remove.

An award of four guineas went to a manservant, working as a husbandman who had the greatest length of service (not less than ten years) with the same employer. A similar award was given to a female servant who worked as a dairy maid.

The best animals; stallions, bulls, tups and breeding cows were shown and judged in March at Saint Cuthbert's Fair in Durham. The awards ranged from five to three guineas.

These awards would entail judging the various categories of farming, farm produce and animals. It would take knowledge to be involved in the judging procedure. A considerable amount of time would be needed to fulfil these judging commitments.

Other categories included; four guineas was awarded to the cottager, usually employed in husbandry, who had the greatest number of legitimate children, not less than six children was specified. The cottager would need to demonstrate that his children had been maintained, educated, and placed in service, without the assistance of the Parish. Two guineas was awarded to the cottager who came second in this category. The more children produced, educated and maintained without help from the parish the more responsible equally hard workers there would be for the land. A father would be liable to support an illegitimate child if paternity could be established. Otherwise an illegitimate child born to a woman in the parish would often need support from that parish. This was not just to encourage supporting legitimate children within the family household it was to limit the amount of relief required by the poor of the Parish and reduce the amount paid by the tax payers, the landowners who supported the poor of the Parish.

The information submitted by claimants of these awards needed to be certified by the Minister, Churchwarden, and Overseer of the Poor, or any two of them where such cottagers reside. The Society would not take the word of the cottager, so he was expected to be truthful as well as hardworking enough to support his large family. The Society had to be certain of the truth of a claim, as apparently there had been several occasions when candidates obtained certificates to which they were not entitled. Four guineas was a considerable amount of money in 1797 and cheating had taken place in the past. Candidates were warned they must be honest in order to make the Society certain they were telling the truth.

The Society insisted on good behaviour of the workforce. It was resolved that, no member of the Society will in future hire any Servant, but who shall produce a Certificate of their good behaviour from their last place of Service. The Society not only awarded prizes to farmers. It also appeared to uphold good behaviour amongst the landowners 'servants', a term then used for those employed by the farmer who worked on the land.

A member of the Agricultural Society would not only need to be informed on agricultural matters but also have sufficient time to carry out his duties. Although Rowland Burdon appeared to spend a considerable time involved in various activities, he did appear to be involved in some business ventures in the North. In 1783, he was listed, along with his father as one of the Proprietors of the Exchange Bank, as a proprietor of the recently opened Fire Office 'for the Assurance of Houses, Buildings, Goods, Wares, and Merchandises, from Loss or Damage by Fire' situated in Sidegate, Newcastle. It is uncertain how much time Rowland Burdon jnr allotted to this enterprise.

He may have been more interested in gaming and hunting than in Insurance. There were several Hunts in the area. The Earl of Darlington and his Raby hounds frequently organised several meets, including events around Newton Hall, Easington, Sedgefield and Lanchester. Advertisements appeared to notify members of the hunt of forthcoming meets. In late September 1783 it was announced that there would be a fortnight long meeting of the fox hounds."

Good hunting country was a selling or letting point for a house. In June 1800 the letting opportunity of Coxhoe Hall in Durham was described as; "The situation" is "in a fine hunting Country, near several Covers, hunted by the Earl of Darlington's Hounds, and within easy distances of others hunted by Mr. Lambton's."[55]

Coxhoe Hall is near Castle Eden, so it too would be considered as being in 'fine hunting country.' The Burdon family appear to have been very interested in hunting. In 1946, items for sale included; china items with hunting scenes, a large number of prints depicting fox hunting, one oil painting from 1849 painted by Gusto Lange entitled 'Stag Hunting in a German Forest', a stag's head and a pair of antlers and a stuffed fox as well as various cases of stuffed birds. The Rowland Burdon may have frequently ridden with the Earl of Darlington's hounds, so he may have known the Earl well. The Earl must have had a good opinion of Rowland Burdon, as he was one of the eminent people who supported Rowland Burdon's nomination for Parliament and helped him get elected.

There were social events around fox hunting like the Gentlemen of the Forest Hunt's Ball on Monday 26th March flowed by a concert the next day.

Although there were functions, concerts and entertainments in the North East of England, these could not compare with the social life of London. There would be no functions like the first party of the season thrown by Mrs. Methuen in March 1801, attended by the Burdon's where they would be mixing with the Prince of Orange and the titled and social elite of the day. They may not have been on the social scale of Lady Hester Stanhope, who attended a function to pay respects to the King on his 67th birthday with Lady Stanhope wearing a white crepe dress, richly embroidered in bright and dead gold, intermixed with chains of amethysts and emeralds which had a beautiful effect; head dress feathers and chains of precious stones

Not only were these men Parliamentary colleagues of Burdon, Dundas was a friend of Rowland Burdon and Burdon had known

John Scott from his youth. Rowland Burdon may have dined in Baker Street amongst this illustrious company.

The trial of Warren Hastings

As well as social functions, Cotsford was interested in politics and current affairs. She boasted that she attended every sitting during the trial of Warren Hastings. She believed she was the only person who sat through the whole of this trial. Mainly because of her father's terrible fate, Cotsford was a great supporter of Warren Hastings.

Warren Hastings was the official Governor of India between 1773 and 1784. During the reading of the India Bill, Hastings was criticised by Charles James Fox, Pitt only giving Hastings limited support. Hastings left India and had returned to England on June 1785. During the voyage he wrote a defence of his conduct in India and on his return to England presented this to Henry Dundas. .

Edmund Burke was the main instigator in bringing a case of impeachment against Warren Hastings supposedly for mismanagement and personal corruption during his time in India.

The trial, held in Westminster Hall, began on the 13th February 1788. The Members of the House of Commons sat to Hastings' right and the Lords to his left. Rowland Burdon would probably have been present.

Cotsford Burdon would have been one person amongst the large gathering of spectators, which included Royalty, who sat in boxes or the public galleries. She would have been quite young at the time It is possible she attended with Lady Hester Stanhope, who wrote; [56] "I can recollect, when I was about ten or twelve years old, going to Hastings' trial. My garter somehow came off, and was picked up by Lord Grey, then a young man. At this hour, I can see his handsome but very pale face, his broad forehead, his corbeau coat, with cut-steel buttons; his white satin waistcoat and breeches, and the buckles in his shoes. He saw from whom the garter fell, but, observing my confusion,[56] did not wish to increase it, and, with infinite delicacy, gave the garter to the person who sat there to serve tea and coffee."

The Hastings' trial began on 13th February 1788, so Lady Hester Stanhope would have been about 12 years old. Cotsford Mathews, as she then was, would have been about 13. They had both attended the trial at a very young age. It is possible they knew each other, suggesting Cotsford may have known Lady Hester before her marriage to Rowland Burdon.

Lady Hester appears to have been more interested in Lord Grey than in the trial. She described his attire so well and gave him perfect manners of 'infinite delicacy'. The serving of tea and coffee suggests a social occasion and this is possibly what some, including Lady Hester, considered the trial to be.

Not so for Cotsford Mathews. She was a 'devoted follower of Hastings' mainly because of the fate of her father and the connection they both had with India. It may have helped her to connect with the father she had lost a few years earlier in such tragic circumstances. The trial lasted for seven years until 1795. Cotsford married Rowland Burdon in 1794 so she was a single young woman for most of the sittings. This does appear to confirm that she was a 'devoted follower of Hastings'.

Hastings had other supporters. Jane Austen's family knew and supported him, as did Fanny Burney, the novelist and playwright and Ralph Broom the pamphleteer and satirical poet. It is possible they too attended the trial.

The prosecutors were Edmund Burke, Charles James Fox and Richard Brinsley Sheridan. It took Edmund Burke two days to read the charges against Hastings. This was a long time but the trial was much longer, taking 148 days, spread over seven years. By the time the verdict was reached in April 1795, one third of the Lords who had attended the trial seven years previously had died. There were only 29 Lords who had attended sufficiently to qualify as acting as a judge. Initially the press portrayed Warren Hastings as being guilty but this began to change throughout his trial

Press and public opinion had changed by this time and the verdict was as expected with Hastings being overwhelmingly acquitted on a majority vote. He had not accrued a vast fortune in India and the £70,000 cost of the trial left him financially ruined.

There had been great interest in the trial at the beginning but interest had waned dramatically during the 148 sittings that took place over seven years. Cotsford Burdon not only supported Hastings but she attended every day to witness the happenings in the trial. Other women did show interest. On 10th May 1788 the following is an advertisement for the April edition of '*The Lady's Magazine*'; "Illustrated with a beautiful large engraving, exhibiting a view of the Court sitting on the Trial of Warren Hastings, Esq., in Westminster Hall. 2. An Historical Print entitled, The Explanation … and a continuation of the Trial of Warren Hastings Esq."

The magazine also included; a beautiful pattern for working a cloak or a gown, a song of Mr. Handel's, letters from a brother to a sister, a letter from an English Gentleman in France, an article about Captain Cook's Voyage, letters on education, a comedy entitled 'The Unreserved Lady', domestic lessons for young ladies, a short account of the Jews, solutions of enigmatical questions, poetry, foreign news, home news, Births, Marriages and Deaths.

This magazine covers a diverse range of topics. There must have been great interest in the trial of Warren Hastings to not only include it in a ladies magazine but to also include a 'beautiful large engraving.'

Cotsford appears to have been interested in political matters such as the Hastings' trial from a very early age. This interest appears to have continued into adulthood. Cotsford was later described by Canon Tristram as being a strong-minded woman. It is possible she did not wish to leave London and the life it offered her to live permanently in a country estate. Rowland Burdon's constituents wished him to continue to represent them in Parliament. This knowledge together with Cotsford's persuasion may have influenced Rowland Burdon to seek re-election.

Early attempts to make Rowland Burdon to reconsider his wish to stand down were ineffective. He had made it known in November 1801 that he did wish to seek re-election.

When Parliament was dissolved, Sir Henry Vane Tempest probably thought he was in line to be the next representative for Durham. Yet Burdon was extremely popular. A campaign to nominate and elect Rowland Burdon gained strength amongst voters in Durham and voters resident in London. It was not until the day before the nomination meeting that Henry Vane Tempest withdrew and Rowland Burdon was successful both in his nomination and along with Sir Ralph Milbanke, an unopposed appointment as Members of Parliament for Durham. There were no election expenses this time when he was again elected as Member for the Durham County Constituency. He was still a Member of Parliament.

The final phase of Rowland Burdon's parliamentary career: The lifeboat

Whilst still an MP, Rowland Burdon achieved a notable thing in 1802 when he presented a petition to Parliament from Henry Greathead, a shipbuilder of Shields for compensation for the invention of a Lifeboat. Many lives were lost at sea. The terrible storm of November 1789 had left a ship stranded on a sand bank in very rough seas off the coast of Shields. Although the ship was close to land the sea was so rough that nothing could be done to save the sailors.

The fierce storm of 1789 that raged down the East Coast is described in a newspaper. [57]

"A few minutes before four in the morning, one of the most violent squalls of wind from the North East came on, which has ever been remembered. It's commencing not less suddenly than violently has been an occasion of a fierce almost too dreadful for description. A large fleet of ships were lying in the Roads, several of which being driven from their anchors and running foul of one another, great confusion took place. Some foundered, many lost their masts, whilst others were obliged to slip or cut their cables, and run to the Southward, which luckily for them, on account of the quarter from which the wind blew, they could do without much danger, so that two only were forced on shore to the Southward of the harbour.

The case however, of those vessels which were caught by the storm to the Northward of the Cockle sand, was infinitely more distressing and fatal. Such of them as were at anchor, waiting for the light to enter the roads, were almost every one of them forced to quit their anchors by the violence of the wind, or by other ships coming athwart them – some sank instantly upon their striking against each other – others perished the moment they were driven on the sand – some having been beaten upon the Cockle, either went down in deep water, or fell upon the Barber – several met their fate on the shore. Nothing can be conceived more dreadful than the morning prospect from this place. The walls of the town were lined with persons of all ages, sexes and conditions. Distress and anxiety painted on the countenance of every one you accosted. On account of the fishing season being at its height , there was not a poor person who had not a father or husband, a brother or son, for whose fate they were not all alarm; nor a rich person who had not some property, either in ships or in boats and nets, for which he felt himself interested ... ships from the Northward were every moment coming in – some with every sail split, hanging like so many pennants – others with only one mast standing –others with nothing but a small piece of torn canvas fasted to the remaining stumps of the masts – others with all their boats and anchors washed away, making signals of distress – others in a perfectly unmanageable state, driving through the Roads at the mercy of the waves, and at last sinking in the sight of hundreds of spectators. But our attention was at length called off from these kind of objects, by a piece of wreck being discovered, on which were decried three men. About ten in the morning the wreck became stationary, from some cause or other, opposite the Chapel, or near a mile from the shore. We could distinctly perceive the poor men at times turn to each other and appear to converse. One of them, who seemed much stronger, and appeared more alive than the others, every now and then clapped his hands, in order to warm them. A little before eleven, one of them disappeared, being either washed away by a wave, or having died through cold and fatigue. Several vessels passed them, apparently very close, at which they were seen holding up in vain their imploring hands- The ebb beginning to make them strong, the wreck was loosened from what prevented it from going to the Southward, and it moved to the Northward.

All hopes of the poor wretches being saved were now given over by the distressed spectators from the shore, when an attempt was made by the ferryman of the Cote, South of the Jetty, to launch a yawl with seven men. It is impossible to describe the feelings of those who were witnesses to this scene. The way in which the attempt was made was this – Two ropes were fasted to the boat, one at the head and the other at the stern – the men were all placed at their oars ready – the oldest ferryman was set at the end of the Jetty, to watch when he thought he perceived a temporary suspension of the toll of the waves, and to give notice of the moment when he judged it expedient to launch the boat. – It was several minutes before he dared to give the signal; during which time a most affecting silence prevailed amongst the spectators. The instant he gave the signal, the boat was pushed off the shore, and the persons on the Jetty who had hold of the ropes, ran with all their force, and gave her as much way as they could – The first wave she met with had like to have occasioned many of those who had hold of the ropes to fall from off the Jetty. Luckily, however, no such event took place, and the boat shipped but a little water. The old ferryman had formed a good judgement about the time of the launching, for there was only one more wave which at all caused any danger to the boat. Having got over this, we had the heart felt satisfaction of seeing her row away in perfect safety towards the unhappy objects of our anxieties. I now hastened to look through the glass at the wreck, in hopes of perceiving to save that of some marks of mutual congratulations taking place between its miserable possessors to the prospect of the boat's approach – Judge of my cruel disappointment, when, upon applying my glass, I could find only one poor wretch existing! – It was not, however, many minutes before I had the comfort of seeing him safely conveyed into the boat, & rescued from destruction. In the moment of excited sensibility, a subscription was set on foot, to reward the men who had thus boldly ventured their lives to save that of a fellow creature."

Although this was a time when there was no specially designed lifeboat with the ability to keep afloat and stable in such treacherous conditions, this story could illustrate the beginnings of the idea of a

R.N.L.I. Although the rescuers used only a ferry boat they bravely set out to save the men. Sadly only one survived. With a lifeboat and brave men such as these, all three may have survived. Subscriptions went to the brave men. They probably did not expect a reward.

Subscriptions in Newcastle and North and South Shields were instigated to raise money for the Widows and Orphans of the 400 seamen from the Port of Tyne who had lost their lives. Many of the ships reported lost in the storm were colliers from the North Eastern Ports mainly from the Port of Tyne. One hundred thousand pounds of shipping from the mouth of Tyne was lost some probably amongst the "Several other ships (that) foundered on the coast between Yarmouth and Eccles; the crews of which, it is feared, perished, a number of dead bodies having been already washed on shore."

The newspaper article concluded with a harrowing story. "On Sunday morning the body of Capt. Joseph Carter, of the ship Peggy of North Shields, was brought on shore in two bags, he having been cut in two in a most extraordinary manner, by being caught, in the hurry of letting go to a second anchor, between the cable and the windlass."

The horrible end of Captain Joseph Carter may have been one of the driving forces for those who formed a committee to design a lifeboat capable of rescue in extreme conditions. Henry Greathead of Shields, a boat builder who had himself experienced a shipwreck, designed such a boat. He did not take out a patent but donated models of his boat to those who asked for them including Scarborough and Lowestoft. Seven boats sailing from or to Newcastle had been lost off Lowestoft so Henry Greathead was probably very willing to donate Lowestoft a model so boat builders in Lowestoft could construct a lifeboat.

By 1802 Burdon brought a petition to Parliament for compensation for Greathead's design reporting to Parliament that Greathead's design for a lifeboat had already saved more than 700 lives. The petition for compensation to Greathead was supported by many including Mr. Rose who mentioned a recent case of people being lost near his country seat when the voices of those struggling to survive could be heard distinctly on the beach but despite the vessel being so close to the shore, the sea was so rough that no ordinary boat dare venture out in assistance.

The petition was carried unanimously and Henry Greathead was awarded compensation of £1,200. Thirty one lifeboats were built, saving many lives.

Rowland Burdon was becoming involved once more in Parliament but this could not continue for much longer.

The failure of the Exchange Bank

The devastating news of the failure of the Exchange bank broke on 30th June 1803. Payments were suspended on June 30th and the matter was to be put into the hands of a committee of several gentlemen to speedily effect the liquidation of the bank. The public who held notes were advised not to part with them for less than their full value. This information did not decrease the alarm especially when Burdon and Surtees announced the bank was to be wound up. The highest amount of liabilities, £85,368 8s 10d,more than three million pounds today, were held against Rowland Burdon, although it was suggested that the failure was caused by the rash speculations of the younger members of the firm. This could include Burdon but he bore the brunt of the financial loss.

This may not be the whole story. Rowland Burdon appeared to be a sleeping partner and not active in the running of bank. His father had served an apprenticeship as a merchant with Surtees. He had worked in commence from a young age, set up and was actively involved in running of bank with Surtees. The older Surtees had died. Rowland Burdon had shown little interest in bank when father alive. He went on his grand tour for two years before embarking in a career in politics. Although he left the running of the Exchange Bank to others the major part of his wealth remained in the bank. The ironic part is he had been intending to draw his capital out of the bank in order to invest it in the Hart Estate. He had left the examination of the title deeds to his friend Lord Eldon who held the title deeds for two years. Unfortunately Eldon had moved with haste. Burdon did not urge Eldon to action so the transaction had not materialised. If Burdon's capital had been withdrawn he would not have lost so much money. There were other factors that led to the failure of the Bank.

The Salvins and the French Revolution

The Salvins, related to Rowland Burdon by marriage, had established manufactories in Durham and Castle Eden making sails for ships. On 29th September 1794, a deed was drawn up between Rowland Burdon and George Salvin, both of Castle Eden referring to land in North Hudworth, South Hudworth, North Mill Hill and South Mill Hill. A second covenant outlines a building in a field in North Hudworth of a residence for George Salvin, two storeys high measuring 88 yards by 55 yards. It is stipulated the roof should be tiled with best Westmoreland slate. A later document, dated 3rd February, 1797, transfers the lease to Jeffrey and Hugh Salvin.

On this land, the Salvins erected a workshop for manufacturing cotton goods, a warehouse and several dwelling houses. On October 22nd 1798, a deed is signed for a 99 year lease. However, the lease was surrendered only seven months later when the business faltered because they were owed a considerable amount of money. The Exchange Bank had advanced a considerable amount of money to the Salvin's for this venture. The prospect was not good. In 1796, George and Henry Salvin transferred machinery from the Factory at Castle Eden to a manufactory in Durham, situated south of St. Oswald's Church. The Durham factory was destroyed by fire in 1804.

The Salvins had given large advances to the Salvins probably considering the firm a sound investment and probably more generous because of relationship with Burdon. The Salvin Manufactory in Castle Eden had secured a contract with the French Government despatching very valuable shipments of sailcloth France. These exports were made immediately before the outbreak of the Revolution. As payment for the goods had not been received, one of the Salvins with his unmarried sister Mary, journeyed to Paris to negotiate payment of the debt amounting to the massive sum of £70,000; around two and a quarter million pounds today. The amount owing was paid to them in assignats (French Revolutionary money) but before they could leave they were thrown into Luxembourg Prison. The Reign of Terror had begun.

Mary Salvin and her brother were imprisoned for some time. Mary began a love affair with a fellow prisoner and they became engaged but their marriage was not to be, as her loved one, along with other prisoners were taken from the prison and guillotined.

The Salvin siblings were apprehensive their fate would be the same. Mary was devastated by the execution of her intended but comfort was at hand when she became acquainted with Andrew Bond, an English surgeon, also imprisoned the Luxembourg.

Andrew Bond had been attached to the 69th Regiment in Toulon. After the siege and defeat of Toulon by the young Napoleon Bonaparte, Andrew Bond, General O'Hara and Major Archbold Campbell were amongst those imprisoned in the Luxembourg.

In prison Andrew Bond and Mary Salvin became better acquainted and formed an attachment. There would be fond farewells when Bond was set free. He would leave for England with his now beloved Mary and her brother, left behind in prison, apprehensive about their fate.

Not long afterwards the Salvins were relieved by their release and made a speedy return to England. Their lives were saved, but the assignats, valued at £70,000, were now virtually worthless. Assignats, paper money issued by the National Assembly of France during the revolution, had been accepted as legitimate currency at the time by domestic and international creditors. Hyperinflation led to assignats losing their nominal value and eventually becoming virtually worthless. The Salvins had lost a huge amount of money.

The business at the Castle Eden factory was ruined and it had to be closed. The Exchange Bank had given a huge monetary advance towards the Salvin's venture. It too was lost.

Andrew Bond and Mary Salvin were reunited, marrying in St. Oswald's Church, Elvet Durham on 20th November 1798.

Andrew Bond practiced as a surgeon in Brigholmston, part of Brighton in Sussex, where they lived in North Parade. His will shows they had quite a wealthy life style. Along with household goods they owned furniture, linen, plate, china, glass, books, pictures, wines and liquors. Mary also had jewels and 'other ornaments of her person.'

The will was written in Brighton but seven years before Andrew Bond the death of, the couple had moved to France. Andrew Bond died on 1st June 1827 in Tours 1827. The codicil of Andrew Bond's will refers to Mary as "my dear wife" and "my affectionate wife" and he sets out delays in order to alleviate any anxiety she should experience if he died in Tours. As the codicil was written in 1827. He may have been aware he probably was about to die in France.

It is uncertain why Andrew and Mary left Brighton to live in France for seven years. They may have favoured the climate. They may have been partial to the wines of the region; wines were mentioned in the Will. Andrew and his 'dear' and 'affectionate wife' Mary may have wanted to return to France where they had met under such strange and harrowing circumstances. They only returned to England once for a few days in the whole seven years they lived in France. Mary returned to England after Andrew's death. She may not have wanted to stay in France without her husband.

The Salvin's had lost money mainly due to lack of payment from France due to circumstances resulting from the French Revolution. The Exchange Bank had advanced the Salvins a huge amount of money, so this loss may have one factors that lead to the collapse of the bank. Although Burdon was solvent when the bank stopped payment in June 30th 1803, his capital was in the bank. The ironic part is he had been intending to draw his capital out of the bank in order to invest it in the Hart Estate. He had left the examination of the title deeds to his friend Lord Eldon who held the title deeds for two years. Unfortunately Eldon had not moved with haste but Burdon had not urged Eldon to action as there appeared no urgency, so the transaction had not materialised. The Exchange Bank collapsed.

Those with money in the bank only eventually received 8s 1d in the pound Under the bankruptcy of Aubone Surtees, John Surtees, Rowland Burdon and John Blandling patrons the Exchange Bank, the final 8d of the 8s 1d in the pound to the bank's clients was not paid until 1832. Many people lost a considerable amount of money. Rowland Burdon had lost all his capital. All that was left was Cotsford's marriage settlement yielding £500 a year interest. Burdon was ruined. He was concerned he would have to sell the estate.

Friends in the county formed a committee to raised money to secure the estate. They were willing to give him the money but Burdon would only take it as a loan at 4%, vowing to repay the money in entirety. Before he died everyone was repaid except Bishop Barrington, who refused, to accept anything. Much later, his granddaughter Elizabeth would say; "This he only achieved by the greatest self-denial and economy. He retired from Parliament and cut down all expenses, living in the smallest possible way at Castle Eden, educating his children and improving his estates. Yet he still remained "much respected and beloved: though always very poor. He was dressed always by the village tailor, and though possibly the whole of his wardrobe would not have fetched 5s at a village auction, at his death many from far and near begged for some of his old clothes as a remembrance of him."[58]

Despite being a bankrupt and now considered a poor man, the above shows how highly regarded he was however Burdon resolved to stand down from Parliament. In a printed leaflet the Chairman of the Freeholders lamented that Rowland Burdon was unable to devote any more of his life to their service. This was expanded in another letter;[59] "Although the unmerited misfortunes to which he alludes has obliged him to decline acceding to the earnest wishes of his friends, you ought not to accept his resignation: you ought to feel for his misfortunes and lessen their weight, you ought to call him again into active life, and not suffer him to retire."

Rowland Burdon replied to these, and other letters begging him to remain their Member of Parliament, in July 1806, from Castle Eden.[60]

"Much as my feelings with regard to matters of a public nature must be supposed to be blunted by adverse fortune, which has late attended me, I cannot but be sensibly touched by your kind and steady attachment which the Resolutions of the respected Freeholders held on November 5th at the Town Hall South Shields... my warmest gratitude is due to them for their too favourable opinion of me. To you for your communication as their Chairman I had hoped that when a Gentleman of high respectability and independent fortune had come forward to the wishes of the County ... I should not have occupied my further attention."

Rowland Burdon was alluding to Sir T.H. Liddell who had expressed a desire to stand in his place. He thought the Freeholders would be satisfied with Liddell as a prospective candidate. It would appear they preferred Rowland Burdon. The second resolution they wrote to him received the following response;

"Your second Resolution describes most duly my extreme desire to relinquish public life. I believe it to be for the credit of the County as well as necessary for my private circumstances that I should be permitted to close. I have quitted the service of the County possessed of its confidence and esteemed in spite of my degradation will be the Balm of my future life."

That last sentence is very revealing. Rowland Burdon felt 'degradation' because of his bankruptcy. He would fell this all his life. However the blow would be softened that, despite his misfortunes, he was still held in high esteem.

After his resignation, merchants and ship owners in his constituency wrote to Rowland Burdon on 30th January, 1807 saying they were;[61] "Deeply impressed with the extensive and important advantages which the Merchantile and shipping interests have derived from your services during the three successive Parliaments which you represented the County of Durham beg leave to send you our grateful acknowledgments for your past services and to assure you that the severe and unmerited misfortunes which Have deprived us of the continuance of your public exertion have in no degree abated the high esteem and high regard which we in common with the public at large entertained for your public and private virtues.

Were we to allow our personal attachment to you to prevail we might content ourselves with wishing that the remainder of your days may be spent in peaceful retirement and in pleasing reflections you have rendered your Country. But as members of the Community and interested in its commercial prosperity we cannot but express an earnest hope that you may again be placed in such a situation as may enable you still to exert those talents, that energy, and above all that genuine patriotism which you heretofore so usefully employed and which we shall never cease to admire.

We avail ourselves to declare our unqualified approbation of the sentiments expressed in your last address to your constituents of the conduct pursued by you in Parliament and of your support of the measure adopted by His Majesty's then Government during the most anxious struggle in which this country was ever engaged, and we most cordially concur with you in the admiration you express of the conduct, talents and integrity of that preeminent Statesman that late Rt Hon William Pitt to whom this country is indisputably indebted for its present existence as an Independent Nation and whose death the public will have daily increased cause to lament and deplore."

The long sentences and turns of phrase in this letter indicate it was carefully composed, probably by a group of people before being finally written in an almost legalistic manner whilst still containing sentiment and praise for Burdon. Burdon was recognised as being a supporter of William Pitt, so his death is referred to in this letter.

The death of William Pitt

William Pitt died on 23rd January 1806. He had suffered bouts of ill health from childhood. Lady Hester wrote in November 1802 that when she first returned to England in April 1801 although her uncle, was thin and still had a cough, the cough appeared to be abating and he was building up his strength.

As well as radicalism of the French Revolution, this was a time of war with the French. There was the great fear of an invasion. Many, including Lady Hester expected to hear of the landing of Napoleon. We are reminded of the fear and panic of the Castle Eden labourers leading to the calling out of the Militia when the butler dressed up as Napoleon. This fear was real and not to be joked about.

As well as the stress of these times, Pitt worked incredibly hard.[62]

"People knew little what he had to do. Up at eight in the morning, with people enough to see for a week, obliging to talk all the time he was at breakfast, and receiving first one, then another until four o'clock, then eating a mutton chop, hurrying off to the House, and there badgered and compelled to speak and waste his lungs until two or three in the morning! – who could stand it? After this, heated as he was, and having eaten nothing, in a manner of speaking all day, he would sup with Dundas, Huskisson, Rose, Mr. Long, and such persons, and then go to bed to get three or four hours sleep, and to renew the same thing the next day, and the next, and the next."

In 1804, Pitt's drinking habits were described;[63] "Mr. Pitt used to come home to dinner rather exhausted, and seemed to require wine, port, of which he generally drank a bottle, or nearly so, in a rapid succession of glasses."

Pitt had problems with his digestion, so these unhealthy eating habits, stress and a penchant for port was not conducive to a healthy lifestyle for a person with this condition.

Cotsford Burdon, supposedly a very close friend of Lady Hester's, was concerned when; [64] "One day she received a note from Lady Hester Stanhope, before breakfast, begging her to come and see her at once. She did so, and found her overwhelmed with grief. Her uncle, William Pitt, had returned from the House the evening before to find awaiting him the despatches telling of the Battle of Austerlitz. He read them, called for a bottle of port, drank the whole of it, and then threw himself on the sofa, calling out to her: 'Hester, roll up the map of Europe (which was hanging on the library wall); it is all over.' He had lain on the sofa all night, and was there still when Mrs. Burdon arrived, as if mentally paralysed by the shock of the intelligence."

The Battle of Austerlitz took place on December 2nd 1805. Napoleon had a great victory when he defeated the much larger forces of the Russian and Austrian armies near the village of Austerlitz in the Austrian Empire, thus ending the Third Coalition against France that had been spearheaded by William Pitt during 1804 and 1805. Pitt would have been devastated.

Hester records an incident on 9th January. William Pitt had returned from Bath in a futile attempt to recuperate in order to attend a meeting in Parliament; [65] "When the carriage came to the door, he was announced, and I went out to the top of the stairs to receive him. The first thing I heard was a voice so changed, that I said to myself, 'It is all over with him.' He was supported by the arms of two people, and had a stick, or two sticks, in his hands, and as he came up, panting for breath – Ugh! Ugh! - I retreated little by little, not to put him to the pain of making a bow to me".

By early 1806,[66] "Mr. Pitt was on his death bed. He had come up from Bath…, very ill and feeble; but it was not till the 19th that he was pronounced to be in danger. His exhaustion was so extreme that hardly anyone was admitted to see him."

This ban included Lady Hester who adds; "On Wednesday January 23rd, Doctors Baillie and Reynolds arrived about three, and gave as their opinions that Mr. Pitt could not live above twenty-four hours. "Mr. Pitt spoke of Hester saying "Dear soul, I know she loves me. Where is Hester? Where is Hester gone?" So Hester saw him before he died. He was Prime Minister at the age of 24 but died, in debt, aged 46.

Lady Hester was now homeless and penniless. The dying Pitt had requested a pension for Hester and her two sisters so Parliament granted Hester £1200 and £60 each to her sisters Lady Griselda and Lady Lucy. Lady Hester took a house in Montagu Square but her life no longer revolved around her being able to resume her life in London and "queen it in society." Lady Hester was reduced to selling her possessions to raise capital including, Tippo Sahib's gold powder-flask, worth £200. The giver of the powder-flask is unknown, but it is possible it may have been a present from her friend Cotsford Mathews, later Burdon, who had obtained the treasure from her father General Mathews.

Rowland Burdon stands down as MP

1806 was a disastrous time for the Burdons. Pitt was dead. Rowland Burdon had lost his wealth through the collapse of the Exchange Bank. He felt he had to stand down from Parliament. Although his friends had rallied round to save his estate, he still had debts so money had to be raised. On 10th January 1807 at the Turk's Head in Newcastle there was an auction of Rowland Burdon's financial interests from the tolls of Wearmouth Bridge. An Act of Parliament was secured for a State Lottery for Sunderland Bridge and to reimburse Burdon with the £30,000 he had invested.

There was a more positive outcome from a meeting in Town Hall South Shields with Joseph Bulmer in the Chair. The meeting resolved unanimously to forward an address to Rowland Burdon to express their very high personal regard and gratitude for the services that he had rendered for the County of Durham, particularly his efforts for the Port of Tyne in particular. The meeting stressed the indefatigable zeal with which he had always attended to their interests in Parliament.

The meeting went further than praise. To raise money Rowland Burdon had to sell some possessions, so the meeting set up a subscription to raise money to purchase the plate, linen and furniture from his home in Castle Eden which Rowland Burdon was going to sell. The Committee raised £1,050, and presented their purchases to Rowland Burdon. They also sent a letter begging him to continue to represent them in Parliament and decided to offer his services again. This offer of support went further. Volunteers offered to campaign on his behalf an encourage others to do likewise.

Rowland Burdon may have at first been encouraged by the support he obtained from his friends and supporters to encourage him to stand again for a fourth term but not everyone was of the same opinion as his supporters. A letter [67] addressed to the *Freeholders of the County of Durham* reads; On the 13th May at Gateshead a similar meeting as that described at Sunderland had taken place. The writer noted that "it is to be wondered at that so few were present, when so many of the Freeholders are yet smarting under the Wounds inflicted on their Families by the Failure of

Messrs Surtees, Burdon and Co. The Friends of Mr. Burdon may talk as they please, but it is highly reprehensible to bring him forward at present as an eligible Person to represent them in Parliament, when the Wounds of the County are yet bleeding, and when so many Thousands must be squandered in securing his Election, but which would be more honourable to Mr. B. and his Friends, were they appropriated to liquidate the Debts of his House.

When Mr. Burdon retired at the late Election, Sir Thomas Liddell was brought forward as the Representative of the County; and it was the Opinion of a Party that he would be easily swayed... (and) give way to Rowland Burdon ....(who is) now declared a certified bankrupt... I cannot help expressing my Indignation at Mr. Burdon again offering himself as your Representative: It is an insult to the County and to the Feelings of his Creditors...the Ambition of Mr. Burdon appears to be boundless...What are the pre-eminent Services we are told Mr. Burdon has rendered his Country? What are those Talents with which he is said to be gifted? Are not his Misfortunes the Consequences of his Neglect, in not looking into his Affairs? And have not we, by a Reliance on his Integrity and timely Interference, been made the Dupes of misplaced Confidence?

"CREDITOR OF SURTEES BURDON & CO, Gateshead May 14, 1807." Rowland Burdon probably had sight of this letter. The sentiments of the letter struck home. Rowland Burdon may have considered standing but did not proceed. There were offers to fund his election expenses but his capital was greatly reduced by the collapse of the bank, so his financial circumstances would have meant holding office an expense he could not afford. By May 1807, Rowland Burdon had children and there would be more so his family commitments may have been a consideration. There is the possibility that sentiments such as those expressed in the disparaging letter, published in a newspaper also affected him very deeply.

He did not seek re-election but the sentiment that he was a good Member of Parliament remained for a long time. In 1886, 'The Hartlepool Mail' did as series of articles entitles 'Durham Old Worthies.' Rowland Burdon was the first person to be written about. The following was included in this article; "The typical M.P.

of to-day comes down among us a week or two before the election, shakes hands with us and greets us much as a three-volume –novel hero does a long lost brother. Two days after the election he screws up his eyebrows – if we are influential he nods a response to our lifted hat, if we have only our vote (he knows it well enough) he may vouchsafe a grunt of semi-recognition. But Mr. Burdon was cast in a different mould. He had an idea – would it were common – that an M.P. towards his constituents stands in loco parentis. And he acted upon this precept. We do not mean he was an advocate of what is today termed as grandmotherly legislation. He became the father of his people by 'directing his energies and talents to the furtherance of their prosperity and that of their country.'

This description of Rowland Burdon's time as a Member of Parliament for County Durham was written 80 years after he stood down in 1806. He must have made a considerable impact at the time to be written about in these terms so many years later. The writer's description of the 'typical M.P.' echoes in many ways of some people's opinions todays.

One may question what may have happened if Rowland Burdon had continued his Parliamentary career. He remained a 'gentleman' but he did not receive any honours, such as a knighthood. This honour may have been possible for him if he had stayed.

He could not stay as he had lost his fortune. His wife Cotsford had her marriage settlement of £40,000, yielding about £500 a year, money she may have spent on buying herself articles like hats or dresses. In 1794 the trustees had been named as; John Scott (now Lord Eldon), Charles Brandling, Jeffery Jackson and William Cooke. By 1806 only John Scott was still alive, so new trustees had to be found.

On 6th July 1809, an indenture was formed between Rt. Hon John Lord Eldon, Rowland Burdon and his wife to appoint new trustees, Matthew Russell of Hardwick, Anthony Munton of Pear Tree Green, Robert Farguhan of Portland Place St. Marylebone and G His wifeeorge Bramwell of Junar Temple, a partner in the banking firm of Dorrien, Magers and Mello, to manage her marriage settlement. On 15th January 1794, the High Court of Chancery had transferred £41,681 12s 9d banked with an annuity of 4%, purchased annuities, money remitted from India, and the authority to sell a leasehold and messuage of land. The contents of this indenture show a large amount of invested money, money from India, and a house with land. Shortly after this indenture of 1809, the interest in the sum of £41,682 in 4% annuities was sold by auction.

Rowland Burdon and his household would be living on a much reduced income, mainly from Cotsford's fortune. By 1811, the £85,368 debts against Burdon's income had been repaid. Burdon and his partners still remained liable for the £280,298 owed to the 3,320 creditors. The fate of this huge number of creditors is unknown but some of them may have lost everything.

The bankruptcy did not pay final dividends until 1836. This probably concerned Rowland Burdon deeply for the rest of his life. People raised money so he did not have to lose his estates. The donors offered it as a gift but he accepted the money as a loan with interest and had repaid all the money by the time he died in 1838, except for that given by Bishop Barrington who absolutely refused any money as he insisted it was a gift.

Bishop Barrington was a close friend of Rowland Burdon. The Burdon's appeared to be a religious family. Rowland's father had seen his first duty as building St. James' Church in Castle Eden when he bought the Estate and Rowland Burdon IV extended the church. He also played an integral part in the conservation of the Galilee Chapel of Durham Cathedral. During the episcopacy of Bishop Shute Barrington the architect James Wyatt was contracted to undertake external repairs of the Cathedral. Wyatt advised the Chapter of Durham to demolish the Galilee Chapel in order to make a carriage drive from the Castle to the College.

Lead from the Galilee Chapel had already been stripped from the roof before John Carter, an architect, draughtsman and anti-quary heard of the intended demolition wrote 'an indignant letter to the Gentleman's Magazine.'[68] On reading this letter Rowland Burdon, "letter in hand went to Lord Cornwallis, the dean of Durham." Although the Dean had "consented to the destruction on advice from Wyatt" he was "stirred" into action by Rowland Burdon to bring a rapid halt to the proceedings, so the Dean "hurried to Durham to save (the Galilee Chapel) from destruction."

Bishop Barrington may have considered this when he refused to take back the money he had given to his friend Rowland Burdon. Paying back the money owed on the collapse of the Bank must have been something which preyed on Rowland Burdon's mind. There are echoes of his feelings in the following letter written in 1837, not long before he died;[69] "It is with pain that I see myself in danger of leaving life with the prospect of having my honest and equitable conduct misunderstood - the management of Castle Eden and Hesleden Estates and their produce as regards the different branches of my family.

Castle Eden I hold without impeachment. Hesleden is held in Trust of George Bramwell Esq .extra profits from scrivenances interest from the sale of land to the Hartlepool Railway. For the moving of stone at the sea site, and timber sold. I hold the Quarry site from the South Dene Quarry receive from Hartlepool £236 173 as a set off against various repair and alterations in the Premises which have lately been made in the Houses and Premises of the Estate and which have caused a great outlay in foreign timber for new roofs at Benridge, Mickle Hill and Hesleden for which the timber grown on the premises is entirely unsuited...besides no fewer than six valuable threshing machines at different farms which are the personal property of myself. Previous to 1833 I have restored several cottages in Low Hesleden done expensive repairs to Little Eden and Cotsford Grange besides the police house Tweddle Farm and others.Under these circumstances I solemnly admonish my sons to avoid acting upon interested motives so far as to differ themselves to interrupt the harmony which might rest between Brethern as they hope to pass through life prosperously."

These sentiments must have been on his mind or he would not have possibly committed these thoughts to paper and have the letter placed with his solicitor. He appears concerned that 'different branches of (his) family' would consider he had mismanaged his estates.' He may have thought the expenses incurred in the management of the estate was, because of the bankruptcy, due to bad management on his part. To alleviate this impression, Rowland Burdon detailed the expenses he had incurred to illustrate he had managed the estate well and spent the money wisely. Repairs and alterations had cost a great deal of money. He had purchased six new valuable threshing machines. These renovations and repairs plus the purchase of expensive agricultural equipment could mean there was less money for his sons to inherit. It is possible this is what is hinted at in the last sentence when he admonished his sons 'to avoid acting upon interested motives so far as to differ themselves to interrupt the harmony which might rest between Brethren." This sentence could suggest the sons had been disagreeing amongst themselves because they could see little prospect of a sizeable inheritance when their father died. He wanted not only 'harmony' amongst his sons but he needed them to consider his conduct had been 'honest' and 'equitable.'

This letter was written about one year before he died, yet it would appear the implications of the failure of the Bank and his bankruptcy had weighed heavy on his shoulders in the years that followed. Yet, he remained highly respected amongst many. The following [70] account written 60 years after the event illustrates this respect. Rowland Burdon, is still remembered in 1883, by George Gray, by then an old man living in the Alms Houses at Bishopwearmouth. This account recalls what happened in 1823.

"On the 11th October, 1823, during a dreadful storm, a ship – the Economy, of Lynn – came on shore near the foot of Castle Eden Dene. She grounded a short distance from the shore, which gave the crew scarcely any shelter from the spray and breaking waves. It was seen by the people on shore that there was somebody fastened in the round top of the mainmast. George Gray got on board, I think by swimming to the ship and the ascending the mast, which lay over at a considerable angle. There he found a poor lad lashed securely. He had been about six hours in that position. Cutting the lashing loose, Gray lowered the lad, through the square hole in the round top to the deck, when he found the poor lad so frozen that he could not render himself any assistance. The water running down the Dene had a deep place near which the vessels stern lay. Taking the lad in his arms, Gray jumped overboard, swam through the water, and delivered him to the people on shore. Gray then got back to the ship and helped five other men who were sheltering behind, bulwarks, cookhouse, or any place they could from the waves that were washing over the ship. Night was drawing on, and it seemed certain they would all perish before daylight next day."

The boy was lashed to the mast, probably in an attempt to stop him being washed overboard. The sailors were huddled together to try to escape the waves. It was possible none of sailors could swim and were reluctant to jump overboard. Night was drawing on, it seemed certain they would all perish before daylight next day. But with the bravery of a good swimmer, George Gray, all the sailors, including the boy were rescued.

Rowland Burdon was so impressed with Gray's bravery that he rode over to Gray's house on horseback to congratulate him. When he was in London Burdon advocated Gray's case to the Royal Humane Society who awarded Gray a silver medal which Rowland Burdon subsequently presented to him.

Gray's bravery was mentioned but so was Rowland Burdon who had sought recognition for Gray. Gray was always grateful.

By 1823, Rowland Burdon's wealth had increased sufficiently for him to be able to go to London. He is still considered a respectable gentleman, as he amongst those who attended a presentation at the Assembly Rooms in Newcastle on January 12th 1818 to present a large tankard to Mr George Stephenson for his services rendered to science and humanity by the invention of the safety lamp. The tankard was an additional form of recognition as Stephenson had already received a donation of £1,000 from the coal trade.

Charles John Brandling, father-in-law of Rowland Burdon's first marriage, acted as Chairman of this presentation meeting. The money raised and presentation tankard probably arose from Stephenson's work on a safety lamp after the disaster at Felling Colliery in 1812 when 92 lives were lost.

Felling Colliery was owned by a branch of the Brandling family. Because the disaster was caused by an explosion of firedamp the

Brandling's were mainly responsible for paying for the invention of Stephenson's safety lamp until 1812

An account of this disaster probably weighed heavy on the Brandling's prompting them to try to encourage Stephenson to invent what became known as the 'Geordie Lamp;'[71] "Nearly the whole of the workmen were below, the second set having gone down before the first had come up when a double blast of gas took place. A slight trembling, as from an earthquake, was felt for about half a mile around the workings; and the noise of the explosion, though dull, was heard three or four miles distance, and much resembled an unsteady fire of infantry. Immense quantities of dust and small coal accompanied these blasts, and rise high into the air, in the form of an inverted cone ... In the village of Heworth, the dust caused a darkness like that of early twilight, and covered the roads so thickly, that the footsteps of passengers were strongly imprinted in it. The heads of both the shaft frames were blown off, their sides set on fire ... As soon as the explosion was heard, the wives and children of the workmen ran to the working pit; wildness and terror were pictured in every countenance. The crowds from all sides soon collected to the number of several hundred; some crying out for a husband, others for a parent or son, and all deeply affected with a mixture of horror, anxiety, and grief. In this calamity ninety-one men and boys perished. The few men who were saved, happened to be working in a different part of the mine, to which the fury of the explosion did not reach."

It took six weeks for the fire to extinguish. The recovery of bodies began on 8th July but the last of the bodies, some buried under 'six or seven feet of stone' was not recovered until 19th September. All the dead, except four, were buried in a mass grave in Heworth Churchyard.

Amongst the list of dead those with the same surname may have been in the same household or relatives. Thomas Gordon aged 8, a trapper was buried like his probable relative, maybe brother, Joseph, aged 10. Robert Gordon aged 40 could have been their father. Mrs. Greener may have lost her husband Isaac aged 65 and two sons Isaac aged 24 and John aged 21. Of the dead the youngest was Thomas aged 8 and the oldest Isaac Greener aged 65. The average age of those who died was 24.

Brandling's mine had until then been considered as one of the safest in the district. Charles J Brandling was probably devastated at the loss of so many lives and because of this gave £1200 to commission George Stephenson to develop a safety lamp.

Hartlepool Dock and Railway Company

Although Rowland Burdon was not involved in funding of Stephenson's safety lamp, he did play an integral part in the scheme to improve the docks at Hartlepool when in 1832, the application of the Duke of Cleveland and Mr. Christopher Tennant's improvement scheme was submitted to Parliament.

Much improvement was needed;[71] "In the summer of 1832, Hartlepool presented the most dreary and desolate prospect that can well be imagined...The pier had been thrown down in an autumn gale several years before, and with the exception of a small piece at the west end, was a mere heap of loose stones...The old harbour had...been the place where any rubbish, which had become inconvenient to the town's people, had been shot for ages. The walls of the harbour themselves, had long been a mass of ruin; and the same air of desolation and decay pervaded the whole area."

The application of the Duke of Cleveland and Mr. Christopher Tennant's submission received some opposition. Rowland Burdon canvassed for its support resulting in the Act receiving the royal assent on the first day of June 1832.

Had that session been lost, it is very doubtful if an act would have been obtained, at all events, for several years afterwards and there if the Hartlepool project been delayed another year, much of the trade resulting from the improvements to the port would have gone elsewhere.

The promoters of the dock and railway secured funds to repair the pier and construct the docks. The docks were opened on 9th July 1835 when coals were shipped from Thornley Colliery, in the 'Britannia'.

Shipbuilding was important in Hartlepool. Mr. Thomas Richardson, of Castle Eden, and Mr. Joseph Parkin, took the lead in 1837, by building the 'Castle Eden.' Rowland Burdon would have been acquainted with Thomas Richardson, who may have sparked Burdon's interest in canvassing for support for work on the docks.

Rowland Burdon was involved in other areas. He had been a magistrate for many years becoming chairman of the bench. He remained a leading Freemason. All these accounts are amongst examples of how he remained a respected leading member of society despite his belief his bankruptcy due to the failure of the Bank led to his feelings of degradation. Many still respected him and remembered his service as an M.P.

CHAPTER SIX

The Burdon family in Castle Eden

Rowland Burdon retired from Parliament but did not retire from his public life and his estate of Castle Eden, where he lived with his family.

Rowland Burdon IV had married his second wife Cotsford Mathews on 20th February, 1794, when he was 37. Rowland and Cotsford's seven children were all born in Castle Eden; Elizabeth in 1800, Rowland Burdon in 1802, Frances in 1805, Mary Cotsford in 1807, Richard Matthews (named after Cotsford's father) in 1810, John shortly afterwards in 1811 and the youngest, a boy called Cotsford in 1815. This was quite a large family. Elizabeth would have been 15 when her youngest brother Cotsford was born and Rowland the eldest son, about thirteen.

Until the Bank of Surtees and Burdon collapsed in 1803, the Burdon family was very rich. All expenses had to be cut but he ensured the boys had a good education. How the daughters were educated is uncertain.

They all attended Durham Grammar School. John in particular appeared to have rather a bad time as his father insisted he wore his "court suits and coloured waistcoats cut down to fit his small person and short legs."[1] These 'court suits and coloured waistcoats' would be completely out of fashion at this time and were probably a remnant of the fashionable attire worn by Rowland Burdon, when dubbed a macaroni manque.

John Burdon, when a small boy of about eight started his education wearing his 'parti-coloured raiment at that period fighting his way through Durham Grammar School......for it was a rough bullying school. The Headmaster was John Carr. He was not a nice man...and a harsh disciplinarian; the food was execrable, and he gave the boys a very poor time. The piece of part-coloured raiment that gave most trouble was a certain scarlet waistcoat that earned its owner the name of 'Cockrobin' – Here's Jacky Burdon coming, Little Cockrobin. The matter, of course, had to be attended to out of hand, but after the first year, whether it was that the clothes wore out or the arms grew stronger, little more was heard of them."[2]

The clothes did not fit. They were probably altered for the boy to grow into and get more wear out of them. Besides being too large and ill-fitting, they would be completely out of fashion with the darker colours worn at the time. It would appear John, and probably the other boys too were bullied at school by some of the other boys and possibly some of the teachers. The clothes would not only look ridiculous but they would be an outward sign of their apparent poverty. John probably stopped wearing the ill-fitting gaudy clothes after a year maybe out of design or possibly because he outgrew them. The bullying appears to have stopped but John had learned to fight and not give in to bullies.

Durham Grammar School is a long established independent boarding school. The Rev John Carr appears to have ensured the boys had a good education. He does appear to have been respected by many as after his death a monument of him was erected in Durham by his pupils.

The Burdon boys boarded at Durham School during the week but came home for weekends. They had to walk nine miles home to Castle Eden and nine miles back to Durham, even when they were quite small.

This was a Spartan regime in every way. The children were forbidden to have pets of any kind under penalty of severe punishment. Naturally, to enterprising young folk, this did not obviate this being done, and for some time a flourishing establishment of owls, thrushes, rabbits and guinea-pigs lived in a cage just over the edge of the Dene to the west of the Castle, tucked away out of sight. Eventually, of course, discovery came, and every one of the pets had their necks wrung. The children must have been devastated but they had disobeyed their father who they thought a "hard man … but one must remember that they were hard times press-gang days, days in which a young woman could be executed for stealing a handkerchief. The child's point of view was of great cruelty in putting his beloved pets to death before his eyes, the man's – an autocrat in his own family – simply the necessary consequence of disobeying orders."[3]

The story of the killing of the children's beloved pets 'before (their) eyes' appears particularly harsh. Elizabeth his granddaughter, tries to defend the action by linking it with 'hard times' where punishment for small crimes was exceedingly harsh.

The children's pets seem an odd collection. The birds, owls and thrushes would have lived in the dene. They may have been injured and nursed back to health by the children. The rabbits may have been wild. Some person or persons must have helped them to make cages for the animals. They may even have helped the children obtain them and look after them. Guinea pigs are not native wild animals in English woods, so someone must have given them the guinea pigs. Guinea pigs, come from the Andes and were first brought to Europe as early as 16th Century by European traders and became popular household pets. They are docile, responsive and if handled from young liked being picked up, seldom biting or scratching. They even recognise their owners and greet them with a whistle. Someone probably gave the children some young guinea pigs. The children probably regarded the guinea pigs in particular with great affection.

The pets were hidden on 'the edge of the dene, tucked away out of sight." Someone must have noticed the children taking food and titbits to the pets and become suspicious. Their father was informed and they were punished, not physically themselves, but by having to undergo the trauma of watching someone kills their 'beloved pets.' John was one of the younger children and this event seemed to have helped form his opinion of his father. His daughter Elizabeth refers to her grandfather as being 'an autocratic in his own family;' probably seeing him through her father's eyes. These may even have been her father's own words. The children's father appeared to use fear and control to obtain their blind obedience to his authority.

Their mother Cotsford ruled 'the household and family with a stern rule'. All the children except John 'feared her' and when older it was 'his delight to tease her.' Cotsford had a 'rather passionate temper.' Her son John once said something to her 'that irritated her more than ordinarily' so she 'ran after him as he was escaping from the room and, catching hold of his coat tails, ripped the coat up to the collar.' Blind obedience of the children appears to have been expected by their mother. She was probably just as autocratic with the servants in the household. The children appeared to fear both their parents. Only John seems to have had the courage to 'tease' his mother.[4]

The treatment of Children

Rowland Burdon v was born in what was considered 'the darkest hour' of the Burdon family. The boys wore their father's cut down clothes. Their father had clothes made at the village tailors. They economised on household expenses. The use of candles was limited. The children were not allowed the expense of keeping pets. Despite these perceived deprivations, the children's lives were still completely different from those of the children in nearby mining villages.

In the early 19th Century there was a rapid rise in coal mining. Wages were higher, so workers from factories and in agriculture left these employments to work in the mines. The work for men was hard but reports circulated of the long hours and hard work undergone by women and children in the mines.

A Royal Commission was set up to gather evidence about the employment of children and young persons in the mines. As well as gathering evidence form those working in the collieries Commissioners gathered evidence from coal owners, mine officials, teachers, surgeons, incumbents and the police.

The Commissioners took evidence to ascertain 'the state, condition and treatment of the children and young people' employed in the mines. A secretary, familiar with Pitman's shorthand, recorded the words of the interviewee. The findings were collated into a Report that was presented to Parliament in 1842.

The following information is taken from the report compiled by James Mitchell LLD of the mines in the South Durham Coalfield, covering those within the boundaries of the River Wear and Tees. James Mitchell describes the changes that have rapidly taken place in the last 10 to 12 years. He says; "During this time an entirely new population has been produced. Where formerly was not a single hut of a shepherd, the lofty steam-engine chimneys of a colliery now send their volumes of smoke into the sky and into the vicinity of a town."

The influx of new workers and the building of the colliery villages had been rapid. These workers gave evidence of work in these collieries. There were no women employed in the South Durham Coalfield, so those who gave evidence were male. James Mitchell outlined the work done by the children and young persons, starting with the work done by the youngest boys.

Conditions at the Pit

(i) **The trapper boy:** Ventilating doors were vital to the mine ventilation. The doors needed to be closed to ensure good ventilation. The job of the trapper was to open a ventilating door to let through any passing tubs of coal. The boys may be seven or eight, although boys of five and six sometimes worked as trappers. The boy would be awakened at about three am, have some coffee and bread and make his way to the colliery to start work at 4am. The small boys would often descend the shaft sitting on the knee of a man, often a relative.

It was a solitary job, often done in complete darkness. Candles were expensive at ¾d each, and it would need more than two candles to last the shift of twelve hours. The child received 10d a day wages. The father would need to buy the child's candles, so this expense would greatly deplete his wages. The only light the child would see would be when a flickering light from a small candle indicate the coming of the putters and their tubs wanting passage through the door. The child would operate the trap door and rapidly close it again after the putters had passed through.

The little boy took food, usually bread and cold coffee, probably eaten in complete darkness. He may hear the squeaks of mice. The mice came down the pit in the hay for the horses, fed on crumbs dropped by workers like the little boy and soon multiplied, resulting in an infestation in the pit.

The little boy probably became very sleepy in the dark. If a deputy caught him asleep, a sharp rap with a stick would wake him up. This was better than falling asleep and stopping the putters coming through because the trap door was shut, as then the little boy would be sharply awakened by a punch in the face. Falling asleep was dangerous in itself. He could fall down onto the tram way causing terrible injury or even death, especially if he was trampled by a horse or run over. The worst punishment for falling asleep would be to lose his employment and the money he earned for his family.

The boy would finish work at 4pm, come up from the pit and be home about 5pm. He would get washed, have a meal, usually baked potatoes and broiled ham and go to bed by about 7pm, ready to rise again about three the next morning. Pay day was once a fortnight on a Friday. The following Saturday would be a day off work. Sunday was always a day of rest. So the little boy, would have a Saturday when he did not have to work. He could play on that Saturday as he would not be afraid of falling asleep at work the next day. On Sunday morning he went to Sunday School before attending morning service. After a midday meal, he went to Sunday School again. He may learn to read somewhat, probably from the Bible, and possibly to write a little. When a little older, the boy may progress to a driver of ponies. This is a higher status than a trapper, but he would not have time to eat his dinner as he could only snatch it when he could.

When the lad was older and strong enough he could be a putter, enabling him to double his wages if he works hard. This could partially explain the apparent cruelty of some of the putters towards the trappers. They are paid, along with the hewers, the work of strong men usually over 21, on the amount of coal they produce. Any delay in putting the coal could mean a reduction in wages.

The putter, once down the pit, collected a tram (a small sled on wheels) on the tramway. He places an empty corve (tub) on the sled and the deputy directs him to his place of work.

Working in a coal mine was very dangerous especially at this time when safety measures did not appear so important. The following information from the enquiry, records some of a boy who was 'lamed', injured twice;

"No 130: James Punton Aged 15. Hoists at the crane. Makes 1s 6d a day. Has been down pits 9 year about. Was six and a half years years old when he went down first. Kept a door for 4 years. Next drove for 3 or 4 years. Has twice wrought double shift; and once 3 shifts together. Has been lame twice, not very bad. Reads very easy words; writes his name. Goes to no school, but got to Primitive Methodist Chapel. Sometimes was brayed if he was caught asleep when keeping a door and the putters knocked him about."

James Punton has been a trapper, a driver and now aged 15 'hoists at the crane.' A shift may have been ten or even twelve hours long. A 'double shift' means working about twenty hours non-stop with three shifts adding another ten or twelve hours to that time. He was 'brayed' if he was caught asleep; physically assaulted for being tired.

James is now 15. He probably aspires to being a putter and eventually a hewer so he can earn more money. This will be his life;

(ii) **The hewers** bring down some coal by working on their sides with a pick so they could drill a hole, insert gunpowder to bring down more coal. The putter and hewer load the corve. It is the hewers responsibility to ensure the corve is filled to capacity or he will not be paid for the coal in that tub. The hewer has to make sure there are no black stones or pyrites amongst the coal as it will assumed he deliberately put in stones to make up the weight. There is only the dim light of a candle, so with no daylight it can be difficult to find the stones and withdraw them. As a combination of fines and perceived underweight tubs can mean a huge loss in earnings.

The hewer has being working since 2am. So he finishes at 11am leaving coal for the putter to fill and sort alone. The putter starts work at 4am and like the trapper finishes at 4pm. After tub has been filled, the putter places it on the tram and pushes the tram along the tramway towards the horseway. The tramway usually varies from 3' to 4', so his back is bent as he pushes it along to the area high enough to be transferred. The tub is rolled from the tram, pushed onto a rolley for the horses to continue the journey with trams on the rolleys along the rolleyway. The putter takes an empty tub and repeats the process. He has no break but eats when he can.

Sometimes boys are too young or not strong enough to manage putting alone so he needs a boy of about 10 or 11 to assist him. This boy is called a foal. The headman, or half marrow, goes in front and pulls the tub along the tramway with a rope over his shoulder. The foal pushes the tub from behind. Evidence collected shows the job of a foal appears to be the most difficult for a young boy. These boys receive less wages than the putters who do this work alone. Not only is it very hard for young boys doing such strenuous work, bent over in a small space, sometimes the foal's back is scraped by the roof as he pushes along. Some boys even resorted to wearing leather protectors on their backs to help prevent such injuries. If the seam was very low, the posture of these boys during working, could affect the way they walked.

These boys are older, so they may stay up a little longer at night than the youngest boys. They too need to rise at three, so they are often in bed at 8pm. These boys and young men would hardly ever see the sun, especially in the winter. There is no time for education as the boys are too tired. Education, apart from Sunday Schools, had to be paid for. Some boys went to night school after work but often fell asleep.

The workers have to buy their own candles so this is an added expense. The hewers also buy the gunpowder and their own picks which could cost up to 2s each. Work is available depending on the price of coal. A low price means less work as the owners halt work until the price rises. These days off are not holidays, as no work means no pay.

Mitchell observes the miners are generally, "not of large stature, but always appear strong and vigorous." Despite the apparent strength of the colliers, "they mostly are not long lived" because their work is "laborious and exhausting." He is a doctor so this is his medical opinion.

James Mitchell includes the opinion from two clergymen;

"The Rev Joseph Tiffen of West Rainton and Rev Frances Thompson of South Hetton, severally express their opinion that the children should remain at school until 12 years of age. No doubt this would be desirable if the necessities of the parents, and the demand for juvenile labour, would allow it to be practicable."

The children did not remain at school until they were twelve. They had to work. The family needed money in order to survive. The colliery needed child and juvenile labour, so the children worked. The children, like others working in the pit, often had accidents.

The following is from William Aldernut, aged 14. It illustrates some of the accidents the children had. William started working at the colliery when he was nine and a half. William now drives at bank head and is paid 1s 6d a day, so he is no longer working underground. He has been injured six times, probably when he worked underground. A stone fell on him and he was off six months. He would need a doctor to certify he had to stay away from work so he must have been badly injured. He was absent for 12 weeks when rolleys (larger trams pulled by ponies) jammed his legs. The ponies were probably going quickly along the rolley way. He may have been in the way and not able to escape quickly enough. The same thing happened twice and he was off work first for four weeks 4 weeks and then six weeks. He was absent for a week when a horse trod him down. His final accident occurred when the corve jammed his leg against a piece of wood on the rolley end. He was off work for another week. William appears to have been either working in a dangerous place or not fast enough to get out of the way of rolleys and horse. The first accident when he was injured by a fall of stone may have left him physically impaired and slowed him down. William probably works above ground now and may be paid less money.

Accidents may happen when children and young people are tired. They sometimes worked an extra, or even two extra shifts and could be down the pit for 36 hours. James Punton did that. Although James does not go to school he does go to the Methodist Chapel. It could be in the chapel Sunday School that he learned to read and write his name. He would go walk home, not from school, from an exhausting day to his home in a colliery village.

Coxhoe Colliery: James Mitchell did a survey of life in Coxhoe, a village close to Clarence Hetton Colliery. Men working at other nearby collieries also lived here with their families.[5]

"The cottages are built with stone plastered with lime, with blue slate roofs and all appear exceedingly neat…There is no yard in front of any of them, or yard behind, or dust-hole, or convenience of any kind or any small building, that is usually considered independent and necessary" Mitchell would probably be referring to some form of toilet facilities. There would probably have been a facility shared by several families. A small cart came every morning to deliver coal and take away the dust to a dust heap. Presumably some the dust from the fires would be placed in the closet and the ashes and waste would also be carted to the dust heaps.

Despite the lack of outdoor storage for coal and dust, Mitchell concluded that there was no unpleasant nuisance, no filth, nor ashes, nor decaying vegetables. All was swept and clean," presumably by the women and girls of the households. Mitchell observed that "most of the women took pains to make themselves as well as their houses look very agreeable."

He describes the cottages as being 'very clean and well-furnished.' The larger of the two cottages has two rooms downstairs. The front room measures 14' by 14' 10". This room often contains a 'chest of drawers with brass handles and ornaments reaching from floor to ceiling (the ceilings were not very high), a four poster bed with a large coverlet." The parent probably used this room and bed and possibly some of the smaller children in a crib.

The smaller room would be where the cooking took place and often had "bright saucepans and other tin-ware displayed on the walls." There would probably have been a table and some chairs in this room. The women cooked on the fire. There were probably no ovens as there were communal ovens fired by coal in the street where bread was baked.

The house had no gardens but there was a field divided into allotments where the men could grow vegetables, mainly potatoes. Some grew flowers as well and even entered them in local flower shows often taking prizes above those achieved by the gardeners of gentlemen.

He considers the miners and their families, including the children to be "substantially clothed." "Both men and boys on Sunday are dressed exceedingly well", the men wearing "black suits". Although there is no Church of England place of worship in Coxhoe at this time, there are Methodist and Primitive Methodist establishment. It is the chapels that provide the Sunday Schools for the children and youths. Between ½ to ¾ of the children and youths attend Sunday School. Mitchell considers the Methodists have brought about a great change in the "respectability of dress and good behaviour in the miners." Methodist did not drink alcohol. Alcohol cost money and with no income spent on alcohol, there would be more to spend on household expenses and clothing. Alcohol consumption was often linked with bad behaviour. No consumption could mean an improvement in some miners' behaviour. Despite the influence of the Methodists, there are 30 beer houses in the village.

Life for the children of a colliery village was hard. It was recommended children should stay at school until they were twelve but this did not happen. They had to work.

The Burdon Children progress with their Education

It may have been perceived the Burdon boys had a hard upbringing because of their apparent lack of wealth but they were well educated. Rowland Burdon jnr went to Rugby for a short period after he left Durham School before he distinguished himself at Oxford. After leaving University in 1822, he travelled for two years 'on the Continent' becoming 'a fine linguist.' Money must have been more available by this time to enable him to do the Grand Tour as his father had done in his youth.

John obtained a 1st Class and afterwards an Open Fellowship at Queen's College, Oxford. He went on to become a cleric, first as curate at Castle Eden.

Richard Mathews Burdon, born on 9th March 1810, left Durham Grammar School aged 13, on 19th May 1823 to attend the Royal Naval College as a midshipman. Richard Mathews passed his examination as Lieutenant in 1829 and obtained a commission as Lieutenant on 'HMS Thunderer' from 20th January 1834, sailing round the Mediterranean under the Captainship of W.M. Furlong Wise.

The youngest son, Cotsford, born in August 1815, after attending Durham School, obtained a B. A. at Lincoln College, Oxford before obtaining articles of clerkship to John Clayton, the family solicitor in Newcastle on 18th July 1836.

The boys were given a good education at Durham Grammar School. Life was not all bad. John appears to have had some notable memories of his time spent there. One story he tells is about [6] a dwarf named Count Borolowski who; "Was living in a cottage by the river-side, near the Prebends Bridge, with two old ladies, Misses Ebdons. He was a Pole and had been brought to England for the purpose of being shown. He was of extremely diminutive stature, and yet as well-proportioned as a fully grown man. The Dean and Chapter had, I believe, pensioned him out of charity. He used to be constantly asked to the Residence Dinners, where I often met him. The cottage is now pulled down. He spoke very good English, and I remember was particularly proud of his gold watch which had been given to him by the Prince Regent. He was very fond of shewing it. It is said that he had several brother, who were all tall and well-proportioned men. Also there was a story that he had been married, but his wife used him very badly. She used to set him on the chimney-piece, where he had to stop till she chose to put him down. He was extremely jealous of his dignity as a Count, and it was said that on one occasion when the street was crowded and he was hesitating about crossing it, a man took him up in his arms and carried him over. He was furious at this act of indignity. He was the smallest specimen of a dwarf I ever saw. Just after his death Dr Green of Durham, had come over to pay my mother a visit, and was full of the disappointment the Faculty had sustained in not being able to get at the Count's body. The doctors had intended to resurrectionize it for the purpose of setting up his skeleton, but it was impossible to get at him, because they had buried him in the Cathedral."

Count Borolowski left Poland to tour Europe under the patronage of a Polish Countess. It would be interesting to discover if this countess was the cruel wife. Borolowski spent a considerable time in Paris but left prior to the French Revolution. Whilst in England he became a great favourite amongst the nobility and gentility, so the gold watch could have be a gift from the Prince Regent He was reputed to be intelligent, good mannered and amiable, so these characteristics would greater enhance his good reputation. He was given a cottage on the banks of the River Weir near Durham in which he spent the last thirty years of his life. He died in September 1837 at the very old age of 99.

The doctors would have considered him unique, as he was only 35 ½ inches high and yet perfectly formed, like a miniature man. It is fortunate he was interred in Durham Cathedral so that he skeleton could not become an exhibit for the doctors. With the fond memories Rev. John Burdon had of Borolowski when he was at school, it is probable he too was pleased the perfect little gentleman was buried in Durham Cathedral. John Burdon was not the only person who remembered him. His death was announced in newspapers throughout the country so John Burdon was not the only person who held Borolowski in high esteem.

The Burdon boys may have considered they had a hard upbringing because of their perceived lack of wealth. They could no longer live to a high standard, the standing expected of a country gentleman and his family. Their father could no longer afford expensive clothes so he had them made by the village tailor. The boys, notably John, had their father's old-fashioned highly coloured clothes altered.

Candles were expensive, so the number of candles they used was reduced, but they still had light. The boys did not have to sit in complete darkness for twelve hours down a coal mine. Little boys working down the pit were too sleepy to attend school after work. School was expensive, so many families would not be able to afford the 2d a week and the equipment needed. What schooling the boys did receive seems to have come from attendance at Sunday Schools run by Methodists. The Burdon boys had a good education. Rowland jnr went on a Grand Tour where he became a good linguist. Richard was educated as a midshipman, becoming a Naval Officer. John, apparently the brightest of all obtained a first at Oxford. Cotsford, first articled to John Clayton in Newcastle, later practised as a barrister in London.

The daughters were probably educated at home. Little is known of Elizabeth, the eldest. Fanny, according to her younger brother John,[7] "seems to have combined in herself all the virtues…and she was gentle, peaceful and greatly beloved." John said that he "never knew any woman equal to his sister Fanny for either ability or goodness, and as a peacemaker she was unrivalled." Mary was just the opposite. John thought his sister Mary had 'inherited a good many of the cranks of the family" as she had a "querulous, censorious disposition." Mary herself considered she was 'the fault finder' and she probably said this with more than a little pride. John appeared to consider these traits as being 'cranks of the family'. Mary was 'censorious'; severely critical apparently as her father and mother had been to her when she was a child. This treatment does not seem to have affected Fanny as her personality differed completely from her sister Mary's.

While her father was alive, the family lived at home in the Castle. Fanny's mother, Cotsford Burdon,[8] 'was a great appreciator of art, both Angelica Kaufman and the well-known sea painter Carmichael used to visit Castle Eden.' Both painters gave pictures to Cotsford. These were handed down to Rowland and John Burdon. The Angelica Kaufman and Carmichael must have been friendly with Cotsford Burdon as they both painted pictures especially for her, which she in turn handed down to her sons Rowland and John.

No doubt Fanny would have been very interested when these artists came to stay. Both Fanny and her mother Cotsford have been described as having ability and being very intelligent. Cotsford appreciated art so much that artists visited her at Castle Eden and painted work especially for her. Angelica Kaufman was famed at the time as a neo-classical artist, founding member of the Royal Academy with her last work exhibited there in 1797. Kaufman left England and died in Rome in 1807. It is possible Kaufmann was acquainted with Cotsford when they both lived in London and there could have been a visit to Castle Eden.

Visits of John Wilson Carmichael are more likely. He was born in Newcastle and lived there until about 1845 when he left to live in London. He painted many seascapes and also exhibited in the Royal Academy. It is uncertain when these artists visited Castle Eden, but things were probably less austere when they were entertained by the Burdons.

The effect of the Bankruptcy

In 1806, news about the bankruptcy due to the collapse of the Exchange Bank appeared in many newspapers throughout the country; for example, 'The Morning Chronicle' dated 19th November 1806, listed Bankruptcy Certificates had been released to various people with the following trades; a bricklayer, a cotton-spinner, a tanner, a victualler, a hatter and two linen-drapers. Bottom of this list reads, "Aubone Surtees, John Surtees, Rowland Burdon, John Brandling and John Embleton of Berwick on Tweed, bankers." Rowland Burdon probably felt more humiliated seeing his names along with that of his partners and friends, listed alongside what they would have considered lower class tradespeople, one of above, a line draper, was a woman who was declared bankrupt.

Announcements like the following, appeared in newspapers at various times for the next thirty years. The 'Newcastle Chronicle' of 1st September 1832, announced the 'Commissioners in a Commission of Bankrupt' of the partners in the Exchange Bank were to meet in the 'Turk's Head Inn, in Newcastle upon Tyne, in order to audit the Accounts of the Assignees of the Estate and Effects of the said bankrupts......and the said Commissioners also intend to meet on the same day, at one o'clock in the Afternoon, at the same place, in Order to make a further Dividend.'

Until the final dividend was paid in 1836, each time a dividend was announced to creditors, notices were printed in the newspaper, being a constant reminder of what Rowland Burdon considered to be his 'degradation.'

Burdon retired from the political life he had when a Member of Parliament, but he still remained involved in life managing the estate. The Estate was mentioned in 1814, as; [9] "Two miles to the south-east of Easington is CASTLE EDEN. This village, with its neighbourhood is the property of Rowland Burdon Esq, whose residence is near the village. The mansion-house is a large elegant edifice, built after an ancient model, and beautifully situated on the top of the woody precipice that forms the southern boundary of the romantic defile, called Castle Eden Dene, and commanding a fine land and sea-prospect."

The estate may have been larger. Prior to the collapse of the bank, as Rowland Burdon had been going to take out capital to invest it in land at the Hart Estate. He put this transaction into the hands of his friend Lord Eldon but "Eldon was well known for procrastination"[10] so he had not examined the deed in time for the transaction to go ahead. This resulted in not only not obtaining the land but also resulted in Rowland Burdon being the only solvent partner when the crash came but by then it was too late absorbing the 'whole of the Burdon's estate excepting his wife's settlement of £40,000."[11]

Fortunately with the help of friends, his estate was saved so the Castle was still in Burdon hands when it was described in 1911 as an 'elegant mansion-house'. There were 42 rooms and a large conservatory so the building would require money for the upkeep as well as servants to help run the place. The tenants' houses would need repair. New, probably expensive farming equipment would be needed. The upkeep of the estate and its buildings would have financial implications.

Rowland Burdon, as well as maintaining his estate, remained very active in the locality. He continued as a magistrate. As time progressed he appeared to become even more involved in local affairs.

In July 1822,[12] Rowland Burdon was one of the pall bearers at funeral of Matthew Russell. Matthew Russell was born in 1765. His father was a merchant and banker at Sunderland who made a considerable fortune from coal mining in Wallsend. In 1796, he bought Brancepeth Castle from Sir Henry Vane Tempest for £75,000. In 1800 Russell contested Durham city as an independent.

Rowland Burdon was Member of Parliament for Durham County at this time. Matthew Russell did not win this election but succeeded in becoming a Member of Parliament for Saltash in 1802. Russell was a supporter of Pitt, as was Rowland Burdon, so they were probably on the same political wavelength.

When Matthew Russell's father died in 1817, he inherited his estate. The newspaper account of his funeral suggested he was a, "truly amiable and benevolent gentlemen" and because of his generosity there would be "lamentations of the poor" and "all classes" would feel "deep regret."

Rowland Burdon was in one of the leading carriages that left Sunderland Bridge accompanied by a 'considerable number of gentlemen on horseback as they made their way to Brancepeth Castle where the body of Matthew Russell was to lay in state for four days before his funeral. Great crowds lined the streets. Church bells rang as they made their way to Brancepeth and as they passed through Durham the Cathedral bells tolled out echoing through the streets lined with people, most dressed in their finest clothes to pay respect to Matthew Russell.

Many came to pay respects and file past his coffin as it laid in state in Brancepeth Castle before he was laid to rest in Brancepeth. Rowland Burdon was one of the pall bearers at this funeral, so he must have known him very well. Although both Russell and Burdon had their political views in common, Russell was a man of great wealth and Burdon's relative poorer state did not seem to have hindered their friendship.

People encountered by Rowland Burdon IV

i. The Duke of Wellington:

Rowland Burdon was also considered worthy of high esteem when the Duke of Wellington visited Durham in October 1827;[13]

"The expected arrival of his Grace in this city occasioned a great influx of strangers, and during Wednesday the kind of bustle usual at elections was observable throughout the town. A commodious platform was erected in front of the Town Hall, on which it was intended to receive the gallant Duke on his entrance into the city, and there to present to him the Addresses from the Corporation and the Inhabitants of Durham. The windows of the Town Hall were taken out, and temporary seats erected within the building, for the accommodation of the ladies; below the windows, and at the back of the platform, were the words; "Welcome to the Hero of Waterloo" in letters of gold, and pink calico. Flags were also displayed from the windows, and having the motto "See the conquering Hero comes," and another "Welcome to England's Hero." An arch, formed of laurels and flowers, attended over the top of the steps leading to the platform, and a profusion of evergreens also decorated the front of the Town Hall. Throughout the city, at least that part of it through which the gallant hero had to pass, there was a very general display of flags, laurels, mottos, and other devices, evincing on the part of the Inhabitants an anxious desire to give a hearty welcome to the man, whose consummate military skill and brilliant achievements had gained for himself imperishable fame, and for his country peace and honour.

There was a huge procession which included; "Lt-Col Tower and a detachment of the Durham Cavalry, with their full band of music", a banner six yards in length with the motto, "Wellington, the conquering Hero, comes! God bless him" was carried by three soldiers who had fought at Waterloo, "banners of the different free trades", "twelve other flags (pink and yellow)," each with their own mottos of various battles and "all carried by soldier who had fought under the gallant Duke". The Duke riding a horse taken from the carriage of the Marquis of Londonderry, "was drawn in triumph into the city, the band playing "See the Conquering Hero comes, the people loudly cheering, cannons roaring and bells ringing. When he reached the Market Place the scene was truly exhilarating, the utmost enthusiasm being expressed by the people, who literally crammed every portion of that spacious area which resounded with their joyous cheers.

"The Duke ascended the platform to join the Mayor, councillors, the Marquess and Marchioness of Londonderry, Captain Chipchase, Sir Henry Harding and others. Addresses were read. Wellington replied.

"The Noble Duke, after bowing to the Hon. Mr. Barrington, Rev. G Townsend, General Seddon, Rowland Burdon; as their names being mentioned to him by the Hon. Mr. Barrington, again re-entered with the Marquis And Marchioness of Londonderry, the open carriage, amid cheering of an admiring multitude, and was drawn by the populace to the Bishop's Castle, where the Duke was received by his Lordship and his Chaplains, and almost immediately after took a hasty view of the Cathedral and College, whilst the Company was assembling in the Castle. A more distinguished party has never, perhaps, been assembled in this county, than that to do honour to the Duke's visit, on this occasion at the Bishop's Castle."

Rowland Burdon was one of this 'distinguished party' mentioned which included, "The Marquesses of Londonderry, Earl Bathhurst, Viscount Bereford and Castlereagh, the Bishop of Gloucester, Lord Ravensworth, Sir Roger Gresley, Colonel Sir Henry Browne, Sir Walter Scott," several high ranking military men, Members of Parliament, clergymen and "nearly 100 of the Principal Gentry and Clergy of the county." Rowland Burdon had not been bunched with the principal gentry. He had been mentioned alongside the distinguished notables of the county. He had also been one of the few introduced to the Duke, the Duke as was the custom, nodding back to him.

As one would expect, once the guests were seated in the "magnificent Hall of the Castle", they were served with "a dinner which united all the sumptuousness of a noble banquet, with the comfort of private entertainment"; followed as usual by various toasts and speeches, one speech being given by the Bishop. This was a visit many, including Rowland Burdon, would talk about for a long time to come. The ladies too, possibly including g Cotsford Burdon, would have also talked about their place sitting in the Town Hall and seeing the Duke in person, possibly discussing things about him other than his military prowess. He did have a certain reputation with the ladies after all.

In December 1825 Rowland Burdon was one of the guests at the retirement dinner of Charles Ogle at the Assembly Rooms in Newcastle [14] organised by the merchants and coal owners. Charles Ogle had recently retired after 34 years as a 'Collector of His Majesty's Customs' at the port of Newcastle. Rowland Burdon, 'a much valued friend', had been acquainted with Charles Ogle for fifty years, so he had known him previous to his involvement with the port. The event was really grand and no expense appears to have been spared.

When the guests entered there was a 'flurry of trumpets' played by the 'King's Own Light Dragoons' followed by a rendering of the 'Keel Row.' The meal had courses which included, "rich West Indian Turtle, venison, lamb and other delicacies as well as a noble baron of beef", followed by a "score of large pineapple, pomegranates 'giving pleasing proof of the skill of British horticulture', and four large pyramid cakes."

There were an exceeding number of toasts including; to the King, the Duke of York and his Army, the Duke of Clarence and his Navy, the health of the Bishop and the clergy of the diocese. The wines to accompany the many speeches and toasts were listed, being described as being 'as fine a wines as could be expected anywhere.' With each toast the cheering and applause became more enthusiastic. The wines were concluded with the passing round an 'honest flavoured old port.'

The response to John Brandling's toast of "The ladies who had that day honoured them as spectators in the gallery" was met with "great applause and three times three", not the only occasion for a "three times three." It is uncertain what the 'Ladies 'thought about being excluded from the sumptuous repast and fine wines. It is to be hoped they had some refreshment.

By the time the Mayor's toast arrived, the applause and cheering was followed by a rendering of the tune "Bonnie Pit Laddie."

Rowland Burdon would have known those present, probably very well. He may have sat next to Charles John Blanding, his brother-in-law from his first marriage to Margaret Brandling. Charles John Blanding was Member of Parliament, having taken oven from his father Charles Brandling when he retired.

ii. Charles Brandling:

Charles Brandling senior had married Elizabeth Thompson daughter of John Thompson of Shotton in September 1756. They owned Shotton Hall in what is now called Old Shotton, very near to Castle Eden. In 1824, Charles' son, Rev. R.H. Brandling is living in Shotton Hall with his family.

Charles Brandling had retired from Parliament in December 1797 after he suffered a severe stroke. His son Charles John followed his father as MP, so would have been in Parliament the same time as Rowland Burdon. Charles senior died in 1802 and Charles John inherited his father's wealth, mainly from coal mining; collieries at Gosforth and Longbenton in Northumberland and Shotton and Felling in Durham.

The occasion was not as happy when Rowland Burdon and Charles Ogle were amongst the twelve chief mourners listed at Charles John Brandling's funeral in February 1826. There were many mourners of a [15] 'truly mournful cortege extended nearly one third of a mile in length."

"At a quarter past 2 o'clock, the procession set out from Gosforth House. It was headed by;

Two beadles with their staves, and

Four mutes on horseback, in long cloak.

The Hearse with the BODY, drawn by 4 black horses

In sable housings

The chariot of the DECEASED drawn by four horses

A train of 25 gentlemen's carriages

(A list of some of the occupants of the carriages is given here. Rowland Burdon is included in this list.)

The carriages were followed by

Forty Tenants on horseback, with rich silk scarfs

Four mutes as before.

This procession was joined by "the Adjutant of the Newcastle and Northumberland Volunteer Cavalry..... on horseback, with about twenty members of the Newcastle Troop, all in mourning."

After this procession had passed other mourners followed, many of the gentlemen wearing 'scarfs and hat bands. This was a grand funeral indeed.

Charles John Brandling had died suddenly.[16] He had been "well on the Monday and enjoying the sports of the field, when inflammation, occasioned by cold hurried him to his grave on Wednesday." He was described as having the "most bland and cheerful manners" who "captivated all who had the honour of enjoying his society, and his kindness to his tenantry and workpeople is proverbial on his excessive estates." As Charles and his wife had no children, Rev. Ralph Brandling of Shotton inherited the estate.

There had been a celebration at Shotton Hall about two years earlier when Ralph's son, also named Charles John Brandling had celebrated his marriage to Henrietta Armytage,[17] when there was "a plentiful repast of roast beef and plum pudding, moistened with libations of strong-ale and punch; of which not only the tenantry of Mr. Brandling partook, but most of the inhabitants of Shotton also." This was a different Charles John's celebration of marriage. His uncle Charles John would be buried two years later.

Later that year, probably in the summer of 1826, John Burdon tells a story, with an accompanying sketch drawn by his sister

Fanny, from later that year, probably in the summer of 1826, concerning Charles' widow Frances Brandling; page 9. There was a birthday party held on the beach at Blackhall Rocks. The tide comes in very quickly and it can be difficult to ascend from the beach if one is caught by the incoming tide and cut off because of the rocks. John Burdon tells the story;[18]

"It would be about the year 1826. Mrs Brandling, the widow of Charles Brandling, of Gosforth House, at the time resided at Shotton Hall, and was very fond of giving parties on the sea shore to visitors and young people who were her guests. The person just coming out of the cave is meant for my eldest brother (this would be Rowland Burdon), carrying Miss Anna Bell, a very pretty Northumberland girl, who afterwards married a Mr. Shaw of some place near Beverley. I think the lady carried by two menservants in a cat's-cradle is Mrs. Brandling. I, a lad of 15, am carrying Mary Wentworth, a daughter of Mr. Wentworth of Woolley Park. My father is the old gentleman on the shore with his stick in hand, looking with evident amusement. The lady leaning against the rock is Charlotte Hildyard, holding her sides and splitting with laughter. I don't remember the other figures, but think the one who has tumbled down is Miss Bowes. The boat is a Hartlepool coble, which, having observed that the party was in distress, being caught by the tide, has come to render assistance. The dog was a favourite spaniel of my brother's named 'Flush.'"

This story could have had a very different outcome if the incoming tide had been fiercer. As it was, they probably made their way round the rocks to safety, especially using the horses to get through the water. The cobble would probably not have been needed for their rescue.

Despite the mishap due to the tide, this story paints a pleasant family picture. Rowland Burdon senior has mellowed. The situation appears amusing. His son Rowland now has a pet dog, a spaniel, unlike the days when they were not allowed to keep pets. Rowland junior, now about 23 years old, is being a gentleman carrying a lady through the water but his brother John reminds us he is carrying the prettiest girl there, a Miss Anna Bell. It is possible there was talk of a romance between her and Rowland but if so it came to nothing as she later married a Mr. Shaw. John himself, although aged just 15, appears from the sketch to enjoying the adventure of carrying Mary Wentworth.

The widowed Mrs. Brandling 'was very fond of giving parties on the sea shore' and the comparatively recent death of her husband has not stopped this practice. She is hoisted aloft looking very elegant in the cat's cradle formed by the two menservants. Charlotte Hildyard, a frequent visitor to Castle Eden, is apparently very amused by the whole adventure.

This incident occurred about one year after Rowland Burdon jnr returned from his two year's abroad. He probably returned for his elder sister's wedding. In April, 1825, Elizabeth Anne Burdon married Lieutenant Colonel Thomas Henry Wagner Browne K.G.H of Bronwhylfor, Flintshire in Wales in St. James' Church Castle Eden. It would have been a great family occasion as everyone would be overjoyed at Elizabeth making such a good marriage and joyous to welcome Rowland jnr home after his two years abroad.

iii. Henry Browne

Not long after Rowland Burdon returned from abroad, in April 1825, the eldest Burdon child, Elizabeth Anne married Lieutenant Colonel Thomas Henry Wagner Browne K.G.H. of Bronwhylfor, Flintshire in Wales. Elizabeth would have been about 23 when she married forty year old Thomas Henry Browne, a considerable age difference. He was a widower, his previous wife dying when their first child was born. The child also died. Thomas Henry probably thought young Elizabeth would give him a second chance of a happy family life. Elizabeth probably thought it was a good match.

Thomas Henry Wagner Browne was born in 1785 in Liverpool, the home of his maternal grandfather Benedict Paul Wagner, a wine merchant. He was commissioned as an ensign in the 23rd Royal Welch Fusiliers in 1805. He served mostly overseas from 1807 to 1816, during which time he participated in the seizure of the Danish fleet at Copenhagen in 1807, the capture of Martinique from the French in 1809 and was heavily involved in the Napoleonic Wars serving at one time in the Adjutant-General Office of Wellington's staff. Browne kept a vivid journal account of his service overseas in which he noted day-to-day events of other units, camps, on the march and events during battle. He gained rank after the defeat of Napoleon in 1815 and retired with a knighthood and the rank of Lieutenant General.

John Burdon wrote an account concerning Sir Henry Browne;[19] "He was a member of the famous Milan Commissioners, whose business it was to collect evidence against Queen Caroline. While engaged in this not very grateful act, an attempt was made to assassinate him in the streets of Milan. As he was walking along one of the streets, a man put his hand on his shoulder behind, saying at the same time: 'Colonel, I have been looking for you a long time.' Browne, looking over his shoulder to see who had accosted him, received a stab in the side. He fell, and was left for some little time lying there, and the would-be assassin escaped – no one venturing to interfere. Colonel Browne always considered that the plot had been devised by Bergami, the Queen's courier, on whom grave suspicions rested that evidence might have been obtained of intriguing with his mistress. A few years afterwards Colonel Browne was knighted, and the King, when about to perform the task, turned to the Duke of Wellington, who was standing by his side, and asked for his sword. A graceful act, indicating that the honour was conferred for gallant conduct in the Peninsular War, and not for dirty work done on the Milan Commission. In speaking afterwards, Sir Henry Browne always used to dwell on the fact that he was knighted with the Duke's sword. Evidently this was regarded with extra satisfaction, though he would not have admitted that he had done any dirty work on the Commission."

Between 1795 and 1820, Caroline was married to George, Prince of Wales. In 1796 soon after their marriage, Caroline had given birth to their daughter Charlotte. Shortly after this rumours circled of Caroline's infidelity with several lovers, with suggestions she had an illegitimate child. An enquiry concluded these rumours were unfounded but Caroline's access to her daughter Charlotte was restricted. Caroline moved to Italy where she employed Bartolomeo Bergami as a servant but soon they became very close companions.

George and Charlotte's daughter died in childbirth. George desperately wanted a divorce, presumably to obtain an heir. The Milan Commission was set up to provide evidence for Caroline's adultery. In 1820 George became king after his father died. Caroline returned to England to take her place as Queen. George IV banned his wife Caroline from attending the coronation in 1821. Three weeks later in July 1821, Caroline died.

Presumably Browne was involved in collecting evidence against Caroline and especially Bergami when he was in Italy. That is probably why he assumed the plot to assassinate him stemmed from instructions from Bergami. John Burdon said that Thomas Browne had been 'engaged' in a 'not very grateful task' in obtaining evidence of Bergami 'intriguing with his mistress' presumably meaning Queen Caroline. The use of the word 'mistress' is ambiguous as Caroline was Bergami's employer, and 'mistress' in that sense but it could also imply Browne had found evidence that Caroline and Bergami were lovers.

Browne does not wish to consider this was the reason for his knighthood. Instead Browne emphasises the story of Wellington's sword as proof in his mind that he received his honour for his unquestioned valour in battle. It would appear the Thomas Henry Browne would rather believe he had obtained his knighthood for his military service rather than for any apparent espionage as a Royal agent.

Browne wrote a comprehensive journal of his military exploits but he was not the only writer in the family. His sister Felicia married Captain Alfred Hemans, an Irish Army Officer. Felicia Hemans had a noted literary career, including several volumes of poetry. She was well known at the time, immensely popular especially amongst female readers and highly regarded by her contemporaries such as Wordsworth. Browne's other sister Harriet Mary, first married to Rev T Hughes and afterwards to Rev W. Hicks Owen was very musically talented and collaborated musically with her sister Felicia.

Elizabeth Burdon married into a literary, musical family. Shortly after her marriage Elizabeth became pregnant. The couple were living in Bronwylfa, near St. Asaph and as the time for the arrival of Elizabeth's baby due near, her sister Fanny left Castle Eden to visit them and stay in Wales with her sister during her confinement.

During her stay Fanny Burdon gave an account of what is described as a 'curious thing';[20]

"A rook came and built in a tree near the front door. Colonel Browne thought it would bring dirt about the place, and had it shot." Browne may have thought the 'dirt' would be dangerous to have around and could endanger his wife's health. His first wife had died in childbirth so he may have been more apprehensive than normal. "The very next day the cock bird brought a second mate, and the nest was continued. Still Colonel Browne would not have it. He shot the mate again, and, singular to relate, again the bird appeared on the morrow with a fresh partner. Such a singular persistence in the rook overcame the Colonel's resolutions. He did not shoot the third wife. They nested and brought up their family."

The reason Fanny thought these event curious was that she may have considered them to be an omen of what was to happen. At the end of February her sister Elizabeth "was brought to bed."

Twin boys were born but they died. A week later, Elizabeth herself died at the age of 24.

The whole family would have been distraught. Good hearted Fanny would have felt the loss keenly, as she was there to witness her sister's suffering both at the loss of her twin boys and her week long decline into her death. Fanny's father Rowland Burdon would not only have felt the loss of his eldest daughter and the two boys who would have been his first grandchildren, but it would also have been a reminder of that tragic year when both his wife and daughter died. It could also have reminded him of the mother he hardly knew when she died in childbirth when he was only two years old.

Fanny may have tried to comfort her father when she returned home to Castle. The whole family, would have felt the loss of their sister Elizabeth.

The following year Sir Henry Browne married a daughter of Ralph Brandling of Gosforth. There was a family with this third marriage and his new wife outlived him. Fanny thought the story of the rooks and Henry Brown's shooting of the female birds was an omen. He had lost two wives, her sister included during childbirth but when he did not kill the bird the third time because it was so persistent, everything went well. Henry Browne was persistent and he finally got his family and a long marriage. It is possible Henry Browne met his third wife, daughter of a Brandling, on a visit to Castle Eden. He was another of the 'distinguished party' attending the visit of the Duke of Wellington in October 1827 and may probably have stayed there at that time, so it is possible he visited after the death of his wife Elizabeth.

iv. Bishop Barrington

There were other visitors to the Castle. Rowland Burdon was close friends with Bishop Barrington so he probably visited Castle Eden. The Bishop was the person who refused to accept repayment of money given to Burdon when he was in financial difficulties so he may have been a close friend.

They had things in common. Bishop Barrington was a patron of architecture and education; architecture especially being one of Rowland Burdon's interests. Both had first wives who had died, the Bishop's in childbirth and Burdon' suddenly of natural causes. The Bishop's child had been born stillborn whilst Burdon's daughter had died when a child. They had both had losses.

Barrington, like Burdon had a hard side to his personality. In 1812, there was a miner's strike in Chester-le-Street collieries on Dean and Chapter land. Bishop Shute Barrington was the penultimate Palatine Bishop of Durham. As such. He had troops under his command and these troops were sent into Chester-Le-Street on New Year's Day, 1812 to break the strike and force the mine work. This was repeated in 1818, when the price of lead fell dramatically at the end of the Napoleonic Wars, reducing the lead miners in the Stanhope area to a ragged and starving condition; the mainstay of their diet being rye Bread with weak coffee or Tea, hardly the diet adequate for heavy industrial work. So the took to poaching to supplement this meagre diet for themselves and their families. The land up the dale had always been a rich hunting ground for the bishops of Durham so the ground was heavily protected against poachers. There was even a law which made it compulsory for local hunting dogs to have three claws removed from the right foot in order to stop them being used to hunt the bishop's deer.

When the poaching of the desperate miners got to the ears of Bishop Barrington he sent out his troops to assist his bailiffs to arrest several of the poachers. Newspaper accounts refer to the Bishop's 'constables' rather than troops.[21]

The constables arrested those they considered to be the "most incorrigible of this fraternity. Their success, however, was of a short duration – the fellows were taken to Chapel, whence the circumstances rang through the hills – the clan mustered their forces, and marched to Stanhope, where the escort had imprudently stopped at a public house with their captives. Here a few of these daring and lawless miscreants, leaving their companions as a corps of reserve at the end of the town, rushed into house armed with guns, and in three minutes affected a rescue, by disarming and putting to flight double their numbers, and most mercilessly beating one or two of the constables who had the courage to remain to do their duty, one of whom, we regret to add, lies at Stanhope in a most dangerous state." It was reported that none of the inhabitants of Stanhope were involved in the fighting and those who were injured were given great care. The injured man recovered.

These were hard times and possibly Bishop Barrington considered it was correct to bring out his 'troops' to confront lawlessness. The underlying cause of poverty due to the low prices of lead at the time was not mentioned in newspaper reports. If more had been done to solve the problem, as one may expect from a bishop, men would probably have not resorted to wide-scale poaching in order to feed their families.

Bishop Barrington died in March 1826 leaving £160,000; a huge amount of money at that time. In 1828, Burdon, amongst many others gave a subscription towards a monumental statue of the Bishop in Durham Cathedral.

Rowland Burdon continued his association with Van Mildert, the next Bishop of Durham. At the end of July 1827, the Lord Bishop of Durham led a confirmation service for 600 young persons at Sunderland Church followed by the consecration of Ryhope Chapel where a "numerous party of neighbouring Clergy and gentry, were very hospitably entertained by Capt. Dale, at his residence in Ryhope. His Lordship proceeded thence to Castle Eden the seat of Rowland Burdon Esq".[22]

Rowland Burdon would have felt the loss of Bishop Barrington in March 1826, as he was probably quite a close friend. A far greater tragedy in would affect him that March. When his daughter Elizabeth Anne died along with his still born twin grandsons.

Rowland Burdon V gets married

Rowland Burdon jnr would also feel the loss of his sister but by the end of January 1829, he had other things on his mind. He was now about 26 and still unmarried, so with a group of like-minded bachelors; John Fawcett of Newton Hall, Gerard Salvin of Croxdale, W.R.C. Chaytor of Witton Castle, R.D. Shafto of Whitworth Park and William Russell of Brancepeth Castle, he sponsored a Bachelor's Ball at the Assembly Rooms in Durham. Two hundred and sixteen people attended, less than intended as unfortunately fifty guests had been unable to attend because of the "very unfavourable state of the weather."[23] Those who did attend were described as "comprising all the rank and fashion" of the county. It was a grand occasion with the "rooms presenting a perfect galaxy and blaze of beauty. The dresses of the ladies were very splendid. The band was full and efficient. Dancing commenced at ten o'clock, and the ball was led off by W. Russell M.P. of Brancepeth Castle with the Marchioness of Londonderry. Supper was announced at half-past 12 ...and was most sumptuous."

It would appear to have been a splendid evening. As it was a 'bachelor's ball' many of the young ladies present would be looking for prospective husbands. The bachelors would be looking for suitable wives to be. Rowland Burdon jnr did not find a good match here.

Rowland junior and members of his family spent some time in Bath. They donated money to causes like the building of new churches in the Bath area. In 1834 they were mentioned amongst the arrivals at Bath; those who had come to Bath for the Season.

In April in 1829, there was a Batchelor's Ball in Bath. If the 300 visitors at the Ball, Miss Burdon and Miss Uhthoff were amongst the selected names mentioned. The Ball was held in the Tea Room, which had been lined with ottomans and chairs for the occasion.[24]

There was brilliant lighting and a 'capricious orchestra.' The festivities began at nine thirty and continued until the early hours of the next morning. There was supper and breakfast from 'a rich costly banquet.' 'Wines of the scarcest description' with 'rich and delicious flavours' were available. The 'numerous and brilliant assembly' probably had a wonderful time.

It is uncertain which Miss Burdon and which Miss Uhthoff did attend the above ball, but it could indicate the young ladies may have acquainted with each other and this may have led to Rowland Burdon jnr meeting Anne Malet Uhthoff.

Rowland and Anne did meet and as a marriage was to be arranged, Anne Malet and (E page 16 of hers) 'a very arbitrary, disagreeable old person in the shape of the old uncle, Uhthoff, who also kept very tight hold of his purse strings', visited the Castle so that Uncle Uhthoff could negotiate Anne Malet's marriage settlement with Rowland Burdon senior. Anne's father Joshua Andrew Uhthoff had died in 1819, so her uncle was acting on his behalf.

An incident occurred which could have greatly influenced these negotiations;

Rowland jnr and Anne Malet were in the morning room learning German together. Rowland was a 'linguist' and may have wanted to learn a new language. They probably chose German because although Anne's father had been born in London, her grandfather and other descendants on her father' side had been born in Bremen Germany. It is possible Anne knew some German already and they had decided to learn German more fluently. While they were possibly not hard at work learning German, Rowland's younger brother John burst into the room. John continues the story; [25]

"I was ordered out instantly by Rowland and told not to disturb them in their studies. Shortly after, as ill luck would have it, old Uhthoff wanted something. He was a very old man…and stooped a good deal. He always walked, as one may say, head-foremost. He was rather a queer–tempered old gentleman, and testy, and his niece stood in great awe of him. Well! He opened the door head-foremost, as I described it, when Rowland, thinking it was me come back again, rushed to the door and banged it fiercely in my supposed face. But it was not my face, but old Uhthoff's forehead with which it came in contact, knocking him down and making a considerable cut, which bled a good deal. There was a pretty go! The Settlements were being negotiated and nobody could tell what might be the consequence. The marriage might even have been broken off! But, luckily, Charlotte Hildyard was staying with us at the time, and she was a prime favourite with the old man. She fetched warm water and bathed his forehead and plastered it up most tenderly and successfully, inveighing all the time against me and my stupidity for being the cause of all the mischief. Having brought the old gentleman round into a good humour by her care and nursing, I was brought forward to make a very abject apology for my stupidity, confessing that I had been the cause of it and begging his pardon for what I had done. So the Settlements were drawn, and the wedding took place, and the couple lived happy ever after."

Charlotte Hildyard appears to be a constant visitor at the Castle and also known to old Uncle Uhthoff that she considered his 'prime favourite'. Due to the tender care of Charlotte and Rowland's brother John's contrite apology for being the cause of the mishap, Rowland Burdon jnr and Anne Malet Uhthoff were married by the Rev. H. Uhthoff on 19th June 1831 at St. Swithin's Church in Walcot, a suburb of Bath. The Church was built on the site of the old medieval church where George and Cassandra, parents of Jane Austen had married in 1764.

Anne Malet Uhthoff's family

Joseph Andrew Uhthoff, Anne's father, was one time the British East India Company's envoy to Goa. While he was in India, the British officers serving in Goa presented him with a gold plate cup and cover. They probably held him in high regard.

Anne's middle name is probably from Sir Charles Warne Malet, also of the East India Company who concluded the treaty of 1790 against Tipu Sultan under instructions from Marquis Cornwallis, Governor General of India.

Anne had two elder sisters, Gertrude Ann and Amelia Fancourt. The household lived in Green Park Buildings in Bath. Jane Austen's family lived in 3, Green Park Buildings between 1803 and 1804. Joseph Uhthoff and his wife also lived in Green Park Buildings, possibly at the same time as the Austen household.

Anne's two elder sisters married in Bath. Amelia Fancourt married George Alexander Hamilton in 1835 and Gertrude Ann married George's brother, Thomas. C. Hamilton in 1840.

Anne and Rowland's brothers-in-law, George Alexander Hamilton and his brother Thomas were Irish. George, born in 1802, lived at Hampton Hall near Balbriggan County. George Hamilton had attended Rugby and Oxford about the same time as Rowland jnr, who had attended Rugby for a short time befor going to Oxford, so it is possible they knew each other before they became brother in laws. George may even have met Anne's sister Amelia through his previous association with her husband Rowland.

George Hamilton became a Member of Parliament. And had a distinguished parliamentary career. In 1837 he presented the Protestant Petition. He became Financial Secretary of Treasury in 1852 and 1858-9. In 1859 he was Permanent Secretary and a Privy Councillor in 1869. He formed the Conservative Society for Ireland.

The Hamilton money came from manufacturing. In Balriggan, George Hamilton's grandfather, Baron Hamilton built two factories to manufacture cotton fabrics like "checks, jeans, calicoes and fustians."(1837 Lewis' topographical history of Ireland.) They were also noted for the manufacture of the finest cotton stockings and men's long john's, which were nicknamed 'balbriggans.' The factories used water mills and steam engines to power its machinery. Coal would be needed for the steam engines.

In1763, Baron Hamilton completed a pier. Balbriggan was a fishing port but by 1837 there were only ten small fishing vessels. Yet in 1833, 134 coal vessels and 29 coasting vessels came to the port.

Anne's sister Amelia had a grand welcome from the folk of Balbriggan when she returned to Hampton Hall with her new husband George Hamilton;[26]

"Mr. George Hamilton and his lovely bride" were welcomed by "all the respectable people of the town" who "walked up to Hampton, to present him with an address" to congratulate him on his marriage. The return of the company back to Balbriggan was headed by Mr and Mrs Hamilton, George's brother Thomas and their widowed mother riding in a horse-drawn carriage in front of the long procession."

Once they reached the town, the "horses were taken from the carriage" and somehow or other, "the carriage was drawn through every street amidst the most enthusiastic and heartfelt demonstrations of affection and regard" as a demonstration of "the love of a grateful tenantry towards a kind and benevolent landlord."

"In the evening the town was most brilliantly illuminated" in even the "poorest cabins in town and suburbs" when "candles" were lit in windows "in honour of the event... Lanterns were suspended from all the masts and riggings of all the vessels in the harbour and bonfires blazed on adjacent hills."

The inhabitants hoped, "The young English bride has got a favourable impression ... that is praiseworthy" of the "Irish character." Amelia was probably highly impressed and touched by this show of welcome and hospitality towards her husband George and herself as his new bride.

Rowland and Anne come to Castle Eden

Rowland v and Anne were probably welcomed to Castle Eden when they returned to live in The Cottage, but it would not have been on the grand scale experienced by Anne's sister, Amelia.

It is to be wondered what Anne thought of life in Castle Eden after she had lived so long in Bath. There were some functions but nothing like the season one would experience in Bath. The following ball sounds as splendid as one may have had in Bath however.

In April 1832, Rowland Burdon V arrived with his wife Anne at a Fancy Dress Ball at the Assembly Rooms in Newcastle accompanied by his mother and two sisters. They wore unspecified fancy dress but others described appear striking; Miss Brandling was dressed as Mary Queen of Scots, R.D. Shafto as a Spanish bullfighter and various people wearing, a Chinese costume, a Swiss flower girl, a gentleman of the last century, a Circassian princess, a Turkish lady, a Quakeress, highland dress, Greek dress and several men in regimental uniform were described. This ball too was highly attended with notable guests. The dancing began at 10 pm with a "lively country dance", followed by "quadrilles, gallopades and waltzes."[27] After a 'sumptuous supper" beginning at half past twelve, dancing was again "resumed at half-past two, and was kept up with unabated spirit until a late hour in the morning." No doubt many of the guests at the ball would be introduced to Rowland Burdon V's young wife.

There were many donors for the ball, including Rowland jnr. It may have been the most "splendid ball" ever "witnessed" but it would appear balls like this were not as frequent or as splendid as those held in Bath.

There were other balls like that attended by Mr. Mrs Burdon and the Misses Burdon. Rowland junior and Anne Burdon do not appear to have attended the Grand Ball and supper to celebrate Matthew Bell's election to Parliament as MP for the Southern Division of Northumberland.

The young couple did not appear to have joined Rowland's brother John on his voyage from London to Tees Bay on the new steam powered vessel the "Majestic." Under the command of James Main the ship left London and reached the Tees in 40 hours despite lying in anchor for three hours off Gravesend because of fog. John was so enthused by his journey that he was one of those recorded in the newspaper as recommending the journey. He probably found the journey on a steam powered ship very exciting and adventurous.[28]

There were visitors to Castle Eden to see Rowland's v's father, mainly about his enterprise at Hartlepool Docks. Rowland and Anne may have been present at dinners when people like Lord and Lady Howden, Captain Dalling and Sir George Shee, Under Secretary for State for Foreign Affairs, came to visit. Rowland Burdon[29] was chairman of the commissioners. There was controversy over building a new jetty. Rowland Burdon [30] "who had seen a great deal of the absurdities of engineers, in his great work, the Sunderland Bridge, immediately gave his sanction to it. The work was begun by sinking old keels, and filling them, with material from the dredger: these were covered with loose rubble stones, in the form of an embankment; the accumulation of sand and shingle, which invariably follows any extension of works from the shore seaward, assisted very materially for the operation; and in this way, in the teeth of all sorts of doleful prophecies and prognostics of failure, the work progressed, and was completed to within twenty-five or thirty yards of its present length, for a sum littler beyond the amount first roughly estimated…In the following year the commissioners erected their light upon their pier, at an expense of about £200."

Rowland v may have been present at these discussions and visits as he was to continue his father's work in Hartlepool.

Rowland v may have been involved in affairs of the estate like the selling of stock or threshing machines, another recent invention, or the letting of the Inn at Castle Eden. This work was more likely to have been handled by the farm bailiff but young Rowland may have had some involvement. His father was getting old and one day he would have to take over the estate.

The death of Rowland Burdon IV

Rowland Burdon remained quite active for a short while during his involvement at Hartlepool. Henry Thomas Liddell was canvassing for support in Easington for the forthcoming election He had served as a Member of Parliament for Northumberland between 1825 and 1830 but he was now contesting Durham.

On 29th May 1837 there was great excitement at his visit when;[31] "He was met by the inhabitants at the end of the village, accompanied by an excellent band of music, and welcomed by a merry peal from the bells of the Church. The procession proceeded through the village playing the most animated tunes, and on reaching the King's Arms, Mr. Liddell was warmly greeted by his numerous friends, who had assembled to pledge him their support. The large room of the Inn was speedily filled, when the chair was taken by

Rowland Burdon Esq of Castle Eden. The venerable octogenarian appeared in excellent health and surprising vigour, and his presence on this occasion seemed to add interest to the proceedings, and to give unmingled satisfaction to his friends and neighbours who are accustomed to look up to him with confidence, respect and veneration.

In opening the business of the evening, Mr. Burdon observed that he had long ceased to take any active party in politics, and that he had not appeared there today for the purpose of mixing himself up with political intention. He had merely come as a country gentleman to tender to his friend, Mr. Liddell, the best support he could give him, for he felt assured that his Honourable Friend possessed every qualification essential to make him a useful Member of the Legislature and unflinching supporter of their rights, privileges and liberties. …For himself, he could only say as a politician, that he was a Pittite – and Englishman who ardently loved his country, and who regarded her matchless institutions with increasing veneration. It had been his lot to serve his country as a representative of this county in Parliament in days of great trial, when the hearts of the boldest men almost quailed before the difficulties and dangers which threatened the Government of that day, and in his heart he believed that but for the master mind of the Immortal William Pitt, our happy Constitution would have been subverted by ambitious foes, who would have reduced this kingdom to the position of a French Province. He had seen much of Parliamentary life, and had reason to know that he in his day had been of service to his country, and had also promoted to the extent of his ability the welfare and prosperity of the county in which he lived, and which he represented. He blessed God in his full old age and he wished for no greater, no other reward, than that which he felt in the satisfaction of his bosom. The consciousness of having done his duty with faithfulness was an ample recompense for all his services; and when the grave, which was fast calling upon him, had removed him from this world, the best remembrance which Rowland Burdon could leave behind him would be the example of his anxiety \and labour to improve and benefit the county in which he had spent his life"

Huge cheers followed this part of his speech. He continued with a canvass for Henry Liddell in the forthcoming election, bringing a cheer when he suggested Liddell deserved to top the poll in the election. Throughout his speech, "Mr, Burdon was frequently applauded and sat down amidst the most gratifying demonstration of applause from his hearers." Henry Liddell did win the election and remained MP for Durham until 1847, becoming a Member of Parliament again between 1853 and 1855 for Liverpool. Although Liddell had been well received at Easington, it would appear most of the applause and respect went to the now elderly Rowland Burdon.

It would be just over a year after this event, on 17th September, 1838, that Rowland Burdon IV died. Rev H. B. Tristram wrote;[32] "Such was Rowland Burdon the fourth, who has been called the 'most illustrious of his race' – a splendid specimen of the high-toned English gentleman; cultured, with accomplishments possessed by a very few of his compeers; scientific, in a prescientific age; throughout a long life of unselfish devotion of time and talents to the benefit of his fellow men; of preserving public usefulness; of constancy under misfortune; of patient self-denial; a bright example in a cold and unsympathetic age, of whose philanthropic and Christian principles which were the mainspring and key of his whole life, public and private."

This is a fine obituary and it is clear he admired the man and his achievements a great deal.

CHAPTER SEVEN
Rowland Burdon V

Rowland Burdon v was born in Castle Eden at about 7 o'clock in the morning of Monday 16th August 1802. He was baptised by the Rev Henry Forster Mills at Castle Eden Church. His baptism was recorded in the baptism book as follows;[1] "Following ladies and gentlemen present at the baptism, Mrs Brandling of Shotton Hall as proxy godmother for Mrs Jodrell, Rev Ralph Henry Brandling as proxy for the Hon John Scott eldest son of Lord Eldon, present High Chancellor of England, his Lordship being the only surviving trustee under the said marriage-settlement, Rev Henry Hildyard godfather, proxy for Anthony Numton of South Hampton Esq the Worshipful Benjamin Page Archdeacon of Durham, Mr Mrs and Miss Robinson, Mrs and two Miss Hildyards, Miss Bowes, Miss Wilson, Mrs Charles Watson, Mr Mrs Silvertop, Mrs Ferguson, Rev James Manisty, Mr Smith of Durham, the officers of the church , attendants with Miss Burdon & c."

A considerable number of women were present at the baptism service. There were three people acting as proxy godparents for Mrs Jodrell, Hon John Scott and Anthony Numton. It is uncertain why these godparents did not attend, although Anthony Numton did live in Southampton. All these people would have been known in the County and probably recorded as they were considered important. Miss Burdon would be Elizabeth, Rowland's older sister, needing attendants as she was only about two years old.

Rowland Burdon went to school at Durham before going to Rugby School for a short time and continuing his education at

Rowland Burdon v

Oriel College, Oxford. He spent two years in Italy studying art and antiquities and afterwards visited other European countries. On his return to England, he soon became a magistrate on the County Bench. He married Anne Malet Uthoff in 1831. They lived in the Cottage until 1838 when at the death of his father Rowland and Anne Malet Burdon moved into the Castle.

The Cottage was not was one usually describes as a cottage. Although it may have changed somewhat from the following description in 1948, one can see from its size it was quite a large dwelling.[2]

The Cottage was later advertised for auction after the death of Col. Burdon, the sixth of that name in in 1944. The following description of "LOT 1", does not appear to fit the description of a cottage, instead being described as a "charming country house."... containing;[3] "Entrance Hall (15' x 13' 6"); Breakfast Room (16' x 16'); Dining Room (22' x 16'); with service hatch to kitchen quarters; Drawing Room (35' 6" x 17'); West Bedroom (13' 6" x 14' 6"); South Bedroom (16' x 15'); with wash basin. Large South Bedroom (17' 6" x 16') with wash basin and bathroom leading off; South Bedroom (16' x 14' 9") with wash basin and built in cupboard; East Bedroom (16' 9" x 12' 6") with built in cupboard; Bathroom with airing cupboard; W.C.; Three Attic Bedrooms and Store Room."

This is a description of a sizeable house. The dining room and drawing room are particularly large. There are five major bedrooms and two bathrooms.

The description moves onto the domestic quarters which include; "large Kitchen with good range and adequate cupboards; Pantry, Scullery, Larder; Maid's sitting Room; Laundry Room; W.C.; Store Cupboard; Bathroom; W.C. Butler's Pantry, 2 Maid's Bedrooms and Bathroom."

The 'domestic quarters' indicate the staff living there in the past; maids, a butler, cook, kitchen maid and scullery maid.

In 1832, shortly after his marriage, Rowland Burdon v[4] "was urgently pressed to enter Parliament as one of the members for the newly franchised borough of Sunderland, where he would have been elected unopposed." Burdon declined the offer and refused to put his name forward. He would later be urged to stand when in 1868, a similar offer was made in North Durham. "He had a strong impression that his father's losses had been caused by his neglect of his own affairs while devoting himself to the needs of his country."[5] There could be an essence of truth in this as he had grown up under the austerity caused by the failure of the bank and probably was aware of his father's possible sense of failure. His lack of fondness for public speaking may have been another contributory factor in his refusal to become a Member of Parliament.

Although he was not fond of public speaking, he had "few equals as a conversationalist. His fund of anecdotes and recollections of political life was inexhaustible, largely derived from his mother…From her too he derived that quiet humour and ready repartee which was one charm of his conversation. Besides his classical and linguistic accomplishments he was also a learned art critic and a draughtsman of no inconsiderable ability." In the 1946 auction at Castle Eden, the architect's table for sale may well have been his.

Like his father this Rowland Burdon was a "sturdy unflinching Protestant"[6] being "looked upon universally as the leading Church layman of the county." He was also political and "was head of the constitutional party in the north division of the county."

With the death of his father, Rowland Burdon v inherited the estates. Although Rowland and Anne Malet Burdon had moved into the Castle, they do not appear to be there in 1841. In 1841, Rowland's mother, Cotsford Burdon, now a widow aged 65, describing herself as independent is living with her two unmarried daughters, Frances (Fanny), aged 35, Mary aged 30 and her son John 25, Perpetual Curate at St. James Church, Castle Eden in the Cottage. They have visitors; Mary Bowes aged 60 and a Miss Hildyard recorded as being above 20. The household has six female servants and two male servants. Miss Hildyard has brought her own, a 15 year old unnamed male and an unnamed female aged above 20. Whoever gave the information did not know how old Miss Hildyard was. Neither did they know the age of the female servants. Even worst, they did not know their names.

Mary Bowes was John's godmother, so she was probably an acquaintance of Cotsford, so she was paying them a visit. She may have been the Miss Bowes who was present at the baptism of Rowland Burdon.

Rowland and Anne Malet were recorded at the Castle in 1851, needing eight servants to maintain the household. Rowland describes himself as a J.P., a landlord and a farmer of 360 acres employing 23 labourers.

Sentencing and Justice

He is first and foremost a J. P. He had been a magistrate for some time but by October 1842 he was appointed Chairman of the Durham Quarter Sessions. This position came about because the previous Chairman, John William Williamson resigned because of hearing problems, so Rowland Burdon was proposed by the Marquis of Londonderry and unanimously accepted as his replacement.

Rowland Burdon's niece Elizabeth[7] said she "had always been told that he was the best Chairman of Quarter Sessions the County ever knew; not many lawyers knew the law better than he, or had it completely at their finger ends. He was not fond of talking, but when he had to speak out, he did. Once when he was walking with Canon Tristram in the streets of Durham, he was accosted by a half-drunken man: 'Mr. Bordun man, when ye're i't Coort, why can't ye speak oop and lets hear what ye ha' to say?' Mr. Burdon, bending his great height down to the man, simply said: 'My good friend, when I have the pleasure of transporting you, you will hear me.' He had barely finished when his friend had disappeared down the street!"

Rowland Burdon did have the reputation of handing out a "grand sentence"; sentences which included transportation. Most of these sentences appear to have been for theft and were given to those who had offended on previous occasions. In October 1845, James Connor aged 18 and John Brown aged 20 were both transported for 10 years for stealing a purse containing; £1 17s 6d.

Another nineteen year old man was transported for seven years for stealing wearing apparel. Like John Harrison, aged 21 they had previous convictions for theft. John had stolen a gown this time so in 1846 he was transported for 10 years as was a young man who stole a pair of boots. Another young man had stolen oilcloth which led to his seven year transportation probably on the same ship as the man who had stolen the boots. They may have met an older man of 37, Archibald Mackay transported for seven years for stealing yards of tartan.

Both John Harrison and Archibald Mackay sailed from Woolwich on board the "Lady Palmira" (Palmyra) on 4th March 1846 along with 310 other convicts. They had a long, arduous journey, not arriving in Van Dieman's Land until 22nd August. On 6th January 1847, James Connor was also bound for Tasmania, but the 289 convicts on board the "Thomas Arbuthnot" disembarked at Port Phillip, Victoria instead on the 4th June that year, after a sea voyage of just under five months.

The majority of the convicts transported to Australia or Tasmania were sent there for what may be considered as petty crimes. Between 1787 and 1868, 160,000 people were transported to Australia. It is not surprising the man who rather cheekily, but probably accurately told Rowland Burdon to speak louder when in court, ran away as fast as he could when Burdon curtly told him he would certainly be heard by the man if he ever sentenced him to transportation. It was a sentence to be feared.

Sentences for first time offenders appear to be harsh. In October 1845, sentences for up to nine months hard labour were given for stealing, frequently articles like apparel and clothing, cloth and linen, metal, a pair of shoes, and a ladder. Most of the offenders were young men. There were women convicted like; Ann Taylor sentenced to one year's imprisonment for stealing china ornaments, Mary Emery given six weeks for stealing two pieces of ribbon and another woman two weeks for stealing two chickens. Rowland Burdon may have considered that woman stole chickens to eat but the woman who stole the ribbons committed the crime just for gain.

Many of those convicted were given one or two weeks of their sentence as solitary confinement. John King, aged 15 was given one week's solitary confinement as his sentence for stealing lead. Fred

Taylor was only 11. He had stolen some satin and was sentenced to one month with the first week spent in solitary confinement. This appears a horrendous sentence for such a young boy. There appears to be an echo of the strictness of Rowland Burdon's father when he forbade the children to keep pets and made them watch while the discovered creatures had their necks wrung in order to teach them obedience.

Those imprisoned were usually given their sentence with hard labour. There was a treadmill in Durham prison so that may have constituted hard labour. Durham Goal had set rules. Drinking, bad language, quarrelling and indecency were punishable by fettering in irons, flogging or birching.

Prisoners had to work. Those in for a short time would take away rubbish, work in the gardens whilst others would pick oakum, picking out old rope for re-use, or possibly work in workshops. The prison was inspected three times every quarter by magistrates, so Rowland Burdon would be familiar with the conditions in the goal.

These prisoners convicted by Rowland Burdon In October 1846, would be in the Durham Goal that began construction on 31st July, 1809, funded by a donation of £2,000 from Bishop Shute Barrington. Due to various construction problems its use as a goal did not commence for another ten years.

Prisoners were still executed in public at this time. The last public hanging in Durham took place on 16th March 1865.

The crime the man committed was particularly brutal.[8] It was reported in many newspapers throughout the country. A miner named Atkinson from Spen, near Winlaton left his home at eleven in the morning to go out to a shooting match at a neighbouring pit village. He returned home at 11 in the evening exceedingly intoxicated. There was no fire blazing in the hearth and no supper on the table, so he became so blind with rage with his wife Ellen, hat she ran out of the house. But he pursued her, giving her a heavy blow and dragging her back in to the house. "Then he began to kill her, a work on which he spent about an hour and a half. He beat her with the poker, the tongs, the fire shovel and a sweeping brush. The shovel broke over her head, and the poker and tongs bent with the violence of his blows." Neighbours did hear her screams and tried to help but they were afraid of Atkinson, especially when he threatened then with his gun, declaring that "he would shoot man, woman or beast, God, or devil, that interfered." Newspapers suggested that amongst the "number of these strong men there was not one who dared to lift his arm in defence of this poor woman." The miners of Spen were branded as cowards but they knew this man Atkinson and believed his threats when he said he would shoot anyone who interfered. The poor woman suffered a prolonged, agonising death.

So, it would seem did her brutal husband. Newspapers throughout the country gave extensive coverage both to the murder and the execution.[9]

"The execution took place in front of Durham Jail, and was witnessed by a vast concourse of people, the principal portion of whom appeared to be miners…..The scene upon the scaffold was of a most sickening character. The Under-Sheriff, followed by Atkinson, the chaplain, the executioner (Askern), and other officials, appeared on the scaffold exactly as the prison clock struck eight. The chaplain then read part of the burial service. Atkinson was quivering in every nerve".[10]

"When all the paraphernalia for carrying out the execution had been adjusted, the bolt was withdrawn, when the rope broke, and the body fell with an appalling sound. Immediately from the crowd around arose the loudest cheers at this untoward event. The unfortunate man was removed within the precincts of the prison until a fresh rope could be obtained. At twenty minutes past eight o'clock, Askern, the executioner, again appeared upon the scaffold with a fresh rope, and facing the multitudes beneath was greeted with a perfect storm of hisses. A few minutes later, the chaplain, followed by Matthew Atkinson, again mounted the scaffold. The latter stepped on the drop, firm and collected, although a blood-red mark round the neck testified to the severity of the terrible tug which it had experienced by the breaking of the rope. Askern, who seemed determined that no new mishap should occur, spent a great deal of time in adjusting the new rope, and pulling the access tight, an operation which drew forth from the mob a perfect hurricane of hisses. The dying struggles of the unfortunate man were horrible and frightful to witness, and they lasted a few minutes, owing to the thickness of the new rope."

This execution was regarded as "one of the most deplorable scenes ever witnessed at a public execution."[11] Several letters appeared in newspapers suggesting the Home Secretary should be made aware of this horrific public hanging. It is possible the hanging of Matthew Atkinson may have been one of the factors leading to the Capital Punishment Amendment Act in 1868 that put an end to public executions. Prisoners sentenced to death would then be executed within the walls of the prison. In Durham the gallows were set up in the prison exercise yard until 1890 when a temporary execution shed was built prior to the construction of an entire block.

Rowland Burdon as a magistrate appeared to be well versed in the law. His friend Colonel Surtees was also a magistrate and acted as Chairman.[12] When "Colonel Surtees had been sitting as Chairman in the Second Court, as he was going down the street he overheard his name uttered by two colliers. Hurrying up to listen, he one say to the other: 'Ah, the Colonel gave him a grand sarment, but had it bin Rowley Burdon he'd ha' given him a gran' sentence.'" It has already been noted the Rowland Burdon was a man of few words but it would appear his friend Colonel Surtees was the opposite, as he would have the man a sermon, a long lecture. In contrast Rowland Burdon would have said little and given the man a stiff sentence.

"He certainly had not the gift of oratory... at the Village School at Castle Eden, when he had to make a presentation, he was so overcome by nervousness at the crowd assembled that he simply said, handing the gift (it was a silver mug): 'The inscription will tell you all I can say', and sat down. I suppose it came over him that he had been somewhat curt and wrote a very eulogistic speech, which appeared next morning in the paper, lest he should give the impression of not being interested in the ceremony." It was not that he was unintelligent or lacking in conversation. The reverse was true. "As a conversationalist he was wonderful... His fund of knowledge was marvellous, and ....he always seemed to know more of his subject than the person perhaps who started it, no matter if it were classics, law, poetry or philosophy. He had a way of taking up a book and idly, as it seemed, turning over the leaves, and in a short time he had assimilated the contents from cover to cover, more thoroughly than the ordinary reader who plodded diligently through."

His brother John Burdon

Rowland Burdon's brother John was also well educated. He may have been the cleverest of the Burdon boys as he obtained a First at Oxford and went onto to a Fellowship. When he left University, he became incumbent of Castle Eden Church. Because the living was only £100 he could not keep up his Fellowship. John Burdon had one advantage over his brother. He was a competent orator, something he would need to be as a clergyman.

John Burdon delivered an "appropriate and impressive sermon" in Castle Eden Church on 25th May 1840[13] to a congregation of Oddfellows, 'clothed in the insignia of their order.' John Burdon's sermon was 'appropriate and impressive'. Much later, when Rector at English Bicknor, he delivered a sermon in Hereford Cathedral to a congregation consisting mainly of clergyman. He was so impressive on that occasion that they requested the transcript of his sermon. John Burdon was not only intelligent but he had the gift of oratory.

Rev John Burdon was well respected in the area. In 1837 he laid the foundation stone of a chapel-of- ease South Hetton by Rev John Burdon Church and was present on October 11th 1838 when the church was consecrated by the Bishop of Durham. Rev John Burdon did more than just lay the foundation stones for churches.

Castle Eden Colliery had chapels but no church or school. John, with financial help from his brothers and sisters paid for the erection of a school and the payment for a curate to look after the folk in the Colliery.

Nearby Wingate Colliery opened in 1839 under the ownership of Lord Howden and Partners.[14] "The owners did nothing for the religious needs of the population thus brought together." Her father used a legacy of £1,000 and a "small endowment under the Peel

Act" to build a Church in Wingate. (The Peel Act was a government measure to encourage the building of churches in industrial areas.) Rowland Burdon, his brother, gave land to build a parsonage and Church Schools. Despite his living at Castle Eden being only £100, Rev John Burdon had used his available finances towards building churches and schools.

Rev John Burdon appeared to a more empathetic nature than his brother Rowland. An incident occurring in Castle Eden in 1842 and written in his own words;[15]

"About one o' clock in the afternoon the atmosphere became gradually darkened; there was no cloud, only a haze which gradually deepened until one could not see without candles. The day had previously been very bright. The storm burst quite suddenly, peel after peel of thunder, with heavy rain. The lightning as well as the thunder was continuous for about twenty minutes. At that time I lived at The Cottage with my mother. I was in the saddle-room, smoking; the groom standing at the open door. I had him shut the door and come in, I was sure we should hear of some mischief done. I never witnessed such a storm in my life. The lightning was of a pale blue colour. The fire ran along the ground (literally the whole of the yard in front was covered with fire, darting about in every direction.) The storm did not last long. It was over in little more than half an hour, rolling away eastward to the sea. I found after wards that two persons in the parish had been killed by the lightning, both of the name of Proud, but no relations. One, a woman at Castle Eden Colliery. The husband had gone out to get his sickle sharpened at a grindstone. He was driven home by the bursting of the storm and on his return found his wife lying dead on the floor in front of the fire. She had had a baby in her arms, which was crawling on the floor, crying. It was blinded by the lightning, but some time afterwards, when they had left the Colliery, I heard that it had recovered its sight. The second death, also of the name of Proud, by the turn of the road from the Turnpike up to Hutton Henry. The lightning had struck the gable of the house close by, killed him, and also the horse he was driving in a cart. Both victims were buried in Castle Eden Churchyard, the funerals being together. The Burial Register records the circumstances of their deaths. They were no relation. I may add that the storm was so fearful that at Wingate Colliery the people all turned out into the streets screaming with terror. They thought it must along the ground (literally the whole of the yard in front was covered with fire, must be the Day of Judgement. My brother and his wife had gone to a fete at Wynyard, not more than 12 miles off, and there was scarcely any storm there at all."

This is a distressing story but it not only informs us of the dreadful storm and some of its consequences but also gives an insight into Rev. John Burdon. In 1842 he is still living with his mother and sisters in The Cottage. He is in the stables when the storm commences so is probably having a smoke after he has been for a ride on his horse. The groom was told to come into the stables and shut the door, so John Burdon was concerned about the groom's welfare. His description of the storm is vivid, almost as if he was describing the Day of Judgement perceived by the screaming inhabitants of Wingate. There is compassion in his description of the poor blind baby crawling on the floor. Even though the man and the baby had left the colliery, Rev. John's concern was such that he made enquiries about the baby to ascertain the condition of its eyesight and appeared relieved its sight had been recovered.

Wynyard celebrations for the Duke of Cambridge

As a comparatively lowly curate, John had not been invited to Wynyard. Rowland Burdon and his wife Anne Malet were there to greet the arrival of H.R.H. Duke of Cambridge who had come to visit Wynyard on the occasion of the twenty first birthday celebration of Lord Seaham, the Londonderry's son.[16]

The Duke and his entourage had taken a special train from York to journey to Stockton. He was met by several dignitaries including; the Marquis of Londonderry, Lord Seaham, the Marquis of Blandford, Baron Brunow, the Russian Ambassador, Captain Fitzroy M.P. and Mr. D. Maclean M.P. There were also, "a great number of other visitors at Wynyard, upwards of 200 of the yeomanry and farmers of the county on horseback, and a long procession of gentlemen belonging to the town and neighbourhood walking two abreast. The party preceded to the Town Hall, where His Royal Highness and the nobility and gentry were received by the Mayor and Corporation in their robes, and two addresses were presented to the illustrious visitor- one by the Corporation and the other by the country gentry, to which his Royal Highness replied in suitable terms. Upwards of 100 gentlemen then sat down to an elegant and sumptuous dejeuner a la fourchette in the long room of the building."

Rowland Burdon was probably one of the gentry who attended this light luncheon. After many speeches some of the party, possibly including the Burdons, made their way to Wynyard to a dinner party to which, "a numerous company of the gentry of the county were invited."

Other entertainments were arranged for the Duke which the Burdons may not have attended. The Marquis of Londonderry owned collieries. A celebration was organised at Penshaw when nearly 2,000 of the Duke's workmen attended a special lunch. A public entertainment was staged especially for the Duke. A "special stand" had been erected for the "grand distinguished party" who accompanied to Duke to Stockton Races.

The celebrations over a succession of days, ended with a Grand Ball to which Rowland and Anne Malet Burdon were invited along with many other highly distinguished guests. Wynyard Hall had just undergone renovations and this was a good opportunity for guests to tour the building.[17]

"The visitors generally, were struck with the grandeur and magnificence of the new apartments, and those who had visited the ruins of the late mansion so lately as March last, expressed their utmost astonishment at the rapidity with which the works must have been carried on to bring the building into its present advanced state. It is now exactly twelve months since the restoration of the roof was commenced, and not more than five months since the completion of any part of the interior was undertaken." A huge amount of work had been completed in this time including work on the Marchioness's apartments which have been considerably enlarged and "decorated with splendid Corinthian Italian marble pillars, other portions of the walls being lined in a corresponding manner with the same marble so as to produce a sumptuous effect, which is much heightened by reflection from large mirrors... In the great dining-room (perhaps unrivalled for its size and propor- tion), the architectual features, which were formerly of wood and plaster , have been executed in Italian marble, which from its high polish adds greatly to increase the splendour of this sumptuous room. The library is beautified by two chimney-pieces of pure white marble, ornamented with bas-reliefs and sculpture. Two large look- ing glasses over these chimney pieces reflect the beautiful prospect seen from the windows.

The extensive work had taken a comparatively short time to complete and the Marquis was delighted not only with work but also it had not cost as much as had been expected. The ball was lavish, so possibility extra money had gone into creating a celebration of Lord Seaham's coming of age, an occasion of "splendour,......that will long be remembered by the people of the County of Durham."

This occasion may well have been a topic of conversation for Rowland and Anne Malet, but Rev. John appeared more concerned about the fate of a blinded baby and the burial of two young people he had to undertake in Castle Eden Church. These people had lived in Castle Eden Colliery. John took his vocation seriously.

Castle Eden Colliery and mining disputes

Castle Eden Colliery was not located in Castle Eden. It was sunk about 1840 on land the boundary of Monk Hesleden leased to Castle Eden Coal Company by Rowland Burdon. The colliery was closer to Castle Eden than Monk Hesleden, so it took this name.

Sinking was still undergoing at the time of the 1841 Census of Castle Eden Colliery. The sinkers village, South Field Colony until 1843 became known as Castle Eden Colony until mid-1847. There were 34 households recorded on the 1841 Census, most of these being the households of the sinkers.

Houses would soon be built to replace the temporary accom- modation quickly erected for the sinkers. There was a church, several chapels, schools and a library reading room.

A Literary and Reading Society was opened in March 1848. And within two months they had received £33 in donations, including ten guineas from Castle Eden Coal Colliery, five guineas from the Bishop of Durham, £2 from Rowland Burdon, Lord Seaham M.P.and R.D .Shaftoe M.P. and £1 from Mrs. Burdon. These donations enabled the Society to open on 6th May 1848. Rowland Burdon and his wife Anne Malet appear to be interested in the education of those living in the new colliery. It would appear that Rowland Burdon probably knew the Bishop of Durham, Lord Seaham and R.D. Shaftoe well enough to ask them to contribute.

In 1844, two years after the colliery opened there was a strike in Durham and Northumberland. The workers at Castle Eden were involved in this strike. Until 1872 miners in Northumberland and Durham were tied to their masters by a bond which they had to sign every year. Buddle, the manager,[18] 'wrote to Lord Londonderry at the time of the Coal Commissioner's enquiries which led up to the 1842 Coal Act. He wrote that:

What we have to guard against is any obvious legislature interference in the established customs of our particular race of pitmen, The stock can only be kept up by breeding- it never could be reinvented from an Adult population – but if our meddling, morbid, humanity-mongers get it infused into their heads that it is cruel and unnatural slavery to work in the dark and to be imprisoned twelve hours a day in the pit, a screw in the system will be let loose."

The miners worked in a system of 'cruel and unnatural slavery.' They were not free men. Every year they had to sign a bond that contracted them by law to the mine owner for that year. The mine owner did not have to give them work. If work at a pit was slack and the men were not paid, they could not seek other employment. If they tried they could receive a prison sentence of between one and two months. If they were employed, the employer could be fined £5. Instead of prison, a man could work out a fine, meaning he could work for a length of time without receiving any wages.

There was a campaign in 1844 to abolish the bond and improve working and safety conditions in the mines. The members of the miner's association wrote to the coal owners of Great Britain and

Ireland, requesting meetings to discuss the bond and the improvement of conditions. This request was not even acknowledged. Meetings were held, like the one at Shadon's Hill near Birtley on March 2nd 1844. A Conference was held in Glasgow when upwards of 70,000 miners attended to discuss a general strike in Durham and Northumberland. It was decided to write a circular to the coal owners but the coal owners took no notice of this circular and the men of Durham and Northumberland resolved to strike.

There were meetings of the miner's; the first one at Shadon's Hill where about 40, 000 attended. There were bands, banners and flags and the 'whole mass seemed in earnest sympathy with the object that had brought them together p 56 F.

Mr. Dent was the first to deliver a speech, when he said,[19] "We will stand together till we obtain our rights. We are determined to be free... the time of reasoning between master and man will take place instead of strikes, and the working man will get a fair day's wage for a fair day's work. Miners as a class are not on with respect from the public, and the great majority of the press seems to be against us. Our employers use every means to oppress us ...But now that there is an understanding amongst us, are we any longer to continue to drag the chains of slavery, to bear the yokes of bandage and toil in the bowels of the earth, as we have done?"

Thomas Pratt from Castle Eden was there to second a resolution. If Thomas Pratt was there, it is likely other men from Castle Eden Colliery also attended this and maybe other meetings. Thomas Pratt moved from colliery to colliery. He was born in West Rainton but his nine children were born in Pittington, Haswell, Castle Eden where his daughter Jane was born in 1845, Shadforth, Sherburn Hill, Wingate, Trimdon and finally Monk Wearmouth where he seems to have settled for a considerable number of years. He may have been looking for better conditions and pay or have been considered an agitator and required to move on.

Those present would have heard the Chairman's speech which included these words;[20] "All their employers thought about was getting as much work done for as little pay as possible, and when they were not able to go any further, to turn them out of doors. If they were ignorant, what was the cause? Had those who had profited out of their labours done anything towards their education?... What school accommodation was there provided for the workmen's children?... The owners sank a colliery, and built houses for their workmen to live in; but they were not houses, and many of them mere hovels, clustered together... Some had from seven to eight children grown up to men and women, all living in one house the whole room only being four yards by five, with a small pantry to keep their provisions in. This was the miner's castle, sitting-room, bedroom, and parlour his family brought up to men and women all in this small space."

This appears radical yet if one considers the perceived hardships of the Burdon family shortly after the bank collapsed there hardships could not compare with these. They lived in a mansion with their own bedrooms. The boys went to boarding school and University.

There were several meetings of the miners and another resolution requesting a meeting forwarded to the mine owners requesting a meeting to discuss their grievances in order to avert a strike. This communication again was ignored. The miners of County Durham and Northumberland went on strike.

The homes where the miners lived were tied to the colliery, so the owners instructed evictions. These were especially bad, especially in Cramlington, Northumberland. In times of strike or times when less work was available, shops in the village would often give miners credit.

In 1844 there were no working collieries in Seaham but shopkeepers and tradesmen in Rainton and Penshaw were ordered by Londonderry to refuse credit to striking miners or he would ensure their business would be blacklisted by him. He threatened the removal of his business from tradesmen in Seaham Harbour if they gave any credit. It was suggested that Londonderry had personally attended and overseen evictions of some of the miners. Miners from his estate do not exactly have pleasant memories of him.

Rev. John Burdon wrote a letter to the miners of the Hartlepool District. He addressed it;[21]

"Dear Friends,

When people's minds are excited as yours are now, it is difficult for anyone to get a hearing who does not hold the same opinion with themselves. "*Nevertheless, I will make the attempt. I will try to show you that the distress among the Pitmen arises from another cause than that to which you have been taught to attribute it.*"

He agreed their wages were lower than they had been 15 years ago. He argued that," Many years ago the number of Pitmen was small in proportion to the demand for coal, and consequently the owners were glad to give higher wages, and they bid against each other to secure a significant number of men to work in their collieries.

But while the trade was prosperous, the number of persons employed in it increased rapidly. Your families multiplied, and from time to time fresh hands from other occupations came to work in the pits. …wages fell and in vain attempt to keep them up to their former rate, you struck work. That was the great strike of '32. And what were the consequences of the strike? More fresh hands were brought into trade, and you found yourself worse off than ever. For, though the collieries have increased, you have increased faster. The sale of coal has increased since then 17%, while you have multiplied 27%."

Burdon argues some of the workmen are bad workmen and other skilful. He argues that only skilful workmen should be employed as they could do the work of two bad workmen… "the good workman should have worked the harder, and then the bad hands must have left the pits, and sought employment in some other business, for which they were better qualified…there would have been more work and better wages for those that remained. The Union…has brought people to the pits who were not wanted, and it has kept people in the pits who ought long since to have sought work elsewhere."

Burdon is blaming the workforce for the low wages. There are too many employed for the work available. Amongst these are men who do not work hard enough. Only the hard workers should remain. These men should work harder. Then they would be paid more and be in continuous work.

Burdon does not take the following into account.[22]

"In 1780, the mines in the north-east coalfields produced three million tons of coal. By 1850, that had increased five times to 15.5 million... a quarter of the national output."

There was a monopoly or 'vend' still practised amongst these northern coal owners.[17] This vend had been widespread in the 18th Century when a "collection of coal owners and merchants known as the Grand Allies operated 'the vend' as a monopoly practice. Output was limited by a series of quotas, on the principle that this would limit competition, maintain prices in the London market and maximise profit. By the end of the eighteenth century however the Grand Alliance had been superseded by a simple alliance between the Lords Londonderry and Durham...these aristocratic capitalists continued the mercantile practice of the vend." Lambton and Londonderry "sought means to extend the vend through land purchase. Collieries were held idle, others brought up to be left unused."

New owners helped change this practice. "The monopoly of Newcastle was broken as coal from the new pits was run by rail to the new ports of Hartlepool, Sunderland and Londonderry's Seaham. "From 1837 to 1868 new docks were opened at Sunderland. Ralph Ward Jackson obtained an Act of Parliament to form Victoria Dock at Hartlepool. By 1862 the two Hartlepools were the largest trading port behind London, Liverpool and Hull, shipping three times more trade than the other North-Eastern ports combined.

Employment for the workforce had been manipulated by aristocrats like the Marquis of Londonderry. There was a depression the coal industry in the 1840's but owners still wanted to maximise profit even if it meant less employment and wages for the workforce. Docks were constructed at Seaham and by 1857 three quarters of a million tons of coal were shipped from the dock. It was now more profitable for the Londonderry's to have their own port rather than having a Grand Alliance with the traders from Newcastle.

The time of Rev John Burdon's letter was 1844. He had more to say to the miner's about their strike. He asked them to reflect what good could come from their strike with warnings about the disastrous troubles caused by the strike of 1832. He asks, "What have the strikes, which have been so common of late years in all branches of trade, yet done for the working classes?"

Rev. Burdon warns them about trusting "to the strength" of their union as the masters will only recruit men from other parts of the country to replace the strikers and these new workers "will continue in the trade" and "take the bread out of their mouths." This would prove to be true.

Agents were sent throughout the country and new workers were recruited, often not knowing they were to be strike breakers.

Rev. Burdon advised the strikers to "resume your work, before fresh hands are brought in, and before you have exposed yourselves to all the privations and all the misery which a protracted strike must bring upon you. Let those who are les skilful gradually find employment in other lines."

Being ordained, the Rev. John Burdon tried a different argument when he said; "In your present refusal to work, you are resisting – not the oppression of your employers – but the will of your Maker – the ordnance of that God who hath said that 'in the sweat of his face shall man eat bread…that if any man will not work, neither shall he eat."

His final words may have appeared stinging. He wished, "That your trade may hands were brought into trade, and you found yourself worse off than ever. For, though the collieries have increased, you have increased faster. The sale of coal has increased since then 17%, while you have multiplied 27%."

Burdon argues some of the workmen are bad workmen and other skilful. He argues that only skilful workmen should be employed as they could do the work of two bad workmen… "the good workman should have worked the harder, and then the bad hands must have left the pits, and sought employment in some other business, for which they were better qualified....there would have been more work and better wages for those that remained. The Union...has brought people to the pits who were not wanted, and it has kept people in the pits who ought long since to have sought work elsewhere."

Burdon is blaming the workforce for the low wages. There are too many employed for the work available. Amongst these are men who do not work hard enough. Only the hard workers should remain. These men should work harder. Then they would be paid more and be in continuous work.

Burdon does not take the following into account;[23] "In 1780, the mines in the north-east coalfields produced three million tons of coal. By 1850, that had increased five times to 15.5 million... a quarter of the national output."

There was a monopoly or 'vend' still practised amongst these northern coal owners.[17] This vend had been widespread in the 18th Century when a "collection of coal owners and merchants known as the Grand Allies operated 'the vend' as a monopoly practice. Output was limited by a series of quotas, on the principle that this would limit competition, maintain prices in the London market and maximise profit. By the end of the eighteenth century however the Grand Alliance had been superseded by a simple alliance between the Lords Londonderry and Durham...these aristocratic capitalists continued the mercantile practice of the vend." Lambton and Londonderry "sought means to extend the vend through land purchase. Collieries were held idle, others brought up to be left unused."

New owners helped change this practice. "The monopoly of Newcastle was broken as coal from the new pits was run by rail to the new ports of Hartlepool, Sunderland and Londonderry's Seaham. "From 1837 to 1868 new docks were opened at Sunderland. Ralph Ward Jackson obtained an Act of Parliament to form Victoria Dock at Hartlepool. By 1862 the two Hartlepools was the largest trading port behind London, Liverpool and Hull, shipping three times more trade than the other North-Eastern ports combined.

Employment for the workforce had been manipulated by aris-tocrats like Lord Seaham. There was a depression the coal industry in the 1840's but owners like Lord Seaham still wanted to maximise profit even if it meant less employment and wages for the workforce. Docks were constructed at Seaham. Rev John Burdon's final words may have appeared stinging. He wished, "That your trade may hands were brought into trade, and you found yourself worse off than ever. For, though the collieries have increased, you have increased faster. The sale of coal has increased since then 17%, while you have multiplied 27%."

Burdon argues some of the workmen are bad workmen and other skilful. He argues that only skilful workmen should be employed as they could do the work of two bad workmen..." the good workman should have worked the harder, and then the bad hands must have left the pits, and sought employment in some other business, for which they were better qualified....there would have been more work and better wages for those that remained. The Union...has brought people to the pits who were not wanted, and it has kept people in the pits who ought long since to have sought work elsewhere."

The time of Rev John Burdon's letter was 1844. He had more to say to the miner's about their strike. He asked them to reflect what good could come from their strike with warnings about the disastrous troubles caused by the strike of 1832. He asks, "What have the strikes, which have been so common of late years in all branches of trade, yet done for the working classes?"

Burdon warns them about trusting "to the strength" of their union as the masters will only recruit men from other parts of the country to replace the strikers and these new workers "will continue in the trade" and "take the bread out of their mouths." This would prove to be true.

Agents were sent throughout the country and new workers were recruited, often not knowing they were to be strike breakers.

Burdon advised the strikers to "resume your work, before fresh hands are brought in, and before you have exposed yourselves to all the privations and all the misery which a protracted strike must bring upon you. Let those who are les skilful gradually find employment in other lines."

Being ordained, the Rev. John Burdon tried a different argument when he said; "In your present refusal to work, you are resisting – not the oppression of your employers – but the will of your Maker – the ordnance of that God who hath said that 'in the sweat of his face shall man eat bread...that if any man will not work, neither shall he eat."

His final words may have appeared stinging. He wished, "That your trade may prosper as it has done heretofore – that your tables may be crowned with plenty – that contentment may dwell among you, and with contentment God's blessing and peace, is the heartfelt prayer of your sincere friend and well-wisher."

The miners did not have 'tables crowned with plenty. After seventeen weeks of strike, 'they were starved back to work. Many were evicted from their homes and blackleg labour brought in. Rev John Burdon, incumbent of Castle Eden may have thought the dispute was solely about wages. He not refer to; abolition of the miner's bond, improved safety measures, the introduction of coal inspectors, weighing machines, a request to pay weekly rather than fortnightly wages. The strikers did get a concession. The bond continued but was renewed monthly rather than yearly. This benefitted the owners as they thought it enable them to rid themselves of perceived troublemakers. This monthly bond lasted for twenty years. The yearly bond was re-instated in 1864 leading to a rise in trade-unionism amongst the miners. The hated bond was finally dropped in 1872.

Rev Burdon was attempting to be conciliatory and persuade the miners against the strike of 1844. He saw only wages as the issue. He did not appear to recognise or be aware of other issues of concern. However, unlike the mine owners, he had tried to bring about a settlement.

Safety measures in the mines were one of the miner's concerns. One of these was improved ventilation. The result of poor ventilation was demonstrated in Haswell pit on Saturday, 28th September 1844.

A huge explosion at Haswell colliery killed 95 men and boys. It was at the end of the shift and the workers were preparing to leave the colliery when the explosion occurred. Men hurried to the scene but the presence rescue of gas prevented immediate rescue attempts and it was about two hours before attempts could be made. None of those underground were alive so 95 corpses were brought out of the pit; the operation extending into Sunday morning.

Carlisle Journal 5/10/1844

"The scenes of despair which the village of Haswell presented was harrowing in the extreme, wives weeping hysterically over their dead husbands, and whole families shedding tears of unavailing bitterness as the relics of them whom so lately they had called fathers and brothers. In almost every house…almost in every place were heard the wails of the widows and fatherless."

The majority of those killed were young men. Many were teenagers and young boys. It was the first time young 10 year old, John Barrass had been in the pit. Both he and his father William were killed.

Funerals followed. Accounts were reported in many newspapers. The following is from the Tipperary Express 12/10 1844; "HASWELL MONDAY…. The funeral of the sufferers took place this day, and was indeed an extraordinarily and melancholy spectacle. Between fifty and sixty carts were employed in conveying the dead bodies to the places of interment. Fifty four were buried in the burying ground of South Hetton church, the others at Easington and Hallgarth. Villages about three miles distant. There were thousands of persons present. The procession to South Hetton church seemed to be upwards of one mile in length. Many families have lost three and four each. The dead belonging to each family were placed in separate carts, and each followed by the friends and relatives of the parties.

Haswell is about 5 miles from Castle Eden, so the local tragedy would be felt keenly. People from surrounding mining collieries would have come to pay their respects. Rev. John Burdon may have been there to witness this sad event.

The disaster was published in newspapers throughout the country. A fund was set up and money for the widows and children.

Money was rapidly raised and soon reached £8,000…Although £100 given reluctantly by Lord Londonderry, it was announced in newspapers with the rider that he disapproved of a relief fund.

There was an inquest to find the cause of the explosion. Doubts to the validity of the verdict were raised, voiced by a Carlisle reporter; "It is perfectly absurd to expect anything at all satisfactory from a coroner's jury, composed of farmers in close connexion with, if not dependent on the colliery owners…especially as evidence comes from viewers, overmen and others anxious to excuse themselves to their employers….We will not call this explosion an accident until it is clearly proved that it could have been prevented by human care and foresight."

There had been many pit explosions causing fatalities in the early part of the 19th century. Those causing greatest loss of life included; 92 killed in Felling in 1812, May of 1815 in Heaton when 75 were killed, in June of the same year 57 lives were lost in Newbottle, 52 were killed in Wallsend in 1821, 1823 saw 59 killed in Rainton, 102 in Wallsend in 1835, 51 in 1839 in South Shields and now 95 in Haswell in 1844.

The Gateshead Observer was quoted as saying;[24] "This is a fearful catalogue – and one, we trust, which will not appeal to science, to benevolence, and to legislature in vain."

The Mines Regulation Bill was passed in 1850. This bill included the appointment of Mines Inspectors, a measure 3rd Marquis of Londonderry had violently opposed.

Visits to Ireland

Alough Rev John and his brother Rowland were involved in local affairs, they did travel. Rowland and his wife Anne Malet frequently travelled to Ireland because Anne's two sisters had married into the Hamilton family. Rev John accompanied them on at least one occasion.

Around 1840 while John Burdon was still encumbent of Castle Eden, he went on a tour of Ireland with his brother Rowland and Henry Hamilton.

They stayed one night at the Lysinan Castle the home of the Macartneys. John Burdon wrote of their visit;[25] "The McCartneys were not there, but Mrs. McCartney had invited Rowland to take it on our route. The Castle was prettily situated on an island in the middle of a small lake. It had just been re-built, and, oddly enough, instead of having the windows looking out on the lake and the pretty scenery beyond, they all looked inwards upon the court-yard of the Castle; the object, evidently, being to make the place defensible in case of it being attacked in some rebellion. If I remember right, we spent a couple of days there, and had a day after the rabbits. I don't think the Castle had been occupied by its owners at that time since its restoration. Not very long after our visit, a dreadful catastrophe occurred. The McCartneys had gone to live there, and one day Mr. McCartney went to a closet in one of the sitting rooms to get some powder out of cask, which was kept in a closet at the end of the room. He wanted it for some workmen for blasting purposes. In filling the can, he had split some of the powder, and Mrs. McCartney, who was sitting in the room, scolded him for his carelessness; and, as he went out, he left her sweeping up the powder with the hearth broom. It afterwards struck him she was sweeping the powder in the direction of the fireplace. He took his can of powder to the workmen and about a quarter of an hour afterwards there was tremendous explosion, by which the whole of that part of the Castle was destroyed. Mrs. McCartney of course was killed; the body, I believe, much mutilated. I had met them more than once during the visits they paid to my brother at Castle Eden. Mrs. McCartney was a very elegant and ladylike woman."

This is an unusual, yet tragic story. The McCartneys appeared to anticipate trouble in Ireland, so built their castle in such a way that it could be easily defended. Yet it was not defended from what appeared to be an accident. It appears unusual to keep gunpowder stored in a house, let alone place it in a container in a room where there is fire. It is thoughtlessness that the split gunpowder was swept towards the fire. The loss of Mrs. McCartney in such negligent circumstances appeared to remain in Rev. John's memory. He would know them quite well.

He would also know the Hamiltons, especially Henry Hamilton and his wife who appeared to be frequent visitors at Castle Eden. Rowland Burdon had a yacht, "The Mayflower". Henry Hamilton often accompanied Rowland and Anne Malet on yachting holidays. They didn't voyage, "very far afield, but explored the coasts of Scotland, Ireland, and part of France very thoroughly. Once, in Dublin Bay...Mrs. Burdon had the ill luck to fall overboard, and was very fond of relating and embellishing the story as to how H. Hamilton, as in duty bound, promptly jumped overboard and fished her out again. He always used to vow that he found the lady seated quite calmly on a stone at the bottom, with her silk handkerchief (without which she was never seen at any time.)...Mrs. Burdon's niece, Gertrude Hamilton was also a visitor in those days."[26]

Both Rowland Burdon and his wife Anne Malet would be aware of the dangers of the sea, especially as Anne Malet had fallen overboard on their yacht and the story may not have been so frequently and enjoyably related if Henry Hamilton had not reacted quickly and the outcome had been completely different.

Castle Eden was very near the coast. Storms resulted in shipwrecks along the North East Coast. There was a particularly bad incident in January 1857 when twenty ships were sunk off Hartlepool, seven of Sunderland and six between Amble and North Sunderland. The Burdons were involved in one shipwreck;[27] "During recent heavy gales, the brig Era, of Rochester, while off Easington, was struck by a tremendous sea, and one of the crew was washed overboard, and unfortunately drowned. The vessel was shortly afterwards driven on shore, between Castle Eden Dene and Horden. There were a number of villagers gathered together on the shore, among whom were Rowland Burdon, Esq JP, and the curate of Castle Eden, who took a leading part on the occasion. The vessel was then between 30 and 40 yards from the shore, the sea was making a complete breach over her, and the whole of the crew seemed to be completely benumbed with cold, with the exception of the mate, who got out a rope, with a cork fender fastened to the end; but after it had drifted for several yards towards the shore, the cork fender got fast amongst the stones. Mr. Burdon urged the crowd to use every means in their power to save the lives of the shipwrecked sailors. He then offered a reward to anyone who could swim through the surf and bring the line on shore, but there was no swimmer bold enough to accept the offer present on the occasion; therefore Mr. Burdon proposed the tallest man should go in first. The proposal was at once agreed to, and a stalwart gamekeeper went first, followed by Mr. Burdon and the curate of Castle Eden, and a train of people reaching up the shore held firmly by each other's hands. They then advanced into the water until Mr. Burdon was up to the shoulders, when they caught hold of the rope and the cork fender, and brought it out, and by that means made a communication between the vessel and the shore. The mate then formed a rope sling with a slip noose, and the crew were speedily drawn safe on to the beach. The captain was the last man to leave the vessel. He was an elderly man, and seemed much exhausted, and while being drawn on shore he completely lost the use of his hands, and fell over and hung by his leg, being in a most dangerous position, when Mr. Burdon, the clergyman, and the gamekeeper again joined a chain of hands. They were up to their necks in the sea, and succeeded in reaching the captain, and speedily brought him safe on shore. Mrs. Burdon had promptly sent down from the Castle a supply of brandy and other restoratives, together with a quantity of blankets for the shipwrecked mariners. A carriage was also in waiting, and the whole of the sailors were driven to the Castle. On their arrival they were hospitably received by Mrs. Burdon, who rendered them every assistance, and they shortly afterwards recovered."

It is understandable no one was brave enough to swim in such a heavy, dangerous sea. Those who went into the sea in a chain of hands were brave, especially went up to their necks in pounding sea whilst rescuing the captain. Rowland Burdon was tall but evidently the unnamed gamekeeper was even taller. The rector of Castle Eden at that time was Charles Robinson Bird. He may have been the 'curate' referred to in the article. Rev. Bird lived in Hudworth House with his family. His daughter Mary, a frail small child born in 1859, became a medical missionary in Iran working for the London Church Mission Society. Bravery appeared to run in the family.[28] "Mary Bird... became a wonderfully successful missionary to Persia – the first woman missionary to Persia and was a perfect saint on earth."

Incumbents at Castle Eden

Rev John Burdon was curate at Castle Eden. He lived with his mother and two sisters in the Cottage. He did not have much wealth as the living was only £100 a year, yet he was a generous man.[29] Nearby Wingate Colliery had no church, so when John received a small legacy of £1,000, even though the Burdon's had no connection with Wingate Colliery, John spent the entire amount in the building of a church in Wingate colliery.

"Somewhere about this time, John Burdon's mother wrote to Bishop Maltby on her son's behalf, detailing what he had done for the Church, as well as his brilliant career, and setting forth that with a living of under £100 a year, he had spent all his private means in Church building, but now he wished to marry, and she trusted he might hope for some preferment on which he could live. The Bishop's reply stated that he fully recognized all that Mr. Burdon had done, but he regretted that 'he had been so unfortunate in patronage since he came to the See and had so many personal and political friends to provide for, that he could not hold out any hope of being able to comply with her request."

This must have been a great blow to the Burdon family and a slight on Mrs. Burdon. Her husband Rowland had been very close to the previous Bishops, especially Bishop Barrington. He had done a great deal himself for the Church. John Burdon was extremely able and should have been considered even without the request from his mother on his behalf. It must have been a blow when the Bishop passed him over for his own personal and political friends.

John Burdon did obtained a living shortly afterwards at English Bicknor, Gloucestershire. It was in the patronage of the Provost and Fellows of Queen's College, Oxford and as a previous Fellow at Queen's College Oxford, his ability would have been given more consideration. Going to English Bicknor meant a move away from County Durham and his family.

English Bicknor was situated in beautiful, yet isolated countryside, eight miles from the nearest station. In 1844 John Burdon had become rector at English Bicknor Church, and also for a time at nearby Welsh Bicknor. English Bicknor in Gloucester is in the Forest of Dean near to Symonds Yat which was a tourist destination even in the time of John Burdon's curacy. It was mainly agricultural but coal mines, ironworks, lime kilns and limestone quarries were nearby.

The area was also noted for the production of apples, particularly cider apples.

When John Burdon became rector of English Bicknor, the living, in the diocese of Gloucester and Bristol, was valued at £300 a year; a reasonably good living. With an increased income of £300 a year, Rev John Burdon could afford to marry, so, on February 13th 1847, he married Elizabeth Ann Hale in Acomb Church near York. Her sister Mary Ann and the two Misses Wynne were bridesmaids. The announcement of their marriage appeared in several newspapers, including the London Standard. Elizabeth Ann's father Henry Hale of the Plantation, Guisborough, had died before the marriage as had her grandfather, General John Hale.

The Hale Family

Elizabeth's grandfather was General John Hale. He was born in 1726 in Guisborough, Yorkshire. John Hale's parents had destined him for the bar but John wanted to be a soldier. At the age of 14, he joined the 47th regiment, the Lascelles. He rose through the ranks and, as Colonel, commanded the 47th at the siege of Louisbourg and also at the decisive battle of Quebec on September 13th 1759.

General Wolfe died during the taking of Quebec. Colonel Hale was a close friend of General Wolfe and Wolfe's dying request was that his friend Colonel Hale be sent back to England with the news of the victory and as it turned out, news of Wolfe's death.[30]

"On October 13th Colonel Hale arrived in London, the bearer of dispatches which set all England aflame with pride and sorrow, for they told how on September 13th 1758, the battle of the Plains of Abraham had been fought, which decided the capture of Quebec and the conquest of Canada. General Wolfe had fallen in the moment of victory, and Colonel Hale, who at the head of the 47th Regiment had taken a brilliant part in the action, and had been selected to carry the news to the King."

Colonel Hale had been "one of the group of officers that stood round General Wolfe in his last moments "

When Benjamin West was commissioned to paint the picture of "The Death of Wolfe" he offered to include General Hale in the picture if he would pay the sum of 100 guineas." As General Hale refused to pay this exorbitant amount even though he was present at the battle, he was not included in the picture.

Benjamin West's painting of the death of James Wolfe was not a realistic portrayal of the event. Lieutenant Henry Browne, portrayed as holding a flag above the dying Wolfe was one of the four men out of the fourteen who were depicted as being present at Wolfe's death. The others, apart from one, Lt. Col Fraser, who was recovering from previous wounds and not even at the Battle of Quebec, would have been elsewhere on the battlefield. An American Indian was certainly not present. The painting gave an inaccurate depiction of Wolfe's death in order to figuratively portray Wolfe's death as being that of a martyr, giving up his life for his country. Including those not present meant he could be financially rewarded by those willing to pay for inclusion in a historically inaccurate portrayal. Prints were made of the painting, notably by a William Woolletts engraving, were sold in large numbers, yielding more returns.

The painting was inaccurate and dramatized, but it could have been even more so if West had taken Joshua Reynold's advice and painted the leading figures wearing togas.

On General Hale's return king George III awarded him a bounty of; £500, 10,000 acres of land in Canada and promotion to Colonel of a Regiment of Light Horse. These newly formed regiments rode smaller, faster, more agile horses. The riders need to be equally as agile, as they carried carbines and were trained to fire at speed from the saddle. They did not carry swords but were equipped with fixed bayonets, pistols and an axe.

Colonel John Hale

Although Colonel Hale was born in Guisborough, Yorkshire and may have been acquainted with the Chaloner family who also lived in near Guisborough, it was when he was quartered in Yorkshire with his Dragoon Regiment,[30] "he became passionately enamoured of Miss Chaloner a daughter of an ancient family residing at Cleveland in a house called the Priory, near Guisborough."

Sir Thomas Chaloner, an ancestor of the Chaloner family, together with his brother James were amongst the 135 commissioners at the trial of Charles I. Sir Thomas was a signatory to the King's death warrant. After the restoration, he fled to the Continent to escape a trial for treason and remained there until his death in Middleburg, in the Netherlands in 1661.

Mary Chaloner, the object of Colonel Hale's affection lived in Guisborough with her parents, William and Mary Chaloner. Both Mary and her sister Anne were considered great beauties. Mary Chaloner was born on January 16th 1744, so she was about 18 years younger than Colonel John Hale. Mary's elder sister Anne made a good marriage on May 12th 1761, when she married Edward Lascelles. At this time, Edward, son of a customs officer in Barbados, was a Whig Member of Parliament for Northallerton. He remained in this position until 1774 being returned again from 1790 to 1796.

The Lascelles family were very wealthy. Henry Lascelles owned interests in 47 plantations in the Caribbean and interests in 21 slave ships. He extended his wealth by importing sugar and going into banking. Using his vast wealth, Henry Lascelles built Harewood House, near Leeds, as his residence. He spared no expense, using designers John Carr and Robert Adam for the house, Thomas Chippendale for most of the furniture and Capability Brown's expertise in the gardens. At his death in 1753, Henry Lascelles's fortune amounted to over £400,000, equivalent to around £34 million pounds today.

Henry's son Edwin Lascelles inherited his father's estate and became the 1st Baron Harewood. When Edwin died childless in 1795, his cousin Edward Lascelles inherited the estate. In 1796,

Edward Lascelles was raised to Baron Harewood. In 1812, he was made Viscount Lascelles and Earl of Harewood.

Although Anne did not know her intended Edward Lascelles would rise to such heights, he was a wealthy Member of Parliament when she married him in May 1761. They were of the same age as Edward was only about two years older than his new wife Anne.

Mary Chaloner was as beautiful as her sister Anne. Colonel John Hale, about sixteen years her senior fell in love with her. The Colonel had a slender fortune, his income being considered, "barely adequate to support his family genteely at that time." General Hale wrote this letter to Mary when on board the ship "Namur" whilst still at sea near Hispaniola in the West Indies.

"May 15th 1762, Perhaps young lady you are ignorant" of how "you have destroyed the Peace of one person…whose first wish is your happiness. And whose greatest merit is that he would risk his life for your service. Whilst I make this declaration I reproach myself, with the possibility of giving you a moment's uneasiness, but my situation is too critical and my Heart too full to keep from you any longer the secret that embitters every hour of my life. You cannot forget that last September chance conducted me to Mrs. Chaloner's house, short as my stay there appeared to be, it was too long for my future repose and I soon found that no time or circumstance could those impressions which the Beauty of your person, the sweetness of your temper, and the strength of your understanding, made upon a heart but too susceptible to 'Love'. In a word (forgive the involuntary crime), I loved you to folly and extravagance. Forgetting the disadvantages of my Person, and the disparity of my age, without a single pretension to such a blessing, I formed and eagerly pursued the vain prospect of making you mine. But your mother to whose care and whose prudence I do but justice in commending them, wisely stood between me and my hope and taught me that her duty must ever oppose any wishes as inconsistent with the Interest and happiness of her daughter. Under this disappointment I took the part with honour and cruel necessity seemed to dictate; I strove by absence to get the better of any unhappy passion and as my last resource, went to seek in foreign climes that tranquillity which my own Country denied me. Fruitless effort! The body feels the change of Heat and Cold, but the firm and constant mind is invariably the same under any atmosphere. A few days may possibly finish my Career, and perhaps I am now taking my last leave of you, but whilst I live I must adore the assemblage of everything available in Miss Chaloner, and in my death alone I can cease to be her most passionate admirer, J. Hale".

The picture painted of Mary Chaloner by Joshua Reynolds demonstrates her beauty. John Hale was also painted by Reynolds and Hale referring to the "disadvantages of my Person" may have considered his looks were not as attractive as those of Miss Chaloner. He also refers to "the disparity of my age" as he was considerably older than her. It would appear he did not consider himself a young, dashing army officer and therefore not a suitable match for a beautiful young woman. John Hale refers to Mrs. Hale with a respect for her views that he is not a suitable match and would not make her daughter happy but he does it in such a way that even Mrs. Hale would consider that he had her daughter's well-being at heart. John Hale's declaration of love and deep devotion appears sincere and extremely romantic. Mary would have shown this letter to her mother. Her mother, probably swayed by John Hale's depth of feeling, relented and Mary and John were married on June 19th 1763. She wore an elegant wedding dress and would have looked extremely beautiful.

Mary's sister Anne had made a good marriage. Ann and Edward Lascelles had four children. Mary and John Hale had[32] "23" children, of whom 17 grew up." She was a clever woman and educated all these children herself. It would have been a considerable expense to pay for education for all those children. Mary is described as;[33] "A peerless woman of her time, virtuous, talented and charming, the delight of all around her, dying at the age of 60 worn out by maternal cares."

It is not surprising that Mary died at a reasonably young age with the suggestion that her early death was due to the effects of childbearing. Her husband John Hale died four years later.

Mary Hale

Their eldest son John Hale was born on 25th March 1764. On 2nd December, 1776, John Hale joined the marines. On 12th May 1779 he became a lieutenant in the 2nd Foot Regiment, rising to Captain and eventually as aide-de-camp and military to Prince Edward Augustus, later the Duke of Kent.

The Duke appeared to have high regard for John Hale and they appeared to keep in touch. On December 4th, 1819, the time of this letter, John Hale was living in Quebec and the Duke of Kent in Kensington Palace.[34]

"My dear Hale, - Your kind letter from Quebec, November the 8th, containing your affectionate good wishes upon the return of that day (which, as you justly observe, you have offered me uninterruptedly for the last thirty years), came to hand this day, and claims my most hearty and cordial thanks. It does indeed appear a dream when we look back upon all that has come to pass in the world since you and I embarked together for Gibraltar on January 27th, 1790. Changes and events have taken place so rapidly one after another during that period as to be beyond all human foresight."

The long letter continues mainly concerning people they both know prior to the Duke relating family matters; "I am on the eve of setting out to Sidmouth in Devonshire, in order to give the Duchess the benefit of sea-bathing during those months in the year that are most disagreeable here; and I the more readily adopted this measure as the delightful air of that part of England will be far preferable for our little Girl, to the fogs that at this season of the year prevail in the neighbourhood of London. If it agrees with both Mother and Child, which are of course my first objects, we shall probably stay till the beginning of April; then just come over here to pack up and return to Germany, where the Duchess's duties as Guardian of her children and Regent of her son's Principality call her. Probably our return to Old England will be governed altogether of her future pregnancy."

The Duke's "little Girl", one of his "first objects" would eventually become Queen Victoria. The Duke appeared to care a great deal for young Victoria.

John Hale, now in Quebec and hoping for a Government post which would take him back to England, probably requesting the Duke to approach Government on his behalf. It was to no avail as the Duke's reply would indicate; "I sincerely wish I possessed that influence with Government, probably asking the Duke to which I do not, to enable me to use it for your benefit."

The Duke's closes the letter with; Pray remember me kindly to Mrs. Hale and all my young friends, and believe me to be at all times with the most friendly regard, My dear Hale, Yours faithfully, Edward."

The letter from John Hale was dated the 8th November. The Duke was born on 2nd November, 1767, so the communication probably wished the Duke a happy birthday, something John Hale had done for the past 30 years. The reply from the Duke, written on the day of its receipt, appeared a letter written to a friend one had known for a very long time.

As aide-de-camp to the Duke, he had not only accompanied him to Gibraltar. He had also served as the Duke's aide in Halifax, Nova Scotia when the Duke had taken command of the forces in Nova Scotia and New Brunswick. John Hale was probably involved in the reconstruction of the Halifax fortifications, instigated by the Duke, then still Prince Edward Augustus. After a riding accident and injury to his leg, the Prince left Halifax in 1798 to return to England. He was created Duke of Kent in April 1799.

John Hale also returned to England in 1798. He married Elizabeth Frances Amherst in London on 3rd April, 1799. They had four daughters and eight sons.

John Hale left England for Quebec with his new wife Elizabeth in June 1799, to take up the post of deputy paymaster to the British troops stationed in Canada. During his time there he was given several commissions, appointed a Justice of the Peace, on a committee to assist destitute and sick strangers, became a member of the Legislative Council from December 1808 to March 1838, serving as speaker three times and sitting on the Executive Council from December 1820.

In 1823, John Hale was one of the three members of a committee investigating the Receiver General John Caldwell. John Hale gives an account of these happenings in the letter to his brother, Rev. Richard Hale incumbent at Harewood, Yorkshire dated December 20th 1823; "One day Lord Dalhousie sent for me and told me that the Receiver General of the Province was a defaulter to the amount of £96,000; that he must immediately be suspended; and his Lordship requested me to accept the appointment till the King's pleasure be known, saying that I should thereby relieve him from great embarrassment. I give up for the time being the officer of Inspector of Accounts, because it is incompatible with that of Receiver General, and I do not at present derive any pecuniary advantage by the exchange – only the Honour. The appointment of Receiver General gives but £400 a year, therefore I hope that I shall be confirmed at home, for there are not many people likely to come abroad for such a salary. If I should be confirmed, I think I stand so well with the Government and the Legislature here that I shall be able to make it a better thing. I have written to Lord Harewood, Mr. Wortley, Mr. Lewin, and Sir Charles who shaves a Lord of the Treasury, pray put in a word for me. I may be called on to find two sureties of £5,000 each, and I do not know who to apply to save Lord Harewood and Mr. Lewin. If Dundas were in England, I should ask him with less hesitation than Lord Harewood."

It would appear that although John Hale would have preferred to return to England in a post with a salary higher than the £400 a year he had written to those with influence to attempt to procure him a higher salary as he was considered his appointment would be confirmed. John Hale needed "sureties" and he appeared reluctant to ask Lord Harewood considering Dundas as more approachable for this request.

Life in Canada

John Hale was appointed as Receiver General and did not return to England. In 1819 he had purchased the seigneury of Saint-Anne de la Perade, an area covering 60 square miles. This was a time of settlers coming to Canada. In the letter to his brother Richard in 1823 he said he had; "answered some enquiries in the Farmer's Journal on the subject of obtaining land in Canada, "as he had "50,000 acres of Forest upon which (he) would be glad to see some Yorkshire Farmers, but no one should come out here who has not enough to live upon until he can cut down Trees and replace them with wheat." As a member of the committee to 'assist destitute and sick strangers,' strangers referring to incomers, John Hale had probably seem the results of prospective farmers arriving in Canada with insufficient funds to fell trees and wait for income from grain harvests. He did not want that to happen to Yorkshire farmers.

The British Government encouraged emigration to Canada by offering free passage and on their landing in Canada, a grant of 100 acres of land and provisions for the first year. These would be emigrants may have taken advantage of this offer when on the 8th July 1823, the "ships Slakesley and Hebe, Captain Johnson and Hare, will sail from Cork, for the new settlements at Canada with 567 Emigrants, chiefly ruined farmers from the South of Ireland." Mr. Robinson, a superintendent appointed by the Government with "very ample powers to encourage the settlers" also sailed on board the 'Slakesley'. [35]

A letter written to the brother of a settler in Canada appeared in the press. (Evening Mail 4th April 1823) The settler, finding "farming so low, and farmers so much in the power of their landlords" had left his family and friends in Scotland to start a new life in Canada.

At the time of writing things had been a "little unfortunate" and he was "at present labouring under some difficulties" he did not regret his decision to go into a "new and strange country." He optimistically considered, provided "his good health continued" he would in a "very few years…be able to surmount" these setbacks. The 567 settlers aboard the above ships would be given support for only one year. The Scottish settler was looking ahead to several years of hard work ahead of him.

The Scot had "purchased "200 acres of excellent land at two dollars and a half or 12s 6d currency, per acre…on the banks of the Chateauguay river, about 50 miles south-west of Montreal, and my brother "is in terms of another 100 acres alongside of mine, on the same river." The Scot is not alone, as one of his brothers has also settled, with the brother staying in Scotland being recipient of the letter.

The Scot describes the River Chateauguay as much "near the size of the Clyde at Hamilton" but unlike the Clyde, because of "rapids" it is "only navigable for canoes or flat-bottomed skiffs which carry 10 to 20 cwt., excepting in Spring when the melting snow raises it so high, that rafts of square timber, oars (and) staves" are able to "float down." Transport of goods by boat appears difficult. The winters must be hard with heavy snow as the spring melts raise the river considerably.

Although he states he has travelled the Scot considers "no place has appeared where the land and situation are so good, and possessing so many local advantages at such a cheap rate." There are "three going sawmills" in the "neighbourhood" where they can purchase "plenty of boards at six dollars per 1000 feet." He is situated about one mile down river from the construction of a "new grist mill." In the same spot, the building of a "carding and fulling mill ….the necessary apparatus for dressing cloth" will soon commence. This area of land is laid out "into half acres for a village, to accommodate mechanics, store-keepers, tavern-keepers & c." A lot is "laid out for a schoolhouse, and I expect a schoolmaster by next winter. We have greatly to lament the want of a Gospel in this Place which is the case in all new settlements for some time. But I expect we shall be able to build a church, and keep a minister before a great while."

The Scot had received letters from his brother requesting information on settling in Canada from their friends back in Scotland. The Scot replied he considered there was "more danger in giving advice" as "so many who came to this country had foolish and extravagant notions of it; and when they find that it is not all that their fertile imagination pointed out to them, they return home sick."

The Scot suggested to "all our friends, who are accustomed to warning, and can bring a little money with them, they are the fittest subjects for America," but they "need not think to find this such a clear country, where agriculture, roads, bridges & c are brought to such perfection as they are in Britain; on the contrary, the more prominent features of this country are woods, the trees measuring from 80 to 1230 feet in height, and in some places measuring 200 feet. "Even after these trees have been "cleared", it takes time before cultivation of the land can begin. Land for about ten miles around Montreal that has already been cleared is mostly "in possession of the original settlers, the French." The Scot considers their methods of farming much inferior to those practised in Scotland, so as they do not farm well and make the most of what could be good farm land and under a Scottish farmer's management could yield three times more. Because of the French seeing little value in their land and "generally part with it to some Scotch farmer for a trifle."

Farms a considerable distance from Montreal could be purchased for a "much lower" price. "A yeoman with a few hundred pounds at his command, upon looking about, can often have very excellent bargains of land, as a little ready money is a very tempting article in this country."

The Scot recommends coming to Canada with sufficient funds to carry him through the time it takes to fully develop his land or with enough money to buy already cleared land. Those who come without money may find it hard to spend considerable time and hard work chopping down trees in land to be cleared before they can make any income from farming. Some of the "ruined farmers" who set sail from Cork may well find themselves in this situation and in need of help from the charity set up to aid "strangers" in "distress."

It can be a good life. Many crops apart from cereals, fruit and vegetables can be grown, including Indian corn, hops, melons, grapes and pumpkins. The juice from the maple tree enabled them to make "plenty of good sugar, molasses and vinegar." Farmers living a distance away from a settlement can be self-sufficient as they "commonly feed their own beef, pork, mutton and veal, make their own soap and candles, and if they choose, make their own cloth." They would not be poaching by gaining food from the river or land as they could "fish, shoot, and hunt without tax or molestation." Any surplus produce could be taken to market and sold.

So, although Canada "may not be as agreeable as the fine clear farm in Scotland, yet the industrious man will soon come to have a very comfortable living in it, and bounty will follow by degrees. Here the man with a few hundred pounds, say from one to four, has nothing to fear. Those who have little can expect hard work for a time. The most of the trades' people, except in the large towns, have to perform, the part of mechanic and farmer alternatively. The blacksmith's is the best – the weaver the worst; for what of his employment is not done by steam power or water, is performed by women."

The Scot has outlined a description of beginning a new life in Canada, emphasising the need for very hard work and preferably financial security. He tells his brother that "I assure you nothing would give me more pleasure than to see all my friends settled around if they were satisfied with the country as I am. But nothing, on the other hand, would give me more pain, than to see any of you coming out and returning home again dissatisfied with the prospects before you."

This letter has painted a picture of those British settlers who came across the Atlantic to start a new life in Canada. There was a huge influx of Irish settlers during the potato famine of the 1840's. In 1847, the ordeals of the long journey of three thousand miles, taking up to forty days was worsened by outbreaks of typhus, spread by lice. The numbers of emigrants was so large that numerous ships waited a considerable time to be inspected in order that quarantine measures at a hospital on Grosse Isle, a small island thirty miles downstream from Quebec, could take place. The bodies of those who died on board whilst the ships were in line waiting, were dumped overboard into the St Lawrence River.

Many of these families were paupers who had left Ireland for a better life or even survival. A considerable number went to Montreal, some quite ill from typhus or malnutrition. Homeless Irish wandered the countryside looking for help but the Canadians were afraid of the spread of typhus and kept away from them. In 1847, one fifth of the 100,000 Irish who sailed to Canada died from disease or malnutrition either on board ship or shortly after they arrived. Many of the men who did survive, walked across the border to settle in America.

John Hale wishes to return to England

John Hale had settled in Canada, as a Government official well before these events. He had wanted to return to England but this did not happen. His mother, Mary would have greatly welcome his return and would have ventured across the Atlantic to Canada to visit her son, his wife Elizabeth and their first child but she, although just in her late fifties, considered herself in "her declining years"[36] so she knew such a voyage could never be, despite the longing for the "happiness of seeing and embracing the dear trio."[37]

Instead letters passed between her and her daughter-in-law Elizabeth who seemed to be very close to her heart, as she always headed the letters with 'Dear Daughter' and addressed her in most affectionate terms.

Mary Hale longed for information on her new grandson, requesting Elizabeth to mention "from time to time the improvement the little fellow makes. Teach him to pronounce Grandmama, and in that word endeavour to convey the full extent of all that Love and affection I am already disposed to feel towards him." Elizabeth was a competent artist but although Mary Hale knew her daughter-in-law sketched mainly landscapes, when a second grandson, Edward was born, she wrote, "I well know the use you can make of your pencil, and I do not despair to have his picture drawn." Mary was to send "by the next month a box to Quebec containing woollen stockings for the baby and some useful pieces of linen for Jack, and one piece of calico for you." Distance may have separated Mary Hale from her growing family but she kept in contact and appeared to have them frequently in her thoughts.

Mary often asked her daughter-in-law for information and even gossip of their life in Quebec. She forwarded her own news of local events writing.

Gossip from England

"Tis quite proverbial that a woman's pen is always the vehicle of scandal. I am not conscious of often deserving this censure, but as an affair has happened in this neighbourhood which is the common topic of conversation, and as you are acquainted with the parties, I shall venture to mention it. Mrs. Markham of Stokesley has been detected in a naughty intercourse with Mr. Fawcett her neighbour, (p85) and there's the deuce to pay. Mr. George Markham has shifted his quarters, and is now with Sir William Foulis till maters are arranged with her Richard Sutton to take her home. He says this affair is to be brought before the House of Lords to obtain a divorce. I commiserate the situation of poor Markham with his nine children. He is deservedly, beloved of us all. His vain, foolish wife, I never liked, and as the vulgar saying is, 'An old ape has an old eye.' I saw this storm brewing some time ago, and the ventured to give this opinion to the ever cautious and prudent Mrs. Gary. The lady's demure looks and affected delicacy deceived everyone! I have always approved the more open heart and innocent unguarded manners in young women which may be seen through."

It would appear from the above that Mrs. Hale, although she says she is not a gossip, appeared gratified that her interpretation of Mrs Markham's "demure looks" and "affected delicacy" as being false had proved correct. Mrs Hale admitted she had never liked Mrs. Markham and it would appear she fully supported her husband.

Elizabeth Evelyn Markham was the daughter of Sir Richard Sutton. She had married Rev George Markham, nine years older than her, in London on June 6th 1789 when she was only seventeen years old. During their 13 years of marriage she had given birth to nine children. Another child, Sarah, would be born later in 1802 after the scandal first broke out.

George Markham and John Fawcett had known one another from childhood. They had both attended Westminster school and were fellow students at Christ Church College, Oxford. After he married, George Markham came to live in Yorkshire when he became rector of Stokesley.

When John Fawcett, a Captain in the militia was later posted nearby, George Markham regarding him "as a brother" welcomed him" into his family as such." Rev Markham was supposedly completely unaware that "the criminal intercourse existed five years antecedent to its discovery."

Witnesses stated Mr and Mrs Markham lived together in a "happy and affectionate manner" before "she became the victim of the Defendant's seductive arts." It would appear from evidence that the affair had been long term. Mrs Elizabeth Boys, who had been the housekeeper and lady's maid in the plaintiff's family, said, she went to reside in the household in 1795 quitted in 1798, "in consequence of suspicions she entertained of her mistress's infidelity." She thought John Fawcett entered Mrs Markham's room at night through the window of her bedroom but she insisted that at that time, Rev Markham "had no idea of his wife's criminal attachment to the Defendant."

This appears somewhat strange, even unbelievable, that an affair could have continued for so long in the house that the lady's husband was not aware of the happenings.

In January 1803, a court case for damages of £20,000 was brought by Rev Markham against John Fawcett. John Fawcett's pleaded for leniency, stating he had to sell his estate due to "pecuniary embarrassment" and "he palliated his offence by ascribing it to the excess of his passions, heated by his constant intercourse with a lovely and beautiful woman." He admitted he acted wrongly but he "hoped the jury in punishing him, would temper their justice with mercy." Because of Fawcett's plea the damages awarded were £7,000, not the £20,000 requested.

The divorce petition was submitted to the House of Lords before going to the Houses of Parliament to pass a Bill to finalise the proceedings. In both instances Garrow, the noted barrister at that time, presented the case for Rev. Markham.

At the time of the incident, Captain John Fawcett, a member of the militia was stationed near the Markham residence. Whilst invited to dinner one evening, a servant who waited at table, probably the butler, gave evidence that from observations he could not help making he began to entertain suspicions that an improper relationship might be taking place between his mistress and Captain Fawcett.

On another occasion Mrs Markham gave a letter to the servant with instructions to deliver to Captain Fawcett. The servant had his suspicions the letter contained and appointment" so he decided to keep watch and that evening when he watched the house he focussed his attention on the ground floor window of the Mrs Markham's room. He saw Mrs Markham, alone, peeping out through a curtain. Shortly afterwards, Captain Fawcett, unaware he was being watched, approached the window, drew the curtain and climbed into the room before closing the curtain once more. The servant quietly approached the bedroom, drew back the curtain of the open window and looked into the room, where he testified under Garrows questioning that he had no doubt that adultery was actually committed.

It would appear unlikely that a servant, even a butler, would take it upon himself to undertake such investigations with his master's knowledge before proceeding to the master with such an accusation of the infidelity of his mistress. It appears probable the Rev Markham had his own suspicions and instructed him to observe his wife and keep him informed.

Garrow, on behalf of Rev Markham, by 1803, Dean of York, insisted on his client retaining property which had belonged to his wife as "he would have ten children the issue of this woman to provide for." Although all the ten children were legitimate in the eyes of the law, the above words appear to suggest Rev Markham may have felt differently about some of them.

After the divorce, Elizabeth came under the protection of her cousin, Lady Bath for several years. Her children would remain with Rev Markham. Lady Bath was the only child of Sir William Pultenay. Her[38] fortune "real and personal" was larger "than almost any individual in England". At her death in 1808, her husband Sir James Pultenay inherited "the interest for his life of all her personal property, amounting to near £600,000." They had no children, so after his death "this immense property is bequeathed to her cousin, who was the wife of the Rev Mr. Markham, son to the Archbishop of York." This fortune "is to descend to her children by Mr. Markham. Sir John Johnson, the Earl of Darlington, and Sir Richard Sutton, all inherit very large estates." Although the will was contested it would appear Evelyn inherited a very large sum of money.

Sir James Pultenay was born James Murray and had taken his wife's name. He died in 1811. John Fawcett and Elizabeth Evelyn Markham married, first becoming Mr. and Mrs. Fawcett later taking the surname Pultenay. In 1841, they are recorded as both being 70 years old, living in St. George's, Hanover Square. Both are registered as being of independent means. They had remained together and appear to have ended their lives in comfort in a very fashionable part of London. Mrs Hale would never know of what could be called a somewhat happy ending.

Mrs Hale, whilst declaring herself, not a gossip, informed her daughter-in-law of yet another untoward incident, this time concerning events at Harewood.[39]

"At present indeed the whole family of Harewood and their relatives have had enough to talk about with a thousand 'I daresays' and 'I wonder', etc., etc. for lo! And behold Miss Lascelles, of famous fat memory, has thought proper to elope with a young man who was either enamoured of her extensive person, or probably with her prospective fortune. His name was formerly Sheepshanks, now Yorke; his father is a merchant at Leeds, who has grown rich by his own industry and had settled £800 a year on his son, who I hear has been educated. Miss Lascelle's left her father's house very early in the morning, and herself opened the door into the Street with a bundle of clothes under her arm, and was married at St. George's Church, from whence the happy couple went to Swansea, where they will remain. I hear Lord and Lady Harewood are more composed than they were, and for my part I think it may all be for the best, for she certainly was a great Plague to them all, and as a Husband has long been her aim, she may in future be more placid."

This story is almost worthy of Jane Austen in its description of the elopement. Mrs Hale describes Miss Lascelles as not only being extremely fat but also of such a temperament as to be a plague to her family. Despite these apparent disadvantages, Miss Lascelles was desperate to be married. The young man appears reasonably wealthy and Mrs Hale scathingly admits she "believes he has been educated", but it is considered he either is 'enamoured' of Miss Lascelles 'enormous person' or is a fortune hunter, the alternative she probably leans toward. Mrs Hale appears extremely surprised at the young lady's initiative in actually opening the door herself whilst carrying her bundle of clothes before venturing into the street unchaperoned.

Mary Ann Lascelles, the Harewood's youngest daughter ran off to London to marry her intended, Richard York in St. George's Church, Hanover Square on 20th April 1801.

Richard's father, Whittell York, formerly Sheepshanks was a prominent merchant and financier in Leeds. He had served his apprenticeship in Leeds after leaving the residence of his father, a yeoman farmer. Richard and Mary Ann did not remain in Swansea. Their son Edward York was born on 5th June 1802 at Harewood House.

Richard and Mary Ann went to live in Wighill Park about 10 miles from Harewood. They had a large estate employing estate workers and large house with many servants for its upkeep.

Mary Ann was only 56 when she died at Wighill in 1831, being buried at Harewood, the service conducted by her cousin Rev Robert Hale who was incumbent at Harewood. Richard was living in his residence in London in 1841 with his son Edward and Edward's wife Penelope Beatrix. After Richard's death in 1843, Richard and Beatrix are in the house at Wighill Park with the five children, two governesses and 17 servants, as well as numerous estate workers.

The Harewood's had recovered from the shock of their youngest daughter eloping with a man they considered unsuitable. The couple were not banished but lived nearby and were probably accepted.

Mary Hale would not know the full outcome of her two scandalous accounts. Mary died on 27th October 1803. Her husband, John did not survive his beloved wife Mary for long as he died on 20th March 1806.

Mary Hale's sister Anne

Their son Henry, who served as a sea Captain for the East India Company, married Elizabeth Hildyard. He died in May 1818, so he too did not live to see his daughter Elizabeth marry the Rev John Burdon in Acomb Church, near York, on February 13th 1847 although Elizabeth's mother did attend the wedding. When John Burdon (The brother of Rowland Burdon v) got his living at English Bicknor, the couple left for a life there to raise up their family.

Henry Baker Tristram

The Rev. Henry Baker Tristram was appointed curate of St. James' Church Castle Eden in 1849. Prior to his appointment he served as a naval and military chaplain in Bermuda. In 1856, when he became ill and was advised to travel abroad to a warmer climate he journeyed to Algeria. Rev Tristram wrote of this time;[40] "I traversed the Sahara about 800 miles from West to East. The Eastern part is far more the interesting, with many shallow salt lakes, low hill ranges covered with sand, and a fair proportion of big game. The lion now (1900) quite extinct in these regions, was then common. One day I left camp with an Arab servant, both mounted, to meet my companions and our party at an indicated spot about nightfall. We were exploring for natural history purposes, and my gun was only charged with small shot for birds. All at once I came upon some broken ground and a nullah,(a small gully) and emerging from behind a bush a good sized lion. Without hesitation I fired right and left in the animal's face as he sprang. As good luck would have it, I blinded the beast, and he rolled over down the side of the nullah. When he got up he shook himself, and, not seeing me, trotted off in the opposite direction. Mr Arab servant made off as hard as he could when he saw what was happening, and I had some difficulty in making him hear my call." Elizabeth Burdon considered this event "thoroughly typical of the Canon, blazing away at a lion with small shot." This turned out to be good for the lion too and would not have added to their extinction if he had killed the lion with a bullet instead of temporarily blinding it with the effects of firing shot.

Rev Tristram's health improved and extended his travelling, publishing a narrative of his journeys in 1860. On his return to England, in 1860 the living at Castle Eden was £242 a year, but Rev Tristram had a growing family and would need a larger income, so he moved onto the incumbency of Greatham Church that had the added responsibility of Master of Greatham Hospital. In 1861 he lives with his wife Mary Gertrude and their six children able to employ a governess for the four elder children and a nurse for the two toddlers. There is also a cook and two housemaids in the household.

Prior to Rev Tristram's appointment as Canon of Durham Cathedral in 1873, he made extensive journeys in Palestine and other neighbouring countries. These journeys led to more publications like, "The Land of Israel" and "The Land of Moab." He also journeyed to the Turkish dominions in Asia, the Canary Islands and Japan.

His interest in Japan arose from his daughter, Katherine Alice Salvin Tristram who became a missionary and teacher at the Church Missionary Society School in Osaka. The school opened in 1879 and Katherine Alice developed the school during her stay between 1888 and 1925. Canon Tristram and several members of the Burdon family were amongst those who made financial contributions to the Church Missionary Society, some of which would have been to open and develop the school in Osaka.

Rev Tristram took a special interest in the study of birds. His interest was such that he had several birds named after him, like the Tristram's Starling, Tristram's Warbler and Tristram's Woodpecker. He was a founder and original member of the British Ornithologists Union. Rev Tristram was made a Fellow of the Royal Society in 1888. He collected bird skins and his collection was sold to the World Museum in Liverpool, several of which are still on display.

Henry Baker Tristram became a friend of the Burdon family. During "his eleven years incumbency at Castle Eden,"[41] Rowland Burdon "used to call for him for him several times a week for a walk round some of the farms or down the Dene."

Rowland Burdon's mother, Cotsford also sought Rev Tristram' company and intelligent conversation. She was now a widow and would appear to need stimulating conversation as she would send for him two or three times a week to visit her for lengthy visits. Cotsford's granddaughter Elizabeth did not know her grandmother. Elizabeth's curiosity prompted her to ask the life-long family friend, the then elderly Canon Tristram about her grandmother's appearance. After some hesitation, possibly to give him some time to think about her question he told her that her grandmother was "rather like a tiger."[42] Elizabeth did not record her reaction to this description of her grandmother. The "tiger" description appears odd, but Rev Tristram would have heard the stories about Cotsford's father, Colonel Matthews and may have associated her with a tiger because of India and the death of the Colonel at the hand of Tipu Sultan, also referred to as Tipu Tiger. He knew so much about the family through these stories that he wrote a short account of the family's history.

Rev Bird and the development of the school

Rev C. R. Bird became Rector of Castle Eden when Rev Henry Baker Tristram moved to Greatham to take up his position as rector of the church and Master of the Hospital at Greatham. Elizabeth describes Rev Bird as [43] "a gentle, worthy little man, of the old-fashioned low-Church type."

Mr Bird showed great interest in education at Castle Eden Boys School. In 1858 there were two National School in Castle Eden, one for boys and the other for girls.

The schools were chiefly supported by Mr. and Mrs. Burdon. Mrs. Burdon was benefactor of the Girl's School, reputedly the "best Elementary School in the county." Miss Urwin, the mistress, remained in the village after her retirement and no such sewing, knitting or darning has been seen since her time."[44] There would be other lessons but it appeared greatly important that girls learn handicraft skills.

Miss Urwin was a pupil teacher at the school under Miss Lumley, receiving her teaching certificate in 1868, becoming a qualified teacher and taking over the running of the school shortly afterwards when Miss Lumley left.

Mrs. Burdon frequently visited the school. At times she taught lessons in arithmetic, dictation and sometimes religious education. Mrs Burdon taught the children some of the time when Miss Unwin was ill but still attending school. During Miss Unwin's absence due to ill health, Mrs. Burdon went into the school for a whole week to teach. Anne Malet Burdon appears very interested in education and is more than willing to be involved in the process.

Mrs. Burdon inspected the school and the reports are recorded. She is most complementary for example on June 18th 1868, part of the reports records that she was much pleased with the work of the school. The children she found to be lively and intelligent.

There is an instance of an inspection by Anne Malet's husband Rowland. His inspection was complimentary but he considered the children read too quickly, possibly more a comment on his own slow, deliberate way of talking. After Rowland Burdon's death, his widow Anne Malet continues to visit the school but her brother-in-law Rev John Burdon continues with the inspections. In July 1881 he remarked that;[45] "The children passed an extremely good examination and the school continues to be in all respects in a high state of efficiency. The spelling and arithmetic were especially well done, and the Grammar too; while the needlework deserves very good praise!"

The curriculum contained a great deal of religious education. It could be considered a Church School. Rev Bird often visited and sometimes Mrs. Bird. They gave missionary tea parties at the Rectory for the children. Rev H.B. Tristram also visited the school on a number of occasions as did Rev R. Taylor. Rev Bird sometimes gave poetry lessons to the children, so his influence was not solely centred about religious education.

Geography lessons were diverse, including; coalfields in Britain, Loughs in Ireland, Friths of Scotland and the Lakes, Plains and Valleys of Europe.

At the Boys' School in Castle Eden, the boys studied mainly drawing, reading, writing, dictation, mental arithmetic, singing, scripture, history and geography. Mr. Bird visited the school to examine the reading; new books having to be bought by the boys themselves. He also examined the boys on the catechism and subjects like New Testament history. Rev Bird also did some teaching, some religious education but notably singing lessons. He appeared very keen to establish a boys' choir in St. James' Church, and frequently visited the school on afternoons to give singing lessons, principally using sacred music.

Education was not statutory or free, fees being paid quarterly. During hard times some children left school when the family could not pay. At times attendance was low. Bad weather meant children from a distance did not attend. Many boys came from agricultural backgrounds and during busy times, like potato picking and hay making they would be absent to work in the fields. Girls would also do agricultural work particularly during harvest and haymaking times. There holidays at harvest time and on the day of the local agricultural show.

There was an annual school outing usually to the nearby seaside. Rev Bird organised Missionary Tea parties for instance, there was a school holiday on the 25th August with a Missionary Tea Party in the schoolroom on the afternoon. Rev Bird's second daughter Mary, aged about four in 1863, later became a missionary, being the first woman missionary in the then Persia. The missionary teas appeared to be an annual occurrence so it probable Rev Bird's interest in missionary work influenced his young daughter Mary.

Boys from Castle Eden Colliery attended the school and to encourage their attendance it was agreed in August 1864 that the boys from the colliery could pay monthly rather than quarterly making payment by the parents easier. These boys left one year later in 1864 when a new school opened in the colliery. A new school was opened in Castle Eden in May 1867. This school was much larger and more convenient.

The boys were not always well behaved. There are reports in the school log book of the class being punished by having to work on compound multiplication and division exercises because they were 'light spirited.' Classes got noisy when they were just supervised by monitors, with the 'little ones' appearing to be the noisiest. It was noted that care needed to be taken with one boy in particular because he was inclined to be disobedient and he had a very peculiar temperament. In November 1864, Mrs Nimmo made a complaint to the school that some boys were throwing stones at the workings at the brewery.

When some boys left the school, the reasons were recorded. Families moved from the area, mainly going to Hartlepool. Boys left school to work. One became a shepherd, two boys went to a place on a farm one farm being at Billingham and another boy left apprenticed to a grocer. One boy's education had been paid for by a Roman Catholic curate. This boy left when a Catholic School opened in Hutton Henry in 1863. Some boys did not attend throughout the year as they were needed to do agricultural work at busy times of year. Weather could affect the boy's attendance especially those boys who lived some distance from the school. Many of the children did not attend school at all.

There was a school at Castle Eden Colliery. Mrs Burdon also visited this school. Miss Burdon made frequent visits and both Misses Burdon sometimes visited together. Miss Burdon was probably Fanny, the sister with the 'generous nature' rather than the 'querulous' Mary Burdon. Miss Burdon repeatedly gave material, like patchwork and calico as wells as sewing cottons to the school for the girls to use in sewing lessons.

The children appeared to mainly sew the patchwork but they also made flannel shirts. It was recorded that a small girl of only six had completed sewing a chemise. Miss Burdon brought in patterns for a bag and an apron, so girls would have other useful articles to sew. The girls also knitted stockings. Sometimes the girls would sew whilst stories, like 'Babes in the Wood' were read aloud, usually by the teacher. Sometimes a child read aloud, one child reading the story of 'Cinderella' to the children as they sewed. It would be very useful for these girls to learn to sew and knit, some seeming very capable at a very young age.

A gift of 10/- was given to the headmistress 'to get some necessary articles' for her room. Miss Burdon gave a basin and towels to school so the girls could wash their hands.

There appear to have been at least two outbreaks of typhoid in Castle Eden Colliery; quite a serious one in January 1868 and less serious recurrence in May of that year. The following January 'many' in the colliery village were 'dangerously ill' with typhus. On January 1868 it was recorded that the pits were working at less than half time and many people had left the colliery. Many other children had left because they were unable to pay the school pence.

Attendances of the children dropped at the school mainly because of the apparent poverty in the colliery. Typhus is often associated with poverty and overcrowding. Typhoid may also be a poverty indicator. There were outbreaks of measles, whooping cough and scarlet fever amongst the children, maybe undernourished if times were hard because work was scarce and money low.

Families were leaving removing to nearby collieries like Wingate, Haswell and Ferry Hill.

Whilst some left, others arrived from local collieries and further afield like Cornwall and the Staffordshire potteries.

The population was fluctuating, as were the pupils' attendance at the school. During times of little work when income was low children left as the parents could not pay. If there was an outbreak of illness, children did not attend as they were kept away from school when there was a "dread of infection" when "more cases of fever amongst children" were reported. Children left for other areas. Incomers brought different children to the school.

Children were absent from school for other reasons. The weather played a huge part in school attendances in both schools. Children frequently had a distance to walk to school. Very heavy rain would result in the children wearing wet clothes in school. Snowstorms posed similar problems with sometimes roads made impassable by high falls of snow. Sunny weather also took its toll as mothers would not send their children back to school in the afternoon but take them to the coast instead.

The children had visited the coast with the school. On July 17th 1863, after the children said prayers at school, they marched down to the sea at Blackhall Rocks and spent the day playing in the sand, throwing stones in the water, singing and playing games before returning to the Colliery at 4pm."

It is possible such an enjoyable day had prompted some children to request their mothers for further such outings to the coast. Children also absented themselves from school on one recorded instance on 18th May 1865 when a menagerie visited the colliery. Girls were sometimes absent when their services were required at home, or they were needed to assist in the cleaning of the house. Sometimes the girls were needed to stay at home when their mothers were hay making and even assisted with the harvest themselves.

Frequently the incoming children did not appear to even know their alphabet. The fluctuating school intake together with incomers who had previously received no education and unstable school attendances resulted in much poorer inspection reports than those recorded in Castle Eden School. Despite these setbacks, the school did appear to improve.

Again the curriculum contained reading, writing, dictation, spelling, arithmetic, sewing, geography and a considerable amount of Bible Study. They also sang, frequently singing hymns. They had moral lessons on topics like disobedience and stealing. One recorded lesson was on soap, so probably the school encouraged hygiene,

The Rev Robert Taylor, vicar of Monk Hesleden, the main visitor, at the colliery school was sometimes accompanied by his wife Elizabeth. They would have known the Burdon family and they called their first-born son Rowland. Members of the Burdon family did support these schools with Miss Burdon their main visitor at the colliery school and Anne Malet more involved in the Castle Eden Girl's School.

The family had been involved in promoting education for some time.[46] In 1843, it was recorded in the press that a special fund had been set up to raise money for the "Society for Promoting the Education of the Poor in the principles of the Established Church".

Money raised was to establish schools in manufacturing and mining districts. Donations from several people, many of them clergymen included £200, from Rowland Burdon, Mrs. Burdon (Dowager) and Rev J Burdon £20 each and Mrs Burdon £10. It would appear £200 would be worth about £20,000 in 1843, £20 equivalent to £1000 and £10 to £500. These are substantial sums of money. It would appear they encouraged education for the 'poor' in industrial areas but linked this education with the teachings of the Church of England, emphasising the need for education to include strong spiritual and moral elements.

This involvement in education extended further than involvement in schools. Good schools needed good teachers. There was training school for male teachers in Durham but none for schoolmistresses. The original idea to set up a training school for schoolmistresses in Durham supposedly came from a conversation between Rowland Burdon and, Rev H.B. Tristram. It is possible the germ of the idea originally came from Anne Malet as she frequently visited the girl's school, did some teaching herself and would see the need for suitably qualified teachers. The nearest college was in York. The campaign to build a training college for schoolmistresses in Durham began in 1853. The idea of the college was to promote Church of England Protestantism; a religious rather than a secular education.

St. Bede was such a college in Durham but this college only trained schoolmasters. Rowland Burdon was on the General Committee of St. Bede between the years of 1839 to 1853. In 1853 he was chair a smaller committee which set up the campaign for a similar training school for schoolmistresses. The venture was not supported by the Archdeacon of York who favoured the college at York. This did not deter the three main advocates of the scheme, Rowland Burdon, Rev H B Tristram and Rev George Hans Hamilton. Burdon was Chairman of the Committee and Rev Tristram became secretary.

Rev George Hans Hamilton began his ministry as curate of Sunderland. He was then appointed chaplain of Durham Prison before becoming vicar of Durham, the Archdeacon of

Lindisfarne from 1865-1882 finally being appointed Archdeacon of Northumberland. He was made an honorary Canon of Durham Cathedral.

His time as chaplain to Durham prison greatly affected Rev Hamilton to the extent that in 1849, he initiated a scheme to provide a refuge for prisoners discharged from Durham prison. This resulted in the movement leading to the Prisoners Aid Society. In Durham this Society evolved into Durham Discharged Prisoners Aid founded by Rev Hamilton, clergy, local magistrates and local people. These initiatives, based on Rev Hamilton's initial model, spread throughout the country.

Rowland Burdon, as a magistrate, probably began his friendship with Rev Hamilton when he became chaplain for Durham Prison. They would have encountered female as well as male prisoners, probably seeing an education with strong religious content would benefit the moral conduct of females as well as males.

All three men saw a need for education, so they campaigned for a training college for schoolmistresses for Durham and Northumberland. Their initial objective was to raise money to buy land, build the college and suitably furnish the building.

Appeals were made in local newspapers. Money was donated, mainly from County Durham. The college was intended to serve Northumberland as well as Durham but donations were slower in coming from Northumberland. Rowland Burdon, Rev Tristram and Rev Hamilton visited various locations and individuals to raise the funds. Land was identified near Elvet School and Miss F.E. Bowlby promised £200 for this site. This land near Elvet School was not taken up. The eventual site of the college was decided in February 1856. The money was eventually raised and the college opened in 1858. This college, the Durham Diocesan Female Training School was later renamed St. Hild's.

Rowland Burdon and the Hartlepool Hospital

The Hospital in Hartlepool was also named after St Hilda; St Hilda's Hospital in what became known as Old Hartlepool. The Friarage Manor House was built about 1605 on the site of a former Francisan

Friarage, believed to have incorporated some of the monastic buildings. The building was described in 1928;[47] "The disused building which was standing in the early part of the last century (19th C), was a large rectangular gabled mansion with mullioned and transom windows, erected probably in the latter part of the 16th or beginning of the 17th century. The walls were tolerably perfect in 1825, but the roof and some of the gables had disappeared. Very little or nothing of this building now remains in the Hartlepool Hospital, which occupies the site and has developed from it. Used at one time as a workhouse, the building was converted to a hospital in 1865 and rebuilt with the exception of a small portion at the east end in 1889. The grounds are enclosed by an old stone wall."

During the early years of the Poor Law (HM 1889) the Friary was used as a workhouse for the district under the jurisdiction of the Poor Law Guardians of Stockton. Hartlepool became a separate Union in 1859 and a new Workhouse on a different site was built between 1860 and 1861. The Friary was left to fall further into disrepair.

Rowland Burdon[48] converted the front part of this building "at his own expense" into a hospital large enough to "accommodate twenty five patients." In order to run the hospital, he applied to the "Charity Commission for a grant of £100, to be allowed on terms proposed" by him "and with several contributions it is thought the hospital will be self-sustaining."[49]

"Part of the funds of the Henry Smith Charity were appropriated to the use of the Hospital. But with the progress of the 'Pools' and the increase of the population larger accommodation was required, and the scheme for the extension of the Hospital was brought before the Governors in April, 1884. Plans were submitted and several subscriptions promised at the time. In consequence of the depressions of trade, however, the matter was left in obeyance for some three years, when operations were again commenced, with the result that the present commodious extension was completed at a cost of £3,600 towards which the Rev J. Burdon, of Castle Eden, and several other friends of the institution have subscribed largely, albeit the whole cost of the enlargement has not yet been met."

Further money was needed to be met by subscriptions, donations and fund-raising events like that described in October 1889;[50]
One of the most successful entertainments that has ever taken
place at the Athenaeum West Hartlepool was enjoyed by a crowded
and fashionable audience last night. The Athenaeum commenced
in October 1851 was completed in the summer of 1852. The large
Italian style building stood in Lynn Street in was then considered
the new town. Inside the building there was a school-room, kitchen,
laboratory, and storeroom on the basement floor. The ground-floor
housed a news-room, library, two classrooms and two rooms for
the house-keeper. On the upper floor there was a lecture-room
measuring seventy feet by thirty five feet. This room had a coned
ceiling, space for a gallery and ventilating arrangements. The upper
floor also had a retiring-room with connected offices.

The cost of the building was about £1,100. The site and stone
materials were contributed by the dock company, through Ralph
Ward Jackson. He also privately contributed £100.

In 1865, Rowland Burdon laid the foundation stone for a New
Mechanics Institute, with the Athenaeum being used for other
functions. He delivered a speech at the ceremony saying that;[50]
"wonderful improvements" had "taken place in Hartlepool which a
few years ago was a fishing village, and now was a most important
place." He thought that a "important change had taken place in the
whole country...a great change had taken place in the working class
that in the estimation in which they were held." There was applause
after this comment. He continued with, "Englishmen had always
boasted of their freedom, though centuries Ago they did not enjoy
the same privileges and advantages they did now...Now, the son of
a blacksmith, or other working man, might elevate himself by his
own exertions and talents independent of the favour of the public.
In all times...there were persons of wealth and rank who used their
influence to obtain privileges not consistent with their talent but he
trusted the remains of the system were dying out. (Hear hear)... In
this country the working classes had risen.... The working classes
were being elevated quietly and slowly but surely. ...By their patient
and good sense the working classes of England had not attempted

suddenly to seize power; and from good conduct on their part, and confidence, the power had come to them. ....the working classes wished to be instructed and the wealthy wished to assist them. (Applause)... The benefits to be derived from mechanic institutions were numerous. They assisted the working class to avoid the scenes of low, debasing pleasures and morally dangerous temptations of the ale house. (Hear hear) Such institutions afforded an opportunity to members of improving their positions, and rising to distinction; and there was now not the slightest opposition to the working classes bettering their positions. In educating themselves the working classes tended very much to increase the prosperity of the country which was much due to such men as Watt and Stephenson... Those were the sentiments in which he entirely participated, and he thanked the members of the institute for permitting him to utter them. (Loud applause.)"

The Athenaeum would still be used for the type of events organised by Mr. Herskind. At the last meeting of the Governors of the Hospital it was announced that Mr. Herskind had offered to give a concert for the benefit of the Extension Fund of the Institution, and the offer was thankfully accepted. The success of the event has realised the highest anticipations. The entire sum realised by the sale of the tickets was devoted to the fund. The patrons include the Marquis of Londonderry, the Mayors of the two Hartlepools, Mr T. Richardson M.P. & c" The amount raised by ticket sales was £72 10s with Mr Herskind adding money to make this up to £150 to be handed over by cheque to the Hospital fund. Mr Herskind not only gave a handsome donation, but he had also arranged and paid for the concert. There were musicians and singers mainly playing classical music including a piano piece by Chopin. Mr Herskin himself along with Herr Eckener and Herr Robert Hansen played pieces on the piano, violin and violoncello. Alfred Eckener was a 27 year old German Professor of the Violin, so he probably played the violin.

Fritz Holger William August Herskin was a born in 1831 in Denmark. He was naturalised in 1870. By 1871 he owned at least seven ships and had a business as a coal merchant in Hartlepool. He died in 1907 whilst living at 19, Lancaster Gate, Middlesex. He lefty £15,085, so he was a wealthy man. In 1889, whilst he still lived in Hartlepool and ran his business from there he wanted to give some of his wealth by making a generous donations to the building of a hospital in Hartlepool.

Later additions to the hospital included the Morison Memorial Wing, costing £10,000 opened on August 1926 by Princess Mary, Viscountess Lascelles.

Mary, Princess Royal was the only daughter of King George V and Queen Mary. She married Viscount Lascelles in February 1922 and became Countess of Harewood in 1929. Their seat was Harewood House.

The Lascelles connection returns to the Chaloner family when Anne Chaloner married Edward Lascelles in 1761. Anne's sister Mary later married John Hale, the grandparents of Elizabeth Anne Hale who married Rev John Burdon in 1847. Possibly this distant family connection influenced such a prestigious lady as Mary, Princess Royal to open the new wing of the hospital in 1926, when John, son of Col. Rowland Burdon was Chairman of the hospital.

Other members of the Burdon family were involved in the hospital. In 1929, the then Mrs Burdon was President of the Hartlepools Hospital Ladies Linen League. As well as monthly meetings, the League held fund-raising event like the Garden Fete held in July 1929. There was a 'large company present" who "thoroughly enjoyed the excellent programme of events,"[51] including entertainment of; popular music by the Old Boys' Band, the Excelsior Male Voice Choir, a conjuror, a ventriloquist, as well as attractions which included; a coconut shy, hoop-la, fortune tellers, a treasure hunt, competitions and tea and refreshments served on the lawn.

The fete was opened by Mrs. Burdon at 3pm. The Mayor, who was also to 'senior honorary physician' to the hospital introduced Mrs Burdon and "paid a high tribute to the excellent work carried out by the Linen League, who, by untiring efforts … succeeded in providing the whole of the linen ,blankets etc rendered without cost" for the hospital. Mrs Burdon followed his introduction with a lengthy speech on the work of the League, not only urging the large numbers present to give generously to the cause but also encouraging others to join the League. The hospital needed a building but running costs even down to blankets and bed linen had to be funded in order to sustain the upkeep.

When Col. Burdon later resigned his presidency of the hospital in 1936 he severed a family link which had been unbroken since the institution was founded and also a personal association with the hospital lasting 42 years.

The hospital had undergone extensions as the two Hartlepools had grown and the population had increased. Old Hartlepool was as Rowland Burdon said in his address at the stone laying ceremony in 1865, had once been a small fishing village.

The Development of Hartlepool

This Hartlepool became frequently referred to as Old Hartlepool. It was an old place with history going back a long time. In 640, an Anglo-Saxon monastery for men and women was founded here by St Aiden. The first Abbess was St Bega. She was followed in 649 by St Hilda who remained there until 657 before moving to Whitby. The connection with St Hilda accounts for the medieval church in Hartlepool being dedicated to St Hilda, the subsequent naming of the hospital as St Hilda's and probably the naming of the schoolmistresses college in Durham as St Hilda's.

The Danes destroyed this monastery in the 9th Century with the Friary being constructed after the Norman Conquest. This in turn was destroyed in the dissolution in 1547, leaving no trace other than masonry in the Friarage field. The Friary Mansion was built on the site of the Franciscan Friary.

Fishing was the mainstay of the town. In the early 1800's it was recorded that;[52] "In summer Hartlepool is much frequented by invalids, and by families from the interior, who resort thither for the benefit of sea air and bathing. There are many good lodging houses for their accommodation, but the want of an inn, upon an extended establishment is much lamented, is most sensibly lamented; a warmbath recently erected, a floating bath, & c offer the usual advantages to be met with a watering place. The Town

Moor, the favourite resort of strangers, affords a most agreeable and interesting promenade…The prospect on the land side gives a rich succession of corn fields, gradually rising to a considerable distance… The 'Fairy Coves', or cells, which are near the north-eastern termination of the wall towards the sea, are circular excavations of about five feet in diameter, and about 12 feet above the shore large enough to admit a human figure.

The visitors would receive a welcome from the inhabitants. They consisted[53] "principally of fishermen, a hardy race, many of whom have not received even the first rudiments of education: their manners are very courteous and civil, especially towards strangers, their mode of life and thinking is characterised by stern and unbending discipline." This mode of life would change as more incomers, not those coming to take the sea air or bathe would descend upon the town to stay and work.

An Act of the Docks was obtained in 1832 to build Victoria Dock and with the building of the railway coal could be shipped from nearby collieries including Thornley and South Hetton first shipping coal in 1835, three collieries in 1839, two in 1840, 2 in 1841, Castle Eden and Shotton in 1842, and seven between the years 1843 and 1850. The population of the town rose. Between 1833 and 1834 there were more than two thousand incomers. In 1831 the population totalled 1,330. By 1851 it had risen to 9,277. Victoria Dock had given an immense impetus to coal shipments at the once small port.

In 1837, an Act allowed Commissioners of the Pier and Port. Rowland Burdon (IV), as one of the members of the old dock company became a commissioner.

This role evolved into the Hartlepool Pier and Port Commissioners. Rowland Burdon V was one of those appointed, eventually chairing the Commission. Ralph Ward Jackson's scheme for the construction of docks in the Slake was opposed by Rowland Burdon probably as new docks may result in less income for the Hartlepool Dock Company but the argument to save agricultural land may have been used.

The land at the west of Hartlepool consisted of a [54] "few scattered huts and brick cottages stood on the edge of sand blown flats studded with small mounds with here and there a patch of green where the long grass lifted itself above the blanket of golden and brown.

A little inland the grey tower of Stranton Church lifted over a few score houses in more orderly pattern, but around and beyond the land lay under the plough, dotted at wide intervals with farm buildings as it swept up to the Elwick hills."

Ralph Ward Jackson put forward a bill to Parliament to form new docks in Hartlepool. This bill received great opposition notably from the Hartlepool Dock and Railway Company, of which Rowland Burdon was a leading figure. This company had invested thousands of pounds into building Victoria Dock so they probably resented and mistrusted the scheme to build a new dock in close proximity to their costly enterprise.

Despite the opposition, in 1844 Ralph Ward Jackson obtained an Act of Parliament to construct the west harbour and dock, on the Stranton shore.[55] "Their plans comprised an outer harbour of about eleven acres, enclosed form the shore, with piers extending seaward to the low water mark of neap tides; and an inner dock of seven acres; the estimated cost of the whole being £52,400. These works were opened for traffic, on the first of June, 1847; and the company having become the Lessee of the Clarence Railway, the whole of the traffic of that line has been brought to Hartlepool since the west dock was opened… Their traffic, in consequence, very largely increased; being, according to their last statement, 578.876 tons for the year ending 30th June, 1851."

Alterations and improvements were made so that,[56] "in a period of less than twenty years the little neglected fishing town of Hartlepool" had a large accommodation for ships, able to afford shelter for "upwards of 1,000 sail of Merchant vessels at once."[57] Hartlepool had once had "no commerce – no trade- no manufacture – everything beyond a country blacksmith's, or a boat builder's shop, had to be provided." With the new docks accommodating such a large number of ships, there was "the want of ships." Ship building was "begun at a very early period of the commercial history of Hartlepool (p 56)… Mr. Thomas Richardson, of Castle

Eden, and Mr. Joseph Parkin, took the lead in 1837, by building the 'Castle Eden'." By the year 1851 they had built four more and along with other five more companies a total of forty four ships had been built.

The illustration, entitled 'West Hartlepool' was published in a book of 1851. Ships are entering West Dock, hence West Hartlepool. The construction of the west dock was the beginning of the two Hartlepools. More docks like the Swainson and Jackson led to greater expansion of the new town of West Hartlepool, an area that was once marshland and cornfields became a separate town.

In 1922, Elizabeth Burdon, daughter of Rev John wrote,[58] "I hope it has not yet been forgotten that West Hartlepool owes its creation entirely to Mr. Burdon" meaning her Uncle Rowland Burdon. Ralph Ward Jackson (1806-1880) (Hartlepool History Then and Now) is credited with the founding of West Hartlepool. Yet, Elizabeth has a point. It Rowland Burdon had gone along with Ralph Ward Jackson's original plans for extension of the port, the town would   probably not have been divided and the port just known as Hartlepool rather than having two separate identities.

Ralph Ward Jackson is regarded as the founder of West Hartlepool. As initially a solicitor, he was the legal adviser first to the Clarence Railway and later for the Stockton and West Hartlepool Railway.

The town of West Hartlepool's growth began around the new docks, soon spreading rapidly. As the population increased. Shipbuilding yards were opened. An Improvement Act was granted in June 1854, recognising West Hartlepool as a town with Ralph Ward Jackson chairman of the Board of Improvement Commissioners until 1870.

There were two now Hartlepools and by 1862 West Hartlepool had become a large trading port, the fourth biggest port in the country behind Liverpool, London and Hull. Population increased and by 1881, there were 12, 361 inhabitants of Old Hartlepool but 28,000 in West Hartlepool.

In 1862 Jackson resigned from the West Hartlepool Harbour and Railway Company. An investigation discovered he had "carried out business dealings which were not allowed under the terms of the running of the company." The business was taken over by the North Eastern Railway. Following legal battles by Ralph Ward Jackson left him almost bankrupt. However he was so respected in the town that he elected their first Member of Parliament in 1868.

It would appear Ralph Ward Jackson was not without controversy. In 1861 he was fined £5 for assaulting the new vicar of Greatham and Master of Greatham hospital, the Rev H.B. Tristram. As vicar of Greatham and Master of the hospital, alms houses for local retired men of good character Rev Tristram was entitled to the residence at Greatham Hall. This entitlement appears to have led to a grievance between them. Ralph Ward Jackson had a twentyone year lease on Greatham Hall and he appeared to suggest that Rev Tristram was about to make him give up his residence at the Hall. It would appear this was not the intention of Rev Tristram but the situation was a cause of conflict. An added factor may have been that Rev Tristram had been curate at Castle Eden and under the patronage of Rowland Burdon before his appointments at Greatham.

A path from the church went across the churchyard towards the wall around the church. A gated gap in this wall led to a continuation of the path towards the Greatham Hospital. It was a long established tradition that this gate gave freedom of access to all who wanted to use the path, even to villagers who wished to make their way across the fields, through the churchyard and into the village of Greatham. There had never been any previous restrictions on vicars using the path to make their way from the church to the hospital. The elderly men said prayers and attended services in the church. It was usual for the vicar to lead the procession of the residents of the hospital in their short journey to the church.

One morning in February Rev Tristram had been reading morning service in the Church. After the service he headed the procession of the residents of the hospital to pass through the wicket gate, down the gravel path and into the hospital. As the procession was drawing near the gate, Mr Jackson proceeded towards the gate followed by an unusually large crowd of people.

Reaching the gate, Rev Tristram found it was padlocked on the other side. By this time Mr Jackson was standing with the group of noisy supporters on the other side of the gate anticipating Rev Tristram's reaction.

Ralph Ward Jackson informed Rev Tristram he would open the gate for the residents, but he, the Rev was not allowed through the gate down the path to the hospital. Rev Tristram was at the head of the accustomed procession to accompany the residents back to the hospital. He was not deterred by Ralph Ward Jackson's comments, so he attempted to climb over the gate so once the residents had been allowed through, he could again lead them to their homes.

As Rev Tristram was climbing over the gate, Ralph Ward Jackson pushed him backwards onto the graveyard with such force that part of the gate was broken off, much to the delight of Jackson's supporters who cheered and guffawed at the Reverend as he lay on the ground.

There was a trial where witnesses testified it was custom and practice to have the gate unlocked for common use. Witnesses for the Reverend testified he had been pushed very roughly from the gate to the ground by Ward Jackson. Some of the Jackson supports disputed this. The bench agreed the incident had occurred as the Reverend stated. Ralph Ward Jackson was fined £5 and instructed to keep the gate open as a right of way.

The dispute may have been over the tenancy of Greatham Hall or there could have been a resentment by Mr Jackson for Rev Tristram's support for Rowland Burdon of Castle Eden. Rowland Burdon did have links with Hartlepool, the railways, docks and hospital. He was on committees attached to these bodies, so would have spent a considerable time in Hartlepool and seen the new town of West Hartlepool grow. These and other mainly local commitments took him away from Castle Eden, but the running of his estate appeared to take up a considerable amount of his time.

CHAPTER EIGHT
Life in Castle Eden in the mid-nineteenth Century

In 1858, Castle is described as having;[1] "Two National Schools one for boys and one for girls chiefly supported by R. Burdon Esq and Mrs Burdon…. (Rowland Burdon v) There is an extensive colliery in this parish, the property of Thomas Richardson and Co., affording employment to a considerable number of persons. There are also brick and tile works, a brewery, malting, and a steam corn-mill, small ropery, and a good inn at the railway station. Castle Eden Castle, the seat of Rowland Burdon Esq J. P. is a castellated mansion, pleasantly situated in a well-wooded park at the head of a deep ravine; it is a square stone building; the interior is elegant, and contains a fine collection of paintings."

Castle Eden Dene is described as "a picturesque spot and is much frequented during the summer by persons from all over the county. The public are admitted every Thursday by the liberal proprietor." Visitors would come to the Dene, then the property of Rowland Burdon.

Sometimes there would be organised visits to the Dene. In 1855, Rowland Burdon was president of the Tyneside Naturalists Field Club and the Dene was one of the places they visited the previous year. In 1854 they also visited places including, Brinkburn, Lindisfarne and Holy Island, Northumberland Lakes, Alnwick and Tynemouth. During a meeting in 1855, Mr. Hancock's ornithological collection was mentioned, suggesting specimens of taxidermy would [2] 'furnish the nucleus of a popular exhibition.' The Tyneside Naturalists Field Club eventually became the Natural History

Society. In 1884 a building they commissioned was opened by the Prince and Princess of Wales and their five children.

The Royal family had travelled by Royal train from King's Cross to visit the area. During their stay they were guests of Sir William and Lady Armstrong at Cragside near Rothbury. Cragside was the first building in the world to be lit by electricity sourced from hydro-electric power. Electricity was still a novelty, so the press recorded that "a light of such brilliance", placed on top of the building "could be seen from a great distance."[3] Sir William Armstrong owned Jesmond Dene Park, the site of his previous home and he bequeathed the park to the people of Newcastle so as well as opening the Newcastle Museum and Free Library, the Prince of Wales also opened Jesmond Dene Park to the public.

Crowds thronged to welcome the royal visitors. Preparations had been made for the visit. The workmen had a holiday so " for once we are all in a position to breathe air comparatively free from smoke and sulphurous fumes. The workmen at other times roughly clad and with smutted hands and face will appear in the most attractive garb. The streets on ordinary days are choked with laden waggons and ringing with a perfect babel of voices and clattering carts, will be thronged in a show with eager sight-seers, and will send forth a buzz of excitement or a loud hurrah as the royal carriage approaches. The factories and places of business have already hidden their architectual beauties or their abominations and monstrosities under flags and bunting so that the whole has the appearance of a fancy fair rather than that of a toiling, struggling manufacturing and trading town.... The decorations of the display no doubt add to the pleasure (of the Prince and his party) but at the same time convey .... a false picture or our river banks and towns. Tyneside is not a part of the globe which enjoys a smokeless atmosphere, nor is it the city it appears today."

The writer appears to be suggesting that after the day of celebration of the visiting royals, the people of Tyneside would have to don their work-clothes return to the toil and manufacture the grime and foul atmosphere that fuelled the wealth of Britain.

The Prince had opened the Museum in Newcastle. John Hancock collection was housed in this museum and the museum was named the Hancock Museum after his death in 1890. Rowland Burdon would have known John Hancock and his collection, probably very well. John Hancock had probably visited Castle Eden Dene as Burdon's guest.

Castle Eden estate consisted of 1,935 acres of land, the soil being sandy and loamy with a subsoil of clay and limestone. The main crops at this time were wheat, oats and potatoes. In 1851, Rowland Burdon described himself as a JP and farmer of 360 acres, the land he used as his own farmland. He was not just a landowner but appeared to be involved in the oversight of his estate and farmland. He considered farming and looking after his estate as his foremost duty. He appeared to frequently walk round the estate to inspect the farms. His walks in the Dene would probably include a degree of inspection into the state of the woodland and game. He probably also had an interest in the produce of the kitchen and flower gardens. At this time he appeared to have a particularly competent head gardener called Livingstone who in 1851 had grown calceolarias, four of which[4] "very beautiful" specimens would have been greatly admired amongst the numerous people who attended the show. Livingstone also won prizes for "fuschias, geraniums, verbenas, balsams, roses, pansies, antirrhinums and stocks.". He won a prize for four heads of lettuce that year but two years later took first prize for the best selection of eight vegetables. He also grew grapes. Rowland Burdon had donated some of these grapes for the seventy five guests at the Sunderland Victuallers Dinner in Hendon Gardens in March 1852. The Marquis of Londonderry had gone one better by donating pineapples for dessert. The gardeners must have been experts to grow grapes and pineapples for consumption in March.

Miss Mary Burdon may not have been such an expert. She exhibited in the pansy section in the Castle Eden Show in July 1854 but her entry was a group exhibited which much puzzled the contributors. Mary frequently walked in the Dene. There is a walk named after her which may have been one of her favourites. On walks near Gunnerspool, wearing a [5] "tremendous pair of boots" she would be "armed with a sort of hooked spud for nettles", so she was probably familiar with hunting round for wild flowers and may have discovered some wild pansies she exhibited in the show much to the bewilderment of the other contributors.

Mary, or probably her gardener, had done much better with the roses as they won first prize. These shows appeared to follow a pattern. As well as displays of flowers and vegetables, there was entertainment of bands playing popular music and an open invitation to visit the [6] "splendid and romantic scenery of the Dene." Visitors, "including all the gentry" enjoyed a special treat in 1854, as Rev H.B. Tristram had included a "beautiful display of stuffed birds" from his collection, "disposed at various conspicuous points." The Burdon's butler Sclater may have begun his collection of stuffed wild birds when he visited the display and saw Rev Tristram's collection.

The Agricultural Show was connected with the land. It would appear Rowland Burdon, carried out many improvements on his land. He appeared to have an interest in exhibiting his chickens and geese in local agricultural shows, frequently winning prizes. He also showed yearling heifers. A ploughing competition began on his land in 1857, with Rowland Burdon presiding at the dinner after the event.

At a dinner after his death a toast given to Rowland Burdon who had been president of the Castle Eden Agricultural Show for many years when it was seen as a great loss that the society had sustained in the death of Mr. Burdon. No doubt Mr Burdon was one of the chief moving powers of the society.

Rowland Burdon sat as a magistrate, being Chairman of the Bench for a considerable time. In more serious cases, he frequently sat at Durham Assizes as Chairman of the jury, sometimes hearing even more serious cases. He was also appointed a Sherriff of County Durham and in 1872 was appointed High Sheriff of Durham. His duties as a magistrate and management of his estate, along with other institutions like the Hartlepool Railway and Dock Company, Hartlepool Hospital and a College for Schoolmistresses appear to have led to him having a full, influential life in County Durham.

There was still reminders of conflict, even in his work as a magistrate when in 1857 Lord Adolphus Vane Tempest M.P. had presented Rowland Burdon as Chairman of the Durham Quarter Sessions[7] "with an interesting souvenir from Sebastopol, an inkstand formed from half a Russian shell mounted on a stalk consisting of three grapeshots."

This seems an unusual item to present as a souvenir and may have been something brought back from the Crimea by Lord Adolphus Vane Tempest. He was the son of 3rd Marquis of Londonderry had served in the Crimean, notably in the siege before Sebastopol whilst serving as a Lt. Colonel in the 3rd Regiment of Guards. He retired from the army on his return, becoming a Member of Parliament. He died in 1864 at the young age of 38.

There was a great loss of life in the Crimean War with the British Empire losing 2,755 killed in action, 2,079 who died of wounds but a staggering over 16,000 who died from disease.

Rowland Burdon's mother Cotsford died at Castle Eden on 6th October 1851 aged 78. There do not appear to be any details of her funeral. Not long afterwards, on 16th October, Rowland and Anne Malet Burdon, along with many other distinguished guests, attended the Annual Sessions Ball held at the Duke of Northumberland's Assembly Rooms in Alnwick.

In March 1851, Cotsford Burdon was living in the Cottage, the Dower House with her two daughters, Frances, Fanny and Mary Cotsford. As well as their eight servants they also had a visitor, Caroline Bowlby in the household. Caroline's maiden name was Salvin. She was born in Castle Eden in 1795. The Salvins were related to the Burdons by marriage, so Caroline Bowlby was more than just a family friend. Caroline was the daughter of Henry and Magdalene Barecroft Salvin, Henry being described as a gentleman.

Caroline married George Henry Bowlby, a Lieutenant in the Royal Navy. His sister Mary was the Mary Bowlby who offered the land to Rowland Burdon for the intended College for Schoolmistresses, although this land was not used. Caroline's husband George Henry's mother was Eleanor Elizabeth Salvin, so

George and Caroline were also related. The ties with the Burdon family were even stronger.

When Caroline visited the household of Cotsford Burdon in March 1851, she too was a widow as her husband George had died in October 1847. She may have been unwell herself as she died shortly afterwards on 24th June, aged 56 whilst at her sister-in-law Mary's house in Durham. Her death was followed later that year by the death of Cotsford Burdon.

Cotsford's son Richard Mathews Burdon had joined the Royal Navy, going to Naval College from the age of about 13. He too was a Lieutenant in the Royal Navy. It is possible he was influenced to join the Navy by contact with the Bowlby family. Richard also died at a comparatively young age on 13th January, 1866.

Richard Mathews Burdon

Richard was born on 9th March 1810. He was engaged to Miss Brandling but the engagement was called off. As a young lady, she rode in a race at Gosforth Racecourse when Jacky (John, Richard's younger brother) was aged just 12. Richard was about two years older than his brother, so he would have been of an age with Miss Brandling.

When Richard was about 13, he entered the Royal Naval College as a midshipman for naval training on 19th May 1823. He passed his examination for Lieutenant in 1829 and obtained a commission on HMS Thunderer from 20th January 1834. Whilst aboard the ship sailed round the Mediterranean under the command of Captain W M Furlong Wise. On 10th July 1834, Richard was suspended and put onto half pay because he was no longer employed as a Lieutenant. The reason for this action by Captain Wise is unknown.

What Richard Burdon did after this date is unclear. He does not appear to be recorded on either the 1841 or 1851 Census Records. The 1861 Census records him as being a patient in the Dinsdale Asylum. This was provincial licensed house situated near Darlington. There are 59 patients, all described as having past employments of note like, surgeons, accountants, army officers, solicitors or ladies or gentlemen. They were probably wealthy or had wealthy relatives to pay for their care.

Dinsdale Asylum, built as a Spa Hotal was a three storey, seven-bayed mansion, with accommodation for 70 visitors. In the 1850's people were declared insane because of mania, dementia, or melancholia. Women were sometimes incarcerated due to infidelity which was diagnosed as moral insanity, post-natal depression or what was known as hysteria. Those with the end stages of syphilis were often in asylums and diagnosed as lunatics.

At this time a more enlightened approach towards those declared as insane was beginning to emerge. In July 1858 it was written that; [8] "Among the mostly important signs of enlightened modern thinking about the proper treatment of the insane where the newly constructed county and public asylums, warmly praised as places where 'everything is done to cheer and comfort the unfortunate inmates....there are long galleries in which they associate, gardens in which they may take exercise; they are encouraged to be cheerful by every stratagem which the most thoughtful humanely can devise."

This was the description of the 'newly constructed county and public asylums'. Richard Burdon was a patient in a country mansion with a licence for looking after those diagnosed as insane. Dinsdale Park Asylum, built as a Spa Hotel, was set in large wooded grounds of 30 acres, near the River Tees; a peaceful and quiet setting.

Dr. Mackintosh the Superintendent, held the licence for Dinsdale Park. At the time of his application he was described as a 'very fit and proper person to be entrusted with the care of the insane. In 1862, Mackintosh wrote; [9] "Insanity, or mental unsoundness, is a positive state. It is a name assigned to a disease or disorder of the mind, but does not mean or imply an extinction of the intellectual powers. There is intelligence, more or less, in all cases of this class of mental disease ....witness the large number of them who are employed at this moment in trades in all the county asylums in this and other countries."

Dr Mackintosh sees insanity as a disease and sees the need for proper care for the sufferers. He probably thinks like some at that time that activities like writing, art, forms of occupational therapy and even learning some sort of trade could help in the health and well-being of patients.

However ill treatment in asylums did continue. In 1862, in the Pauper Lunatic Asylum in Sedgefield harsh treatment by one of the attendants led to the death of patient. In September 1866 there was an incident of neglect at Dinsdale Park. The attendants were brought to court charged with wilful neglect. One attendant, in charge of an 18 year old prone to fits along with another supposedly in charge of a man with suicidal tendencies, had left their charges without leave at 8pm one Thursday evening, returning to work the following Monday morning in a state of intoxication. Dr Mackintosh fined them £5 each as a punishment for neglect. These patients were put at risk but not treated so brutally that they died as the man had in the Pauper's Asylum. This may indicate Dr Mackintosh expected the best care for his patients. They would be paying patient s and he had his good reputation to uphold.

Richard's name is hardly mentioned in the family records so it is uncertain whether they visited him whilst he was in the asylum. Darlington is near enough from Castle Eden to visit. The asylum may have been chosen with care as Dr Mackintosh appeared to have a good reputation and the building with its pleasant surroundings would have contributed to the Burdon family considering Dinsdale Park a suitable place for Richard as a patient.

Richard died in Dinsdale Retreat on 13th January 1866 aged 55. His death certificate was signed by Dr Mackintosh, who was there when Richard died. He gave the cause of death as 'inflammation of the submaxillary glands two weeks certified'. Richard had only been physically ill for two weeks with an inflammation of the salivary glands that probably led to abscesses that became gangrenous or seeped into the blood stream causing sepsis. There were no antibiotics to give early treatment to such inflammation.

The address on his death certificate is given as Park Retreat Dinsdale. Dr Mackintosh probably did not like to refer to his hospital as Dinsdale Asylum. He saw the mansion as a retreat where patients could live in quiet surroundings with the possibility of being cured. Richard Mathews Burdon had been a patient for some years, so it would appear there was little hope of a cure for his mental illness. It was the inflammation that ended his life with the end being short and probably painful.

Richard Mathews left no will. His illness was short and probably unexpected but it is uncertain whether he would have been considered of sound mind and unable to make a will. His assets of £8,000 were put into administration with his brother Rev John Burdon named as executor. Richard's brother Cotsford was a barrister, trained in law. Rowland was the eldest brother. The four siblings followed a pattern familiar at the time: the eldest taking on the estate, the second going into the armed forces, the third the church and the youngest a profession – in this case the law. Yet it was Rev John who was named as executor. It is uncertain whether any family member visited Richard at Dinsdale retreat. John would have had to travel a considerable distance from English Bicknor. No family member was recorded as being present when Richard died. He had a very sad end.

Not long after the untimely death of their brother Richard, their sister Frances, Fanny, also died. In February 1867, Fanny and Mary were visiting Cheltenham to spend the winter. Fanny developed a bad case of laryngitis and she died on 3rd February in her 63rd year, again something which may have been cured by antibiotics.

Fanny like sketching but she also wrote poetry. The following is a short poem from her pen;[10]

> *"I envy no one birth or fame,*
> *Their title, train, or dress,*
> *Nor has my pride e'er stretched its aim*
> *Beyond what I possess.*
> *I ask not, wish not to appear*
> *More beauteous, rich, or gay;*
> *Lord, make me wiser every year,*
> *And better every day"*

Fanny was the kind, gentle person who everyone loved. The sentiments in her little poem give a sense of her caring nature and religious beliefs.

Fanny left effects of £20,000, bequeathing the estate of Little Eden to her brother John, her interests in the Stockton estate to her brother Cotsford and the residue of her property to her sister Mary. She did not forget her goddaughter Jane Boydell who received one hundred pounds Jane was the daughter of Rev Boydell, the vicar of Win gate who would have been about eighteen when Fanny died. She also remembered her servant, Susannah Dawson who received an annuity of £12 a year for her life.

Rowland Burdon died on Monday April 19th 1876 after what was described as a long and painful illness from cancer of the stomach. An obituary appeared the following day.[11] The article referred to the downfall of his father's fortune after the collapse of the bank but continued with; "Under these circumstances it was perhaps natural that the young man should have applied his whole soul to the acquisition of money, in order to free his ancestral estates from the debts which embarrassed them. Thus early compelled to take a keen interest in money-making, the pursuit of wealth became to him, if not a master passion, at events one of the great objects of his life. He made money enough to clear off the debts of his father. He made more money and still more money, until he had acquired a large fortune, but still the money making continued. Not that Rowland Burdon was a money grabber. He never lent himself top the pursuit of gold. He never forgot what was due to him who held the hall at Castle Eden, and who was the living representative of the ancient, honourable family of Burdons. Nor was he merely a country gentleman, a justice of the peace and a country magnate, than he filled a foremost place in the County of Durham.

His father had gained great esteem throughout the North by his munificent subscription and generous support to the erection of the Sunderland Bridge, he had also taken a warm interest in the prosperity of Hartlepool. His son concentrated his attention on Hartlepool when he succeeded his father as Chair of the Port and Harbour Commission, a post which he, with a few breaks, held up until the day of his death. Mr Burdon thus officially connected with the port of Hartlepool, laboured zealously to serve the town to the best of his ability. He made one mistake in opposing Mr. Jackson's scheme for making docks in the Slake.... Even after West Hartlepool had opened up around the docks, (he) maintained his self-appointed vigil as guardian of the Slake. In all the county of Durham there was not a more faithful concern.... With the grim correctness of a Puritan – if a Puritan can be imagined as a Tory – he used the whole of his influence – and it was vast – on the side of the Conservative Party. He was a great landlord, and it was to him a conscientious duty to exact the uppermost jot and tittle in the rights of property.

There is something of antique grandeur in the way which Mr Burdon ruled with patriarchal authority all those who surrounded him. He impressed upon all that belonged to him the stamp of his own individuality. In the county he long held one of the forward positions of influence of power...he has filled too long a place in the governing classes of Durham... Rowland Burdon was a tall, vigorous, well-made man, with the eye of one born to command. He was possessed of great administrative ability. He saw things clearly, expressed himself with lucidity, and never lost his self-control. He will succeeded by his brother the Rev. John Burdon, of English Bicknor, Coleford, Gloucestershire."

Rowland and Anne Malet had no children. His niece Elizabeth, John's daughter had always been very fond of her uncle. She wrote she was [12] "very much attached to my Uncle Rowland, and I believe it was a great disappointment that he never had a son to succeed him." Because of that Rowland's brother John had to leave his incumbency at English Bicknor in order to take over the running of the estate.

After the death of her husband Rowland Burdon V, Anne Malet decided to build a new residence in the parklands at Castle Eden. According to Elizabeth [13] Anne Malet was [13] 'somewhat of a doctrinaire, a lady of indomitable will." Much against advice from many the costs spiralled up to £30,000 when "aided and abetted by an unprincipled architect, to build herself a large house known as

Parklands close to the Upper Lodge in the Park. "She only lived in it two years, but she was thoroughly pleased with her work, which certainly showed tenacity of purpose. After her death it stood empty till 1887, when my brother Rowland resided there for a time after his marriage."

Rowland Burdon v had died without any children. Elder brother Richard had died so Rev John inherited Castle Eden Estate. The family had to move from English Bicknor and begin a new life in Castle Eden. They had many friends in the parish. Elizabeth Burdon had lived there since her marriage. Her children had grown up there. They would feel a respected part of the community.

Rev John Burdon and English Bicknor

The church of St. Mary where John Burdon became incumbent stands on the site of an outer courtyard of an ancient motte and bailey castle. The rectory with stables and kennels, is adjacent to the church. When two bridges were built in the mid 19th century to provide access to the churchyard, part of a ditch was filled in to enlarge the rector's garden. John Burdon may have used the extra garden to provide an orchard and grow apples.

The rectory was small, but in time Rev John managed to enlarge the house. He also continued building and restoring Churches in the area, including the Church at Lydbrook which he began in 1851.

English Bicknor is on the border with Wales, near the Forest of Dean. The area around English Bicknor was mainly agricultural. When John Burdon was there, there were large flocks of sheep, small herds of beef and cattle, pigs and some crops like wheat, barley and turnips. The 1871 Census is only 12 pages of records. This means there are few people living over a wide area, so he would have a widespread parish. There are farms and agricultural workers and three domestic gardeners. There are workers like sawyers, woodcutters and labourers in the forest who are employed in the wood industry in the Forest of Dean. A number of carpenters probably obtain work connected with this.

Charles Heugh, a proprietor of an iron mine lives here. There are iron and coal mines nearby like Coleford where the inhabitants are chiefly employed in collieries and iron mines.

English Bicknor was close to Symonds Yat, already a tourist destination at the time John Burdon was a Rector. John Burdon was also sometime rector of Welsh Bicknor which lies on the high ground between Symond's Yat and Lower Lydbrook.

In 1871 John Burdon now 59 and his wife Elizabeth, aged 54 are living in the Rectory with their daughter Elizabeth Ann aged 19 and her brother Rowland aged 13. They have sufficient income to employ six servants and sufficient room in the rectory to house them.

John's daughter Elizabeth gives an indication of the work Rev. John did in English Bicknor.[14]

"Lydbrook was his first venture (in 1851). This he built and paid for entirely himself; next came Welsh Bicknor. In this he had the help of ,the resident Squire, Stephen Allaway, but as the gentleman became insolvent before the church was finished, it is questionable whether Mr. Burdon had not to foot most of the payments after all. He also helped largely in the renovation and restoration of Ruardean and English Bicknor Churches."

An example of his help around 1873 or 1873 at Ruardean is recorded by Elizabeth;[15]

"My father went out one afternoon after luncheon, as was his wont when visiting many distant part of the scattered parish. He came back rather late, and my mother asked him, quite casually in the course of the evening, 'Where were you this afternoon, John?' 'Oh,' he replied cheerfully,' I have been putting the new weather-cock on Ruardean steeple.' 'What?' was her horrified rejoinder. 'Oh, the new weathercock', he repeated. 'But how did you get up?' (For Ruardean is one of the highest if not the highest spire in the neigh-bourhood, and stands at the top of a high hill, seen from all the 'four airts that blaw!') 'Oh, well, of course I went up inside most of the way, but the 60 feet we went up a ladder outside, and I had had a littler square scaffolding made at the top, and after we had put the cock on we had a little service there at the top, knelt down and said a few prayers, you know, and then – well, we came down again.' "There are not many old gentlemen of 60, which was his age at the time, who would have cared for a similar experience, and thought so little of the performance. It was greatly due to his exertions and help moreover, that Ruardean was restored at all."

As well as restoring churches, Rev John Burdon was greatly involved in his work in the parish, sometimes dealing with happenings in an unorthodox but effective manner.

There was a great deal of drinking amongst some of the locals and Elizabeth says that [16] "he had a good deal of trouble with the little public house near the Alms houses and nearly opposite the Rectory gates." The pub appeared to encourage drinking after hours and Rev John had repeatedly,but to no avail, warned a chap called Marshall the main offender against such practice. Not to be deterred, Rev John devised a plan. He was still a good runner, as he demonstrated at school by, keeping up with the older boys in the hare and hound chase.

Rev John waited outside the pub and Marshall rolled out just before midnight, well after closing time. Marshall took flight as he did not want a scolding from the Rector, running as fast as he could across the Churchyard. The Rev easily out ran Marshall, "and caught him by the scruff of the neck. Now, Mr. Marshall, sir, if you please, you will take your coat off (as his assailant did),

"Besides ministering to the spiritual needs of his parishioners, John Burdon and we will see which of us two is the better man.' That matter being settled, there was no more trouble afterwards."

This behaviour would appear effective but somewhat drastic and not what would expect of a Rector. Rev John had fought bullies at school. Now he fought who he considered a trouble maker. He must have put up a good show as there was no more trouble, from Marshall or anyone else. That is indeed an unusual way to look after the moral needs of his flock.

Elizabeth says that her father not only looked after the spiritual needs of his flock but he [17] "also attended to their corporal ones. Inside the porch door in the front hall at English Bicknor, stood a shabby little high cupboard with many divisions replete with many nostrums and drugs. How often have I seen him on his knees on the little mat by the table adjoining, weighing out ginger, 'colocynth and henbane', carbonate of soda, quinine, and even blue pill … doing them up into quite professional little twists of paper to be given to the waiting applicants. The summons generally came at dinner time, as being the most favourable moment for finding him in. 'If you please Mrs. Goodwin has come to ask you if you'd be so kind, etc.' and the symptoms were then fully described. Of course dinner was left to cool, and he remained glued to the mat till the weighing-out process was complete and the mixture administered. A good many of the old recipes from the other side of the family came in very useful on these occasions…. One of his parishioner-clients once came to him and complained of having swallowed an unusual substance (I think it was a pin). What should she do? 'You can either take a large dose of medicine or a large meal – I will provide either.' The suffering one chose the meal, and the next morning all was well!"

The above account demonstrates the generosity of John Burdon both in spiritual and material matters. He offered the woman a large meal which she readily accepted. Times were often hard in agricultural areas. The labourers had insufficient resources to visit an expensive doctor.

Rev John's brother Richard was a patient in Dinsdale Retreat, a hospital for those diagnosed with mental illness. The following story, by Rev John, demonstrates the sympathetic attitude John had towards those with such illnesses, and maybe the reason why he was chosen as Richard's executor.[18]

"I great many years ago (I forget the date) I had a singular interview with an insane person at English Bicknor. A parishioner by the name of Grindal had been sent to the asylum at Gloucester, suffering from a violent attack of insanity, but, at the expiration of several months, the symptoms had so completely abated that it was thought he might safely be sent back to his home in Joyford lane. A few days afterward, one Saturday night, I was busy with my sermon, about 12 o'clock, when my wife, who had been going round to see if all was safe, came into the study and told me she was certain she heard someone outside the front door – she could hear him breathing. I armed myself with a life preserver, went to the door, undid the fastenings as quickly as I able, and went out. There was nobody there, but in the distance, near the front gate, I saw something white. It seemed to be moving towards the house. I called to my wife, 'Get upstairs as quick as you can and keep out of sight.' I had a sort of suspicion of what it was. Presently, who should come up but the man just sent back from the Asylum. He was in the same condition as Saint George, the Patron Saint of England, is depicted, 'with never a rag on, fighting with the blood old dragon.' 'Well, Grindal,' I said very quietly, 'and what has brought you out at this time of night?' 'The Lord sent me,' was his reply. 'Oh, if that is the case please walk in!' Close to the door in the passage were two oak chairs, opposite each other, I pointed him to one, and sat down myself on the other. 'Rather a cold night, Grindal.' It was December, and the bushes were covered with rime. 'Yes,' he says, 'it is.' 'I have got some clothes that would fit you commonly well, we are about the same height; but what do you say?' 'Well,' he says, 'I have no objection.' So upstairs I went, leaving him sitting in the passage. My wife (who had been listening at the top of the stairs) soon helped me find an old frock coat and a pair of trousers, with which I returned. Grindal put them on, and seemed mightily pleased with his own appearance, I commenting on the fit and the turn-out altogether. 'Well, now what do you say to walking home; I'll go with you?' He made no objection. I then suggested we should start, that he might show his wife what a grand suit he had got on, so off we set, he making no difficulty. About a mile off, near the entrance to Joyford, we met some of his neighbours, who had just discovered that after leaving his house he had deposited all his clothes on a bush by the door, so wherever he had gone he must have been in a state of complete nudity. Here was a pretty state of things. They immediately proceeded to search in all directions, when they stumbled upon me. It must have been an immense relief. I left him with his friends and returned home. Of course we had to send Grindal back to the Asylum on the Monday morning and I am sorry to say that he died there two or three years later."

Rev John Burdon appeared to have a very empathetic manner towards Grindal and probably also towards his brother Richard. Rev John appeared to be able to steer Gindal into doing things without causing him distress. Without Rev John's help Grindal may have died from exposure and hypothermia on such a cold evening. It is possible Grindal came to Rev John saying that the Lord had sent him because in his confused state of mind, he knew he would get help from Rev John.

Burdon's predecessor at Welsh Bicknor did not have such generosity.

John Burdon wrote [19]; "My predecessor at Welsh Bicknor was a very singular man. Among other eccentricities he had a swing hung down from crooks in the ceiling, and when he was tired of reading (for he was a great student) he would ring the bell, and his wife, who understood the summons, used to come in and swing him. It was a casement window, so his legs appeared outside periodically every time he was swung. One day, Mr. Partridge, of Bishopswood, was calling on me (in nearby English Bicknor) and had witness this extraordinary phenomenon of legs showing at periodic times out of the Rectory window, from the other side of the river. He could not make it out, and was much exercised in his mind, till I explained matters. Old Segar was a great miser. When he died £5,000 in gold was found in the house, £1,500 in powder canisters behind the books in a glass bookcase; but not under lock and key; and the rest of the money in an iron safe where the registers are kept, underneath the registers, but neither was this under lock and key..... Latterly he kept no servant, his wife having died years before, and he used to put a penny on the doorstep outside, which a little girl used to pick up every morning when she left the milk. He always paid with a cheque, no matter how small the bill, that it might not be supposed he had any money in the house."

As well as this money in the house. Rev. Segar had money in two bank accounts, the amounts only coming to light when he died about 1845, not long after John Burdon came to English Bicknor as rector. He was certainly not a miser. He appeared to have similar qualities as a rector as his father reportedly had as a Member of Parliament. As a rector Rev. John Burdon appeared to have 'directed his talents and energies' towards looking after the people of his parish.

Rev John had friends in the neighbourhood. Squire Machen, older than John was a particular friend. Edward Machen owned the Eastbach Estate and lived in Eastbach House. On a Sunday afternoon in Summer Rev John used to walk with his friend along the Walks to Symond's Yat. Sometimes Elizabeth would accompany her father and Squire Machen. When they reached a 'small School House under the lee of the Crag', Rev. John held another service. They often did not return until 7.30pm for their late supper. Squire Machen looked after the Walks not only because he liked to walk but also to ensure they were well kept. To this day there is a tree near Edge End called the 'Machen Oak'. He may have planted this tree.

As owner of the Eastbach Estate, in 1851 Edward Machen improved the road between Eastbach and English Bicknor. During this time many farm labourers were unemployed, so to give them work John Burdon employed these men to build several new roads in the area to replace the old tracks. The road up from Lydbrook was a dangerous lane so Rev. John financed the building of the two miles of new road. It was completed in 1853 and became to main thoroughfare from that part of the Forest to Lydbrook Station. Rev John's wife supervised the erection of a stone drinking trough half way up the hill. Another road, from English Bicknor to Stowfield was finished in 1855. Rev John financed the enterprise to provide work for the unemployed farm workers. He chose to build new roads. His friend Edward Machen may have given him the idea but he would also recall the turnpike roads built by his father. This too would have influenced his decision to spend his money building roads.

Rev. John Burdon gave work to the unemployed in the building of roads, financed the building of churches, administered to the sick of the community who could not afford medical care and even chased an unrepentant drunkard across the churchyard before confronting him, so that he and his fellow trouble makers made no more trouble in the inn across the street from the Rectory. He appeared to care for the needs of his parish.

Rev John was very involved in his work of the parish making frequent visits to his parishioners. This work increased when he was made Rural Dean. He was involved in two clubs; the Men's Benefit Club and the Women's Clothing Club. Like most Men's Benefit Clubs they held an annual service. Theirs was on Whit Monday, when Rev John would officiate. A dinner followed the service and he most likely attended this also as it probably a very good dinner.

In 1868 Rev John Burdon became one of the original sharehold-ers in the Ross and Monmouth Railway becoming the first man to walk through the tunnel from Kerne Bridge to Lydbrook. He was also a visitor at Monmouth Grammar School, Rev. John was also a preacher of note. On April 18th 1860, during the Archdeaconate of Lord Saye and Sele, Rev John Burdon delivered the Archdeacon's Visitation Sermon in Hereford Cathedral, the subject being 'Unity in the Church.' His sermon was described as adding[20] "another discourse of great merit to those admirable contributions of 'sermon literature', which from time to time have been preached on this occasion."

After the service, at the luncheon of upwards of 70 clergy-men and several laymen, Rev John Burdon sat on the left of the Archdeacon with Lord William Graham MP on his right. During the usual toasts and speeches, the Archdeacon gave the health of the 'Preacher of the Day... alluding to the gentleman's scholar-like attainments as a first class man of Oxford, his liberality as having, together with Mr Allaway rebuilt, at great cost, and in a most beautiful manner, the Parish Church and his sound doctrine and eloquence displayed in the feeling discourse he had that day deliv-ered in the Cathedral Church. The clergy present wished him to request the publication of that sermon, and he felt great pleasure in making that request." The sermon was published very shortly after this request, a request that demonstrates Rev John Burdon's ability as a preacher.

When the news of the death of his brother Rowland arrived, he would be greatly saddened but he and his family, including his wife would probably have felt sadness at leaving the place which had been their home for so long. They would leave their friends and relationships built up over many years. Rev John would leave his parish and have to begin a new life in Castle Eden overseeing the estate.

Rev John Burdon in Castle Eden

Rowland Burdon V had died without any children. Elder brother Richard had died. Rev John inherited Castle Eden Estate. The family had to move from English Bicknor and begin a new life in Castle Eden. They had many friends in the parish. Elizabeth Burdon had lived there since her marriage. Her children had grown up there. They would feel a respected part of the community. In 1876, they decided to move to Castle Eden. Daughter Elizabeth says her mother [21] 'was not in good health, and she keen felt the wrench,' when they had to leave.

They took until May, 1877 before the move was organised. Elizabeth observed 'the change to a harsher climate and somewhat uncongenial surroundings' may have been a factor in the sudden demise of her mother about one year later. Elizabeth's account of her mother's sudden death is moving, as is the strange event witnessed by her brother Rowland.

"On Sunday, May 26th 1878, my father was taking the evening service at Wingate for Mr. E. W. Boydell. He had ridden over after tea, leaving the house about 5.30. The evening service at Castle Eden was at 6.30. I was to play the harmonium, up in the gallery. When we had finished our tea, my mother left the room, saying, "Now don't be late, Bessie" I was deep in a book and (to my sorrow) did not answer, but presently went and dressed and went on ahead. From the gallery you could see nothing of the pew where my mother sat, and I heard nothing further until at the conclusion of the service, I was beginning the Chants for the Choir Practice, when someone came to fetch me, saying, "Mrs. Burdon is ill" When we got to the Castle, I found her sitting on the ottoman at the foot of the bed in her room, quite dead, her hands stiff in the act of tying the strings of her hat, where the housekeeper had found her. Of course, the doctor could do nothing, but the saddest thing was having to go and meet my father and break the news to him.

My brothers were at Repton School at that time. It had been a beautiful warm day, and was naturally light till nine o'clock or after. My brother John was in a dormitory with four other boys in the Headmaster's house, and all were in bed. He became aware of a grey figure which came across the room from the door, and came and sat down on the edge of his bed (he felt as well as saw it.)

It bent over him, but he was too frightened to look up, and kept his eyes tight shut. When the weight moved, he looked up, and saw the figure going the same way it had come. In those days one could not telegraph on Sunday, but about 8.30 the next morning, the Headmaster (Dr. Peers) sent for the two brothers, and told them what had occurred at home the evening before. My brother never would speak of this occurrence to anyone at the time, and it is known to few even in our own immediate family."

It would appear that John jnr, and the family members who eventually knew the tale, thought John had seen the ghost of his dead mother. She was in poor health but had died suddenly apparently in the act of tying her bonnet before going to evening service. Elizabeth had felt distressed because she hadn't realised her mother was about to die and was so engrossed in her book she did not answer her. Her mother was probably used to this lack of response from the bookworm Elizabeth. All the while Elizabeth was playing the harmonium, and throughout the service, she was unaware her mother had not come to church but instead had died alone in her room, probably a quick and painless death. The worst thing for Elizabeth was having to meet her father and tell him that his poor wife had died at the time he was con ducting a service at nearby Wingate.

The two boys were told by the Headmaster the next morning in his office. John would have had a sleepless night, apprehensive about the incident in the night. He may have felt his mother had tried to say goodbye to her youngest child. Let it be hoped this may have been some comfort.

Death of Anne Malet

Sometime later, on the 10th March 1885, young Rowland's aunt, Anne Malet Burdon died. Her gross effects amounted to £80,903 8s 8d. This amount would have been much greater if she had not spent so much building herself Parklands. Anne Malet left her nephew Rowland the whole of the manor farms at Horden. John Caldwell Uhthoff, the grandson of her first cousin Edward Uhthoff received ten thousand pounds. Mary Gertrude Holland, once Trisram, also daughter of Canon Tristram, inherited five hundred pounds whilst Canon Tristram's son Thomas Henry Barrington received two thousand pounds.[23]

There were other large inheritances, including Rowland's sister Elizabeth Anne and his brother John George who both received two thousand pounds. Two thousand pounds was a substantial sum in 1882, but others unrelated like Fanny Anne Brent and Jane Mary Ann Boydell inherited five thousand pounds. Anne Malet may have considered her relatives had sufficient wealth and gave money to those she considered needier, or she may have just favoured them more than her nearer Burdon relatives.

Her niece Gertrude Uhthoff Hamilton did much better. She lived at Hampton Hall Balriggan Ireland. Gertrude was left £20,000 by her aunt but she also received all her jewellery, plates and a gold cup presented to Anne's father Joshua Uhthoff.

Anne Malet possibly admired Canon Tristram's son Henry Barrington and that may have why she left him £2000. Henry was clever, going to Oxford with a BA and an MA. He would become a classical master at Loretto School in Scotland rising to be Headmaster by 1903 before moving to London to become Headmaster of St. Pauls' School in London. Not only was he clever, he was also good at sporting activities. He played cricket for Durham County and Oxford University. He was even more skilful at rugby, playing for England between 1883 and 1887 and being capped five times.

Anne Malet had more to bequeath. The Cancer Hospital at Brompton had a huge legacy of £20,000. There were also substantial legacies to the Meath Hospital in Dublin, the Incurable Hospital in Dublin, the Consumption Hospital in Brompton Road London and the National Refuge for the Homeless and Destitute Children based in Holborn.

As well as large inheritances, Anne Malet left the smaller sums of five hundred pounds each to three servants; John Sclater the butler, Anne Roberts the housekeeper and Jane Darling the cook. Anne Roberts, now able to live on her own means, returned to Bedlow, Buckinghamshire the place of her birth to live with her independent unmarried brother George, a retired master of an industrial school. The cook Jane Darling also retired comfortably, returning to Amble near to Craster the place of her birth.

Elizabeth Ann Burdon who inherited £2000 and the kitchen crockery from her Aunt Ann Malet, [24] had some interesting things to say about the butler Sclater who inherited £500. Elizabeth called him "a most disagreeable person (except to his master and mistress), with a not very clear perception of the difference between 'meum' and tuum'; a clever old reprobate and a collector and curer of wild bird's skins, of which a large assortment graced the big table in the front hall, under a glass case. He shot or snared them on the sea shore, and got a great quantity of the migratory race in that manner." He did not appear to take his collection with him when he used his £500 to set up in a tobacconist's shop in Warwickshire with his family. Elizabeth says that, "one of my brother's first acts in his turn was to transfer all of these, 'lock, stock and barrel' to the Museum at Durham.....(so) they could no longer offend the eye and the nose of those entering the front door of the Castle."

When Rev John Burdon came to Castle Eden in 1877, he no longer had a parish to look after. He did, it appears, conduct services in other local churches when he was needed. Apart from those occasions, he felt he had make best use of his time. He decided to make improvements to the Dene by 'opening new paths and views, revealing the great natural beauties of the Dene.'

Jacob's Ladder and Gunnerspool had 'become quite wild' and almost inaccessible'. He designed a footbridge to cross the deep chasm. The bridge was made in pieces at Hartlepool and transported to the Dene. The pieces were put together and 'pulled across into position by chains and ropes.' This designing and building of a bridge, albeit on a much smaller scale, had echoes of his father's achievement in the building of Wearmouth Bridge.

The final stages of the building of the bridge occurred in June 1877. Friends, including Mr. Edward Boyd, gathered to watch the framework of the bridge being thrown across the chasm. Once this was complete and the framework in place, although there was no planking on the bridge, the bridge could still be crossed by stepping along the iron framework. The chasm is very steep so this is not a task to be undertaken lightly even though Elizabeth suggests;[25] "There was no danger in this whatever, if only due caution was observed (if you had a fairly good head, be it understood.) Rev John had a 'good head'. At the age of 60, he had clambered up a ladder on the side of a high church steeple to fix a weathercock on the top. Not only that he conducted a service, kneeling down for prayers on the small platform they had erected. His daughter Elizabeth probably considered stepping along the iron framework across a very deep chasm as something fairly simple, as she and others had done it quite frequently previously. The workmen had started laying the planks across the framework to enable the men carry red hot rivets to complete the laying more quickly. Mr. Boyd decided to cross the bridge, one hand on his stick and the other in his pocket. He stepped on the first plank, probably forgetting it had not been fixed by rivets and it was still loose. The plank tilted. He lost his balance, dropped his sticks, made a failed attempt to grab the iron rails so his legs fell through the opening between planks Although he dislocated one shoulder, he hung onto the framework with the other hand.

During this incident, Rev John had his back to the bridge, talking to Mrs. Hildyard, when she suddenly 'turned deadly pale.' He turned round rapidly only to see a man's hand clinging desperately onto the framework of the bridge, the 'body not visible.'

Rev John dashed to the rescue and started hauling up Mr. Boyd. Three of the workmen, at the other side of the bridge rushed across the unplanked framework to come to his assistance. They hauled Mr. Boyd to safety. Rev John admitted without the aid of the workmen, he alone could not have rescued Mr. Boyd. Rev John says that his friend, 'had a marvellous escape, and did not recover from the shock for a good many months.'

Elizabeth and Mrs. Hildyard witnessed the event. Elizabeth said it seemed like an 'eternity' before the men came to the rescue. All she could see was her father lying astride the framework desperately trying to hang onto Mr. Boyd, terrified that they both would fall through the framework before the workmen could come to their aid. She remembers the deathly silence followed by the panic in trying to bring round Mr. Boyd, who had fainted with shock upon his rescue. Someone sent for a horse and carriage. He was probably carried by the men to the point in the dene where the carriage could reach. Once transported back to the Castle, where he was swiftly despatched to bed rest for a fortnight. Elizabeth, recalls how 70 year old Mr. Boyd 'most looked picturesque in a red nightcap with a white tassel," the nightcap probably brought by his daughter when she came over to look after him. It is good the escapade had a happy ending, as the consequences could have been fatal for Mr. Boyd and Rev. John.

This incident does not appeared to have perturbed Rev John's confidence. Elizabeth says her father 'was always absolutely fearless.' She used to worry about him when he returned home very late because she knew he had been in the 'forefront of superintending operations, felling of trees, etc, and clearing down below the bridge to the edge of the chasm.' He saw no danger in this and 'could never understand people being nervous,' despite a precipitous drop of 110 feet down the chasm to the water below. Despite his ordeal Mr. Boyd did recover and so did his stick. When returned to him he had a plate engraved with the date of the accident fixed onto the stick. It was given, no doubt with gratitude to Rev Burdon.

Rowland and Mary Arundel get married: The trip to the South of France

About ten years after this incident, Elizabeth's brother Rowland (John's son) married Mary Arundel Slade on 17th February 1887. The wedding took place in St. George's Church Hanover Square,

London. (This Rowland Burdon will be referred to as Rowland Burdon VI when he inherits the estate.) Family members probably attended the wedding. Two days after the wedding and as they were probably already in London, visited the South of France, travelling via Paris and Avignon. Elizabeth accompanied her father Rev John. Whilst just about to board the train at Avignon to continue their tour, they felt a slight shock but thought nothing about it. They arrived at Marseilles and were amazed to see a 'tremendous crowd on the platform in a most excited state but could not make out what had happened.' They were informed there had been an earthquake. The tremors they experienced as they were about to board the train at Avignon were the much more severe in Southern France and Northern Italy when a severe earthquake occurred. Cities posted telegrams via Reuters and reports of devastation and fatalities appeared in newspapers throughout the country. Italy appeared to have fared worse. Villages were completely or nearly destroyed. Three hundred of the terrified inhabitants of a hilltop village, Bagado, rushed to the Church after the first tremor to seek refuge inside. The next tremor was more severe and the already damaged church collapsed, burying all three hundred inside its ruins. None survived. Three hundred of the 821 inhabitants of Caroo were killed or buried.

In Nice the Carnival Season had begun that had attracted many visitors, a great number of them English. There had been a torch-light parade the previous evening through the streets, some wearing elaborate fancy dress. The parade was followed by a masked ball. Some would hardly have returned to their hotels or lodging houses when disaster struck.

About 6 o'clock in the morning, houses, buildings and hotels rocked and shook. Walls cracked, some buildings collapsed. In panic, people, some in a state of partial undress, ran out into the streets. The second, more severe shock brought greater panic and alarm.

"Other two more shocks were experienced, and the panic deepened and extended. The squares were crowded with terrified fugitives, some of them on their knees praying for Divine mercy.

The wealthier residents and visitors hurried to the railway station as best they could, with a view to seek safety in flight from the stricken town, but up to the present traffic is impeded, owing, it is understood, to landslips on the line. Many of the hotel keepers and others dependent upon the pleasure and health seekers for their livelihood are half crazed with grief, and seem reckless to further disaster. The season is ruined and with it their fortunes. A few hours ago their prospects were of the brightest. Within the past week over 1,000 visitors have arrived in the town and most of them had arranged to stay over the carnival fetes. Now everybody is hurrying away, and intending visitors will give Nice a wide berth."

Not so for Rev John and his daughter. They were bound for Nice. They travelled on to Nice. Arriving in Nice, there were mountains of luggage with only one porter on the station. An 'excited old gentleman' rushed up to Rev John and 'assured him it was madness to go to a hotel there, as the shocks had been fearful.' Rev John did not heed this advice. Elizabeth said, "My father was, however, not at all the man to be turned aside from his purpose, so we went to the hotel, took rooms, and after a somewhat scrappy dinner, prepared to pass the night as usual, but there were several very severe shakes, and it was not altogether pleasant."

It would appear an understatement to suggest 'several sever shakes' were 'not altogether unpleasant'. It would appear Elizabeth was made in the same mould as her father.

They stayed in Nice for several days before driving along the corniche, a road running along the sea to Mentone. Mentone with its many luxurious hotels and villas was a town popular with English and Russian Tourists. Unfortunately a small tsunami caused by an offshore landslide had killed scores in Mentone. Nevertheless they stayed in Mentone. Not surprisingly they were amongst the very few people staying at the time.

Elizabeth decided to walk on the high ground above the hotel, maybe to better appreciate the view. To her surprise, when looking down on the hotel, she noticed part of the roof was missing. It is impossible to know whether there was any other structural damage. The church in Mentone had been badly damaged, so the early Sunday service was held outside under a large cedar tree in the grounds. At the service the Mayor gave information on the earthquakes and tries to calm the people, probably mostly towns people as most of the tourists would have left. They stayed in Mentone, despite the partially roofed hotel, for about ten days before leaving for San Remo, the approximate seismic centre of earthquake.

When they were in San Remo in March, they visited the village of Colla;[26] "a small mountain town, containing some 1,500 inhabitants, which is about 1,000 feet above the Mediterranean, and overhangs it. The road is a series of zigzags up the steep mountainside, very picturesque, but not altogether pleasant driving."

This description was written by Rev John Burdon and his daughter Elizabeth adds that this is "a wonderful thing for him to admit." Driving would involve a horse drawn carriage. The hill was very steep with many zig-zag bends in the road. Presumably the horses and their driver would be used to this journey but it must have been an ordeal driving up such a road getting increasing higher with a steep cliff on one side heading down towards the sea.

There had been no tremors for a few days, so they probably thought the danger was over and they were probably looking forward to their visit, guided by a young boy they had hired, to "see a gallery of pictures belonging to an old priest."

They alighted from the carriage at the edge of the town, following their guide along the extremely narrow streets. They were shocked at what they saw; "the walls of the houses, which had been dreadfully shaken by the earthquake, were shored up by timbers kept in place by other timbers stretched across the street."

As they walked through twisty side lanes they became increasingly apprehensive, as some of the buildings looked ready to collapse. They finally reached a small square where a crowd of about 50 people were assembled. A gendarme in the square appeared to on guard. Rev John approached him and pointed towards the side street they needed to go along to continue their journey. He shook his head in reply, implying they should not venture along that lane but should stay where they were.

Rev John continues the story of the earthquake

"Suddenly there was a great rumbling as of falling masonry, which at the moment I supposed was caused by workmen pulling down some house shaken by the earthquake, and which had now fallen bodily. But in a moment there was a loud screaming, and a steady stampede of all the people. I looked round for Bessie, and could see her nowhere. So I ran with the crowd, supposing she was among them, but still not realizing there had been an earthquake, and supposing it was only a falling house. In a minute or two Bessie was at my side, and we proceeded more leisurely, returning as we had come....We thought no more of pictures, and were glad enough to get away."

Although Rev John had not realised what he had experienced, but Elizabeth (Bessie) had realised. She described the earthquake; "the noise was awful, like a clap of thunder, combined with a sort of roar, no doubt partly from falling masonry, but the actual shaking of the ground was very severe. My own first impulse was to get as much into the centre of the little square where we were as possible, away from the houses; and when I had recovered from the 'scare' and looked round (one's first feeling was of being glued to the ground with fear), I found nearly everyone out of sight, papa just vanishing round the corner of the street up which we had come, so I ran too; and very thankful we were to be out of it."

After this frightening experience, they would have to board their carriage and return down the zig-zag bends towards the bottom of the high hill and back to San Remo.

The people who had lost their houses and those escaping from the earthquakes camped in the fields outside the villages until the threats of more earthquakes had finally gone. In San Remo and Alassio, inhabitants who had lost their homes camped out in spare railway carriages. Nearly 2,000 lives were lost, most in Italy but many in France were also victims.

The Return to England

On 3rd March, 1890 Rev John's sister Mary died. At this time she was still living in the Cottage in Castle Eden. Effects of £37,683 were left in her will. The joint executors were her brother Cotsford and Eugene Wethey of Coatham. Mary bequeathed one of her River Tyne warrants for five hundred pounds and £50 to Eugene Wethey for acting as her executors.

Her niece Elizabeth was given all her 'articles of furniture and all articles of kitchen crockery" as well as a five hundred pound share on the River Tyne. Elizabeth now had a great deal of kitchen crockery as she also inherited some from her Aunt Anne Malet. Mary's nephews, Rowland and John George Burdon (John's sons) and Cotsford Mathews Burdon (Cotsford's son) all received River Tyne shares.

Mary's servant Hugh Hodgson was given one hundred pounds. Charlotte Tristram, Canon Tristram's daughter inherited £100 which was invested in the Artisan and Labourer Company.

The rest of her wealth and effects Mary gave to Agnes King, her companion. Agnes received, "money invested in Railway and other shares, stocks, debentures or securities and all ornaments in (her) drawing room and elsewhere and (her) Copeland dinner service and other china ware and (her) plate, linen, pictures and books."

Mary appeared to have had a considerable number of shares that contributed to her wealth. Most of her effects were left to Agnes King, her companion. When Agnes herself died on 28th November, 1898 whilst living in Bilborough House Yorkshire she left effects of £37,651 with Rowland Burdon named in the probate. Agnes' effects were of similar value as those left to her by Rowland's Aunt Mary.

Aunt Mary had not lived long enough to celebrate the marriage of her nephew John George Burdon. In February 1892 Rev John Burdon youngest child, John George married Blanche Louisa Somerset, sixth daughter of General Somerset of Troy House Monmouth. Troy House was about 11 miles away from English Bicknor. It is possible John and Blanche had known each other from the time Rev John was Rector of English Bicknor.

The engagement was announced in November in various newspapers throughout the country. The wedding that took place in February the next year in the 'ancient church' of Mitchel Troy was also reported nationwide, frequently headed a 'fashionable wedding'.

The bride entered the church accompanied by organ music, on the arm of Lord Edward Somerset. She wore a; [27] "white Duchesse satin dress' trimmed with 'Brussels lace'. Duchess satin, shiny and lustrous was made from silk. Handmade Brussels lace was well known for its delicacy and beautiful designs. This would have been an expensive dress. Blanche Somerset wore a 'white tulle veil, fastened with a diamond start, a gift of the bridegroom;' an expensive present.

Blanche and Lord Somerset were followed by the four bridesmaids, her sisters Lilian, Muriel and Hilda and her cousin Miss E. Bright. The bridesmaids wore 'white pompadour, edged with rose ruching, white felt hats with ostrich tips and rose ribbon." It was February and probably cold so the bridesmaids were wearing stylish, attractive outfits that would probably help keep them warm, White pompadour is a very soft three ply yarn, frequently used to make delicate clothes for infants. It would appear that ostrich feathers were still fashionable. The bridesmaids all wore pearl and turquoise bangles, again a present from the bridegroom.

The bouquets carried by the bride and bridesmaids consisted of lilies of the valley and pink carnations; both flowers having a delicate perfume. The pink ribbons tied from the bouquet would add to the theme of white and pink.

As Blanche's father was dead, her mother gave her away. Blanche's cousin, Rev. Plantagenet Somerset, rector of Raglan conducted the ceremony assisted by the Rector of the church.

There were a large number of guests assembled in the Church for this 'fashionable wedding'. The couple received 'numerous and costly' wedding presents. After the ceremony, the guests made their way to Troy House for the reception. The bride and groom did not stay long because they left at 3.30pm to catch a train to travel to their honeymoon on the Riviera.

The bride's going away outfit was a dress of 'Roseda cloth'. Roseda was a shade of green; roseda being a plant popular with the Victorians. The new Mrs. Burdon wore a 'white embroidered waistcoat of the time of Charles II' on top of her dress. This waistcoat allegedly had been in the 'possession of the Burdon family' since the time of Charles II. It may have been a waistcoat worn by the Rowland Burdon who was seven times Mayor of Stockton and allegedly prevented Oliver Cromwell from entering Stockton. Blanche added a 'Tudor cloak and hat to match' to complete the outfit. Presumably this would be cloak in the Tudor style.

It is uncertain whether Rev John was at the wedding as by this time he was not too well. He had undergone a severe operation in the summer of 1891. As he was 80 at the time the operation was a cause for great concern. After the operation rev John was not allowed to walk much and this led to frustration as he had always been a very active man. He spent a great deal of time reading took great interest in politics and 'in all the many affairs of life going on around him'. He prophesised;[28] "If you children live to the second decade of the new century you will see the whole of Europe in a blaze, marks my words!"

He used to sit in his 'chair by the fireplace, always cheerful, always the courteous host, always ready to lay his book down to take part in the chatter around him always ready to greet old friends, and the centre of all family and social life.'

Rev John did attend the baptism of his grandson, another Rowland Burdon, the seventh of that name. (He will be referred to as Rowland Burdon VII) He was baptised on 25th March 1893, Annunciation Day in St. James' Church Castle Eden. Rowland was the oldest son and second child of Rowland and Mary Arundell Burdon. He was born on Monday 6th February at 7pm.

Those who were present at the ceremony included; Rev. Canon Tristram DD Canon of Durham, Rev F. J. G. Robinson, Rector of CE (officiating clergy) Mr. and Mrs B, (father and mother) Mr. Mrs JG Burdon (aunt and uncle) Miss E.A. Burdon (aunt), Miss F M. Burdon (sister), Miss Elsley and Miss Fanny Elsley, Mill Mount House York, (cousins) , Mr. John Stonehouse agent, Miss King, Mrs

Robinson and all the workmen, villagers etc. The service was fully choral. The godparents were Lt Colonel Mitford and Mr J. Arundell Hildyard and Mr. F. M. Davison, proxies being Mrs R Burdon, the Rev John Burdon and Miss Elsley.

After the ceremony three trees were planted in the Park, one an oak, on the Knoll near the Lodge, under which was buried a glass bottle containing a parchment with an account of the ceremony, with names of those present, a copy of the 'North Star' of the day, a 6d and a 3d bit of the year 1893, with copies of the invitation cards to the workmen's dinner And fireworks; and a pine near the Crossroads, and a yew on the south east side of the Castle. In the evening there was a display of fireworks in the West Park, which was witnessed by hundreds of spectators, and further enlivened by the strains of the Castle Eden Colliery Brass Band. It was exceptionally fine hot day for that time of year, and in the evening a beautiful meteor was noticed, which was regarded as a very favourable omen for Rowland the 7th.

On Tuesday, April 6th (ten days later) a dinner for the workmen and employees on the estates was given at Parklands, when a sumptuous repast (one of the chief features of which was a huge christening cake) terminated by speeches.

The cake having been cut by Miss F. M. Burdon (Fanny), the baby's sister, still a young girl herself, the Rev John said that they might suppose it gave him very great pleasure to be able to be present with them that afternoon and to propose the health of the seventh Rowland Burdon of that name in his own family. He was afraid the remarks he was about to make were to some extent egotistical, being chiefly connected with the family. Some of those present might remember his father. Rev Burdon then went on to speak of how his father had been connected with the Bank at Newcastle which broke after which he had spent the rest of his life quietly amongst them in Castle Eden, In point of public usefulness he was, however, a man of mark, and although he had many peculiarities and odd habits, was much respected and beloved, although always a very poor man, he was dressed always by the village tailor, and though perhaps the whole of his wardrobe would not have fetched

5s at a village auction, at his death many, far and near, begged for some of his old clothes as a remembrance of him. Mr. Burdon then touched upon the subject of squires generally, and expressed a wish that though they were supposed to be out of date, the young man whose health whose health they had just drunk might grow up to be as useful a member of Society as any that had gone before him.

After this toast had been drunk, Canon Tristram responded on behalf of Rowland 7th and in an eloquent address, in the course of which he touched upon various points of the politics of the moment, remarked that the first owner of that name of any note was the one who kept the town for Charles 1st in 1664, being Mayor that same year. RB the second moved from Stockton to Newcastle, and established the first private bank there. He was the man of large commercial grasp and enterprise, but in no way connected with the annals of CE. It was his son, Rowland the third who was to be connected with that place who bought the estate from a Mr. Bromley, planned and built the castle. There were about 90 people in the parish then, no enclosed land, and grouse and black game abounded. He partly restored the Church (then endowed to the amount of £12 5s od a year for a perpetual curate) He used to stay at an old farmhouse while the Castle was building, situated near the 'Knoll' with groups of trees in it, near Laidlaw's Lodge.

It was he who was the first resident squire, and who rebuilt the Church. He was a great inventor, spent both time and capital to a great extent on the place, being in early life a rich man and representing the County in Parliament. There was an old pack-horse road, which he converted into a turnpike road practically all the way from Thirsk to Newcastle. The bridge at Sunderland was his invention, and he paid for it chiefly. He was a great personal friend of Pitt's. Of his son, Rowland Burdon v someone very tersely said that he was a man who had given to his county talents heaven destined for his country, but being a man singularly free from ambition, preferred to devote all his energies to doing good in his own immediate neighbourhood. No man more conscientious than he in doing his duty, and he was one who never stooped to pander to truth. In conclusion, Canon Tristram said it was unnecessary to remark upon those so well known to them as his good friends Mr. John Burdon, and his son, both with them today. If there was anything in a 'good strain' as applied to racehorses, then there was a good deal in a pedigree, as applied to families. As long as England is England, the best men always come to the top in the long run, and he hoped that the name of Burdon may long remain connected with Castle Eden, and that this RB the seventh of that name, may long live after all of us have gone, to carry on the work, and the good name of those who have gone before him. In conclusion, he proposed the health of Mr. John Burdon, grandfather of the infant, which having been responded to in a few suitable remarks, the proceedings terminated with a good deal of clapping and lusty cheers for all the Family. Master Rowland Burdon was a silent but appreciative spectator pf the proceedings. The party then adjourned to the hall door, where they were all photographed. After renewed and hearty cheers they separated.

The above reported account of Master Burdon's birth and christening contained many references to his Great Grandfather Rowland Burdon, more so than to the new born baby. There appeared to be still great interest in Rowland Burdon v.

The baptism of Master Burdon in 1893 was a joyous occasion. However, like the story about his great grandfather, 1893 would not be a joyous year.

There were some good occasions. In April, tenders were advertised for refreshments for the Whitsuntide sports in Castle Eden when it was estimated between five and six thousand people would attend. A great bazaar was held in a marquee in the grounds of his grandfather's estate at Castle Eden. The Marchioness of Londonderry, accompanied by her daughter Lady Helen Stewart opened the event held to raise money to establish a Darlington Branch of the Durham Diocesan Society for waifs and strays; a fate no must have loved his first wife Elizabeth very much as he was t destined for baby Rowland Burdon. Nor would he suffer the fate of a[29] "little boy, aged 5.... Summoned for doing wilful damage to turnips. The child was carried into the dock by his father, sobbing loudly." The child was considered too young to be tried so he was released by the court on the condition that his father whip him, to which the father agreed.

Hartlepool Show was also in August and people from Castle Eden probably attended. Rev. John Burdon, amongst others was one of the sponsors for the Show so members of the Burdon family would probably have been there to see the [30] 'vegetation' described as being 'unusually luxuriant.' The 'flowers' in particular were 'magnificent…some blooms…more like tropical productions than the growth of our variable climate.' There were prizes for the twenty eight classes of exhibits; industrial exhibits like model sailing ships and yachts, locomotives, marine engines, cases of stuffed animals and birds, models of buildings, fretwork, oil and water colour paintings of landscapes, animals, fruit or flowers and drawings in sepia or chalk." Most of the exhibiters were reason ably local but some came from as far away as Scarborough. The description sounded as if it was quite a spectacular show.

There would be some who probably would not be able to afford to visit the Hartlepool Show. There had been trouble at Castle Eden Colliery since 1892.

Benyon says that 1892 [31] "was the year in which the Durham miners became locked in a titanic battle with the coal owners," when "the Durham employers had insisted on a reduction in wages." Strike action was voted for and "on 12 March the 'Durham Lockout' began."

The "Durham Lockout" and Castle Eden [32]

"Castle Eden Colliery was a large colliery that employed 1,300 workers. During the strike management including the clerks made up the twenty one men who were on duty; "whose hands, I hear, are likely to suffer, from the unusual manual employment they are experiencing …some men from Hartlepool come to render assistance…because of) the considerable amount of water."

Pumps needed to be continually working to keep the pit from flooding. This was probably the main task of those who the reporter considered were not used to manual work. The strike affected everyone.

Three men from Castle Eden were greatly affected. Castle Eden Colliery was a wet colliery and constant pumping was needed to safeguard the workings from flooding. The men would not do this work, in the hope that management would seek an early resolution of the dispute. Management would not negotiate, so blackleg labour was brought in the work the pumps. This action prompted what was called a riot of [33] "several hundred men headed by a county councillor."

One man had been injured but the three brought to justice were not accused of this offence, they were tried and convicted for; "With a view to compel a person to abstain from doing an act which he had a legal right to do wrongfully and without legal authority following such person with several other persons in a disorderly manner in a public road."

The three men, Michael Forbes, Thomas Jones and Thomas Henry Cann appear to have been singled out for conviction of being amongst those who were "in a disorderly manner in a public road."

Thomas Henry Cann was the County Councillor for Greatham, elected as a miner's delegate. He won the seat over Major Burdon whom Tristram considered to have a 'natural right' to the seat and had only been rejected because "the miner's union throughout the county ordered its members to vote only for the pitman's delegates." One may question whether the trial may have been prejudiced. The events had occurred in Castle Eden Colliery, land owned by the Burdons. Major Burdon, his father John who was still alive at this time and his brother Cotsford were all J.P.s. sitting at Castle Eden Magistrates Court. They would have been known by the officials at Durham Assizes.

On the morning of the trial, Thomas Cann [34] "felt concern... not because his conscience told him that he had done anything wrong, but because he knew that there were a certain number of men – men of position and influence- who would do their level best to put him and his two friends who stood beside him in the dock, under lock and key."

William Forbes was sentenced to four weeks in prison, Thomas Jones six weeks and Thomas Henry Cann two months, all with hard labour.

Thomas Cann and his two friends were imprisoned on Friday July 15th 1892. Thomas spoke of his imprisonment. Once alone in his cell, awaiting the allotted time of 8 o'clock when it was time to pull down his plank bed from the ceiling, "he walked up and down, thinking of his home and his friends at Castle Eden."

Thomas made his audience laugh when he told them the warder had instructed him to "Sleep with everything off except (his) shirt," so he duly undressed and prepared to sleep on the plank bed, supplied with "a blanket, two sheets and a rug." He said he would never forget trying to sleep in that bed. Again his audience laughed when he told them, "He was only a spare man, and he soon found that his bones and the boards did not agree. He turned from side to side, but found no comfort. It was very painful, very painful indeed."

For he was sore all over. After enduring this misery for two or three nights, he...employed one of his socks in a sort of fender to prevent his bones chafing against the boards." This appeared to help a little, or maybe he just got used to these uncomfortable sleeping conditions.

One thing Thomas did appreciate in prison was listening to the good sermons of which there were many. He may have been a Methodist himself as this statement, in the New Connexion Church, raised a "Hear, Hear" from the audience. There was one sermon however, he did not really enjoy; the sermon of the feeding of the 5,000 with the loaves and fishes. Throughout his imprisonment, he, like the rest of the prisoners, was underfed, so he was constantly hungry so much so that hunger pangs kept him awake at night.

Despite being fed little, he had to endure hard labour. He spent six hours a day for six weeks on the treadmill, describing it as "very distressing work" before spending the rest his imprisonment in the arduous task of oakum picking, unravelling old rope.

On his release he had lost weight and as he was a "spare man", of slight build, Thomas probably looked haggard and tired. He would soon recover physically but he admitted "the mental pain" of his imprisonment would "always be in his memory."

Thomas Henry Cann was released about seven o'clock in the morning of September 10th. Men from the Miner's Union were awaiting his release. A deputation of his work colleagues, fellow union officials, together with his friends Michael Forbes and Thomas Jones, now released, were awaiting him outside the gates of Durham goal.[33] They made an "enthusiastic rush" towards Thomas and after "hearty hand-shaking" they all made their way to a "hostelry" for "breakfast." Thomas would be overjoyed to his friends, but probably equally overjoyed to enjoy a hearty breakfast.

The party then drove back to Castle Eden in carriages where "they were met by several thousand miners and their wives belonging to Castle Eden and other collieries. The enthusiasm was very great, the horses being unyoked from the carriage in which Cann was riding and the carriage drawn by a number of men through the village. A band of music and the lodge banner preceded the throng of people, and on their arrival at the Station Hotel Square speeches congratulating Mr. Cann, who having replied, the crowd dispersed."

Cann's friends, Michael Forbes and Thomas Jones, also charged with intimidation had been released earlier. They too had a tumultuous welcome back to Castle Eden with bands playing, lodge banners, processions through the village and speeches. The speech-making insisted that the "imprisonment of Forbes, Jones and Cann was strongly condemned."

Their imprisonment was not condemned by everyone. Rev. Tristram [35] was scathing about the county councillor and others" being met by "bands of music, banners, and carriages," and even more so about Thomas Cann who resumed his seat as county councillor instead of Major Burdon, especially as the Major and his family had "funded" the feeding of "hundreds of children for months," a notable deed in itself but not one hopefully for which the Burdon family sought any reward. They probably did have the gratitude of the villagers for such paternalistic generosity but the miners had not elected Major Burdon as county councillor. They now had a voice of their own in Thomas Henry Cann.

Not only men took part in the welcome home processions for the three returning prisoners. Women and children were involved too. They had suffered during the strike and even some of the children may have been aware of their parents' condemnation of the men's imprisonment.

The apparent injustice of the 1892 strike and the reduction of wages was considered by Jack Lawson as being "desperate and savage."

Lawson, as a child, had seen that [36]; "The men and women had fought for months. Although unconscious of it, I had, even as a boy of 11, become class conscious. A national strike is a calamity and arouses strange feelings, but a county strike is savagely bitter because it effects are more directly devastating…as the sense of defeat deepened, passions rose until the women and children were as bad as the men. Indeed, the women were the worst, as they always are on such occasions."

The strike action lasted 12 weeks. The miners "refused to settle or to give their officials freedom to negotiate." This made the employers "more severe on their demands for settlement." A settlement was reached mainly because of the actions of the Bishop of Durham.

The Bishop of Durham had been to Parliament to discuss the strike with Thomas Burt MP. The Bishop of Durham wrote a letter to the Secretary of the Durham Miners' Federation Board urging the miners to return to work with a reduction of 10% of their wages in anticipation that no further reductions would be made without the matter being referred to a Wages Board to be established that would have full powers to negotiate. The Bishop suggested representatives of the "masters and men" should meet with him at the Bishop's Palace "to discuss the details." Dundee Courier 28th May 1892. The Bishop had already visited Parliament to discuss the strike with Thomas Burt MP for Morpeth Northumberland; the first working miner to become a Member of Parliament.

Mainly because of the Bishop's intervention, a settlement was reached. The employers had demanded a reduction of wages and at the end of the twelve weeks of strike the employers got their way and the miners returned to work with a reduction of 10% of their wages.

When the men returned to work, the problems arose. During the strike the pumping of water from the workings was probably inadequate. Part of the mine flooded; [37] "causing considerable anxiety both to the owners and also the men employed in the pit… In some portions of the workings the water is up to the roof and covers the workings for a distance of between 300 or 400 yards. The result of the disaster is that close upon 300 hands are still unable to get to work. Strenuous efforts are being made by the officials to keep the water under. Nine-inch pipes have been laid

From the now pit bottom to the Nesbitt engine-plane, and a large new pumping engine is to be added to the powerful apparatus already employed for removing the water."

The trouble did not end there. In 1893, the first major national miners' strike, involving 300,000 miners lasted 16 weeks. Durham and a few other counties were not involved in this strike. There were still problems at Castle Eden Colliery. Miners were accused by the management of violating their contract.

There was a special sitting of the Castle Eden Police Court before Major Burdon (John's son), Rev John Burdon and Mr. R M Hudson. The Castle Eden Coal Company had brought a summons against 187 of their workers. The company were claiming compensation of 10s per man for allegedly restricting the output of coal on 24th and 25th April and thus violating their contract. The case of William Appleby was to be [38] "taken to decide the lot."

William Appleby, the man named for the test case had gone down the pit to work but instead of filling from five to six tubs as expected, had only filled three tubs, thus producing only half of the expected amount and making him in breach of his contract. Because all the 187 workers had undertaken similar action, only one third of the usual quantity of coal had been extracted and the owner had sustained a 'considerable loss.'

The manager of the colliery Mr. Thomas Shipley told the court that if more than 30 lbs of stone is found in the tub when it is picked out in the screens, then the entire tub is forfeited and the worker not paid for the coal in the tub. Apparently there were 'certain classes in the various seams in which stone or other foreign substance appears in the coal.' This stone 'is called fish stone' as it is 'embedded in the coal' and is 'difficult to detect.' The men had met with the colliery manager in February as there had been increasing numbers of rejected tubs that the previous manager would have allowed. The new manager instructed the men to screen the coal as carefully as they could so that there would be insufficient stone in the tubs to render the tub rejected. The court decided the men had not violated their contract but insisted they work with management to achieve a compromise.

Thomas Shipley had come to Castle Eden colliery after working for 18 years at his previous employment. His job at Castle Eden was lost when the mine flooded despite the lessee of the colliery spending many thousands of pounds on new machinery in an attempt to cope with the influx of water. The mine closed and went into voluntary liquidation in December 1893. No buyer could be found so dismantling of the colliery took place in March 1894, ready to be auctioned in April.

The colliery was abandoned with a loss of 3,000 jobs and an estimated 80,000,000 tons of coal still in the seams. Thomas Shipley, manager was one of those who lost his job. He did get other employment; still in mining as a general manager in the Transvaal about 30 miles South East of Johannesburg.

The death of Rev John Burdon

Rev. John Burdon was ill at this time, but he did not live to see the closure of Castle Eden Colliery. He died after a recurrence of his illness, not wishing to undergo another operation. Obituaries like the following appeared in newspapers; "At half past two in the morning of November 12th 1893, the Rev. John Burdon died. He had apparently had a serious internal illness for eighteen months but had only been seriously affected by it in the days previous to his death.[39]

"The deceased gentleman was a well-known figure in the Hartlepools, where the Hospital of which he was president, largely benefitted by his munificence. He was born at castle Eden in 1811, and was the third son of Mr. Rowland Burdon MP. He was a fellow of Queen's College, Oxford, and at the age of 23, took holy orders and was appointed curate of Easington. He was subsequently presented to the living of English Bicknor, Gloucestershire, which he held until 1877, when he succeeded his brother Mr. Rowland Burdon, the owner of the Castle Eden Estates. He deceased gentleman married in 1847 Elizabeth Ann, daughter of Mr. H. Hale JP of County Durham and granddaughter of General Hall (Hale). Mrs. Burdon died I n 1878. Mr. Burdon leaves two sons and a daughter. He will be succeeded by Major Burdon of the 1st Durham Volunteers. The deceased gentleman was chairman of the Castle Eden Bench and president of the Hartlepool Branch of the Lifeboat Association."

His death was announced in many newspapers including the Bath Chronicle which covered English and Welsh Bicknor where he had been incumbent for many years before coming to Castle Eden. This may have been where he and his family were happiest. In the 1891 Census, his son Rowland had recorded his occupation as 'living on his own means'. Not so his father. John Burdon recorded his occupation as 'Clergyman without the care of souls." Despite inheriting the estate of Castle Eden from his brother Rowland, John Burdon still regarded himself as a clergyman even though he was not responsible for a parish church and parishioners. He frequently covered for local sick or absent clergymen, being at Rev Boydell's church when his wife died.

His funeral took place on 16th November at Castle Eden Church;[40] "the funeral being largely attended by relatives and friends of the deceased, including most of the leading residents of the district...."The church was completely filled. The chancel was decorated with camellias, chrysanthemums, violets, arums and ferns."

After the service, the coffin was carried by twelve workmen to the grave situated just outside the church. The grave itself was lined with "evergreens, flowers and ivy, and the bottom covered with moss." He had made great improvements to Castle Eden Dene and these tributes may have been a reminder to that. Before his internment, a short service was conducted at the graveside.

Later Rev. Burdon's death was announced at Castle Eden Police Court,[41] "in the business of which, for many years, the deceased gentleman took a prominent part. Mr. Burdon died at the age of 83, and was apparently in the full enjoyment of life up to within a few days of the end. His genial and happy disposition manifested itself in many ways, and was ever expressed by a kindly smile, which showed that advanced age in his case was anything but a burden. In stating that as a magistrate Mr. Burdon invariably tempered justice with mercy."

The above description gives some description of the man rather than his deeds. He was 'genial' and 'happy' with a 'kindly smile.' He showed 'mercy' in his administration of justice.'

Rev John's daughter Elizabeth wrote this of him[42];"Such was John Burdon parish priest, administrator, church builder, engineer, politician, staunch friend and earnest Christian and servant of God, fearless both orally and physically, and the most absolutely unselfish of men, simple indeed, and truthful to a fault. Many-sided indeed, and happy those, who like myself, lived in his society for half a lifetime."

This is a wonderful tribute from his daughter. He did not appear to seek praise for good works as the following would suggest; "About six months after his death, an advertisement appeared in the Durham paper. 'Would any gentleman come forward and take the place of the Reverend John Burdon and contribute the sum of £100 a year to the 'Poor Clergy Fund'; and then for the first time it became known that had been in the habit of contributing for many years."

The Rev John Burdon would have been sorely missed by his family and many others.

CHAPTER NINE
Rowland Burdon VI – The Colonel

In 1893, John Burdon's son Rowland,then Major Burdon, took over the estate. His sister Elizabeth wrote;[1] "We children had a very retired life in our earlier years. I suppose the young one nowadays would scarcely be able to 'stick it', but having known nothing different we were quite happy. We had a black pony, 'Billy', about 12 hands high, and later 'Jaquetta', also black and used to ride about the woods and enjoyed ourselves amazingly."

Elizabeth had one chore which she 'loathed'. She had to 'write a resume' of her 'father's sermon every Sunday afternoon.' When she was 13 she had to teach Sunday School on the morning and afternoon. She did have treats as she had a 'faint recollection' of being taken by her parents to London for the week to see the Great Exhibition in 1862. One thing she did remember "with most wonder and pleasure is the big fountain playing scented water."

Her brother Rowland was not born until she was six years old and she remembers that time when every evening her father used to take her "on his knee" and "spin the most marvellous yarns" for her benefit.

Her brother Rowland, when older was 'entrusted to the care of old Mr James, the organist for afternoon's fishing on the river.' Elizabeth never heard of anything being caught but they always returned supremely happy. Old James used to appear on the scene, very rotund, with rod, spectacles, and umbrella and one felt very happy about them[2].... At other times the river for us was 'taboo'. We were never allowed to go near it or on it, chiefly, I suppose, be-cause of the yearly toll it took in life from its many dangerous rapids."

One such death was recorded by Elizabeth;[3] "There is a simple little tombstone in the Churchyard at Welsh Bicknor, on which the following epitaph is inscribed, in memory of a girl who was drowned in the Wye. The girl, who was a servant at the Rectory, had taken the boat across the river, which was in flood. She fell overboard in trying to land, and was swept away.

John Burdon wrote the inscription on her gravestone, as he was also Rector of Welsh Bicknor, so he would have known the servant girl. It is a very moving verse;

"Cold and relentless was the grasp
That did thy shuddering form enclasp,
When thy young life was quenched beneath the wave,
And there arose one sad wail,
Echoing through the Wye's peaceful vale:
That cry for help, when none was nigh to save,
But was there then no Saviour near?
No hand to help, no voice to cheer?
He saw thy spirit's agony, poor maid,
Whose arm the sinking soul can keep,
Whose voice can answer from the deep
And whisper, 'It is I, be not afraid."

This inscription on a gravestone in the churchyard may have been of some comfort to the girl's grieving parents and friends.

Elizabeth was educated by her father but her brothers Rowland and John George went to Repton School. They were probably there during the headship of Stuart Adolphus Pears who was Headmaster from 1854 to 1874. Headmaster Pears was responsible for massive improvements in the school including the building of more classrooms and extra boarding facilities. He raised the status of the school so it became one of the leading Public Schools in the country.

Headmaster Pears paved the way for a reputation of sporting excellence at the school. He believed, a healthy exertion of body and spirit together which is found in the excitement, the emulation and the friendly strife of school games"

Rev John had been athletic at school. This emphasis on sporting excellence may have been a deciding factor to send his sons to Repton.

From Repton, Rowland VI followed in the family tradition and studied at University College Oxford. By 1881 his Uncle Rowland had died and as there were no heirs to inherit the Castle Eden Estate Rowland's father John left his parish and returned to Castle Eden.

The Castle had 43 rooms. In 1881 there are nine servants in the household; a housekeeper/cook, a ladies' maid, a laundry maid, a dairy maid, an under housemaid, a kitchen maid, a groom and a 15 year old page boy life in Castle Eden would be very different for the life they had known in English and Welsh Bicknor.

Rowland Burdon married Mary Arundell Slade in February 1887. Mary Arundell was the daughter of Wyndham Slade of Monty's Court in Taunton, Somerset. Mary had lived with her family in 70, St. George's Square London and at the family home in Montys Court near Taunton in Somerset.

After the wedding the newly-weds travelled to Castle Eden to live in Parklands Hall which was to be their new home. The day before their arrival at the station, preparations were made to give them a 4 "hearty welcome." The day before their arrival they began decorating the station with flags and banners. These must have been numerous as the decorating continued into the day of their arrival. They had received many wedding presents including; "a silver candelabra from the tenantry, presents from the Volunteer Corp, the county constabulary stationed at Castle Eden, the workmen on the estate, the school children, and from Major Burdon's own Horden and Shotton tenantry."

They would receive presents from the Volunteer Corp as Rowland Burdon was a Major in the Volunteer Battalion of the D.L.I. He would eventually command the 1st Volunteer Battalion and rise to the rank of Colonel. He was appointed Deputy Lieutenant of County Durham in 1900 and High Sheriff of Durham in 1907, also serving as a Justice of the Peace. He is often known as "Colonel Burdon".

Rowland Burdon commanded the 1st Volunteer Brigade of DLI as Lieutenant Colonel becoming Honorary Colonel of the 5th Battalion in 1911. He was awarded the Volunteer Decoration, an award for long and service of merit for officers in the Volunteer Force.

Rowland Burdon had been made a magistrate in his early twenties, so he would have known the county constabulary stationed at Castle Eden, so they too bought a wedding gift.

The couple arrived in Castle Eden on the evening of the 18th and were probably pleased at their welcome. Life in Castle Eden would be very different from life in London, so they eventually had two residences, Castle Eden and a house in a fashionable part of London.

In June of 1887, Queen Victoria's Jubilee took place. The Burdon family and some members of the Nimmo family who owned the brewery in the village contributed towards a knife and fork tea for adults from the village held in the grounds of The Castle. The afternoon included sports for adults and juveniles making it a 'lively and enjoyable afternoon.'

This event was followed by the Horticultural Society Flower Show held in the grounds in August, of which Rowland Burdon was President.

These were village events. There were more prestigious social events like the Grand Ball for the debut of Lady Helen Stewart at Wynyard Hall when members of the Burdon family attended along with a large company of the leading inhabitants of County Durham.

Much had happened in the two years before this ball. In Castle Eden there were strikes at the colliery between 1892 and 1893. In 1893, there was the joyous occasion when Master Rowland Burdon, the seventh Rowland Burdon the son of the young couple was born and baptised. Later in 1893, on November 11th John Burdon died, so the joyous year was tinged with great sadness.

More concern was to come. Despite the purchase of new pumps to alleviate the water influx problems at Castle Eden the mine flooded and had to be closed. The Castle Eden Coal Company Ltd was wound up voluntarily and went into liquidation.

Castle Eden Colliery employed 1100 men and boys. They would need to find employment elsewhere. The workers and their families all lived in the 600 colliery houses in the colliery village. These houses would be empty. St John's Church and the rectory had only been erected ten years previously in Monk Hesleden. Now a lack of congregation would make the church redundant. The lessee had gone into liquidation. The colliery workings were dismantled and all the machinery and materials were sold. There was no reason for the colliery village to exist. It became desolate.

Canon Tristram, who had been incumbent at Castle Eden for eleven years, wrote a letter to the editors of several national newspaper decrying what had happened and laying blame directly at the doors of the Miners' Union whose actions had produced "untold and far spread misery."

Tristram sets out his case by venerating the Burdon family as one of the "foremost among the county families in Durham in public enterprise and philanthropy" who had built schools and a church at the colliery and supported the curate. They were generous. They had "daily fed hundreds of children for months" during the strike and unrest.

It appeared 'unnatural' that Major Burdon had lost his County Council seat to Thomas Henry Cann, the miners' delegate from the union. To Tristram, it appeared the Miners' Union did not respect what should be the natural order of things that the landowner Major Burdon should be in a position of political power rather than a miner.

To make matters worse, this miner, Cann had been to prison for his part in the unrest at the colliery and had been greeted on his release as a hero when in Tristram's eyes it was his leadership that had caused the mine to flood and not only lost the men their livelihoods but also forced the lessee into liquidation, the dereliction of the village and the loss of a newly built church. To make matters worse, Tristram informed the readers that the Burdon "family mansion which had been for generations the centre of charity and munificence is to be closed and its proprietor returns to the South of England."

It is possible the Burdons wished to return to the South of England and would have gone anyway. They had not been brought up in Castle Eden and may have preferred to have their main residence elsewhere.

Rowland Burdon and his wife Mary Arundel did live in London. They had both lived there before their marriage in St George's Church, Hanover Square; a fashionable church for high society weddings, on 16th February 1887.

Their four children were born in London, probably at 14, Sloane Gardens, where the children; Frances Mary (1890), Rowland (1893), Joan (1898) and Lettice (1900) were living in the 1901.

The 1901 Census records the children living in this family home in Sloane Gardens. Their parents are not recorded living in the household. There are seven servants including a nurse and nursemaid in the household. Presumably the nursemaid is responsible for looking after eleven month old Lettice and the nurse responsible for the rest. Their mother, Mary Arundell Burdon does not appear to be recorded on this census. Their father, Rowland Burdon is recorded in the Station Hotel, York on the night of the census.

They moved from fashionable Eaton Square to an equally fashionable area. The Electoral Register of 1918, places them at 44, Hans Place in Chelsea. Hans Place is a residential garden square immediately south of Harrods. The address was named after Sir Hans Sloane. Jane Austen lived in 23, Hans Place in the early 19th Century. The address remained fashionable and is now considered one of the most sought after addresses in Chelsea. The Burdon's appear to have lived here for some time.

44/45, Hans Place appear to have been converted into apartments. The following is a description of such an apartment, recently sold (June 2015) for £3,595,000, with a service charge of £4,600 per annum.[5]

"With everything at your fingertips, Harrods is your local store which once sold everything from a toothbrush to an elephant! There is easy access to all the wonderful museums, theatres, restaurants and night life this great city provides. The vast acres of Hyde Park are but an easy ride away. The apartment, which has its own private entrance from the street has been redeveloped to the very highest of specification. The drawing room with high ceilings and triple aspect windows which, at the flick of a switch, may be dulled by intelligent glass, looks out to give a panoramic view onto the private gardens."

The above description gives an indication of the grandeur of the house and surroundings that the whole of 44, Hans Place, before it was turned into apartments with its neighbouring house at number 45.

In 1938 Rowland Burdon is living in an apartment at 3, Lyall Street, Westminster. Mary Arundell died in 1930, so he may have moved somewhere smaller after her death.

Although it would appear their main residence was in London, the Burdon family did not abandon living in Castle Eden.

The 1ˢᵗ Volunteer Durham Light Infantry

Rowland Burdon was still very much involved in his work in County Durham and Castle Eden. He was still very much involved in the Durham Light Infantry.

The Second South African War began on 11ᵗʰ October 1899. There was a move from the Government to raise Volunteer Regiments throughout the country to swell the ranks of the army. Rowland Burdon was made Lieutenant Colonel of the 1st Volunteer Regiment of the Durham Light Infantry. He was also highly involved in fund raising to supply equipment for the newly formed volunteer regiment.

Volunteers needed training. In 1900, there was a government funded initiative for special training on Salisbury Plain in which volunteers had to participate. As this training was compulsory, the men were paid at Army rates for the fourteen days of their attendance.

In June 1900, the 1,200 strong volunteer force of the 1st Battalion DLI attended Bulford Camp, a mixture of tents and huts erected in 1897 on Salisbury Plain, to begin their training. The weather was very hot; the men wearing their grey shirts rolled up to the elbows and white caps with neck protectors during drill.

The second week saw the weather break with very heavy showers and thunderstorms. It was still very hot with the weather reaching 83 degrees even in the shade of the tents. It was extremely hot on the ranges where there was no shade and not a trace of breeze. Drills in this weather were fatiguing. There were battalion manoeuvres, extension movements, skirmishing, and class firing, all undertaken in extreme heat. This weather would be a foretaste for those who eventually served in Africa.

Life during this fortnight was not all hard work. There was some recreation. On 13th June all the men in the first were given a holiday from third parade so many of the men journeyed into Salisbury. The sergeants of the 4th had given a 'smoker' to the sergeants of the rest of the brigade the previous evening. Other battalions would be giving 'smokers' during the week before leaving camp. [6]

A 'smoker' referred to a smoking concert, a Victorian term for a male only get-together where men smoked, talked while listening to music, singing or instrumental, probably performed by some of the men themselves as a way of entertainment.

Training of the Volunteers continued. As well as local training, another extended training session took place away from the locality. There was a training camp set up for a week at Scarborough Racecourse, three miles from the centre of Scarborough. This was not compulsory, so those who attended needed to take time away from work without pay. Despite this drawback, one thousand of the 1,250 volunteers attended. The officers used the permanent buildings at the race course for their mess. They camped inside the race enclosure. The rest of the men camped on the race course. The previous year had been very hot. This year it was so cold in late May at first the men paraded not in rolled up shirt sleeves, but in their greatcoats. The weather did improve, but again there were thunderstorms.

As well as the training that Colonel Burdon intended "to ram in as much practice and instruction in reconnaissance and outpost duty as possible." 27th May 1901 Yorkshire Post and Leeds Intelligencer. There were lectures every evening. The Commanding Officer Colonel Burdon appeared to allow the men no time to visit

Scarborough, the "most seductive of watering places" or even give time for 'smokers'.

The men were well fed during this week's training. Sergeant Walker saw to that. He had been on a training course at the Army School at Aldershot so the quality was good. Each day a large quantity of food was consumed including; 900lb beef, 900 lbs of bread, half a tons of potatoes, 40 gallons of milk, 420 eggs and 90 lb ham. Apparently the consumption of beer was low as half of the men were teetotallers, probably Methodists who abstained from alcohol.

Colonel Burdon appeared to be involved in training, exercises and drill inspections of the newly formed Volunteer 1st Battalion, both locally and further afield. During the local training he, and probably his family lived would live in Castle Eden.

The Colonel was also a Justice of the Peace. He would hear several cases at Castle Eden. In 1900 he was appointed a Deputy Lieutenant of County Durham in 1907, he served as High Sheriff of Durham. These positions would take up a considerable amount of time in the locality necessitating residence in Castle Eden. There was also estate work.

Parklands

Colonel Burdon's Aunt Anne Malet had commissioned the building of Parklands between 1875 and 1878 at great expense only living there until her death in 1885. The Colonel and his young wife lived from 1887 until 1893 moving into the Castle on the death of John Burdon, the Colonel's father. Shortly after this the Colonel had the building gutted as a Drill Hall for the first Volunteer Battalion of the D.L.I. The coach houses and stables were converted into the armoury and clothing stores with accommodation above these buildings. In 1901, three households, a soldier, the head woodman and his wife and a cattleman whose wife is a dairy woman live in this accommodation.

The 1st Volunteer Battalion DLI

The soldier living above the armoury with his family was probably responsible for the safekeeping of the buildings and the equipment stored inside. As well as training in the Drill Hall at Parklands, Colonel Burdon's uncle, Rowland Burdon V had installed a rifle range in the grounds. During his time this range was used mainly for practice and shooting competitions of the Rifle Club. The rifle range was now used by several together DLI Battalions as well as the 1st Volunteer Battalion to train soldiers for battle.

The Colonel had also given permission to instigate a Cyclist Brigade. This brigade would be 100 strong. Horses needed rest and food and could be injured or killed in combat. A bicycle was readily available, so cyclists were used to carry messages, telegrams, mail, despatches and stores. Cyclists were used for reconnaissance and patrols, especially to patrol railway lines.

A parade, inspected by Colonel Burdon took place on the afternoon of Saturday, 20th January 1900 at Stockton Drill Hall and was inspected by Colonel Burdon. Those about to go on active service were to spend two weeks at Newcastle before leaving for South Africa. The Colonel appealed to the [7] "inhabitants of Stockton, Thornaby, Darlington, Castle Eden and Middlesbrough" from where the Battalion was raised, as he had done on many previous occasions, for subscriptions to "augment the grant of £9 a head made by the War Office for the purpose of providing the men with a proper outfit and additional comforts."

Public dinners, concerts and other events were held to raise money for those about to enter active service. Colonel Burdon frequently officiated at these events. Sometimes more intimate fund raising events took place like the smoking concerts held for a man called Greenwell of the 1st DLI who had been chosen for active service so the organisers of the smoking concert presented him with [8] "a diary to record the events of warfare from day to day, together with a substantial sum which had been subscribed by his numerous friends and acquaintances."

Mrs Burdon also played her part in raising gifts for the men about to go on active service. She collected [9] "a number of parcels from various friends in response" to her "appeal ... for comfort for the men of the first V.B.D.L.I., who are going on active service" which she presented to the Mayoress of Hartlepool. There were also collections at Chapels and Churches throughout the area.

Despite the training, the men were not trained for the guerrilla tactics of the Boers. The Cycle Battalions were not as effective as had been anticipated as tyres frequently punctured in the rough South African terrain.

There were heavy casualties on both sides with many British soldiers dying or being wounded not only in combat but also dying from disease. The War ended on 31st May 1902.

Other uses of The Drill Hall

The Drill Hall was used for concerts to raise money for Church Funds. There were Balls, especially to raise money for the first Volunteer Battalion like the one held by members of the F Company when [10] "Dancing commenced at 9 pm and was indulged in by 61 couples up till 6 am." That appears to be an exceedingly long time to dance through the night. There was supper provided by Mrs. Claxon of the Castle Eden Inn. Colonel and Mrs Burdon attended the Ball along with Captain and Mrs Tristram, who by this time were living at The Cottage Castle Eden, and other named guests.

There were other balls as well as those organised for the 1st Battalion DLI. Mrs Burdon appears to have organised balls in December, in the [11] "Drill Hall, kindly lent by Mr. R. Burdon," when Mrs Burdon, "assisted by other ladies" promoted these balls, probably as a pre-Christmas celebration. In this instance the Hall was "tastefully decorated by the head gardeners, Messrs. Fulford and Charlton. Over 250 persons were present at the opening dance at 8.15 pm." A "sumptuous supper" subscribed by several attendees at the ball was served at 10 pm.

Amongst those present were the members of the Trechmann, Nimmo, Claxon, Hutton and Snowdon households. Apparently this ball "was a great success."

Fund raising balls also took place like that organised in aid of the Church Restoration Fund with another [12] "very successful" event with the Drill Hall decorated with evergreens, an "excellent orchestra" and a "splendid supper."

The Burdons attended other balls some on a much grander scale like those organised by the Marchioness Londonderry at Wynyard Hall. These balls were not on the level of those attended by Rowland VI's grandmother Cotsford and grandfather Rowland in London that included descriptions of the grand setting, clothes, jewellery and food. Unlike the balls in the Drill Hall where local people, farmers, the military and friends attended to enjoy themselves, the balls organised by the Marchioness were much grander with many titled personages in attendance.

Mr. and Mrs. Burdon, along with Cotsford Burdon, Rowland's uncle, members of the Nimmo and Trechmann households, attended a [13] "grand ball at Wynyard" to celebrate the "introduction to society of Lady Helen Stewart the daughter of Lord and Lady Londonderry."

The occasion was even grander in 1899 to mark the occasion of the 21st birthday of their son, Lord Castlereagh. The Ball had already been postponed because he had an accidental fall from his horse whilst hunting. As he was still convalescing he could not attend his birthday ball but it went ahead without him.

Some of the guests, mainly from their titled closest friends were house guests. They had spent the day at Stockton races and had dined prior to the ball on a sumptuous meal of many courses, all of which were written in French. French chefs were popular, so it is possible they employed a French chef or one who knew something about French cooking.

The one thousand two hundred guests who attended the ball experienced an exceptionally grand affair. To accommodate the servants, marquees were placed in the grounds. As the guests had arrived by carriage, two huge marquees were erected to stable about six hundred horses.

Beacon fires were lit for the carriages to light their way down the long, winding drive approaching Wynyard Hall. Once near the Hall, [14] "great trees festooned with fairy lamps, illuminated by electricity could be seen along the margins of the lake." Outside the Hall was a "flood of light" from "four large arc lamps of 2,000 candle power, and supplemented by innumerable smaller illuminations, some hundreds of which also leant colour to the scene by being enclosed in tinted semi-transparent lanterns."

Dancing commenced at 10pm to the "orchestra under the baton of Mr. H.G. Amers of Newcastle." Military brass bands were very popular. The military brass band by Henry Amers, appeared to be in great demand at several functions over a wide area like; the Percy Hunt Ball at Alnwick, Morpeth Cricket Club Ball, a Mayoral At Home at Wallsend and several fund-raising event like that held in Berwick.

As in the times of Cotsford and Rowland v attendances in fashionable balls in London about one hundred years earlier, the fashions of many of the ladies and descriptions of their jewels was recorded in the newspaper. These included Lord Castlereagh's sister, Lady Helen Stewart, "was attired in a gown of rich white watered poplin, prettily edged with a design of white satin ribbon. The corsage was trimmed with chiffon and fine cream lace, with bouquets of La France roses. Her ornaments were pearls and diamonds." Lady Helen had experienced a grand ball, but not on this scale at her debut in December 1894 attended by a "large company of the leading inhabitants of County Durham" including members of the Burdon family to be present at Lady Helen's "introduction of society." Amer's Band played here too including a special waltz called "Lady Helen's Waltz" that had been composed for the occasion by Major R. Irvine of Norton.

Miss Caplin, the fiancée of Lord Castlereagh, was also a prominent guest. She "was attired in white tulle, embroidered with silver spangles over a white satin gown. Her ornaments were turquoise and diamonds."

The reader of the newspaper article could attempt to visualise the grandeur of the occasion and the expensive clothes and jewels of the ladies present.

Supper was served at midnight. The food was again written in French, so unless the reader was familiar with the language and cuisine, the reported menus could only appear exotic and probably very expensive.

Rowland Burdon's Uncle Cotsford attended this ball, along with Mr. Mrs and Miss Trechman from Castle Eden. Colonel and Mrs. Burdon were probably invited but were probably in London at the time.

The Castle Eden Estate at this time.

Colonel and Mrs Burdon were not living in The Castle in 1901. There appears to be no-one recorded as living in this building in this census. It is not recorded by the enumerator at all except in the description of the enumeration district. An uninhabited building is usually recorded so this may have been an oversight.

The Foundry is recorded in the enumeration description next to The Castle. Houses have replaced what once was the site of the iron foundry owned by the Richardson family who established a ship building business in Hartlepool in 1832. These were wooden ships but bolts, hinges and anchors were manufactured at in Castle Eden. Brothers Thomas and John Richardson inherited the foundry business from their father. In 1854, they built 'Sir Colin Campbell' the first iron ship constructed in Hartlepool but they stopped ship-building in 1857 to concentrate on making marine engines. The foundry in Castle Eden had closed by this time and houses were eventually built on the site.

The Foundry, although now consisting of houses, retained its name. Railway and brewery workers and a mason who works on the estate lived here.

The Factory, also retaining its former name, now consists of houses. The 'Manufactory' began about 1794. An early deed from the 29th September 1794 between Rowland Burdon and George Salvin, who were related by marriage, designated the land on which the Factory was to be built. A second covenant describes the land intended for the building of brick house for his dwelling place. Houses were built on the site when the Factory was demolished.

There are houses called The Bleachery, a reference to the time when the Salvins had a bleachery on this site for their sail-making business. Workers mainly at the railway and brewery lived there. There is still a ropery in 1901, operated by Robert Smith, ropemaker who lives on the premises.

Harry Dent, a civil engineer lives in Hudworth Cottage. He born in Liverpool, son of a civil engineer so after he studied at Rugby School, he followed in his father's footsteps. In 1891, aged 27 he was living in the Trevelyan Hotel in Darlington whilst working as a civil engineer. He married Charlotte Elizabeth, his wife in Harrogate in 1897 when he was 33 years old. BY 1901 they have two very young children, so a nurse is employed to look after them. The household also had a cook and a housemaid. In 1911, the household has moved to 'Southleigh', an eleven roomed house in Forest Hall Newcastle. Harry Dent has now become a civil engineer employed by the North Eastern Railway.

In 1901, when he was living in Castle Eden, it is possible Harry Dent was involved in the opening up of the railway for the expanding coal field in South Durham. Pits were to be sunk in the villages of Horden, Easington and Blackhall. Railways would be needed to transport coal once it was mined. Navvies came into the area, mainly living in huts in the area where the railway next to the coast was to be constructed. In 1902 it was estimated there were 100,000 navvies in the country working on railways, reservoirs, water tracks, docks, sewerage and other similar works. There were no navvies living in Castle Eden but the railway contractors had provided a mission worker for the navvies, Mr Thrift who lived and was based at Castle Eden.

Civil engineers would be needed for the railway construction which included three viaducts, tunnels and embankments as well as lines of track. Harry Dent may have been one of the civil engineers who worked on the construction of the new railway. Unlike the navvies he lived in Castle Eden.

Work on the railway was well under way by June 1901, when a party of civil engineering students from Newcastle first visited the new docks works at Seaham before they rode over part of the track of the new railway. From Seaham,[15] "the party mounted a couple of trucks and commenced a journey along the route of the new railway to Hartlepool. Notable features of the route are four large brick-built viaducts, the largest of these, that which is to span Castle Eden Dene – is about half finished. Another large viaduct of Crimdon Dene appears to be almost entirely finished. The quantity of earth to be excavated for the cuttings of the line is 700,000 cubic yards. Among other features of the work are the aerial cable (Henderson's) along which all the material is carried and lowered in to position where it is required. The wire cable itself is 2 inches in diameter and it carried a load of three tons. The cable which spans Castle Eden Dene has a span of 300 feet. The construction of the railway is being carried out by Messrs. Walter Scott and Middleton Ltd, a contract price being £200,000."

The students would have been amazed at this construction but their uncomfortable ride in a truck was softened by a 'pleasant interval at Dene House in Dene Holme, where luncheon was served."

There was an even more distinguished visitor to the railway in July that year. His royal Highness the second son of the King of Siam was studying civil and mechanical engineering, so[16] 'accompanied by his attendants', he was 'gathering information concerning the laying of a railway." As a 'fluent speaker of the English language' the Prince would be able to converse with those involved. He was 'most courteous, agreeable in manner and intelligent', so those involved in his fact finding mission would have found him a willing listener.

This young Prince of Siam would be the son of King Chulalongkom. He had spent four years studying at Harrow and was about to enter Cambridge to study engineering. He was probably interested in the construction of this railway as Siam had just opened its first railway that year, 1901, running between Bangkok to Kiat. As an engineer the Prince would be able to help Siam before he began his studies at Cambridge.

Prince Purachatra Jayakara was born on 23rd January 1881, son of King Chulalongkorn (Rama the Great) in the Royal Palace in Siam. He was educated first in Siam before attending Harrow and Trinity College Cambridge. He continued his studies in France and the Netherlands concentrating mainly on the construction of dams and canals. He returned to England and entered the Institute of

Engineering before returning to Thiland in 1904 where he worked as a military engineer as an officer in the Siamese Army.

Prince Purachatra became head of the Northern railway department, developing and expanding the railway system. He brought the use of the diesel engine to Siam, the first country in Asia to use a diesel engine.

The Prince expanded his expertise into creating roads and bridges throughout Siam. He was responsible for the building of the Kasatsuk and other railway bridges. By 1921 he commanded the railway department. He also commissioned a geological survey to find coal and crude oil.

Prince Purachatra brought broadcasting communication to Siam as well as countrywide telegraph offices, mailing services, parcel and postal services. He became Minister of Commerce and Transport in 1926. The Siamese revolution of 1932 disrupted his plans to bring television to Siam. The visit to Horden and Crimdon viaduct and sight of the construction of the new railway to Hartlepool may have influenced his young mind a little and encouraged him to great engineering projects in his own country of Siam.

This Prince of Siam was not the only royal personage from Siam who visited Britain. In August 1903 we are informed that [17] "The Royal Family of Siam is a numerous one." Prince Purachatra's father King Chulalongkom had 92 consorts throughout his lifetime and fathered 77 children. In 1903, on a visit to England by the King; "With him came an astounding assortment of sons dressed in Eton suits. His majesty turned up at all sorts of places at which he was not expected. Students and readers in the reading room of the British Museum, the very capital of silence, were horrified one day by a sudden outburst of howls and shrieks. There stood the King of Siam, with all his hosts of sons round him chorusing after the manner of the East at their surprise at the number of books they saw."

There appears to be a superior, condescending attitude in this report. Those in the reading room were 'horrified' by the 'howls and shrieks' of the young boys. The writer appears to suggest their noise was due to the 'manner of the East.' The party did not stay long in the reading room. They probably caught the chill of the disapproving atmosphere because they were so thrilled to see such a centre of learning. The readers should have been delighted at the boys' outbursts of glee in seeing so many books in the library. This delight, and the delight the boys must have felt on the visit to the British Museum led to the development of a museum and library in Bangkok. The visitor to the new railway in Durham appeared to have a more gracious welcome as he was described as being 'courteous, agreeable and intelligent." Possible the railway engineers were much more used to visitors than the readers in the British Museum.

In 1901, the railway in Castle Eden in 1901 employed several people.

The Brewery

There was a brewery in Castle Eden which employed a great number of workers in 1901. The brewery had expanded from quite modest beginnings. In 1841 John Nimmo was living and working as a brewer in the house attached to the Castle Eden Inn where he had set up his business in 1826 at the young age of about 25. This 'Capital Inn' was advertised to let in October 1835; [18] "With upwards of 90 acres of good GRASS and ARABLE LAND (Free from small tithes), which may be increased, now in the occupation of Mr. Robert Rollins.

Well situated for Posting, on the Turnpike from Shields and Sunderland to York & c, by Stockton, Thirsk and calculated for the accommodation of travellers.

The Inn contains, 5 parlours, 9 good Bed-rooms and Servant's rooms, 2 kitchens, convenient Bar, good Cellars; also good stabling for 23 Horses, Chaise-House, Corn and Hay Barns, Byers, Granaries, Garden, and other Conveniences for carrying on an extensive business.

The Sunderland to Stockton coach stops here daily.

None need apply but such as are capable of serving the public and genteel families in the best manner.

Further particulars may be known by applying to Mr BURDON, or Mr JOHN NIMMO, Castle Eden."

It would appear the Castle Eden Inn was a thriving business with a good reputation and customer service especially for 'genteel families.' The accommodation sounds spacious with rooms for servants who would travel with the genteel customers. Stabling for 23 horses seems extensive but horses needed to be changed several times on a long journey. From the description of the storage facilities it would appear the animals would be well fed, probably with food grown on the grass and arable land to let. The brewery run by John Nimmo would provide ale for the premises.

The Nimmo family

In 1851, John Nimmo is a brewer and a farmer of 200 acres. His son William, also in the household is employed as a road surveyor.

William Nimmo did not remain in this employment. By 1861, he has married Anne, and has taken over the brewery, employing two men, one boy and a land surveyor. His father John lives nearby but dies in 1867.

In 1871 he is recorded as a brewer, wine merchant and spirit dealer employing 25 men and 2 boys. The household has four servants, including a young governess.

William Nimmo expands the business even more. By 1881 aged 53, he is recorded as a brewer, maltster and spirit dealer, employing 42 men and 8 boys. His farm had greatly increased in acreage to 520 acres, giving employment to 15 men, 5 boys and 4 women.

At home, he is wealthy enough to employ three servants in the household of himself, his wife Anne and two of his daughters, Eleanor and Wilhelmina. His son George aged 28 is involved in the brewing business and also runs a farm.

In 1892, the business becomes a limited liability company trading under the name of J. Nimmo and Son Ltd.

William Nimmo died from pneumonia on 27th April, 1901 aged 73 years. Yorkshire Post and Leeds intelligencer 29th april 1901 Obituaries appeared in several newspapers each saying that he was 'greatly esteemed' in the district. "He was the oldest native inhabitant of the Parish of Castle Eden, and by shrewdness and business capacity had largely extended the business founded by his father in 1826. He took a great interest in agricultural matters, and was a frequent prize winner with his pedigree cattle, his specialities being

West Highland, polled Angus, and Galloway stock. In politics he was a Conservative, and he was a generous supporter of Church work and philanthropic movements. He is survived by his wife, to whom he had been married for 49 years, and with whom he had looked forward to the celebration of their golden wedding anniversary in March next. Two sons and four daughters also survive him."

At his death in 1901, he left a gross sum of £100,322 8s 1d, becoming £95,277 14s net; a huge amount of money for that time.

William Nimmo was one of the local gentlemen. He attended agricultural shows like the ploughing and hedging competition held by the Castle Eden Agricultural Society in January 1860 on Rowland Burdon's land. Rowland Burdon was President of the Society and William Nimmo acted as Hon. Secretary, so they would probably attend the competition, Rev. H.B. Tristram was one of those who gave congratulatory speeches, so he too would be well known to William Nimmo.

These occasions continued with later generations. Three of the Burdon family and William Nimmo were amongst the local gentlemen who sponsored a knife and fork tea for the locals to celebrate Queen Victoria's Jubilee.

The Nimmo and Burdon women were also acquainted, running fund raising events like bazaars in the Castle Park often to raise money for the parish church. These bazaars were opened by one of the Burdons.

Rev. John Burdon assisted in the ceremonies of the marriages of both Elizabeth and Margaret Nimmo, William's elder daughters. Eleanor married Rev. F.G.J. Robinson, later incumbent of St. James' Church, Castle Eden. Wilhelmina, the youngest daughter married Dr. Duggan, the local doctor in April 1883. Both Motherwell Duggan and Wilhelmina Nimmo sang in fund raising concerts in various local churches. Dr. Duggan's father, also Motherwell Duggan was incumbent at nearby Cornforth church. It is probable Dr. Duggan and Wilhelmina became better acquainted during the singing events and church attendances. In 1891, they are living with their three children and servants in Hulam Lodge.

In December 1894, the Burdon and Nimmo families were both amongst those invited to the ball at Wynyard in celebration of the debut of Lady Helen Stewart. Members of the Trechman family also attended. These families were considered gentlefolk of the area worthy of being invited to such a grand occasion. They probably knew each other well.

They probably knew the farmers in the area, at farms like Headshope, Wellfield, Catchgate, Stone Leazes and Fir Tree. Rowland Burdon employed workers on his agricultural land. James Henderson, whose father was a farmer was born in Castle Eden, worked as a shepherd for his father became steward for Rowland Burdon whilst also rearing sheep.

Amongst the agricultural workers, as steward, James oversaw the work of several woodsmen on the Burdon land.

The Nimmo and Burdon family shared the same politics. In March 1898 a large attendance, presided by Rowland Burdon, had gathered to nominate a seat for the Parish Council. William Nimmo, a Conservative was one of those nominated by a show of hands. The families appeared to have considerable connections.

The Trechmann family

Charles Otto Trechmann, who in 1917 lived in Hudworth Towers, Castle Eden would also be well known by Rowland Burdon. Charles Otto Trechmann was born in 1851 in Hartlepool. His father, Peter Otto Edward Trechmann was born in Wilster near Lagerdorf, Germany in 1820. Moving first to Seaham as shipping agent, he became a shipowner in Hartlepool before setting up the Warren Cement Works in Hartlepool. For many years he served as German Consul in Hartlepool.

Peter's eldest son, Charles Otto had a scientific education, including studying chemistry to PhD level under Dr Bunsen at the University of Heidelberg before returning to England to manage the business. In June 1879, he was married to Getrude Elizabeth Taylor, daughter of Rev Robert Taylor vicar of Hesleden with her father performing the ceremony.

The wedding was described as being [19] 'fashionable', the church at Hesleden was a "pretty little edifice had been decorated with exceedingly good taste the day before by the bride's numerous lady friends. The whole village, in fact, presented quite a holiday appearance, and the greatest anxiety was manifested to get into the church."

The outfits, as usual, were described with the bride wearing a 'rich white silk dress, having as head dress a veil and wreath of myrtle and orange blossom," and the four bridesmaid wearing, "pale blue cashmere trimmed with blue satin, white chip hats with feathers."

After the ceremony and reception the couple left Castle Eden colliery Railway Station for a honeymoon tour of the Rhine. Charles Otto was probably keen to show his new wife the sights of Germany. The couple had a good send off when the "villagers cheered most vociferously until the trained steamed out of the station."

They set up home in Hudworth Tower, Castle Eden. Charles Otto Trechmann eventually took over the business. In 1911 Charles Otto and his wife Gertrude have been married for 31 years. They had four children but two died leaving son, Charles Taylor a chemist at the Portland Cement works and daughter Hilda Gertrude. They employ two housemaids and a cook in their 12 roomed house.

Charles Otto developed an interest in minerology, becoming a member of the Institute of Mineralogists of Britain and Ireland. He amassed a huge collection of minerals, numbering about 5,000 specimens which he displayed in two cabinets in Hudworth Tower. After his death, most of these specimens were eventually donated to the British Museum. In 1905, a mineral trechmannite was named after him.

By the time of Charles Otto Trechmann's tragic death in 1917, the family had re-invented themselves as being of Danish extraction. Charles Otto Trechmann had been ill for some time prior to his death so he underwent a serious operation at Leeds. He had a relapse some time afterwards. He was probably in a great deal of pain, as he was [20] "found at about noon in his bedroom dead with a bullet wound in his forehead, and a small rook rifle by his side."

Medical opinion at the inquest determined because of seriousness of his physical health, he could not have lived much longer, yet, because the inquest was he had died from suicide whilst temporarily insane.

The immediate cause of death is not referred to by Col Burdon at a meeting of magistrates, when, as Chairman he paid tribute to Charles Otto Trechmann saying; "He was a man whom they all admired, an eminent man in his own profession, and a very good friend. He did an immense amount of unseen work willingly and in a straightforward manner. Many of them knew of his loyalty and support to the King. He was a great supporter of the volunteer movement and had forseen the happenings of the past three years and urged upon them what must happen if war broke out and Britain was not prepared."

Col Burdon stresses that Trechmann was a "very good friend." He goes on to emphasise the patriotism of Trechmann towards Britain, in the knowledge the Trechmann's father was German rather than Danish, possibly to expel any anti-German feelings some may foster against his friend.

This suicide was tragic but Charles Otto was a very sick man. His was not the only suicide to occur, this time near Hudworth Cottage. In December 1900, an inquest was held into the death of twenty one year old Jacob Irving.[21] At about three o'clock in the afternoon of Christmas Eve, Jane Thompson a servant employed at Hudworth Cottage had heard a gunshot outside. Jane ran out and found Jacob lying on the road just outside the cottage with a revolver in his right hand and blood pouring from a wound in his head.

Jacob Irving came from Hesleden, No reason could be given for his suicide but it was suggested he had been behaving strangely prior to his death, so just a verdict of suicide was recorded. Charles Otto Trechmann had killed himself with a rook gun. Jacob Irving had used a revolver. The origin of this weapon was not disclosed. There appears to have been a considerable number of available guns at that time.

John Joseph Candlish

Charles Otto Trechmann had been a magistrate. Rowland Burdon would have known John Joseph Candlish, another fellow magistrate who lived in Shotton Hall. By this time, Shotton Hall was owned by the Burdon family, so John Joseph Candlish would have been a tenant on the estate.

John Joseph Candlish had moved to Shotton Hall about 1887. His uncle John Candlish began the bottle works in Seaham in 1853 erecting a building for the manufacturer of black bottles. Candlish extended the business over twenty one years, so when he died in 1874 there was a thriving business of seven bottlehouses that exported bottles to many parts of the world.

After John Candlish's death, his brother Robert took over the business and in 1886 introduced the continuous gas furnace to replace the less efficient coal furnace. When Robert died in 1887 his son Joseph John Candlish took over the business. Further expansion of the business introduced more continuous glass furnaces which enabled continuous production throughout the two twelve hour shifts and consequently employing many more men, women and boys, eventually manufacturing 20,000 bottles in one day. The demand was there, especially for the paler glass bottle manufactured by the continuous gas boiler.

In 1913 Joseph John Candlish merged with others to form the United Glass Bottle Ltd Company, becoming one of the largest companies in the country with Joseph John Candlish as Chairman of the Directors.

He did live in Seaham in the Tempest Hall but in 1887, he moved to Shotton Hall on the Castle Eden Estate. In the 1901 Census Joseph John Candlish, now aged 46 is recorded as a "glass bottle manufacturer." He and his wife Jane had no children so probably enjoyed the company of their two nieces, sisters Jane and Florence Laing aged 21 and 23. They have servants in the household; a cook, housemaid, laundrymaid, kitchen maid and groom. There are domestic gardeners; one living in Shotton Hall dwellings and in small village of Shotton. A horse-keeper, maybe responsible for the Hall's horses lives in Shotton Hall dwellings as does his neighbour, a domestic coachman.

Shotton Hall was a place of [22] 'hospitality' where he 'lavishly' entertained his personal friends and also held "huge picnics of his people from the bottleworks (who) were invited to spend the day and have tea on the lawn." Like his father Robert and his Uncle John, Joseph John Candlish was considered a good employer and a generous man known for his philanthropy.

Unlike staunch Conservative Rowland Burdon, Joseph Candlish was a Liberal. His uncle John Candlish had been M.P. for Sunderland, so it was a political family. Politics came to Shotton Hall as Joseph Candlish entertained both the Sunderland and South East Durham Liberal Associations here on their frequent annual outings. The quarterly meetings of the South East Liberal Association were held in the Castle Eden Inn, followed by a lunch-time meal and on 27th August 1900 this followed this by a "Stroll through Castle Eden Dene.. Colonel Burdon having kindly given permission." Mr. Candlish had arranged tea for the group once they reached Dene Holme. This appears a pleasant day out but one which Rowland Burdon, a staunch Conservative would probably not attend. Despite this, he gave permission for the group to visit the Dene.

Both Rowland Burdon and Joseph Candlish were magistrates and frequently sat on the bench at the same time. They were also on Easington Board of Guardians and would attend meetings. The Board of Guardians were responsible for overseeing the business of the Union that covered the parishes of Castle Eden, Dalton Le Dale, Easington, Kelloe, Monk Hesleden, Seaham Seaham Harbour, Thornley and Wingate grange. The Ladies Visiting Committee was a sub-committee of the Board. Both Mrs Burdon and Mrs Candlish were co-opted onto this committee, probably making regular visits of inspection of the conditions in Easington Workhouse. They may have been present on Christmas Day December 1900 with other members of the Board when the inmates had their Christmas meal of an [23] 'ample supply of roast beef and vegetables, plum-pudding & c' and the" old folk received supplies of tea and tobacco, the boys and girls useful gifts, and the infants toys." The children's gifts were 'useful'. Possibly the Burdons and their friends extended this celebration as in 1902 the Christmas festivities included a [24] "plentiful supply of tea and cake and a Christmas tree, the gift of Colonel Burdon. "To prolong the festivities the Board and Guardians along with a few friends provided a tea for all the inmates, and gifts of toys for all the youngsters on New Year's Day.

Both Rowland Burdon and Joseph Candlish were councillors on Easington Rural District Council. Candlish represented Seaham Harbour on Durham Council.

Both men were prominent freemasons. The Rowland Burdon Lodge was formed in Castle Eden. Joseph Candlish had membership of the Fawcett Lodge in Seaham.

Candlish was very interested in agriculture and frequently visited county and local shows. He was also a keen naturalist, Vice-President of the Sunderland Naturalists Society. Fond of hunting, he was a member of the North Durham Hunt and subscriber to the Essex Hunt.

It would appear the only thing that separated the two men was politics. They seemed to have so much in common as well as their political views. Joseph Candlish was a [25] "popular and genial speaker on all sorts of topics, whether on the political platform, in the Council Chamber or at public dinners he could always suit his remarks to the occasion" and he was reportedly "possessed of an exceptional attractive personality."

Joseph Candlish was also very interested in agriculture and frequently visited county and local shows. He was also a keen naturalist and Vice-President of the Sunderland Naturalists Society. He was fond of hunting; was a member of the North Durham Hunt and subscriber to the Essex Hunt.

Mr. and Mrs Candlish were also invited to many of the society occasions attended by the Burdons, like the Grand Ball in 1894 when Lady Helen Stewart, daughter of Lord Londonderry was introduced into society at Wynyard Hall. Both the Burdons and the Candlish family were considered amongst the leading gentry of County Durham.

It would appear that apart from their different political persuasions, Rowland Burdon and Joseph John Candlish had much in common. It is possible they knew each other very well.

The Burdons travelled but Joseph Candlish and his wife were great travellers. They travelled around the world twice, the last world tour being in the Spring of 1913.

Other Castle Eden Residents

Others of note were in Castle Eden in 1901. The civil engineer, Harry Dent and his household are living in 'The Cottage', the house that was the home of Colonel Burdon's two aunts, Mary and Fanny, and at one time his grandmother Cotsford Burdon.

The Cottage is near The Rectory, the home of the incumbent, Rev G. J. Robinson and his wife Eleanor. Rev Robinson was born in York but Eleanor and Ralph, their eight year old son were born in Castle Eden. Ralph is educated at home by a young governess with the household being looked after by a cook and a housemaid.

Fredrick Godwin Johnson Robinson was born in York. His father William was a barrister and could afford to send Fred to Harrow School. From there he entered University College Oxford. When aged 24, Fred has gained his B.A. but is still a student, studying theology. In 1881 he is in LLandaff, Glamorgan Wales, lodging with a fellow theology student. St. Michael's theological college was not founded until 1892, but it probable Fred Robinson was training to become ordained in an establishment in LLandaff.

LLandaff was in the midst of the South Wales coalfield. The experience may have influenced Fred Robinson into coming to Castle Eden as incumbent; South Durham also increasingly expanding as an area of coal mining.

Whilst in Castle Eden, Rev. Fred Robinson met Eleanor Nimmo, third daughter of William Nimmo of the family of brewers in Castle Eden. The event was reported as being another fashionable wedding in Castle Eden. The village, including the station was again decorated with flags for the occasion.

Rev Robinson's cousin, Rev. G.C. Fisher from Beverley Yorkshire conducted the ceremony assisted by Rev. Oldroyd of Haswell. Many turned out to witness the wedding. The church was crowded long before the hour announced for the ceremony, and a large number of would-be spectators had to content themselves with a peep from the outside. Villages may have been anxious to see what the bride's attire which included a dress of white satin, trimmed with white net and branches of orange blossom, and a toulle veil. She carried a bouquet of choice flowers given to her by the bridegroom. To complete the outfit, Eleanor Nimmo's Uncle, Mr. T. C. Thomson of Ashton Park had given her a diamond bracelet. The four brides-maids, including the bride's sister carried bouquets of Marcechal Neil roses, all the bridesmaids wearing dresses made from cream embroidered cashmere, trimmed with sapphire blue velvet and matching hats. Castle Eden villagers would flock to see such a grand affair in such a small village.

There is no mention of the guests, but the Burdon family were well acquainted with the Nimmos and would probably have been amongst the large party who assembled at the house of the bride's father for the wedding breakfast. After the reception, the newly married couple left for Durham at 2.55 in a carriage and pair in order to board the 4.10 train south to spend their honeymoon in North Wales. Rev Robinson may have visited North Wales during his time in LLandaff, and liked the scenery there, so they may have decided to visit Wales on their honeymoon.

The couple would be well on their way when a large ball in the new hall adjoining Mr. Nimmo's residence began. More than forty couples were expected to attend, probably including some of the Burdon family. The ever popular Mr. Amers was engaged to provide the music.

When the newly married couple returned from their honey-moon on 29th April, they were given [26] 'a hearty welcome by the parishioners, who assembled in strong force.' The station was again decorated with a 'handsome arch of evergreen.. tastefully decorated with primroses, daffodils etc' and containing 'a motto bidding the Rector and his wife welcome' was erected at the approach to the platform'. The parishioners and friends of the couple presented them with a present of a cabinet they had purchased for them.

Although the Rector must have been highly respected to afford such a welcome, Eleanor, his new wife born in Castle Eden was a daughter of the local brewer, a major employer, so the workforce would want to show a 'hearty welcome' to both of the newly-weds. Other villagers also turned out to greet them. Many would be estate workers employed by Rowland Burdon.

Agriculture on the estate: James Henderson's diaries (1900-1902)

James Henderson' diaries gives some indication of the cycle of agricultural work done on the estate. The estate farming appeared concentrated on Oakerside farm. A farm manager, John W Lockey in 1901 oversees the running of Oakerside farm. George Johnson, born in Scotland lives in a farmhouse at Oakerside with his wife and family. George is a farm hand, an agricultural worker who usually has charge of horses. His eldest son John, aged 15, is a domestic gardener probably employed at Shotton Hall, whilst Carlyle, aged 14, is a shepherd boy, so even at such a young age, Carlyle would have looked after the flock of sheep in the fields around Oakerside.

James Henderson grew up on his father's farm in Castle Eden and worked as a shepherd on this farm from an early age just like Carlyle Johnson. Henderson was considered a local expert on sheep and lambs using his skill to judge animal at shows like Easington Agricultural Show held on the 7th August 1901 there was a large attendance at this show, possibly partly due to the fine weather. There were many competitors and much to see. [27] "There were 19 classes for horses, cattle and sheep, and about 120 entries. In addition, there were driving classes, open horse racing, pony racing, block tests for beasts and a sack race." James Henderson together with Mr. Best of Sheraton were responsible for judging, "ewes, lambs, cows, heifers, bullocks & c", so he was considered an expert on animals other than sheep.

James Henderson bought and sold animals, like the seven fat ewes sold at Haswell Market that belonged to Colonel Burdon. There were stock markets held at Castle Eden where he traded animals. He visited Tow Law and purchased a roan cow for £16 10s

3d for the Colonel, on 5th Jan 1900. In 1908 he was still visiting Tow Law to buy sheep. Four fat bullocks were sold at Sunderland Crows Mart for £84 1s. Other stock sale like those in Chester-Le-Street, Ferryhill Station and Hexham were also probably visited. Animals purchased would probably be transported by rail from the nearby station to Castle Eden.

James Henderson visited some stock sales with J.W. Lockey, farm manager of Oakerside Farm. In August 1900 he gave a sale catalogue for the stock sale in Rothbury to J.W. Lockey prior to sending him to the sale to buy ewe lambs for Oakerside. Catalogue shopping began in the middle of the 19th century. Many things, like farm machinery, seeds, clothing, furniture and furnishings could be purchased by mail-order by 1900. The catalogue Lockey had probably listed the animals for sale at the stock sale. He could peruse the catalogue and have more idea of the stock he needed to purchase. Lockey bought thirty five Bradford Edge lambs. This could be a reference to the Bradford system; an indicator of the spinning capacity of wool. These ewe lambs were possibly to increase a flock of sheep kept for their wool. Sheep had been sheared and the fleeces sold in August 1900. It is possible a good price was obtained for the fleeces and a decision was made to increase the flock of sheep for shearing, hence the purchase of 35 ewe lambs with suitable wool producing capacity. Henderson and Lockey possibly had a copy of the flock book produced by the Shropshire Sheep Breeder's Association in 1883 that listed sheep and the prizes they had won at shows, enabling purchasers to identify reputable breeders. This book may have improved their knowledge of sheep and influenced purchases of new stock.

Dogs would be used on the farm to herd the sheep. A young collie dog called Sam was bought for 45/- in 1913 from John Middlemass in Berwick, a considerable way to go to buy a young dog. The dog would probably need some training before it could be used in the fields to herd the sheep raised for wool and meat.

Some of the lambs raised for meat were sold at the Castle Eden sales. Meat also appears to have been slaughtered and sent to

London by train. This meat was probably mutton rather than lamb as mutton was a cheaper cut of meat popular at this time.

In October, the Shearling tup was 'among the ewes'. It may have been the first season for this young male ram to be put 'among the ewes'. This ram may have been bred to produce either better meat or finer quality wool.

Henderson appeared to have knowledge of horses. He records the names of horses used to serve various horses on the estate. On various occasions, the cart horse Flower was served by Gallant Robert, Prince of Currah and the grand sounding, 'Prime Horse Count Cedric of Glaswick.' These stallions were show winners. Gallant Robert was described as a massive Clydedale stallion nearly year years old. In February 1900, Mr R. Darling and Mr Shaun as representatives of the Castle Eden Cart Horse travelled to Scotland to select two horses to travel to their district during the ensuing season. Gallant Robert was one of those selected. Fifty pounds premium was given by the society for each horse.

The Castle Eden Cart Horse Society, which commenced in 1869, held an annual competition with a prize that had now reached £100. Horses were entered from many parts of the country including; Cumberland, Newcastle, many parts of Scotland and Yorkshire. The winning horse would travel the district in order to serve mares and sire foals. 'Corswell's Grandson', the winner in 1894 had won the previous year but had since 'both thickened and improved, and what is more, left a record of fully 70 per cent of in-foal mares.'

Flower did produce foals, as did the chestnut mare who had been served by 'Little Wonder' and 'Belsille.' James Henderson used embrocation when one colt had a sprained leg but Alfred Peele, the veterinary surgeon from Hartlepool, was called in when another colt was injured. Alfred Peele also castrated some of the animals; a colt and some of the lambs.

James Henderson bought horse for the estate. In March 1900 he travelled to nearby Fishburn to look at horses. He also recorded buying a saddle from John Hudson saddler 5, Finkle Street, Stockton. On the 28th March 1900 he went to Fishburn to look at horses but did not appear to purchase any. In April 1900, Henderson and Lockey went to Newcastle to buy a cart horse, selecting one on trial. This cart horse was unsuitable so it was returned and another horse bought later in the month. James Henderson appears shrewd as he probably recognised the first cart horse may have had faults so he only purchased it on the understanding that it could be returned if found unsuitable, which it was, so that horse was returned. There are later accounts of buying horses. He appeared to frequently buy horses on trial, as he bought a carthorse from Mr Clark of Hardwick Hall in May 1911 one on month's trial. It would appear this horse was suitable as it was not returned.

There were also cattle on the estate. The bull used to serve the cows was replaced in October 1914 when the old bull fat dairy bull on the farm was killed and sold to Mr. Scott of Easington. A young shorthorn bull from Cotherstone replaced the old bull at Oakerside. A red and white bull from Mr. Angus of Sheraton Hill was also used on the cows. These new bulls give an indication of the type of beef and dairy cows at Oakerside, and probably other farms on the estate.

In May 1900, four bullocks and eight hoggets' young sheep, were 'put into the Garden House fields' They were maybe put into this field to fatten them up ready for the Castle Eden Christmas Show and sale of fat cattle and sheep in December. Roast been appeared to have been a popular dish at Christmas. The fattened animals for sale at Christmas would not have to be overwintered. Those cattle overwintered in cow barns would be fed from stored fodder crops inside the barns throughout the winter. The animals' condition would not deteriorate by exposure to winter weather.

The weather could be severe during the winter. In February 1900 a snowstorm prevented the transport of sheep from Oakerside to market. The ice froze on ponds. In late March there was another severe snowstorm. Severe weather occurred in late June when the roof of one of the malt kilns at the Brewery was struck by lightning. In late October, a storm of sleet and rain during the night was so heavy that dene beck swelled and carried away the culvert near Red Slide. The foundation of the flat bridge near dungeon rocks was also damaged. There were several landslips down the steep sides of the dene due to this heavy flood of rain. Winds were fierce too and a chimney of a cottage in village blown down. Stormy weather continued with fierce storms at the end of March the following year. Animals would require overwintering in this extreme weather. As well as stored fodder food was bought in, like cotton cake to feed the cattle two tons being bought from North Agricultural Supply Association, Alnwick at a cost of £11, possibly ordered by mail from their catalogue.

The cotton cake was bought at the same time 20 quarters of 'finest Scotch potatoes' at a cost of £20 10s.

Manure from overwintering the stock would be used as fertiliser but this was complimented by a deliveries of superphosphate, nitrate soda and other chemical fertilisers early in the season, usually in March. In May 25, 1901 carts of nitrate soda were delivered to Oakerside farm. In February 1912, 25 tons of gysum were purchased for Oakerside farm. Supplementary methods of fertilising the land were being introduced. In 1911 a liquid manure tank and pump, probably ordered from a catalogue were delivered to Horden Station for transport and installation at Little Eden Farm for Mr. Scurr, one of the tenant farmers on the estate

Fields needed ploughing prior to sowing seeds. In February 1903, James Henderson records a 'ploughing day' at Blue Leazes farm for Mr. Coates. There were 35 pairs of horses with one draught coming from Oakerside Farm. This 'ploughing day' resulted in the ploughing of "Tree Field, Fulwell Low Field and Fulwell Bank Shank." There were also ploughing days which included hedging competitions.

The Mole Catcher

There appears to have been a problem with moles. In 1907 Alf Patterson was the mole catcher employed to catch moles on estate. Alf Patterson lived in 2, Providence Place Gilesgate Moor so he would have to travel from Durham. He was replaced at a later date by Fred Bushby. Mole traps were made for use on the estate. At the end of February 1902, two dozen new mole traps were made. It is possible elimination of moles was usually dealt with by estate workers, but there may have been a needed for more expert intervention when the outside mole-catchers were called in.

According to some moles could be a pest in agriculture. In April 1882 it was written that;[28] "This is the time of year when moles begin to start their mischief. Some fields are dotted from end to end with hillocks thrown up these subterranean delvers. Mole-catchers are in demand now and are doing brisk business on light lands. On stiff clay soil, moles are said to do good by pulverising the tenacious earth but in loose loamy soil they still do much harm. Mole catching dexterity appears to run in families. I know a man with several sons who inherited the paternal skill in capturing these little animals. In addition to the fee paid by the farmer, the mole-catcher claims the moles which he skins and a moleskin waistcoat is warm and so durable that it will last an average lifetime. For some reason neither dogs nor cats can be persuaded to eat the carcases of the moles after they are skinned, and it is said that ferrets will refuse them. Yet foxes esteem moles as delicacies, and will spend much pains in digging them up."

It would appear foxes had an ally in their liking for moles. In 1899, a farm manager at Fodderty, Dingwall observed [29] "a curious mole catcher at work. A large and handsome sea-gull attracted his attention by the graceful way it floated over the drill, intensely scanning the surface of the ground. Suddenly, steadying itself a minute, it dropped, dug its beak into the heaving ground, and rose with a mole as its prey."

Moles which were considered a pest were becoming more expensive to eliminate. In 1893, there were complaints that fees paid to mole catchers had increased by 200% during the previous thirty years, so a fox or a sea gull which enjoyed a mole may be preferable to exorbitant costs to get rid of them. There was a move amongst naturalists that moles were beneficial to the land, by destroying 'noxious insects'.

Despite these objections it was found necessary to exterminate moles on the estate land. Some catchers may skin the moles to sell the skins whilst others hung the dead moles on a fence supposedly to deter the underground animals away from the area, or possibly to advertise to other local farmers how good they were in catching moles in order to drum up more business.

The mole catching would probably be done prior to sowing seeds. Oats were sown in the Oakerside flat field in April, followed by the sowing of barley at Burnt Lands. Hay was cut at Oakerside, some of the grass culled and hedging took place particularly in Oakerside. Wheat was also grown. In 1900 48 sacks of wheat, 24 quarters, was sold at Stockton corn market for 29/- a quarter to the Co-operative Mills.

In July 1901 the turnip field was attacked by diamond back moths. The caterpillars were brushed off by sacks attached to poles, an arduous task.

From Henderson's diary there is evidence of growing potatoes, turnips, barley, oats and wheat as well as hay for overwintering the stock. In February 1917 40 stones of seed beans were carted to Haybarns. Some of these may have been for use in the Burdon gardens.

In 1903, Mr. Adamson's thresher was at Oakerside. This portable threshing machine would be hired out to farms, making threshing quicker and more effective. Three days hire £8. os od Additional costs of £1 18s 7d were paid to provide refreshments for the men.

Lambing commenced in March. The sheep were dipped in the autumn. In October 1914, Mc Dougal's dip was used prior to the later use of Jeyes fluid.

There were pig sties at Parklands and the Castle. James Henderson bought pigs frequently from a nearby farmer, George English. In April 1910, he bought four young pigs for 24/- each. That was the same year that the old sow Tarbuck Pattie V111 pigged 10 piglets. Four of these piglets died and poor old sow Pattie took ill shortly afterwards and she too died despite the vet being sent for. They appeared to rear Middleton White Yorkshire pigs and sold them often at Haswell Mart. Pigs were not always sold. A pig was raffled at Haswell Mart probably for some charitable cause. The lucky winner, Mrs Faulkner promptly sold the pig for £2 16s 6d probably thinking she would be better off with the money.

When pigs were sold the money was paid into Mrs. Burdon's account. It is possible she was interested in pig breeding and raising and saw this venture as her project. In 1914 the sale of eight Middle White Yorkshire pigs yielded her £19 5s 6d. Many other results of sales went straight into Mrs. Burdon's bank account. Some of these pigs were probably sired by 'Wharfedale Valour', the middle white boar purchased in May 1913. It is possible she may have some input in the purchase of this and other pigs. Mrs Burdon did appear to have some interest in agriculture as in Feb 1916 she was reported as because of a [30] "response to an urgent request, has kindly undertaken woman's agricultural matters with reference to the war in some 15 parishes in South East Durham and Houghton-Le-Spring."

The Contribution of The Women's Institute

The National Federation of Women's Institute, as a committee of the Agricultural Organisation Society was founded in 1915 to help the war effort. The First Women's Institute, a concept originating in 1897 in Stoney Creek, Ontario, was founded in Britain in September 1915 in Llanfairpwll in Anglesey. Madge Watt had mobilised Canadian women to maximise food production. She toured Britain to inform women about the W.I. when Britain was threatened by food shortages due to the German naval blockade.

Information soon spread and it was only a few months later in February 1916, Mrs Burdon had volunteered to undertake women's agricultural matters in 15 parishes and Houghton-Le-Spring. These parishes contained a great deal of agricultural land so this work would be vital. The Women's Institute movement was very in a short time and by December 1918 their work reportedly [31] "continues to make excellent progress. Many of the institutes are doing very useful work of various kinds in connection with food production and conservation". For example, at Witton-le-Wear Durham the Women's Institute had organised the" co-operative for buying and selling of poultry food, seeds, manures, etc., and carried out the distribution of 7,000 fruit-conserving bottles for the Women's War Agricultural Committee as well as many gross for its own members." Mrs Burdon appears to have "undertaken women's agricultural matters" throughout South East Durham and Houghton-Le-Spring for the Women's War Agricultural Committee, probably similar achievements occurred in her area.

There were a considerable number of farms in South East Durham and Houghton. In the 1911 Census there were many tenant farmers on the Castle Eden Estate; including J.R. Alderson at Low Hills farm, Benjamin Scurr at Acre Rigg, Thomas Simpson who farmed at Dene House, Ralph Clarks dairy and arable farm at Howletch, George Cowan farming at Cotsford Grange, Frank Cowan at South Field and Mary Jane Coates who ran the farm at Dene Leazes.

Mary Jane Coates had been brought up on her father's farm. Her husband Robert Jackson Coates was about 15 years older than her when she married him, a widower with children in the summer of 1900. When Robert died on 8th December 1904, she continued running the farm with Robert's children and her brother.

Other women were involved in farming activities. Poultry was kept on the estate including at Oakerside Farm, Haybarns and Parklands. Prior to George Proudlock's arrival as farm bailiff at Oakerside Farm, Mrs Norman, then at Oakerside Farm with her husband, was paid for chickens and eggs. Mrs Proudlock, along with her husband, continued this work. They appear to increase production to include not only chickens and eggs but also ducks and geese.

Some of the chickens and eggs from the estate were sold over many years to Mrs. Jane Ann Corner, a shopkeeper in 49, Northgate, Hartlepool who specialised in the selling of game. She was a widow and her husband William had sold game and fruit in the same shop. Mrs Corner carried on the business after the death of her husband. Raising poultry like Mrs Norman and running a shop like Mrs Corner appear to have been acceptable occupations. It would appear Mrs Burdon's interest in pigs and her work in the Women's War Agricultural Committee was not only accepted but highly valued.

If Mrs Burdon was involved with the pigs she would have been sad when the old sow died despite the vet being called in. Although

Henderson did manage simple care of the animals, like purchasing embrocation for a colt with a sprain, there were times when veterinary help was needed. In January 1902, a colt died from tetanus. In April that year, Mr. Peele, the vet from Hartlepool treated a cart horse taken ill with colic. In 1905 a new vet Mr. Walker was consulted on two ewes from Cottage field with inflammation of the udder. One of the ewes died. There was a case of sheep scab in Castle Park in September 1905. Although vets were called in, measures were taken to care for animals themselves like the purchase of a cattle thermometer for Oakerside in April 1905. Many of these country folk knew a great deal about animal welfare and only consulted the vet when necessary. A cattle thermometer was one of the many innovations in advancing agricultural methods. Visitors to agricultural shows often saw new equipment and labour saving machinery.

Sales and Shows

In April 1900 it was time for the Easter sale at Castle Eden. The County Agricultural Show took place in July 1900. The estate workers were probably working during the Easter sale but they were give one half day's holiday to attend the County Show at Hartlepool. The report in the York Herald begins with[32]; "The grimy touch of the coal and iron industries has tarnished the once fair face of Durham County, but agriculture if not now pre-eminent is still a force to be reckoned with."

This was 1900, just before the deep mines on the coast were sunk but even at this time it was evident that the once predominately agricultural county of Durham was becoming increasingly industrialised. Agriculture itself was becoming more advanced in the production of food. On January 3rd workers spent half a day working with a steam threshing machine. Threshing had been time consuming but had supplied employment during the winter. Now threshing took only half a day. On 26th March 1900, James Henderson obtained a Horsier Corn Drill for Oakerside Farm. This was an American seed drill, horse drawn and far superior to methods like broadcasting for sowing seeds. Sickles were still used, probably to cut long meadow grass in the garden in July 1901 by the sickles James Henderson had purchased for two workmen. Despite the sickles, Castle Eden estate was moving towards modern farming machinery and methods. New machines would be advertised in catalogues. They may have been exhibited at various shows or events.

Durham County Show took place in West Hartlepool but apparently the County Show was a 'migratory institution, settling one year on the verge of the moorlands, coming to the ancient stronghold and capital city itself another, and again visiting one of the coast towns. On Wednesday the exhibition – the 56th held by the society – took place on a level piece of grass land just outside West Hartlepool, rejoicing in the name of "Cold Knuckles."

The weather was sunny throughout the day and a considerable number of people, including the estate workers from Castle Eden, came to see over 1,000 entries in the show, including cattle, horses, poultry, pigeons and rabbits. The luncheon, to which the estate workers would not have been invited was held on the show ground and presided over by Lord Henry Vane Tempest.

Farmers, including tenant farmers and their families from the Castle Eden estate may have attended this and others agricultural shows.

Little Eden[33]

"The Manor of Little Eden lies to the South-East of Easington, and includes a portion of Eden-Dean, lying to the North of the rivulet which divides it from Hardwick." When Rowland Burdon purchased most of this land, he demolished the remains of an oblong tower the 'Turris de Parva Eden' in 1800. A field adjoining the site of this tower 'bears the name of Chapel Hill, where some traces of foundations are still visible." This was probably the site of a medieval pele tower and chapel.

Eden Hall Estate included the land east of Blunts Dene and east to East Dene. The Manor House and its estates were sold to Rowland Burdon in 1800.

Although a greater part of Little Eden was part of the Burdon Estate, the western part of Little Eden still belonged to the Ellison family in 1911. William Ellison had died in 1906. His son, another William now ran the farm with his wife Mary, brother Luke, five farm workers, including two horsemen a cowman and a milk lad who all, together with the domestic servant Elizabeth all lived in the eleven roomed farmhouse.

There were farmers at Horden Hall. Horden Hall had a history stretching back to the 16th century. Until 1313 the manor was owned by Fitz-Marmaduke before passing on to the Conyers. Rowland Burdon bought this estate in 1767. In 1872 Horden Hall farm, was run by Mr. Peacock, included a residence, five cottages and very extensive good farm buildings. The farm consisted of 543 acres, 378 of which were used as arable land suitable for growing crops like turnips and barley. These cultivated fields were large enough for 'steam cultivation'. Cattle sheep and horses grazed on some of the 179 acres of grass land, the rest being used to produce quantities of hay.

The 1881 Census description of part of Shotton Township includes "Shotton Village with the Hall…together with the following Farms – Oakerside, Garden of Eden, Dene House, Dene Cottage, Cotsford Grange, Black Hills, Eden Hall, Little Eden, Howletch, Acre Rigg, (and) Low Hills. There was also a 216 acre farm at Shotton Hall, run by George Sweeting. Hill Top Farm was run by Penelope Clark a 47 year old widow, who was born in Shadforth. Strawberry Hill was also the site of a farm.

Dene House Farm goes back a long way. In 1655 a messuage (Palatine) called Deyne House had a garden an orchard and certain closes. A farm at Shotton Village is run by Emily Smith a widow with Shotton Hall Farm worked by Thomas Robinson. Farm workers, housing a hind and a horseman have cottages for Shotton Hall Farm. A farm had existed on the site of Shotton Hall Farm since at least 1649 with the old village of Shotton dating back to the year.

Howletch, Acre Rigg and West Horden farms were developed in the 18th century. Acre Rigg and Howletch Farms were on church land until 1830 and 1867 respect. The two plantations east and northeast of Acre Rigg were planted by Rowland Burdon as game covers.

Shotton Mill was built on an old foundation of 1724 and abandoned in 1903. Foolish Hill was named after the man, Fullish, who ploughed the land. Edderakers was Ethered's acres. Many of these farms had history spanning hundreds of years.

In the immediate locality, there was a large number of farms, many in the Burdon estate. As well as overseeing the running of the agricultural concerns on the estate, James Henderson collected the rents from the tenant farmers living on the estate. Rents were usually collected monthly. One entry in January 1900 records a 'fat pig from Mr. Boulton'. It is uncertain whether the pig was part of Mr. Boulton's rent. Tenants in cottages also paid rents to be collected. Sometimes repairs or alterations were needed. These were frequently supervised by James Henderson with estate workers like masons, plumbers and painters carrying out the work. When a workmen left a tied cottage, that residence was usually repainted or decorated before a new workman moved into the property. Gamekeepers, watchers and woodsmen were amongst those who moved out of properties. Some of the gamekeepers' homes were in quite isolated places, like the property called the Garden of Eden, situated within Castle Eden Dene itself.

Gamekeepers

Wild rabbits could severely damage crops so a man was employed to keep the rabbits under control. In 1900 Aitkin was engaged to kill rabbits from September 1st to April 1st and to work in the woods the remainder of the year at a wage of £1 a week and journey expenses. He was replaced in March 1903 when Charles Kidd arrived by the 8.25 pm train to take over as rabbit catcher. Although the estate employed rabbit catchers, others who caught rabbits were guilty of poaching or trespass if they were caught. Rabbits were usually poached using nets and ferrets. In October 1893 four miners were prosecuted for poaching 21 rabbits, 15 of which were still alive when they were caught. One miner was fined £5; the other three were fined £3 each. They also had to pay costs. If they did not pay they would spend one month in prison.

A similar incident occurred in September 1898 when three men, miners from Station Town, were charged with poaching for rabbits with a large sweep net on a farm near Castle Eden. A game-watcher John Hedley of Sheraton Hall gave chase. They stopped until he neared them, then one threw a stone that felled Hedley to the ground, kicking him in the body and legs where he lay. Hedley lay in the field injured for some time before he could may his way home and could be tended to by a doctor. The poachers were convicted and sent to jail for two months with an additional 14 days for the default of costs.

It would appear it was considered that[34] "colliers were seen as the most innovative, cunning and dangerous poachers." The greatest threat to game preservation as occurring on estates close to significant urban settlements or coalfields." There no nearby 'significant settlements' but there were coalfields and by the early 1900's there would be more colliers as deep mines were being sunk in the vicinity. Those caught by gamekeepers would be prosecuted for trespass in pursuit of game. It was a more serious offence to be caught trespassing at night.

In December 1865 it was commented that,[35] "The district of Castle Eden, the estate of Mr. R. Burdon, appears to be infested with poachers." This appeared to be the case at this time. There had been a serious affray in Castle Eden Dene at night in early December 1865 when a number of gamewatchers, their assistants and policemen were lying in ambush to apprehend a gang of about eight poach-ers.[36] "Frequent firing of guns was heard at a short distance off, the sounds becoming gradually nearer, until at length the footsteps of the party could be heard, and their forms dimly seen in the dark-ness of the night. The party sprang forward on the [poachers, who at once took to their heels, closely followed by the watchers .They had not gone far before the poachers cried out that they would fire if the pursuit was kept up." This threat was unheeded. "One of the poachers then fires, striking P.C. Lowrey in the cheek, arm and side." Another shot was fired, hitting the son of Robinson, one of the keeper's; fifty pellets lodging in his back, arms and legs. At first it was thought the injuries to Thomas Lowery were not serious, but some pellets had entered his brain resulting in bouts of insanity which results in admission to Sedgefield Asylum.

Rowland Burdon offered a reward of £50 for evidence that would lead to the arrest of the poachers. Only two men both, of them miners, one being a miner from Shotton Colliery apparently a notorious place for poachers, were prosecuted and given prison sentences.

The use of guns appears to have led to other problems. Earlier in 1865, in June William Harrison, a cabinet maker, and his young son were out for a stroll in a plantation on Mr. Burdon's estate at the same time as Mr. Robinson, gamekeeper was in the vicinity ferreting and shooting rabbits. A rabbit pursued by the ferret ran into the direction of a footpath which was completely out of sight being obscured by bushes.[37] "Robinson levelled his gun at the rabbit and fired just as it was entering among the bushes a distance of about twenty-five yards, and the shot had gone through the bush and struck Mr. Harrison and his son several places about the body. Harrison shouted out immediately he had found himself shot, fearing that another barrel might be fired. Robinson at once proceeded to the spot and was horrified to find that such an accident had occurred. The poor lad, who was the more seriously injured of the two, was at once conveyed home, and Dr Watson was sent for. On the doctor arriving it was found that the shot corn had gone in at the side of one eye, and it was afterwards extracted at the back of the ear. It was also discovered that five corns had penetrated into the breast and two into the forehead none of which have been extracted. The youth, although suffering from the pain of his wounds, passed a pretty favourable night, and his injuries are not such as would terminate fatally. Mr. Harrison received only three shot wounds, which were in the fleshy part of his back, and although it is painful, are happily not of a serious nature."

The latter case was accidental shooting, hopefully with a good outcome. The first case of poaching occurred the day after two Wingate men were convicted of poaching by Rowland Burdon and sentenced to ten and twelve months imprisonment. These sentences did not appear to act as a deterrent as incidents of poaching appeared to be more frequent.

A case of desperate poaching affray appeared before Rowland Burdon in February 1875 when two men were charged with night poaching at Wingate on the land of Major Wilkinson of Durham. The men were also charged with [38] 'cutting and wounding Police Constable Carruthers and a game watcher… at the same time and place." The policeman "appeared in the witness box with sticking plaster on various parts of his head, and bore other traces of serious suffering." The policeman and game watcher were passing through a gate on the Durham road when they "met with a white dog, and at the same time two men came forward." The policeman took hold of one of the man and the game watcher the other. Six or seven men then "rushed forward" knocking the policeman down with sticks before stabbing him in the side with a spear. After this attack the policeman lost consciousness and the assailant escaped. The spear was part of the gear which included 300 yards of netting and huge sticks the poachers intended to use for salmon poaching. The three prisoners identified by the policeman were committed as prisoners to appear before the next Durham Assizes.

Game watchers appeared to have a difficult and sometimes dangerous job. Gamekeepers lived in Warren House, near Horden Hall and Holm Hill Farm. On 17th September 1900, William Smart arrived at Warren House from Lumley Thicks, followed by the arrival of his furniture on Mon 24th. He did not stay long as on 14th February 1901, John Mc Phail underkeeper for Warren House arrived by 2.15 train. His furniture removed from station to Warren House on 16th. John Mc Phail is 37 on the 1901 Census. He was born in Scotland as were his wife Agnes and four children.

There was a keeper's cottage at Fulwell. On Friday March 21st 1902 Andrew Taylor, underkeeper arrived. As his furniture was nor arriving until the next day, he stayed overnight at Mr. Claxon's Inn.

The head-keeper and his family were based in a six roomed house in Oakerside. Charles King, the new head-keeper arrived on the estate in March 1903. Charles was born in Norfolk and had lived for some time in Suffolk, the birthplace of his wife and children. Coming from such an agricultural area, he appeared to have knowledge of pheasant rearing. Only one month after his arrival a new rearing shed was built and pheasants were bought to begin rearing more for the estate. The birds were fed on maize. James Henderson records regular large supplies of maize being delivered from Tyne Dock and Hull. The pheasantries were kept clean with flowers of sulphur to minimise disease.

The pheasants were raised to shoot. There was a 'shooting party' at the east end of the Blunts in November; the participants taking lunch at Dene Cottage. Shoots continued, usually in November. A particularly successful shoot on November 14th 1905, in Fulwell Plantation, and the south side of the dene from Mossy Bridge to Butts Bridge, resulted in 425 birds being killed. This seems a huge amount of birds shot in a single day. It is possible some were kept and distributed amongst the participants and friends, others may have been sent to Mrs. Corner of Hartlepool as she sold game as well as chickens and eggs.

Mrs. Burdon would sell some at charitable events like the fete to raise money for the Waifs and Strays held in the Drill Hall, Sunderland on 18th November 1902. (SESG Sunderland echo)There were several stalls with articles for sale including; flowers, refreshments, craft, toys, art work, needlework, fancy goods, baskets and glass. Mrs Burdon ran stall 11 which sold butter and game, the butter too probably made on the estate. Raising money for 'Waifs and Strays' through the Church of England Waifs and Strays Society. The Mayor of Sunderland gave a speech on the first day of opening saying; [39] "In every large town, unfortunately, there was a great amount of slum properties; and there was a great number of waifs and strays." He urged those present, including many dignitaries, to see the need to "lift up and improve the condition of the life of these little mortals… In the police courts…cases of little urchins brought up for small offences such as begging…(like the) case of a small boy who had been brought up for begging four or five times….(The) parents of such children sent children out to beg on the streets for the purpose of getting a conviction so that the children might be sent to school (meaning an industrial school), and the parents get rid of the responsibility."

Lieutenant Colonel Challoner added he saw, "a real need... to get at the root of the matter, and deal with the children before they become acquainted with the vices of the streets and before they formed habits they could not name." The response to such fund raising events resulted in the Highfield Cottage Homes being erected, north of the Workhouse in the early 1900's in Sunderland to provide children with accommodation in small family groups supervised by an appropriate adult. These cottages were probably better than the Workhouse and Industrial Schools. The sale of pheasants from Colonel Burdon's shoots were going to a good cause.

Shooting continued on the estate, accompanied by refreshments and a lunch at a nearby location.... On the 22nd more shooting took place in the Hardwick Denes and inside the Castle Dene from the sea to the Garden of Eden. In each event there were 5 guns. It was a frosty day in November 1911 when Colonel Burdon, Colonel Darwin, Richard Gardner and J.F.B. Baker went shooting in the Blunts, Oval Plant, Little Eden, and the North side of the dene from the Garden of Eden. Colonel Darwin was the only man who self-loaded his gun. The keepers loaded the rest. They were familiar with guns and probably carried them in their line of work.

The shooting party probably stayed overnight at the Castle as they were out again the next day, another fine frosty day, to shoot in Fulwell covers. Shooting during the season, especially during November appeared popular for Colonel Burdon and invited guests.

Carrying a gun would have a tragic consequence for one newly arrived gamekeeper. On 26th July 1900 Robert Hunter Storey arrived to work as an under gamekeeper. He took lodgings in the village. He left his lodging at 1pm on Sunday 2nd August, a few days after he arrived but did not return to his lodgings. He had still not been heard of by Tuesday, so an extensive but unsuccessful search to find him that day. The following day, his body was found in the dene near the Garden of Eden. The inquest, held in Castle Eden inn, disclosed Strong's head was[40] "shattered by gunshot." The gun lay by his side. At first it was thought he was the "victim of foul play" but "evidence given by Sergeant Scott and Gamekeeper Hogg and others pointed to the fact that Storey...took his own life...while temporarily insane." Robert Hunter Storey was buried in Easington Church. Robert had been brought up on a farm. His father Henry and mother Elizabeth still ran the farm at Newton Park Northumberland. His death was announced in the Morpeth Herald on 11th August but he was buried in Easington Church. Some of the Castle Eden Estate workmen attended. It is to be hoped his parents also attended their tragic son's funeral.

Robert Storey's funeral was different from that of another keeper who lived in the cottage in the part of the dene known as the Garden of Eden. Featherstone English died in the cottage on 13th March 1903. On Sunday the 16th he was carried by bearers through Castle Eden Dene to St. James' Church Castle Eden. The family and friends would have followed behind. The procession would have to walk about two miles over through fairly rough ground through the dene to a steep bank that led to the church.

Woodsmen

Woodsmen worked in Castle Dene and other parts of the estate where there were plantations. Castle Eden Dene, covering 221 hectares, is the largest natural woodland in the North East of England. It runs from Castle Eden 3 ½ miles down to the sea at Denemouth. There are many paths crossing the dene, created by the Burdon family some giving views of magnesium limestone cliffs, deep gorges, one crossed by Gunner's Bridge and many ancient trees including yews and beech. There are huge varieties of flowers, insects and birds as well as roe deer and foxes. As well as ancient woodland, some plants like sycamore and rhododendrons were introduced.

In March 1905, James Henderson recorded that "Two trucks of rhododendrons arrived from Knowsley". "Trucks" probably meaning railway trucks arriving at the station. It is uncertain where the plants came from but Knowsley may refer to Knowsley near

Liverpool and possibly the landscaped gardens at Knowsley Hall. Both ivy and rhododendrons were very popular plants especially in late Victorian times and considered suitable for planting in Castle Eden Dene at this time. Gertrude Jekyll had published "Wood and Garden" in 1899 and described how in the "third week of May", her garden in Munshead Wood near Surrey the "rhododendrons are in full bloom on the edge of the copse." This book may have been the inspiration for the introduction of the exotic looking rhododendrons into Castle Eden Dene. Visitors would have been able to admire the display when the dene opened to visitors on Saturday May 16th 1908. Notices were erected the week prior to the opening and may have directed visitors to the places of interest and routes to follow.

Ivy was also planted. Other planting took place. In March 1900, creeping ivy was planted on the banks near the Castle, an area of heavy shade, ideal conditions for the growing of ivy. Hollies were planted in March 1909, so holly and ivy would provide greenery for decorating the Castle at Christmas.

Whellan's 1894 Directory describes the dene saying; "Great improvements have been effected here of late years, and Castle Eden Dene has been rendered one of the most romantic spots in the north of England. A recent writer speaking of the dene says, A winding and safe road, throughout the extent of the defile, serves admirably the purpose of displaying its endless beauties to the many hundred visitors, who during the summer, are admitted by the liberal proprietor to the enjoyments of this magnificent region, containing some of the finest scenery in the county of Durham. Seen from the upper part of the dene, not far from where a stream of water springs from the crevice of a rock, and, forming a natural cascade, falls into Gunner's Pool, the road can be traced to a considerable distance through the valley below. Snake-like, and in broad coils, it rushes down the steep sides towards the bottom of the dell, which is too much steeped in gloom to reveal its own secrets.... A tubular bridge has been placed across Gunner's Pool, rustic bridges erected, the grounds laid out, and many improvements effected by the owner Mr. Burdon."

The dene was not the only wooded areas. There were plantations mainly of pine trees throughout the estate. Some timber was
felled and hauled in the various plantations before being sold, so
new planting was necessary to replenish the existing woodland and
create new plantations. In March 1900, 1,500 Austrian pine trees
were ordered from Joseph Robson and Son Hexham. Later that
year in October a one acre plot at Acre Rigg was measured out to
plant with young trees. Robert Scurr the tenant farmer of Acre Rigg
was paid to plough and harrow this land prior to planting. A new
plantation of just over six acres was begun in January 1903 ready
for tree planting in March. In 1904 many young trees; 1,300 larch,
2,000 Scotch pines and 1,500 Austrian pines were planted in Fulwell
plantation. In 1905, the woodmen moved to West Plantation with
even more trees; 4,800 larch, 4,800 Scotch, 2,000 Austrian, 2,500
Corsican, 250 Italian Poplar and 250 alder. Six thousand trees,
including 12 horse chestnut and 50 silver firs were planted to 'fill
up' in Dene Leazes. A great number of trees must have been felled
if it took six thousand trees to 'fill up' in Dene Leazes, only one of
the planting areas. Records of planting more trees, usually conifers
continues throughout James Henderson's records. Most of the trees
mentioned for planting were pine trees yielding soft wood timber.

Tools were bought in June 1904, giving an indication of the
tools used to fell trees and work with the timber on the estate; 2
hand-hammers cost 3s, 2 augers size ½ and three eighths were also
3 shillings, two strong hand saws at 9 shillings, 2 workmen's axes 9s
6d making a total of £1 4s 6d. Felling and preparing trees for hauling using these tools would be extremely hard work.

Tree felling could be difficult and dangerous John King, a
woodman was slightly injured by a falling branch at the east end
of Fulwell plantation. The woodmen erected several wooden fences
throughout the estate but in 1904, they put iron fences at the bottom
of East Dene Bank.

In October 1905, woodman G. Gibson was injured by a "blow
from a pointed end of a fence post at Little Eden, in unloading the
cart containing the fence posts and rails, by C. Scurr's boy, one of

the posts struck Gibson on the inner part of the thigh in front of the body."

Other smaller jobs were undertaken like one woodman who was given the task of repairing the cattle feeder boxes at Horden Hall Farm in 1911. These men must have been skilled at working with wood as well as felling and planting. They were also skilled at hedging, doing work in September 1900 hedging at Oakerside.

The woodsmen's work was hard and strenuous for six days a week until 15th August 1908 when they were allowed to finish work at 1pm on a Saturday before having the Sunday free. The men did leave and move elsewhere bringing new workers into the estate. In 1917 under-woodman Edward Robson "moved from Blue Cottage to Burnmoor Village Fence Houses to work for the Earl of Durham." He must have been a good worker and had good references. When Andrew Taylor left in 1905, E. Scriven from Consett took over from him, moving his house at West Lodge. When Edward Scriven himself left in 1908, Ernest Jones from Yarm took over his job. 1910 was the year James Armstrong left Blue Cottage to be replaced by William Hepple. Hepple arrived at Horden Station from Hexham. Like other workmen, his train fare and removal expenses were paid. The cost from Hexham was £1 4s train fare and £1 13s 10d for his furniture and luggage. Half the total of £2 7s 10d would be paid on arrival. William Hepple would have to wait one year for the remainder. This appeared to be common practice, may be to ensure the men did not come to work and leave before at least one year. Edward Ridley's furniture had a more complicated journey when he moved into Dene Cottage from Rowlands Gill. His "furniture was removed by motor rolling to the top of the bank of Cotsford Grange field and carted from there by George Cowan to Dene Cottage," a complicated journey.

Looking after the Workmen

The estate workforce appeared to be looked after to some extent. In 1911 Jacob Urwin had an accident and was absent from work for some time. He had another misfortune when his "boy died "on 13th January 1913 and he was "interred at Ryton on Tyne." This was probably the place the Urwin family had come from because in February Henderson records that Urwin removed his "furniture from house in the village to Ryton on Tyne." C. Hoggett took over from Mr Urwin but James Henderson records his child too developed a 'serious illness.' The illness of children must have been of some importance for Henderson to make a note of it in his records.

In March 1913, Joseph Swindley took ill while he working at the back road at the Garden of Eden. He returned home but it was some time before the family called for a doctor, maybe to spare the expense. When Doctor Russell arrived, appendicitis was diagnosed and urgent transport was needed to take him to Hartlepool Hospital, so he was taken to hospital in the Castle motor car, driven obably by the chauffeur.

Estate workers employed for a long time received a small pension when they retired. Sometimes servants were left an annuity or payment on the death of their employer. Anne Malet had left a considerable sum to her companion Agnes King as well as small amounts to some of her servants. The Burdons were probably considered good employers as well as good landlords who appeared to keep their cottages and farm dwellings in good repair and decorative order.

CHAPTER 10

Life in Castle Eden in the Early Twentieth Century

In 1911, the Castle is described as having 42 rooms. There was also an extensive conservatory running alongside the building.

Some of the Burdon family are at home at the time of the 1911 Census; Colonel Burdon is now 54 and described as being of private means, Mary Arundell aged 46 his wife of 24 years, daughters Francis aged 21 and Lettice aged 10. Francis has probably completed her education but Lettice has a governess, Agnes Marshall aged 35 born in Edinburgh. Joan Burdon, now 15 is at boarding school; the Manor House Boarding School, Brondsberry Park in Willesden. Rowland Burdon, junior, now about 18, does not appear to be recorded on the Census. He may still be at Eton, where he played cricket several times for the XI but an accident injuring his knee prevented him getting his colours. From Eton, Rowland went to Oxford to continue his studies.

Joan Burdon appears to have had an interesting education at the Manor House Boarding School with Lucy H.H. Soulsby as Principal. Miss Soulsby' obituary in 1927 gives an insight into her beliefs and character.[1]

"The death took place somewhat suddenly at Reading last week of Miss Lucy Soulsby, who for many years had been a leader in educational and religious movements among women. Miss Soulsby, who was 70 years of age, spent some years of her early life at Leamington, residing with her mother in Heath Terrace and no doubt many old Leamington residents will recall she did much good work in St. Mark's parish during the time the Rev. Carus Wilson was vicar of the "Pepperbox" Church. During the few years she resided in Leamington – she left in 1879 to take up residence at Salcombe, Devonshire, Miss Soulsby made many friends....

After residing in Devonshire for five years, Miss Soulsby joined the staff of the Ladies College, Cheltenham. In 1887, she was appointed head mistress of the Oxford High School for Girls, and quickly made her mark as one of a brilliant band of head mistresses belonging to the Girl's Public Day School Trust. On leaving Oxford in 1897, Miss Soulsby took over from Miss Clarke, a private girl's school at Manor House, Brondsbury. She retired in 1915."

A fine tribute is paid to Miss Soulsby's character by a Times correspondent, who writes: 'She inherited from her father the splendid physique of an old Northumbrian family; from her mother a wonderful power and capacity for building up an developing character. An arresting personality, she transfused and infused in all she met light, energy and enthusiasm. With a man's power of grasping essentials, she had a woman's greatness of heart, an unerring sympathy with every human need and a child's enjoyment of every little pleasure'. It is interesting to note it would have been considered a compliment to suggest that Miss Soulsby 'had a man's power of grasping essentials' almost suggesting it was outside the power of a woman's intellectual ability to be able to 'grasp' any 'essentials' at al all.

Miss Soulsby retired from Brondsbury in 1915, but, like Cortez,' new planets swam into her ken' and she then set out for the United States of America. There an intended visit of two months stretched out into two and a half years of crowded life, travelling and making friends everywhere, from east to west. Americans opened their hearts and homes to her, and it may be said that she did more than many travellers to realize one of her great desires in bringing the two nationalities together. Her book, 'The America I saw in 1916-1918', which came out in 1920, revealed her great gifts of understanding and sympathy. But the strenuousness of her life had begun to tell, and after her return from America she lived very quietly, though ever ready with counsel and advice to all who sought her. 'Her children shall rise up and call her blessed', and all who knew her 'felt the wind on the heath.'

The book Miss Soulsby wrote about America was not her sole published work. She wrote prayer books, including "*Suggestion on Prayer*" and "*Short Prayers.*"

These would indicate the extent of her strong religious beliefs. She also wrote five books on "Stray Thoughts"; one each for 'Girls', 'Mothers and Children', 'Reading', 'Character', and 'Invalids.'

The book entitled "*Stray Thoughts for Girls*" gives an insight into Joan's education. She wrote, "At school you are reminded constantly of Prayer, hard work, tidiness, regularity (and) self-control."

The girls were taught subjects like Mathematics, Languages, including Latin, History, Geography but Miss Soulsby appeared to greatly encourage them to read what she considered suitable books. Her book, "*Stray thoughts for Girls*" was dedicated to "Girls at an Awkward Age," presumably including the 14-17 year old who attended her school. In her book girls were warned not to read, "Society novels that make you live with flippant, irreverent or coarse people, or those who take sin lightly." The reading of "sentimental and passionate poetry" is like a weak self-indulgence similar to a 'greedy love of pastry.' Miss Soulsby conceded girls may read a few novels that are "exciting and romantic" but they should read many of "Scott, Thackeray, Dickens, Miss Austen and Mrs. Gaskell."

Miss Soulsby considers family duties more important than reading when she writes, "You know that I care very much for your reading…you will have plenty to do if you read all the books I have begged you to study – but if it gave your mother pleasure for you to be the stupidest garden-party, I should think you were wasting your time terribly if you spent it over a book instead." Although Miss Soulsby values education and especially reading, she sees family duties, and pleasing your mother more important. She comments that; "Higher education often makes girls feel it a waste of time to write notes for their mothers, and to settle the drawing room flowers," but these are the duties of a "Virtuous Woman" and she encourages the girls to aspire to this goal.

"Girls should aim" to become "fit to manage your house and to teach your children." Before this can happen they need to marry. She even has some advice on this, "to marry for money is degrading, but a woman may redeem it by being a good wife: to marry without money (supposedly she means to marry for love) means debts, which is irretrievably degrading, and is altogether selfish instead of romantic." This idea could feed her passion of dissuading the girls from reading romantic fiction. The idea of marrying for love without money she saw as 'selfish' rather than 'romantic' as it would only lead to 'debts' and presumably unhappiness.

The "Virtuous Woman" always did her 'duty' and was 'industrious at home.' This industry includes organising the servants to "give them full work and insists on its being done, at the right time and in the right way, but she is careful never to overwork them, and to remember that servants have rights and feelings.... But she never does her servants work, nor spoils them."

The Servants

It would be interesting to know if the servants at the Castle in 1911 thought their employers knew they had rights and feelings. They may have felt overworked at times as servants' hours were very long.

The Butler, in 1911 Frank Henry Lockyear aged 48, was the highest ranking servant being responsible for the servants and answerable to the Burdons.

Frank Henry Lockyear was born in St. Marychurch, near Torquay in Devon in 1863. His father, Henry, was a coachman. In 1891 when Frank Henry was 27 and still unmarried he was employed as a footman in Escot House in the household of Sir John Henry Kennaway, Member of Parliament. The house was large so there was a large number to servants living in the house. Gardens outside designed by Capability Brown in the 18th century gave employment to many gardeners living on the estate.

By 1901 Frank Henry has risen from footman to butler for the Burdon household, not such a large household as Sir John Henry Kennaway's, but a very responsible position to have attained.

In 1911, Lockyear, the butler is now married to Eliza who was born in Suffolk. They have three children, Louisa, Frank Henry and Ellen all born in Castle Eden. The family live in a four roomed house in the Village near to the Castle. His house and coal would be part of his wages, which in 1901 would be about £60 a year.

Elizabeth Anne Burdon tells of a previous butler, Sclater, who worked in the household of her Uncle Rowland and Aunt Anne Malet Burdon. Elizabeth considered Sclater a most disagreeable person, a 'clever old reprobate'. Henry Baker Tristram had been an expert in his collection of bird skins. Possibly Sclater thought he could emulate Rev Tristram and also start a collection. It is possible he had not perfected the technique as Elizabeth considered Sclater's collection extremely unpleasant and probably smelly. When Elizabeth's brother the them Major Burdon took over running of the estate one of his first acts in his turn was to transfer all these 'lock, stock and barrel' to the Museum at Durham.

By this time fashions for displaying cases of wild birds had changed, so Elizabeth's brother Rowland got rid of them. The subsequent fate of Sclater's macabre efforts are probably long since destroyed, although there is still the possibility they are hidden away in some remote corner in Durham. This Sclater, as butler appeared to show deference to all but his master and mistress. He also pursued a hobby he considered suitable to his position of butler on a large estate.

Elizabeth may have been mistaken when she thought her brother Rowland had transferred all the cases of stuffed birds to Durham as many such items were for sale in the auction of 1946. There was a stuffed eagle in a glass case for sale in the entrance hall, as well as a stag's head with antlers and a pair of antlers. There was even more of a collection in the smoking room including 18 cases of stuffed birds and a stuffed fox in a case.

Mr. Lockyear the butler in 1911 was replaced by Mr. Hawkes in May 1914, moving into the house in the Village previously occupied by the Lockyear household.

At this time there was no housekeeper at the Castle, so Mrs. Burdon as mistress of the house would be, according to Miss Soulsby, expected to give; "her servants full work and insist on it being done, at the right time and in the right way, but she is careful never to overwork them, and to remember that servants have rights and feelings…but she never does her servants work, or spoils them."

As the Castle had 43 rooms and a large conservatory there would be a considerable amount of work for the housemaids to do. Three housemaids; Clara, Ethel and Alice lived in the household.

There are two ladies maids. Annie Dobson aged 42 is probably the servant of Mrs. Burdon whilst another Annie, aged 28, probably referred to be her surname Thompson may look after Francis Burdon now aged 21. There is another maid, Lily Jones the parlour maid. She lives in the Village with her family, her father Ernest working as a woodman on the estate.

Mrs. Burdon may have met Annie Dobson whilst visiting a relative of her husband's mother in 1901. She was in the household of land agent Giles William Lloyd, who was a member of the Hale family. Rowland Burdon's mother was Elizabeth Ann Hale prior to her marriage to his father John. Both Rowland and Giles William Lloyd are named as two of the executors of the will of George Hale, land agent to the Earl of Derby who died in January 1903.

In 1901, Annie was a cook in the household of relative by marriage Giles William Lloyd. Mrs. Burdon may have requested Annie become her lady's maid instead of working as a cook because Annie is in the Burdon household as lady's maid in 1911.

There are two other male servants in the household; twenty year old Alfred the footman whose father is a woodsman living in the Village and William Henry North a seventeen year old hallboy.

It is not known how long Alfred the footman remained in the Burdon's employ.

Elizabeth Anne Burdon recalls what she describes as a 'funny story' told to her by her Aunt Fanny Burdon about a footman in the time of her grandparents; Rowland and Cotsford Burdon. [2]

"A footman they had, and rather valued, appeared at the drawing-room door one day rather awkwardly, and hung about as if wishing to attract attention.

Mrs. Burdon turned round. "Well Thomas, what is it?"

"Oh, if you please, Mum, I am wishing to leave."

"Well, Thomas, I am sorry to hear that; and what is your reason?"

"Well, you see, Mum, it's like this. I am wanting to get into a more respectable family."

Thomas achieved his ambition "in the family of Sir James Weir-Hogg, which he adorned for many years. In those days a title was of greater value than now!"

Sir James Weir Hogg was an Irish born business man and Liberal Member of Parliament. He was not from a long line of nobility, but he had a title, so Thomas the butler must have considered him more 'respectable' than the Rowland Burdon who descended from a long time of distinguished Rowland Burdons. Although the above account is written as a story by Elizabeth, the word "respectable" is probably the one used by Thomas. Respectable appears harsh and cutting but Rowland Burdon did not have a title and because of that he was not deemed 'respectable' by a servant and possibly those who were titled. If the unfortunate circumstances resulting in the failure of the Exchange Bank had not occurred, he would have probably remained as a Member of Parliament. John Scott, Burdon's friend from youth was knighted Lord Eldon. His brother William became Lord Stowell. John Scott, like Rowland Burdon supported William Pitt. Although Rowland Burdon was reportedly not an accomplished orator, he may still have been knighted and become more 'respectable' in the eyes of servants and gentility.

The Servants' Work

In 1911, the cook, Mary Stewart will be in charge of the kitchen staff; Mary the kitchen maid, and Minnie aged 17, the scullery maid.

Around 1901, the following account[3] of "Life in Hitching-brooke", appeared to be the typical daily life for servants in a large house. There may have not been much change by 1911.

Minnie, the scullery maid would be in the kitchen at 6.00am getting 'the kitchen range hot enough to boil water for tea.' Throughout the day Minnie would have endless washing up, sweeping and cleaning in the scullery and kitchen

Early in the morning the hallboy would be cleaning boots. Mrs Beeton is specific on the cleaning of boots and shoes;[4] "three good brushes and a good blacking must be provided;: one of the brushes hard, to brush off the mud; the other soft, to lay on the blacking; the third of a medium hardness, for polishing…The blacking should be kept corked up, except when in use, and applied to the brush with a sponge tied to a stick, which, when put away, rests on a notch cut in the cork. When boots come in very muddy, it is good practice to wash off the mud, and wipe them dry with a sponge, then leave them to dry very gradually on their side….Much delicacy of treatment is required in cleaning ladies' boots" so they have a "fresh appearance" and the "lining is free from hand-marks, which are very offensive to a lady of refined taste."

In times when there were no flush lavatories, the hallboy's job would have also included emptying the chamber pots. He would be expected to fetch and carry throughout the day as well as doing chores like chopping kindling for fires.

The three housemaids, Clara, Ethel and Alice would get dressed in their attic rooms, at 6.30, hurry downstairs to prepare 'tea and toast' for the ladies maids, Annie Dobson and Annie Thompson. As their forenames were the same, Annie Thompson may have been known by a different forename or possibly her surname. Clara, the senior housemaid, delivers the ladies maids their tea before commencing cleaning the main downstairs rooms. Ethel would also be involved in this cleaning work. Alice, as the youngest house-maid would fetch kindling previously chopped by the hall boy and coal from the coal hole and light all the fires before commencing cleaning.

After finishing their tea and dressing, Annie would help Mary Arundel dress and do her hair. Thompson would go to Miss Francis' room for similar duties.

One of the maids would probably have taken tea to Agnes Marshall, ten year old Lettice's governess. Agnes may have super-vised Lettice in getting ready on a morning and retiring at evening as well as being responsible for her tuition.

Meanwhile Minnie, the scullery maid would tidy up the kitchen and sweep the floor. She is joined by Mary, the kitchen maid who makes breakfast for the servants. Mrs. Stewart, the cook would spend most of the day cooking the family meals. If there were visitors this would mean a considerable amount of extra work.

Lockyear the butler at Castle Eden, who lived in the Village would be ready about this time, to attend to Colonel Burdon morning role as his valet. Whilst the family is getting ready and after the servants have had a quick breakfast, probably of porridge bread and butter and tea, Alfred, the footman lays the table in the dining room.

Mrs. Beeton describes the domestic duties of the butler include bringing;[5] "in the eatables at breakfast, and wait on the family at that meal, assisted by the footman, and see to the cleanliness of everything at table. On taking away, he removes the tray with the china and plate, for which he is responsible. At luncheon, he arranges, and waits unassisted, the footman now being engaged in other duties."

These duties, Mrs. Beeton suggests include;[6] "cleaning cutlery and also furniture, answering the door to visitors, answering drawing- room bells, trim lamps, brush his master's clothes and do all errands. His duties include carrying letters and messages to friends, the post or tradespeople.

At dinner, the footman places the silver and plated articles on the table, sees that everything is in its place, and rectifies what is wrong. He carries in the first dish, and announces in the drawing room that dinner is on the table, and respectfully stands by the door until the company are seated, when he takes his place behind his master's chair on the left, to remove the covers, handing them to the other attendants to carry out. After the first course of plates is supplied, his place is at the sideboard to serve the wines, but only when called on."

Mrs Beeton continues with what appears to be a rigid, discipline formula for serving the various course of the meal in the correct manner. The butler, where[7] 'only one footman kept will be required to perform…duties of the valet, to pay bills and to superintend other servants." He should be "competent to advise his master as to the price and quality of the wine to be laid in." He keeps a book on the contents of the cellar and is responsible for all contents of the cellar and their distribution. Mrs Beeton emphasis that "nothing spreads more rapidly in society than the reputation of a good wine-cellar" so she lays great store on this part of the butler's job with many paragraphs written on the subject of wine.

There are so many other duties Mrs. Beeton suggests for the butler and footman. These greatly increase in events like receptions and evening parties. Especially in these occasions, [8] "Attendants in the drawing-room, even more than the dining-room, should move about actively but noiselessly, no creaking of shoes, which is an abomination."

The Housemaids' Work

Clara, Ethel and Alice, housemaids in the Castle, had forty three rooms and a large conservatory to keep clean. The auction catalogue listed some rooms as; the entrance hall, drawing room, morning room, dining room, staircase and landing, smoking room, billiard room, library as well as bathrooms and a boxroom.

There was the kitchen and scullery, a housekeeper's room, a butler's pantry and bedrooms for the maids. There may have been other rooms not mentioned.

Many of these rooms would have fires. Some of the guest bedrooms may have only been used when visitors came to the Castle. Fires would have to be lit in these rooms on such occasions. Lighting so many fires would be difficult work for the housemaids and hallboy. Huge amounts of heavy coal would be needed, so scuttles would be filled and carried often up flights of stairs.

The catalogue lists various items of furniture to be sold. Some like the; Hepplewhite mahogany settee, a Sheraton inlaid mahogany table with a matching cupboard all displayed in the drawing room, a Chippendale mahogany settee and an antique rosewood writing desk in the morning room appear to be valuable pieces of furniture. There is much more furniture for sale, a considerable amount of it being made from mahogany. This furniture would need polishing and dusting probably frequently if dust gathered from the lit fires in the various rooms.

There were 147 items of china listed for sale including; a tray of 'early morning tea and coffee' items on a tray. Early morning tea and coffee would be carried upstairs to family and guests. There were items of china which would need careful handling and cleaning such as: various flower vases, a crown derby dessert service, items of Worcester, Staffordshire, Wedgewood, Coalport and Crown Derby china and a 'pair of Copeland Parian China Busts of Wellington and Napoleon under glass domes.'

Sixty eight items of glass were also included, again more careful handling and cleaning. Amongst the above lots were four were pig patterned flower vases and a bottle in the form of a pig. It is possible these had belonged to Mary Arundel as she appeared to have been an expert on pigs.

There was also a large quantity of brass, copper, pewter, silver and cutlery to clean. The kitchen stew pans were copper. These, and other copper kitchen equipment would be in constant use but also expected to be sparkling clean, as would the copper coal box in the shape of a hippopotamus in the drawing room.

There were many carpets itemised in each room including Axminster and Turkish. James Henderson had noted that carpet beating took place in the Castle on 11th June 1913. This would be only one of the many occasion when the Castle carpets would beaten. A carpet sweeper had been invented by Bissell in 1876 but the carpet would need a vigorous beating outside with a carpet beater to remove collected dust and grime. The carpet beating probably took place when the Burdons were at their London residence, so that the family would experience no disruption. The housemaids had a considerable amount of work to do.

Three new baths were installed in the early summer months of 1908 when the family were in London by Hardy and Longford at a cost of £130 8s 5d including pipework and connections. There would have been more work before the installation of bathrooms in the Castle. Slipperbaths were amongst the lots for sale in the auction and would have been used in the past with containers of hot water being carried upstairs to fill them. These baths were for sale in the maid's rooms so it is possible they were still used by servants.

A heating boiler for hot water was installed in the Castle, making life easier for the maids. A heating boiler was installed under the conservatory in 1904. These boilers would need stoking, maybe by one of the gardeners or an odd job man.

In 1911, also in the absence of the family, electric wiring was installed to the Castle by Drake and Gorham of London. The work was completed by October when electric lights were switched on at the Castle by Cleveland and Durham Electric Power Company. Prior to electric lights, gas lamps would have been used. These would often have to be lit manually. They were probably not fitted throughout the house. Oil lamps were for sale in the billiard room in 1946, so these must have been used at some time in the house.

In earlier days candles were used which could account for the numerous candlesticks for sale in the auction. There were candle snuffers with Georgian silver handles, a reminder of earlier days in the Castle.

After the earlier collapse of the bank, the Burdon family had to cut down on expenses and life became a [9] "Spartan regime in every way." Young John Burdon "suffered at Durham Grammar School from having to appear in his father's Court suits and coloured waistcoats cut down to his small person and short legs." The children were not allowed pets because of the extra expense. The use of candles was limited; [10] "the habit of the family on winter evenings was to sit round the light of one solitary candle, placed in the middle of the large table in the drawing room." They would still have servants at this time, so life for them in a darkened household would be even more difficult. Well before 1911, the family fortunes had been restored and now electric lights could be installed to illuminate winter evenings instead of one solitary candle.

Colonel Burdon had electric lights installed in the Castle in 1911. Work to extend the cables must have continued later because on the morning of 16th September 1917, electric lights were switched during morning service. This may have been a special service when the church was lit by electricity for the first time.

The Kitchen Work

The cook would plan and cook the family meals aided by the kitchen maid. The kitchen maid probably prepared food for the servants. The scullery maid would have to cope with endless washing up.

Pigs and poultry were kept on the estate. Young pigs were bought in but it is possible they were intended to be fattened before sale. Game from the estate was shot or killed. Some of the above may have been used for consumption in the household. James Henderson does record many instances of sheep from the estate or others being bought in 'for house killing.' One recorded instance in August 1913, '12 scotch wethers were bought from W. Collingwood Tweddle Farm for house killing' with a further '15 more scotch wethers' bought from Tweddle Farm shortly afterwards. In September 30th 1914 "30 Scotch wethers" were bought at Barnard Castle for "house killing." A great deal of mutton appeared to be consumed. Mrs Beeton includes a considerable number of recipes for mutton including many recipes for braised, roast and boiled mutton, curried mutton, Irish stew, rolled loin of mutton and less familiar recipes nowadays cooking kidneys for breakfast, sheep's feet or trotters, lamb sweetbreads and singed sheep's head. It would appear very little of the sheep was wasted.

Mrs Beeton also included many recipes for game which could be used after shooting parties. As well as recipes for birds like grouse, pheasant and partridge, she also included various dishes made from hare, including jugged hare and potted hare, another breakfast dish.

Animals were also taken, alive or dead it is unsure, to the Burdon's house in London, probably for consumption. On 23rd February, "Mr. Burdon left the Castle for London" accompanied by "one fat hog" weighing "45 lbs."

Desserts could include fruits from the garden or something much grander. In extremely cold weather in January 1900, James Henderson describes taking ice from the South Fold Pond to place in the Ice House at the Castle. Ice and snow would be packed into the ice house and insulated and may last until the summer. Desserts like ice cream, rice pudding and sorbet. Mrs. Beeton's ice cream was a pint of fruit juice and a pint of ice cream with sugar to taste, a considerable amount of whisking and freezing the mixture in a freezing-pot, presumably containing ice from the ice house.

During the five course family dinner, the Ladies maids would be hard at work once again clearing up the bedrooms after the family and any guests have spent an hour getting changed in them. After picking up the clothes she would draw the curtains and lay out the night wear.

"Life in Hitchingbrooke" suggested that the footman would clear the table about nine o'clock after dinner. Clean napkins and table cloths would be needed for every meal, so the maids would start on the crockery and laundry. Meanwhile the footman would clean the glass, silver and cutlery.

The ladies maids would need to stay up until the bell rang when the ladies were ready to retire. They would go to help the ladies get ready for bed. The butler had the last task of a long day when he checked the lights were out and the doors secured.

The typical yearly wages in 1901, quoted in the Channel 4 programme, seem low; the Butler, £60, (housekeeper £45, none in the Burdon household in 1901), Chef £80 (a cook in the Burdon household would be paid less than this), Ladies maid £32, Kitchen maid £24, first footman £26, (second footman not in Burdon household £24), first housemaid £28, second housemaid £22, scullery maid £12, coachman £18, and hallboy £16. Although household servants had board and lodging as well as their wages, the wages still appear very low. Those who lived in other accommodation received a tithe cottage with a coal allowance.

Wages may have seemed low in 1901 but were even lower in 1796. A list of the then Rowland Burdon's employees and their wages were recorded on 12th May 1796.

"Husbandman ... Wm Taylor ... £16: o. o. pr. ann. Meat and lodging" William Taylor would be the live in farm servant responsible for looking after the animals on the estate.

"Gardener ... Thos. Parrison ... £21 :o. o. pr. ann. House and 15/- for coals."

The gardens must not have been so extensive in 1796.

In 1911, "Gamekeeper ... Geo. Handcock ... £22: 0. 0. Cowgait, house and 32/- for coals". A cowgait may mean an area of land where he could keep cows. There was only one gamekeeper at this time. This had increased over the years not only to watch the game against poachers but because the Burdon's raised more game for shooting and trapping.

"Butler: Peter Walton ... £30: 0s 0d pr. ann. Meat and lodging." There is also an under-butler, Peter Strong who receives £10: 10: 0. Per annum plus meat, lodging and £2:2s for washing. The footman, Daniel Toombs receives £16 : 16s 0d, more wages than the under-butler, so presumably Daniel is of higher status than Peter. Daniel also receives meat and lodging.

Coachman, William Pearson earns £18 guineas a year whilst the postilion, George Stonehouse gets seven guineas. George was probably a strong young man as he was employed to sit on the lead horse of the carriage, driving the horse more quickly. He would get dirty, so he was allowed an extra 30/- a year for washing. The groom, George Clark earned £14 a year to look after the horses. They also receive meat and lodging.

The under-butler, footman, coachman, postilion and groom are supplied with frocks and liveries and £2: 2: 0. Each for boots and breeches. This is particularly relevant for the postilion as he had to wear high, rigid boots to protect his legs from injury.

Andrew Drysdale, as under-groom got £13 a year, plus meat lodging and a frock for his work in the stables. There was only one woodman, George Clark. His wages of seven shillings a week were paid jointly by Mr. Burdon and Mr. Brandling. The woodland management of the dene and various plantations had not commenced at this time, so George Clark would be mainly responsible for maintenance of the various woodland areas.

Only two of the women servants are named; Mrs. Barlow, housekeeper and cook and Mrs. Cook the ladies maid, who both receive £26. 5s per annum. It would appear they are of equal status, and valued equally in the household. Two unnamed housemaids received each five guineas a year, the laundry maid six guineas, the under-cook nine guineas and the kitchen maid five guineas. All the female servants received meat, washing and lodging. The names of the maids and under-cook were not known. They would be invisible to their employers, keeping out of the way and knowing their place as they went about their duties, working very hard but virtually unnoticed by those upstairs.

There would be a considerable amount of laundry if most of those employed received "washing" as part of their wages. The laundry maid lived in the household at this time.

Servants changed over the years. In March 1900, Mrs. Best came to Parklands to work as a laundress at a wage of £70 a year, paid £1. 6s. 11d a week or £2. 13s. 10d a fortnight. Seventy pounds a year was a better wage than the £60 paid to the butler in the Channel 4 programme. There were no set wages for domestic staff in 1901, so wages would depend on the employer. Seventy pounds a year may have been considered a good wage for a laundress, even though it was a very skilled job. Rowland Burdon may have been a good employer, paying his employers better wages than some.

Mrs Best was a widow with four young children. Her husband Joseph, an assistant in a chemist's shop in Hartlepool had died in October 1897, leaving £189 2s 3d in his will to his wife Ann. By 1900, Ann may have needed to find work to support her family, so she obtained employment and a place to live for her and her family. She did not remain at Parklands for long because in early 1901 she had met and married an Irish coal miner living in Monk Hesleden. They remained in Hesleden and by 1911 had an eight year old daughter of their own.

The estate would need a new laundress. By 1907, Mrs Conroy is the laundress at Parklands. Mrs Beeton described the laundry establishment as consisting of; [11]. "a washing-house, an ironing and drying room, and sometimes a drying closet heated by furnaces." There would be a "range of tubs, either round or oblong....an ironing board...a strong white deal table, about twelve or fourteen feet long for ironing blankets, a mangle in one corner and clothes horses for drying and airing, cupboards for holding the various irons, starch, and other articles used in ironing."

"The laundry maid should commence her labours on Monday morning, by a careful examination of the articles committed to her care, and enter them in the washing book, separating the white lined and collars. Sheets and body-linen, into one heap, fine muslins into another, coloured cotton and linen fabrics into a third, woollens into a fourth, and the coarser kitchen and other greasy cloths into a fifth. Every article should be examined for ink – or for grease spots, or for fruit, – or wine stains." Mrs Beeton continues with information on how such stains should be removed prior to washing before detailing the lengthy washing procedures which in some instances entails soaking and boiling some articles.

Much of the washing appears to include hand-washing where linen especially is "rubbed over in every part" in water that is as "hot as the hands can bear."

Each of the groups of washing described by Mrs. Beeton has a different washing procedure which she describes in minute detail.

She also includes how to make starch, a "process by which stiffness is communicated to certain parts of linen," prior to giving details on the skill of ironing with flat irons, including the use of an Italian iron used on 'frills and plaited articles.'

Laundry work appeared a very time consuming, labour intensive procedure but one that needed skill and knowledge particularly when laundering fine or expensive articles. Labour saving devices were being introduced and Mrs. Conroy probably used the Syracuse Easy Washer probably ordered by catalogue and sent to Castle Eden Station by North East Rail from Marshall and Phillip furnishing and wholesale ironmonger, 179, Union Street Aberdeen. The innovative machine, that "washes fast, washes clean, washes everything" cost 35/-. It was on rollers so could move about easily. This machine would be a hand-operated machine as the Easy Washing Machine Company in America did not make their first machine operated by an electric motor until 1918. The machine delivered in 1907 to Castle Eden would still be great improvement on the time consuming process of hand washing. She would still have used a flat iron to smooth the clothes once washed and dried.

After the Conroys left Parklands, the seven rooms are occupied by David Garrie a dairy man, his wife Mary skilled as a dairy maid, and son aged 19 who is a student. There are four servants in the household, another dairy maid and three laundry maids. It would appear there may have been increased facilities for the laundry work installed at Parklands. The other occupants of Parklands are in the Drill Hall where the sergeant instructor for the 2nd DLI Sergeant Harry Webb lives with his wife Mary.

The Gardens

The Castle had large gardens. There was what was called the Peach House a heating greenhouse for growing fruit such as peaches nectarines, grapes, melons, figs and if you were wealthy enough like the Marquis of Londonderry, pineapples.

In the 1860's Rowland Burdon's head gardener, Mr. W. Laidler won prizes at Horticultural Shows for grapes grown in the vinery. Peaches would have been grown it the building was called a peach house so the family would enjoy fruits like these for desserts at mealtimes.

Miss Mary Burdon appeared to be interested in gardening. She frequently won prizes in agricultural shows as in 1854, when she won first prize in the Castle Eden Horticultural Show for her display of pinks, picotees and carnations. Mary did sometimes baffle competitors and judges at times on her exhibits with the example of some pansies which left everyone extremely puzzled.

In 1911, there are dwellings in Castle Eden Gardens. William Charles Fulford, the head gardener, aged 42 lives in a four roomed cottage with his wife and six month old son. In 1914, he is replaced by James Machar who arrived in May on a train from Ferryhill.

In 1913, Albert Kingscote, gardener, left and was replaced by T. W. Weston who took up residence in Church Lodge. There were a number of gardens on the estate where gardeners would be needed. Other gardens in the area would be managed by the several domestic gardeners who lived in Castle Eden, many recorded on the 1901 Census. James Caplin, a gardener originally from Sussex had lived and worked in Castle Eden for many years. In 1891 he was recorded as a farmer and gardener living in Fir Tree Farm. James Henderson noted in his diary that James Caplin had died on 29th March 1900 and was interred in St. James' Church Castle Eden on 1st April. James Caplin was sufficiently well known to the agent of the estate, so it is possible James Caplin was responsible for some of the gardening work done on the estate. He must have been well known both as gardener and person if James Henderson noted him in his book.

Substances ordered at that time for garden improvement may not be used today. In February 1901, James Henderson ordered two cwts of sea salt for the gardens on the estate. Apparently when used in the correct quantities, the minerals in sea salt are beneficial especially for flowers, particularly roses.

In October 1903, one wagon load of sand was carted from Horden Colliery for use in the gardens. Another load was sent to Mrs Tristram who was living in the Cottage. Horden Colliery was undergoing sinking operations at this time and the sand would be from these excavations.

Gardeners changed over the years. The foreman gardener Mr. Abbots was replaced in 1914, Victor Grimes, foreman gardener arrived on the 5.32 pm train. The house must not be ready for his arrival as he lodges with James Henderson.

A larger dwelling is a boarding house run by Mary Greener, a 42 year old widow. The four young men boarding are all domestic gardeners on the estate.

In October 29th 1915, "three lady gardeners leave Castle employment Miss Whitton, Stowell and Reece."

Gardeners change again in 1916 when Lewis Webster, from Burn Hall Easingwold arrives, lodging with James Henderson before moving into a small cottage near the school when his furniture had arrived. His wages are 30/- a week plus the small cottage and coal.

These gardeners would grow vegetables for the household. On 22nd October 1917, gardeners had 'finished taking up potatoes at the Cottage. Parklands very good crop." These potatoes were stored in the "cottage coach house."

There was a gardener's bothy in the gardens and, although small is sometimes occupied. In October 1901, clerk to the Mr. J.F. Baker of Middleton Tyas, Rowland Burdon's land agent is staying there, probably whilst he is conducting his business on the estate.

The First Motor Car

Other servants live in the Village like Thomas Richard Hooper the chauffeur. He has a wife and baby daughter. His 16 year old assistant boards with the family in their four roomed house.

On May 22nd 1903 at 8pm, a motor car arrived at the Castle from London.

James Henderson had even noted the time the car arrived, so its arrival must have been significant and quite an event in the village.

In 1903 Rowland Burdon's car had probably been bought and licensed in London, where he also had an address.

According to a writer in 1900; [12] "Newcastle was the first town to have motor cars paving the streets and roads in omnibus fashion." This omnibus would have referred to public transport by means of a horse drawn omnibus running on a steel or iron tramway... The city 'bus driver has to squeeze into an already over-gorged street, and worm in and out of the traffic with calculating coolness. That the motor car driver in Newcastle can seize every little opportunity to gain time by escaping when he rushes forward through the gap." The omnibus would be horse led, like other forms of transport. The motor car, a new innovation had to find a way through all this traffic. The drivers must have been somewhat of a risk-taking adventurer eager to experience the new technology.

The streets would be crammed with numerous kinds of vehicles including carts, coaches and omnibuses. People may be trying to cross the street. The motor car driver apparently can weave in and out of this apparent chaos. Not everyone would this this form of transport and even, "Even minded, unexcitable persons might find locomotion by spurts of this kind jar upon their nerves, but it is the ideal sort for those who love adventure."

There must have been many who loved adventure on the streets of Newcastle if a great number of residents had witnessed motor cars weaving in and out of the traffic. So many that the writer included what he considered a witty remark;

A boy who was asked by his teacher at one of the Newcastle Board Schools for the definition of an autocrat, promptly replied, 'the driver of a motor-car.'

One wonders at what speed these motor cars wove in and out of traffic.

The speed limit was increased in the 1903 Act to 20 mph. Those exceeding the speed limit were prosecuted like Basil Withy, a ship builder from Hartlepool who was fined 10s in October 1910 for speeding at an estimated 29 miles an hour. Despite this apparently low speed, accidents did happen. HM 18th August 1910 reported that;[13]

"An accident occurred near the Parklands; last night at about 8 pm, when a car belonging to the Sunderland Forge and Engineering Company, and driven by a man named Raine, was in collision with a pony and trap owned and driven by Mr. Conroy, bill-poster, Haswell. The car was going to Sunderland and Mr. Conroy to Hart. One of the pony's legs and a shaft of the cart were broken. The pony was subsequently shot. The car proceeded to Sunderland. The driver of the cart, who was accompanied by two little boys, escaped with a severe shaking."

It is uncertain whether Mr. Conroy was recompensed for the loss of his cart and the death of his pony. His loss does not seem to have affected his livelihood. James Conroy stills lives in a four roomed house in Mary Street Haswell, still working as a bill poster. His wife Mary was probably very upset at the accident, especially as her two little boys, James now eight and Albert aged three, were so shaken up by the accident. They have a baby brother now, probably the reason for them being in the cart in the first place but it is to be wondered whether Mary lets the boys go out in the cart with husband James again.

Despite concern about accidents, motor cars were on the increase with 'motor cars in the shape of omnibuses' also on the increase which would be[14] "very useful to the masses" and not 'only enjoyed by the privileged few."

Cars were useful. The chauffeur took an ill estate worker to Hartlepool Hospital in the Burdon's car. Their use was rare in 1903 and noted in newspapers. (SDESG 22 June 1903) There was a great interest in speed walking in 1903, the press going as far as to call it 'the walking craze.' In June 1903, a race of 21 miles commenced at 4.33 pm from West Hartlepool Town Hall, finishing at the Grangetown Terminus of the Sunderland Tramways. Sixteen of the twenty six entries began the race accompanied by three referees riding bicycles and Dr. Durward Brown and Mr. R.H. Mushers riding in a motor car and probably a driver, kindly lent to them by Mr. F. Taylor.

The route went through Castle Eden and Old Shotton. Villagers may have turned out to see the speed walkers. One competitor's 'knees gave away' at Seaham Hall and 'had to be lifted in the motor car.' The race was won by a bank clerk from Hartlepool in the staggering time of 3 hours 31 ½ minutes; exceedingly fast for walking a distance of 21 miles. Those who finished under five hours received a medal. Two clerks, who came in last and did not receive a medal, had walked more leisurely, stopping for tea on the way, so did not finish until 9.15pm.

The car had proved useful for the walker whose 'knees gave way'. He would be grateful for the ride and attention from the doctor.

Thomas Richard Hooper came to Castle Eden as the Burdon family's chauffeur. He was born in 1873 in Paddington London and began working in large households as a stable-helper in Hertfordshire. In 1901, he was valet in a large household in Berkeley Square, London. He appeared enterprising as he learned to drive and became a chauffeur, possibly being hired by the Burdon's whilst they were living in their London residence. He stayed with the Burdons for some time, being replaced in March 1916 by chauffeur, Mr. Beer. This time the removal of his effects was not by rail or cart. Mr. Beer moved into a house in the Village from Wolsingham travelling with his effects in a motor van at a cost of £8 6s 3d, much more expensive than the previous rail removals had been.

By this time work had been done in July 1907 and in 1913 to resurface the Castle coach road with 1910, presumably to stop animals grazing in the parkland straying onto the coach road.

Although the family had a chauffeur to drive their car, they still needed a coachman to drive the coaches. William Henry Mc Endoo, born in Ireland, was their domestic coachman in and his large family all live next door to the chauffeur in their four roomed house.

According to Mrs Beeton a coachman should not only have skill in driving, he should also[15] "possess a good general knowledge of horses...see that the horses are regularly fed and properly groomed, watch over their condition, apply simple remedies to trifling ailments in the animals under his charge, and report where he observes symptoms of more serious ones...He has either to clean the carriage himself, or see that the stable- boy does it properly."

William Mc Endoo must have been very good at his job as coachman. He lived in Castle Eden for 35 years, thirty two of which he was in the employ of Col. Burdon, after which he worked for four years for Durham County Council. Col. Burdon probably had no need for a coachman around 1930 but it is possible he was able to secure him a suitable position working for the Council.

William McEndoo died in early January 1934 aged just 59 after a very short illness. A large congregation gathered for his funeral as he[16] "well known in the district." There would be many members of the Church present as William had been a "member of St. James's Church Choir for 33 years." He also "took an active interest in all the sports clubs of the village. His sons, George, Len and Henry are all well-known members of the Castle Eden Cricket Club."

Cricket

The Mc Endoo family would have been known to Col. Burdon. He was patron of Castle Eden Cricket Club and William's son George was a member of the Committee. Colonel Burdon was probably interested in cricket as his own son Rowland had been a promising cricketer at Eton until an accidental leg injury stopped him playing.

Col Burdon may have encouraged the McEndoo boys in playing for the Castle Eden team. He may even have watched them play.

The team had been in existence for some time. In February 1903 the cricket ground in front of the Castle was being levelled so by April of that year the cricket ground could be measured off. It was probably from this time a serious team for Castle Eden was established. Rowland Burdon jnr, about ten years old at this time was at Eton where he developed an interest and had ability in playing cricket. It may have been young Rowland's idea to have a cricket team in Castle Eden. A photograph taken in 1908, shows players at that time. Rowland Burdon jnr, aged 15 and probably still at Eton, is one of them.

Frederick William Landale, the umpire, was a clerk for a timber merchant. He lived with his widowed mother Eleanor in Eden Street Hutton Henry. John George Heslop was a surveyor who lived in Castle Eden. Rowland Johnson Stonehouse was a draughtsman for a marine engineering firm in Hartlepool. Thomas Mowbray Stonehouse was a clerk in 1901 becoming the secretary of a Hartlepool Brewery in 1911. John Austin Leo Magee, then known as Leo, lived in Burnside Castle Eden with his family, including father John Magee, an owner of merchant shipping vessels. Leo became a doctor but moved away from is birthplace of Castle Eden to the south of England to practice. Charles Judson was a former member of Sheffield United cricket team. He had fine scores for Sheffield and was a good bowler but was now playing for Castle Eden. Charles was a brewer at Castle Eden Brewery so would have been known by William Nimmo also of the brewery. Andrew Dixon was a clerk at the brewery, so three cricketers had connections with the brewery. Francis Herron was the registrar of Birth Deaths and Marriages. They all lived in Castle Eden.

Other Sports

The cricket team of 1908 did not appear to have any estate workers playing for them at this time. Some of these cricketers appeared to work as clerks. In 1911, Anne Dewhurst, Colonel Burdon's private secretary lodges with the estate bailiff James Henderson and his

wife in the Village who live in a six roomed house so there is sufficient room for James' elderly father-in-law to live in with them.

Cricket was not the only sport the Burdons participated in.
Indications of some others were the items in the entrance hall of
the Castle put up for sale in the auction. There were; riding crops,
archer's bows and arrows and golf clubs in a canvas bag. There were
also four shepherd's crooks and seven walking sticks.

One or some of the walking sticks may have been used by
Colonel Burdon's Aunt Mary. Mary Cotsford Burdon liked walking
in Castle Eden Dene. A walk in the dene, 'Miss Mary's Walk' was
probably a favourite of hers as she tramped along wearing a large,
muddy boots which she would probably not have to clean, although
there was a boot scraper up for sale, so some of the mud may have
been eliminated before more intensive cleaning.

There would be horse riding. Prints of fox hunting for sale in
several rooms indicate an interest in fox hunting. A gun case with a
leather outer case was one lot here, a reminder of the shoots held on
the estate. Two fishing creels and a pair of waders meant an interest in fishing. Elizabeth Burdon told how her brother Rowland had
fished at English Bicknor from a young age, so he probably continued with the sport.

There was a tennis court at the Castle but on December 13th
1913, work was commenced on a new court made from ashes from
Hartlepool Gas and Water Company Works which supplied material to surface the court to a depth of ¾.

Whether one can consider greyhound coursing a sport, even
in 1911 is unlikely but James Henderson made a memorandum in
his diary to remind himself that the first greyhound coursing event
took place on January 23rd at Little Eden. Although it was a damp
day there was "good sport and a good company attended."

The Village

Some of those who attended this meeting at Little Eden may have
come from the Village in Castle Eden. Workers like joiners, painters
and bricklayers live here and in other parts of Castle Eden, nota-

bly The Factory. These are workers employed in maintenance and building work on the estate.

Robert Craman, born in Castle Eden and in 1911, aged 44 is one of the estate joiners. He lives in The Village in quite a large house of six rooms with his wife and two children. Robert Craman[17] had this article written about him many years later in 1949.

"Sixty eight years working on the Castle Eden Estate and 72 years uninterrupted service in the Church choir, is the proud record of Mr. Robert Craman (82), who has lived all his life in Castle Eden. With him in Castle Eden Church choir, is Mr. Andrew Dixon, secretary of Nimmo's Brewery, who has nearly 50 years service to his credit. These two are the only male voices now in the choir."

Andrew Dixon was one of the cricketers in 1908. Now he is secretary at Nimmo's Brewery. He still sings but can probably no longer play cricket.

"Mr. Craman started his apprenticeship as a joiner with his father on the Castle Eden Estate at the age of 14, and continued in this work until the death of Colonel Burdon four years ago. He is now estate bailiff, which he considers 'heavy enough work for me now.'

"I would retire, but the business won't allow it," Mr. Craman told a Northern Daily Mail reporter, so I will go on as long as I can."

Mr. Craman's younger daughter keeps house for him whilst his elder daughter occupies a house across the road – the house in which Mr. Craman was born. He was christened, confirmed and married in Castle Eden Church.

Much of the woodwork done in the Castle was done either by Mr. Craman or his father, who also handled the joinery and masonry work for the Hartlepools Hospital opened in 1870.

Mr. Craman recalls when he joined the choir, which was under Colonel Burdon's sister, there was no accompaniment except for a fiddler! "The choir is not what it used to be," he commented regretfully.

Mr. Craman, a widower for the past 19 years, attributes his long life and excellent health to a quiet and peaceful living in the country, and says that he, at the time of Rowland Burdon and Anne

Malet, when his son Robert was four years old lived in number 6, The Village."

James Henderson, then a shepherd, lived in number 10. Sclater, the supposedly ill-mannered butler at the Castle who shot and stuffed wild birds, lived at number 12. Young Robert would have grown up knowing all these people.

"R Craman Senior worked on Hartlepool Hospital, renovation work paid for by the Burdons. They had along involvement with the Hospital, both in raising money and serving as President of the Board."

Colonel Burdon had continued work on the hospital begun by his Uncle Rowland and later his father Rev. John. In December 1923 the following notice appeared in the "Hartlepool Mail"; "With a view to raising greater interest and increased support for the two local hospitals, the following letter has been sent by Colonel Burdon (president of the Hartlepools Hospital) and Sir William C. Gray (president of Cameron Hospital) to many leading Churchmen, including the Free Church."

Money had to be raised to sustain the hospitals in this time before the National Health Service. Colonel Burdon writes;

"May we ask you to help us to revive the very laudable custom of Hospital Sunday when sermons may be preached, and collections made on behalf of the local hospitals."

Colonel Burdon remained President of the hospital until 1936. There had been a family link with the hospital from the founding of the institution in 1865 when his Uncle Rowland Burdon was original chairman and part founder. Extensions were completed in 1889 at a cost of £3,000 to Rev. John Burdon, Colonel Burdon's father who was also chairman or president. Robert Craman senior would have been involved in the masonry and joinery work undertaken in the hospital. John Thomas Smith, a plumber, glazier and painter who also lived in the village was also probably involved in the later work.

Robert Craman junior became apprentice joiner to his father. When a young man called David Brown finished his five year apprenticeship on September 17th 1904, he received a bonus of £10, quite a reward. Young David Brown may have been the joiner who lifted Mrs. Hatton's dining room floor and found the dead rats that were creating the bad smell.

It would seem that workers who had been in long service on the estate were given a pension when they retired. James Thubron was given 7/6d a week when he retired in July 1903. William Stranghair, a retired mason received 10/- a week until his death in 1902.

When employees left their situations, their cottages are often repaired and redecorated. Similar work is done for the tenants, for example two rooms were papered for Mr. Robinson at Shotton Hall Farm in March 1902. The painters then moved on to decorate Eden Vale in May the same month as the boiler was fixed in Dene Leazes. New ovens were installed in various properties over the years. Kitchen floors were layered with cement. In 1902, the ceilings of the Boy's school were whitewashed.

Mill Hill Cottage was decorated before being let to Mr. John Hunter Auctioneer. This included the drawing room, dining room, breakfast room, kitchen, scullery and pantry downstairs with four bedrooms upstairs containing a bathroom in the 4th bedroom. There were also out offices, a stable, a coach-house, a hay and straw loft with a boy's sleeping room above.

Building work began in July 1902 to erect four new cottages in The Village. Captain Francis Thomas Tristram had moved into The Cottage so the Bothy House was whitewashed and papered for his gardener. The painting and decorating, repairs continued throughout the years. It would appear the estate cottages were well maintained. In 1910, new cottages at the south end of the foundry were built by the estate workmen. Two more were built in 1911 the same year as a new farm house was built at Howletch. Stable roofs were raised. In 1913 and 1914, joiners and masons made alterations to the Drill Hall. These estate workers were kept busy.

The cottages and farms where the tenants lived needed upkeep and maintenance. There were estate workers like joiners, a mason and his labourer and painters employed to carry out work like whitewashing and papering a room in Oakerside farmhouse in May 1900, wallpapering Fulwell cottage in June 1900. In February 1900, a new boiler was installed in Wellfield Farm. The Police Station needed a white basin fixing in May 1900. In December the appointment of a new cartman meant his cottage needed papering. Also in December a new closet pan and 'fillip' was installed in Mayes cottage At Burnside. Work to install a new heating boiler and bath at Meadow Bank was beyond the expertise of the estate workmen, so it was installed by Langland and Hardy.

Meadow Bank was the home of John Stirk, schoolmaster and his family. His two elder daughters, Edith and Mabel were pupil teachers at the nearby National School. It may have been seen as a luxury to have a boiler, probably a gas boiler to heat water for a bath in the bathroom.

Next door on one side of the Schoolmaster's house, Mrs Mary Forster and her niece Jane who ran a grocer' shop. The Superintendent of Police, Anthony Heslop and his family lived on the other side. There was a young police constable, Albert Walker and Mary, the 16 year old servant also in the household.

Work was done on John Edgar's cottage Garden House in Old Shotton. He had died and his widow had moved into Castle Eden to live with her son, so the cottage was empty. In January 1900, the water pump was moved to the bottom of the garden. A new kitchen range was installed in May of that year. The land at Garden House was taken over by Mr. Burdon from May 13th.

The joiners did other work as well as estate work like putting up rails and posts in various places on the estate. In September 1900, they put up a stage in Parklands for Mr. Lambton's political meeting with a fee of £2.20 for the use of the hall, paid by cheque in late October by Mr .J. Stonehouse, agent for Mr. Lambton. By this time Lambton had been re-elected Member of Parliament.

Parklands needed redecorating, so estimates were obtained from Mr. Wright Painter in West Hartlepool in July 1900. T.W. Stokeld gave an estimate of £1.9s.6d to wallpaper the staircase.

There appeared to have been fencing erected in 1900. The estate employed carters or paid others to cart. In 1901 John Edgar was paid for carting 2,000 bricks manufactured by Straker and Love of Brancepeth Colliery to Little Eden. A wagon of sand and building lime from Aycliffe was carted. It would appear some building work was occurring in Little Eden. Wagons of coke breeze, probably for boilers, were carted to the Castle in November and January. In March there was a delivery of two loads of coke to the Church.

These items, and many others, may have been transported to the station and carted from there.

It would appear sometimes outside contractors were used for some jobs especially those that required more expertise or what could be considered more refined such as decorating Parklands. Apart from contracts like this, the estate workers did a huge amount of work.

Castle Eden in 1900 was considered as a summer resort when visitors came to lodging and dwelling houses to stay for the summer. They came because the district had many [18] "attractions to recommend it, the famed Castle Eden Dene being the chief, and the air is most enjoyable."

Rowland Burdon and Magistrates' Courts

Although a great deal of time may have been needed to manage the estate, Rowland Burdon was still greatly involved in his work as a magistrate. The annual report for the year ending 1901 by Superintendent Heslop of the Castle Eden Petty Sessions was published in January 1902. It included;[19] "Indictable offences: - Wilful murder, 1; attempted murder, 1; manslaughter, 1; wounding, 1; rape, 1; indecent assaults, 2; burglary, 1; horse and sheep stealing, 7; larceny from the person, 2; simple larceny, 39; false pretences, 1; receiving stolen goods, 1; destroying railways.

There were 44 persons apprehended of whom 22 were convicted, 16 sent for trial and 7 dismissed. There were 12 persons summoned, 2 of the cases being dismissed, 2 sent for trial, and 14 were convicted. The number of non-indictable offences was 1,532. Of these 105 were apprehended, 1,512 summoned, 815 being for drunkenness. The conviction for permitting drunkenness was 4, and illegal sale of drink 1."

There appears to be a large number of cases of drunkenness.

The case of attempted murder took place in Shotton Colliery involving a young couple married for only four months who constantly argued. There was an argument over who should get some cinders for the fire. When the husband refused, "She called him a lazy beast and he struck her in the chest and she hit him back. He then struck her a heavy blow between the shoulders and she picked up a chair and threw it at him. He had got his knife out. He remarked that she had a thin neck, and now after bolting the door he knocked her down and thrust the knife into her neck on the left side. The woman got hold of the knife and got her finger and thumb out. He then attacked her again and thrust the knife a second time into the wound, and, after struggling, stabbed her on the right side of the neck."

Although he had used a pocket knife the wounds were 'very serious.' The husband was sentenced to twelve months in prison. Oddly enough the couple appear to stay together, maybe under better terms. After he came out of prison they moved to Coxhoe, then Rainton and finally Gilesgate where he worked as a miner. In 1911 they are living in Gilesgate with three of the surviving five children. It is to be hoped they settled their differences.

The wounding with intent involved two miners at Castle Eden Colliery when one miner inflicted two serious wounds on the head of the second with a coal rake. The attacker was sentenced to three months in prison.

The murder case involved a herbalist from Hartlepool who subjected a heavily pregnant woman to an illegal operation which proved fatal. He was at first sentenced to hang but this sentence was reduced to imprisonment on appeal.

The manslaughter case was that of a young woman from Heselden who drowned her new born illegitimate baby in a wash tub. She did not know why she had drowned the little boy. She was sentenced to twelve months in prison. In 1911 she is working as servant in the household of a miner in Tudhoe.

The man who stole the horse and cart at Castle Eden was sentenced to 12 months in prison for his crime.

These are outcomes of a few of the crimes committed. A newspaper article in January 1901 suggests that at this time there was a[20] 'more humane system of dealing with criminals' with the intention of 'giving the criminal an opportunity for reform rather than punishing him as severely as possible for his crime.' The article gives examples when the death sentence was passed by Justice Littledale at Durham Assizes in February 1831. Those sentenced to hang were, "a young man of[21] for stealing two pieces of broadcloth, two women for stealing wearing apparel, a man for killing a sheep with intent to stealing the carcase, two boys of 13 and 14 for stealing six silver spoons, two blankets and wearing apparel, a man and wife for shopbreaking, a man for horse stealing, four youths of 17, 18 and 19 for house-breaking, and a youth of 19 for wilful murder, the only capital charge in the list."

The above list of people hanged for what would appear minor crimes of stealing, especially those where children were executed, appears horrendous.

It was not until 1861 that the death penalty was restricted to the punishment for only "wilful murder and high treason." The article reminds the reader that the Quaker Sir Joseph Pease had "laboured so long, though unsuccessfully, in endeavouring to secure the abolition of capital punishment altogether."

Joseph Pease was a Liberal politician. His father, also Joseph, was a Quaker industrialist and railway pioneer of Darlington with his son Joseph becoming a banker and owner of coal and ironstone mines in Durham and Yorkshire. Member so the Pease family would have been known to the Burdon family. They moved in the same social circle as members of both families attended the ball at Wynyard Hall in 1894 for the daughter of Lord and Lady Londonderry. It is uncertain what views on capital punishment were held by the Burdon family, but as Quakers, the Pease family were against the practice.

Colonel Burdon did not deal with serious cases other than to refer the more serious cases to the Durham Assizes. His cases as a JP involved the cases for drunkenness and an increasing number of applications for the licensing of premises to sell alcohol including

John Prest who was given a licence to sell alcohol in the Workmen's Club in Horden and Nimmo's who were granted licences for premises in Easington, Deaf Hill and Blackhall Rocks.

At Castle Eden Sessions there were many cases involving drunkenness. In October 1903, a man was fined 7/6 for being drunk and disorderly. Another man, in his drunken state, attempting to jump onto a moving train and falling from the footboard onto the platform. The man's defence was that he had been mesmerised on stage. This was not believed as he was fined 20s plus costs. A driver of a horse and cart was fined 7s 6d for being drunk in charge. Some women were also drunkards. A woman was sent to prison for one month for being drunk in charge of a child under seven.

In July 1901, a woman was charged with selling drink without a licence. A police sergeant went to the navvies huts on the New Coast Railway. He was dressed as a farmer pretending to look for some lost sheep. During a conservation with a woman at the hut, the police sergeant asked her if she had any beer. On receiving and paying for a pint of beer from the woman, he asked her who she was. When her house was searched, more beer was found. The woman was fined £20 plus costs, a large amount of money, so this have been considered a serious crime, especially as it would be assumed she was selling beer to navvies who had a bad reputation for heavy drinking.

Even landlords were not exempt from being charged. The landlord of the Colliery Inn, South Wingate was fined 17s and costs for being drunk and disorderly. Another landlord was fined 5s but given a one month's prison sentence for assaulting a police officer.

Colonel Burdon, as chairman of the bench at Castle Eden, recognised the increased cases of drunkenness. At the annual Brewster Sessions for Castle Eden Police Division in August 1900. Superintendent present the police report to the three sitting magistrates; Colonel Burdon as chair, Mr William Armstrong and Rev. R. Taylor. The report stated that the population was 32,009 and the number of licensed houses being 75. This appears a large number of licensed houses. Those premises holding existing licences had their licence approved apart from three in Shotton Colliery who were given one month to improve their sanitary conditions prior to the renewal of their license. There were three new applications, one for a hotel at Blackhalls which had originally opened as a temperance hotal, one at Deneholme and one at Deaf Hill.

Members of the public were present, including a large body of teetotallers, members of various church denominations and shopkeepers. They probably had concerns as convictions for drunkenness had increased to 881; an increase of 120 from the previous year. These people would be please when the magistrates denied the three new applications for a licence.

There were still cases of poaching or trespassing in pursuit of game as it was called with fines usually between 7s and 10s. The RSPCA was gave evidence resulting in a 19s fine for cruelty to a pony. Two other men were fined 13s and 8s for cruelty to a horse.

The SPCA was formed in 1824 by three men including William Wilberforce. The society was given the royal charter by Queen Victoria in 1837, becoming the RSPCA. In 1835 Joseph Pease (the senior, born in 1799), was responsible for the Peases Act, prohibiting cruelty to dogs and other domestic animals, and the outlawing of bear baiting, dog fighting and cock fighting.

This Joseph Pease was elected to Parliament for South Durham in 1832. He was the first Quaker to sit in Parliament. As such, he was allowed to affirm rather than swear the Church of England oath of office and was also permitted to wear his hat in the chambers. He was a Whig and he campaigned for the end of slavery. He retired from Parliament in 1841. In 1860, he became President of the Peace Society.

Joseph Pease bought a small riverside farm in the small hamlet of Middlesbrough with a population of 30 people in 1829 with the intention to develop this farmland site into a new port on the River Tees. The extension of the Stockton and Darlington Railway reached Middlesbrough on December 27th 1830. By 1831, the population of Middlesbrough was 154. In January 1831, shipping coal from the staithes began. By December, 151,000 had been shipped from the new port.

At the same time, in 1831, Rowland Burdon together with Christopher Tennant of Yarm commences development of Hartlepool into a coal port. Lord Seaham saw the first shipment of coal from the new port of Seaham Harbour. In 1835, Hartlepool Dock opens shipping coal from its deepened harbour. The whole area begins to grow in population. Crimes would increase. Both the Burdon and Pease families were magistrates and successive members of these families would have to deal with crime.

In 1901 there crimes other than those related to drunkenness.. A man was fined 15s plus costs in 1901 for travelling on a train between Newcastle and South Hetton without a ticket. In June 1901, Colonel Burdon heard a case when a traction engine driver for Vaux brewery was charged with driving a traction engine attached to some brewery drays, without lights about midnight in Easington.

Other crimes appeared somewhat more serious as they resulted in short prison sentences. A thief stole a Yorkshire terrier worth £4 so he received one month's hard labour. A man was admitted to the Workhouse pretending to be an army deserter. The pretence to enter the Workhouse appears more serious than claiming to be an army deserter, so this man was imprisoned for one month. A larceny case resulted in a three month prison term. Larceny of a lamp valued at 3s warranted a 30s fine. Two miners who stole apples and pomegranates were remanded for eight days. A fifteen year old who stole 10s from a house was sent to a reformatory school for four years.

Crimes and punishments had changed from 1831. Attitudes appeared to be changing too. It would be a different outcome in 1831 for the four small boys who, in 1903, stole a pony, trap, and harness from a man in Shotton Colliery. The three boys all pleaded guilty and they were ordered to each receive six strokes of the birch. Even this sounds brutal but the outcome may have been hanging at an earlier time.

Attitudes towards children appear to be changing. By this time the Church of England waifs and Strays Society, begun in1881, had established homes for destitute children. Sunderland had a Waifs Rescue Society and Street Vendors Club fund raising events. Many children, some very young, were brought repeatedly to the courts for minor offences like begging. Others began a life as a street vendor as soon as they left school. It was suggested that parents appeared to encourage their children's activities for the money they raised Sunderland, like most large towns had a 21'great amount of slum properties.' These 'little mortals' came from such backgrounds.

It was seen necessary to tackle this problem before children became "acquainted with the vices of the streets and before they formed habits." The Society sought residential care other than work-houses in order to "raise" these young "out of the submerged state" and help them in a "very practical way". The Church of England Society had three methods to achieve this end; young children were boarded out, it had homes of its own and 'thirdly it achieves its end by emigration."

Whether it was right to separate children from their parents is debatable, but young children of 13 and 14 were no longer hung for stealing silver spoons and clothes. A change in attitude towards the welfare of children had taken place. There were other changes in the area at this time.

The Sinking of the Collieries

The sinking of three coastal collieries began first with Easington in 1899, followed by Horden and later by Blackhall. The land on which Horden pit was to be sunk was owned by the Hulem Coal Company. Company members included the Ecclesiastical Commission and Rowland Burdon and his brother Cotsford. In late December 1899, a new company, Horden Collieries Ltd bought the syndicate rights of about 16,000 acres of land from the Hulem Coal Company in order to sink a deep mine that would go out under the sea and land enough to construct houses and other facilities for prospective incoming workers.

Much of this land was densely wooded and had to be cleared. There was no direct road to then potential sinking site so equip-ment and machinery had to be transported by aerial flight from Castle Eden across the chasm in Castle Eden Dene.

Pit sinkers occupied huts around the sinking site. The navvies, also living in huts, were building the railway along the coast. By 1901, incomers were occupying land once belonging to the Burdon Estate. The colliery village of Horden was under construction. By December 1902, it was reported that;[22]

"The success attending the putting down of Horden is phenomenal, a record having been made in the history of shaft-sinking by dealing with a flow of close upon 8,000 gallons of water per minute without a loss of a day's work. Mr. Prest, the manager, is pushing the work forward with a real energy. A new village is being created by the erection of something like 600 miners' cottages."

The huge amount of water influx was managed successfully with pumps, so work on the sinking was progressing rapidly. The construction of cottages was already underway.

In 1901, some colliery workers are lodging in farms like Horden Hall and Paradise Farm. Many navvies are living in Blue House. By 1911, rapid growth of the colliery village had replaced huts with row after row of terraced housing resulting in 1,500 houses being built by 1920. The population grew rapidly. By 1911, land, once covered by trees or farmers' fields, was now a colliery village with a church, chapels, shops and a school.

In 1900 Shotton Colliery was reopened by the Horden Coal Company. The pit village had been disbanded for 23 years so a new influx of workers would come here. By 1906, Shotton had 1,163 workers producing 472,000 tons of coal. Brickworks were opened in 1905. The old beehive coke works were re-opened in 1907.

Easington Colliery was also well established by 1911 and Blackhall Colliery well underway. By July 1910, Colonel Burdon had commissioned the construction of a properly laid and railed footpath from over the two miles from Horden to Blackhall. This was great improvement as previously travelling between the two places was a choice between a circuitous route along the beach or a journey involving trespassing along the railway risking life or legal proceedings. The land around Castle Eden had seen considerable change by 1911.

There were changes in the Burdon family too. In April 1900, Colonel Burdon's Uncle Cotsford Burdon died at the age of 85. Cotsford had also served as a magistrate at Castle Eden Petty Sessions. He was the owner of the Monk Hesleden Estate, bequeathed to him by his brother Rowland. Cotsford Burdon died at his residence Parkhurst, Haslemere, Sussex where he had lived for some considerable time.

Cotsford Burdon was born in 1815 and educated at Lincoln College, Oxford, graduating in 1836 when he was articled to the family solicitor, John Clayton Attorney of Newcastle on 18th July, 1836. He was called to the Bar at the Middle temple and Lincoln's Inn in January 1842 where he practised as an equity draughtsman and conveyancer.

In June 1852 Cotsford Mathews Burdon married Eleanor Margaret Jane Pemberton Thompson in Malton, Yorkshire. They had three children; Rowland John born in 1857, Cotsford Mathews in 1860 and Francis in 1862. It is interesting the names chosen for the children. Rowland the eldest had a second forename of John, who probably looked after him at his days at Durham School which he attended as a very small boy. He was probably very fond of his sweet natured sister Frances, or Fanny as she was known. From what his brother John had said their lives as children had been quite harsh, so both his brother John and sister Fanny may have been especially fond of their little brother Cotsford and looked after him. Cotsford may have called his third son Frances, but unfortunately, little Frances died the following year whilst still a baby.

Cotsford Mathews Burdon had two surviving sons; Rowland John and Cotsford Mathews. In 1911, Rowland John Burdon is an unmarried clergyman living in 54, West Street Chichester with four servants in his 13 room house. Rowland John had attended New College Oxford where he had obtained a 1st class honours degree in Modern History, receiving his MA in 1882. He took up a curacy at Midhurst before moving to posts including, Brighton, Oving and Rural Dean of Arundel before becoming vicar of St. Peter's Church in Chichester.

After 18 years at Chichester, Rev Rowland John Burdon retired in June 1923 During a Church Council Meeting, he was wished[23] "farewell and God-speed". The PCC considered that, "in losing Preb Burdon they were losing a scholar, a gentleman, and a good churchman who had always discharged his work in an efficient manner. They would remember him, and hoped the Vicar would remember them in a deservedly happy retirement." A presentation was made of a silver salver to which Rev Burdon thanked them "their kindness in making him this handsome present."

Rev Burdon did have a reasonably long retirement at Parkhurst, Haslemere, Sussex. He died aged 83 in Llandudno, probably going there for his health.

His younger brother Cotsford left England in 1902 to settle in New Zealand in a house called 'Parkhurst' in Woodbury, South Canterbury. Cotsford established a sheep farm at Woodbury. He died in 1920, a wealthy man.

In the Anglican Church of St Thomas in Woodbury, New Zealand, there is a window dedicated to the memory of Cotsford Mathews Burdon by his wife Mildred showing Christ as the Supreme Angel with St. Wendelin and St Elizabeth of Hungary. St Elizabeth is regarded as a symbol of Christian charity. St Wendelin is the patron saint of herdsmen and depicted carrying a book in one hand and a shepherd's bag and crook in the other. He is usually surrounded by feeding livestock, including sheep and lambs, appropriate for and Englishman who came to New Zealand and set up a successful sheep farm.

The following April, in 1901, a long-time associate of the Burdon family, William Nimmo, also died. William Nimmo was 73, and at the time the oldest native inhabitant of the parish. His father had begun the brewery business in 1826. William was a shrewd business man so he largely extended the business. Like the Burdons, he attended and competed in Agricultural Shows. However, William Nimmo was a frequent prize winner at leading shows with his West Highland, rolled Angus and Galloway cattle. Like Burdon, William Nimmo was also a Conservative and a generous supporter of the church and philanthropic movements. The families had much in common.

Mrs Nimmo, along with other leading ladies of the area assisted Mrs Burdon in the organisation of a highly successful ball in the Drill Hall in December 1901. The head gardener William Fulford and young assistant gardener, William Charlton had decorated the hall. These decorations would probably have been of greenery suitable for a near Christmas festivity. It would have been much admired and appreciated by the attendees. In some ways it would have been a more congenial occasion than the grandeur of the Wynyard Ball in 1899, set out to impress with the way lit with beacons, festoons of electric fairy lamps in the trees and large floodlights outside the Hall. The guests wore their best finery and the ladies were festooned with jewels; a ball to impress.

The 250 guests at Castle Eden probably enjoyed the much simpler occasion where they met friends and socialised with people they knew. This may have been less grand but more enjoyable. Dancing commenced at 8.15 pm with supper served at 10 pm. This grand occasion, though not nearly as grand as those organised by the Londonderrys, would have been much enjoyed by the guests.

There were other events held in the Drill Hall. In January 1902, the Rev F. G. R Robinson was now incumbent at St. James' Church Castle Eden. He organised a concert to augment funds for the village reading room. This concert attracted a large and influential audience, hopefully raising much needed funds.

Events in the village in August 1902 would have been greatly enjoyed. A free tea and sports were arranged on Coronation Day. Mr. John Hutton of Eden Vale gave over 500 coronation mugs to all the children of the parish including those living at Castle Eden Colliery. At Hesleden, tea and sports were held in an eight acre field belonging to farmer Mr Walker. At 9 pm a bonfire was lit on the old pit heap. Celebrations were held all through the country for the coronation of King Edward VII and Queen Alexandra.

In late September 1902, October Colonel and Mrs Burdon were amongst the 700 guests, headed by the Marquess and Marchioness of Londonderry who attended an afternoon garden party at Auckland Castle where the Lord Bishop of Durham and his family had recently taken up residence. As well as refreshments, the guests were entertained by the band of 2nd Voluntary battalion of the D.L.I. As it was October, the guests, received in the spacious drawing room of the Castle, may have found a garden party a little chilly, but the 'principal residents' and the clergy in practically the whole of the diocese were there.

The villagers at Castle Eden had tea and sports. The principal residents including titled people, mayors and mayoresses as well as other 'principal residents' of the diocese went to a garden party in a grand castle to welcome the Bishop of Durham. The children of Castle Eden and Castle Eden colliery were probably more pleased with their tea, sports and coronation mug.

A more sombre but well attended occasion took place in St John's Church in Hesleden on Sunday 7th September, 1902 when the vicar of the parish, the Rev G Little unveiled and dedicated a new stained glass east window in memory of the late Rev John Burdon. Rev Burdon had been a generous benefactor to the church and parish for many years. The windows had been erected by public subscription and Col Burdon, Mrs Burdon, their family and private friends were amongst the large congregation who attended the morning service of dedication.

Many of the subscriptions for the window depicting the Ascension of Jesus, came from working people who had been helped in the strike of 1892 by Rev John Burdon providing school dinners for their children, the year before he died. The figures in the three windows are almost life-size and harmoniously coloured. At the base the inscription reads, 'To the Glory of God, in loving memory of Rev. John Burdon, of Castle Eden, Benefactor to this Church and parish. Erected by subscription A.D., 1902.'

There is a sad note to this account. Hesleden Church closed in the early 2000's. It is now (2016) advertised for sale as a private dwelling. To date some stained glass windows are still intact but it is uncertain whether the Rev Jon Burdon window is still there.

Another sad event followed in 1906 when Canon Tristram, the life-long friend of the Burdon family since 1849 when he became curate of Castle Eden Church, died on 8th March aged 83. As well as his work in the church, Canon Tristram had been a great traveller and author of many works dealing with countries associated with the Bible. He had also explored little visited areas of Japan where his daughter was a teacher in a missionary school. At that time he also visited China.

Apparently [24] "one of Canon Tristram's most treasured possessions was an ordinary soda-water bottle which played a not unimportant part in his adventurous career. Once when on his travels he seized upon what he thought was a lizard in the sand, but which proved to be a deadly horned viper. His Greek boatman, scared almost out of his life, proffered no assistance. Suddenly espying an empty soda-water bottle the canon with consummate presence of mind, forced the head of the reptile down the neck and slowly uncoiled from his hand the remainder of the anatomy. When he regained his ship, he filled the bottle with whisky and from that day to this, paradoxical though it may appear, the viper has been in good spirits." This appears a most unusual, almost Indiana Jones story, but it demonstrates the courage, coolness and quick thinking of Canon Tristram.

His funeral took place in Durham Cathedral officiated by the Bishop and Dean of Durham. Reports of his death had appeared nationwide and a huge congregation gathered to pay their last respects.

There were many clergy including Preb H E Fox who had missed a meeting of the Church Missionary Society in Gloucester to attend the funeral of his life-long friend whom he considered to also have been a life-long friend of the Church Missionary Society.

As Deputy Provincial Grand Master of the Freemasons since 1885, Canon Tristram's funeral was attended by numerous high-ranking officials in freemasonry, including Lord Barnard the Provincial Grand Master.

The under-sheriff of the county was in attendance. Dr Forbes from Liverpool, Director of the Museums Committee was there in recognition of the valuable ornithological specimens donated by the Canon to the Liverpool Museum. Two boys from Durham School laid a wreath at the side of his coffin in recognition of a famous old boy of the school. Students and staff of Durham University as well as old students of St Hilda's College, where he was still a governor all attended the funeral.

It was also a family affair, with his wife of over fifty years, family members and close friends. They may have been comforted by the celebrated turnout for the Canon's funeral.

Canon Tristram had not only been a noted freemason like Rowland Burdon, he was also a, again like Burdon, a convinced conservative in his politics.

In December 1906, there was a Unionist Ball at Chester-le-Street in aid of the Chester-Le-Street Conservative and Unionist Association. Despite the rough weather there was a large attendance including Lord and Lady Ravensworth, Sir Lindsay Wood and party and Sir Slingsby Duncombe Shafto, of Beamish Hall. Colonel and Mrs Burdon were amongst these guests and as a leading conservative, Colonel Burdon was probably acquainted with these guests.

Canon Tristram had a long and interesting life but on October 16th 1906, 24 lives were cut short when an explosion caused by shotfiring ignited coal dust and air in Wingate Colliery near Castle Eden. The explosion killed four men outright but it also caused the release of firedamp, quickly killing another twenty. Two more died later as a result of the explosion.

Men were trapped underground and the rescuers had to proceed cautiously as there was still a quantity of deadly gas. (TIMES 16/10/1906"The rescue party had much to contend with, but, as is usual in cases of this bent, the miner's heroism is brought into true play, and nothing will prevent him making a gallant attempt to help his fellows underground. There was, therefore, no lack of willing helpers. While the ninety six men and boys alive but trapped underground in various places in Harvey seam they sang hymns and songs to raise their spirits. The rescuers, in places crawling on their hands and knees, took thirty six hours to bring the living to safety. After the rescue, much more debris had to be cleared away to reach the bodies of those killed. Rescuers discovered more signs of the violence of the explosion everywhere. The dead they found were much burnt and disfigured.

As the bodies were brought to the surface the scene presented a most distressing one. Mr. Armstrong, the manager, and medical men were quickly on the spot. By noon twenty four of the bodies had been brought to the surface. There was also the distressing task of bringing dead horses and ponies to the surface."

William Peat, an old pitman was one of those rescued. A while after the explosion, William and three of his comrades came across four men they knew well who had died from firedamp, the inhalation of poisonous gas. William and his three comrades, distressed at the scene, hurried away from the area to reach pure air. It was now two hours after the explosion. They waited for some time until William Peat discovered the wire controlling a signal rapper which was used for signalling to the wagon-way man to start the tubs. William started rapping and persisted until to the men's joy they saw the lights of the rescue party approaching. They were weary and hungry as they had to wait for eighteen hours before they were rescued in very dangerous area where timbers had fallen down and there were great falls of the roof everywhere.

Rescue work continued for some time with some of those rescued being underground for over forty hours. When William and his three comrades came to bank, they like others rescued would be joyously greeted by their families and friends.

Rescue work continued during the night. As day broke people again began to gather from all parts of the district. Many had assembled by the time the dead were brought to the surface. The Bishop of Durham was unable to come immediately but he sent a telegraph of condolence and he preached in Wingate Church the following Sunday. The Bishop of Jarrow did come to the village and visited the houses of the mourners.

On 18th October, thousands of people gathered in Wingate in heavy rain on the day fifteen of the dead were carried to the church for burial. Every shop in Wingate was closed.[25]

"Women and children, some of the former carrying pale-faced infants in their arms, pattered through the muddy thoroughfare to cemetery and churchyard, eager to lose none of the incidents of a day that will long hold a place in saddened memories. Soon after three o'clock the main street of the village presented a most striking appearance, pathetically sad and happily rare. Fifteen of the dead were carried onwards in a long and melancholy cortege that took three quarters of an hour to pass a given point. How many thousands of people composed the avenue of humanity through which the mourners wound their way it would be very difficult to say. Despite the dreary atmosphere and the pitiless rain, they came from all the pit villages for miles around. Some were in the procession itself, or in the churchyard in a representative capacity."

Representatives were there from the owners of the colliery, including Mr. William Armstrong, owner and agent for the mine. "The Hon. F.WE. Lambton, M.P. for South-East Durham was at the graveside. All the local miners' officials walked with their banner, and Mr. John Wilson, M.P. for Gateshead, and others were there specially to represent the Durham Miners' Association."

Other colliery bands were present including Shotton, Murton and Wheatley Hill bands. Each band played alternatively until through the village and up the hill towards the church.

Some of the bodies were conveyed up the hill in glass-sided hearses. The rest were borne shoulder-high by pitmen comrades of the dead. The church bell tolled and bands played a psalm outside the church gates while the chief mourners entered the church. The church filled rapidly with even the aisles crammed with mourners. One coffin was not taken into church as prayers had already been said for this man at the Primitive Methodist Chapel but the other fourteen coffins were carried along the north aisle into the chancel with some being placed across two of the front pews. "The careworn look of some of the bereaved women, and the tremulous cry of young children carrying bunches of chrysanthemums and ferns and marguerites in their hands, made a deep impression, and moved many to tears of sympathy." Whilst the service was conducted inside the church, two clergy conducted a service from the porch of the church for the benefit of those who could not enter the already packed building.

Eleven of those buried were interred into two separate trenches, whilst four others were placed into the graves of their departed relatives.

Nine were buried elsewhere and left the village at various times for the places of their internment. The first to leave, was "William Studholme, a man of 54, who has left a widow and a family. Outside the door of his house in Mill Row there assembled at noon, a small crowd of neighbours, and close by, in the dripping rain, stood a group of his old comrades rapidly forming into file under the lodge banner, with the Wingate Silver Band at their head. In this neighbourhood are line upon line of cottages with green doors and shutters. Here, as everywhere else in the village, the blinds were drawn, and hats were raised as the coffin was lifted out of the house and placed on a couple of chairs at the door. Then there was a touching little incident. The Primitive Methodist Choir gathered round and sang Cardinal Newman's beautiful hymn, "Lead kindly light," and above the harmony one could hear the half repressed sobbing of the near relations. Widow, mother, and two daughters rode in the first carriage carrying flowers to lay upon the grave. Studholme was buried at Pelton Fell, a pit village some 10 or 12 miles away, which accounted for the cortege making so early a start. An escort was given to a spot called the Near Lane Ends, about a mile outside the village, and the band and others making up the processions then returned."

All the men who died lived in the village and would have been well known. The majority of those who been killed were older men like stonemen and shifters. These men had families, leaving widows and children. A nationwide fund was set up. The King sent a message of condolence and a cheque for £100 guineas to add to the fund which had been set up to aid the widows and children of the men killed. As the disaster had been reported throughout the country donations were widespread with one anonymous donation of £25.

One lady from Settle offered to take three of the orphaned children of George Smith and place them with her tenant farmers. George Smith, born in Shotton and aged 47, had seven children.

His wife Elizabeth Maria died in the spring of 1906, so with the death of their father, the children were now orphans. The children were split up but none left the area to probably work for Yorkshire tenant farmers, they all went to live with relatives. Uncle George and Aunt Mary Partridge, living in Horden with their one surviving child, John Henry, took three of the children; Valentine, Maria and Matilda who would have been only two years old when her father and mother died. John Thomas Smith, the eldest boy married and in 1911, he too is living in Horden with his wife ten month old son and his 13 year old brother Edward. George William is 18 in 1911 and living in Ryhope with Aunt Rose and Uncle Leonard and their seven children. Jemima, orphaned when she was six,travelled further afield, but not too far to visit, to North Ormesby, to live with Uncle Henry and his wife. As they had no children of their own Jemima was probably cared for as if she was their own. The children had no need of the probably well-meaning offer of re-locating to the countryside in Settle. The family kept together although they lived in different households.

As well as the money was raised to help the widows and children, a fund raised money for a monument to be erected in the main street of Wingate. The memorial cost £155 of which £100 had already been raised by the time it was unveiled on 21st December, 1907.

That day a procession began at the Miners' Hall headed by the band and banners and marched towards the monument. A prayer was given by Rev. W. Barton. The monument was unveiled by the Hon. F.W. Lambton M.P. who said[26] "when the calamity occurred the people of Wingate had the sympathy not only of the district but of the county and country." He considered the monument "would bring to mind the dangers which beset a miner's life...Those who saw that monument would look upon it as a record of heroism, and think that it was a heritage of which they must be proud, and which they must do their best to be worthy of."

John Wilson M.P. and John Johnson M.P. were there amongst the many present to witness the ceremony, as were Colonel Burdon and William Armstrong, the agent of Wingate Colliery.

Mr. John Wilson M.P. said he "had never in his experience seen such sympathy shown" not only by "by all hands at the time of the disaster, not only on the part of the workmen, but on the part of those in authority at the colliery...Mr. Lambton had mentioned the miners courage, and he could say that if action were needed, no Durham pitman would have to be asked twice."

William Armstrong, the agent, "thanked Mr. Wilson for his kind words, and for the assistance rendered by him, and everyone associated with him, in the Durham Miners' Union, at the time of the disaster. If all leaders of men approached the management of a mine as they did, the kindly feelings engendered would make the relations of capital and labour much more pleasant. Mr. Armstrong concluded by announcing, amid applause, that the deficit on the amount raised to defray the cost of the monument would be made up by Colonel Burdon and Himself." Colonel Burdon had already donated the land on which the monument stood.

John Wilson, a Primitive Methodist, was a Liberal trade union sponsored Member of Parliament. He was born at Greatham in 1837. His mother died when John was four years old and his father died from cholera when he was ten. He could speak with authority about miners as he had worked in a mine from a young age. He did spend four years as a merchant seaman before he returned to Durham to work again as a miner in 1860. In 1864, he journeyed with his wife Margaret to America to work in coal mines in Pennsylvania and Illinois. Before returning to Durham in 1867.

In 1869, John Wilson was one of the founders of the Durham Miners' Association which led him to being black-listed for work in coal mines. In 1878, he became a full-time organiser for the union becoming general secretary in 1896. In 1885, he was elected as Liberal-Labour MP for Houghton-Le-Spring but the seat was lost in 1886. In 1890 he was elected for the Mid Durham in a by-election. He was a Member of Parliament for more than twenty five years.

Colonel Burdon and Politics

In 1910 Colonel Burdon stood as the prospective Parliamentary candidate for the Conservative Party in the General Election. It was the second election that year. The Chancellor of the Exchequer David Lloyd George and his ally Winston Churchill had spearheaded the People's Budget in order to distribute wealth in the country by increasing taxation on the wealthy in order to fund what was consider by some as radical social welfare programmes. The House of Lord's rejected the People's Budget so Asquith called an election in order to receive a mandate for these reforms. The outcome was a hung election with the Liberals remaining in power supported by the Irish Nationals.

The seat was fought between Frederick William Lambton, 4th Earl of Durham, Liberal Unionist and Evan Hayward Liberal. Lambton had been the Member for South Durham since 1900, but he was soundly beaten in the election in January 1910 by the Liberal candidate. Lambton did not wish to stand in the election called later that year to attempt to obtain an overall majority for the Liberals.

As a Liberal Unionist, Lambton had supported the political alliance with the Conservative Party. He did not wish to stand again, so Lord Londonderry supported Colonel Burdon in his bid to stand as candidate for the Conservative Party.

After the death of the president of the South East Durham Conservative Party

In September 1910, Colonel Burdon was elected as his replacement at a meeting in Parklands, Castle Eden attended by Lord Londonderry and[27] "a number of other prominent conservatives of the constituency" including Mr. J.J. Prest manager of Horden Colliery.

Mr. Prest lived in Hardwick Hall, five miles north of Hartlepool. The estate had been bought for £16,000 on behalf of Colonel Burdon and the Horden Collieries Company in September 1907. The estate comprised what was consider a mansion house, Hardwicke Dene, two farms, and Dene Holme Temperance Hotel all comprising a total acreage of 683 and annual rents of £716. Mr Prest lived in the mansion house but Colonel Burdon probably added the rest of the acreage and farms to his estate.

At the meeting in September 1910, Colonel Burdon delivered a speech, that would turn out to be a prophecy of events that may have influenced the outcome of the forthcoming election, when he referred to the effects of the Eight Hours Act saying that," There were four of their largest collieries up in arms, not only against their employers, but against all law and order. An agitation against law and order always went against the Conservative Party."

At this September meeting Lord Londonderry spoke highly of Colonel Burdon, saying he "had pulled the party together and provided Unionist principles in everyone in East Durham." He agreed with Colonel Burdon that although it would be "an arduous task," it was not impossible task the seat could be won for the Conservatives especially if they made known "the real principles and policy" of the Liberal Party who he described as being a "Radical party" whose policies were "nothing but mere socialism." This comment raised a loud "Hear, Hear" from those assembled indicating the Conservative depth of feeling against the against the People's Budget.

Lord Londonderry praised the previous MP Mr. Lambton but as he had decided not to seek re-election, he indicated the "representative of South East Durham should be a gentleman who was well-known, popular, who lived in the constituency, and who was identified with the interests of the constituency." Londonderry then proposed Colonel Burdon as such a man who would enable them to "join with the vast mass of anti-Socialists in fighting against this Socialist Government at the next election." With much applause and general assent Colonel Burdon was duly selected to represent the Conservative Party in a forthcoming election.

The election was called to be held between 3rd and 19th of December. Prior to those dates there were many meetings throughout the constituency organised so voters could hear the policies of Colonel Burdon and his opponent Evan Hayward. Mrs. Burdon appeared to attend many meetings in support of her husband.

An example of a meeting held in support of Colonel Burdon was held on Saturday 10th December in the Theatre Royal, Seaham Harbour. HM 12th December 1910 where about 2,000 people were present of which the vast majority were enthusiastic whilst the opposition appeared to be "confined to a small section of the gathering. One persistent offender was ejected by the police."

There had been more trouble at Wheatley Hill when Colonel Burdon had addressed a crowded meeting in the Miner's Hall when[28] "in the audience a large number of youths, who were responsible for a great deal of noise," frequently interrupted Colonel Burdon's speech.

At this meeting he defended the policy of the veto of the House of Lords, something the Liberals wanted to abolish. He was also in favour of the Tariff Reform which he saw as having advantages and would not increase the cost of living. Colonel Burdon considered the Tariff reform gave a bargaining power "with foreign nations who had erected tariff walls" against the country and this in turn bring the "greatest advantage as would "steady employment." The Chairman in his support of the Tariff reform, gave the example of the manufacture of glass bottles as these were manufactured in Seaham at that time when he said "Last month the Board of Trade's value of imported glass bottles was £61,952. This meant the working man in this country was deprived of £7,700 in wages every week. It would have given 5,000 men 30s a week." This speech went down very well with the audience.

As well as supporting the Tariff reform, the Colonel was against the Liberal policy of taking the veto from the House of Lords. He had been nominated by Lord Londonderry so he did frequently emphasise this viewpoint. This view was supported by Lady Londonderry in a speech of support for Colonel Burdon at a meeting in Hartburn on 10th December. Lady Londonderry informed the meeting they[29] "were told by Mr Winston Churchill that the Radicals were going to do away with the Veto of the House of Lords, disestablish the Church of England and Wales, and pass Home Rule. Her defence of the House of Lords emphasised, the House had "always...gone to the people to enable the country to consider things calmly, and the Radicals (were) now proposing to do with the Constitution what no trade union could do with society. No trade union would give its executive full power for five years without reference to its members, and yet the Radicals proposed to do away with the House of Lords and have only a Single Chamber."

As well as meetings a statement was printed in the Hartlepool Mail stating Colonel Burdon gave[30] "his assurance to the Electors of the Division – and those who know him know his word is his bond:'I give my pledge that if elected as your Representative to Parliament I will not vote for any measure which will increase the cost of food to the people."

The liberal candidate, Evan Hayward also had many meetings. He reminded the voters that the Liberal had reversed the increase in the price of tea and sugar levied by the previous Conservative Government. The press statement on behalf of Colonel Burdon was probably a reaction to the suggestion by Hayward of the possibility that the Conservatives would increase the cost of food if they got into power.

At a crowded meeting in Dawdon, his fifth meeting that day, Hayward reportedly said;[31] "there was no doubt whatsoever that the voters the voters of South-East Durham were all convinced that the veto of the House of Lords should be done away with." There was great applause when Hayward said if the Liberals were returned to power the "Veto Bill would be law in a few months."

Hayward thought it was the 'greatest honour' that he had been part of the Government that had passed the Budget of 1909 which was now passed into law. It was "doing some excellent work for besides providing for old-age pensions and making it possible to remove the pauper disqualifications, it had provided a nest egg for insurance against sickness and unemployment… The Government had to find the money and they got it from those who could afford to pay it…They got some from the royalty owners – people who did nothing to earn the money except to sign an agreement. Money got in that way ought to be taxed for the benefit of the community." This last statement would directly refer to those, like Lord Londonderry who owned the land on which coal was mined. The colliery owners had to pay a royalty to the land owners for coal extracted. These people according to Hayward did nothing to earn this money."

There were huge differences in the policies between the Conservative and Liberals. There was one policy of the Liberals that had not gone down well in mining areas. Colonel Burdon when he warned there may be trouble over the Eight Hours Act. The 1908 Eight Hours Act came into effect in Durham in January 1910. There was no consultation when the Durham Miners Association agreed with the implementation of the Act with the owners. The hewers already worked seven hours ten minutes, so they were not affected. Putters were affected as their hours were reduced from ten to eight, meaning less income for them.

Coal owners, like those on the Durham coalfields, changed the shift pattern, from two to three shifts. This change affected the livelihoods and wages of the putters, often young men. Local collieries looked to the Durham Miners Association for support but some probably felt these officials were more interested in negotiation than settling the dispute in favour of their members. The County Durham miners were usually considered traditionally moderate but in this instance some collieries went on an unofficial strike, meaning no strike pay. By 14th January 1910, fifty one pits in County Durham were idle. Thirty nine were working under protests whilst over 100 mines accepted the new agreement.

The Government was aware of this unforeseen consequence of the Eight Hours Act as the effects were debated in Parliament. Hansard [32] records that Winston Churchill, then Home Secretary was asked about the number of seams closed as a consequence of the Act and "if so, whether he can say what mines there are, and how many men have been thrown out of employment owing to the closing of the mines."

Churchhill had could not answer this question. He had "addressed this enquiry to the Inspector of Mines" but he did "not know how long it takes to get an answer, but he would consider the matter."

It is uncertain whether he received an answer. After a while Lodges at individual collieries reached agreement with the management on the operation of the Act. Shotton, Horden, Murton and South Hetton collieries continued the strike. After a mass meeting in April, the miners at these collieries agreed to end the strike and returned to work that month.

It was a particularly harsh winter and the coal allowance for miners had been stopped. Money was low so food and the means to cook it was scarce. During this time "a fund was opened by Colonel Burdon of Castle Eden by a strong and enthusiastic community effort being put forward by the Colonel to see that no child goes short of food." From Thomas Hill's school log. During the strike, the Free Meals Canteen fed hundreds of children, over 850 on the 6th February, each morning at 8.30 am and each afternoon at 3.30pm, even on a Saturday and Sunday. The Headmaster, Thomas Hill, who himself was heavily involved wrote,[33] "It is the intention of Colonel Burdon (who is holding himself responsible for the major expense, by supplementing subscriptions received through myself) to continue these efforts during the prevalence of the unfortunate dispute, over a local difficulty respecting the working of the nearly operative in Northumberland and Durham".

"Nearly operative" refers to the young men who were putters and not yet able enough to be hewers. They were greatly affected by the new system. So too were the women with many workers in the house. The three shift meant workers in the household leaving and returning from work at many different times. This greatly increased women's work and some in large household found they could only go to bed to sleep on a Saturday night when there was no work on the next day, the Sunday.

The trouble at Horden came to a head on Election Day; Wednesday 26th January 1910. This was the first election that year. Lambton was standing as Liberal Unionist against Evan Hayward the Liberal. The pit had not worked all of January, so as money was running out most of the population was short of food. Election Day roused political feeling and greatly increased the ill-feeling against the mine owners and management who the workers considered were the main cause of their predicament.

Some men were drinking in the Colliery Club constructed by the owners. The Steward and Stewardess were reportedly wearing rosettes in support of Lambton, whom the men regarded as being a supporter of the Conservatives, derided the men for their politics. This incident reportedly ignited the trouble.

Men began smashing casks of beer, drinking the contents. Spirts and small casks of beer were looted and carried away. The now drunken men headed towards Lambton's committee rooms and smashed the windows.

The men from the club soon became a crowd sand this crowd headed down towards the colliery offices, smashed their way in and ransacked the building. Stones were thrown at the manager of the colliery and the cashier.

The crowd became a mob as some headed the short distance towards the pit head and threw shaft tubs, a huge metal girder, baulks of timber and anything else they could lay their hands on down the pit shaft. Police were called in to prevent further destruction and damage.

There was trouble the next day when a grocery shop was raided and a window broken. The rest of the shops closed quickly. Credit for food would no longer be available. It was decided to speak to Mr. J.J. Prest in an attempt to resolve the situation but this idea backfired, because as reported by Thomas Hill, there was "some grievance against the mining agent Mr. Prest."

On the morning of 27th January, up to five hundred men and boys left Horden and marched to Hardwick Hall, the seventeen roomed home of Mr. Prest and his household which included two small children. The mob threw stones at the windows, destroyed greenhouses and garden ornaments, threw a vehicle probably a car down a cliff and threatened to set the house on fire with petrol stored in the coach-house. Mr. Prest fired a shot gun into the mob severely injuring one 14 year old boy. A man wrested the gun from Mr. Prest, broke it so it could not be used again.

By this time the police who had been drafted into Horden reached Hardwick Hall and began a severe baton attack injuring several men. They arrested the ringleaders and calmed the mob.

Meanwhile the police had left Horden and despite efforts by some to calm the situation a mob of between 1,500 and 2,000 outside the Workmen's Club. Three young men entered the club and started a fire with piled up furniture. The large building and the house next door, the home of the Steward and his wife, were soon ablaze, destroying the buildings.

More police were drafted in by train from far afield as Newcastle. Early the next morning some of the ringleaders were arrested, tried and sent to prison.

Thomas Hill, the Headmaster lived in Horden. He wrote the following in School Log Book; "This week will be referred to as "Riot Week" in this villager, for years to come. Excesses have been committed by young, irresponsible miners exasperated by being out of work, through some grievance against the mining agent Mr. Prest. The Club has been ransacked, then burnt down and the safety of the village has been generally jeopodised. As a consequence the school attendance had been affected. I am pleased to be able to report that by tactful management my staff and myself were saved any display of the local unrest in school. To the unsettled state of public safety may be added the wretched winter weather, as a factor of attendance disturbance."

4th February 1910, "The village is quieter than one would have expected from last week's excesses. Police in the number of two hundred are quartered in the schools, village and colliery. The attendance is still low at school, and many of the residents have temporarily left the village taking their children with them."

It was after this riot that Colonel Burdon began the fund to feed the children "to see that no child goes short of food." Lambton had just lost the election. He did not withdraw as prospective candidate until much later. Colonel and Mrs Burdon's motive was to look after the children in the village.

That winter was cold and hard. Thomas Hill reported attendance at school was low on April 8th because the children were "coal-seeking"; looking for waste coal on the pit-heap.

Coal-seeking, looking tiny pieces of coal the size of a pea took place in nearby Murton. A large pit heap consisted of coal the size of a pea, unfit for sale, was used for ballast and railway embankments. It would burn, so when pilfering from the heap became widespread security was called in to stop the theft. These men were intimidated so police were drafted in, some from as far afield as Ireland. This action resulted in conflict between the police and those desperately attempting to have a fire in their homes.

Colonel Burdon knew of these incidents when he warned the meeting of the bad feeling that had arisen because of the Eight Hours Act. This could have been one of the factors that helped return Evan Hayward to Parliament in December 1910. Rowland Burdon managed to halve Evan Hayward's majority but he could not defeat him. (There were two elections in the one year).

Another factor in his gaining votes, may have been due to a meeting in March 1910 when an application for a licence for a public house was requested in Horden. The Workmen's Club was the only place to legally purchase alcohol as the nearest public house was about two miles away. By March, this club had been burned to the ground, leaving no official supply of alcohol in the village. Colonel Burdon, speaking as a magistrate was of the opinion that,[34] "the result of drink being supplied to the place had been seriously prejudicial to the morality of the place. There had been more drunkenness in Horden, with no public-houses than there had been in Thornley which had six or eight. When the original lease was made with himself as landowner and the Horden Collieries Ltd, he inserted a clause – and he thought it was as well that it should be known –that no drink should be supplied in the whole of Horden without his permission or the permission of his successors and the directors of the company. He had been in communication with the directors and it had been decided that there should certainly be at least three public houses in Horden. The one to be put before them that day was the first and it would be followed by others in the course of a year or two... (however) no licences could be granted without consent."

The logic appears to be that public houses decreased the amount of liquor brought into houses, which appeared to be happening in Horden, and the amount of drunkenness. At least one public house would be granted a licence and two more could follow soon. The miners at Horden may have liked the idea of three public houses instead of having to drink in a club owned by their employers.

The striking miners had not threatened Colonel Burdon but had threatened the colliery manager, Mr. Prest. Like Rowland Burdon he was a Conservative. They appear to have a different reason for their animosity towards him, probably linked with his management of the colliery and treatment of the workers. Rowland Burdon on the other hand had ensured their children would not starve during the time of the strike, so they probably respected his help in their time of trouble.

However, during the campaigning of the December 1910 election, a letter was published in the "Sunderland Daily Echo and Shipping Gazette" accusing Colonel Burdon of only providing food for the children of Horden in order to secure support in a possible forthcoming election. Charles Bowles, Colonel Burdon's agent replied to this letter saying that Col. Burdon did not have [35]"this election in his mind when he and his wife so generously led the way to relieving the hungry and distressed at Horden and elsewhere… it was not until September 10th that the invitation to accept the seat was given to" Colonel Burdon.

In July 1910, at the quarterly meeting of the Horden Lodge of the Durham Miners' Union, examined the statement of accounts in relation to the strike at the beginning of the year. The total expenditure had been £837 0s 6d. Money from subscriptions and in goods amounted to £117 5s 10d. Apart from the Miners' Union Relief Fund, a separate fund called the Colonel Burdon Fund had been set up. The balance of £719 14s 8d needed to balance the books was paid from the Colonel Burdon Fund. That amount would be the equivalent of nearly six thousand pounds today. It is uncertain whether this amount was the total amount of expenditure of the Colonel towards relief of the miners, especially the children but even six thousand pounds is a large amount.

The agent further defended Colonel Burdon stressing that whether he won the election or not would not stop Colonel Burdon from "living the life of an English country gentleman, whose position gives him the opportunity and privilege of helping when necessary his less fortunate neighbours."

This last statement could have been said of the Colonel's father John Burdon who had not only helped the members of his congregation when incumbent at English and Welsh Bicknor but had also fed children during the miner's strike at Castle Eden Colliery. Many other members of the Burdon family had in the past helped those who were their "less fortunate neighbours." In these times of a growing feeling amongst the working class that society should be more equal the statement in defence of those who could live ' the life of a country gentleman' and helping their 'less fortunate neighbours' may have had the opposite effect on some.

Colonel Burdon did help the community of Horden in a more tangible way. He funded the building a new Anglican Church. The church was situated on a prominent position in Blackhills Road. It would be a large church, planned to seat 600 people. The building was 160 feet long, with a nave 28 feet 6 inches wide. The lantern tower, 28 feet by 22 feet, rose sixty five feet above the nave.

Until that time the Mission Church of St. Hilda's was used for worship. This small building later became the Church Hall. By February 1911, the foundations were practically completed. On 11th October 1911 Mrs Burdon laid the foundation stone.

The church building cost Colonel Burdon £9,000. Money was raised by the congregation for the fabric of the church and a church organ. One thousand pounds was raised by fund raising activities like bazaars. Three pounds were spent on the furnishings of the church and £700 on the organ. There were many who donated items of furnishings including Mrs. Burdon who gave the dorsal and side wings of the altar and brass candlesticks and a brass cross.

The dedication of St. Mary's Church by Dr. Nickson the Bishop of Jarrow took place on Saturday 26th April 1913. Colonel and Mrs Burdon were present together with the Colonel's sister Elizabeth, and daughters Joan and Lettice. There was a public tea after the ceremony in the mission hall. Rev C.J. Thurlow was appointed as the first vicar.

The church building was described at the time as [36] "a handsome structure, standing on a commanding site in Blackhills

Road….The imposing pile is quite a landmark and can be seen for a considerable distance towering all over the village."

Other churches opened new buildings. Colonel Burdon and a fellow magistrate performed the opening ceremony of a new Sunday School and institute for the Wesleyan Church at Thornley in December 1910. The building contained a billiard room, games room and reading room on the ground floor with a Sunday School with five classrooms that can be converted into a large hall on the second floor.

The Colonel still found time for his involvement in the Newcastle Farmers' Club at Newcastle. There was a large attendance in January 1911 when he was elected as president for the ensuing year. He then presided over the annual dinner held at the Crown Hotel, supported by notables including the Duke of Northumberland and the Bishop of Newcastle. There were the usual large numbers of toasts but none to Parliament as they seemed a little aggrieved that no member was parliament was present at the event.

As well as the building of churches in the new colliery villages, the Durham Aged Miners' Homes Association built retirement homes for aged miners. In October 1912, Colonel Burdon and Mr. J.J. Prest, manager of Horden colliery opened the John Johnson Memorial Home and Institute at Haswell Moor for single men, widowers or bachelors.[37] "Mr Prest made a strong appeal for generosity from royalty owners in connection with the work. One farthing one very ton of coal in the County of Durham would in ten years provide comfortable homes and sufficient coal for every aged miner without hurting anyone. Colonel Burdon remarked that he had been considering for some time how he could best help miners who had ceased work, but who had been contributing all their lives to the wealth which he and others had the spending of, and personally he should be very glad in the future to give his quota to this work. (Applause.)

Colonel Burdon did live his life as an English country gentleman, and it would appear he did use his position to help when necessary those he considered his less fortunate neighbours.

Colonel Burdon and his family did not always live in Castle Eden as a country gentleman. They frequently had a London address and at the beginning of March 1911, it was announced they had [38] "taken 45, Cadogan Place London for the season and will arrive with Miss Burdon directly after Easter. Mrs. Burdon will give a ball on the 2nd June at the Ritz Hotel."

Cadogan Place is in Belgravia. William Wilberforce lived at number 44 for the final two years of his life. Harold Macmillan was born in number 52 spending his childhood years there. In 1913 The Burdon's London address is 59, Cadogan Gardens. There are other fashionable London address where they took up residence. In his diary, James Henderson refers to Mr Burdon's visits to London. He also records a French hotel, the Hotel Splendid Aix-Les-Bains in Savoie. Aix-Les- Bains is a French spa town in Southern France, 60 miles from Lyon. There is a large fresh water marina, thermal baths and views of a nearby mountainous area. It is possible the family went to this part of France for health reasons.

The family had cause for celebration in February 1912 at the silver wedding of Colonel and Mrs Burdon. They were given many gifts on the occasion from more than 180 subscribers, including the tenants, workpeople and friends. The household staff gave Mrs Burdon a tortoise-shell and silver jewel box and a silver ring box. They were probably pleased at such high regard from so many people.

In January the following year, their eldest daughter's forthcoming wedding was announced in newspaper society pages. On 23rd June 1913 Frances Mary Burdon married Major, the Hon Walter Dashwood Sclater-Booth, youngest son of Lord Basing, in St. Peter's Church Eaton Square London. St Peter's is in Belgravia and probably the church attended by the Burdon's when they resided in London. The ceremony was conducted by the Bishop of Jarrow and Rev F G T Robinson, rector of Castle Eden

The bride's wore a dress described as stylishly simple but of distinctive dress made mainly in satin but embroidered with pearls and crystals and a train coming down from both shoulders. She wore a tulle veil with a wreath of myrtle leaves and orange blossom.

There were eleven bridesmaids, five of them young girls, but her two sisters Joan and Lettice headed the bridal team.

Major Scalter- Booth was in the Royal Horse Artillery, so the church was decorated with dark blue hydrangeas and crimsons roses, the colours of the regiment.

After the ceremony, the reception was held at 59, Cadagon Gardens where the Burdon's were residing at the time. The couple left the reception later in the afternoon for a honeymoon in the West of Scotland.

There was a huge number of wedding presents from relatives, many titled personages including the Marquess and Marchioness of Londonderry, friends, tenants, and the household staff of both houses. Many of the presents from the bride's relatives were items of expensive jewellery containing gems like diamonds, pearls and sapphires. The bridegroom had given his new wife several items of such expensive jewellery. One of the smallest presents held a nice touch; a silver photograph frame and a caddy spoon from the school children in Castle Eden.

At another celebration in April 1914 the couple's first child, a daughter, one of three children they would have had recently been born. This celebration in the Drill Hall at Parklands, Castle Eden, was to mark the 21st birthday of Rowland Burdon the seventh. There were many guests as well as relatives including the Nimmos, the Trechmanns, the Hendersons, tenants and estate workers. This was not the grand affair organised by the Londonderry's on their son's coming of age. Instead it appeared to be a ball of a friendly, genuine but less formal affair.

The tenantry and employees on the estate presented Rowland jnr with a solid silver rose bowl decorated with acanthus leaves and grapes, inscribed with; "To Rowland Burdon, from the tenantry, workpeople, and friends at Castle Eden, on the occasion of his coming of age, February 6th, 1914."

The bowl was accompanied by an illuminated address which read;[39] "To Rowland Burdon Esq: We, the tenants and friends at Castle Eden, desire to heartily congratulate you on the attaining of your majority. Your family have had a long and honourable association with Castle Eden, alike as Lords of the Manor and as large property owners. Their connection has been cemented by many kindly deeds, which are on this auspicious occasion recalled with great pleasure. We feel sure that the traditions of your family will be fully maintained by you, and we trust that you may be granted many years of health and strength to fulfil your responsibilities which will ultimately devolve upon you."

The presentation was made by William James Nimmo during an interval in the dance programme who commented that he "was delighted to know that Mr. Rowland Burdon was not only doing exceedingly well in his scholastic training at Oxford but was on the way to becoming a fine athlete. In running he had shown good form over the hurdles and he had achieved distinction in the long and high jump. Further, he showed promising form as a cricketer."

Mr Nimmo "hoped it would be a long time before young Mr Burdon was called upon to step into his father's shoes, but he had no doubt when the time came Mr Burdon would prove to be a worthy son of a worthy father. Meanwhile, he was going into the Army, bearing a name which had had been writ large in the history of the county of Durham for the last 100 years. (Loud Applause.)"

"Mr. Burdon briefly replied, and expressed his thanks for this kindly feeling which had always been extended to him on the estate."

There followed various toasts and cheers, one being a toast to the health of the new baby, the first grandchild of the Colonel and Mrs. Burdon. This was a happy time but times were about to change.

CHAPTER ELEVEN

Wars and the Durham Light Infantry

Colonel Burdon's late Uncle Rowland was the chief instigator of the 16th Durham Rifle Volunteers (Castle Eden) in 1860. In 1894, the strength of this company was 100 and it constituted the F Company of the 1st Durham Reserve Volunteers with the then Major Burdon as commander.

The volunteers underwent training like the event in 1886 when there was a week's training under canvas in Redcar. At that time the total strength of the 1st Battalion was 840, and 700 of these men were able to train at the camp on Ings Farm, about a mile and a half from Redcar railway station. This was the first such camp of the volunteer battalion. Colonel Sadler was in overall command with several officers, including Major Burdon also in the camp.

By the time of the beginning of the 2nd Boer War on 11th October 1899, Rowland Burdon was promoted to Lt Colonel and the command of the 1st Volunteer Battalion of the DLI. In 1898, he had been awarded the Volunteer Decoration.

In late January 1900, 43 volunteers from the 1st Battalion, joined with another sixty seven to make up the 110 men who had been selected from the Durham Volunteer battalions to take the train from Stockton to Newcastle to begin further training. An inspection took place before the men left the Stockton Drill Hall, with Col, Burdon looking 'fine, smart and soldier-like' as he inspected his men.

After his inspection, Col Burdon addressed the men who were going to the barracks in Newcastle and also wishing them good luck hoping 'to Heaven they would see some service. If they did he hoped they would take as much care of themselves as possible and have a safe return. (Cheers)'

The men marched through the town amidst cheering crowds of people lining the streets. Once at the station, the band played "patriotic airs including 'The Girl I left behind me' and 'Rule Britannia'. As for the cheers they were long, loud and enthusiastic passing all description…. People cheered and cheered again, and handkerchiefs were waved the more."

There were many casualties in this war which had ended by 31st May 1902. Over 20,000 British were killed and 28,829 wounded. All those killed did not die in battle. Over 13,000 died from diseases, mainly typhoid, dysentery and other enteric diseases but 86 were killed by lightning and one was eaten by a crocodile.

Because of the guerrilla-type tactics used by the Boers, the British destroyed farms and settlements. They also introduced concentration camps where it is estimated 26,000 Afrikaans, mainly women and children, died mainly from malnutrition and disease.

By 1911 Rowland Burdon was made Honorary Colonel of the 5th Battalion of the Durham Light Infantry. In August 1914, his son Rowland joined the Northumberland Hussars as a despatch rider. Rowland jnr was only there for a short time as, he was gazetted (promoted) as a lieutenant into the 18th Battalion of the Durham Light Infantry.

War between Britain and Germany was declared on 4th August, 1914. The Regular Army and the Territorial Force made up what Kaiser Wilhelm II is alleged to have called, 'a contemptible little army'. Numbers may have been small compared with the numbers of German troops but these men were highly trained and many regulars had served in the Boer War and were used to conflict. The Battle of Le Cateau between August 25th and 26th was a rearguard action fought by British soldiers. Although this battle delayed the German's advance on Paris the British had casualties of 7,812 highly trained troops.

Colonel Burdon's son-in-law Major Walter Sclater-Booth was one of those who experienced these very early days of the war.

This was written by him in a letter to Colonel Burdon;[2] "For days and nights we never got any sleep fighting from daylight till dark followed by a long night march and never arriving at billets till after dark. Everyone is so tired they positively could not keep awake... The attack came from across country and was begun quite close with guns – machine guns and rifle fire. We never got a dog's chance – three guns were manhandled into action – and everyone with them was killed or wounded. I was bowled over as I was running towards the battery. I knew nothing for six hours during which time the shells and bullets must have been flying around me. Heaps of men have been killed stone dead without a mark on them from the shells. The German artillery is very good indeed as are their machine guns... The British Cavalry is very good, but we expose ourselves too much and suffered in consequence."

His letters of 24th and 26th of September, were written from a hospital bed in King Edward VII's Hospital for Officers, 9 Grosvenor Gardens, London, so by this time he must have returned to England.

His account of events in Paris appear somewhat confused. His head injury must have been worse than he thought, especially as his opening line in the first letter reads; "My head is infinitely better and I should very soon be quite well." It is uncertain whether this is the case.

The end of the second letter gives an insight of his ordeal; "I suppose I ought to be thankful to be alive and I am really but it has worried me a lot that I did not get exterminated with all the others. One of the most awful parts of the retreat was after Le Cateau. We fought that day a pitched battle from daylight to dark."

The Germans had been successful in their offensive during the Battle of the Frontiers. The Battle of Le Cateau was a rearguard action. Although it delayed the German advance on Paris, there were 7,812 British casualties. This retreat Sclater-Booth described as being 'one of the most awful parts.' He continued with; "After the battle we returned at night and the next day to St. Quentin and we (1st Brigade and my Battery) were ordered to keep the Germans at bay until the 29th to enable the infantry to retreat...De Lisles fight on the 24th August was a bad show. My battery was fairly in it and the last to leave. The men were magnificent under an absolute hail of shells…We had several batteries playing on us but I never located any of them and confined myself to the infantry and fairly mowed them down. We lost two ammunition wagons and several men hurt. One shell burst in front of me and the bullets hit all over and never went in."

A newspaper account of the battle gives more information;[3] "Major the Hon. W. D. Sclater-Booth was in command of the battery, which numbered 200 all ranks with six 13-pounder guns, when it went into action at Mons, where it did good service and at several points in the retreat.

The morning of September 1st dawned thick and misty. A heavy fog overhung the countryside, rendering objects indistinct at over 300 yards. By 5-30 the mist lifted a little, and the battery prepared to march. Guns were limbered up and teams hooked up. Just then a patrol of the 11th Hussars galloped into the bivouac with the news that the Germans were advancing in force as they had ridden into the advance cavalry in the fog and almost got away without loss. Almost immediately a group of cavalry appeared on a ridge some 300 yards away, and a minute later a storm of shell swept through the battery, 12 enemy guns having been brought into position like lightning.

Caught in massed formation, men and horses fell in real butchery. Major Sclater-Booth hurrying from headquarters was knocked out by a shell explosion and badly hurt. Captain E.K. Bradbury the next senior officer took over command. The guns were hastily unlimbered and manhandled into position, but only three of them could only be brought to bear on the German guns, which – supplemented by machine-gun and rifle fire continued to deal death and wounds among our gunners. Two of the guns were knocked out of action almost immediately, Lieu J. Giffard fighting one of them gallantly till he fell dead, with every man of the gun killed or wounded. Lieut. Mundy, standing in the open as observation officer, was killed, Lieut. Campbell was shot down, brave Bradbury fighting the only 13-pounder left agaiInt 12 guns, went down with a shattered thigh, yet even on the ground he retained command

and directed the fire of the solitary gun. Another storm of shell fell round the group, killed Bradbury and killed or wounded every man on his feet round the gun."

Major Sclater-Booth was in command of 'L' Battery of the Royal Horse Artillery at Nery, during the retreat from Mons. In the early hours of September 1st 1914, he was badly wounded and saw no further active service. For the rest of the war he served in England. He was awarded the DSO. Captain Bradbury was post-humously awarded the VC as were Battery Sergeant Major Durrell and Sergeant Nelson both of whom were commissioned.

Reading the account of the battle, where the British were taken by surprise in the attack and so many brave men and young officers killed or wounded, one can understand Scalter-Booth's feelings as he lay in his hospital bed thinking of the 'extermination' of his men and it 'worried' him 'quite a lot' that he did not get 'exterminated with the others.'

Paxman suggests that whilst [4] "the British Official History of the war claimed later that the force sent across the Channel made up 'the best trained, best organised and best equipped British Army that ever went forth to war', he points out that "even the Official History conceded that although "each battalion might have a couple of machine guns…in heavy guns and howitzers, high explosive shells, trench mortars, hand grenades and much of the subsidiary material required for siege and trench warfare it was almost deficient."

The Durham Pals (later the DLI)

This poorly equipped, 'contemptible little army' held back huge numbers of highly equipped Germans until new troops could arrive. Propaganda and recruiting drives quickly raised thousands of volunteers for Kitchener's Army. "Pals" battalions of men from the same town or workplace were encouraged. Men recruited in local recruiting drives would be fighting alongside colleagues, friends or neighbours.

The idea for such a battalion in County Durham originated from a suggestion in a letter from Major F. T. Tristram to Col

Burdon. Rowland Burdon took up the idea and along with Lord Durham they raised the 18th Battalion D.L.I.

When Lord Durham called a committee including Colonel Burdon, Sir William Gray and H. Pike Pease M.P. it was agreed to raise and equip a County Battalion, as it then called, mainly from Durham, Darlington, the Hartlepools, Stockton, Middlesbrough, Sunderland and Bishop Auckland. Money was raised by subscription with The Earl of Durham, W. Cresswell Gray and Rowland Burdon all donating £1,000 each with others donating amounts ranging from £500 to £5.

At first the idea for such a battalion funded by subscription, was opposed by the War Office but Colonel Burdon persevered with the project until official sanction was obtained. In a speech in Seaham Harbour in early September, he told the audience an application had been made to the War Office. He travelled to London, possibly to present the case and wired back not long afterwards that Lord Kitchener was looking at the proposal and he was confident it would be given his approval.

By September 18th the "Pals Corps" was making headway in forming the first and second companies of Lord Durham's County Battalion D.L.I. From that date the battalion would be recognised as an official force and attached to Lord Kitchener's Army. Parades and drills had already been arranged for the volunteers until they could go to the training ground. A rifle club was established with H. Pike Pease as its president.

Some who volunteered to enlist in the services at the outset of the War were refused. Many were turned down on medical grounds. Others were too old. Nevertheless by 18th September 1914, it was reported that over 4,500 men had been recruited to various regiments in the Hartlepools, nearly half of these enlisting in the Durham Light Infantry.

On the same date, Winston Churchill had the following message printed in newspapers; "The German Emperor has urged his soldiers to exterminate the 'treacherous English' and walk over General French's 'contemptible little army'. Counties to arms! No peace until Prussian militarism is pulverised and German truculence abashed."

Messages like this would stir more men into volunteering and by early October, the 18th Battalion had its full establishment of about 1,300 strong. The battalion had selected mainly clerks, shop assistants, teachers, trades people and students,- men considered to be intelligent. There was a height restriction of initially five foot nine, then five feet six inches even this height being tall at that time, height being an indicator of physical strength and strong constitution.This height restriction was later lowered to five feet four inches if the man was found particularly suitable. This was taller than the height needed to enlist for other Kitchener's Army recruits throughout the country. Lord Kitchener summoned Colonel Burdon to London to thank him for such a fine battalion. It was the only Pals unit in the country formed by subscription, other such battalions had expenses refunded by the Government.

The cost of equipment amounted to £10,000. Lord Durham gave the use of Cocken Hall as a training centre and billet. Huts were built on this site to accommodate the recruits. This use of Cocken Hall saved the expense of between six and seven thousand pounds.

The country mansion of Cocken Hall, about five miles from Durham City, was on one of Lord Durham's estates. The Hall was surrounded by woods had extensive grounds with the River Wear running through. The men were housed in wooden huts lit by electricity installed by electrical engineers amongst the recruits.

Recruits underwent rifle practice and a range was prepared for this purpose. A large field adjoining the hall was used as a parade ground. Drill and physical exercise increased the recruits' physique and stamina. "But (DGM 6/10/1914) the most striking feature of the whole battalion is the fine 'esprit de corps' which exists in the first place amongst the ranks, and in the second place between the men and their officers. The men are all 'pals' and extend to one another the best of good fellowship and bonhomie. Though a couple of weeks ago they were complete strangers. A local newspaper suggested the battalion should be called 'Comrades' rather than

'Pals'. The men recruited did not come from the same workplace or neighbourhood but they had bonded so quickly they were now comrades in arms.

In this respect they have an excellent example set them by Colonel Bowes,(a serving soldier), who is at present acting as Commanding officer, for as he moves about the barracks – as the hall must now be styled – and grounds he has a pleasant word to every salute.

From the men he expects strictest discipline and good behaviour, but he is ever ready with words of commendation and encouragement, and he has attained as high a measure of popularity as he possibly could, whilst all the other officers are all exceptionally well liked."

By late October Lord Southampton had taken over command of the battalion with Major Tristram as second in command. By this time after "barely a month's training the battalion has reached to quite advanced manoeuvres, and is daily occupied in outpost, skirmishing and extended order drill."

There were at this time billets in West Rainton and Newton Hall but Cocken Hall was the main centre of training.

Other recruits were needed; pioneers, cooks, men to carry out sanitary and water duties, men for the regimental police, men for transport duties and members of a military band. Sergeant J.D. Muscrop set on a company of cooks whilst a fine band was formed under Sergeant W. L. Allen.

Colonel Burdon' son Rowland was a Lieutenant in the 18th Battalion of the County Regiment. Rowland's cousins would also enlist. Noel Edward Burdon was a Lieutenant in the Durham Light Infantry. His younger brother John was a Lieutenant in the 1st Battalion of the 63rd Foot in the Manchester Regiment.

Noel and John were the sons of Colonel Burdon's younger brother John George and his wife Blanche Louisa. Blanche was the daughter of General Edward Arthur Somerset. During his military career, John's grandfather General Somerset had been appointed Colonel of the 1st Battalion of Worcestershire Regiment in December 1881. John probably joined this regiment to remember his deceased grandfather, while Noel George enlisted in the D.L.I. because of his Uncle Rowland.

Rowland's brother, John George Burdon was educated at Repton with him but he studied at Oriel College Oxford. John George became a mechanical engineer and worked for many years for the Newcastle ship-building firm of Hawthorn, Leslie and Co Newcastle. John George became a trained engineer, echoing his grandfather's desires to be a bridge builder.

Rowland Burdon's son-in-law Walter Sclater-Booth was an Army Officer. His son Rowland had intended to entry the Army but his two nephews Noel Edward and John Burdon enlisted as volunteers. Both Rowland and Noel were Lieutenants in the DLI. The DLI were to experience combat on British soil.

The Bombardment of Hartlepool

On December 15th Colonel P.H. Hammond who was in command of the Tyne and Tees Defence, received information from the War Office of the probability of a raid on the coast by enemy warships.

About 8.30am on the following day, soldiers from the 18th Battalion of the DLI were entrenched in West Hartlepool with the rest of the detachment, under command of Captain Tristram, were stood to. Out in the sea, shrouded in mist, a gunboat and two German destroyers lay off the shore. The poor visibility enabled the vessels to close in close without being detected. The enemy ships displayed British signals and fired out to sea. As battle practice had taken place previously in that area, these actions misled the coast batteries into thinking the vessels were British Ships. The enemy ships drew nearer and were recognised as enemy ships. Sailors got underway and prepared for action. Before they had got out of the harbour, the bombardment had commenced with the shore batteries returning fire. The ship was slightly damaged just as they got out of harbour. Undeterred, they opened fire on the enemy ships but their small four inch guns were of little use against the heavy guns of the warships. Three more shots struck the vessel forcing it to sheer off and take refuge in the Tees. Despite such attempts to disable the enemy ships by a British flotilla of small craft, they were no match for the warships.

The entrenched soldiers were in the process of changing guard. The enemy ships drew nearer and opened fire. Five of the soldiers were killed outright with eleven wounded, one of whom later died. Fishermen were out at sea. They had hurried inshore and as they were trying, to land their smacks on the beach the soldiers observed one fisherman was wounded. Sergeant Heal and Corporal Brewerton left the trench, raced down the beach and brought the fisherman to safety.

Derfflinger 12 inch shells burst in and around the battery. In forty minutes, 1,500 shells were fired from the ships. The enemy ships moved down the coast to shell Old Hartlepool, West Hartlepool and the docks. There were 119 deaths and over 300 wounded. Houses were damaged or destroyed. Churches, hospitals, the workhouse and schools were struck. This was the time little children were going to school accompanied by mothers with babies in their arms. These too were among the victims. A whole family of father, mother and six children were killed.

The worst shelling took place in the vicinity of the Heugh Battery at Old Hartlepool. Whole rows of houses were demolished. Hartlepool Hospital escaped damage but the nurse's quarters at the hospital were wrecked. A sister at the hospital on night duty was standing at the window looking out, when she saw a flash of light at sea, followed by a thundery noise. She too at first thought it was battle practice, so she continued to watch until a nearby explosion made her realise this was something really serious. She went outside and saw the battery guns returning fire. She saw the shot as it hit and damaged the roof of St Hilda's Church. The gable of the rectory was blown off. She had witnessed enough and speedily returned to the safety of the hospital.

The gasworks was shelled with one shell striking a gasometer, causing a million cubic feet of gas to burst into flames, demolishing the gasworks. Many ships in the harbour were damaged. Two workmen were killed at Richardson and Westgarth's shipyards and two vessels under construction were damaged. Three workmen nearby in the street were also killed.

Mines had been laid. Fishing vessels still out at sea found themselves surrounded by mines. They made for the Tees to escape the hazard. Shortly after the bombardment, on the weekend of 26th – 27th December, mines were laid by enemy ships around the east coast of Britain. Several ships were sunk causing the loss of lives. Mine laying continued. In February 1915, a West Hartlepool Tramp Steamer 'Wavelet' struck a mine in the English Channel and was badly damaged. The vessel appeared to be floundering and eleven men, including the first officer, got into one of the ship's boats. The sea was rough and heavy causing the boat to capsize, drowning all eleven men. The captain and the remaining eleven crew members remained on board the damaged vessel as it took in water but still managed to safely reach shore.

Destruction and death caused by mines and the shelling of Hartlepool and Scarborough was good news to the Germans with a German newspaper reporting;[5] "This time it is not merely a daring cruiser raid, or mere throwing of bombs, but a regular bombardment of fortified places. It is further proof of the gallantry of our navy."

In his war history of the battalion Lieutenant Colonel William Douglas Lowe wrote; "The inhabitants behaved extremely well, and the girls in the Hartlepool Telephone Exchange worked steadily through the cannonade. The German aim had been to create such a panic in civilian England as would prevent the dispatch of new armies to the Continent, and to compel Sir John Jellicoe and the Grand Fleet to move the base nearer the East Coast. Both hopes completely failed."

The 18th Batallion goes overseas

On May 20th 1915, at Newcastle, the 18th battalion and other North Country troops were reviewed by the King, Lord Kitchener, the Duke of Northumberland and the Earl of Durham on the Town Moor at Newcastle. Those taking part would be proud when they read press reports of praise by the King for the progress they had made, the high level of physical fitness and the smart soldierly bearing of the troops.

More training took place in September 1915. They were inoculated against cholera. On December 5th they with 5,000 men on board, they set sail, using a circuitous route to advert the dangers of submarines. This combined with the

heavy weather on the Bay of Biscay meant it took six days on an overcrowded ship to reach Gibraltar before moving onto Malta. A collision with an empty French troop ship resulting in some damage meant two days was needed in Malta for repairs. The ship left Valetta on December 17th. Two attempted, but unsuccessful, submarine attacks later, the ship reached Alexandria on the 19th, arriving at Port Said on December 21st where a tent camp was set up just outside the town.

Drill was continued but they had the pleasure of bathing parades in the warm sea. There was no pleasure at Christmas as the troops were on hard rations and as no Christmas supplies arrived, there was no Christmas dinner.

On December 28th, the battalion trained with the rest of the Brigade before setting off in open trucks for Kantara where they met with Sikhs, Gurkhas and the Bengal Lancers, making camp on the east bank of the Suez Canal.

Work began on constructing trenches, building light railway tracks and unloading barges. Between work details there appear to have been a lot of football played. There was even a Kantara Derby where Major P.G. Neville won all the flat races. The Mysore Lancers gave exhibitions of tent-pegging and horse lancers to music. There was a tug-of-war between teams mounted on mules, camel races and bathing in the canal.

The canal was left behind as they marched across the sand to defend the troops of the Mediterranean Expeditionary force, camels carrying their stores along with them. Unfortunately some of the water carriers leaked leading to a shortage of water.

Lt Col Lowe made a poignant comment at this time; "During our early days in Egypt Arab refugees, homeless and generally starving, who were being squeezed out between the British and Turkish fronts, used to attempt to enter our lines. At first this was forbidden, as it was perfectly easy for Turkish spies to enter with them, and arrangements were made to send out grain to their camps in the extensive No Man's Land. Later when they were allowed to come through our lines they would sweep up any grain even from the horse lines or any scraps of food lying about. They were passed farther back and housed in compounds and rationed by the British."

This account had a familiar ring. Refugees such as these are the victims of conflict in their suffering.

The battalion was relieved in late February, reaching Spit Point on the east bank of the canal where they again began to build railways, roads and lay water pipes. They had what was referred to as 400 'coolies' under Arab command to probably do most of the heavy work in this venture. They then left Mesopotamia.

Death of John Burdon

John Burdon, Colonel Burdon's nephew, did not leave Mesopotamia. He had also gone to school at Repton like his cousins. Intending to have a career in the army, John entered the Royal Military College at Sandhurst. He was gazetted on the 13th January, 1915 as a 2nd Lieutenant into the Manchester Regiment becoming a temporary Lieutenant the following September. John went to France in 1915 before going to Mesopotamia to serve with the Kut Relief Force. During this time he was mentioned in dispatches for operations undertaken between 19th January and the 30th April, 1916. He was killed in action on the 8th March, 1916 near the Turkish Redoubt at the battle of Es Sinn while leading his men to attack the Turkish trenches. At first he was reported missing presumed wounded on the 8th March but when found it was confirmed he had died in action on that day. He was buried at Basra Memorial Cemetery, Basra, Iraq.

The 18th Batallion arrives in France

The 18th Battalion DLI left Mesopotamia and arrived in Marseilles on March 11th in floods of rain. In Citerne their billets were poor. It was now snowing and big change from the heat of Egypt. Marching on sand may have softened their feet as marching on roads in France felt hard on their feet. They moved forward through incessant rain, sleet and a snowstorm. On March 29th an enemy aeroplane dropped a bomb at two of their howitzers, leaving one man killed by a splinter.

In May they were often under heavy fire, so working parties marched out at night, marching back again to camp before daybreak. By June 4th they had reached Courcelles.

Lt Col Lowe wrote that; "The whole of the countryside was stiff with high velocity guns:these had to be hidden and a bird's eye view of the country gave out the impression of a series of large mottled tortoises sprinkled freely about....all credit is due to our airmen who kept the enemy aeroplanes at such a height that those strange objects were not spotted."

Colonel Burdon's son Rowland, now a captain in the Royal Flying Corps of the D.L.I., may have been one of those airmen who kept enemy aircraft at a height where they would be unable to iden-tify the big velocity guns.

It was now June 1916. Observations from planes helped deter-mine areas for continuous heavy bombardment on German trenches. During the last few days of June preparations were made for what would be a long and bloody battle.

The Battle of the Somme[6]

"Since the winter of 1914, a continuous line of trenches had stretched from the Belgian coast to the Swiss border, creating a war of attri-tion amid the wire, mud and trenches. The Gallipoli campaign of 1915 had been an attempt to outflank the Western Front, but it had failed. At the Chantilly Conference of December 6, 1915, Allied Strategy for the coming year was agreed upon: large scale offensives would be carried out on every front... And so, in early 1916, prep-arations began for an Allied push along the Somme front. These preparations did not, however, take into account the possibility that the Germans might be making plans of their own.

The Battle of the Somme began on 1st July 1916. Aeroplanes patrolled the fourteen mile front. At 6am it would appear the enemy guns were inferior to those of the British. A great mine had taken months to construct at Beaumont Haimes. At 7.20am, this great mine was detonated. Debris and a mushroom of smoke rose high in the air.

The British began firing but the huge explosion alerted the Germans into action "and with one roar their guns broke out into a bright fire-curtain…hurling a deadly avalanche of shells of the highest calibre, and with absolute accuracy of aim poured hell and destruction on to our trenches, crowded with men who were now on the point of climbing out our front line trenches, Russian saps and advanced communication trenches literally disappeared and with them the major portion of the two leading Battalions and D company. A few of our men broke past the wire, fewer still crossed No-Man's Land, and only a mere handful reached the German lines. Some of D Company struggled on and launched onto Pendant Copse and were never seen again, and these stout hearts will now be buried there.

Meanwhile the hostile trenches could be seen thick with men, who, immediately the barrage had lifted and passed beyond them, stood breast high to repel our assault…the remainder of our troops being mown down in swathes as they lay in the open and stood in the trenches. The ferocity and volume of the Boche batteries was as overwhelming as it had been unexpected… About this time very heavy casualties began to pour in from the whole Brigade in to our Regimental Aid Post – Lieut J.W. Macfarlane and his medical orderly and staff did heroic work in spite of devilish fire."

Private Frank Raine of the 18th Battalion DLI describes his experience; [7]

"Oh, my God! The ground in front – it was just like heavy rain; that was machine-gun bullets. Up above, there were these great 5.9-inch shrapnel shells going off. Broomhead and I went over the top together. We walked along a bit. A terrific bang and a great black cloud of smoke above us. I felt a knock on my hip which I didn't take much notice of. I turned round, and Broomhead had gone. I walked on and I could not see a soul of any description – either in front of me or behind me. I presume they got themselves tucked into shell holes. I thought, 'Well, I'm not going on by myself,' and I turned round and came back."

Those who had gone over the top with Private Raine were probably not 'tucked in shells holes' as he thought. They, like his comrade Broomhead had probably fallen or were wounded.

Sergeant A.S. Durrant was wounded. He says this of his ordeal;[8]

"I reached the German trenches, but I was wounded, and I saw the entrance to a dugout. So I dragged myself along to the steps of the dugout, and I thought, 'Let's see if I can get in there'.... I dragged myself to the steps of the dugout, and I managed – somehow- to get myself into a half-sitting, half-lying position, on the steps leading down to the dugout. Suddenly, the mouth of the dugout fell in. A high-explosive shell must have burst very nearby, and I was thrown into a doubled-up position. I didn't seem to be hurt any further, but the entrance to the dugout was blocked so I dragged myself out and rested in the open. This went on until the evening, and I gradually dragged myself in the right direction, to the British lines, and eventually I crawled to safety. And, on arriving at what I thought was safety, I saw an old college friend of mine, nicknamed 'Whiskers'. I shouted, 'Whiskers!' He came along, 'Hello! What are you doing here?' He was in the Royal Army Military Corps, and he took charge of me, put me on to a stretcher and conveyed me to a medical shelter."

Arthur Swaby Durrant , born in Chester-Le-Street, but living in Sunderland in 1911 had attended Bede College as a student teacher and this is probably where he met 'Whiskers'. At the time of this incident he would still have been only about 23 years old. His actions and determination to survive seem extraordinary. He did not remain in the DLI but was commissioned as a 2nd Lieutenant in the Notts and Derby Regiment.

These stories give a small insight into the horrendous Battle of the Somme when regiments including the 18th Battalion, A and B Companies were violently shelled and lost heavily" Only ten men from D Company survived. The West and East Yorkshire Regiments also had appalling losses in their exposure to the inferno of fire.

The Battle of the Somme was the main Allied attack on the western front in 1916. On the first day the British suffered 60,000 casualties, 20,000 of whom were killed. Sixty per cent of the officers involved in the first day were killed. The battle was mainly fought by the volunteer armies raised in 1914 and 1915. Many of these volunteers were 'Pals' Battalions, men from the same town or workplace. They suffered catastrophic losses when whole units died together. The Official History of the War, writing of the first attack, says; "For the disastrous loss of the finest manhood of the United Kingdom and Ireland there was only a small gain of ground to show.... Never again was the spirit or the quality of the officers and men so high, not the general state of the training, leading and, above all, discipline of the new British armies in France so good. The losses sustained were not only heavy but irreplaceable." There were more than a million casualties on both sides by the end of the Battle of the Somme on November 1916.

While A and B Companies lost heavily due to violent shelling, only ten men from D Company survived. The West and East Yorkshire Regiments had "appalling losses in their exposure to the inferno of fire."

On October 17th 1916, "the Brigade began to move forward slowly by stages in bad weather along water-logged roads, and many of us began, if not to sigh for the flesh-pots of Egypt, which had certainly not been attractive, at least to remember longingly the warmth of the previous months."

Wet weather could lead to trench foot. Icy weather could result in frostbite in the feet. The men were instructed to rub their feet daily with whale and change their socks every day with the result that "trench foot and frostbite was practically unknown in Regiment trenches."

These trenches were described by Lowe as being "much high in porridge-like mud" and even in the better trenches a [9] "gum-boot once securely sucked in by mud thigh deep, was as good as lost." This mud is described by Captain Alexander Stewart; "Mud is a bad description: the soil was more like thick slime. When walking one sank several inches owing to the suction, it was difficult to withdraw the feet."

Henry Williamson described the effects of extremely cold weather in December 1915; [10]

"One afternoon, before Christmas, a harder frost settled upon the vacant battlefield. By midnight trees, bunkers, paths, sentries' balaclavas and great coat shoulders became stiff.... Lying with unprotected boots outside the open end of a bunker, one endured pain in one's feet until the final agony – when one got up and hobbled outside, seeing bright stars above the treetops."

As well as the cold there were rats in the trenches that[11] "abounded in some parts, great loathsome beasts gorged with flesh."

The trenches were notoriously bad but they did save lives as they offered some cover. Hebuterne was a place with little cover. "It was at best a spot where few people dawdled, as the enemy used to send all his spare ammunition there, and the village had a somewhat unhealthy reputation. The most dangerous spots were the crossroads and the west entrance, which went frequently hit, the pond which quite as frequently went up into the air, and the church which, lying between communication trenches, was smashed up, only two thick walls remaining. Behind this ruin lies the cemetery with its graves gashed open by shells. In the debris of the school hard by were found the school register of 1891, and old copy books."

In the horrors faced by those in conflict one can forget these battles occurred in villages where people once lived and worked. The village of Hubuterne was almost completely destroyed and had to be rebuilt in the 1920's. The people had left to an uncertain destination. Often they would have to leave suddenly. In agricultural areas this would mean leaving animals and livestock behind, many of which died in the devastation. Burying parties may have found they would have to inter decaying livestock as well as their own comrades.

There is a cemetery at Hebuterne where over 750 war casualties were buried, nearly fifty of these being unidentified. Private Wallace Featherstone of the 18th Battalion DLI was one of those who was identified. One soldier buried there after he was killed in action on the 1st March 1917.

Castle Eden men lost in actions

Sergeant John Alexander Gorrie was killed in action earlier that year, on 28th February, 1916. He was a sergeant in the 18th Battalion DLI. He was a clerk at Blackhall Colliery and enlisted on 17th September 1914 when a fine young man of almost twenty three; five foot seven inches tall, a well-built 145 pounds with a fresh complexion, hazel eyes and dark brown hair.

John was born in Scotland but he had moved with his parents David Sword Gorrie and mother Mary when his father became park-keeper at Castle Eden. They lived in Parklands. His parents would have been proud of their only son when he completed his education at the Technical College, Hartlepool, going on to Skerry's College Newcastle before obtaining employment as a clerk, then obtaining the post of Chief Clerk at the new colliery of Blackhall.

John Alexander volunteered and enlisted in the 18th Battalion on 17th September, 1914. He trained at Cocken Hall before being stationed at Hartlepool, being there at the time of the bombardment on 16th December 1914. John Alexander went to Egypt on the 7th December, 1915 and from there to France on the 11th March 1916. He was on the front line by the 22nd March and was killed in action on the 27th July, 1916 during the repulse of a German raid at Neuve Chapelle. He was buried in the Military Cemetery at Richebourg, St. Vaast. Lieut Col Bowes, his commanding officer[12] wrote; "His death has been a severe blow to the battalion, for he was so well liked by all ranks, and everyone knew him, officers and men alike, and his sterling good work and grit on every occasion brought him to notice so frequently" and the Adjutant said he showed, "conspicuous bravery when on the night of 2 July, opposite Serre, having been granted permission, went out again and again into 'No Man's Land' under considerable rifle fire and machine-gun fire and brought in wounded men."

John Alexander was the only child of David and Mary Gorrie. Lieut John Hutchinson Tristram was also killed at Neuve Chapelle.

He was the only son of Major F. T. Tristram who helped set up and served in the 18th Battalion DLI. John Hutchinson had followed his father into the army and was already stationed at Cairo in the Worcestershire Regiment at the beginning of the war. He was killed in action near Neuve Chapelle on 12th March 1915, aged just 22.

On 23rd July, 1919, Private William Christopher Thubron of the 1st Battalion Yorkshire Hussars was killed in India. William had worked at Castle Eden Brewery with his father William and his brother George. William was not the only person linked with the brewery to be killed. 2nd Lieut William Leslie Nimmo, son of William John Nimmo, the brewer also died. In 1911 Will enlisted in the 1st Battalion of Northumberland Fusiliers and would only be about nineteen when he was killed. He was buried at Nord-Pas-de-Calais, Neuville-saint Vaast, four miles north of Arras.

The war continued with many lost, including those in the 18th Battalion DLI.

The Home Front

Those back in Britain helped in ways they could without really knowing the full extent of the horrors of the conflict. Lowe recalls this help; "For Christmas dinners they were very much indebted to the continuous generosity of friends at home who had subscribed with such a free hand"

Press appeals for contributions towards Christmas dinners for the troops were often in the form of letters written by Col Burdon to encourage donations to provide a Christmas dinner for the 18th.

Lowe thanked others. "In the same way owed are very much indeed to the 'Lady Anne Lambton Fund' for mufflers, socks, gloves, badges etc." Lady Anne Lambton was the figurehead for motivating women into supplying much needed articles for the 18th. The organisation was set in the early days of the war in 1914. Information was reported in the press of items and those who donated them. For example, from August 1915 to August 1916, 2, 246 articles were donated including; shirts, towels, handkerchiefs, mufflers, mitts, soap gloves, helmets and laces.

Most articles including gloves, socks, handkerchiefs and shirts were hand made by women. Organisations like; ladies working parties, church societies and sewing parties, shirt committees, Durham needlework Guild, teachers and scholars from schools, even infant schools, readers of various newspapers, the Lambton household, Co-op employees, and colliery working parties, had been set up throughout the county. Donations of money were generously given to purchase the materials necessary for the mass production of essential items. Clean, dry socks could prevent trench foot and frostbite. This too was essential work.

Money was also donated for items like; tobacco, reading matter, oxo cubes, malted milk tablets and soap. Other monies were needed for hospital use for bandages, linen, nightshirts, bed jackets, towels and slippers.

Others, like Lady Londonderry collected for other DLI Battalions. By November 1916, she had collected over 25,000 articles. Her organisation had also sent seventy-six wheeled stretchers to the DL1 at the front.

Organisations like these, run by women to provide essentials and 'comfort parcels' would be duplicated throughout the country. As Lowe said, "It was all these kindnesses, continued so regularly and for a long time, that had made life under the stress and hardship of war still bearable and reminded so often the thoughts of those in England were with us."

Throughout the war, Colonel Burdon and Captain B. S Roberts looked after the Battalion funds and "they never failed to give any assistance asked for, keeping and supervising the accounts at very considerable trouble to themselves."

The War Ends

On 27th May 1919, the Colour Party of the 18th Battalion Durham Light Infantry entered Durham City in order to lay up their colours, adorned with a laurel wreath in the cathedral.[13] "The Mayor of Durham welcomed the soldiers and "Lord Durham said they were all proud when they thought of the work the battalion had done. Some of them had known the battalion from the first day it was raised, and they knew with what zeal and energy they devoted themselves to make it one of the most efficient battalions in that gallant army which had saved them from ruin and devastation and rescued the whole world for civilisation." Col Burdon reminded the congregation that Lord Kitchener had personally requested him to thank the County of Durham for raising such "an extraordinarily good battalion as the 18th Durham".

The soldiers at this ceremony had survived the war. Many did not. Col Burdon may have looked at the survivors in the cathedral that day, remembering his own son Rowland who had not survived.

CHAPTER TWELVE
Rowland Burdon VII (Captain Burdon)

Rowland Burdon jnr joined the Northumberland Hussars as a despatch rider in August 1914. On 21st September 1914, he was gazetted as a lieutenant in the 18th Battalion Durham Light Infantry, being promoted Captain on the 1st June 1915. He is usually known as Captain Burdon.

On 5th September, 1915, after tuition at the Military School, Norwich, Captain Rowland Burdon obtained his flying certificate taken on a Maurice Farman Biplane. This plane was developed by the French prior to the onset of war. It was used for reconnaissance early in the war but by this time was used for training purposes.

Paxman calls the young men of the Royal Flying Corps, [1]"dare devils." He suggests the organization attracted "more than its fair share of reckless young men and teenagers who drove too fast and drank too much. Military aviators were conscious of being an elite who, as they climbed and swooped at speeds of up to 200 miles an hour, lived in a permanently intensely exhilarating present." They were "trained with one object – to kill." They "had one hope – to live…. In 1916 the life expectancy of a combat pilot could be three weeks. On the other hand at the end of their patrols they returned not to a sodden dugout but to an airfield with beds and baths and decent food. The glamorous, rakish lives of these young men careering about the sky could not have been in greater contrast to the dank terror of trench warfare."

Rowland Burdon jnr may have one of those who gathered in May 1914 to witness the squadron of nine aeroplanes of the Army Flying Corps during the fourth stage of a relay test journey from

Montrose to Salisbury Plain. The nine plane had landed overnight at Seaton Carew and were preparing for an early morning start to York City. By five o-clock in the morning there were already several thousand people gathered to witness the departure of the airmen.[2]

"Captain Dawes was the first to ascend at 5.25. The other officers rose and winged their way southward at brief intervals, but it was not long until news arrived that trouble was being encountered." One plane, in the air when about five miles out to sea, suddenly experienced engine trouble, turned round to attempt a landing at Seaton Carew. The plane did not reach its original take off point as about a mile away from this destination, the pilot was forced to attempt to land at the golf links. By this time, a sudden heavy fog had obscured the pilot's view and the plane, at tremendous speed, struck a sea bank about 15 feet high smashing the undercarriage and two bottom wings and reducing the propeller to splinters. The pilot and mechanic were both killed. A repair lorry had to be telephoned for to remove the damaged aeroplane.

An aerodrome was opened at Seaton Carew in June 1916, shortly after the Zeppelin attack on Sunderland that May. On 27th November, a patrol of B.E. 2cs planes took off from Seaton Carew to intercept two groups of Zeppelins, probably returning for another attack on the North East Coast. Lieut I.V. Pyrott destroyed one of the Zeppelins and the other airships turned back across the sea.

Rowland Burdon jnr may have witnessed events at Seaton Carew in May 1914. This, and later newspaper accounts of bombings by enemy aircraft and the successful bringing down of German airplanes reported in the press, may have influenced him to become one of the 'daredevils' and learn to fly an aeroplane.

By the time Captain Burdon obtained a certificate to fly, great advances had been made in the production of aeroplanes. Selmer Fougner, an American journalist who covered WW1 until 1917 for the 'New York Sun' observed;[3] "Formerly aeroplanes in England were made by the dozen, now they are made by the hundred. Great sections of the English countryside have been turned over completely to the training and practice of flying men; huge works previous engaged in the production of automobiles are now turning out aeroplanes, and vast armies of men and women devote night and day to making the various parts entering into the construction of the latest models. After seeing the factories I was granted the privilege of making an ascent in the latest British Army bi-plane – the first civilian to whom such a trip has been granted. This machine achieves better results in speed and climbing ability than any other previous model and it is fitted with a gun of marvellous precision.

Through the raging winds and in the biting cold of a November evening, the machine took us soaring through the clouds at tremendous speed, yet answering perfectly to the touch of its youthful pilot. Sitting in the observer's seat, I had at no time the slightest cause for anxiety despite the gale and the fast oncoming darkness.

Not a tremor did I perceive beyond the roar of the motor, so wonderfully stable is this car. The pace at which we ascended worked out at almost 1,000 ft per minute. We encircled the surrounding country at a great height and then descended gracefully."

This experience appeared exhilarating to the writer as it would to the 'young pilot' flying the latest model aeroplane. This experience would appeal to young men like this. Captain Burdon probably had similar experiences in models like this. He was not demonstrating a new machine in England to an American journalist. In November 1915, he was serving in France.

Captain Rowland's Aunt Elizabeth relates an account of her nephew's time in France; 4 "Colonel and Mrs. Barrington Kennet of 19, Cheyne Gardens, have lost three sons in the War; the third son, Victor, was in the Royal Flying Corps, and his family were for a long time without certain news of his end. Rowland Burdon, my eldest brother's only son, determined to set the matter at rest one way or the other. He accordingly wrote a note asking for information, and fastened it securely to a football, and, equipped with this, flew over the German lines, and dropped his football in them. He himself was, of course, under fire all the time. He returned in safety to his own base. An answer was sent to him at once, but unfortunately Victor Barrington Kennett had been killed."

The Barrington-Kennetts' aviation exploits

The Burdons knew the Barrington-Kennett family. When Rowland Burdon's eldest daughter married Sclater Booth, they received a wedding present from Col and Mrs Barrington-Kennett. As the wedding was in London, they may even have attended the wedding.

The Barrington-Kennetts may have heroes of Captain Rowland, and possibly an inspiration for him to learn to fly an aeroplane and join the Royal Flying Corp as the Barrington-Kennetts had a long association with aviation. Before the invention of the aeroplane, an uncle, Sir Vincent Kennett-Barrington had died in a balloon accident. Basil, the eldest won the Mortimer-Singer prize of £500 in 1912 and [5] 'established in one flight a world's record for duration in the air with a passenger." In 1911 "he was beaten into the North Sea by a snowstorm while attempting to cross to Holland by night, and was rescued by a tug boat after being over three hours in the water."

In 1911, Basil H Barrington-Kennett was flying an F8 (Bristol no 38) biplane. In late August 1911, at Hardwick Military Camp, near Cambridge, he gave a demonstration of flying before large crowds of people from Cambridge and the surrounding area. The Sunday after these days of demonstrations, Victor Barrington-Kennett's biplane had to be moved to Colchester so the aeroplane was loaded onto an Army lorry. Unfortunately as the overloaded lorry was overtaking a cyclist on a bend in road, the poor cyclist was thrown from his bicycle, luckily escaping with minor injuries. It seems so unusual that the aeroplane at that time could not travel from Cambridge to Colchester and had to be transported by lorry. The cyclist would have had a great surprise but after recovery would have had a great story to tell.

Air races took place in the summer of 1911. One of these was the Circuit of Europe with one of the stages being from Calais to London, landing at Hendon aerodrome and returning again to Calais. Early on the morning of 5th July ten of the aviators took off in intervals from Hendon for the return journey across the Channel to Calais by way of Shoreham, Dover and Amiens.

Huge crowds, many of them French had gathered, some sleeping in the field overnight to watch the aviators leave again for France.

The crowds were still there when a [6] "Bristol biplane appeared in the west, and came slowly toward the ground. It was travelling at about 1,000 feet and the crowd cheered and cheered again as it descended. Many climbed over the barriers, and swarmed on to the ground." Lieut. Barrington-Kennett and his colleague Lieut. H. R.P. Reynolds climbed out of the aeroplane with Lieut. Reynolds commenting that they were "just jogging around and we thought we would come up as it is such a perfect morning, and see the start."

Apparently the two lieutenants had been "going about for weeks, one practising sketching whilst the other driving. Two days ago they had a little adventure which serves to illustrate the national temperament and the quiet courage of these men. Their engine was working badly and they thought it advisable that one should descend and relieve the machine. They tossed a penny to decide which it should be and Lieut. Barrington-Kennett won. Near Uxbridge the petrol pips began to leak, so he descended in an orchard, and having repaired it temporarily with the help of Lieut. Reynolds, who had turned up, "they jogged along" yesterday morning to Hendon."

In May 1912, Barrington Kennett was flying a Nieuport monoplane. Four other pilots, including Mr. De Havilland as well as himself were introduced to the King and Queen at Farnborough Common before the five airmen gave an hour long flying display of aerial manoeuvres for their Majesties.

They did on at least one occasion encounter problems. In June 1914, whilst flying from Larkhill at Salisbury Plain to the manoeuvre area at Cambridge, now both Majors, Barrington- Kennett and Reynolds were caught in a bad thunderstorm near Bedford. Major Barrington-Kennett was piloting a monoplane when turbulence hit him so badly that he was tossed out of his seat so badly that the seat broke. Yet he still landed safely. Major Reynolds was following in a biplane. A fierce gust of wind caught the airplane at about 1,500 feet, turning it over three times in the air, before landing upside-down with Major Reynolds gripping the wires to hold himself on, luckily escaping with only cuts and bruises. As one would expect the airplane was reduced to 'matchwood.'

Basil H Barrington-Kennett was in the Royal Flying Corps at the beginning of the war but transferred into Grenadier Guards.

Victor Barrington Kennett graduated from Balliol College Oxford in 1910. In 1911 he joined the London Balloon Company of the Royal Engineers as a 2nd Lieutenant. On an afternoon in May 1911, he and a fellow officer were flying a balloon with two ladies and another gentleman near Southfields Station, Wimbledon.

The balloon began to descend and observers in the street below saw the two aeronauts throwing out large quantities of ballast. Despite this, the balloon continued to descend. The car of the balloon descended onto the roof of a stationer's shop, dislodging slates and tiles as it continued downwards. Quick-thinking men in the streets below grabbed the attached ropes and guided the balloon safely to the ground. The occupants, apparently undeterred, stepped out of the car of the balloon.

The death of Victor Barrington-Kennett

Victor Barrington-Kennett received his flying certificate in 1912 and joined the Royal Flying Corp Special Reserve in 1913. In August 1914 he was a Flying Officer. On 7th March 1915 he left for the St Omer, his base in France. His bombing attacks included special aerial operations in the Battle of Loos when he targeted moving trains. In January 1916, be became Commanding Officer of the 4th Squadron.

Major Victor Barrington-Kennett was an ace pilot and it needed the German ace pilot, Max Immelman, the Blue Max to have enough skill to shoot him down on March 13th 1916. A note was delivered to the Royal Flying Corp by German aviators which read "Flying machine with Major Victor Barrington-Kennett has fallen near Serne. Pilot dead." It would appear there could be some truth in Captain Burdon's football story. He dropped a note attached to a football behind German lines, probably at the German aeroplane base, enquiring of the fate of Barrington-Kennet who had been posted missing on March 21st 1916. Official reports of his death did not appear in the press until 8th June. This is a long gap, so his parents would have been extremely concerned, as would his flying colleagues. Captain Burdon was probably at the same aeroplane base and he and fellow aviators would have been anxious of the Major's fate. Captain Burdon, note attached to the football, apparently dropped it in the vicinity of the German aeroplane base. They appear to have reciprocated by delivering a note to the Royal Flying Corps, possibly attached to the same football.

Major Barrington-Kennett had two other brothers killed in the war with only his third brother surviving. His brother Basil, who was an air enthusiast but became a Major in the Grenadier Guards was thirty years old when he was killed in May 1915, leading his men. He was in command of the 4th Brigade and was leading his men to the front line at Festubert. Under heavy fire and shelling, they had trudged through heavy rain and muddy ground full of shell holes, reaching their trench by nightfall. The following morning, leading the 1st platoon the Major took his men over the trench in an attack on enemy lines at Cour Lavoue, a farmhouse heavily protected by German machine guns. The platoon was mown down. The 2nd and 3rd platoon suffered a similar fate, barely advancing 100 yards. Many were killed including Major Barrington-Kennett and several other officers.

The youngest brother, Aubrey was the first to die. He was a 2nd Lieut. In the Oxford and Buckinghamshire Light Infantry. On September 19th, he and his men were sheltering in caves when they were ordered to the trenches. Under heavy artillery fire, thirty five men and two officers were killed. Lieut. Barrington-Kennett was badly injured and died later of his wounds.

The family must have been devastated at the loss of three of their four sons.

The death of Captain Burdon

Shortly after the death of aviator Barrington-Kennett, Captain Rowland Burdon was injured. He was invalided home in June 1916. It was probably then he told the tale of the balloon and the note to discover the fate of his fellow aviator.

He did not return to France. After he recovered, he was sent to Bramham airfield at Tadcaster as an instructor.

Captain Burdon's Aunt Elizabeth writes about what happened to her nephew on January 10th 1917;[7] "He had been flying one of the big new machines, and he had been up for half an hour, and came down into the aerodrome, just touched land, and then opened up his engine and went up again, and went straight for a wood, which he meant to 'jump', as he had done dozens of times before; but something was wrong, pace I expect, and one wing caught a tree and they could not recover, and the machine crashed to the ground in a nose-dive, and both Rowland and the other lad (Turner) were killed instantly. The machine caught fire, but they were both dead, and that did not matter, but for the fact that they were burnt badly. All the Flying people have been most kind about it. He was a very good pilot, and both he and the other boy will be missed sadly, and people were very fond of him."

Elizabeth's account is moving. It was an accident in a "big new machine". Something went wrong and despite being a good pilot, he and Taylor were killed. The family appear to have derived some comfort from thinking they were both killed instantly. Elizabeth had put this word in italics to stress it did not matter when the aeroplane caught fire and they were dead already and not trapped in a burning plane unable to escape.

On Saturday the 13th January, Captain Burdon's badly burned body was taken back to Castle Eden by ambulance with the funeral taking place on Monday the 15th.[8] "Thus ended, shortly before his 24th year, the young and promising life of the seventh of his name, to the unutterable sorrow of his parents and friends."

On a day when the ground was covered with deep snow, "a large and representative gathering of mourners from various parts of the county of Durham," attended Captain Burdon's funeral. In a snowstorm, a procession headed by the buglers of Yorks Regiment followed by the bearers, members of the Royal Flying Corps holding the coffin, covered with a Union Jack as they carried it "aloft from the Castle along the winding carriageway to the church."

Walking alongside the coffin were six 'old servants' of the estate who would have known Rowland Burdon since he was a small child.

Crowds of people gathered outside the church door to pay their respects as the cortege passed through the doors of the church to the organ playing and the congregation singing "Lead Kindly Light." After the service and singing of hymns, the choir "gave a solemn rendering of Nunc Dimittis." The organist played Chopin's Marche Funebre. The "procession reformed and wended its way to the graveside, which is near to the grave of the late Rev John Burdon (grandfather).… At the conclusion of the service at the grave the buglers sounded the Last Post."

The family were the chief mourners of course and they must have been distraught. There was a large military presence, local notables, magistrates, tenants, conservative representatives and many others. Some from the Castle household and estate workers were present, including Mr. James Henderson, head bailiff who also would have known Rowland since his birth. There were many wreaths including some from those who attended but also from "the tenants of Castle Eden Estate, from the workpeople on Castle Eden Estate, the members of the Mother's Union, from the schools, the directors, officers and employees of the Brewery."

Later that year, on Sunday 23rd September, in St James' Church, a memorial window, commissioned by Rowland Burdon and his wife Mary Arundell, was dedicated by the Bishop of Jarrow. In July, earlier that year, John George and Blanche Burdon had erected a window in memory of their son, John who was killed in Mesopotamia on March 6th 1916. A third memorial window in the church is dedicated to Lieut. John Hutchinson Tristram, the grandson of Canon Tristram. Lieut. Hutchinson died, aged 22 years, at the battle of Neuve Chapelle on March 12th 1915.

A War Memorial was erected on a plot of land outside the entrance to Parklands. Subscriptions of £600 were raised including £100 from Rowland Burdon and £25 from his wife. Thirty men's names, including Captain Burdon, from this small parish serves as a memorial for their deaths in World War I.

In May 1917 it was announced that;[9] "Colonel Burdon, as is well known, was the prime mover in raising and equipping the "Pals" Battalion of the Durham Light Infantry in 1914, a body of men which has greatly distinguished itself during the war. In 1916 he devoted his energies to the initiation of the new Volunteer movement in the County of Durham, a work he pursued with the same personal zeal and generosity, and with singular success. It is with much regret that he finds himself unable to continue his patriotic work."

The loss of his only son may have led to this decision. He may have felt he no longer had the 'zeal' to recruit other young men to go to war. So many had died. He still continued raising money for the 1st Battalion DLI. A letter from him in late October 191712; "The coming Christmas will be the third which the battalion I am interested in has spent on service abroad, and the committee propose to acknowledge the fact by making certain that the men have a good Christmas dinner, and one which shall be worthy of the occasion so far as the circumstances permit. It is no exaggeration to say that a good Christmas dinner is an event which has a valuable and lasting effect on the morale of the men, and the committee feel that any effort which they and other friends of the battalion in the country can make to ensure this is the best proof of our respect and admiration for those brave men who have left all to fight for our protection and some attempt to alleviate the discomfort under which they do their duty. The amount required will be £200 and any subscriptions – however small – will be gratefully accepted."

When Rowland Burdon wrote this letter he would know his son would never "have a good Christmas dinner" as he had died while doing his 'duty'.

The end of the war and the aftermath

Not only men died. Horses, many requisitioned for use in the war, had been slaughtered in huge numbers. After the war, not only men returned home, but some horses too were restored to their original owners. Elizabeth Burdon includes a story of "Susette's War Career 1914–1918" written by Venetia D. Hildyard in her book.

"Susette was bred from a 14.2 hh. Roan pony called "Susan" hunted 10 years by Venetia D. Hildyard with Bedale, Husworth and Zetland Hounds. When Susan's hunting days were ended she was mated with 'Simon Hampton', a polo pony, sire, belonging to Mr. Herbert Straker and the result was 'Susette', a roan filly born 1905. She was hunted by V.D. Hildyard and also C.F. Hildyard until the year 1914. 'Susette' was a strong 14.2 hh. Pony of the polo pony type – very active and clever. She was purchased by the Army buyers in August 1914, and went to Northallerton to the 4th Battalion Yorkshire Regiment, with whose transport she went through the war; first of all as a pack pony and later as an officer's mount. She went to France in April, 1915. She went through all the second Battle of Ypres in April and May, 1915, when conditions were especially difficult for transport animals, as the town and canal bridge, through which all transport had to pass, was always under shell fire. When ridden by Mr. Hutchinson (of Catterick's Manor House Farm), she was hit in the near fore by a bullet, near the Ration Dump at Sanctuary Wood. The extent of the wound could not be seen, as it was dark and it was dangerous to strike a light. Mr. Hutchinson took her to a Field Dressing Station in a house in Ypres, and the wound was dressed by a doctor. The night was very dark and wet, and she had to limp seven miles, led by Mr. Hutchinson, to the 4th Yorkshire Transport lines. She mended in a few weeks.

On two other occasions she was scratched by shrapnel, but nothing serious. She was with the Battalion through the French warfare of 1915 round Armentieres and at Ypres again in January and March 1916. She took part in the prolonged Battle of the Somme in July and October 1916, and was with the Battalion when they took over part of the line from the French troops in February 1917, in the Peronne –Amiens road district on the Somme. She was in the third Battle of Ypres, 1917-19187, and in the first, second and third German attack on the Amiens, Armentier and Aisne Front, after which she had no further active service. When the 4th Yorkshire Battalion was absorbed into other Battalions, she was sent to the Welsh Fusiliers, from which she was sent to England, went up to Aldridges for sale, and was bought back by V.D. Hildyard, who was informed of the sale by wire, and who travelled down by train with her from King's Cross, and rode her up from the station at Northallerton to Hutton Bonville, in April 1919. She was fit and well, but the wound in the near fore prevented her hunting again…..' Susette is enjoying a run out as a pensioner."

That account is an amazing 'war horse' story. She would be pleased to be back to her former owner who appeared to care a great deal about her.

The returning men would also be pleased to return home, but they too, like Susette would have gone through terrible times, suffered and experienced dreadful things. They returned to Britain, a country now suffering under food shortages as it had done throughout the war.

Food was in short supply. In 1917 even the King called for a national reduction in bread consumption. It was reported in April 1917[11] that; "Lord Beresford suggested that the Food Controller, having taken over the mills, should also take over the bakeries, and there should be a further reduction in the import of unnecessary articles. The people should be gravely warned, and he thought the situation would be better realised if the display of foodstuffs in the shop window was put an end to.

The Archbishop of York said the want of knowledge and imagination rather than the want of patriotism was largely responsible for the unnecessary consumption of food."

Even the King called for a reduction in the national consumption of food.

The situation became so bad that food shortages led to voluntary rationing. Consumption of bread was greatly reduced. In 1917, a severe problem was caused by "the entire absence of potatoes and the long and severe winter. These two factors had an extra-ordinary effect on bread consumption." (As above)

Many agricultural workers had joined the armed services leaving a shortage of workers on the land. Transporting supplies to Britain became a great problem due to lack of shipping. Not only had Germany's submarine campaign sunk many ships but ships were needed to transport military requirements. There was also a world- wide shortage of food. Shipping was being depleted every day resulting in less imports of food. It was considered the only way forward was the diminution of consumption. Lord Beresford considered that if everyone exercised "sufficient self-denial in bread consumption" then the country "should surmount the perils that lay ahead." If not, the country would "not get through until next harvest without severe privations and all that involved. Lord Beresford suggested "that people who could afford a wide variety of food should eliminate bread entirely from lunch and dinner, and so preserve bread for people who must depend on it. To ask the agricultural labourer to subsist on 43lbs of bread a week would be a mockery but to be safe the average must be brought down to 4lb per head, and every individual should try to reduce his consumption below that amount."

Four pounds of bread a week may appear an adequate amount to consume, but at this time much more bread was eaten, especially by manual workers. There were no potatoes to replace bread. There was also a shortage of fats like butter and margarine. Meat was in short supply and very expensive. During the four years of war food had doubled in price. Soup kitchens were set up in London and National Kitchens set up over all the country to provide cheap meals.

The Involvement of Women

The ideas taken from the successful Canada Women's Institutes in Canada were first used in 1915 in Wales. At the end of May 1916, a conference took place in Durham Town Hall to discuss the production of agricultural produce. The Permanent Secretary of Agriculture addressed a meeting with representatives from the County Durham War Agricultural Committee, made up of men and the Women's War Agricultural Committee. Colonel and Mrs Burdon were amongst those present. The Chairman, a man, "alluded to the splendid work that was being done in the county of Durham by the various local organisations, and especially the women's organisation, which had Lady Anne Lambton as president, Lady Boyne as chairman and Mrs. H.G. Stobart as vice-chairman."

The main topic of the conference was around the difficulty of obtaining agricultural labourers. Even with increasing use of machinery, farming was still highly labour intensive at this time.

In Britain over 300,000 men had left agricultural work to enlist in the services, leaving, including the farmers, under a million men to cultivate the land.

The possibility of employing school children had been considered but the Permanent Secretary considered this a 'short sighted policy', "Some counties had 'liberated children' of 11 years of age from school" to work in agriculture but the Secretary was pleased Durham County had not followed this practice.

The Secretary said that, "whether they liked it or not, he must say that the main source of auxiliary labour to help the farmers through was going to be the women, though he did not think that anyone would pretend that women could take the place of the skilled agricultural worker.... The indispensable skilled men must be left" Women should not be employed as an" excuse for taking away more men. (Applause) Women should be paid wages corresponding to the work they did, and surely the farmers would pay them when they were trained, the same wages as the men who did the same work."

In February 1916, the Durham County Women's War Committee had been set up, split up into 15 unions with a representative from each. Mrs. Burdon was the representative for Easington. Women were needed to work on the land. Two hundred and seven women had been recruited to register the names of all women willing to work on the land and 'keep in touch with the farmers in their districts with a view to supplying them with women workers when they require them." As the representative from the Easington District, Mrs Burdon would have been highly involved in this process. By early June 1916 information on their progress was published; [12]

"The total number of women at present on the register 4,893

Number with experience 2,438

Wholetime workers 2,878

Number willing to leave home 360

Number on register who are actually working on farm 1,044"

Easington had succeed in registering 831 women in their union by far the highest. Hartlepool had only 79 and Weardale a very low 27. Mrs Burdon and her fellow registrars had worked hard.

At a meeting of Durham Women's War Association in late November 1917, Lady Boyne reviewed the work over that year. There were now "157 National Volunteers" employed in "the county on the land in forage and timber work." The Land Army was praised. Miss Wright the travelling inspector to the Board of Agriculture "dealt with the new schemes shortly to be introduced by the Food Production Department." Mrs Watts from Canada "spoke on Women's Institutes and the necessity for the reconstruction of country life." This movement was the beginning of the Women's Institute. Mrs Burdon was there from the very beginning.

During the war 23, 000 women were recruited to work full time on the land. There was an excellent wheat harvest in 1917. Food production increased. Despite the work of agricultural workers, including the women, shortages continued. Imported supplies were lost by the sinking of shipping by German submarines. By the end of 1916, an average of 300, 000 tons of shipping was being destroyed each month. In February 1817, 230 ships bringing food and supplies to Britain were sunk.

Wealthier people could still afford food but many amongst the poor suffered from malnutrition. In an attempt to make the situation fairer, food rationing was introduced in 1918, sugar being the first item rationed in January 1918. By the end of April, meat, butter, cheese and margarine had been rationed. Butter remained rationed until 1920. Ration cards were introduced and everyone had to register with their local butcher. Men returning from war came back to a land of rationing but although there was scarcity, the regulations ensured a sufficient food supply.

Rowland Burdon's daughter's wedding

It is to be hoped there was a sufficient food supply for Rowland and Mary Arundell Burdon to cater for the reception when their daughter Joan married Captain Mark Sykes M. C. at Brampton Parish Church, London on 16th November 1918. Nigel Charles Mark Sykes was born in 1894 at Kirk Ella, near Hull. His father Charles Percy Sykes died in 1899 when Mark was about five. In 1901, he was living with his widowed mother and siblings in Hastings. During World War I, Mark Sykes served in the East Riding of Yorkshire (Queen's Own) Yeomanry 4th Hussars Machine Gun Corps. He was awarded the Military Cross.

Joan Burdon's dress was 'of cloth of gold, embroidered with pearls. She wore a wreath of gold leaves and a tulle veil, and carried a bouquet of pale yellow malmaisons, a type of carnation. These were popular winter flowers, grown in country house glasshouses. This attire sounds stunning but gold appears somewhat different from the usual white. Joan's sister Lettice was dressed in white chiffon velvet. It was November and would probably have been cold. Her brother-in-law had given her a present of diamond and jade earrings as a bridesmaid's gift. She too carried yellow carnations. Mr .Rolland of the East Riding Yeomanry was best man. Rev G. K. M. Evans who was at this time the rector at Castle Eden officiated in the ceremony.

There were many titled personages and Hons at this society wedding as well a military presence of high-ranking officers and their wives. After the reception, hopefully with enough delicacies to tempt the illustrious guests, the couple went to Taunton for their honey moon. Col and Mrs Burdon would be happy for their daughter on her wedding day but this would have been tinged with sadness at such a strong military presence with many probably in uniform, as it would have been a reminder of their son Rowland who could not celebrate his sister's wedding.

CHAPTER THIRTEEN
Towards the end

The family wedding took place shortly after Armistice Day. By this time a General Election had been called and Parliament was dissolved on 25th November. The General Election took place on 14th December. This was the first election where women over 30 and all men over 21 were able to vote. Col Burdon stood as coalition unionist candidate for the newly formed seat of Sedgefield.

Colonel Burdon in Parliament

Col Burdon had unsuccessfully contested the South East Durham seat in December 1910 against the Liberal candidate Evan Hayward. As a popular candidate he managed to halve Hayward's majority to 1,182 votes but this was not enough to win the seat.

In 1918 Col Burdon stood in a three way contest against John Herriots, the Labour Party and Sir Charles Starmer, Liberal.

John Herriots, nominated by the Durham Miner's Association, was a checkweighman at Windlestone Colliery. Although considered a[1] 'capable labour man, with some experience in local administration' he did not have the 'support of all the miners in the division.' Sir Charles Starmer urged 'priority of claim from the fact that the old division was represented by a Liberal.' It was considered that "a fair proportion support Colonel Burdon, whose statesmanlike appeal to all sections of the electorate to sink party differences in national aims is receiving a gratifying response."

Colonel Burdon's position can be ascertained in a speech at a crowded meeting in Ferryhill in November 1918 when he reportedly said; "It was very important that they should all think seriously upon matters of government from their own independent opinions, and act accordingly, irrespective of party and with no other object than that of desire to do the best for the people and the Empire. Thank God, our 'Contemptible little Army', which had grown to the finest in the world, had saved Britain, Europe and the world from the most terrible danger ever experienced.

Germany must pay for iniquities and robberies. Vengeance was not ours, but we must see justice done. Our soldiers and sailors and their dependents, some of whom had bled and died for us, must be generously and properly provided for. We must not allow any Parliament to forget its duties to the people. (Hear, hear) With regard to the land; Parliament must see that it was cultivated to the best advantage in food production."

Speeches like these gained Colonel Burdon support. He appealed to patriotism and provision for the dependents of those killed or injured in the war. More than 41,000 men had their limbs amputated during the war. Another 272,000 suffered injuries to arms and legs not needing amputation. There were 60,500 wounded in their head or eyes with another 89,000 sustaining serious bodily damage. Col Burdon's family had suffered loss in the war, including the death of his son. Many would know of the good work Mrs Burdon did with others to increase food production in agriculture.

Col Burdon was successful this time, beating the Labour Party John Herriots by 826 votes. There was a landslide victory for the coalition government. Although the Conservatives had the gained the largest number of seats, making them the largest party, Lloyd George remained Prime Minister.

During his time in Parliament, Col Burdon appeared to concentrate on agricultural matters. Speaking at an agricultural show in Coatham Mundeville in August 1919, he appears to be dissatisfied with progress made to secure an agricultural policy. He is reported to have said that;[2] "As a supporter of the Government, he was not satisfied with their agricultural policy. In fact, they had not got one. During the war, farmers, at the request of the Government, for the sake of the country, did a great many things they did not like to do, and they made sacrifices in many ways. It had been shown that the safety of the country depended upon agriculture, and he thought it was a very grave mistake that greater efforts had not been made by the Government to formulate and establish a district agricultural policy. The Members of Parliament representing agricultural constituencies had done what they could, but it was evident that the whole of the agricultural community must be united in their effort, if they were to obtain what they wanted – a real agricultural policy on the part of the Government. Unless something definite was done before the next session, the agricultural members of the House of Commons, backed up by their constituents, would have to take steps to impress upon the Government the absolute necessity of agriculturalists – farmers and landlords, and their employees also – to lay before them a policy on which they could frame their farming to national needs and to meet any emergency."

In 1921 the Burdon's London residence is Hans Place. They probably spent more time in London during his time as a Member of Parliament. Col Burdon was very ill with pleurisy in November 1920, so ill it was reported in the press. In February 1921, the Colonel was advised by doctors to leave England for a few weeks. In December 1921 Col Burdon's agent announced he will not be seeking re-election due to his health, in particular problems with his eyes.

In a speech he delivered in September 1922, he referred to his "pending retirement from the representation of the constituency, and said it was entirely due to physical causes. He was glad if he had been of service to them either collectively or individually. He could honestly recommend Mr. Waddington to the electors as his successor, He urged them to maintain their Unionist principles and warned them against the Labour party extremists. Who, he asked, was responsible for all the ambassadors of Communism who were going about the colliery districts. Nobody had got any money to pay them except the Bolsheviks and the Germans."

Col Burdon is warning of the rise of the Labour Party, linking them with the threat of Communism. He urges his supporters to "maintain their Unionist principles" and recommends Mr.

Waddington as a candidate. Mr Waddington lost the election to the Labour candidate, John Herriots. Col Burdon did not seek re-election due to his health. However, he had lost an election once in 1910. He saw the rise and influence of the Labour Party in his and other neighbouring constituencies. He may have contemplated his defeat if he stood for re-election, so this may influenced his decision to stand down.

The Colonel and his wife remained staunch unionist supporters. In August 1923, returned to Castle Eden, a meeting and tea was held by the Seaham Division Unionist Association in the grounds at Castle Eden. It was a sunny day and many from the division had come along to have a long ramble through the dene, view the lovely gardens and greenhouses before having a picnic on the grass in the grounds. Col and Mrs Burdon probably enjoyed the afternoon with people they both knew well.

After this pleasant afternoon, a meeting was held with address given by Major Ronald Ross M.C., a barrister from London. Ronald Deane Ross was the only son of the last Lord Chancellor of Dunmoyle, County Tyrone. During the war he served in the North Irish Horse. In autumn 1914, he was in the retreat from Mons and fought throughout the war, receiving both a Military Cross and the Croix de Guerre.

Major Ross stood against Sidney Webb for the new constituency of Seaham both in 1922 and 1923. Sidney Webb won on both occasion with a large majority, although Major Ross did manage to increase his vote in 1923. At the meeting after the garden party,[4] Rowland Burdon gave Major Ross some encouraging words. He said that he, like Ross knew what it felt like to lose an election; "Nobody in the room, he ventured to say, with the exception of Major Ross and himself, knew how unpleasant a thing it was to contest an unsuccessful election. Major Ross had started the campaign with the knowledge that the chances of success were 100 to 1 against him, and throughout the whole election he had been a very plucky fighter. (Applause) Not only had he held his own, but he had increased to 11,000 the people who would not bow the knee to Baal. Major Ross, he added, had endeared himself to all with whom he had come in contact, and they were exceedingly sorry they were going to lose a man who had succeeded in ingratiating himself with all classes of community."

As President of the Association, Lord Londonderry also addressed the meeting at Castle Eden. He said he "could claim to have been instrumental in persuading Major Ross and his charming wife to come amongst them and to fight what was perhaps, the hardest electoral battle in the whole country.

He felt that they did indeed owe Major Ross and Mrs Ross a deep debt of gratitude. Nothing could really repay the candidate. No one could have fought a more splendid fight than he did. (Applause)

In Mr. Webb he had a redoubtable opponent. Apart from his ability altogether, he was a fetish with the Labour Party and the ignorant people who thought that in the doc trines he expounded, and which he made an ambiguous and obscure as possible, there was something which they ought to follow. The obscurity and ambiguity he had used in persuading ignorant electors were wonderful.' As Col. Burdon had said, the winning of mining constituencies was simply a matter of education, and if they adopted the means of propaganda used by the Socialist Party, they would see quite a different complexion on the mining constituencies throughout the United Kingdom…Major Ross had fought two splendid fights, and he only hoped that, with the valuable experience he had gained here and with the claims he certainly had on the Union Party, they would see him in a short time in the House of Commons. (Cheers)"

Ronald Dean Ross had not win this time, but these words of praise from Lord Londonderry and Col Burdon encouraged him to fight again. He was elected unopposed to Parliament in 1929 in a by election for the Londonderry constituency, a seat once held by his father. Lord Londonderry would have been pleased.

Activities for local children

The Unionists appear to have enjoyed their garden party and meeting at Castle Eden. Others visited too. In August 1921 of the children of the Hartlepool Members of the Buffaloes came and nearly three hundred adults who accompanied them. The children must have been very excited as they marched behind the Hartlepool Old Boys' Band from the Barracks at Baltic Street, along Durham Street, Corporation Street and Warren Street to the station at Hartlepool. Once there thy boarded a special train for Castle Eden. They left the station and proceeded to a field for an afternoon of sports. At four o'clock, each child received a bag of cakes and three pennies. After prizes were presented to some children, the party made their way back to Castle Eden Station and home to Hartlepool. This would have been quite a treat for the children.

Some children may have had other treats at that time. In 1921 and other years, land suitable for camping situated between Dene Holme and Blackhall Rocks was let out by the Horden Collieries Ltd. for six months. It is possible Scout Troops in the area used this site for camping at some time. There were troops in surrounding villages, including the collieries. Lettice Burdon went along with her father in February 1923 to open the annual sale of work for the 1st Troop of Scouts in Wingate. A large number of people present helped raise £38. Some of these funds may have been used for camping trips for the boys.

The new coast road

With a new road access to these camps sites would be easier. In March 1921 Durham County Council had decided to construct a new road from Easington to West Hartlepool at a cost estimated at £271,000. The idea for the road was first mooted in 1909 and it had taken until 1921 before it reached the stage of practicality.

At this time there was no straight road from Easington Colliery to Horden or from Horden to Blackhall making journeys between the collieries circuitous and much longer journey. There was a beach road between Horden and Blackhall but this was only suitable for very light traffic. This journey was via Old Shotton, Castle Eden and Hesleden, a journey of about six miles. From Blackhall to West Hartlepool, instead of a straight line between the two along the coast, the journey inland went through Castle Eden and Sheraton doubling the distance travelled.

The bulk of the labour was concentrated in the excavation and filling up at Crimdon Dene and Castle Eden Dene. In December 1921, the work had the use of one mechanical digger but there were hopes for more mechanical appliances when funds would allow. Work had begun on the new coast road on 23rd April 1921. The road was completed in 1925. It was opened by Mr. Hugh Goshing, Minister of transport. It had been a great work of engineering. The road was nine miles long with a width of 60 feet and carriage way of 24 feet. There were stream running through the denes. Huge concrete culverts, up to 15 feet wide and 12 feet high had to be built to carry the water. The ravines in the denes had to be filled by embankments to the level of the cuttings. The use of mechanical diggers was vital. Even navvies may not have been able to do the work without machinery.

This road would benefit not only people travelling between the colliery villages and Hartlepool, it would also benefit Castle Eden as it would reduce through traffic in the village. Some motorists drove fast, for those days, through the village, and well above the speed limit. This was still a rural area with sheep being led down the roads. A driver was fined three pounds for speeding at 50mph, running into a flock of sheep, injuring three and killing one animal. A motor cyclist, also going too fast through Castle Eden who knocked a cyclist off his bicycle was fined 10s. Luckily the cyclist, although shocked was only slightly injured. The new road would probably reduce such incidents.

Colonel Burdon the Magistrate

These drivers were fined. Colonel Burdon was no longer a Member of Parliament, but he was still a magistrate. The crimes that came before and their punishments seem minor compared with those which came before his grandfather and uncle. Transportation had long disappeared. In 1923, a farmer was fined 10s because his milk was deficient in fat. Men trespassing on the railway, very dangerous at any time, were fined 40s. Bookmakers were fined £5 for street betting. Warrants were issued for those who had not paid their rates. Men were charged with stealing timber from Col Burdon's estate but as he did not wish to press charges, the case was held over. However, men charged with the theft of coal from the colliery were fined 10s. Two pit lads were fined £10 each for having cigarettes in their possession and smoking in the mine. This may seem a stiffer fine but smoking down a mine was extremely hazardous and could lead to an explosion and loss of life.

There was a confectioner fined for selling mineral water without a licence. Possibly more mineral water was being drunk as there did not appear to be so many incidents of drunkenness causing disorderly behaviour. Colonel Burdon appeared to agree drunkenness was on the decline when he said;[5]

"As far as this district was concerned, if the improvement was not great it was gradual. As he had the privilege of sitting on the Bench year after year it had been a great pleasure to him to hear the evidence that in the County of Durham – and this part of the county in particular – sobriety was more and more prevalent."

Hartlepool Hospital

As well as seeing some changes in behaviour through all his service on the Bench, in 1923, Col Burdon also had plans for improvements in the buildings at Hartlepool Hospital, where he had also served as President for over thirty years; his Uncle Rowland being the first President then followed by the Colonel's father Rev John Burdon. Because Col Burdon considered the hospital was easily reached by car, he envisaged the catchment area of the hospital could be widened from the Hartlepools down to Stockton as the hospitals at Stockton and Middlesbrough had also reached their capacity. He advised the Governors to work together to ascertain whether they could enlarge the accommodation at Hartlepool to provide for increased requirements.

Dr Morrison seconded the proposal made by Col Burdon emphasising that if they built more available beds the hospital would probably be recognised as a State training centre for nurses.

Great efforts were made to raise £10,000 to fund the new wing. On 10th August 1926, H.R.H. Princess Mary Viscountess Lascelles opened the Morrison Memorial Wing. The wing of 37 beds was dedicated to the now late Dr A.E. Morrison who had served the hospital for so many years.

Col Burdon and Capt. Sir William Gray met Princess Mary at Hartlepool station on behalf of the Governors of the Hospital. Despite the heavy morning rain, crowds thronged the route they took to the hospital. The opening ceremony took place at 12.30 with a small girl on the children's ward presenting the Princess with a bouquet of flowers.

The party proceeded to the Borough Hall for lunch. The weather greatly improved in the afternoon with yet more crowds anxious to greet the Princess as they visited St. Hilda's Church before placing a wreath on the War Memorial and visiting the spot where the first soldier was killed on British soil.

The Princess appeared to show great interest when she visited the Central Marine Works and the engine works of Richardson and Westgarth and Co. From there, she went to Seaton Carew to open a new pier, 600 yards long with large shelters along its width. After a busy day, the Princess returned to the station to take the train to Harrogate. From there she would journey to Harewood House.

The Girl Guides

There was a distant family connection between Col Burdon and Viscount Henry Lascelles, the husband of Princess Mary. Henry Lascelles would become 6th Lord Harewood when his father died in 1929. The first Lord Harewood was married to Anne Chaloner sister of Mary, who married General Henry Hale, an ancestor of Col Burdon's mother.

Princess Mary had an interest in hospitals. In the War she had visited many hospitals and welfare organisations with her mother Queen Mary. In 1918, she did a nursing course at Great Ormond Street Hospital and worked for two days a week on the Alexandra Ward. In 1926, the Princess became Commander in Chief of the British Red Cross. This interest may have led her to come to Hartlepool to open the new wing of the hospital.

Princess Mary was made Honorary President of the Girl Guides in 1920. The Girl Guide movement had expanded in the district with troops in places like Horden, Blackhall and Shotton as well as Castle Eden. Miss Sadie E Hall was in charge of the Castle Eden Guide Company, which covered the district.

Sadie Hall lived in Hardwick Hall, Castle Eden. Her father Joseph Percival Hall was aget for Horden Collieries Ltd, later becoming managing director. Many of the Girl Guide fund raising activities took place in Horden like the dance Miss Hall organised in December 1929 which took place in the Co-operative Hall Horden. Over two hundred people attended and Miss Hall's brother who later became under-manager at Horden, acted as compere.

In December 1929, Miss Hall was present at the 20th sale of work organised by the members of St. Mary's Church Horden, when she supported Lady Eden, of Windlestone Hall who opened the event. Sadie E. Hall appeared to be much involved in the mining community.

Hartlepool Division held a Rally in May 1929 in the Borough Hall Hartlepool. The event had been organised for four reasons; Empire Day was approaching and this could be used as a celebration; to use the event to demonstrate the work of the guides to parents and friends, to urge guide companies to raise money for the appeal to raise £74,000 to build a new headquarters in London and to present the District Shield.

According to Miss Dillon ARRC, the County Commissioner there had been a huge increase in numbers of girl guides in the area. The guides present were very neat and orderly as they were inspected prior to the salute. Displays followed of ambulance work, musical drill, signalling, national dances in costume including a Scottish reel accompanied by a bagpipe, and backward drill which the audience found amusing. The guides were reminded if they did small things and did them well, this would equip them to "do the bigger things for the good of their country and their fellow men" when they grew older. They were also encouraged to look after their health, particularly their teeth, "doing all in their power to make themselves strong and healthy citizens."

The girls went camping too. The following is advice given by a Girl Guide Captain in May 1929;[6]

"Every year the camping holiday appeals to more fresh-air devotees. Quite apart from the question of health, this kind of holiday has the advantage of being inexpensive, for a party of girls can club together and hire a tent and other apparatus for quite a reasonable sum. Even if there should be any difficulty in hiring, it must be remembered that purchasing may prove a good investment, since the gear may afterwards be hired out to other parties and a nice little interest made on the original outlay.

The equipment obtained, the question of a site arises. If the seaside is preferred, the nearest local council to the favoured spot will supply particulars of camping sites, and also of fresh water supplies etc. If the country is chosen it is best to find a site near a stream so that bathing is assured. It should be remembered however, that tents should not be pitched near a river Bank nor on a slope where the wash of a rainstorm can flood them. They should be on well-drained level, ground.

Not every farmer is partial to campers on his land, but most of them are very reasonable if a promise is made that no damage shall be done. Remember that breaking branches off trees may be accounted damage unless permission has been obtained. The owner of the land will usually mention where fuel for the camp fire may be obtained.

A spade should be included in the camping outfit so that a trench of a spade's depth can be dug round the tent; as run-way should be cut in the lowest portion of this trench. This, of course, is to drain off rain water. Without it campers are likely to have some uncomfortable nights if the weather proves inclement.

Never try to economise by doing without camp beds. Ground sheets for sleeping on are worse than useless. Lie on a good thick blanket, for both damp and cold strike upwards rather than down.

Above all things do not trust to camp cookery. Take ample supplies of good tinned food. There are times when the primus will not burn and the camp fire smokes without producing flame.

Take supplies of simple remedies such as carbonate of soda or your indigestion tablet, oil of citronella to keep away the midges, carron oil for burns or scalds, boracic crystals to make a solution for bathing eyes or minor injuries, plenty of antiseptic plaster and two or three bandages."

Other activities for young people

This may be advice for a camping holiday for Girl Guides and presumably also Boy Scouts. It does not sound altogether pleasant with ideas on how to brave stormy weather and the cold, using tinned food to avert indigestion, lighting camp fires and a primus stove that does not work, the possibility of irate farmers who object to camping or any damage done to the site, midges, burns, scalds, cuts and bruises.

However the possibility of youngsters camping on a holiday demonstrates how times have changed for young people. Boys would have been working underground in collieries from a very young age. There was now much more for young people to do other that work.

There were football, cricket and tennis clubs in Castle Eden and the surrounding area, including Castle Eden. There were also junior football and cricket teams for the boys. Even children in the Children's Home at Easington had an easier and happier time. At Christmas, 1926, Mr Joseph Percival Hall, colliery agent, donated a Christmas tree. This tree was laden with presents for the children. Councillor George Walker, of Easington acted as Santa Claus. After the presents were distributed the children had tea and a party. Children were having more fun and being treated as children.

Another Burdon Wedding

Colonel Burdon had cause to celebrate in June 1925 when his youngest daughter Lettice married Captain Giffard Loftus Tyringham of the Scots Guards in the Guards Chapel at Wellington Barracks. The Bishop of London and the chaplain of the Guards' Chapel officiated.

It was a grand affair. The bride wore a dress of gold and silver lace, a dress probably similar to that worn by her sister Joan at her wedding. Her tulle veil had a coronet of orange blossom and small gold lilies. She had a train of gold tissue shot with silver and her bouquet consisted of Madonna lilies. Her mother had given her a pearl necklace with diamond clasps but the groom's present was long diamond earrings with pearl drops and the regimental badge of the Scot's Guards set in diamonds.

Her elder sister's two young children, Mary and Nora, were two of the five bridesmaids. They all wore similar gold and silver dresses as the bride but each carried small bouquets of red roses and blue delphiniums. The two pages wore gold tunics and silver breeches.

The chapel was decorated with red roses and blue delphiniums. The Scots Guard band provided the music with four pipers from the bridegroom's regiment playing out the couple as they and the guests left the chapel. The guests included many titled personages and high-ranking military personal.

Now all three daughters were married but sad times were coming.

Funerals

Col Burdon's nephew Noel Edward Burdon was a 2nd Lieut. in the Durham Light Infantry during the war. He had fought in France where had been injured. His brother John had been killed. Their father and mother would be devastated when their remaining Noel died suddenly as a result of an illness contracted in the war. The service was conducted by The Archdeacon of Northumber, aged just 34 at his home in Kensington on 15th March 1928. Noel was buried on 19th March in St James' Church, Castle Eden. Col Burdon and Anne Malet could not attend as they were abroad at the time, and would probably not have been able to return in time. Noel's widow was there, his mother and father and Captain Fenwicke-Clennell of Wigton who was married to Noel's sister. Brigadier General Walter D Sclater-Booth had travelled from Newham, Hook in Hants. His wife Frances, Noel's cousin had not accompanied him.

Other relatives attended the funeral, along with Lt Col Rogers from Newcastle; and many from Castle Eden including Mr W.J. Nimmo, Supt Bennett D.C.C., the estate bailiff Mr. R. Craman. Noel's coffin was carried by eight employees of Castle Eden estate. Many wreaths were sent including those from family members.

The death of both of his sons may have affected John George Burdon enormously, because he too died suddenly, aged 70 on 15th January 1930 at his home at Spital Hill Mitford, Northumberland. John George was also interred in Castle Eden Church. The service was conducted by the Archdeacon of Northumberland and Rev Nelson, the Rector of Castle Eden. On this occasion Col and Mrs Burdon attended.

Colonel Burdon's wife dies

Col Rowland Burdon had lost his only son, his brother John George and his two nephews John and Noel. Tragedy struck again in February 1930 when his wife Mary Arundell died aged 62.

On Monday 25th February, her coffin was conveyed to St James' Church by estate workmen accompanied by members of the family and household for a private ceremony. After the family had paid their respects, the doors of the Church were open for mourners. They assembled in the church to the music of Chopin's funeral march and music from the Messiah. A very simple and moving funeral service was conducted by Rev. Nelson, the Rector and Rev. Little, Rector of Monk Hesleden.

Many notables were present, including the wife of the Bishop of Durham. The Master of Sherburn Hospital Canon Boutflower attended with his wife who was the President of Durham Diocesan Mother's Union. Other Mother's Union representatives came from Hartlepool and Castle Eden, where she was a member. Wreaths were sent by the Mother's Union groups of local churches. Mary Arundell Burdon was probably highly involved in the work of the Mother's Union.

There were representatives from the Hartlepool Hospital Ladies Linen League. At a later meeting of the Hospital her work as President of the League was praised, reminding the meeting that in the previous year Mrs Burdon presented above £700's worth of linen and money with many of the garments coming from the Mother's union at Castle Eden and the Women's Institute had also recently become involved, probably due to her encouragement. Her funeral took place very close to the day of the annual Governor's meeting at the Hospital Col. Burdon was re-elected in his absence with agreement that a letter of sympathy should be forwarded to him.

Mary Arundell Burdon had been a founder member and worker for the Women's Institute during the War. The W.I. had grown and expanded and she was still involved in the organisation at the Branch in Castle Eden. Many W.I. organisations sent wreaths.

As well as being involved in this work during the War Mary Arundell Burdon had also organised a V.A.D Convalescent Home for officers and men at the Drill Hall Parkland. As the V.A.D. received only 3s a day for each man convalescing, those organising the facilities had set up fund raising activities to aid the running of the convalescent home. Many women, like Mary Arundell Burdon were involved in this type of work during the war.

There were representatives from the Bench of Magistrates; representatives from organisations in West Hartlepool like Foster and Armstrong, the Gas and Water Works Company who may have had more of a connection with Col Burdon rather than with his wife but were there to show their respects.

Local people attended especially those from Castle Eden, the Church and Police. There were many wreaths sent including; wreaths from the churchgoers of Horden Church, which had been built by money from the Burdons,, Castle Eden Women's Union, Castle Eden Young Men's Club, the tenant farmers on the estate, Castle Eden Girl Guides, Hesleden Nursing Association and Castle Eden Parish Council. Servants sent floral tributes, including one from the butler and a wreath with the words' from an old servant' written on the card.

Many people appeared to have been touched by the loss of Mary Arundell Burdon. Her family would be greatly affected, especially Col Burdon. His daughters were married and not living nearby. He was no longer a young man but age did not stop his involvement and activities.

In 1932, Col Burdon expressed his sympathy at the retirement of Superintendent Joseph Atkinson observing that the Superintendent had always been not only very kind to him but had also considered the public as well as the Bench. Col Burdon expressed his good wishes on behalf of the bench, hoping that he hoped the Superintendent would have many years of happiness but that he had something to do in his retirement as some people go downhill when they do nothing. The Colonel would be older than the retiring Superintendent. This was good advice and something which the Colonel himself adhered to. He appeared to have more than something to do.

Colonel Burdon continues as a Magistrate

As a magistrate he was still Chairman of the Bench. Crimes had changed over the years. Drunkenness and disorderly behaviour had dropped considerably. As Vice Chairman of the Durham Licensing Committee Col Burdon would have the statistics to verify these statements.

There were now few instances of poaching. One more serious offence of night poaching occurred in September 1935 on Col Burdon's land. Four men, heard and seen poaching, were chased for about one quarter of a mile by two of the Colonel's gamekeepers. As the men ran away they dropped five bags containing 58 rabbits and a long net.

The four men climbed to the top of a hill, turned round and threatened the two gamekeepers as they rained stones down upon them. Undeterred, despite one of the gamekeepers being cut on the lip by a stone, the gamekeepers caught up with the poachers. A poacher struck one of the gamekeepers on the head with a stick. There was a struggle with one of the poachers being held down on the round. The other three poachers ran away. The gamekeepers recognised three of the men. They were charged with poaching in Castle Eden Dene at five minutes past midnight. Each man was bound over in the sum of £5 and ordered to be of good behaviour for twelve months.

Many who came before Col Burdon and the Bench had previously offended and were warned they would be imprisoned if the offended again. Children were no exception. They were warned with being sent to an industrial school. Boys were whipped when caught stealing. Two boys aged 11 and 12 were whipped when they stole pigeons from the Drill Hall in Horden. Similar punishments were given to boys who stole from shops. One boy who had stolen some brawn, probably for his mother for the family to eat, had stolen before. He was warned he would sent away if he re offended. On this occasion he was put on probation for two years ordered to pay 2s 6d costs.

There were many driving offences at this time, mainly speeding, careless or even dangerous driving. People were injured, even killed. In May 1933, a man and his brother were walking on a road through Ryhope about 11pm when a motor cyclist knocked them both down. One of the brothers was knocked unconscious with a fractured skull and internal injuries. He died in Sunderland Infirmary, leaving a widow and two children. Col Burdon frequently warned of the dangers of reckless driving, emphasising care was need as bad driving could endanger lives, especially the lives of children. Yet children were whipped.

The Hospital work continues

Col Burdon, as President of Hartlepool Hospital attended many meetings and fund raising activities like garden parties and fetes. He did resign in 1936 but remained President of Castle Eden Nursing Association.

In 1937, Col Burdon laid the foundation stone of a new £57,000 extension being built to the hospital. A grant of 75% of the cost had been awarded by the Commission for special areas, leaving the remaining 25% to be raised. The building would have three floors and a basement. The boilers, dispensing on mortuary would be in the basement. The ground floor would house outpatients, orthopaedics and offices. Extra wards would include E.N.T. with accommodation for a second operating theatre.

Mr. J. W Nimmo was now president so he introduced Col Burdon to the guests, matron, nurses and hospital patients listening to the broadcast of the event. He reminded the audience of the long association between the Burdon family and the hospital. Col Burdon had been President of the Hospital for 43 years. In the early days there were 12 beds. This rose to 95 and with the new extension there would be 130.

Before laying the foundation stone, Col Burdon was presented with a silver trowel as a memento. After the ceremony, prayers were said led by the Rector of Hartlepool and a vote of thanks was given to the Colonel. He replied pointing out that since the hospital had first opened in 1812, a great deal had happened in Hartlepool. He reminded the listeners that the hospital was formerly the prior of St. Francis who had come to Hartlepool in about 1300; the monastery finally becoming a hospital about the time of Henry VIII. The mansion house the building became gradually deteriorated until it looked more like a barn. Because there was a garden in the old days, celebrated for its fruit, the Colonel presented two fruit trees to be planted in the garden and suggested every year, on the anniversary of St. Francis, the matron of the hospital should take him some fruit, have tea with him and he would present her with a gold sovereign.

Col Burdon then praised the work of the hospital, reminding the audience how the staff had gone on working during the bombardment of Hartlepool in the war. Thanks were given before he and the guests left for tea.

The Old Comrades

Remembrances of the war were rekindled, especially memories of the Somme, when the Colonel, as President, attended the reunion dinners of the Old Comrades, the 18th Battalion DLI, the 'Pals'.

In November 1931 when the Old Comrades held their annual reunion in Hartlepool where part of the battalion had been billeted in the war. Members from all parts of the country and further afield attended. Two hundred officers and men assembled in the Borough Hall before marching to the Battery slope where the battalion first went into action killing four members of the battalion, the first soldiers to fall on British soil. About 150 members of the British Legion and a detachment of the Artillery Brigade joined with the 'Old Pals' in a short remembrance service, including the words;[7]

"It is now difficult to imagine the waste and desolation of the battlefields. One sometimes wonders now how flesh and blood stood the mental stress and the terrible privation of those days. It was a marvellous spirit of self-sacrifice that carried you through."

After the service, tea was the served in the Borough Hall followed by a social gathering of the Old Comrades.

In September 1932 a special open-air service for the British Legion was held in the Welfare Park Horden. A large number of representatives from various branches gathered for the dedication ceremony of the standards of the Blackhall Branch, Horden Branch and Women's section of the Horden Branch were dedicated. After the dedication the standards were draped on a floral cenotaph which had been erected near the bandstand in the park.

After the service, the legion members marched from the park with Colonel Burdon taking the salute from a base in Thirteenth Street. The march past concluded at Eden Street with band playing the 'March of the Standards.' After the ceremony, tea was provided in the Drill Hall in Horden.

In 1933, the Col inspected the new British Legion standards for Wingate and Station Town. In 1934, 246 members of the 'Pals' old comrades, including Col Burdon met for their 15th annual reunion.

Colonel Burdon attended a DLI Ball, to raise money for regimental charities, at Durham Castle that year. The centre of attraction at the ball appears to have been the food; an oyster bar in the crypt and a supper served in the 15th century kitchen and buttery. He probably enjoyed the food and company but possibly did not dance. Although still president of the Old Comrades, he did not attend their reunion in 1938, due to ill health.

The RNLI

During a thunderstorm in July 1937, along with the Marquess and Marchioness of Londonerry, the Colonel was well enough to attend ceremony when the Marchioness named Seaham's new lifeboat, 'Elizabeth Wills Allen.' This new lifeboat replaced 'Elliot Galer', which had served Seaham for about twenty five years.

As Colonel Burdon had by this time, been president of the Hartlepool Branch of the RNLI for almost fifty years, he presented the new boat to Seaham on their behalf, the boat being built with money from the will of Miss E.W. Allen of Northam, Devon, on behalf of the Royal National Lifeboat Institute. The new boat, able to carry 30 passengers, was considered almost unsinkable.

Col Burdon would be present at Central Hall, Westminster on May 13th 1931, together with the Mayor of Hartlepool together when Coxswain Robert Hood of the Hartlepool lifeboat, 'Elizabeth Newton', was presented a service award by His Royal Highness the Prince of Wales.

The award was for the rescue of nine sailors aboard, the Danish auxiliary schooner 'Doris' in September 1930. That September day, there was a fierce gale and heavy seas as the schooner attempted to steer towards Hartlepool Harbour but was in danger of being driven off course towards the Longscar Rocks by the force of the wind.

The motor lifeboat made its way through these heavy seas and howling winds towards the schooner, now anchored but pitching and rolling violently near the dangerous rocks. Once alongside but with heavy seas sweeping it away it from contact, it took four attempts before the lifeboat crew could get near enough to the schooner to secure a rope.

Once secured, the nine men were helped to safely jump across from the schooner onto the lifeboat. Nine men rescued, the line was cut and the journey through heavy seas was made safely to harbour.

There were five other brave men who received awards from the Prince in May the following year. On behalf of the lifeboat team, Robert Hood the Coxswain received the bronze medal for gallantry with each member of the crew given monetary awards.

In July 1932, another award was given, this time by Rowland Burdon in his capacity of Chairman of the Bench. A large public attendance gathered in Castle Eden Police Court when Mrs Rhoda Jopson of Trimdon Colliery and 11 year old George Shannon from Blackhall were presented with silver medals of the National Canine Defence League for the rescue of a dog at Blackhall Rocks on June 22nd.

Somehow the dog had become stranded on a ledge, 30 feet up a precipitous cliff. Mrs Jepson was at the bottom. Several men at the top of the cliff, improvised a rope from ties, belts and towels and threw this rope down the cliff towards the dog. Undeterred by the dangerous climb, Mrs Jepson made her way up this cliff towards the dog. Once on the ledge, Mrs Jepson shouted to the men that the rope was too short to reach the dog. Young Shannon took hold of the rope tightly in his hands. The men held the boy, still grasping the rope, over the edge of the cliff. The rope was now long enough to be attached to the frightened dog. Once secure, the dog was hauled to safety and Mrs. Jepson could make her arduous descent to the foot of the cliff. The dog, Mrs Jepson and young Shannon would be overjoyed to return to safety. They deserved the recognition of silver medals.

Work for the Guides and Scouts continues

For many years Hartlepool received gifts rather than medals through the Girl Guides. Mrs. Sclater Booth, the Colonel's daughter Frances Mary lived in Basingstoke where she was the Captain of the Basingstoke Division of the Girl Guides. In August 1939, a number of the guides from 1st Crondall Company were lucky enough to enjoy a camping trip with her as Captain at St Helen's on the Isle of Wight. Some of the cost of the trip may have come from funds from money raised. Mrs Sclater-Booth, again as Captain, organised things like the jumble sale held in March 1939 in aid of the Guides and |Brownies funds.

Funds would be raised for other causes. For many years, before Christmas her division collected toys, parcels, Christmas stockings full of presents, children's garments and various other items for the needy children of Hartlepool. These gifts were forwarded to Hartlepool Guides and were distributed on Christmas Eve by the Mayor of Hartlepool.

In July 1934, Col Burdon had been invited to attend a garden party in the grounds of the residence of Mr. and Mrs Leeds. The was unable to join the large number of Girl Guides and Boy Scouts as they celebrated the 21ˢᵗ birthday of the 1ˢᵗ Wingate Troop known as the Colonel Burdon's Own.

The company who did attend include Lord Barnard the County Commissioner and Lady Barnard as well as other Scout and Guide Commissioners from the County, including Miss Kathleen Nimmo District Commissioner, members of the local clergy, and other local notables. Although he could not attend, he sent a letter of congratulations.

The Women's Institute

Col Burdon helped Castle Eden Women's Institute. In 1932, he presented a Christmas tree to the Castle Eden WI for a children's party. WI members had decorated the tree with Christmas gifts which were distributed by Mrs. McCallon, suitably dressed as Father Christmas. The party may have been held in the new hut in the Foundry that the Colonel had donated earlier that year for their new headquarters.

The Church

The Anglican Church played a great part in the life of Col. Burdonas it had done his forebears. He was church warden at St James' Church Castle Eden for over 50 years. As such, or because of his late wife's connexion with the Mothers' union, he wrote a letter to Wingate Mothers' Union congratulating them on raising the money to purchase a lawnmower for the churchyard at Wingate.

His daughter, Lettice Tyringham presented prizes at the Castle Eden Mothers' Union whist drive when on a visit to her father. She too may have been involved in the Mothers' Union.

Col Burdon had donated the Church at Horden. Blackhall was raising funds for a church. He did not fund this building but donated quite considerable sums towards replacing their temporary tin built mission with a church. These and other donations were insufficient. The colliery villagers held many fund raising activities like a sales of work and bazaars before the money was raised.

Such an event for the new Church Building Fund occurred in early November 1930 organised by Mrs J. P. Hall of Hardwick Hall who and her team of parishioners in the ladies working party. This successful event raised £265 1s 4d, a large amount of money at that time.

The new church of St Andrew's was finally dedicated on 30th November 1930. Although the church was new to Blackhall, it was not a new building. A church built in a smoky part of Stockton was bought for £300. Tons of bricks were transported by road to Blackhall. These bricks were dirty on the outside, so when the church was rebuilt in Blackhall at a cost of £6,000, the blackened bricks were placed inwards, leaving apparently clean looking bricks on the outside. This was the 'inside-out' church.

Freemasons

The Freemasons held services in Anglican churches, like St. James Castle Eden. Funerals of fellow masons were especially well attended when many masons gathered to pay their respects.

Canon Tristram, who came to Castle Eden as incumbent in 1849, had been a mason from 1844. In 1900 it was his golden wedding. By this time he was the Right Worshipful Provincial Grand Master of Durham and Northumberland. Masons throughout this area presented the couple with first a gift of an antique silver loving cup and two antique silver gilt fruit bowls with Mrs Tristram being given a diamond brooch. A further presentation of a silver tea service and a gold bracelet for Mrs Tristram was made in the Masonic Hall Durham. These presentations were followed by a service of thanksgiving in Durham Cathedral.

Elizabeth Burdon, the Colonel's sister writes of this celebration;[8] "In the year 1900, on February 5th, I attended with great interest the Golden Wedding celebrations of the dear old couple at Durham. The Cathedral was densely packed – you could not have dropped the proverbial pin anywhere. All sorts and conditions of men, their own personal friends in ranks and of all ages. We all stood up when the wedding party came in. The Canon and Mrs Tristram arm in arm and the original best man, the late Chancellor T.H. Tristram, and original bridesmaid Miss Bowlby, and their eight children, and then we sang "Oh God, our help" (which I have always called Canon Tristram's hymn, though on how many pathetic and stirring occasions has it been since used, during the past ten years). A good many wept, notably an old pupil of the Canon's who sat just in front of me. After the service, we most of us adjourned to the reception, and I think the huge drawing room in the house in the College had never been so full before. Dear old Mrs Tristram was the only one who looked a little overwhelmed. She only lived some 18 months after. They were wonderful people. Canon Tristram died on March 8th 1906."

Canon Tristram's funeral took place in Durham Cathedral. He had a long masonic career, holding senior posts and having connections with other degrees of the Order. Hundreds of members of the Masonic order, some wearing buttonholes of acacia or carrying larger sprigs of the Masonic emblem attended his funeral. Others, including the Mayor his robes, his colleagues and corporation officials, clergy, representatives for the University sat in the reserved seats. There were so many members of the public in attendance that they not only filled the empty seats but crowded into the aisles.

The Burdon's also had long connections with the Masonic Order. On 24th September 1919, a new Masonic Lodge, situated in the Drill Hall Parklands named as the 'Rowland Burdon Lodge' was consecrated in Castle Eden in an impressive ceremony attended by a large number of Masonic officers of the Province of Durham. It may not have been a co-incidence that the date chosen was September 24th, as it was this date in 1793, when the foundation stone of the Wearmouth Bridge, funded by the Colonel's grandfather, had been laid: a day full of Masonic honours.

On 24th August 1932, Sunderland opened a new Masonic Hall situated at the junction of Burdon Road and Park Road. This was regarded as a magnificent building and had been built at the cost of £27,000. In July that year, the Freemasons of Sunderland were present when Colonel Burdon unveiled a memorial tablet to his grandfather that read; 1796-1929, "To the honoured memory of Rowland Burdon M. P., who built the first bridge upon this site.

He laid the foundation stone on 24th September 1793. The Bridge was opened to the public by him on the 9th August 1796. This tablet was unveiled by his grandson Col. Rowland Burdon V.D. D.L. J.P. of Castle Eden, and presented to the town by the Freemasons of Sunderland July 13th 1932. E.H. Brown Mayor. Nil Desperandum Auspices Deo."

These Latin words had been the motto of Sunderland since 1849. They were placed on large panels on the bridge in 1857 when major reconstruction work was conducted by Robert Stephenson. The dates refer to the period when the bridge was in use.

In 1929 because of a huge increase in traffic a new Wearmouth Bridge was opened by the Duke of York, accompanied by the Duchess. The Duke hammered a silver rivet into position with a pneumatic riveter handed to him by a riveter who wore his working clothes and a red muffler.

The first Wearmouth Bridge, opened in 1796 was at that time by far the longest single span iron bridge in the world. Since that time there has been great controversy about the design of the bridge. Rowland Burdon paid for the construction of the bridge but he was also credited with its design. So was Thomas Paine.

In July 1932, at the memorial tablet presentation the history of the first bridge was again related. The old bridge had stood for 133 years and the Freemasons did not appear to want the old bridge to become just a memory. They wished the old bridge to remain in public memory. Not only had Freemasons had been involved in this opening ceremony but Thomas Wilson, engineer of the bridge had also been a Freemason.

In the unveiling ceremony, Col Burdon reminded those gathered that his grandfather had close associations with Sir John Soane, the eminent architect saying;[9] "Sir John is certainly one of the men whom you must thank for the fact that you actually got a bridge over the Wear. As you probably know, the forces ranged against my grandfather were tremendous: no one thought it possible that the scheme could be carried out successfully and more than once he was tempted to throw it up.But Sir John was constantly behind him in this matter, urging him to carry on: and to that encouragement Rowland Burdon owed much."

Col Burdon added "that his grandfather had always lived up to the words he uttered when the bridge was opened: 'Nil Desperandum Auspices Deo' which afterwards most fittingly became the motto of Sunderland."

The controversy about the design of the first Wearmouth Bridge had raised its head many times after it was built. There is still a debate going on the press in the 1950's. In November 1950 the following said the bridge was; [10] "Built on plans which owed much to Paine's designs, this bridge earned the praise of Robert Stephenson, the great engineer as 'A Structure which the small quantity of material employed in its construction will probably remain unrivalled."

Thomas Paine did not pay for this bridge so he did not have to keep the cost down by using as little material as possible. Rowland Burdon did pay most of the cost of £30,000 and the total cost was just over £4,000 more than this amount. Keeping down the cost may have been a consideration.

Plans for a bridge were exhibited by Thomas Paine in Paddington for 12 months and had attracted considerable public attention. Rowland Burdon had seen Paine's Bridge so he was familiar with its design. However the span of the two bridges were completely different. Burdon had the Wearmouth Bridge constructed in cast iron. Paine's plan was for a malleable iron bridge which would have had to have been re-wrought for the Wearmouth Bridge.

The controversy continued in 1954 with various letters to the newspaper and concluding that although Rowland Burdon paid for the bridge the question of its' designer would probably remain a controversy.

The first Wearmouth Bridge, c 1800

Colonel Burdon and the Depression

This bridge had a life of 133 years. Traffic has again increased a new 3 span cable-stayed bridge over the River Wear began construction in May 2015.

In 1935 Col Burdon had a much smaller bridge constructed in Horden. Men collected sea coal in sacks washed up by the tide on Horden Beach. The sacks were loaded onto their bicycles for an easier journey home. Men living in Blackhall had a long tedious up the new road pushing a laden bicycle up a steep hill. Some men may have been using the viaduct as a shorter route which could be a dangerous journey. The LNER Company contacted Col Burdon for his permission for the men to use a footpath running up to the viaduct so they could walk alongside the viaduct to shorten their journey. The Colonel decided to make a footbridge across a burn, nearly a foot deep in places at the mouth of the dene. Men who braved across this burn without rubber boots get wet through, so Col Burdon decided to build this bridge with the permission of Easington Rural District Council.

The bridge at Deneholme was completed by October 1935. The North Eastern Railway Company was informed it would be no longer necessary for the men to carry coal along the footpath attached to the viaduct.

The Council agreed to the construction a small bridge across a burn. It also gave permission for Col Burdon to erect a wooden bus shelter on a site near the Factory for the benefit of the public.

In 1933, the Colonel wrote to the Easington Rural District Council to inform them that he was employing previously unemployed men to repair a short road at Wingate, known as Moor Lane, running between North Road and Wellfield Farm. The Colonel's father Rev John Burdon had instigated a similar initiative when he was rector at English Bicknor. The Colonel may have had memories of this and followed his father's example.

In May 1933, there was meeting of the Easington Area Unemployed Association held in Horden. Col Burdon had offered the Association some land near the Labour Exchange which could be used to erect an occupational centre for those men currently unemployed, as many were in the 1930's.

This was the time of the Great Depression, probably one of the reasons men were collecting sea coal for use on their fires. The effects of the Depression were keenly felt in the industrial North of England especially in shipbuilding, iron, steel and coal mining areas. Because of the Depression the demand for ships collapsed so shipbuilding areas like Sunderland, Newcastle and Middlesbrough suffered greatly. Less iron manufacturing and demands from a heavy industry cut by half resulted in the loss of demand for coal.

Occupational centres for the unemployed were instigated throughout the country. There was one in Windsor visited by the Prince of Wales in January 1934. The Prince was pleased that in the space of three months the men had repaired over 700 pairs of boots. He also praised the workmanship of those who made cabinets and desks. The Prince also talked to some of the unemployed.

After this visit, accompanied by the Mayor and Mayoress, the Prince visited the soup kitchen encouraged by the sight of the eighty children present who were enjoying their meal. This was not the Prince's first visit to an employment centre or soup kitchen. He received a tremendous welcome when he made a surprise visit to unemployment centres in Slough. He also dropped in at the British Legion headquarters in Slough he dropped into the soup kitchen where 150 children were having tea. When the Prince requested to look at the big boilers in the kitchen where soup was made daily for the unemployed men, he noticed a woman cutting potatoes if he could have a try. His try resulted in him cutting the potatoes into fancy slices which the women workers requested to keep as souvenirs.

The Durham soup kitchens did not have visits from the Prince of Wales, but like those in Slough many of them were run by the British Legions and other religious bodies particularly the Salvation Army. A soup kitchen in Murton was run by the Salvation Army and events like concerts helped to raise money to keep it functioning.

The employment centre in Horden was to serve the needs of Easington, Horden and Blackhall and in May 1933 was in the

535

process of applying for a Government grant. At this time this was the National Government of Ramsey Macdonald, Stanley Baldwin and Neville Chamberlain. Ramsey Macdonald was the Member of Parliament for the Seaham Constituency.

Col Burdon a staunch Conservative was Vice President of Seaham Conservative and Unionist Association. The Marquess of Londonderry was President and William J. Nimmo was another officer.

When the annual meeting of the association took place in Easington Village in April 1935, and address was given by Mr. Hugh Molson, a Conservative MP who represented Doncaster. Mr. Molson paid tribute to the work of the Labour Party MP, Ramsey Macdonald, because he was the head of the Government that the Conservative party supported. Mr. Molson believed that the policy the Government had followed was one which would commend itself to the fair-minded and reasonable men and women of all three political parties. He hoped that when the general election came, everyone would rally once more to the support of the National Government and that the Prime Minister would be returned once again.

Col Burdon appeared to have agreed with these sentiments. On a sunny Saturday in July Col Burdon was present to greet his guests and visitors who had gathered on his estate for a demonstration in support of the National Government.

Wheatley Hill Prize Band played. There was a magician, a display of Alsatian dogs and various sports. Tea was served by the 'mesdames', the women Conservative supporters. In 1933 these women had organised 36 social events like dances and whist drives to raise money for the Association. Other women were in charge of cakes and sweets. Miss K Nimmo was in charge of ices and two of the Nimmo girls were amongst those in charge of flowers.

As well as the garden party atmosphere, there were speakers at this event, the principal one being Colonel L. Ropner M.P. A dance was held in the evening at Parklands.

Peter Lee and The Labour Party

Ramsey Macdonald had the support as Prime Minister from Mr. Molson. The Labour Party had grown from strength to strength in the Seaham Constituency.

Peter Lee was one of the leading Labour figures at this time. He was born in Trimdon Grange in 1864. As a child, he did not learn to read but he attended night school from the age of twenty and from there became a self-educated man. In 1886 he left England for America where he spent two years working in the coalmines of Ohio, Pennsylvania and Kentucky.

At this time Peter Lee described himself as being a 'wild man.' He had little education, was a heavy drinker and smoker. In 1888 Peter Lee returned to England and worked in Wingate pit, being first elected as a delegate to the Miner's Conference and then elected by the miners as checkweighman for the colliery.

In 1896, he left Wingate for South Africa. It was in South Africa that he became a Primitive Methodist. He stopped drinking and smoking and from that time became a dedicated Christian. In 1900, aged 33 on his return to England, Peter Lee became checkweighman at Wheatley Hill Colliery.

He preached in local Methodist chapels and was the Sunday School Superintendent at the Pelton Street Methodist Church in Wheatley Hill. As a voracious reader of the Bible, he was well equipped to conduct Bible classes. He was also much in demand as a lay preacher.

Peter Lee became a parish councillor in Wheatley Hill, becoming Chairman of the Parish Council, the local Co-operative and Durham County Water Board.

Peter Lee was elected as a member of Durham County Council in 1909 becoming Chairman in 1919, the first Socialist chairman to be elected to that position on Durham County Council.

As Chairman of Durham County Water Board Peter Lee spearheaded the building of a reservoir at Burnhope, in the upper reaches of Weardale to bring an adequate supply of water to the area. The reservoir, costing one million pounds, was completed, but not until after the death of Peter Lee.

He was General Secretary of Durham Miner's Association and eventually became the President of the Miner's Federation of Great Britain.

Peter Lee was one of four men who met Prime Minister Ramsey Macdonald at Durham station on 7th January 1931. The Prime Minister was destined to address meetings at Dawdon and Deaf Hill. In October that year, Peter Lee's opinion of Ramsey Macdonald was given to those gathered in Silksworth Miners' Hall;[11] "I am not charging MacDonald with cowardice but at least I believed that Ramsay Macdonald had a little gratitude. I remember when he was getting a bit shaky in Wales, the miners of Durham and their wives succeeded in giving him a safe seat and this is his gratitude to try to split them.

He knows – no one knows better – how we overcame the forces against us by united effort, how we worked together and got every seat in Durham for Labour, how we got the County Council and the rural districts for Labour, and he comes and throws a bone of contention amongst us and tries to split us from top to bottom."

In 1929 thousands had cheered MacDonald. By 1935, the same thousands did their noisiest to stop him speaking. Peter Lee, like many others considered Ramsey MacDonald was too much in line with the Londonderrys. As early as February 1930 some Labour Party [12] "followers in industrial centres and rural districts" were "a little bit puzzled to read that he sat at Lady Londonderry's side a few nights ago at a brilliant party at the Londonderry mansion in Park Lane."

In 1932 the Marchioness of Londonderry voiced her support for Ramsey Macdonald as she did so on several occasions when she addressed a massed meeting in support of the National Government when she said; "The interests of the women is that of the home and they know that Mr MacDonald's policy was the only one to make life possible for the working classes and the unemployed…. The leading members of the Socialist Party who are the loudest in their condemnation of the National Government are precisely those who brought this country to the very brink of ruin and when they saw the precipice that confronted them, they ran away."

Ramsey MacDonald's support by the Londonderrys proved dangerous for him. They praised him but savagely attacked his political party. Emmanuel Shinwell defeated Ramsey Macdonald in standing for the Labour Party in the Seaham Division in the next election.

The Conservatives and Labour Party were poles apart, as were Col Burdon and Peter Lee in their politics. Yet, there were similarities between the two men. Both men were dedicated Christians, the Colonel in the Anglican Church and Peterlee in the Methodist. Both were highly respected in the area. They opened events and new constructions, delivered speeches and were involved in public works.

Although Peter Lee said the following, it is probably that Col Burdon would also believe this;[13] "Every person should have five opportunities – the opportunity of living, of working, of knowing God, of learning what God had made in the world and of reading and seeing what had been written and made by men and women of all ages."

He earlier emphasised in 1927 the need for man to fulfil his duty.[14] "The power that is needed by the highest to the lowest, is that we shall recognize God and our duty. That is what is needed in these days – the Fatherhood of God and the Brotherhood of man... Sometimes we think there can be no good outside the Labour Party or the Conservative Party or the Liberal Party. What is needed today is that we shall look for the best in all. Let us aim the highest by stooping down to lift the lowest.... If everyone would do their duty to their fellow men the rights would follow naturally."

Although Colonel Burdon and Peter Lee inhabited opposite poles there was much common ground. Peter Lee died in June 1935 after a long illness. Reports of his death featured in many national as well as local newspapers.

Although Peter Lee devoted his life to the service of the miners he was held in respect and admiration by all classes. On the day of his funeral the cortege left his home in Durham for the service in Wheatley hill. Crowds stood in the pouring rain as the procession wound its way through the mining village. There were many women, some with tears in their eyes, lining the streets to show their respect.

The funeral was held in Patten Street Methodist Chapel, a chapel too small to accommodate all those who wished to attend so others stood outside. Inside the chapel gathered prominent trade unionists from all parts of the country, representatives from local government and administrators and noted local people. Police constables carried his coffin into the chapel. Rousing Methodist hymns were sung in the service, including 'Fight the Good Fight.' Outside all sections from the mining community gathered at his graveside including mine owners, deputies, hewers and local trade union leaders. Peter Lee was highly respected for all the good work he had done for the mining community.

Another funeral

Col Burdon did not attend this funeral but he would have been aware of Peter Lee. It is uncertain as to his opinion of the man. He would have felt the loss of his sister when she died in the December of that year, 1935. Elizabeth Anne Burdon was 85 when she died. She never married and wrote the following in April 1922;[15] "I have, since 1893, the year of my father's death, spent a great deal of my time in wandering in many lands, for travel has always held me fast in its spell. I might fill pages with my experiences, but the places visited are for the most part well known, though full of beauty and interest. I invariably met with kindness and courtesy, and have laid up a store of pleasant memories, on which to dwell when the grey days come. I migrated to Herefordshire in 1901, to within 20 miles of my birthplace, and it had been a great amusement to me planting and making my surroundings here in this fertile and fruitful land. I go over sometimes to English Bicknor, and there are several people who love to talk of the old days there and Mr. Burdon's beneficent and wise pastorate. But here I must come to a stop, a full stop, the main object of this little book having been to gather together family traits and incidents. Mine has been a very happy, peaceful life, singularly free from most of the 'ills which flesh is heir to', and is now fast approaching the time when my own turn comes to be laid on the shelf."

This is a fitting end to her life. Elizabeth Anne Burdon did give insights into 'family traits and incidents.'

The Colonel, attended another funeral in January 1938 of someone he and his late wife Mary Arundell would have known well, Mrs Helena Rosa Duncombe Shafto. Mrs Shafto's late husband had been Chairman of the Durham County Bench of magistrates. She was the only woman magistrate in Durham City. Mrs Shafto was president of the Durham Division Women's Unionist Association and Governor of Sherburn Hospital. During the war she sponsored the Durham Light Infantry Prisoner of War Fund, which sent food, clothes and comforts to the men in captivity in Germany. Mrs Shafto was awarded the O.B.E. and given the freedom of the City of Death.

The Colonel Retires

By the time of Mrs Shafto's death, Rowland Burdon had decided to retire. He too may have felt, like his sister had, that he was approaching the time when it would be his turn to be 'laid on the shelf.'

In July 1935, he had resigned as Chairman of St. Hild's College in Durham after serving in this position for forty years. In 1936, he resigned from being President of Hartlepool Hospital. In March 1937 after being a magistrate for 56 years, the Colonel retired from the chairmanship of the bench, an office he had held for forty years.

In 1936 he was not well enough to attend the 17th reunion of the 'Pals' Regiment of the DLI. There was a fear of War at this time. In November 1936, the vicar of Hesleden and a committee had plans to convert the Hesleden Parish Hall into an air raid station complete with ambulance, clearing room for accidents, showers baths and cubicles. It is uncertain whether these plans materialised but they demonstrate the fear of war which existed at the time. At the Pals Reunion, the members were informed of a letter the Colonel had written to the War Office on their behalf offering their services in the event that trouble might arise. The Adjutant General had replied that if there was any work the men could do in the Home Defence scheme their services would be acceptable. Their services were not required at that time, but probably many of these Old Comrades would be involved in Defence work a few years later.

The End of the Burdons

Colonel Burdon would not be able to offer his services when war did come. His health deteriorated. He died in August 1944. He had requested a private funeral without flowers or mourning, so his body was cremated at Darlington and the ashes brought back to Castle Eden. A casket, made from elm grown on the Castle Eden Estate containing his ashes were placed in St. James Church overnight before a Memorial Service was held on 5th August. Representatives from all the organisations he had so loyally served over the years attended this memorial.

The Colonel's son-in-laws Brig General Sclater-Booth and Col Mark Sykes could not come as the Brigadier was ill and Col Sykes was on active service. Tenant farmers, household staff and employees on the estate came to pay their respects, probably thinking it would be difficult to imagine Castle Eden estate without a Rowland Burdon and possibly wondering what would happen to the Estate now that the Colonel had died.

After the choral service the congregation left the church and proceeded to the graveside of Mary Arundell, where his casket of ashes were placed next to his late wife.

A memorial window to the last Rowland Burdon was later unveiled in St. James' Church, Castle Eden containing the words; My sword I give to him that shall succeed me in my pilgrimage. And my courage and skill to him that can get it. In loving memory of Rowland Burdon 1857 – 1944, sixth and last surviving of his name and of other members of the Burdon family who were also Lords of the Manor of Castle Eden from 1758."

CHAPTER FOURTEEN
The end

After the death of Colonel Burdon there was no male heir to take over the estate. His eldest daughter Mrs Francis Mary Sclater-Booth donated the claw beaker to the British Museum. Rowland Burdon's collection of Sunderland pottery, 264 items in total, was donated by the family to the Sunderland Museum. This collection included many fine examples of copper and silver lustre ware, jugs, frog mugs and inscribed plates. Some of these items had illustrations of the first Wearmouth Bridge. In 1945 many of the items were sought by collectors and a subsequent exhibition in August 1945 attracted many people from all over the country.

In 1946 there was an auction of furnishings and household items held in the Castle. Hundreds of items were in display in various rooms in the house including; mahogany furniture, antique furniture, carpets, settees upholstered in silk, oil paintings, portraits including a half-length portrait of Dorothy Forster of Bamburgh, tea sets and other items of crockery including Wedgewood and Coalport, glassware, china busts of Napoleon and Wellington under glass domes, Chinese vases, sporting equipment including riding crops and archers bows and arrows, 'an iron coat of arms of Stockton in a wrought iron frame from the Town House Stockton', a cello, a gramophone, wall mirrors, candlesticks, cutlery some of which was silver, a lady's silver embossed hand mirror, a grandfather clock and other timepieces, brass and pewter items, telescopes, a court sword and a pair of swords, five cases of stuffed birds, fox hunting prints, oil lamps, and a billiard table. There was a huge number of books including some in French, Rousseau, the History of Walpole, Matthew Arnold, the Encyclopaedia of Sport, History, Shakespeare, Cook's Voyages to the Pacific Ocean, the History of Electricity, copies of the 'Gentleman's Magazine and the Life of William Pitt."

These were just a few of the many items up for sale but they appear to range through the whole history and lives of the Burdon family, even before they came to Castle Eden. One would not know which lady was the first owner of the embossed silver hand mirror or which of the men first owned the swords. The 'Life of William Pitt' returns us to the Rowland Burdon who according to the family was a close friend of William Pitt. During the ceremony of the Freemason's dedication of a plaque to the Colonel's grandfather in Sunderland in 1932, the Colonel reminded those present of his grandfather's friendship with William Pitt, adding that if Pitt had not died when he did, his grandfather would have been raised to the peerage. It is uncertain whether this would have come about, but the family must have believed it to be true for the Colonel to say this to an audience of his fellow freemasons. Friends of the Colonel's grandfather had been raised to the peerage; John Scott was raised to Lord Eldon with his brother William given the title of Lord Stowell. John Soane was knighted becoming Sir John Soane. Rowland Burdon suffered a huge financial blow. William Pitt died and he declined to continue serving in Parliament. He was not raised to the ranks, something his family must have discussed over several years for it to be highlighted in a speech by his grandson so many years later.

Now all these possessions which belonged to so many members of the Burdon family and the memories they all held were sold in an auction and scattered away not to be discovered again. Many unnamed portraits were for sale, including those of a gentleman in a dark wig and a lady in a red dress. These people, now unnamed, had already been forgotten.

The estate was split up between the heirs. The Colonel's daughter Francis Mary, now Mrs Sclater-Booth died in 1949 at the young age of 53. Announcements appeared in the press in July 1950 of an impending auction from the estate of Mrs Sclater-Booth, deceased to be held on July 25th 1950. The sale, part of the Castle Eden Estate included;

"LOT 1: That attractive country house known as the COTTAGE (followed by a description)

LOT 2: The LODGE (plus description)

LOT 3: The CASTLE GARDENS: Two well built brick houses containing (1) Kitchen, back kitchen, sitting room, pantry, 2 bedrooms, usual outhouses and (2) Kitchen, sitting room, scullery, 3 bedrooms and usual outhouses, Both houses have electric light and water laid on: large walled garden in excellent state of cultivation and containing 11 greenhouses, potting sheds, store shed, tool houses etc. Large orchard and vegetable garden and woodland and in all extending to approximately 7 ½ acres …..Note – If this is not sold it will be offered for sale as three separate lots.

LOT 4: ACCOMODATION FIELD…..situated Moor Lane Wingate….containing 4,336 acres …at present in the possession of Mr. Harrison.

LOT 6: ACCOMODATION FIELD situated near the village of Old Shotton containing 7,206 acres…….at present in the occupation of Mrs Scurr.

LOT 6: ARABLE FIELD situated near to the village of Old Shotton containing 6 acres……at present in the occupation of Mr. T Wilson…..and includes the land let to E.D.C. for a sewerage tank."

The estate was being broken up and sold. Land and buildings were being sold.

New Houses

The population had increased dramatically in County Durham especially in the Easington area due to the expansion of the three coastal colliery villages. From 1911 to 1921 the population of County Durham increased by more than 100,000. There was a smaller increase of 7,142 in the years between 1921 and 1931 because of the depressed condition of the coal trade during these years. In 1932 Castle Eden had a population of 1,562. Shotton, which included Horden, was by now 19,529.

There were many colliery houses in the three villages of Easington, Horden and Blackhall. These houses had no gardens or indoor bathroom facilities. Many of these houses had been built very quickly to hurriedly accommodate incomers for the new collieries. The population of Easington District had increased from 40,000 in 1900 to 70,000 in 1914 so houses were need rapidly. In Horden the contractor Henry Bell supposedly erected 365 houses in 365 days.

During his time as Member of Parliament for the Constituency, Sidney Webb observed that the housing was not only bad but the houses themselves were 'ugly' and in 'hideous colliery rows'. He advocated the building of "pleasant garden villages", decent quality homes in a healthier environment probably not so close to the pit. This did not happen, so the colliery houses remained alongside the subsequent erection of council houses with gardens. In the 20 years after World War 1 Easington Rural District Council built 4,500 houses at a rate of 220 houses a year.

Many of the houses in the district were overcrowded. In 1935, Durham County Council had the highest percentage of over-crowding in the country. This was not just due to large families. Households took in lodgers as single men could not be allocated a colliery house. Due to the housing shortage, young couples who married frequently had to live in with in-laws, sometimes even when they had families of their own.

By the 1930's some of the older houses in the district were over a hundred years old. In 1939, the council designated over 100 slum clearance schemes.

There were drawbacks in building more new houses. The payment of Government subsidies was uncertain. They had no powers, like compulsory purchase. Rent collection proved a prob-lem. Many of the better paid miners lived in tithed colliery houses.

Renting a Council house, especially on low wages was difficult, as some of the tenants found paying rent proved problematic.

By October 1936, the Housing Act of 1930 (Slum Clearance) had resulted in 1,836 clearance orders and compulsory purchase orders by Easington Rural District Council. One thousand three hundred and twenty two of these had been confirmed by the Ministry of Health and due for demolition. Easington District Council planned to provide 5,000 new houses in the district. The Council considered to date they had done more for housing than any other Rural or District Council in County Durham as they had an extensive programme to replace demolished sub-standard houses. They had erected 1,049 houses using their direct labour staff and the North-Eastern Housing Association very shortly to commence the building of 743 houses.

However there was still a housing shortage. Seven hundred people were on the waiting list for a council house in Horden. Some had resorted to living in sheds erected on allotments, the land belonging to Col Burdon given to Horden Parish Council. In January 1933, a report from a Council Inspector, informed the Council there were 47 huts and caravans on the Parish Council allotments at Horden occupied without authority from the Council. The huts had wells dug in the gardens, unsuitable for drinking so there was no proper water supply. This had to be obtained from nearby residents of houses. Heaps of manure surrounded the huts.

Some of these huts were just crude wooden erections. The tenants of the huts were being charged rent from the allotment owners, one owner having erected four huts on his allotment, received 14s 6d a week rent for the four huts. Several of these huts were grossly overcrowded with one hut of two small rooms occupied by an invalid man and his four daughters. The inhabitants of the huts were being exploited because they had nowhere else to live. If they were evicted, they would become homeless and get into trouble with police.

By the 1930's some of the older houses in the district were over a hundred years old and deemed unfit for habitation. By 1939 the Easington Rural District Council had designated over 100 slum clearance schemes. This added to the severity of the districts housing problems.

In 1943 the Ministry of Health asked local authorities to assess their housing needs. EDC decided on a long term strategy, so C.W. Clarke, the Council's Engineer and Surveyor, produced the planning document, "Farewell to Squalor". The plan was for a large development and avoid building in villages, especially where the colliery had a short predicted life span. Clarke's proposal was accepted and the outline survey for a new town was unanimously accepted in December 1946.This project was accepted by Government as being suitable for the application of the New Towns Act.

Clarke's preferred site was considered by Government to have major drawbacks. The principal access from Horden was very steep. The chosen area was undulating. The proposed situation of the town centre was too close to the northern boundary. The site itself was very exposed. The second choice of a site near Shotton was criticised as being in the proximity of a 'drab derelict village.'

The Ministry of Agriculture recommended a site around Easington Village and Easington Colliery because it was near existing housing, joining a railway, considered suitable for drainage and development and offered good facilities for the development for industry. The NCB saw difficulties in building anywhere near Easington.

After a tour of the proposed sites by the Minister, he opted for the site preferred by Clarke. There were no pits heaps in the vicinity. The Minister proposed the new town should be built by a Development Corporation rather than the Council.

It was proposed approximately 2,350 acres should be developed under the New Towns Act. Before this could proceed a Public Local Enquiry was necessary. This took place on 27th January 1948.

Under the New Towns Act a Corporation was empowered to acquire land for building and provision of services within the new town area. The Development Corporation were entitled to possession of the land immediately without having to obtain the permission of the Ministry of Agriculture. Objections were raised from farmers and those with agricultural interests. The designated

area was prime agricultural land which farmers had cultivated for
years and on which their livelihood depended.

Much of the land was owned either by the National Coal Board
or by the Castle Eden Estate. Because Rowland Burdon had died in
1944 this land was already being dispersed. There was no Rowland
Burdon on the estate to make a case for the retention of this prime
land and champion the farmer's livelihoods.

There were objections from adjacent parishes who considered
a development costing 14 million pounds in order to accommodate 30,000 people would have effects on the adjacent parishes.
The Minister appeared to have no plan of the future for the existing
communities. The Clerk representing Thornley Parish Council told
the inspector that the building of a new town would rob the older
villages of their amenities and new industry could be brought to the
district without building a new town. Some considered the existing
townships should be developed stage by stage instead of building a
new town.

Concern was raised that woodland areas would be destroyed.
Managed woodland had produced timber, a good resource for the
local coal mines.

The Minister decided in favour of the development of a new
town. In 'Farewell to Squalor', Clarke had referred to the new town
as Peterlee. Peterlee Development Corporation was soon established setting up its headquarters in Shotton Hall.

The new town estates took on the names of the farms and farming areas which they replaced like Lowhills, Dene House, Howletch,
Passfield and Oakerside.

Although Castle Eden Dene was passed to English Nature, at
this time it was taken over by the Development Corporation. The
Castle became the local Headquarters for the National Coal Board
(NCB). It has now reverted to private dwellings. The brewery closed
with the once coaching inn becoming offices and a restaurant and
the site of the brewery is now occupied with houses aptly named
Burdon Walk. Shotton Hall is now the premises for Peterlee Town
Council. The building has functions rooms named the Burdon

Suite and the Brandling Suite. St. James' Church Castle Eden closed its doors as a place of worship at the end of March 2016.

It was not that long before there were no pits heaps anywhere in East Durham. The pits closed. Communities disintegrated. Some of the colliery villages, like Horden, are now run down and neglected with little chance of fulfilling Sidney Webb's vision of becoming 'garden villages.'

It seemed Peter Lee had taken over from Rowland Burdon. Agriculture had given way to industry and mining. Housing needs were pressing. There are no 'what ifs' in real life, but what if Captain Burdon had not been killed in that aeroplane accident and the last Rowland Burdon had not been Colonel Burdon, the sixth of that name, there might still be gimer hogs on the fields at Oakerside Farm inside of a housing estate. There may have been garden villages with smaller but still thriving communities. But there are no 'what ifs'. There are no more farms or farmers to raise the loyal toast to the farmer and the plough, which was inscribed on one of Rowland Burdon's toad mugs;

> "Let the wealthy and great rule in splendour and state.
>
> I envy them not I declare it.
>
> I eat my own lamb, my chicken and ham,
>
> I sheer my own sheep and I wear it.
>
> I have land, I have bowers
>
> I have friends, I have flowers,
>
> The lark is my morning alarmer.
>
> So jollyboys now, here's God's speed and plough
>
> And long life and success to the farmer."

BIBLIOGRAPHY

Durham records office

D/CG5/133, D/CG5/134-40; D/CG 4/3, D/X 1934/1/2, DX1934/1/1, DX 1934/1/3; D/CE 54 to D/CE 71; D/CG42; D/CG4/1-5; D/CG 4/6; D/CG 5/1; D/CG 5/5; D/CG 5/8; D/CG 5/9; D/CG 5/11; D/CG 5/12; D/CG 5/15; D/CG 520/ D/CG 5/24; D/CG 5/34; D/CG/5 106-115; D/CG 5/1312; D/X 210/1; D/C45/1273-82; D/CG 5/2 -9,12; D/CE 99; D/CE 100; D/CG 5/46; D/CG/15/1; D/CG5/194; D/CG5/119-31; D/CG5/132-140; E/E3 1863-1900; E/E8 1863 -1872; D/X 210/1; E/E2 1892-1906; D/CG5 23-27 and 31-45; D/CG5/2-9 and 12-13; D/X 1234/1-2; D/CG4/57-72; DCG 5/49-104; DCG 52; DCG5/10; D/CG 5/11; D/CG 5/12; D/CG 5/18; D/CG 5/19; D/CG 5/20; D/CG 5/30; D/CG 5/34; D/CG 5/46; D/CG 5/104; D/CG 5/106; D/X 123/1; Leaflet J. Bell 1/11/1806

"Before My Time And Since", Elizabeth Anne Burdon

"The Lewin Letters: a selection from the correspondence and diaries of an English family, 1756-1884. Printed for private circulation" Thomas Herbert Lewin

"Vanity Fair", William Makepeace Thackeray

"Lady Hester Stanhope, The Unconventional Life of the Queen of the Desert", Joan Haslip

"Lady Hester Stanhope Queen of the Desert" Virginia Childs

"Star of the Morning, The Extraordinary Life of Lady Hester Stanhope", Kirsten Ellis

"William Pitt the Younger" William Hague

"Aycliffe and Peterlee New Towns 1946-1988" Garry Philipson

"Rhymes of Northern Bards" by John Bell

"Mrs Beeton's Household Management", Isabella Beeton

"The Napoleonic War Journal of Captain Thomas Henry Browne 1807-186" edited by Roger Norman Buckley

"Great Britain's War," Jeremy Paxman

"Forgotten Voices of the Somme", Joshua Levine

"The Letters of Sidney and Beatrice Webb" Edited by Norman Mackenzie

"Records of the family of Burdon, of Castle Eden, County Durham a Pedigree", Henry Baker Tristram.

"The Miners of Northumberland and Durham" Richard Fynes

"The History of Hartlepool" Sir Cuthbert Sharp with a Supplemental History to 1851 inclusive, Hartlepool printed and published by John Proctor 1851; Republished by Hartlepool Borough Council 1978

"The Coalminer's of Durham", Norman Emery

"Masters and Servants," Huw Benyon and Terry Austin

"Hidden Chains, the Slavery Business and North East England 1600-1865" John Charlton

"A Fly on the Wheel or How I Helped to Govern India", Thomas Herbert Lewin

Church Magazines; Magazine 5 and Magazine 8, Rev FGT Robinson MA about 1915

"The History and Antiquities of the county of Palantine of Durham Vol 3 Stockton and Darlington Wards" Robert Surtees

"Songs of Innocence and Experience," William Blake

"The History of Newcastle Upon Tyne" Henry Bourne

The Will of Rowland Burdon 1786

Scots Magazine 1/10/1784

Encyl. Britannica Vol 12 (1790) and 1803

Will of Richard Mathews

Banks, Bankers, and Banking in Northumberland pages 27, 385-7, 391, 395

Will John Graham Clarke

"Early History of Psychiatry" John Le Gasside (1972)

British Journal of Psychiatry Vol. 120 pages 419-420

"The Guinea Voyage a poem in three Books," Sunderland Museum Neil Sinclair 2007

Baltoni Portrait of Rowland Burdon, Beamish Museum

Will Edward Cotsford

Stephen King "Poverty and Welfare in England 1700-1850

"The Cathedral Church of Durham" George Bells and Sons first published 1899

"Remarkable Occurences Connected With the Counties of Newcastle-upon-Tyne, Northumberland and Durham" M.A. Richardson published 1844

Report by James Mitchell Esq LLD on Employment of Children and Young Persons in Mines of the South Durham Coalfields between the Wear and the Tees and on the State and Condition and Treatment of Such Children; Edited by Ian Winstanley

Geographical Journal Obit. Canon HB Tristram

1858 Post Office Directory

Seaham Harbour the First Hundred Years 1829-1928 by Tom McMee and David Angus

"History of Castle Eden" Moyes

"Rural England and Urban Poaching in Victorian England" Harvey Osborne

Edwardian Life in Hitchingbrooke: adapted extracts from a Channel 4 programme 'The Edwardian Country House'

Wisden

Whellans 1894 Directory

"War History of the 18th Battalion Durham Light Infantry" William Douglas Lowe published 1920

"The Life and Letters of Lady Hester Stanhope" Duchess of Cleveland

Will of Anne Malet Burdon

Hansard

"A Very Unimportant Officer" C A Stewart

Guardian Booklet, Memoirs and Diaries (WW1)

The Christmas Truce 1915

De Vichy Roll of Honour

REFERENCES

Two books have been extensively used, so they are just referred
to later as Elizabeth(Before my time and since by Elizabeth Anne
Burdon) and Tristram.(Records of the family of Burdon, of Castle
Eden, County Durham, a pedigree by Henry Baker Tristram) This
book was loaned from the British Library.

Chapter One
1) Tristram page 4
2) Ibid page 4
3) Ibid page 6
4) Ibid page 7
5) Ibid page 8
6) Morpeth Herald 27/12/1879

Chapter Two
1) Newcastle Chronicle April 1758
2) Newcastle Chronicle Jan 1762
3) Ibid Jan 1758
4) Ibid Feb 1794
5) Sussex Advertiser 18/10/1786

Chapter Three
1) Rev Robinson Magazine May 8th
2) Elizabeth, letter by Rowland Burdon
3) Newcastle Journal 3/12/1757
4) Ibid 16/9/1786
5) Oxford Journal 18/9/1784
6) Scots Magazine
7) Caledonian Mercury 24/10/1786

8) Newcastle Chronicle September 1786
9) Ibid February 1755
10) Ibid 14/3/1829
11) Leeds Intelligencer 31/10/1786

Chapter Four
1) Pompeo Batoni portrait of Rowland Burdon 1V
2) Elizabeth
3) Newcastle Chronicle 24/1/1789
4) Ibid
5) Ibid 13/1/1789
6) Ibid November 1789
7) Ibid July 1790
8) Daily Gazette fort Middlesbrough 29/4/1893
9) Newcastle Chronicle 7/1/1792
10) Ibid 21/1/1792
11) Ibid 13/8/1796
12) Sunderland Echo and Shipping Gazette 9/11/1885
13) Rhymes of Northern Ballads page 285 'Sunderland Bridge' by MW of South Shields
14) Newcastle Chronicle 13/9/1796
15) Ibid 27/8/1796
16) Durham Records Office
17) Ibid
18) Ibid
19) Ibid
20) Liverpool Mercury 10/9/1840
21) Dublin Monitor 6/5/1841
22) Durham Records Office
23) Elizabeth page 12

Chapter Five
1) Morning Chronicle 4/6/1810
2) Will of Edward Cotsford
3) Will of Richard Mathews
4) Durham Records Office D/CG5/1277

5) Indian Gazette March 22nd 1783- extract from letter from Madras March 3rd

6) Hampshire Chronicle 13/12/1784

7) National Archives currency converter 2005

8) Northampton Mercury 29/123/1784

9) Elizabeth page 13

10) 'Vanity Fair' William Makepeace Thackeray page 89

11) Durham Records Office

12) Tristram page 31

13) Ibid page 32 "Lady Hester Stanhope" page 5 Duchess of Cleveland

14) Ibid page 47

15) "William Pitt the Younger" William Hague, 19,5,519

16) Elizabeth

17) Tristram

18) "Hidden Chains, the Slavery Business and North East England 1600-1865" John Charlton pages 25, 78

19) Newcastle Chronicle December 1791

20) Ibid 28/1/1792

21) Illustration from 19) ibid page 35

22) Newcastle Chronicle July 1788

23) Ibid 3/3/1793

24) Caledonian Mercury 24/3/1798

25) Newcastle Chronicle 12/1/1788

26) Gloucester Post 18/2/1888

27) Chester Courant 4/11/ 1800

28) Ibid 7/3/1800

29) Lewin Vol 1 pages 84-85 "The Lewin Letters Vol. 1"

30) Newcastle Chronicle 18/1/1800

31) Ibid December 1799

32) Tristram page 23

33) Aberdeen Journal 4/3/1799

34) Bury and Norwich Post 23/2/1803

35) Aberdeen Journal 4/3/1799

36) Newcastle Chronicle 15/1/1791

37) National Archives letter re seaman's strike

38) DRO

39) South Shields Gazette November 1792

40) Newcastle Chronicle 29/9/1798

41) Tristram

42) Morning Post 14/2/1801

43) DRO Lord Eldon's letter

44) Morning Chronicle 17/7/1802

45) Morning Post 19/7/1802

46) Ibid 13/6/1803

47) Ibid November 1801

48) Ibid October 1802

49) Ibid 18/9/1801

50) Ibid 7/1/1801

51) Ibid 4/12/1804

52) "Vanity Fair" William Makepeace Thackeray page 584

53) Encyl. Britannica 1830 ed

54) Newcastle Chronicle 7/6/1800

55) Derby Mercury 5/11/1789

56) "Memoirs of Lady Hester Stanhope" Vol 11 page 4

57) Elizabeth page 7

58) DRO

59) Ibid

60) Ibid

61) The Life and Letters of Lady Hester Stanhope Vol 2 Duchess of Cleveland page 13

62) Ibid 63

63) Elizabeth

64) "Lady Hester Stanhope Vol 2" Duchess of Cleveland page 16

65) Ibid page 132

66) Newcastle Chronicle 16/5/1807

67) Tristram page 24

68) D/CG5/2-9,12 DRO

69) Sunderland Daily Echo and Shipping News 11/10/1883

70) Durham Mining Museum

71) "History of Hartlepool" Sir Cuthbert Sharp page 6

Chapter Six
1) Elizabeth page 20
2) Ibid
3) Ibid 142
4) Ibid
5) Report by James Mitchell Esq LLD edit Ian Winstanley
6) Elizabeth page 22
7) Ibid
8) Ibid
9) Durham County Advertiser 31/12/1814
10) Tristram page 21
11) Ibid page 25
12) Stamford Mercury 7/6/1822
13) Durham County Advertiser 6/10/1827
14) Ibid 10/12/1825
15) Ibid 18/2/1826
16) Leeds Intelligencer 9/2/1826
17) Durham County Advertiser 13/11/1824
18) Elizabeth page 157
19) Ibid page 11
20) Ibid page 10
21) Guardian 15/3/2012 Alan Sykes
22) Durham County Advertiser 12/12/1818 / and 28/7/1827
23) Ibid 31/1/1829
24) Bath Chronicle and Weekly Gazette 2/4/1829
25) Elizabeth
26) Bath Chronicle and Weekly Gazette 16/7/1835
27) Newcastle Chronicle 14/4/1832
28) Durham County Advertiser 6/11/1835
29) Newcastle Journal 4/10/1834
30) "History of Hartlepool" page 38
31) New castle Journal 3/6/1837
32) Tristram page 31

Chapter Seven
1) Tristram page 33
2) Picture of Cottage
3) DRO description of cottage
4) Tristram page 34
5) Ibid 35
6) Ibid 37
7) Elizabeth page 17
8) Newry Examiner and Louth Advertiser 11/3/1865
9) The Souther Reporter 23/3/1865
10) Belfast Morning news 24/3/1865
11) Newcastle Guardian and Tyne Mercury 18/3/1865
12) Elizabeth page 17
13) Newcastle Chronicle 5/6/1840
14) Elizabeth
15) Ibid page 19
16) Yorkshire Gazette 27/8/1842
17) Durham County Advertiser 26/8/1842
18) "Masters and Servants" Hugh Benyon and Terry Austin page 27
19) "The Miners of Northumberland Durham", Richard Fynes page 5
20) Ibid page 61
21) Tristram
22) "Masters and Servants" Hugh Benyon and Terry Austin page 15
23) Ibid page 17
24) Gateshead Observer quoted in Manchester |Courier and Lancashire General Advertiser 12/10/1844
25) Elizabeth 28
26) Ibid 18
27) York Herald 17/1/1857
28) Elizabeth 45
29) Ibid 27
30) "The Lewin Letters" page 119
31) "The Lewin Letters" page 120
32) Elizabeth page 30
33) "The Lewin Letters" page 58
34) Ibid page 188

35) Southern Reporter and Cork Commercial Courier 8/7/1823
36) "The Lewin Letters" page 77
37) Ibid page 78
38) Bury and Norwich Post 3/8/1805
39) "The Lewin Letters" page 85
40) Elizabeth page 44
41) Ibid 15
42) Ibid 8
43) Ibid 45
44) Ibid 20
45) DRO
46) Newcastle Journal 10/9/1843
47) "History of County Durham" Vol 3 1928
48) New castle Journal 21/2/1863
49) Hartlepool Northern Mail 25/9/1889
50) Newcastle Journal 27/9/1865
51) Hartlepool Northern Daily Mail 15/7/1929
52) "History of Hartlepool" page 170
53) Ibid 176
54) Hartlepool Northern Daily Mail 29/9/1833
55) "History of Hartlepool" page 41
56) Ibid 42
57) Ibid 55
58) Elizabeth page 20

Chapter Eight
1) Post Office Directory 1858
2) Durham Chronicle 20/4/1855
3) Shields Gazette 20/8/1884
4) York Herald 12/7/1851
5) Elizabeth page 6
6) York Herald 12/7/1851
7) Teesdale Mercury 14/1/1857
8) Times (DMM)
9) New castle Journal 15/4/1862
10) Elizabeth page 100

11) Sunderland Daily Echo and Shipping Gazette 20/4/1875
12) Elizabeth page 17
13) Ibid 20
14) Ibid 28
15) Ibid 40
16) Ibid 28
17) Ibid 35
18) Ibid 31
19) Ibid 35
20) Hereford Journal 23/5/1860
21) Elizabeth page 34
22) Ibid
23) Will of Anne Malet Burdon
24) Elizabeth page 46
25) Ibid 48
26) Will of Anne Malet Burdon
27) Western Daily Press 5/2/1892
28) Elizabeth page 44
29) Daily Gazette for Middlesbrough 19/8/1893
30) Hartlepool Mil 7/8/1893
31) "Masters and Servants" Hugh Benyon and Terry Austin
32) Hartlepool Mail; 15/3/1892
33) Manchester Courier and Lancashire General Advertiser 10/1/1894
34) Daily Gazette for Middlesbrough 3/10/1892
35) Sunderland Daily echo and Shipping Gazette 12/9/1892
36) Manchester Courier and Lancashire General Advertiser 10/1/1894
37) "Masters and Servants" Hugh Benyon and Terry Austin
38) Daily Gazette for Middlesbrough 1/12/1892
39) Ibid 13/3/1892
40) Ibid 17/11/1893
41) Ibid 27/11/1893
42) Ibid
43) Elizabeth page 55

Chapter Nine
1) Elizabeth p 30
2) ibid page 31
3) Ibid page 36
4) Hartlepool Mail 17/2/1887
5) "Miners of Northumberland Durham" Richard Fynes
6) Northern Echo 13/6/1900
7) York Herald 22/1/1900
8) Daily Gazette for Middlesbrough 5/2/1900
9) Ibid
10) Sunderland Echo and Shipping Gazette 10/2/1902
11) Ibid 4/12/1901
12) Ibid 17/1/1903
13) Ibid 21/12/1894
14) Ibid 18/8/1899
15) Ibid 19/6/1901
16) Ibid 25/7/1901
17) Western Times 26/8/1903
18) Durham County Advertiser 30/10/1835
19) Hartlepool Daily Mail 26/6/1879
20) Newcastle Journal 30/6/1917
21) Daily Gazette for Middlesbrough 31/12/1900
22) Sunderland Daily Echo and Shipping Gazette 18/11/1913
23) Ibid 27/12/1900
24) Ibid 29/12/1902
25) Ibid 18/11/1913
26) Hartlepool Mail 30/4/1887
27) Sunderland Daily Mail and shipping Gazette 8/8/1901
28) Western Times 1/4/1882
29) Hull Daily Mail 4/7/1899
30) Newcastle Journal 28/2/1916
31) Daily Gazette for Middlesbrough December 1918
32) York Herald 28/7/1900
33) History and Antiquities of the County Palantine of Durham , Hartlepool Section

34) "Rural England and Urban Poaching in Victorian England" Harvey Osborne and Michael Winstanley
35) Kendal Mercury 23/12/1865
36) Newcastle Journal 8/123/1865
37) Newcastle Chronicle 9/6/1865
38) York Herald 6/2/1875
39) Daily Gazette for Middlesbrough 9/8/1900

Chapter Ten
1) Leamington Spa Courier 27/5/1927
2) Elizabeth
3) Edwardian Life in Hitchiongbrooke
4) Mrs Beeton p921
5) Ibid 918
6) Ibid
7) Ibid 919
8) Ibid 927
9) Elizabeth page 7
10) Ibid page 6
11) Mrs Beeton page 968
12) Newcastle Chronicle 6/1/1900
13) Hartlepool Mail 18/8/1900
14) Berwick Advertiser 20/10/1906
15) Mrs Beeton p 900
16) Hartlepool Mil 10/1/1934
17) Hartlepool Mail 27/12/1949
18) Sunderland Daily Echo and Shipping Gazette 17/8/1900
19) Ibid 10/1/1902
20) Shields Daily Gazette 21/1/1901
21) Sunderland Daily Echo and Shipping Gazette 18/11/1902
22) Ibid 29/12/1902
23) Portsmouth Evening News 21/6/1923
24) Sheffield Evening Telegraph 10/3/1906
25) Yorkshire Post 19/10/1906
26) Ibid 23/12/1907
27) Hartlepool Mail 10/9/1910

28) Sunderland Daily Echo and Shipping Gazette 6/10/1910
29) Hartlepool Mail 12/12/1910
30) Ibid
31) Ibid
32) Hansard HC 24/2/1910 vol 14
33) DRO
34) Sunderland Daily Echo and Shipping Gazette 12/3/1900
35) Ibid 20/12/1910
36) Ibid 23/4/1913
37) Yorkshire Post and Leeds Intelligencer 28/10/1912
38) Newcastle Journal 2/3/1911
39) Sunderland Daily Echo and Shipping Gazette 15/4/1914

Chapter Eleven
1) Daily Gazette Middlesbrough 24/12/1900
2) DRO
3) Larne Times 8/9/1934
4) "Great Britain's War" Jeremy Paxman
5) Western Times 18/12/1914
6) "Forgotten Voices of the Somme" Joshua Levine
7) Ibis p112
8) Ibid p 155
9) "A Very Unimportant Officer" C A Steward
10) The Christmas Truce 1915
11) Memoirs and Diaries Guardian Booklet
12) De Vichy Roll of Honour
13) Sunderland Daily Echo and Shipping Gazette

Chapter Twelve
1) "Great Britain's War" Jeremy Paxman 121
2) Newcastle Journal 16/5/1914
3) Hull Daily Mail June 1914
4) Elizabeth 71
5) Birmingham Daily Gazette 11/5/1916
6) London Daily News 6/7/1911
7) Elizabeth 171

8) Newcastle Journal 16/1/1917
9) Yorkshire Post 22/5/1917
10) Newcastle Journal 29/10/1918
11) Sunderland Daily Echo and Shipping Gazette 26/4/1917
12) Newcastle Journal 9/6/1916

Chapter Thirteen
1) Yorkshire Post and Leeds Intelligencer 13/12/1918
2) Ibid 8/8/1919
3) Ibid 12/9/1922
4) Hartlepool Northern Daily Mail 22/8/1925
5) Hartlepool Northern Daily Mail 10/2/1923
6) Ibid 16/5/1929
7) Ibid 16/11/1931
8) Elizabeth 45
9) Sunderland Daily Echo and Shipping Gazette 14/7/1932
10) Ibid 21/11/1935
11) Ibid 15/10/1931
12) Hartlepool Northern Daily Mail 10/2/1930
13) Ibid 6/5/1931
14) Ibid 5/12/1927
15) Elizabeth 94